THE PSYCHOLOGIST AS EXPERT WITNESS

Second Edition

Theodore H. Blau

JOHN WILEY & SONS, INC.

New York • Chichester • Weinheim • Brisbane • Singapore • Toronto

Library of Congress Cataloging-in-Publication Data:

Blau, Theodore H.
    The psychologist as expert witness / Theodore H. Blau. — 2nd ed.
        p.   cm.
    Includes bibliographical references and index.
    ISBN 0-471-17870-5 (cloth : alk. paper)
    1. Evidence, Expert—United States.   2. Psychology, Forensic—
United States.   I. Title.
KF8965.B57   1998
347.3'67—dc21   98-2523

Printed in the United States of America.

10 9 8 7 6 5 4 3 2 1

Preface to the
Second Edition

It has been approximately 15 years since the publication of the first edition of *The Psychologist as Expert Witness.* At the time of the original edition, it was proposed that forensic psychology was one of the most rapidly growing areas of professional specialization in psychology. Today, this continues to be so, perhaps more than ever. Psychologists have developed a more extensive and binding relationship with American (as well as European and Australian) jurisprudence.

Although psychologists provide their research and clinical wares in a variety of venues, it is in the area of expert opinion that most professional psychologists become involved with the law. Psychologists have rendered and continue to render good service in civil, criminal, and family courts. Black-letter law (basic principles generally accepted by the courts) has emerged during the past decade and a half that specifically targets professional psychological services as part of judicial decision making. The areas of neuropsychology, clinical psychology, psychotherapy, police selection, mental disability, psychological syndromes, psychological profiles and a variety of issues in marital and family law have all been addressed in court.

Organizationally, the American Psychological Association (APA) has become increasingly interested in forensic psychology. Division 41, the Division of Psychology and the Law, has grown from an interest group to a major division of the APA. The American Board of Professional Psychology now sponsors the Diplomate in Forensic Psychology, offering advanced credentialing for psychologists practicing as expert witnesses.

Throughout this book, the reader will find a wide variety of legal citations. Some of them are classic, some are relatively final Supreme Court decisions, while others are very specific, and limited to circuit and appellate decisions. The reader should be aware that almost any legal citation may be out of date shortly after it is cited. For this reason, when any issue arises that requires support from legal references, the reader is encouraged to pursue this either through his or her own legal research or with the aid of an attorney. Where research citations are made, each study must stand (or fall) on its merits.

It is likely that professional activity involving psychology and the law will continue to grow. Educational and training opportunities have lagged behind actual practice, not an unusual situation but it is hoped, only a temporary one. Developments in training have far exceeded developments in education (see Appendix B). The great Wigmore's prediction in his last volume published in 1937 applies today: "The law is ready for psychology when psychology is ready for the law."

A special thanks to Ms. Peggy Barnes for her creative and thoughtful help in producing this manuscript.

THEODORE H. BLAU

Preface to the First Edition

A burgeoning interest by psychologists in the application of psychological principles and practice to the field of jurisprudence seems to have occurred during the past decade. I use the term *seems* advisedly. Efforts to make psychology available to the bar and the bench go back 100 years. Although in the present era most of the contact between psychology and the law is between those professionals in psychology who apply the science and those attorneys and judges who wish the benefit of professional psychology, the origins of the interface between psychology and the law rest firmly with the academicians and experimentalists.

Some psychologists see their role in relationship to the courts as that of ancillary psychiatrists or alienists. Issues of sanity and competence, however, represent a rather small portion of psychology's potential to promote human welfare through the American system of jurisprudence.

There were few guidelines for the use of psychology in the courts. As a result, psychology and law "just grew." It is doubtful that any one individual can define the field. The purpose of this book is to make an attempt at defining psychologists' current and future potential as expert witnesses. An attempt will be made to delineate the ways in which psychology has come into contact with the court, where we have done well, and where we have done badly. Primary emphasis will be on standards for practice and practical training in providing expert testimony to the courts.

In no way can this book be considered definitive. Psychologists who intend to make themselves available to the bar and the bench should understand that the law is much more dynamic and changing than psychology. By the time this book goes to press, many of the citations will have been replaced, enhanced, or challenged in various jurisdictions. This is the nature of the law. Lawyers accept it, and if psychologists are to practice within the framework of the American court system, it behooves us to understand and to accept this dynamic system.

The interaction between psychology and the law can have a salutary effect on the quality of psychological concepts and services. The burden of proof always lies with the expert witness. As psychologists function in the role of expert more frequently, there will be a tendency to emphasize quality of supporting data in terms of traditional reliability and validity.

Clinical and professional psychologists may find it difficult to adapt to the extremely open adversary system practiced in our courts. In a sense, academic and experimental psychologists are likely to fare better than clinicians because they are accustomed to being challenged, and to supporting their conclusions with precedent and relatively substantial data. Clinicians and professionals, however, are likely to do better in the practical requirements of the courtroom since they are more practiced in rendering opinions, within reasonable psychological probability, in their everyday clinical work.

I will venture to risk the statement that there is a place in the court system for almost anyone in psychology. I would certainly hope that more psychologists will prepare themselves and invest their skills and talents in helping to forward the purposes and goals of American jurisprudence. One need only travel to other countries to come to understand the fairness and openness of the American system of jurisprudence.

This system is in dire trouble insofar as court dockets are concerned. It is extremely difficult to apply the constitutional guarantee of early trial and early justice when there simply are not enough places on the docket for the number of cases that require attention. Psychologists will find that when they are retained by attorneys or the court as expert witnesses, in civil or criminal matters, adversary issues tend to become clarified, settlement or plea bargaining occurs, and the case is frequently removed from the docket. If psychologists, by being available to the courts, are able to do anything to help clear the crowded dockets, psychology will have made a significant contribution to the promotion of human welfare.

A wide range of situations in which psychologists have appeared as expert witnesses is addressed in this book. In those areas where psychologists are likely to be called frequently and/or where there are current controversies, details of the law, procedures, and samples of testimony will be more extensive than in areas where psychologists are not so involved. Where pertinent reference works are available, efforts have been made to refer the reader to appropriate sources. In areas where the average attorney may be somewhat unsure about the appropriate use of psychological experts, case law is cited so that the psychological expert can make reference to the appropriate precedent. Common legal terms are introduced and defined throughout the text. A glossary is provided to define most legal terms that the psychologist is likely to find in functioning as an expert witness.

This volume is more of a cookbook than a learned treatise. The objectives are to introduce psychologists to the world of the psychologist in the courtroom, identify current and emerging areas of application, and prepare the psychologist to function credibly as an expert witness.

Acknowledgments are in order at this point. My colleagues in psychology who were helpful and generous with ideas, critique, manuscript evaluation, and encouragement include Linda Coleman, James Crumbley, L. G. Daugherty, Sheldon Freud, F. Girsh, D. Grossman, Blaze Harkey, Florence Kaslow, Elizabeth Loftus, Paul Lipsitt, Robert Leark, Orin McEuen, Maria Martinroe, Maurice Pavlow, Elliott Rapoport, Edwin Shneidman, Sherry Skidmore, R. Bob Smith, and Gretchen White.

Members of the bar whose ideas, guidance, suggestions, and influence have contributed to the tone and content of this book include C. Richard Baker, Charles Baldonado, Donald Bradshaw, Bernard H. Dempsey, Jr., Frank Glinn, J. Bert Grandoff, Mark Horwitz, Bennie Lazzara, Mark Luttier, Ed Ratiner, Robert Scott, Patrick Sirridge, Harrison T. Slaughter, Jr., Tom Tweedy, and Dewey Villareal.

Special recognition and immeasurable thanks are due to Jeffrey Alan Blau, Esq., and Richard Michael Blau, Esq., for their generous help in defining points of law, procedure, and in obtaining legal citations.

Ms. Ann Dimity and Ms. Susan Davenport were extremely helpful in the preparation of this manuscript.

Dr. Lili R. Blau deserves special recognition for loss of consortium during the preparation of this manuscript.

Finally, to all the colleagues and students who have attended my classes and workshops on the psychologist as expert witness, for their support and continuing feedback, many thanks.

THEODORE H. BLAU

Contents

1

Coming of Age

In early English law, experts were not really utilized. The courts relied on the oath taken by witnesses, tests of ordeal, and sometimes conflict in the form of combat to settle an issue. Beginning in the 13th century, courts were privileged to join experts as well as jurors to help in the jury's decision making. There are records of physicians and surgeons called into court to give advice to judges. In the 16th century, it was decreed in English law that when matters arise which concern sciences or faculties other than the law, the aid of science or faculty is an honorable and commendable thing for the law. In the famous Salem witchcraft trials in the 17th century, a Dr. Brown was heard as an expert of great knowledge to help in the judicial decision. By the early 18th century, physicians were appearing regularly in the English courts; their testimony primarily focused on homicide prosecutions. Educationally, it wasn't until the end of the 18th century that English legal texts began to focus on issues concerning the testimony of experts. In the United States, following the English experience, the 19th century saw a good deal of testimony by medical experts, primarily in criminal issues (Landsman, 1995).

The first instance of a psychologist acting as an expert occurred in 1896. An experimental psychologist, Dr. von Schrenk-Notzing testified in a murder trial utilizing the experimental psychology that he had learned in the Wundt laboratories. He testified concerning memory and suggestibility on the issue of pretrial publicity. He suggested this publicity resulted in retroactive memory falsification, an issue that remains with us today. James M. Cattell published an article in 1897 describing a study in which students were asked questions that were paradigms of those that might be asked of a witness (Blackburn, 1996).

The psychologist as expert witness in the United States is not a topic that has developed easily and reached fruition in the 20th century. It has been over three-quarters of a century since lively and often controversial debate began in scientific journals and law reviews all over the world on the psychology of testimony and the value of psychology to the judicial process (Goldofski, 1904; S. Jaffe, 1903; Lobsien, 1904).

Munsterberg brought together a number of essays on psychology and crime, initially publishing these in the *Times* magazine and then as the book *On the Witness Stand* (1908). In his enthusiasm, Munsterberg stated:

> The lawyer and the judge and the juryman are sure that they do not need the experimental psychologist. They do not wish to see that in this field pre-eminently applied experimental psychology has made strong strides, led by Binet, Stern, Lipmann, Jung, Wertheimer, Gross, Sommer, Aschaffenburg and other scholars. They go on thinking that their legal instinct and their common sense supplies them with all that is needed and somewhat more; and if the time is ever to come when even the jurist is to show some concession to the spirit of modern psychology, public opinion will have to exert some pressure. Just in the line of the law it therefore seems necessary not to rely simply on the technical statements of scholarly treatises, but to carry the discussion in the most popular form possible before the wider tribunal of the general reader.

Munsterberg then goes on to state:

> [M]y only purpose is to turn attention of serious men to an absurdly neglected field which demands the full attention of the social community.

Following this, Munsterberg presented a series of essays on illusions, the memory of witnesses, the detection of crime, untrue confessions, hypnotism and crime, and the prevention of crime.

Munsterberg's effort was interesting, enthusiastic, and predictive of things to come for psychology and law. It was, unfortunately, somewhat premature. Munsterberg's work did not go unnoticed. John H. Wigmore, professor of the law of evidence at Northwestern University, wrote a scathing parody about *On the Witness Stand* that was published in the *Illinois Law Review* in 1909. The critique took the form of a report of a mythical suit filed in the city of "Windyville, Illiania" against Munsterberg for having "caused to be printed, published, and circulated in Illiania and throughout the country . . . which said book contained . . . certain assertations, erroneous, incorrect and untrue concerning the said plaintiffs, in their capacity as members of the bar."

Wigmore went on to present a mock trial in which Munsterberg's allegations that "the lawyer alone is obdurate" formed the basis of a mythical civil suit brought by several lawyers against Munsterberg. In his parody, Wigmore confronts Munsterberg on the lack of published evidence to support the claim that the law is ready for psychology. (In truth, Munsterberg cited no references in his pioneer text.) The article cites 127 learned treatises to justify the proceedings. The mock trial ended with a finding against Munsterberg with the jury assessing damages at one dollar.

Wigmore's attack was telling. Few references to psychologists as expert witnesses appeared for a quarter of a century.

In 1931, Lewis M. Terman, then professor of psychology at Stanford, appeared before the Los Angeles Bar Association to present the address "Psychology and the Law." Terman took pains to refer to Munsterberg's *On the Witness Stand* and Wigmore's scathing response. He suggested that Munsterberg's error was in exaggerating the importance of psychology's contributions based on research then at hand. He went on to suggest that in light of significant scientific advances the ultimate importance of psychology for the legal profession could not be overstated. Terman emphasized the value of experimental psychology in clarifying errors of testimony. He ranged broadly in his presentation suggesting that psychology might be helpful, among other things, in lie detection, evaluation of eyewitness accounts, and clarification of the vagaries of the insanity pleading and jury selection. Terman ended his presentation with a critique similar to that presented by Hugo Munsterberg a quarter of a century before: "Our laws, like our proverbs and adages, are the product of folk-thinking and like those they are a mixture of shrewd wisdom, childish error, superstition, and folly" (1935).

By this time, Wigmore's *On Evidence* was considered the definitive work being used and cited by attorneys and judges in America. Psychology's bitterest critic in the law modified his position in the last edition of his master work (1940), just before his death. In this, Wigmore opined:

Nevertheless, within the limitations of these special judicial rules (pertaining to partisan presentation of evidence in an adversary proceeding), judicial practice is entitled and bound to resort to all truths of human nature established by science, and to employ all methods recognized by scientists for applying those truths in the analysis of testimonial credit. Already, in long tradition, judicial practice is based on the implicit recognition . . . of a number of principles of testimonial psychology, empirically discovered and accepted. In so far as science from time to time revises them, or adds new ones, the law can and should recognize them. Indeed, it may be asserted that the Courts are ready to learn and to use, whenever the psychologists produce it, any method which the latter themselves are agreed is sound, accurate and practical. If there is any reproach, it does not belong to the Courts or the law. A legal practice which has admitted the evidential use of the telephone, the phonograph, the dictograph, and the vacuum-ray, within the past decades, cannot be charged with lagging behind science. But where are these practical psychological tests, which will detect specifically the memory-failure and the lie on the witness stand? There must first be proof of general scientific recognition that they are valid and feasible. The vacuum-ray photographic method, for example, was accepted by scientists the world over, within a few months after its promulgation. If there is ever devised a psychological test for the valuation of witnesses, the law will run to meet it. Both law and practice permit the calling of any expert scientist whose method is acknowledged in his science to be a sound and trustworthy one. Whenever the Psychologist is ready for the Courts, the Courts are ready for him.[1]

Wigmore was demonstrating the flexibility, awareness, and practicality psychologists are likely to find among lawyers and judges when presented with psychological data, techniques, and methods generally accepted by colleagues and concordant with the standards of the profession.

One of the earliest reviews of the legal and psychological literature regarding the psychologist as expert witness was published by Louisell in 1955. An appendix to this article presented the testimony of Kenneth E. Clark in the case of *Robinsdale Amusement Co. v. Warner Bros. Pictures Distributing Corp. et al.*[2] Dr. Clark was qualified as an expert in public opinion techniques and so testified.

During the 1950s, psychologists were sometimes qualified as experts and sometimes dismissed by the judge. In 1954, Dr. Michael H. P. Finn, then chief psychologist at the Springfield State Hospital, appeared in *Hidden v. Mutual Life Insurance of New York.*[3] The judge refused to allow Dr. Finn to testify. On appeal, the U.S. court of appeals reversed on the grounds that Dr. Finn was qualified to give expert testimony.

One of the most important instances where psychological testimony in the form of psychological research was utilized in a highly significant decision was Kenneth B. Clark's work on the effects of prejudice on children, which was used in *Brown v. Board of Education* in 1954. In this case, the Supreme Court of the United States gave credibility to the significance of such research.[4]

In the earliest formal text on private practice in clinical psychology, Blau (1959) included a chapter titled "The Clinical Psychologist and the Legal Profession." Blau suggested that psychologists would do well to prepare themselves to be competent expert witnesses within their field. Court transcripts were included to illustrate direct examination and cross-examination of psychologists in a personal injury suit and a matter of competence.

The role of the psychologist as expert witness in matters of mental disease or defect was spelled out in considerable detail in the landmark *Jenkins v. United States* in 1962.[5] Jenkins, after indictment, was committed to the District General Hospital, Washington, DC, for a mental examination on September 4, 1959, to determine his competence to stand trial and his mental condition at the time of the alleged offense of housebreaking with intent to commit an assault, assault with intent to rape, and assault with a dangerous weapon. Jenkins was given a series of psychological tests by staff psychologists under the supervision of Bernard I. Levy, Ph.D. Jenkins was also examined by several psychiatrists, who informed the district court that Jenkins was incompetent. He was then committed to St. Elizabeth's Hospital until mentally competent to stand trial. At St. Elizabeth's, he was tested extensively by Lawrence Tirnauer, Ph.D., who concluded Jenkins was schizophrenic. Two psychiatrists found no evidence of mental disease or defect. Margaret Ives, Ph.D., administered additional tests and concluded that Dr. Tirnauer's diagnosis was correct. The trial court, *sua sponte* (on its own motion), instructed the jury to disregard the testimony of the three defense psychologists that the defendant had a mental disease when he committed the crimes charged.

On appeal, Bazelon, circuit judge of the U.S. Court of Appeals, District of Columbia Circuit, held that the lower court erred on several points, including the rejection of qualified psychologists as experts on the presence or absence of mental disease. This decision was rendered despite an amicus curiae brief submitted by the American Psychiatric Association urging the court not to allow psychologists to qualify as experts. Judge Bazelon's scholarly opinion defined the fully trained psychologist. In a rare concurrence, Judge Burger (later Chief Justice, U.S. Supreme Court) agreed with Bazelon (see Appendix A).

The court thus affirmed that titles or degrees are insufficient to qualify a witness as an expert. Quoting eminent authority, the court underscored the conditions under which experts are qualified:

> An observer is qualified to testify because he has firsthand knowledge which the jury does not have of the situation or transaction at issue. The expert has something different to contribute. This is a power to draw inferences from the facts which a jury would not be competent to draw. To warrant the use of expert testimony, then, two elements are required. First, the subject of the inference must be so distinctively related to some science, profession, business or occupation as to be beyond the ken of the average layman, and second, the witness must have such skill, knowledge or experience in that field or calling as to make it appear that his opinion or inference will probably aid the trier in his search for truth. The knowledge may in some fields be derived from reading alone, in some from practice alone, or as is more commonly the case, from both.[6]

Since the *Jenkins* decision, the rejection of psychologists by the court as experts in their field of specialization has been considered to be trial error.

It is important to understand that all psychologists are not likely to be accepted by the court as expert witnesses in all areas of psychology. The psychological expert must first be qualified before the court in the matter about which he or she will testify. The rules of jurisprudence are specific: An expert is one who is so qualified by study or experience that he can form a definite opinion of his own respecting a division of science, branch of art, or department of trade concerning which persons having no particular training or special study are incapable of forming accurate opinions or of deducing correct conclusions.[7]

The second issue determining qualification by the presiding judge concerns the expert's ability to render an opinion that will assist the jury: Expert opinion may be or may not be admissible, depending on whether the subject matter is within common experience or is in a special field where the opinion of one of special skill and experience will assist and be of greater validity than that of the ordinary juryman.[8]

As legal scholars have pointed out, the issue must be such that the expert may answer by giving an opinion that is a reasonable probability, rather than conjecture or speculation (Ladd, 1952).

The credibility of any expert's testimony in many jurisdictions follows the admonition delineated in *Frye v. United States*, where the court opined:

> Just when a scientific principle or discovery crosses the line between the experimental and demonstrable stages is difficult to define. Somewhere in this twilight zone the evidential force of the principle must be recognized, and while courts will go a long way in admitting expert testimony deduced from a well-recognized scientific principle or discovery, the thing from which the deduction is made must be sufficiently established to have gained general acceptance in the particular field in which it belongs.[9]

For almost 70 years, the general acceptance test that was first presented in *Frye* was the determining standard for the admissibility of scientific evidence. In 1975, Congress enacted the *Federal Rules of Evidence*, and Rule 702 appeared to provide a more liberal approach to the admission of scientific evidence. The rule stated, in part:

> If scientific, technical, or other specialized knowledge will assist the trier of fact to understand the evidence or to determine a fact in issue, a witness qualified as an expert by knowledge, skill, experience, training, or education may testify thereto in a form of an opinion or otherwise.[10]

Frye and Rule 702 provided different standards for deciding whether to let the jury hear scientific evidence. In 1993, the case of *Daubert v. Merrell Dow Pharmaceuticals Inc.*[11] resolved the conflict in favor of Rule 702 and rejected the *Frye* test. Federal Rule 702 mandates that the trial judge is to act as a gatekeeper. The judge must assess whether the reasoning or methodology underlying the testimony is valid from a scientific point of view and whether it can be applied appropriately to the facts at issue. The details of this major decision are discussed in Chapter 5, and the *Daubert* decision itself can be found in Appendix A.

The American Psychological Association, in Principle 701 of *Ethical Principles of Psychologists* (1992), broadly defined the qualifications of forensic psychologists:

> Psychologists who perform forensic functions such as assessments, interviews, consultations, reports, or expert testimony must comply with all other provisions of this Ethics Code to the extent that they apply to such activities. In addition, psychologists base their forensic work on appropriate knowledge of and competence in the areas underlying such work, including specialized knowledge concerning special populations. (American Psychological Association, 1992)

In recent years, considerable concern about the ethics and standards for expert witnesses has emerged. These issues are discussed in Chapter 15.

Since the *Jenkins* decision, psychologists have appeared more frequently in the courts as experts. Most published reports of psychologists as expert witnesses have to do with competency evaluation, and the insanity pleading. In these narrow areas of expert testimony, psychologists have invaded the province of psychiatry. Although there is some tendency for psychologists to regard themselves as "second-rate" experts in these areas, the data suggest that psychologists as expert witnesses in matters of competence and sanity are successful and well regarded. Perline (1980) reports three studies comparing the thoroughness and quality of psychologists' performance at a forensic center. Serving as judges, a prosecuting attorney and a law school professor evaluated reports and testimony of psychologists, psychiatrists, and social workers. Ratings of quality of report and of trial testimony indicated that the work of psychologists was consistently rated equal to or better than that of psychiatrists.

Judges are becoming increasingly aware of the potential psychologists have for the courts. Patricia McGowan Wald (1982), circuit judge for the U.S. Court of Appeals, District of Columbia, stated: "I find that after a decade or more of increasing awareness among psychologists and lawyers about what litigation can and cannot accomplish, the era of their most productive relationships built on mutual respect and realistic idealism may be only just beginning."

The psychologist who functions as an expert witness should be competent. There is a growing movement to set standards, and the California State Psychological Association (1980) proposed requirements for expert witnesses. Since that time, impelled by the burgeoning of forensic practice, the Committee on Ethical Guidelines for Forensic Psychologists of the APA Division of Psychology and the Law as well as the American Academy of Forensic Psychology have prepared and revised Specialty Guidelines for Forensic Psychologists (1991). These guidelines may be found in Appendix F of this volume.

Professional recognition of forensic psychologists is now well established. The American Board of Forensic Psychology was originally formed in 1978. Since that time, this board has come under the credentialing umbrella of the American Board of Professional Psychology (ABPP). The Diploma in Forensic Psychology is the only postdoctoral specialty certification in the area of forensic psychology that is recognized in the American Psychological Association Directory.

Few graduate schools at this time prepare psychologists to function as expert witnesses in the courts. Psychologists who expect to function in this role must acquire education, training, and experience ad lib or from continuing education at the postdoctoral level. Interest in this area is burgeoning, and it seems likely that doctoral students in professional training programs in the future will have a greater opportunity for preparation as experts in the courts. Within the past decade, joint Ph.D.-J.D. programs have emerged for psychologists who want roles in policy development. Such programs produce psychologist-lawyers who, it is hoped, will bridge the gap of knowledge between the two professions (Wolinsky, 1982). Appendix B presents detailed information as to specific education and training opportunities.

At this writing, then, psychologists must take the initiative to become aware of the many areas in which expert testimony can be offered and must engineer their own study and training programs to become competent, effective, ethical expert witnesses. The following chapters present guidelines and information to help achieve such goals.

NOTES

1. 3 J. H. Wigmore, *Wigmore on Evidence,* 367–368 (3rd ed. 1940).
2. Civil #4584 (4th Division, Minneapolis).
3. *Hidden v. Mutual Life Insurance Co.,* 217 F.2d 818, 821 (4th Cir. 1954).
4. *Brown v. Board of Education,* 347 U.S. 483 (1954).
5. *Jenkins v. United States,* 307 F.2d 637 (D.C. Cir. 1962).
6. C. McCormick, *Law of Evidence* §13 (1954).
7. 31 American Jurisprudence 2d *Expert and Opinion Evidence* §1 (1967).
8. *Id.* at §16.
9. *Frye v. United States,* 293 F. 1013 (D.C. Cir. 1923).
10. *Fed. R. Evid.* Rule 702, 28 U.S.C.A.
11. *Daubert v. Dow Pharmaceuticals,* 113 S. Ct. 2786, 2795.

2

Present and Future Roles of the Psychologist

Psychologists have served in several roles as expert witnesses, especially during the past four decades. Until now, the courts have used a minute part of the information that the science of psychology has generated. The scarcity of psychologists willing and competent to serve as expert witnesses to present this knowledge to judges and jurors has been a barrier in the past to providing useful information that would be helpful during court proceedings.

As psychologists have become more aware of the opportunities and, thus, more available as experts, a broadened involvement between psychology and the law has taken place. The increase in numbers of psychologists who have served as experts in a judicial setting and the wide-ranging consultations between psychologists and attorneys that have developed in the past decade suggest that the anticipated burgeoning of interaction between psychology and the law has started (Kerr & Bray, 1982; Landsman, 1995; Saks & Hastie, 1978; Sales, 1981).

The purpose of this chapter is to present a brief overview of some roles psychologists have filled as expert witnesses and to describe testimony or testimonial strategy that has as yet been used infrequently with psychologists as experts. Later chapters explore some of these roles to illustrate the ways and means by which psychologists may serve effectively, ethically, and professionally as experts.

TRADITIONAL ROLES

Competence to Stand Trial

Constitutional safeguards guarantee a defendant the right to a fair trial. Essentially, the law requires that a defendant must be able to understand the nature of charges against him or her, must be able to understand the proceedings and the participants in the trial, and must be able to cooperate with his or her attorney to a reasonable degree. When the court is in doubt about a defendant's competency in any of these areas, expert opinion is sought to aid the court in deciding whether to postpone the proceedings until the defendant is found competent. Traditionally, psychiatrists have conducted relatively brief examinations at the request of the court and reported their findings to the judge, who then decides to proceed or postpone.

More recently, psychologists have been appointed by the court, or privately retained by counsel (usually for the defense), to conduct psychological evaluations in order to render a report or an opinion to the presiding judge as to the defendant's psychological capacities under the competency criteria in the jurisdiction where the issue occurs. Again, the judge makes the final decision, accepting or rejecting the report of the expert witness.

The Insanity Pleading

During the past 50 years, again following psychiatry in the courtroom, psychologists have been called on to render expert opinion as to the sanity of the defendant. Previous to that time, psychiatrists, physicians, examiners (called *alienists*), and lay witnesses had been used to help the triers of fact (judge and jury) decide whether a defendant should be excused from a criminal act either because he or she lacked the ability to understand that the act was unlawful or because some defect or illness rendered the defendant unable to act in an expected or lawful manner. Sometimes the burden falls to the defense to prove by *preponderance of evidence* (something better than chance) that the defendant was insane at the time of the offense. In some jurisdictions, the law is such that when a plea of innocent by reason of insanity is filed by the defense, it becomes the burden of the prosecution to prove *beyond reasonable doubt* (90% or better) that the defendant was sane at the time of the crime. Weights of evidence and other technical considerations are presented in greater detail in Chapters 5 and 8. Contrary to the prevailing belief within the lay public, very few defendants plead innocent by reason of insanity, and few of those who so plead are exculpated of guilt. There is much public concern as to the practicality and fairness of this small but important aspect of American jurisprudence (Leo, 1982b). In the past 20 years, psychologists have served more and more frequently to help clarify issues involving insanity (Perline, 1980).

Competence to Manage One's Own Affairs

Because of innate deficiencies, illness, injury, or deterioration due to age, some people become unable to adequately deal with the normal demands of daily living. When this happens, relatives, associates, friends, or even interested citizens may file a civil petition for the court to appoint a guardian or conservator to protect the defendant from his or her own incompetence. It is usually the burden of the plaintiff to prove *beyond reasonable doubt* that the incompetence exists since the courts are reluctant to deprive anyone of constitutional rights without considerable evidence that this is in the defendant's best interests. Psychologists, often using standardized tests to measure cognition, reasoning, planning ability, and personality integration, have begun to appear more frequently in conservator or guardian hearings to testify as experts in the matter of the defendant's competence to govern his or her own life (Spar, Hankin, & Stodden, 1995).

Involuntary Commitment

People sometimes become so emotionally disturbed because of disease or psychological dysfunction that the courts must decide if it is in the person's best interests to undergo evaluation, treatment, or custodial care whether the individual agrees to this or not. The essential rule of law focuses on the question of whether the individual is a danger to himself or herself or to others. Although research evidence suggests that prediction of dangerousness is quite unreliable, the courts are required to act on such petitions while bending every effort to guarantee the defendant due process and the least restrictive environment. Psychologists testify at initial pleadings where the issue is first brought before the court. In this phase, the judge decides whether to dismiss the petition or to remand the defendant to a mental health facility for a specific period, usually not exceeding 30 days, so that experts can observe and evaluate the defendant and decide whether to recommend involuntary commitment. Most states give the defendant the right to hire independent mental health professionals to perform the examination and report the results to the judge, who will then decide for or against commitment. Many psychologists work in mental health facilities where such evaluations are conducted, while private evaluations requested by the defendant's attorney are likely to be conducted by psychologists in independent practice.

Dangerousness and Treatment Potential

During the past half-century, psychologists have frequently served as experts in determining how convicted felons should be classified in terms of placement in minimum-, medium-, or maximum-security facilities, as well as their potential for rehabilitation, and appropriate treatment procedures while the prisoner serves his or her sentence. In those states where capital crimes are dealt with in bifurcated procedures (a guilt-determination trial followed by a penalty trial if convicted), psychologists together with other mental health professionals have been called on to give evidence as experts to help the triers of fact determine the likelihood of rehabilitation when considering whether to invoke the death penalty.

Psychologists who serve as experts in these settings are often part of a *forensic evaluation team* ordinarily set up under state jurisdiction as a special diagnostic clinic or as part of a broader mental health facility.

MIDCENTURY DEVELOPMENTS

As professional psychology emerged as a growing profession following World War II, opportunities to serve as expert witnesses in a wide range of civil, regulatory, and legislative settings grew. The law had been ready for psychology for some time, and with the great growth of research findings in behavioral science, training, and involvement in applied areas, psychologists began to appear as experts, testifying to a broader selection of issues than ever before. Psychologists began leaving the psychiatric model to appear as experts in the science of psychology, providing testimony to the triers of fact about many issues involving human behavior (Louisell, 1955).

Product Liability

Civil suits claiming injury, deficit, or death as a result of insufficiencies or defects of products represent a common type of litigation. Sometimes, liability hinges on how the consumer sees a product, interprets directions for its use, or responds to its feature description or advertised qualities. Psychologists have been called on to testify as experts in advertising, perception of products, evaluation of the merit of research findings concerning a product, and other matters. Sometimes psychologists testify before governmental committees as experts in matters of product liability.[1]

Personal Injury and Wrongful Death

When a person is injured or dies as a result of negligence on the part of an individual or corporate body, the law provides the opportunity for remedies or compensation through civil litigation. As part of the legal proceedings (see Chapter 11), experts may be called on behalf of the plaintiff (the one who seeks remedy) or for the defendant (the party accused of negligence) to testify as to the psychological factors in either the negligent act or the results of negligence. Most frequently, such testimony has been about psychological deficits following physical injury. Psychologists have a wide range of knowledge and instruments to evaluate a person's intellectual, neuropsychological, and emotional status as well as potential for recovery and rehabilitation. In personal injury matters, psychologists are often asked to render their expert opinion as to an individual's current psychological status compared with estimates or measures of functional level previous to the injurious event as well as the individual's rehabilitative future (Lees-Haley, 1990).

Labor Relations, Workers' Compensation, and Equal Opportunity Issues

Civil suits, regulatory hearings, and administrative judgments may require presentation of evidence about such issues as tests and their proper and fair application, skills required for certain positions, performance criteria, and individual vocational capability. Psychologists can be called on during such proceedings to submit reports or give testimony concerning the results of psychological evaluations, the nature and quality of psychological tests, and the likelihood that an individual is able or unable to perform safely and effectively in certain vocational settings. Procedures for this type of testimony are usually mandated, by statute or regulatory decree, in some detail, including the types of tests and procedures psychologists are permitted to use.[2]

Patent and Trademark Infringement

A civil suit may be filed accusing a defendant of using a process, a logo, or a descriptive phrase that has been registered by someone else and who, by dint of patent and trademark laws, "owns" the process, the device, or the written or illustrated material. During the judicial deliberations, evidence is usually presented to support the plaintiffs' claims that their rights have been infringed on, while defendants seek to convince the triers of fact that the claims have no merit. Testimony by psychologists—concerning the impact of trademarks, logos, advertising, and such on the general public or the similarity of devices or materials and other matters that can be measured scientifically through consumer surveys and laboratory experiments—has become relatively well accepted.[3, 4]

Child Custody Issues

It is generally agreed that divorce is bad for children. In 85% of divorce cases, primary custody of the child is awarded to the mother without contest by the father as a result of a century-old tradition known as the *tender years doctrine*. This unspecific shibboleth (judge's rule) suggests "the child of young and tender years belongs with the mother" (Weitzman & Dixon, 1979). More recently, fathers have been successful in gaining sole custody of the child or children in contested custody cases (Orthner & Lewis, 1979). In traditional adversary custodial issues psychologists, together with other mental health professionals, are often called on by the judge and/or the adversary parties to conduct psychological evaluations of the children, the parents, and even the custodial home setting in order to testify as experts on how the best interests of the children and the parents may be served.

Currently, most states have rejected the tender years doctrine and mandated instead that the divorcing parents attempt to share custody and/or responsibility for the children in ways that will best serve the needs of the children. In cases where conflict arises, the judge will usually order professional mediation, which frequently involves a psychologist. If mediation fails, the psychologist is likely to be asked by the court to serve as an expert witness to aid the judge in making the Solomonic decision in awarding sole custody to one parent. Chapter 10 presents a review of expert psychological testimony in issues of family law.

RECENT AND EMERGING ROLES

A keynote for the increasing use of experts was sounded by Melvin Belli, past president of the American Trial Lawyer's Association. He suggests that experts can be found in the most esoteric fields, and although their cost may be high, the cost may well be higher *not* to employ experts appropriately. He admonishes trial lawyers to understand that choosing to proceed without an expert may be "flirting with malpractice" (Belli, 1982). This attitude seems to be increasing among trial lawyers, and psychologists are being summoned as experts in an ever-broadening range of issues (Landsman, 1995).

Some of the newer areas of expert testimony have resulted in the appearance of academic and research psychologists as experts. This, in a sense, is a recapitulation of origins since the first psychologist "experts" were academicians and researchers (Blackburn, 1996; Loftus & Monahan, 1980).

Eyewitness Testimony

The weight of credibility that has traditionally been given to the testimony of individuals who say they saw or heard something is unparalleled in the field of legal evidence. "He is the one who did it!" is perhaps the most powerful statement a witness can make, pointing to a defendant. Although triers of fact have always had the right and responsibility to evaluate the credibility of eyewitnesses, the focus of concern has been on the witness's personal background, style, and degree of certainty about the testimony. Research now casts serious doubts on many aspects of eyewitness testimony (Buckhout, 1974; Egeth, 1993; Loftus, 1979). Experts in matters of eyewitness identification are usually psychologists who have conducted research in memory and cognition or are very familiar with such research. They generally have a strong academic and research background. Testimony generally focuses on research that demonstrates that various environmental conditions influence reliability and validity of the testimonial statements of witnesses. Experts also testify (which in a sense means educate the jury) about personal characteristics of humans that influence accuracy of recall. Such testimony may be arranged by the defense in criminal cases for the purpose of increasing the probability that the triers of fact will evaluate eyewitness testimony of the prosecution's witness with increased caution and sophistication.

The quality of eyewitness research is generally considered quite good, but the courts have been reluctant to allow testimony about this research.[5] Appellate review may result in changes in this exclusionary response if lower-court decisions are reversed with sufficient frequency.

A specific area of expert testimony as to the credibility of an eyewitness has to do with child witnesses. During the past 10 years, a great deal of attention has been directed toward issues in this context. Not only has there been research interest in whether children are able to testify with credibility, at various ages, but the question of the impact or trauma that may result from having a child participate in the legal process has raised legitimate concerns. Considerable research and opinion have emerged concerning these areas (Quas, De Cicco, Bulkley, & Goodman, 1996).

Penalty Phase Testimony

In many states, capital offenses may be tried via a *bifurcated trial.* In this type of trial, the issue of the defendant's guilt or innocence is first decided by a jury. If the defendant is found guilty, then a second trial may be held to decide whether the death penalty should be imposed. Often the same jury that considered the evidence and rendered a verdict in the first trial, or guilt phase of the proceedings, will hear further pleadings and evidence in order to recommend the death penalty or a lesser alternative. During this second trial, attorneys for the defense usually present evidence that the death penalty will amount to cruel and unusual punishment and is contrary to constitutional safeguards.[6] They may also argue that the defendant, though guilty, is not dangerous, has suffered sufficiently to deserve a lesser punishment, or is capable of rehabilitation. Psychologists may be called as experts to render an opinion about the defendant's psychological state of repentance, potential for dangerousness, or potential to lead a reasonably stable life in prison and possibly in society after a period of incarceration. Different states allow widely divergent degrees of leeway in the kind and extent of testimony allowed in presenting mitigating circumstances during the penalty phase of a trial.

Behavioral scientists may also be retained by the prosecution to testify in penalty phase trials. As part of the prosecution's attempt to convince judge and jury that the defendant is not only guilty but should pay the supreme penalty, behavioral scientists may be called to present opinions, as experts, that the defendant is unrepentant, without conscience, and likely to be a danger to others not only in society at large but within the prison system. Given the subjective nature of testimony about dangerousness, psychiatrists in the past have more frequently been found in this testimonial role than psychologists (Tierney, 1982). As dangerousness has become more thoroughly understood and more accurately predicted, psychologists have begun to appear in court to testify about dangerousness and its predictability.

Composition Challenges

The Constitution guarantees each defendant the right to a fair and impartial trial.[7] If there is reason to believe that an impaneled jury does not meet this important criterion, an attorney may challenge the composition of the jury. After arguments and sometimes evidence have been presented, the presiding judge rules on the attorney's motion (usually to dismiss). Psychologists have served as expert witnesses where the *composition,* or makeup, of the jury is at issue. Most frequently, this occurs when a jury is "death qualified."

A death-qualified jury is one in which no member of the panel has stated any serious reservations about voting for capital punishment. In *Witherspoon v. State of Illinois,* the Supreme Court ruled that disqualifying a juror for this reason is acceptable during the *guilt* phase of the trial and is not an abrogation of Sixth Amendment rights to an impartial jury but that such disqualification is unacceptable during the *sentencing* phase of the trial.[8] Thus the Supreme Court decided that a jury from which all those on the original venue or panel who are generally opposed to the death penalty have been challenged and excluded is acceptable in the initial phase of a dual, or bifurcated, trial where the guilt or innocence of a defendant is determined. To exclude those philosophically opposed to the death penalty for any reason or with any degree of personal conviction results in a jury more prone to recommend the death penalty. This, according to the *Witherspoon* ruling, deprives the defendant of fundamental constitutional guarantees to an impartial jury. In reaching these conclusions, the court considered as part of the petitioner's brief the research findings which suggested that jurors who have no concerns against the death penalty are likely to be more prosecution prone than jurors who object to the death penalty. During the original trial, Wilson, Girsch, and Zeisel testified as experts in this matter.[9] Since then, psychologists have been called as experts in similar matters.[10] This kind of testimony by social scientists reflects the growing interest in social science research as one frame of reference from which judicial decisions can be made objectively and fairly. Research in this area has been reviewed by Haney (1984).

Prison-Conditions Defense

There is a deep and pervading concern about the purpose, usefulness, and potential danger of the prison system in the United States. To be in prison is rarely an experience likely to rehabilitate. Certainly, prison is a punishing, cruel, and dehumanizing experience in most instances. Much crime is committed in prisons, including murder. When prisoners commit crimes, they are culpable under the extant laws of the land and must be brought to trial (Anderson, 1982).

In recent years, psychologists have testified as experts in the trials of prisoner-defendants about the effects of prison conditions on human behavior. In such matters, the psychologist or sociologist, testifying for the defense, (usually) opines that the conditions in most prisons can make people deeply disturbed and thus not responsible for their acts of violence (Cox, Paulus, & McCain, 1984; Haney, Banks, & Zimbardo, 1973).

Evaluation Testimony

Evaluation concerns itself with the *assessment of merit.* Since all research is subject to interpretation, evaluation scientists attempt to act as objective evaluators of research findings and identify the degree of confidence one can place on research findings. Evaluation science has been a growing area of research and practice during the past three decades. Participants include psychologists, biostatisticians, mathematicians, and social scientists from several disciplines. In the legal setting, evaluation scientists may serve as educators, bringing to judge and jury information and concepts that may help them weigh and judge the quality of findings placed before them by other experts. Thus, following a psychologist's testimony based on test results, an evaluation scientist might be called as a *rebuttal witness* to discuss the standards and limits that are ordinarily applied to the test instruments under consideration.

Psychologists who qualify as evaluation scientists may testify as experts before juries making decisions in civil and criminal matters or in regulatory and legislative hearings where the interpretation of research data is a significant aspect of the process (Barkdoll & Bell, 1989). As lawyers and judges become more aware of the extensive research done in the behavioral sciences, it is likely that psychologists trained and experienced in evaluation science will be sought to provide triers of fact with help in the interpretation of complex data.

Repressed Memory

The past decade has seen an eruption of criminal and civil litigation based on adult individuals' alleged recall of previously forgotten memories of childhood sexual abuse. The validity of the concept of "repressed memories" has received considerable attention in the psychological literature. The concept continues to be a source of much controversy (American Psychological Association, 1994). Whether psychologists should serve as experts in these matters and the appropriate limits of such testimony remains a hotly debated issue (Kazdin, 1996). The psychologist who is called on to testify in a recovered memory case is faced with the expectation of rendering an opinion as to the credibility of the remembered memory. Although there is much that an expert can say about the research in this area, it is incumbent on the expert to avoid the role of the "Thirteenth Juror" and not opine as to the ultimate question of whether the alleged recovered memory is true or false. Pressure from attorneys or the judge for the expert to pursue the issue of the truth or lie of the recovered material suggests that the psychological expert should be an investigator or detective. This is a role best avoided.

This area of expert testimony is addressed in detail in Chapter 14.

Addiction

In both criminal and civil law, the judiciary has taken note of and responded to issues involving individuals who claim that they are not in control of themselves because they are "addicted." Classically, the concept of *addiction* has been specifically reserved for conditions in which an individual ingests some material, becomes intoxicated, quickly develops a powerful craving for the material, and responds with serious physiological withdrawal consequences if the material is not available. Thus, opiates, cocaine, alcohol, and some prescription and nonprescription drugs have fallen into this category.

In recent years, the definition of addiction has been changed by various researchers and in particular by government agencies that have attempted to define excessive appetites and the consequences of such behavior as *addictions.*

In general, the law has taken a very conservative view of the redefinition of this classic condition, and in most instances has focused on the intoxication aspects of addictive substances and the degree to which these substances cause a loss of *will* or competence (Akers, 1991; Burk, 1986). A detailed exploration of this complex issue can be found in Chapter 9.

Malingering

Psychiatric classification labels malingering a "condition" (American Psychiatric Association, 1994). The essential feature of this condition is said to be the intentional production of false or grossly exaggerated physical or psychological symptoms motivated by external incentives.

Whether a defendant in criminal proceedings and plaintiffs or defendants in civil matters are faking psychological conditions is a matter of considerable interest and importance to judges and juries. The task of identifying the defendant pleading insanity while presenting feigned symptoms has fallen into the province of forensic psychologists. Neuropsychologists now regularly include tests of malingering, deception, or "faking bad" in the test batteries administered to those involved in criminal and civil litigation. Testimony about malingering by psychological experts may be supported by extensive and sophisticated assessment procedures at one extreme or by simplistic interview indicators.

The validity and reliability of expert opinion as to the presence or absence of malingering is a complex issue. Such testimony must survive challenges as to admissibility as well as vigorous and pointed cross examination. Testimony regarding malingering brings the expert witness close to being the Thirteenth Juror. Chapter 12 presents a detailed review of this issue.

The question as to whether expert testimony influences jury decisions is beginning to be addressed in psychological research. Early efforts indicate that although juries may hardly discuss the expert testimony itself during their deliberations, the expert testimony influenced the interpretation of case facts (Brekke & Borgida, 1988).

FUTURE ROLES

The acceleration in the use of psychologists as experts by attorneys is likely to continue if the work of such experts is useful in forwarding the purposes of American jurisprudence. Behavioral research and its expert interpretation are of growing significance in criminal, civil, and regulatory decision making. Between 1958 and 1982, approximately 14% of U.S. Supreme Court cases cited social science research (Acker, 1990). Psychologists have a very good record to date. The limits as well as the potential for psychological testimony will be determined by the future content and quality of research in the behavioral sciences.

NOTES

1. *See Smoking Prevention Education Act: Hearing on H.R. 1824 Before the Subcomm. on Health and the Environment of the House Comm. on Energy and Commerce,* 98th Cong., 1st. Sess. 76, 76–78 (1983).
2. 6 Mental Disability L. Rep. 438 (1982).
3. Rogers, *An Account of Some Psychological Experiments on the Subject of Trademark Infringement.* 18 *Mich. L. Rev.* 75, 99 (1919).
4. *Robinsdale Amusement Co. v. Warner Bros. Pictures Distributing Corp. et al.,* Civil #4584 (4th Division, Minneapolis).
5. *Dyas v. United States,* 376 A.2d. 827 (D.C. 1977).
6. U.S. Const. Amend. VIII.
7. U.S. Const. Amend. VI.
8. 391 U.S. 510, 20 L. Ed. 776, 88 S. Ct. 1770 (1968).
9. 36 Ill. 2d 471, 224 N.E.2d 259 (1967).
10. *Hovey v. Superior Court of Alameda County,* 616 P.2d 1301, 28 Cal. 3d 1, 168 Cal. Rptr. 128 (1980).

3

The American
Court System

In 1913, Chief Justice Oliver Wendell Holmes, Jr., touched on the judicial system's need for expert psychological testimony when he opined:

> Judges are apt to be naïf, simpleminded men, and they need something of Mephistopheles. We too need education in the obvious—to learn to transcend our own convictions and to leave room for much that we hold dear to be done away with short of revolution by the orderly change of law. (Bartlett, 1968)

In no way will an extensive treatise on the development and function of the American court system help an expert witness. A warning in this regard is in order: Do not become an attorney by association. Those psychologists who become so involved in learning the lawyer's tradecraft can become impediments to the judicial process. The psychologist as expert must be a psychological expert.

A general knowledge of the system within which expert testimony plays a significant role can be helpful as well as reassuring. To know the framework within which one must operate will tend to enhance the psychologist's skill as an expert.

The American system of jurisprudence has developed from over 5,000 years of human experience in the search for justice and equity. Elements of the Hammurabi Code, Talmudic principles, Roman law, Judaic and Christian philosophy, Anglo-Saxon jurisprudence, and, finally, the U.S. Constitution, with its articles and amendments, form the base for justice in the United States (Kerr & Bray, 1982; Sales, 1981).

The bureaucratic system, within which rules, mandates, principles, decision making, and remedy operate, is dynamic and tends to change with changing times. The rules may change by legislative action at either the state or federal level or by appeals to higher courts on points of law that one side or another in an original adversary issue considers to be in error.

Courts are formal settings where issues of law are debated and settled. Judges are elected or appointed to arbitrate adversary issues in the legal arena; the gladiators are the attorneys, who are officers of the court. Decisions are made by the judge or by a jury (or *venire*) of 6 or 12 members who listen to all evidence in an issue and then render a decision called a *verdict*. (A glossary is provided at the end of this book to provide the reader with a more complete definition of some of the terms employed by the members of the legal profession.)

Courts may be sponsored by the state or the federal government. Many of the procedures and rules are shared by both, while some procedures are unique to federal courts and some to the courts of individual states.

A civil case may be brought to the courts (or *filed*) by an attorney representing a client with a grievance (the *plaintiff*) against a person or body of persons (the *defendant*). In domestic court, essentially a civil court, a parent (the *petitioner*) may seek custody of a child from the defendant (a custodial parent or the *custodian of record*). In criminal court, a state attorney, or prosecuting attorney, or a *grand jury* may decide there is sufficient evidence to charge a person with a major crime (*felony*) and may present a formal charge (*indictment*) to a judge requesting that the defendant be kept in custody until the trial. A defendant who the judge is convinced will not abscond before trial may be released without bond (*on his or her own recognizance*) or may be required to post a sum of money (*bail*) to ensure an appearance at trial. The judge may believe the defendant is unreliable or dangerous and may, instead of setting bail, require detention at a local jail until the time of the trial.

Lower courts (*municipal* or *magistrate courts*) are more informal and deal with minor infractions of the law (*misdemeanors*), such as vehicular violations, disorderly conduct, and so on, or minor civil matters (*small claims* or *people's courts*). No jury is present at these lower-court hearings, all decisions being made by the presiding magistrate. If the issue is of major proportion, the presiding judge may move the case to a higher court for adjudication. A person whose case comes before a judge in a lower court may request a jury trial, which requires that the judge move the case to the jurisdiction of a higher court (the case is "bound over"). Figure 3.1 shows the various state and federal courts in the U.S. judicial system.

It is unlikely that a psychologist will be called as an expert witness in a magistrate or lower court. If the case becomes that complex, it is usually bound over to a circuit or district court. It is conceivable that a psychologist would testify at traffic court, but it is highly unlikely. The same is true in federal magistrate courts where initial charges are brought (the defendant is *arraigned*) and a decision is made as to whether there is sufficient evidence to move the case to a grand jury for further consideration or to a higher court for trial. Except in the rarest of instances, psychologists will appear only in circuit or district courts to give evidence.

Appellate courts are the places in the judicial system that consider appeals after a decision has been rendered by a lower court. Not every request for a rehearing is granted. The judges of the various appellate courts must

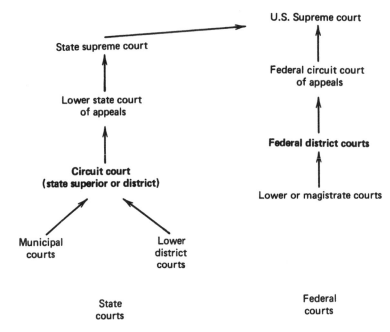

FIGURE 3.1.   State and federal court systems.

be convinced that there is some reasonable doubt that the decision of the lower courts was entirely fair and properly arrived at. Errors of fact, conduct, and procedure by attorneys, witnesses, jurors, or the judge may be grounds for appeal.

Witnesses occasionally appear before higher courts, usually to present evidence as experts. More frequently, the results of research are presented to the appeal judges by attorneys for either side in the adversary process or as a brief of *amicus curiae* (friend of the court) by interested third parties. (The American Psychological Association has supported or prepared briefs as *amicus curiae* in a number of landmark Supreme Court decisions.)[1, 2] Experts usually participate in the preparation of such briefs and may testify on occasion, usually in special hearings before federal judges.

Chapter 13 outlines the details of a legal case moving through the court. The procedures are formal and differ from the handling of both civil and criminal cases in other parts of the world. In keeping with basic principles of democracy and fair play, the American system of jurisprudence is extremely humanistic by world standards. Constitutional safeguards for the individual are extensive; standards for the nature and quality of evidence that may be presented are high and designed to protect the accused, who is deemed innocent until proven guilty. Varying weights of evidence are required to ensure equity and justice.

Certain aspects of the philosophy, rules, and standards of the American jurisprudence system must be understood if a psychologist expects to be regarded as a credible expert witness. In no way does the following cover all the issues involved in the presentation of evidence.

The Adversary Model

The legal model and consequent procedures for the discovery of facts and the administration of justice may puzzle and even disturb some psychologists when they first serve as expert witnesses. This is likely to be more a reflection of the psychologist's naïveté than the law's inadequacy. Most scientists and professionals work on the basis of an Aristotelian model of cause and effect; they make empirical observations and collect or aggregate data in standard ways using field and laboratory research methodology; they attempt to discover meaningful relationships that, when sufficiently clear and replicable, allow for prediction to a greater degree of statistical accuracy. The probability model is the essence of psychological data.

The adversary model of fact seeking begins with the assumption on the part of the judge and jury (the *triers of fact*) that no crime or civil inequity exists. The prosecutor in criminal cases and the plaintiff's attorney in civil cases vigorously present information to suggest as strongly as possible that the defendant is guilty of a crime or liable for damages or remedy. Defense counsel, with equal intensity and vigor, will argue that the criminal defendant is innocent of the charges as drawn or that the civil defendant is without liability in the issue at hand. Each side takes turns in making presentations of arguments and witnesses. It is obvious that each side is out to win at almost any cost. Tempers flare, and accusations, recriminations, and heated debates are common. The intensity of the presentation may reach such a point that the presiding judge may admonish an attorney who has become too loud, too abusive in his or her language, or too leading or manipulative with a witness. If the judge's admonishment is not heeded, the judge may recess the trial and bring the attorneys for both sides to his or her chambers to deliver a more severe admonishment to the offending attorney. Should an attorney continue to act in a manner deemed inappropriate to the proceedings, a judge may fine or even jail the offender for *contempt of court*. The degree of the judge's control of the interchange may vary from judge to judge, but the judge's power in the courtroom is close to absolute.

Unless a psychologist serving as expert witness is fairly experienced, each trial brings new insights about the adversary model. Psychologists who are serious about becoming competent expert witnesses would do well to attend a number of civil and criminal trials early in their career in order to better understand the process. The psychologist may not agree with the adversary system as a philosophical concept, but certainly any psychologist who intends to serve as an expert witness must understand the mechanics and logic of the process. The expert witness is part of the process.

A general review of the terms in the glossary of this book will give the aspiring expert witness a view of some of the concepts and terms likely to be encountered in dealing with the court system.

In addition, there are certain concepts that require clear understanding on the part of those who expect to perform credibly as experts giving testimony in judicial settings. These concepts significantly influence the style and language of the experienced expert's testimony as well as his or her method of collecting and examining information. An expert who does not understand these ground rules may be prevented, on technical legal points, from doing a proper and credible job. Some of the most important and more frequently encountered concepts that should be understood by experts giving testimony include the following.

Hearsay Evidence.   Frequently encountered in TV and movie presentations of testimony, this concept refers to the exclusion of information that comes to the witness through another person. Should a police officer testify, "Mr. Jones told me he had seen the stolen vehicle in Mr. Smith's garage," opposing counsel would rise to object on the grounds the testimony was "hearsay" and not admissible. The judge would sustain the objection, cause the testimony to be stricken from the record, instruct the jury to ignore the officer's remarks, and caution the witness to testify only about those matters in his or her own experience.

If an *expert* in behavioral sciences is the witness, the rules of hearsay are somewhat less stringent. As long as the expert indicates clearly that secondhand information is necessary to come to a conclusion concerning a person or event, the court will usually allow it. This includes information gathered from a defendant's friends, family, employer, hospital records, police reports, school records, the statements of survey participants, and so forth. The witness can be challenged on these matters and can expect to be questioned closely about the degree of reliability, validity, and acceptance of such methods in usual and customary professional practice (Ziskin, 1991). The judge may refer specifically to the use of such quasi-hearsay issues while instructing the jury at the end of the trial or may provide a more general caution to jurors such as, "You may accept or reject the opinion expressed by experts in this case, using your own judgment as to the worth and quality of the information upon which the expert's opinion is based." Once again, *Frye v. United States* was for more than 70 years a sound and conservative test an expert could and sometimes still may use in presenting information leading to the opinion.[3] The expert witness can expect the *Daubert*[4] decision of 1993 to supplant or modify *Frye* in the future. Professionals whose testimony is based on a generally accepted set of procedures and explanatory theories and whose testimony concerns a proper subject matter in the case can usually feel assured that they are functioning within the proper framework of judicial rules for expert witnesses.[5] The issue of hearsay evidence should be discussed with the retaining attorney during the pretrial conference, after the expert's report has been submitted. In short, hearsay evidence is information obtained from another person and is considered secondhand evidence unless the expert can justify its use as reliable, valid, and customary practice.

Exclusionary Rule.   Sustained by the U.S. Supreme Court in *Miranda v. Arizona,* no information obtained against a defendant, from the defendant, may be admitted as evidence unless at the time the information was obtained, the defendant was made aware of his or her rights to remain silent and to have counsel, and that any information revealed could be used against the defendant in court.[6] Failure to read the defendant his or her rights is now a common basis for requesting exclusion of a defendant's admissions and confessions from the trial process or reversing the decision of a court that convicts after allowing such evidence to be admitted during trial.

The Supreme Court has ruled that information obtained during a standard mental health examination comes under the exclusionary rule. In *Estelle v. Smith,* the Court opined that unless the defendant was informed of the purposes to which examination results might be put, the testimony of the expert is to be considered inadmissible.[7] Figure 3.2 shows a written form

---

Apprisal of Rights

Name of Examinee _____ Date of Exam _____

This psychological examination to be conducted by _____
was scheduled at the request of

_____

_____

This agency retained _____ for this
examination.

The examination will consist of questions and psychological tests. These will be
used by _____ to write a psychologist report for the individual
or agency requesting this examination. The information in this report may be used
against me. The report and the tests will be available to my attorney(s).

This statement has been read to me and I understand it. I understand I have the
right to consult with my attorney if I have any question about this.

Signed _____

Examiner _____

Witness _____

FIGURE 3.2.   Appraisal of Rights form to be used with a defendant before conducting an evaluation.

useful in ensuring that the expert's opinion will not be excluded on the grounds that the defendant was deprived of constitutional safeguards against self-incrimination. Figure 3.3 presents the same rights material in Spanish. It is the responsibility of the examiner not only to read such rights but to ensure that they are understood by the examinee.

Since few attorneys provide experts with both the information and the forms to make sure that the examination of a defendant is not excluded from evidentiary consideration, it is important that experts be aware of this important issue and be prepared to protect the viability of their examination and anticipated testimony.

Some mental health experts suggest that their evaluation will be a step in obtaining professional help for the defendant with his or her problems. In a well-meaning effort to establish rapport, a mental health expert may suggest that he or she can try to obtain other professional services for the defendant. Even a promise of trying to get help for a defendant with emotional problems can result in evidence being excluded.[8] The expert must be very clear as to the purposes of the examination and to whom the report will be sent. No effort should be made to disguise or avoid the potentially negative adversary nature of the expert's examination.

Aviso de Derechos

Nombre del Examinado _____ Fecha del Examen _____

Este examen psicólogico, el cual sera conducido por _____
fue fijado a petición de

_____

_____

Esta agencia empleó _____ para conducir este examen.

El examen consistirá a la vez de preguntas y pruebas psicológicas. Basandose en estos datos _____ escribirá un informe psicológico para la agencia que ha pedido este examen. Los conocimientos contenidos en este informe podran ser usados en contra mía. El informe y las pruebas seran puestas a la disposición de mi abogado(s).

Me han leído esta declaración y yo la comprendo. Si tengo alguna duda acerca de esto, entiendo que yo tengo el derecho de consultar con mi abogado.

Firmado _____

Examinador _____

Testigo _____

FIGURE 3.3.   Appraisal of Rights rendered in Spanish.

Weights of Evidence.   Almost every intelligent layperson is familiar with the phrase "beyond a reasonable doubt." Few are familiar with the concept "weight of evidence" and how this forms a cornerstone of American jurisprudence.

Although decisions of small and large import are made by judges and juries, such decisions are not accidental or loosely developed. Among the structures and concepts that guide, shape, or restrict decision making in the courts is the *quality* or *weight* of the evidence relating to the decision to be made. The more serious the consequences to the defendant, whether in criminal or civil issues, the more stringent are the rules for weighing the quality of the evidence. The benefit of the doubt almost always falls to the defendant, especially in criminal cases, to ensure the fairness of the proceedings for the accused.

The lowest or weakest quality or weight of evidence is called *preponderance of evidence.* Although concepts of weight are not defined with mathematical precision, most jurists seem to accept the probability concept of "slightly better than chance," or "about 55% sure," as the defining parameter of preponderance of evidence. Although this parameter is rarely used against a defendant, a judge will decide or instruct a jury to decide if the weight of evidence is better than chance in such matters as whether the defendant was insane at the time of an alleged crime. Thus as much benefit of the doubt as possible is given the defendant.

A somewhat heavier weight of evidence is called *clear and convincing evidence.* In this instance, the statutes require that the judge and/or jury decide that the evidence is clear-cut in the direction of their decision. Some jurists are informally willing to define clear and convincing evidence as "75–80% sure." Again, numbers are seldom, if ever, used in defining this weight of evidence. In civil commitment hearings, such as whether an individual is incompetent to handle everyday affairs or is a danger to self or others, the standard for weight of evidence sufficient for a judicial commitment is now considered to be "clear and convincing evidence."[9]

The better-known *beyond reasonable doubt* represents the most stringent test of the quality of evidence. Evidence that is deemed of sufficient weight or validity so as to be virtually certain falls in this category. Some jurists are willing to say that beyond reasonable doubt means that the facts supported by evidence are "90–95% sure." Some judges instruct juries in such a way as to suggest that *any* doubt is reasonable doubt.

In some jurisdictions, a defense plea of innocent by reason of insanity places the burden on the state to prove, beyond reasonable doubt, that the defendant was sane at the time of the alleged crime. This is considered a more conservative requirement, increasing the probabilities of acquittal over the situation where the defense must prove the existence of insanity by the preponderance of evidence (Leo, 1982a). This is explored in greater detail in Chapter 8.

The Decision-Making Process.   Experts do not make judicial decisions. At no time is the expert witness to render an opinion as to the guilt, innocence, or liability of a defendant. When an expert does render an opinion regarding the key issue of guilt or liability, he or she is testifying to the ultimate question. This, in essence, makes the expert a Thirteenth Juror. Although this is allowed in some jurisdictions, it is strongly advised that expert witnesses avoid rendering such opinions. These decisions belong to the triers of fact. The judge and the jury deliberate and decide.

Juries are impaneled to hear cases, weigh evidence with the guidance and instructions of the presiding judge, and render a decision in the matter at hand. At bench trials, judicial hearings, and appellate reviews, judges alone render decisions and opinions.

Research suggests that most decisions by judges and juries are based on the quality of evidence (Kalven & Zeisel, 1966), although many tangential factors may influence decisions, such as the judge's bias, community standards and expectations, and individual prejudice among jurors. Since the quality and clarity of the evidence are the most powerful variables behind the decision-making process, the expert witness is in a key position to enhance this process through careful, substantial, clear, and appropriate testimony.

NOTES

1. *Addington v. Texas,* No. 77-5992. Brief for the Appellant. S.C. October Term, 1978.
2. *Parham v. J.L.,* No. 75-1690. Brief for the Appellant. S.C. October Term, 1977.
3. *Frye v. United States,* 293 F. 1013 (D.C. Cir. 1923).
4. *Daubert,* 113 S. Ct. 2786, 2795.
5. *United States v. Amaral,* 488 F.2d. 1148 (9th Cir. 1973).
6. *Miranda v. Arizona,* 394 U.S. 436 (1966).
7. *Estelle v. Smith,* 451 U.S. 454, 101 S. Ct. 1866, 68 L. Ed. 2d 359 (1981).
8. *People v. Hogan,* 647 P.2d 93 (Cal. 1982).
9. *Addington v. Texas,* 441 U.S. 418, 99 S. Ct. 1804, 60 L. Ed. 2d 323 (1979).

4

Preparing to Serve as an Expert Witness

$\mathbf{A}$s noted in Chapter 2, psychologists are called on to play many roles as experts in the courts. Procedures, techniques, and professional styles are bound to vary. The following recommended procedures will be appropriate for most situations in which the psychologist is asked to serve as an expert witness. Variations will undoubtedly occur, but they should stand the tests of being in the client's best interests and falling well within the expectancies and constraints of professional ethics, the law, and standards for the delivery of professional services. Although the expert may review literature, write a learned treatise, and serve as a rebuttal witness to attest to known and/or accepted scientific principles, the usual role of the expert is to perform a study or evaluation and render an opinion as to the meaning of the results in respect to issues in the legal case under consideration. The procedures outlined in this chapter should fit virtually all situations in which psychologists are asked to serve as expert witnesses.

GETTING STARTED

Sources of referral vary considerably, but a psychologist is most likely to be sought out by an attorney who has heard of or observed the psychologist's performance as an expert witness in another case. This means that getting started as an expert witness may be somewhat of a problem for a psychologist who has never served in this role. Experience as a member of a forensic center staff, juvenile or family court, or community agency where staff are called on to conduct forensic evaluations is helpful. An expert should have appropriate education and training in forensic matters through courses, workshops, and internship experience. An apprenticeship served as an assistant to an experienced forensic psychologist is the most direct modus operandi of entrance into a forensic practice.

Psychologists who have attained status and recognition in neuropsychology, behavioral medicine, child clinical psychology, marketing research, evaluation science, and other professional subspecialties may be approached to serve as experts by attorneys seeking a professional or scientist whose work and publications are related to significant issues in a particular case. It is easier for a psychologist who has achieved a measure of status and recognition in his or her subspecialty to become known as an expert witness than it is for an entrance-level psychologist, recently finished with education and training and anxious to enter the field of forensic psychology. Although entrance-level psychologists may be qualified to render expert opinion in their special area of professional skill or knowledge, attorneys tend to be drawn to known and/or tested experts.

Young, aspiring forensic psychologists need not be excluded. After acquiring the fundamental professional skills and postdoctoral training in forensic psychology, which is available through continuing education workshops and postdoctoral training institutes, neophyte experts can increase their visibility in a number of ways.

Becoming a part of the forensic psychology establishment will put the psychologist in touch with colleagues who can serve as mentors, sponsors, and sources of referral. Such opportunities include the Division of Psychology and the Law of the American Psychological Association and the Psychology-Law Society. Many state psychological associations have formed sections on psychology and the law. The professional psychologist who wishes to receive referrals for work with the courts must make his or her interest known to colleagues, attorneys, and the courts. A professional card sent out to announce one's interest and qualification can be helpful. Such announcements should be accurate and conservative. Figure 4.1 illustrates a general announcement that might be sent to selected colleagues, lawyers, and judges by a psychologist trained and prepared to offer forensic services.

The highest level of accreditation that can be achieved by the psychologist who intends to practice as an expert witness is the Diplomate of the American Board of Professional Psychology (ABPP). ABPP is the umbrella organization that grants the diploma in several areas of psychological

---

JANE W. DOE, Ph.D.
takes pleasure in announcing the addition of
FORENSIC CONSULTATION
to her practice of clinical and child psychology

Custodial evaluations	*Marital dissolution mediation*
Competency evaluation	*Assessment of psychological deficit*
24 Oak Ridge Parkway	Hours by appointment
Suite 127	
[Phone number]	

FIGURE 4.1. An announcement of forensic services by a professional psychologist.

practice. The Diplomate in Forensic Psychology attests that an established and accredited organization of peers has examined and accepted the psychologist as functioning at the highest level of excellence in his or her field of forensic competence. The qualifications for the Diplomate include good moral character, high professional standards, the doctoral degree in an accredited institution, and licensing or certification in the state in which the psychologist practices. Applicants must have 1,000 hours of experience in forensic psychology over a minimum of 5 years. Four of these years must be postdoctoral. Should the applicant have a law degree, this may substitute for 2 of the 5 years of experience. The applicant must have at least 100 hours of specialized training, supervision, or continuing education in their particular area as a forensic psychological practitioner.

The American Academy of Forensic Psychology is the education and training branch of the American Board of Forensic Psychology (ABFP). The Academy operates a continuing education program for forensic psychology, as well as providing a forum for the exchange of scientific information among its members. Acquiring the necessary hours to apply for the Diplomate in Forensic Psychology can be done through attendance at the ABFP workshops that are provided on a regular basis. These workshops are generally sponsored by the American Academy of Forensic Psychology. The entire membership directory of the American Academy of Forensic Psychology can be accessed on the Internet homepage http://www.abfp.com//aafp.

Each community has legal organizations that are interest groups (often referred to as the "criminal bar," the "matrimonial bar," etc.); these meet regularly, and an educational program is usually presented at each meeting. The forensic psychologist seeking recognition and referrals from the legal community can enhance visibility and offer a professional service to the various bars by offering to make presentations about psychology and the law to these groups.

Work that is carefully, ethically, and professionally done is the best source of referral and continuing respect from colleagues and the legal profession.

Academic psychologists generally become expert witnesses in the courts as a result of their being known as specialists in an area of behavioral science that attorneys have found to be useful in clarifying evidence. Academic psychologists are sought as experts in such areas as eyewitness identification; visual perception; and evaluation of the merit of research, memory, and opinion surveys. Publication and collegial respect are the usual routes by which lawyers seek out academic psychologists.

Part of the training leading to the doctorate in psychology is the ability to do research. This graduate training, which many professional psychologists believe ceases to be useful after graduation, is of great value to psychologists who intend to perform as an expert witness. Opinions rendered by expert witnesses in general must be supported by research and/or theory of a high quality. In addition to this psychological research that the psychologist has been trained to retrieve, it is sometimes useful for the expert witness to be familiar with legal research techniques (Knapp, Vandecreek, & Zirkel, 1985). It is important for the expert witness in psychology to understand that whatever statutory limits or constraints that may exist at any one time may change through legislative action or appellate court decisions. Thus, being familiar with the research techniques and facilities of the legal profession can be very useful in being able to support and set parameters on an expert psychologist's opinions.

At what point is the psychologist ready to be an expert witness? There is no distinct line of demarcation for this. The American Bar Association (1989) has established some standards and qualifications for appointment of experts by the court to perform forensic evaluations. These standards mandate that the expert have sufficient professional education and sufficient clinical training and experience to establish the clinical knowledge required for the specific type of evaluation being conducted and sufficient forensic knowledge gained through specialized training or an acceptable substitute to understand the relative legal matters and to satisfy the specific purpose for which the evaluation is being ordered.

For a general set of guidelines and constraints, the psychologist seeking to function as an expert witness would do well to be familiar with the various codes of ethics and principles of conduct that are currently available (Heilbrun, 1996). This will be discussed in greater detail in Chapter 15, with the various codes and principles available in Appendixes D, F, and H.

Of paramount importance in functioning as an expert witness, the psychologist must keep in mind that primary responsibility lies in conducting one's self in an ethical manner. Psychologists should never attempt to cope with the adversarial pressures of the legal system by imitating the attorneys and being adversarial in report writing and testifying (Cornell, 1987). Expert witnesses are visitors to the court, and not advocates.

STARTING A CASE

The Initial Interview

The initial contact in a forensic case is usually made by telephone. The attorney who wishes to retain the psychologist will ordinarily make a telephone call to discuss the case and to determine whether the psychologist is able and willing to participate as an expert witness. Occasionally, the telephone call is made by the attorney's paralegal assistant or secretary. In most cases, however, the psychologist can expect to hear directly from the attorney. If the psychologist is too busy to talk at some length (usually 15 to 30 minutes), the psychologist should arrange to call the attorney back when there is sufficient time to discuss the case and make an informed judgment based on the facts. In this situation, the psychologist should be sure to set a specific time to call the attorney, the same day if possible. As a courtesy to the attorney, the psychologist should decide early on whether to participate in the case.

During the initial portion of the telephone contact, the attorney ordinarily gives the psychologist a brief synopsis of the litigation in the form of "the facts of the case." This is legal terminology for the bare essentials that would be required to understand the source of the litigation and the remedies sought. It is important that the psychologist obtain the following information during this initial interview.

The Facts of the Case.   Psychologists will be pleased to find that most attorneys are quite expert at summarizing the essential facts of the case. If this does not occur during the initial phase of the telephone interview, the psychologist need only ask, "Could you please tell me the facts of the case, counselor?" In response, the attorney will ordinarily tell the psychologist the situation under which the case came about; whether the attorney represents the plaintiff or the defendant; the essential issues; and the kind of information, testimony, facts, or opinions that the attorney seeks to support the litigation effort. Exact details are usually unnecessary at this stage, since if the expert is willing to serve, volumes of material will be provided to help the expert understand the facts of the case in detail. During the initial interview, the expert must have sufficient information to decide whether his or her scientific or professional skills can be appropriately applied.

The Anticipated Court Date.   Depending on the kind of case involved, considerable time may be required for the psychologist to make appointments to conduct an examination, review literature, compose a learned thesis, or prepare in other ways. Some attorneys may call on their experts one or two weeks before the anticipated trial date. Some attorneys exert a good deal of pressure to convince the potential expert that his or her help is unique and very much needed. The psychologist should politely but firmly reject any efforts that would result in hurried evaluative procedures or the cutting of corners in any respect. Each expert must develop his or her own sense of how much time is necessary to work up a case. It is far better to err on the long side than the short side in requiring time to prepare properly. The expert should remember that it is usually necessary to consult with the attorney one or two times before a trial, and some time must be available for depositions to be taken by opposing attorneys. This should be discussed and clarified at the time of the initial interview.

Hypothetical Questions.   When a professional or scientific expert is retained by an attorney, no matter what the expert's skills or talents may be, the result planned by the retaining attorney will be the presentation of testimony by the expert that concludes with an opinion. The opinion is elicited by one or more *hypothetical questions* presented by the attorney.

The hypothetical question brings together and focuses all the issues in which the expert is involved and presents the jury with a simple, straightforward opinion or conclusion. Attorneys cannot tell exactly what their hypothetical questions will be before they have completed preparing their case, but they can certainly present some general statement that will help the expert understand the focus of the information to be provided. The reason for discussing this during the initial contact with the attorney is to ensure that the expert knows approximately what is expected. This allows the expert to determine whether to participate in the case. Examples of hypothetical questions might include: "Doctor, given all the facts of the case, as you know them and as they have been presented to the jury, within reasonable psychological probability is the defendant, Ms. Jones, suffering neuropsychological deficit?" Another example might be: "Given all the information that is available, and calling on your own background and research, doctor, is it your opinion that the witness, Mr. Smith, could make a clear, reliable eyewitness identification in this case?" And yet another: "Given the information that has been provided you, doctor, as well as your own extensive examination, is it your opinion as a professional psychologist that Mr. Green is able to understand the nature of the charges against him and the consequences that will accrue to him if convicted?" The purpose of asking for anticipated hypotheticals early on is to ensure that the psychologist understands what is expected and can state the likelihood of being in a position to render an opinion in the matters at hand.

The Condition and Availability of the Plaintiff. In the event that a psychological examination of a plaintiff or a defendant is required, the psychologist should determine from the retaining attorney whether there will be any difficulty having the individual come to the expert's offices for examination. At times, the attorney may require the psychologist to conduct the examination elsewhere. The place may not be conducive to a proper examination under standardized conditions. In some cases, a judge may have limited the number of hours that a plaintiff or defendant is available for evaluation, restricting the psychologist's opportunity to perform in an ethical, professional manner. Any such limitation should be known at the beginning of the consultation to ensure that a thorough and professional job can be done. If the proper conditions cannot be arranged by the retaining attorney, the psychologist should refuse the consultation.

Retrieval of Records. The opinion of the expert in any matter of litigation is but a small part of the entire process. Considerable information will have been collected by the time the psychologist is asked to consult. Although the expert will take a history in most instances, the analysis of records can form an important part of the process of coming to an opinion. Whether the matter involves a personal injury suit, product liability litigation, or exculpation because of mental status, background is important.

Hospital charts, school records, work records, and military records can be helpful in the evaluation process. During the initial interview, the psychologist should ask the attorney to obtain and forward such records. A letter from an attorney is much more likely to bring forth records from a bureaucratic organization than a request from a psychologist. The psychologist should encourage the attorney to pursue this promptly, so that the records are available as quickly as possible. It is helpful if lawyers know where to retrieve certain records. Current military service records can be obtained from:

> Commander
> Reserve Components Administration Center
> Attention: PAE-E
> 9700 Paige Boulevard
> St. Louis, MO 63132
> Telephone: (314) 263-3901

For those who have been in the military, and have received service from the Veterans Administration, these records can be obtained from:

> Records Processing Center
> P.O. Box 5020
> St. Louis, MO 63115
> Telephone: (314) 263-3772

If the litigation involves examination by other behavioral scientists, the lawyers should be encouraged to make the reports of these examinations available, particularly in respect to when they occurred. If testing is to be done, the expert must be sure that sufficient time has elapsed to avoid test-retest problems such as practice effect. Axelrod, Brines, and Rapport (1997) have studied the minimization of the effects of practice effect on the Wechsler scales and propose methods of estimating accurate intelligence scores on repeated tests.

Figure 4.2 presents the forensic intake form, which has been found to be useful for taking down significant information during the initial telephone interview and will allow the expert to have basic facts about the case readily available in the case folder. During the initial interview, the psychologist should ask the attorney whether he or she wishes to be called at home in the evening in the event some question arises or should the expert come to some conclusion during the evaluation. Many attorneys devote themselves intensely to their cases and have no objection to this.

Knowing the judge who will try the case and the jurisdiction of the litigation may be helpful in determining the kind of setting in which the litigation will take place. Judges are extremely individualistic, and as one becomes experienced as an expert witness, one comes to understand that

	Date _____
Attorney _____	Telephone _____
Firm _____	Home _____
Address _____	Fax _____
Case style _____	_____ Plaintiff (pros., pet.)
	_____ Defendant
Facts:	_____ Amicus curia
	_____ Court-appointed
Schedule:	To do:
Hypothetical questions:	Fees: Ret. $ _____
	DR. _____
	TR. _____
	Res. _____
Anticipated trial date _____	_____ Discuss fee structure
Judge _____	_____ Request initial letter
Court _____	_____ Designate as consultant
Assistant secretary to attorney _____	_____ Fees paid on 30-day basis
Additional:	_____ Will send agreement letter
	_____ Suggest retrieval of records and information
	_____ Discuss pretrial meeting
	_____ Confirming letter
	_____ First appointment
	_____ CV sent

FIGURE 4.2. Forensic intake form.

each judge conducts the courtroom in his or her own particular way. Part of being a competent expert involves understanding the expectancies of the court in terms of such matters as dress, decor, and style of presentation. This is explored in some detail in Chapter 13.

Most lawyers depend on a secretary or a paralegal assistant. During the case, the expert may want to know all kinds of information about the case that is more readily available from the lawyer's assistant than from the attorney. Knowing who the secretary is can be quite helpful. Ordinarily, the lawyer's secretary is aware of changes in court dates, availability of witnesses, and unusual aspects of the case and is the person with whom the expert can establish a working relationship that in some instances is extremely helpful in clarifying issues and avoiding misunderstandings. The psychologist or the psychologist's assistant usually will contact the attorney's secretary to make arrangements for the examination of litigants. All kinds of minutiae arise during litigation, and to deal with this, a close working relationship between the psychologist's office and the attorney's immediate assistant can be a helpful liaison.

Fee Arrangements.   It is important to discuss fee arrangements during the initial telephone interview. The expert should be sure that the retaining attorney understands the kinds of fees the psychologist will be charging and that the financial arrangements required by the expert are agreeable. During this interview, the expert should indicate his or her hourly fee for work to be done during the case. This may include research, constructing reports, conducting examinations, appearing at depositions, pretrial meetings, and the trial itself. Where the expert uses assistants, such as psychometricians or research associates, the attorney should be told of the fees for such services. It is strongly recommended that the psychologist charge the same fee for forensic work that is charged for any kind of clinical or professional work. During the course of a cross-examination, in open court, the opposing counsel might be very happy to find that the psychologist charges more for forensic work than for other professional work. This issue could be brought to the attention of the judge and jury, with intimations that the psychologist's presence is less a matter of objective, professional opinion than of an opportunity to increase his or her fees. By charging the same amount as for usual professional work, a psychologist can avoid this situation.

Any objections to the expert's fee structure should be stated at once by the attorney. Some attorneys work on a contingency basis and are reluctant to pay professional fees before the case is finished. This could take three or four years and places the psychologist under a considerable financial burden. Of more importance might be the issue of the expert being owed a large sum, unpaid at the time of testimony. To avoid this, once the fee arrangements are found to be acceptable, the psychologist might ask the attorney to forward a letter stating that the psychologist is retained as a consultant and that "all invoices forwarded by the expert will be honored on a 30-day basis."

The expert should beware of such reassurances as "Don't worry," "I will protect your fee," or "You will be paid promptly." Telephone agreement is insufficient. To avoid building large accounts receivable with various attorneys, forensic psychologists must insist on such a letter. If a lawyer is unwilling to do this, the psychologist should withdraw from the case. Figure 4.3 presents an attorney's retaining letter. Many experts prefer a more formalized agreement between the retaining attorney and the expert. Figure 4.4 presents a standard retainer letter as well as an accompanying terms of engagement.

During the initial telephone conversation, it is wise to mention to the attorney that after the report is submitted, a pretrial meeting is required before going to court. Although the attorney may have great confidence in the expert and believe such preparation unnecessary, it is extremely important that the kind of direct examination to be conducted should be thoroughly discussed before it takes place. The reasons for this are presented in detail in Chapter 13.

Jones, Farnham, Abercrombie, and Zilch
Attorneys at Law
Post Office Drawer 1276
Waukegan, Illinois 47209

Re: *Mulligan v. Consolidated Box Corp.*

Dear Doctor Jones:

Pursuant to our telephone conversation of June 7th, our firm would like to retain you as consultant in clinical psychology in the above-captioned matter. We represent the defendant in this case. Please send all invoices to this firm, and they will be honored within thirty (30) days of receipt.

Pursuant to our further discussion, copies of medical records, psychological reports, hospital records, and military records will be forwarded as they are received.

Thank you for agreeing to assist in this matter.

Very truly yours,
Albert B. Abercrombie

FIGURE 4.3.   Example of attorney's letter retaining a psychologist as expert witness.

PREPARING THE CASE FOLDER

Psychologists who are unfamiliar with the forensic area may begin their practice by setting up clinical folders similar to those they have used in their professional work. They will soon find that this will not do in forensic work. Attorneys produce large quantities of documents and frequently send copies to the expert, who must classify and file them.

Some attorneys use 8½-by-14-inch (legal-size) sheets in their work. It is hopeless to attempt to fit such documents into a standard clinical folder. The psychologist who intends to become a practicing forensic expert is urged to begin setting up legal files to ensure efficiency and accuracy. Attorneys have developed all kinds of helpful filing materials and equipment. It is strongly urged that psychologists activate a legal case folder after the initial telephone call has been completed and the case has been accepted.

A recommended type of case folder, either a legal-size, or standard-size two-partition, hardboard folder, as shown in Figure 4.5. As can be seen, this large folder has two inner partitions. The front cover, the back cover, and both sides of the two partitions have metal clips to hold paper that is punched at the top. This allows the psychologist to sort and classify the large variety of materials received during a legal consultation. During the depositions and at the court trial, the psychologist will be grateful for the time spent classifying and organizing the folders. It is embarrassing to search through a folder of loose papers when a specific question is asked. Preparing such a folder from the beginning will ensure that the expert can find and review materials about any aspect of the case at any time. Beginning in the early 1990s, many courts (and consequently attorneys) began to arrange

Ben A. Johnston, Ph.D., P.A.

DIPLOMATE, CLINICAL PSYCHOLOGY, AMERICAN BOARD OF PROFESSIONAL PSYCHOLOGY   CLINICAL PSYCHOLOGY

DIPLOMATE, AMERICAN BOARD OF FORENSIC PSYCHOLOGY   CHILD PSYCHOLOGY

DIPLOMATE, AMERICAN BOARD OF PROFESSIONAL NEUROPSYCHOLOGY   NEUROPSYCHOLOGY

789 East Ashley Boulevard   Doeville, USA 12345   Ph:(213)256-3579   Fax:(213)258-5106

December 30, 1997

R. B. Smith, Esquire
213 Elm Tower, Ste. 101
Anytown, IN 40176

Re: Engagement as Expert

Dear Counselor:

Thank you for retaining me to serve as an expert in connection with *Jones v. Smith.* My professional services will involve consulting with you and possibly conducting psychological evaluations in the referenced litigation. I hope that my work in this matter will lead to a mutually satisfactory relationship with you.

The purpose of this letter is to confirm my engagement as an expert and to provide you certain information concerning my fees, billing, and collection policies as well as other terms that will govern our relationship with you; I have found it a helpful practice to confirm with my clients the nature and terms of the arrangement.

My engagement as an expert began on December 21st, the date on which I was first contacted by your assistant, Ms. Brown, regarding this matter. Our engagement will be terminated at will by either of us, subject to payment of all fees for services performed and costs advanced through the date of termination.

Attached to this letter is a summary of my standard terms of engagement for services as an expert. Please review these policies and let me know if you have any questions.

I require a retainer in the amount of $3000.00 against which initial billings will be made. Fees for my personal time spent on this case will be billed at $350.00 per hour. Should examinations be required, test room time is billed at $100.00 per hour.

If the terms described above and in the attached summary are satisfactory to you, please so indicate by signing the enclosed copy of this letter and returning the signed copy to me.

Again, if you have any questions at all concerning the information contained in this letter or the attached summary, I would be pleased to hear from you.

I'm grateful for the opportunity to be able to work with you and your firm in connection with these matters. I look forward to hearing from you.

Sincerely yours,

Ben A. Johnston, Ph.D.

APPROVED: This _____ date of _____ , 1995.

BY: _____

BAJ/pab

(continued)

FIGURE 4.4.   Standard retainer letter and terms of agreement.

Ben A. Johnston, Ph.D., P.A.

DIPLOMATE, CLINICAL PSYCHOLOGY, AMERICAN BOARD OF PROFESSIONAL PSYCHOLOGY   CLINICAL PSYCHOLOGY
DIPLOMATE, AMERICAN BOARD OF FORENSIC PSYCHOLOGY   CHILD PSYCHOLOGY
DIPLOMATE, AMERICAN BOARD OF PROFESSIONAL NEUROPSYCHOLOGY   NEUROPSYCHOLOGY

789 East Ashley Boulevard   Doeville, USA 12345   Ph:(213)256-3579   Fax:(213)258-5106

TERMS OF ENGAGEMENT

I appreciate your decision to retain to me as your expert. My engagement is limited to the matter identified and the letter to which these terms of engagement are attached. The following summarizes my office's billing practices and certain other terms that will apply to our engagement:

1. We send our bills monthly throughout the engagement for a particular matter. Monthly statements are due when rendered. In instances in which we represent more than one attorney with respect to a matter, each person that we represent is jointly and severally liable for my fees with respect to the representation. My statements contain a concise summary of each matter for which professional services were rendered and a fee was charged.
2. When establishing fees for services I render, I am guided primarily by the time and labor required. I require a retainer in an amount which is appropriate with respect to the proposed professional tasks. Unless otherwise agreed, the retainer will be applied to the last statement rendered in connection with the professional work, with any unused portion being returned to the client.
3. I invite my clients to discuss freely with me any questions that may arise concerning a fee charge for any matter. I want my clients to be satisfied with both the quality of my professional services and the reasonableness of the fees that I charge for these services. I will attempt to provide as much detailed billing information as may be required in any customary form desired. I am willing to discuss with my clients any of the billing formats my office uses and that may best suit the client's needs.

In determining a reasonable fee for the time and labor required for a particular project, I take into account the skills, time demands, and other factors influencing the professional responsibility required for each matter. My internal allocation of values for my time as well as for my psychological assistant, research assistant, and other personnel changes periodically to account for increases in cost of delivering professional services and other economic factors.

Services based on hourly rates are applied perspectively as well as to unbilled time previously expended. My office records and bills time in one-quarter hour (15-minute) increments.

In addition to my professional fees, my statements may include out-of-pocket expenses that my office has advanced on behalf of the client or the client's project.

During the course of my service, it may be appropriate or necessary to hire third parties to provide services on behalf of the project. These services may include such things as consultation with other experts, psychological assistants, or research assistants.

If my monthly statements are not paid within 60 days after they are rendered, I reserve the right to discontinue services until the account is brought current. Additionally,

FIGURE 4.4. *(Continued)*

if my statement has not been paid within 30 days from the date of the statement, I automatically impose an interest charge of 1.25 percent per month (15 percent annual percentage rate) from the 30th day after the day of the statement until it is paid in full. Interest charges apply to specific monthly statements on an individual statement basis. Any payments made on past due statements are applied first to the oldest outstanding statement. I am entitled to attorney's fees and costs if collection activities are necessary.

I will provide my services as an expert in accordance with the engagement letter that accompanies this attachment. You will provide me with such factual information and materials as I require to perform the services identified in the engagement letter. I will keep you advised of developments as necessary to ensure the timely, effective, and efficient completion of my work.

Regarding the ethics of my profession that will govern my behavior, several points deserve emphasis. As a matter of professional responsibility, I am required to preserve the confidence and secrets of my clients as well as my patients. This obligation and the legal privilege for our communications exist to encourage candid and complete communication. I can perform truly beneficial services for a client only if I am aware of all information that might be relevant to my work as an expert. Consequently, I trust that our relationship with you will be based on mutual confidence and unrestrained communication that will facilitate my proper service to you.

Because my professional activities are national and international in scope, I may be (and sometimes am) asked to represent a client with respect to interests that are adverse to those of another client who I represent in connection with another matter. During the term of this agreement, I agree that I will not accept representation of another client to pursue interests that are directly adverse to your interests unless and until I have made full disclosure to you of all the relevant facts, circumstances, and implications of my undertaking two representations and you have consented to my representation of the other client. In turn, you agree that you will be reasonable in evaluating such circumstances and you will give your consent if we can confirm to you in good faith that the following criteria are met:

1. There is no substantial relationship between any matter in which I am serving you and the matter for the other client.
2. My delivery of professional services to the other client will not implicate any confidential information that I have received from you.
3. My work for you and the discharge of my professional responsibilities to you will not be prejudiced by the other client, for the other client has also consented in writing based on full disclosure of the relevant facts, circumstances, and implications of my undertaking the two representations.

By making this agreement, we are establishing the criteria that will govern the exercise of your right under applicable ethical rules to withhold consent to my representation of another client whose interest is adverse to yours. You will retain the right of course to contest in good faith my representation that the criteria have been met, in which event I would have the burden of supporting my representation to you.

Upon completion of the matter to which this agreement applies, or upon earlier termination of our relationship, the relationship will end unless you and I have expressly agreed to continuation with respect to other matters. The representation is terminable at will by either party subject to ethical restraints and the payment of all fees and costs.

Your agreement to this engagement constitutes your acceptance of the foregoing terms and conditions. If any of them is unacceptable to you, please advise me now so that we can resolve any differences and proceed with a clear, complete, and consistent understanding of our relationship.

FIGURE 4.4. *(Continued)*

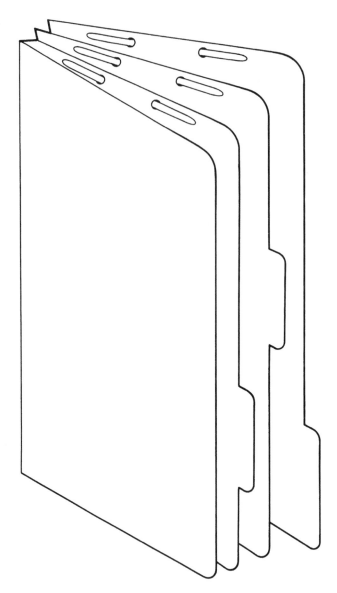

FIGURE 4.5. Legal case folder.

their paperwork in the 8½-by-11-inch format. Thus, the necessity of a larger file folder has begun to disappear. If the case involves legal matters extending back a number of years, the larger folder will be necessary for the psychologist to classify and organize materials; otherwise, the same type of folder is now available for the 8½-by-11 format.

Setting up classifications within the case folder is a matter of individual taste. For a professional clinical psychologist, the tabs might be:

1. Tests, working notes, and final report.
2. Initiating documents and letters from retaining attorney.
3. Reports and records from other sources.
4. Depositions and conference notes.
5. Subpoenas, case chronology and material delivery, and other correspondence.
6. Fees and miscellaneous matters.

Figure 4.6 shows a charge schedule that has been found to be useful. Experts should understand that lawyers keep such a charge sheet for their own billable hours and understand it thoroughly. By submitting a copy of such a charge sheet with invoices, the expert provides the lawyer with a clear picture of exactly what the expert did and how much time was spent on each task. It should be noted that the federal identification number is

Theodore H. Blau, Ph.D., P.A.
213 E. Main St.
Tampa, Fla. 33808
Fed. ID No. 00-0000000
Charge Schedule

Case _____ No. _____

Date	Staff Person	Function	Time	Amount

FIGURE 4.6.   Charge sheet for recording and summarizing fees.

included since some firms have checks issued by insurance companies that require such a number. Providing it on the charge sheet avoids unnecessary correspondence and delay in payment.

Psychologists ordinarily do not charge for telephone time in their professional practice. In forensic matters, the expert will find that lawyers often consult by telephone since it is convenient and practical. When such consultations take place, it is perfectly legitimate to place a charge on the charge sheet based on the amount of time actually utilized. Attorneys do this, and they expect it of their consultants.

Useful Forms

There are no standards, as such, for the forms and procedures to be used by the psychologist in preparing to serve as expert witness. The forms recommended here were designed to ensure an orderly preparation of materials and procedures as the consultation develops. They are products of experience, both positive and negative. The psychologist who intends to perform at a high level of professional skill, competence, and efficiency should be aware that, when consulting with attorneys or working within the court system, a much greater degree of detail and supportive documentation is likely to be necessary than in the conduct of general professional practice. Lawyers and judges are usually very concerned about when things happened, what was said, who said it, and where it happened. The expert-aspirant is well advised to err in the direction of excessive detail at the beginning, later developing forms, procedures, and systems dictated by personal experience.

As a rule, all contacts relating to the litigation should be noted, dated, and initialed by the person who made the contact, whether it be the psychologist, secretary, psychometrician, or receptionist. There is no way of predicting just what information will be required of the expert when he or she is finally called on to be deposed or to testify at the trial, so it is wise to have all this information available.

Case Chronology Form.   Once the initial lawyer-psychologist contact is made, there are various styles in which a case develops. Each consultation is somewhat different. The expert can expect to be called on, by either the retaining attorney or the attorney for the opposition, to specify how the expert was retained and by whom. Questions are commonly asked during trial about when the expert did things, received information, or forwarded reports. Figure 4.7 presents a form that has been found to be useful in keeping a record of the chronology of events in a case.

Beginning with the intake call, all telephone calls, conferences, receipt of materials from the retaining attorney, examination sessions, report writing, and report forwarding (including letters) should be noted as each event occurs. The psychologist should record how much time was spent during those contacts in which any work was done on the case or any discussion

Case Chronology

Case _____ Number _____

Date	Contact	Time

FIGURE 4.7. A form to record all significant events as the case develops.

with the attorney or key figures took place. Again, it is a matter of personal style, experience, and judgment as to the detail recorded on this form.

Case Material Delivery. In a complex case or one that extends over a period of time, the psychologist may wish to abstract from the case chronology a sequential list of materials received and forwarded. Hospital records, academic transcripts, professional reports, and legal citations are commonly forwarded to experts by legal counsel. The psychologist may return some of these, and send research reprints or other learned treatise material and reports to the retaining attorney.

Copies of material may be sent to the adversary attorney (in response to a subpoena). These exchanges should be noted for quick reference if the information is required during a deposition or the trial. Figure 4.8 presents a case material delivery log or record. Parenthetically, all important material, such as reports, should be sent by certified mail, with a return receipt requested.

Pretrial Checklist. As a forensic case develops, the psychologist may find that while the trial date approaches, important preparatory steps can be forgotten. In a complex case, preparing for trial can be a busy and demanding experience. To ensure that the psychologist is indeed prepared to perform as an expert, a checklist of necessary procedures and preparations

Case Material Delivery

Date	Material	Sent by or Received by

FIGURE 4.8.   A case material delivery form.

can be helpful. Finding oneself on the witness stand looking for something that was not done or was not prepared is a disconcerting experience. Such embarrassing moments are viewed by most attorneys as evidence of poor professional competence. Figure 4.9 presents a checklist that covers most of the important tasks in preparing to testify as an expert and is useful in reviewing the status of the case.

The nature and purpose of items that seem unfamiliar at this point will become clear as they are addressed in subsequent chapters.

COLLECTING PRELIMINARY DATA FOR DECISION MAKING

The psychologist retained by an attorney to function as an expert is expected to produce an opinion. The most credible expert opinions are usually the result of a process in which the expert collects extensive materials, conducts necessary evaluations under properly controlled conditions, and prepares, with great care, a document stating opinions or findings in a thorough, reasonable, and supportable manner. The findings may not always be to the retaining attorney's liking. When the expert's findings are not supportive of the attorney's case, the retaining attorney may thank the psychologist and tell him or her that the findings and opinion will not be used. This is proper and ethical. The decision as to whether the psychologist's findings will be used lies entirely in the hands of the attorney who is in charge of the case. This in no way should influence how thoroughly the

Pretrial Checklist

Preliminary
____ Referral letter from attorney received.
____ Hypothetical questions.
____ Curriculum vitae sent to attorney.
____ Vitae annotated for this case.
____ All appointments checked and verified.
____ Case chronology form started.

Process
____ Reports and records annotated and indexed.
____ All interviews and examinations completed.
____ All background material reviewed.
____ Observation notes complete.
____ All materials dated and initialed.
____ Preliminary report to retaining attorney.
____ All test scoring double-checked.
____ Report written and forwarded.
____ Conference with retaining attorney to review findings.

Preparation for Court—Preliminary
____ Review all materials.
____ Review own deposition.
____ Prepare special items for cue book (test reviews, learned treatise support).
____ Prepare charts and illustrations (rough).
____ Prepare qualifying questions for attorney.

Preparation for Court—Final
____ Prepare charts and illustrations (final).
____ Final conference with retaining attorney.
____ Prepare direct-examination questions for retaining attorney.
____ Location of courtroom and time expected.
____ Last-minute check with attorney's assistant to ensure case has not been settled or postponed.

FIGURE 4.9.   A pretrial checklist.

psychologist prepares. All legal consultations should be conducted with the expectancy that the psychologist will be prepared to render an expert opinion based on his or her best professional knowledge and skills.

Psychological evaluations prepared properly for court are frequently more extensive and detailed than customary psychological assessments. Time constraints are usually less stringent in forensic work than in professional practice. Extensive background data and materials are often available to the forensic psychologist, which would be difficult, impossible, or unnecessary to obtain during a usual psychological assessment. Often, but not invariably, financial resources are available for sophisticated or unusual procedures (a full battery of vocational aptitude tests, sequential repetitions of neuropsychological assessments, preliminary rehabilitation procedures, or retrieval and analysis of military or school records). Much of this may have little to do with the assessment process but is necessary to ensure that the expert can respond to even tangential questions by an adversary attorney during trial.

Facts of the Case

Although the psychologist has been given a summary of the facts of the case by the attorney, the expert can expect an array of materials from the attorney that will provide details of the circumstances that led to the civil or criminal action. The materials may include a detailed patent or copyright search in a trademark suit, police and emergency room reports in a personal injury case, or police reports in a criminal case. The more thoroughly a psychologist understands the facts of the case and the issues to be resolved in the litigation, the more effective he or she can be as an expert witness. Some attorneys forward legal citations, rules of evidence, judge's instructions, and other materials to help the expert witness understand more clearly the facts of the case and the legal issues involved. If such material is not forthcoming, it is always appropriate to ask the attorney who retains the psychologist to forward such material when it is likely to be helpful.

After reviewing the records associated with the facts of the case, it is suggested that the psychologist write an abstract of these facts to ensure that the expert's services are being utilized with appropriate understanding and focus. The following illustrates such an abstract.

FACTS OF THE CASE

Wright v. Alameda Power Co.

James Wright, age 12 at the time, climbed a tree in his backyard to retrieve a lost kite. While reaching for the kite, his arm touched a high-voltage electric line. The electrical charge threw Jim from the tree. He dropped approximately 25 feet to the ground, unconscious from the electrical shock. His friend, who watched these events, called Jimmy's mother. They put the dazed boy in the family car and drove him to the emergency room of the local hospital. Though conscious on admission, Jim was in severe shock. Burns to his right arm were so extensive that the surgical team at the hospital amputated the arm just above the elbow. Jim seemed to recover well from the trauma and the surgery.

Jimmy is now 15 years of age. During the two years subsequent to the accident, Jimmy's family reports that he had become a very aggressive behavior problem. He bullies younger children. He is passing none of his school subjects. He seems to have memory loss and confusion at times. The family says he is "very changed" since the accident.

The firm of Sloane and Witty, representing James Wright and his parents, has filed suit against the Alameda Power Company claiming Jim is irreparably brain damaged and severely disturbed emotionally as a result of this accident.

It is sometimes helpful to check the summary with the retaining attorney to ensure that the details are accurate and complete. When the expert's final report is written, this statement can serve as an introduction to the report.

Records

In many instances, particularly in personal injury cases, when the expert is asked for an opinion, it is in reference to a plaintiff's or defendant's previous status. In the facts of the preceding case, the plaintiff's attorneys claim that James Wright is brain damaged and emotionally disturbed as a result of his accident. This assumes that these conditions did not exist before the accident. School records, records of guidance counselors, family physicians, and other sources may shed light on premorbid status. Treatment records before and after the accident, reports of neurological and psychological examinations, and standardized school tests—before and after the accident—can be of value in determining psychological status at different times in a subject's life.

The psychologist may wish to retrieve consumer survey reports in a trademark infringement suit or sunset tables in an eyewitness identification issue where the relation of visual acuity to ambient illumination is important. In the insanity defense, police records; statements of friends, relatives, and casual observers; treatment records; and other behavioral records of the defendant's activities and demeanor before, during, and after the crime can be useful to the expert preparing to give an opinion as to a person's probable mental state. The more objective or replicated the records or observations, the more useful they tend to be. All available records that are associated with the facts of the case should be retrieved, reviewed, and analyzed.

As with the facts of the case, records may be summarized to advantage and may serve as part of the final report. Such a summary of records was made for the case of *Wright v. Alameda Power Company.*

SUMMARY OF RECORDS

Wright v. Alameda Power Co.

Medical Records.   Jimmy Wright was brought to the emergency room of Alameda Community Hospital at 2:40 P.M. on June 29, 1977. Emergency room records indicate that he was conscious but dazed and apparently in shock. A very severe electrical burn of the right arm extending from the wrist to above the elbow was treated by the triage team, and the boy was immediately sent to surgery. James E. Watts, M.D., orthopedic surgeon, headed the team which amputated Jimmy's right arm. Postoperative course was indicated as normal, and the physicians' notes state that Jimmy "tolerated the procedure well and recovered with no unusual sequelae." Postoperative visits with Dr. Watts note good progress.

Reports from rehabilitation services indicate that Jimmy has been resistant to learning to use a prosthesis. Consultants urged no pressure in this issue in view of Jimmy's rapid physical growth during the past two years.

At present, medical reports state that Jimmy is a healthy 15-year-old, ready to be fitted with a prosthesis for his right arm. He seems more interested in this now than last year and plans are proceeding to arrange for fitting and training.

Academic Records.   School records from the Alameda School District, the McFarlane School, are quite complete. Jimmy started the first grade at age 7 years. He did poorly and was referred to the school psychologist for evaluation. A WISC-R at age 8 years, 1 month, dated November, 16, 1973, was reported as follows:

Factor	Deviation IQ	Percentile
Verbal scale	77	7th
Performance scale	81	10th
Full scale	77	7th

In the second grade, Jimmy was placed in a class for slow learners. Notations on the school records indicate that his teachers saw him as aggressive, unsociable, and bullying. The school psychologist notes "family problems." He failed and repeated the third grade.

Jimmy was returned to regular classes in the fourth grade. He repeated the fourth grade and entered the fifth grade at age 12. Standardized Metropolitan Achievement Tests reported on the school record during the fifth grade showed the following:

Factor	Grade Equivalent
Reading comprehension	2.6
Arithmetic	2.7
Language	2.2

After he entered the sixth grade at 13, three months after his accident, his record shows "satisfactory" progress. He entered the seventh grade, moving to LaBrea Junior High School. A referral to the school counselor for aggressive behavior in the classroom was followed by an assessment by the school psychologist. A WISC-R dated November 14, 1982, when Jimmy was 14 years, 1 month, of age was reported as follows:

Factor	Deviation IQ	Percentile
Verbal scale	81	10th
Performance scale	87	20th
Full scale	83	14th

The record shows that Jimmy passed shop, physical education, and American history. He failed functional math and English.

Psychological Records. Jimmy was examined by Arnold W. Pallac, Ph.D., at the request of Jimmy's attorneys during spring 1983. His psychological report includes the following results of a WISC-R:

Factor	Deviation IQ	Percentile
Verbal scale	84	16th
Performance scale	88	21st
Full scale	85	18th

Dr. Pallac also indicates that a Halstead Reitan Neuropsychological Battery (partial) indicates "signs of significant brain disorder." No Impairment Index was reported. Wide Range Achievement Test results were as follows:

Factor	Grade Equivalent
Reading	5.8
Arithmetic	5.6
Spelling	5.1

Dr. Pallac administered an MMPI as well as Draw-a-Person and Sentence Completion tests. He reports that Jimmy is depressed, withdrawn, and "suffering a severe posttraumatic depression." Dr. Pallac makes no mention in his report of having examined previous school records or other data. Dr. Pallac opined that all of these defects resulted from the accident and that Jimmy was of "at least normal intelligence before his accident."

These summaries make it quite clear that a careful review of academic and psychological records can be critical to a proper professional evaluation. Dr. Pallac's omission became the source of considerable embarrassment when he was cross-examined in court.

Literature Review

The psychologist who intends to act as an expert witness will be expected to be reasonably familiar with the scientific literature associated with the case at hand. Guesses, vague recall, and evasions are unacceptable. The reliabilities and validities of all test instruments that make their appearance in the case should be known. A photocopy of the *Mental Measurements Yearbook* (Conoley & Impara, 1933–1995) citation of each test given in the case should be made part of the case folder for reference at the trial. The psychologist will be put forth as an expert at court and must make every effort to meet this expectation. In the case of *Wright v. Alameda Power Company*, the psychologist retained by counsel for the plaintiff claimed that Jimmy's condition is best described as that of a "brain-disordered youngster suffering a chronic posttraumatic neurosis." As either a collaborating or opposing witness, one would be remiss not to review the *DSM-IV* descriptions of these conditions (American Psychiatric Association, 1994) and the more recent research concerning these diagnostic categories.

THE NEEDS-ASSESSMENT

Given the information and materials which have been collected, the psychologist should be able to formulate a needs-assessment of his or her role in the case. This "gap analysis" (Kaufman & English, 1979) identifies the scope of the assessment task. The general basis of the needs-assessment is found in the retaining attorney's original request for consultation, which, in turn, should be made clearer by the hypothetical questions the attorney suggests during the initial contact. The needs-assessment is a formal or informal process whereby the psychologist determines the gap between currently available information and the information that will be necessary before an expert opinion on the matter at hand can be rendered. The strategies chosen to fill the gap represent the psychologist's skill and expertise. They also will represent the basis and justification for the expert's opinion.

The needs-assessment may result in a relatively simple gap as in a disability determination, "Is there objective evidence that the plaintiff is mentally retarded?" Complex gaps are more the rule than the exception and can include various issues, such as the insanity defense (Chapter 8), "At the time of the crime, was the defendant able to appreciate that what he did was unlawful?" or in change of venue issues (Chapter 14), "Is community awareness and prejudice such that the defendant may not be assured of a fair and impartial jury?"

The character, quality, and extent of the opinions the psychologist is expected to render in court should be as clear as possible before deciding on and implementing strategies to reach those opinions.

STRATEGY SELECTION AND IMPLEMENTATION

It is here that solid psychological background and assessment skills are required. There is rarely "one and only one" approach to psychological assessment or evaluation. The experienced, competent professional psychologist will be prepared to review all strategies and select those most appropriate and available for the task at hand. Whether the strategic options involve testing procedures to be used in determining the presence or absence of psychological deficit in a personal injury case (Chapter 11) or the kinds of interviews, evaluations, and record review required for an opinion in a child custody matter (Chapter 10), certain guidelines are helpful in selecting the strategies to be implemented:

1. **Are the Strategies Available?** In a jury evaluation project, the psychologist may recommend a sophisticated procedure, such as a base-rate demographic study of the voters' registration list in a community; however, if the local laws forbid using that list, the strategy may not be used.

2. **Are the Strategies Ethical?** The psychologist must be sure that any procedure, test, evaluation, or assessment done is well within the American Psychological Association (APA) code of ethics (APA, 1992) and the APA standards for the delivery of psychological services (APA, 1977). The expert witness should be especially aware of the Specialty Guidelines for Forensic Psychologists formulated by the Committee on Ethical Guidelines for Forensic Psychologists (1991). (For details, see Chapter 15 and Appendixes F and H.)

3. **Are the Strategies Professionally Acceptable?** Anything that the psychologist chooses to do in order to come to an opinion will be reviewed and possibly challenged during a deposition or at the trial. All procedures should be such that they have general acceptance in the profession and represent acceptable practice and procedures.

4. **Are the Strategies Practical?** Such factors as cost, personal agreeability to all parties, and time constraints must be taken into consideration. In some cases, the psychologist may feel certain procedures are vital to support an expert opinion, whereas the attorney or the attorney's clients may see them as unacceptable. In such cases, the psychologist should ordinarily withdraw from the case. An example of this might be when a psychologist is asked to render an expert opinion on prison conditions and the attorneys for the state are unwilling to agree to release pertinent records.

No set of procedures can create or replace training, experience, and good judgment. Guidelines presented here must be used or adapted intelligently by the psychologist, choosing among various strategies and techniques to gather sufficient information to formulate and support an expert opinion. The competent professional will avoid redundant or unnecessary strategies. In choosing a strategy, the psychologist must always keep in mind the question of how the information resulting from the procedure will relate to the requirements for the expert's opinions at court in the matter at hand.

Implementation

Once the psychologist has decided on the test battery, the evaluation study, or whatever procedure will constitute the data collection phase of the preparation, it is essential that these be carried out in such a way that the procedures cannot be reasonably assailed by an opposing attorney. Tests should be administered in standardized style in an appropriate setting. During the implementation stage of the psychologist's work, preliminary results should be analyzed and, where appropriate, communicated to the retaining attorney. In some instances, interim or formative results may suggest additional strategies. In some cases, early results may suggest that the expert's opinion will *not* add support to the retaining attorney's case. The decision whether to continue lies with the retaining attorney. Some experts become indignant when an attorney decides the expert's services and opinion will not be used when the initial or final results indicate information adverse to the case at hand. A clearer understanding of the adversary process in American jurisprudence would be helpful for psychologists who react in this manner. The expert's job is to provide an attorney with an opinion on some psychological matter related to the case at hand. If that opinion is not supportive of the attorney's legal efforts on behalf of the client, the attorney may choose not to use the psychological expert.

OUTCOMES

Whatever the type of case for which a psychologist is retained as an expert witness, there must be an outcome or a product. In a forensic consultation, the outcome is presented in the expert's testimony during a deposition or in a court of law. At that time, the psychologist identifies himself or herself, states what he or she has done, and renders an opinion. Before this happens, the psychologist will ordinarily finish a series of psychological tests, examine documents, review research, or conduct research or evaluative studies. The psychologist will come to conclusions and form opinions. A report of all of this constitutes the objective summary of the expert's work.

As soon as the outcomes, carefully checked and reviewed, are available, the psychologist should call the attorney and discuss the findings. This preliminary report should be rendered as early as possible so that the attorney who retained the psychologist can begin to consider the most appropriate trial strategy for using the psychologist's information. Many personal injury suits are settled once the experts' opinions are available.

Following the preliminary report, in clinical assessments, a written report is mandatory. Some attorneys may ask the psychologist not to write a report until late in the judicial proceedings. This strategy is questionable, and the psychologist should simply tell the attorney who suggests it that the report must be written as part of the psychologist's professional and ethical requirements. Four guidelines for such reports may be helpful:

1. **Focus.**   The introduction, procedures, and conclusions of the report must focus on the issues of the case.
2. **Clarity.**   Jargon, obscure terms, and erudition should be avoided.
3. **Validity.**   The psychologist must render no findings in a forensic report that cannot be substantiated and supported in a relatively objective way.
4. **Opinion.**   The forensic report must conclude with an opinion or opinions based on the information in the report and responsive to the hypothetical questions posed at the beginning of the case by the attorney retaining the psychologist.

Because of the many areas of knowledge and professional activity in psychology, there is a consequent variety of needs-assessments, strategies, and outcomes available to deal with the expectations of lawyers and judges in the rapidly developing relationship between psychology and the law. Basic principles will apply but an ever-widening range of forensic applications of psychological knowledge and practice can be expected.

5

Admissibility

The expert witness is one whose education or specialized experience results in superior knowledge about a technical or scientific subject. The role of the expert is to render information that will enable those on a jury or a judge without the expert's training or experience to form an accurate opinion or a correct conclusion. For the triers of fact, the expert witness serves as a teacher during the trial process.

Whether an expert, no matter his or her qualifications, will actually testify is determined by the *admissibility* of the information, inferences, and opinions the expert intends to present. The presiding judge makes the decision as to whether an expert (or any witness) may testify.

THE *FRYE* RULE

For the better part of the 20th century, the admissibility of expert scientific or technical testimony was governed by the *Frye rule*[1] (Appendix A). *Frye* is known as the "general acceptance rule." Briefly, this rule required that an expert's opinion be based on information, data, or conclusions that were generally accepted by the majority of those in the expert's field.

THE *FEDERAL RULES OF EVIDENCE*

Beginning in 1973, the *Federal Rules of Evidence* began to address the admissibility rules with specific application to evidence presented by experts. The issues are delineated in Rules 401, 402, 702, and 703 (see Appendix C).

Rule 401. Definition of Relevant Evidence.   "Relevant evidence" means evidence having any tendency to make the existence of any fact that is of consequence to the determination of the action more probable than it would be without the evidence.

In this rule, we see the acknowledgment of the federal courts that probability is a viable and necessary component of evidentiary matters.

Rule 402. Relevant Evidence Generally Admissible: Irrelevant Evidence Inadmissible.   All relevant evidence is admissible except as otherwise provided by the Constitution of the United States, by Act of Congress, by these rules, or by other rules prescribed by the Supreme Court pursuant to statutory authority. Evidence which is not relevant is not admissible.

This ruling enables federal judges to impose basic limitations on the admissibility of relevant evidence. An example would be where an expert, while examining a defendant, elicits an incriminating statement in violation of the accused's right to counsel.[2]

Rule 702. Testimony by Experts.   If scientific, technical, or other specialized knowledge will assist the trier of fact to understand the evidence or to determine a fact in issue, a witness qualified as an expert by knowledge, skill, experience, training, or education, may testify thereto in the form of an opinion or otherwise.

This rule addresses two very important aspects of expert testimony: *technical* as well as *scientific* expertise is ruled acceptable and the right of the expert to formulate an opinion is acknowledged. These issues are explored later in this chapter.

Rule 703. Bases of Opinion Testimony by Experts.   The facts or data in the particular case upon which an expert bases an opinion or inference may be those perceived by or made known to the expert at or before the hearing. If of a type reasonably relied upon by experts in the particular field in forming opinions or inferences upon the subject, the facts or data need not be admissible in evidence.

This rule allows the expert to generate an opinion based on information other than that obtained first hand in the traditional procedures of his or her profession. This could include information gleaned from observations in the courtroom as well as from numerous sources that may be relied on clinically or professionally.

These *Federal Rules* raised questions as to the sufficiency of the *Frye* rule. Some courts depended on the new *Federal Rules* while others continued to be guided by the traditional and long-standing general acceptance position (Racine, Lindeman, & Davis, 1995).

ENTER *DAUBERT*

In the summer of 1993, 70 years after their earlier brethren enunciated *Frye,* the Supreme Court rejected the general acceptance rule in *Daubert v. Dow Pharmaceuticals Inc.*[3] (see Appendix A). The Court's position in *Daubert* emphasized the primacy of the *Federal Rules of Evidence* in determining the admissibility of expert testimony. "Reliability and relevance" was to be required. Four factors would be the litmus tests of the admissibility of expert scientific testimony:

1. Whether a theory or technique has been or could be tested.
2. Whether the theory or technique has been subject to peer review and publication.
3. The known or potential rate of error.
4. The "general acceptance" of the theory.

Daubert rejected the standard of *Frye* and replaced it with a more flexible view emphasizing the methodology and theoretical bases of expert opinion rather than conclusionary statements. The *Federal Rules of Evidence* would hereafter apply (Mack, 1994).

There has been no general agreement as to whether *Daubert* loosened or tightened *Frye* requirements for expert scientific testimony. For example, in *Joiner v. General Electric Co.*[4] the court said:

> In analyzing the admissibility of expert testimony, it is important for trial courts to keep in mind the separate functions of judge and jury, and the intent of *Daubert* to loosen the strictures of *Frye* and make it easier to present legitimate conflicting views of experts for the jury's consideration.

In a contrarian opinion rendered in *Cavallo v. Star Enterprises,*[5] the court opined:

> Prior to *Daubert,* courts presented with this situation may have been more inclined to admit the expert testimony and allow the jury, aided by vigorous cross-examination, to sort out the relative reliability of opposing expert opinions. But *Daubert* recognized the danger in this approach. . . . *Daubert* assigned district courts a more vigorous role to play in ferreting out expert opinions not based on the scientific method.

It is clear that the *Frye* rule is no longer definitive at the federal level, but the concept of *general acceptance* will continue to be considered when judges decide as to the admissibility of scientific or technical expert testimony. Since judges are rarely scientists, they are bound to have some difficulty in determining scientific questions (Simon, 1993).

ADMISSIBILITY AND EXPERT PSYCHOLOGICAL TESTIMONY

Testimony by psychologist-experts may range from purely subjective clinical opinion to research-based pronouncements. Often psychological testimony is a blend of these. The courts may not apply *Daubert* to expert opinion of a subjective nature. This is particularly true in state courts.

Some choose to use the *Federal Rules* as their guideline while others are free to adopt their own standards (Rotgers & Barrett, 1996).

Sometimes experts present clinical opinion as "scientific." The guidelines set forth in the *Daubert* ruling will probably be used more frequently in the future to question such assertions.

Where the expert testifies on the basis of technology, the *Daubert* standards may or may not apply. In such cases, the expert witness may be expected to state what standards promulgated by the expert's professional organization were adhered to in formulating an opinion. An example would be an opinion rendered by a psychologist as an expert "within reasonable psychological probability" based on psychological tests. The court may expect the expert to justify the testimony based on the tests' validity and reliability as defined by standards recommended by the American Psychological Association and other testing groups (American Educational Research Association et al., 1985).

GUIDELINES FOR PSYCHOLOGISTS TESTIFYING AS EXPERTS

How is admissibility to guide psychologists as they prepare to render expert testimony and opinions? This will depend to some extent on the kind of psychologist as well as the content of the testimony and opinion. Testimony based on clinical experience alone is more likely than ever before to be ruled inadmissible. Clinical psychologists who testify as experts are likely to be expected to refer to the most scientifically tested theories and methodologies in formulating opinions (Goodman-Delahunty, 1997; Rotgers & Barrett, 1996). Experimental psychologists who testify as experts represent a group that more frequently refers to rigorous empirical research conducted with due regard and adherence to generally recognized scientific methodology. Even here, anomalies may occur. One example is the area of testimony involving the accuracy and reliability of eyewitness identification. A respectable body of psychological research on the credibility of eyewitness testimony spans more than 100 years of psychological literature. Well-regarded experimental psychologists have been retained to present these research findings to judges and juries. Although the quality of research cited by these psychologists is outstanding, the expert testimony has been ruled inadmissible in some jurisdictions, including appellate courts. In *U.S. v. Amaral*,[6] the United States Court of Appeals for the Ninth Circuit ruled that expert testimony regarding the credibility of eyewitness identification was properly ruled inadmissible. The court opined that it is necessary neither to instruct a jury that they should receive identification testimony with caution nor to suggest inherent unreliability of eyewitness identification. The court, in essence, decided the judge and jury needed no help from scientific experts in weighing and judging eyewitness testimony. This is not to say that judges in the future, in other venues may not decide to admit expert testimony regarding the reliability of eyewitness identification testimony.

Expert testimony regarding "psychological syndromes" (i.e., "parent alienation syndrome," "sexually abused child behavior syndrome," "repressed memory syndrome") have not fared well when challenged as to admissibility (Morse, 1995).[7,8] The courts tend to differentiate between "diagnostic" and "nondiagnostic" syndromes. The legal view is that diagnostic syndromes can provide relevant evidence of *historical facts* in litigation. An example would be the "battered child syndrome." In this case, the diagnosis also provides objective evidence that a child's injuries could not likely have been accidental. A nondiagnostic syndrome doesn't have evidentiary value in establishing *historical facts*. Examples include the so-called child sexual abuse syndrome (Myers, 1996). If and when scientific evidence appears to support such descriptive categories, admissibility constraints may be modified.

One early decision essentially resting on *Daubert* has rejected flexible battery neuropsychological testing. The court held that the entire reasoning process on which the expert neuropsychologist derives a conclusion must reflect scientific methodology (J. Reed, 1996).

Admissibility Rules of the Road

Although admissibility is to the largest extent determined by the court, the psychologist should be aware that his or her style and preparation as an expert witness can enhance or interfere with the admissibility of the expert testimony and opinion. The "Rules of the Road" shown in Figure 5.1 may prove useful.

Rules of the Road

- Never agree to be an expert in any area in which you are not an expert.
- Be familiar with current research in the area you claim expertise.
- Ensure that any test or procedure you use passes the "General Acceptance" rule.
- Be prepared to defend any procedure you use in terms of the reliability and validity of such procedures as supported by research published in respectable scientific sources.
- Discuss admissibility with the retaining attorney in the pretrial conference.
- Remain current as to the rules of admissibility for the court jurisdiction in which your testimony will be offered.
- When referring to normative data in your testimony, be prepared to discuss the similarities and differences between the normative subjects and the person about whose test results you are rendering an opinion.
- Be prepared to explain conclusions and opinions using scientifically supported theoretical positions.
- Avoid making statements which are speculative or personalistic.

FIGURE 5.1. Admissibility.

The law being a complex, dynamic, ever-changing set of rules, procedures, and guidelines, the expert witness is well advised to remain current on issues of admissibility. The American Psychological Association has begun to publish a Law and Mental Health Professional Series edited by B. D. Sales and M. O. Miller. The series presents the laws of various states relating to mental health issues. As of 1998, volumes for Arizona, California, Florida, Massachusetts, Minnesota, New Jersey, New York, Texas, Washington, and Wisconsin have been produced. The expert witness will find such compendia useful but should be aware that they can quickly become out of date as appellate decisions and legislative changes modify existing statutes and precedents.

NOTES

1. *Frye v. United States*, 293 F. 1013 (D.C. Cir. 1923).
2. *Massiah v. U.S.*, 377 U.S. 201, 84 S. Ct. 1199, 12 L. Ed. 2d 246 (1964).
3. *Daubert v. Merrell Dow Pharmaceuticals Inc.*, 113 S. Ct. 2786, 1993.
4. *Joiner v. General Electric Co.*, 78 F. Ed. 524 (11th Cir. 1996).
5. *Cavallo v. Star Enterprises*, 892 F. Supp. 756 (E. D. Va 1995).
6. *U.S. v. Amaral*, 488 F. 2d, 1148 (9th Cir. 1973).
7. *Hadden v. Florida*, No. 87, 574 (Fla. Sup. Ct. Feb. 6, 1997).
8. *Ohio v. Nemeth*, No. 95-JE-32 (Ohio Ct. App. Jan. 30, 1997).

6

Psychological Tests in the Courtroom

Testing is a major part of psychology's contribution to the promotion of human welfare. Although tests are now a major aspect of activity in education, industry, the armed forces, and other venues, the bulk of testing theory, research, and practice during the past hundred years has been developed and applied by psychologists.

After the development of testing instruments used for officer selection in World War I, psychology built the art and science of testing on a foundation of scientific research. Lewis Terman (1931) resurrected Munsterberg's position after almost a quarter of a century and suggested that the use of psychology in the courts be reconsidered in light of developments in the science of psychology since the publication of *On the Witness Stand* (Munsterberg, 1908). His work came to the attention of the legal profession (Terman, 1935).

There is no question that many psychologists qualify as experts in American courts (Perline, 1980). At issue is the scientific quality of the testimony and the degree to which it is accepted in the scientific community. In this matter, guidance was for the 50 years of the mid-century clearly given within the framework of *Frye v. United States.*[1] Although the *Frye* test does not inquire into the essence of the merit of scientific evidence—the internal and external validity of that evidence—it states clearly that to be admissible, the evidence should be generally accepted by the scientific community of which the expert claims membership. Under this test, a technique, a procedure, or a finding must have been available for a fairly long period to have a history of general acceptance or utilization (Suggs, 1979). It has been suggested that *Frye* is most applicable if a device or standardized methodology is being considered and if the average juror would

An early version of this chapter appeared as "Psychological Tests in the Courtroom," 1984, *Professional Psychology: Research and Practice, 15*(2), pp. 176–186.

view the results of a "test" as fairly infallible when so purported by a qualified expert.[2] The various standards of admissibility of scientific evidence have been relatively vague. Psychological tests, when presented as a basis for expert opinion, particularly in state courts, may have to withstand cross-examination based on constraints within *Frye v. United States.* The effects of the *Daubert* decision, especially in federal courts, are addressed in detail in Chapter 5.

As psychologists began to appear on the witness stands of America, frequently using psychological tests to explain or justify their opinions, opportunities for lawyers to learn to probe the credibility of such testimony began to appear (Blau, 1959; Poythress, 1980; Ziskin, 1981). Psychologists who represented themselves as experts and used psychological tests to justify their opinions were asked to delineate the merit and limitations of such tests.

TESTIMONY INVOLVING PSYCHOLOGICAL TESTS

Where psychologists have testified as expert witnesses in a wide range of civil and criminal issues, psychological tests, inventories, or surveys have often formed an integral part of their testimony. If the test instrument is specifically constructed or adapted to the issue or questions involved in the psychologist's testimony, challenge as to the appropriateness of the instrument tends to be minimal. This kind of acceptance occurs most frequently in patent, trademark, and other cases where opinion surveys are conducted and reported as part of the expert's testimony.[3] Most testimony supported by psychological tests focuses on the psychological state of an individual who is either plaintiff or defendant in a civil or criminal matter at issue. The range of psychological instruments that have become available in the past 75 years is considerable, as is the range of quality and applicability of those instruments (Conoley & Impara, 1933–1995). Testimony by psychologists about tests and test construction, as such, has been fairly narrow. Such testimony usually focuses on civil rights issues in which the courts become arbiters of testing practice in schools, agencies, and employment practices (Bersoff, 1981).

In recent years, the use of psychological test data to support expert opinion has increased significantly. Over two-thirds of both psychologists and psychiatrists perceive psychological testing as "essential" or "recommended" in criminal responsibility issues (Borum & Grisso, 1995). Application of specific test instruments to the forensic venue has become a matter of considerable attention (McCann & Dyer, 1996; Pope, Butcher, & Seelen, 1993).

Over the years, a myth has emerged that personality tests such as the Rorschach are inadmissible as instruments whose findings can support expert opinion. In reality, in 7,934 cases in which psychologists presented testimony based on Rorschach findings, only six resulted in a challenge as to admissibility. In only one case was the testimony excluded (Weiner, Exner, & Sciara, 1996).

Computerized Personality Tests

During the second half of the 20th century, the computerized administration, scoring, and interpretation of psychological tests, particularly but not exclusively personality tests, has increased exponentially. Concern as to the reliability, validity, and ethical appropriateness was addressed early on by the American Psychological Association (1986). Subsequent attention has been directed to the question of the equivalency of computer administration and traditional tester-presented formats. When the testing process is changed from the examiner-presented and observed interaction to a computer screen, key-press presentation mode, validity and normative data developed from the traditional method may be jeopardized (Honaker, 1988).

Automated interpretation of test data is now routine. Software is available from many sources so that a psychologist may generate an algorithmic interpretation on his/her own computer immediately after the subject's responses are entered into the database—either directly by the subject or from traditional answer sheets. Proponents praise these mechanical/electronic procedures as accurate, objective, rapid, efficient, and reliable (Butcher, 1987). A majority of practicing clinicians use and approve of computer-based testing. There remains serious concerns about the quality of the clinical decision rules on which narrative interpretation statements are made.

Most computerized interpretation systems include a cautionary note in the narrative, before interpretive statements appear. This admonition warns the clinician that the computerized results should be viewed as adjunctive to other assessment techniques and the clinician's overview of the diagnostic issues. Forensic psychologists would be especially well-advised to heed such warnings in preparation for an opposing attorney's attack on computerized testing. A segment of a cross-examination at trial illustrates this point:

Attorney: Well, Doctor, your report of Mr. Smith's personality is based on a computerized analysis of his MMPI—is that not so?

Dr. Jones: Well, yes.

Attorney: In fact—looking at your written report, the personality description is an exact replication of a computerized test interpretation sent to you by NCS, the firm that developed the MMPI interpretive program—is that not so?

Dr. Jones: Well—yes.

Attorney: This computer—up in Minnesota I believe—never met Mr. Smith, did it?

Dr. Jones: No—but . . . .

Attorney: Yet this computer is telling you what *it* thinks about Mr. Smith and you've swallowed this—whole hog. You expect this jury to believe that a machine in Minnesota can analyze Mr. Smith? That computer has never even met Mr. Smith.

Dr. Jones: Yes—but . . . .

Attorney: No further questions for this. . . . *doctor!*

The competent psychologist would not use a computerized personality interpretation alone to describe a subject. The psychologist as expert witness should help the retaining attorney to blunt such a cross-examination attack by addressing the issue during direct examination:

Retaining Attorney: Doctor—in the course of your examination of Mr. Smith, were any of your tests scored, profiled, or interpreted using a computer?

Dr. Brown: Yes, they were.

Retaining Attorney: Is this standard procedure or usual and customary practice?

Dr. Brown: Yes, it is.

Retaining Attorney: Are there professional standards for the use of computer scored and interpreted tests?

Dr. Brown: Yes, there are.

Retaining Attorney: Who formulated these standards or rules?

Dr. Brown: The American Psychological Association.

Retaining Attorney: In your use of tests taken by Mr. Smith did you follow these rules?

Dr. Brown: Yes, I did.

Retaining Attorney: In your interpretation of these tests and reaching your conclusions, did you accept as printed the computerized interpretations?

Dr. Brown: No. This information simply presented a variety of research-based interpretations. The usual and customary proper clinical procedure is to evaluate the research-based statements with the history, collateral information, other tests and the clinical interpretation of the specific test based on education, training, experience, and the latest research regarding that test.

Retaining Attorney: In your use of the tests given Mr. Smith did you follow all of these procedures?

Dr. Brown: Yes, I did.

Issues of direct and cross-examination will be presented in more detail in Chapter 13.

Ethnic and Racial Bias

The issue and questions surrounding concerns about racial and cultural biases in the use of psychological tests are complex and as yet not settled. The key underlying concept is one form or another of fairness. Although the bulk of research and commentary relates to fairness of tests in selection, promotion, and educational issues, it is in the forensic arena that the individual and society may suffer the most extensive unfairness and damage if test results are not applied with careful recognition of sources of bias based on race, gender, or ethnicity. Official and research concern about this issue has appeared in the literature for several decades (American Psychological Association et al., 1974; Humphreys, 1973).

The most popular research strategy for investigating racial bias, particularly in personality testing, is to compare racial or ethnic subgroups in convenient samples of racial subgroups on respective test score means. Such comparisons ignore the essence of the testing-psychopathology. The most appropriate kind of study would test the accuracy of predictions made in racial or ethnic subgroups (Cleary, Humphreys, Kendrick, & Wesman, 1975; Pritchard & Rosenblatt, 1980). In a few instances, ethnic or racially representative test instruments have been developed. The results of these efforts have been recommendations for continued research and development efforts to decrease or eliminate ethnic and racial bias in psychological tests (Lopez & Romero, 1988).

The expert witness should be well aware that the courts have expressed judicial concern regarding the use of psychological tests in decision making, particularly where an individual's condition of employment may be affected by his or her performance on a psychological test in which the individual's racial or ethnic status is not represented in the norming process. In *Firefighters Institute v. City of St. Louis, Mo.*, the court opined:

> The use of a testing device although neutral on its face, which has a racially disparate impact on members of minority groups and which has not been properly validated by the employer constitutes a discriminatory act.[4]

In preparing to testify on the basis of test results, the expert should seek normative comparisons closest to the subject in terms of not only age, sex, intelligence, socioeconomic level, and education but also the subjects' status of membership in ethnic, racial and, in the case of correctional institution subjects, even incarceration status (Selby, Yuspeh, Ririe, & Quiroga, 1994).

Use of Tests in Predicting Violence

The courts have traditionally vested almost unlimited power in psychiatry to aid in judicial decision making by identifying or certifying those likely to act in violent ways toward themselves or others. The judicial issues generally involve involuntary commitment, and psychological tests are frequently used to support such predictions (Robitscher, 1980). The deficiencies of psychological tests in these matters have been well documented (Slovenko, 1973; Ziskin, 1981). Ziskin suggests that failure of research to support any method of predicting violent behavior should deter sensible psychologists from responding to the demands for opinions in this matter. Some have suggested that "the past is a prologue" and that dangerousness can be best predicted from a history of violence (Monahan, 1981; Wenke, Robison, & Smith, 1972). Recent evaluation of the violent history paradigm does not support this concept. It is suggested that violence is frequently due to transitory psychological states that emerge in response to atypical circumstances and is a fairly poor indicator of future violence (Holland, Holt, & Beckett, 1982).

In practice, testimony concerning potential dangerousness is generally accepted by judges and jurors if opposing counsel is insufficiently versed in challenging the merit of the research and its methodology and is unable to conduct a rigorous cross-examination (Suggs, 1979). The degree to which unsupported opinions concerning dangerousness can become a travesty of justice has been chronicled (Tierney, 1982). All studies to date that relate psychological measuring methods or instruments to violent behavior are subject to methodological critiques. The most important problem preventing accurate predictions of dangerousness remains the issue of stable, acceptable, measurable, and uncontaminated criteria by which to assess the strength of the predictors. If a model of accurate prediction of dangerousness is to be developed, long-range studies of experimental subjects in natural settings using stable and valid behavioral measures are necessary. On careful evaluation or replication, most currently available instruments fail in prediction. Projective techniques, objectively utilized, show some promise as predictors of violence (Mullen & Dudley, 1981).

Hypothetically, psychological tests could be useful in providing the court with probabilities concerning the future occurrence of dangerous acts by individuals. Considerable longitudinal research, with large samples, adequate designs, and careful replication would be the first step in bringing the use of psychological tests in the prediction of dangerousness to a level acceptable to the requirements of admissibility. Although much general psychological information may be admissible without meeting the stringencies of the *Frye* and *Daubert* tests, the specificity of the concept of dangerousness carries it beyond McCormick's assertions that for some expert opinions a lower standard of admissibility, such as "general scientific acceptance," is sufficient (see Figure 6.1).[5]

In truth, although testing for violence risk has a fairly established place in clinical practice (Borum, Swartz, & Swanson, 1996), research supporting accurate predictions of violence from the test performance of individuals is as yet insubstantial (Monahan, 1996; Otto, 1992).

Competence to Stand Trial

Competency statutes represent one of the safeguards for protecting the constitutional rights of a defendant to a fair trial. The U.S. Supreme Court in 1960 ruled:

> [I]t is not enough for the district judge to find that the defendant is oriented in time and place and has some recollection of events but that the test must be whether he has sufficient present ability to consult with his lawyer with a reasonable degree of rational understanding—and whether he has a rational as well as factual understanding of the proceedings against him.[6]

Common-law criteria for competency include an ability to cooperate with one's attorney in one's own defense, an awareness and understanding of

Rules of the Road

- Be sure the tests used measure states or traits relevant to the issue at hand.
- Refer to normative data closest to the basic characteristics of the test subject and his/her milieu.
- Be prepared to present cautions and/or concerns where appropriate, regarding the applicability of the tests used.
- Be prepared to discuss the standardization of all tests used in the forensic assessment as well as subsequent research, reviews, and critiques.
- Be prepared to discuss alternative interpretations of test results and explain why a particular interpretation was selected.
- Assume that the opposing attorney has retained a psychologist to review your choice of tests, administration, scoring, interpretations, and conclusions. Review your own work with this in mind.
- Be prepared to advise the retaining attorney of the strengths and weaknesses of the tests that form the bases of your expert opinion.
- Be prepared for the rare occasion where the presiding judge may ask questions concerning the reliability, validity, and error rate for your tests.

FIGURE 6.1.   Using tests to support expert opinions.

the nature and objectives of the proceedings, and an understanding of the consequences of the legal proceedings. If a defendant does not meet the criteria of competence, the speedy trial rule is laid aside and the proceedings are postponed until the defendant is found to be competent.

Thus if a defendant lacks minimal effective and cognitive resources to assume the role of defendant, he or she is deprived of the due-process right to testify in his or her own defense, to confront adversary witnesses, and to maintain an effective psychological presence in the courtroom beyond mere physical presence. The issue is legal, not psychological or psychiatric. Mental health professionals are sought as experts to *assist* judges and juries in settling competency issues. Psychologists, psychiatrists, and lay witnesses may present informed or expert opinion—they do not make the competency determination. This remains a formal judicial procedure (Lipsitt, Lelos, & McGarry, 1971).

Psychiatrists tend to view psychotic patients and mentally retarded individuals as incompetent to stand trial. Rarely are objective tests or criteria used to assess the validity of the psychiatric opinion (Roesch, 1979). Psychologists have developed competency screening instruments to supplement standardized tests of intelligence, brain dysfunction, and personality for determining competence to stand trial. Promising replication and validation have been reported (Nottingham & Mattson, 1981).

Each state specifies, with a greater or lesser degree of exactness, what is required in the way of an opinion or a report from an expert appointed to advise the court on the competency of a witness to stand trial or to proceed. Under Federal Rules of Procedure, the court may request expert testimony as to the competency of a witness.[7] As with other issues of competency, psychological tests can be useful in supporting expert opinion. Should the presiding judge decide a defendant is incompetent to stand trial, the proceedings will be delayed and appropriate treatment mandated by the judge. A specific time will be set for reexamination to determine whether the defendant has become competent to stand trial.

Standard psychological tests of intelligence, neuropsychological function, and personality offer an opportunity for the psychologist to measure a wide range of responses and capabilities that could address the issue of an individual defendant's competence to stand trial. Competency to stand trial is considered in greater depth in Chapter 7.

Not Guilty by Reason of Insanity

The insanity issue has an entrenched place in Anglo-Saxon law and probably dates back to pre-Biblical codes of conduct. Since the 14th century, English common law has excused offenders mentally unable to control their conduct. In 1843, a psychotic Scot, Daniel M'Naghten, murdered Edward Drummond, secretary to the prime minister of England, Sir Robert Peel, who was the real object of M'Naghten's homicidal and delusional impulses. M'Naghten was acquitted, touching off a national furor similar to that which developed when John Hinckley, who attempted to assassinate President Ronald Reagan, was acquitted by reason of insanity. Following M'Naghten's trial, Queen Victoria commanded all 15 high judges of England to appear before the House of Lords in an effort to clarify the confusion around this issue. The legal guidelines that emerged have been known as the *M'Naghten Rule* ever since. The rule states:

> It must be clearly proved that, at the time of the committing of the act, the party accused was laboring under such a defect of reason, from disease of the mind, as not to know the nature and quality of the act he was doing; or, if he did know it, that he did not know he was doing what was wrong (see Appendix A).[8]

During the 1950s, jurists began to believe that psychiatry could provide clear guidelines regarding the limits of responsibility in criminal matters. As a result, broader tests of responsibility or its lack developed. The major alternative to the M'Naghten Rule, developed in the mid-1960s, is the test proposed in the Model Code of the American Law Institute (ALI) which states:

> A person is not responsible for criminal conduct if at the time of such conduct as a result of mental disease or defect he lacks substantial capacity either to appreciate the criminality (wrongfulness) of his conduct or to conform his conduct to the requirements of the law.[9]

The M'Naghten Rule is a "right-wrong" test to which the ALI Model Code adds volitional elements. The M'Naghten Rule recognizes no degree of incapacity, while the ALI Code permits consideration of a wide range of mental impairments. At this writing, 26 states use a version of the ALI "substantial capacity" rule; 22 states adhere to the M'Naghten Rule. Utah, Idaho, and Montana have abolished the insanity plea.

Despite the general familiarity with the term, the plea of not guilty by reason of insanity is only invoked in about 1 of 1,000 trials. The issue becomes one of general concern when famous people are involved, as in the *Hinckley* case. In 1835, Richard Lawrence, a house painter, was acquitted of attempted murder for shooting Andrew Jackson, as was John Schrank for shooting Theodore Roosevelt in 1912, after an insanity pleading. Each highly publicized case is usually followed by a public outcry demanding elimination of this pleading (Leo, 1982a). In all likelihood, the plea of innocent by reason of insanity will remain a small but important aspect (and problem) of American jurisprudence.

Psychiatrists generally seem willing to render opinion as to the legal, mental, and/or moral status of defendants at the time of a criminal act. As a group, psychologists are less willing to speculate on a person's mental state at a time other than when they examine an individual. Some join psychiatric colleagues in using imprecise science to make absolute moral judgments (Tierney, 1982).

It has been proposed that there are no valid diagnostic tests of insanity and that both psychiatric and psychological testimonies on issues of sanity are questionable since neither distinguishes between a defendant "unable" and one "unwilling" to control unacceptable impulses (Ziskin & Coleman, 1981). It is suggested that it is "risky" to make a statement as to a defendant's psychological state at the time of a crime (Ziskin, 1981).

Neuropsychological assessments may, in the future, provide objective, more valid data to help the courts decide the merits of an insanity defense. Recent court rulings, appealed and sustained, affirm that expert neuropsychological testimony stating that minimal brain dysfunction destroyed a defendant's capability to choose right and refrain from wrong does establish a connection between defect and behavior.[10, 11] The insanity pleading is considered in greater detail in Chapter 8.

Personal Injury Issues

In civil proceedings, attorneys representing clients who are suing for injuries or attorneys representing estates or survivors in cases of wrongful death frequently seek psychological testimony to substantiate claims by the plaintiff. Defense attorneys use psychologists to challenge such claims. In both instances, psychological tests may form a substantial segment of the psychologist's testimony. Traumatic cerebral damage is a frequent issue as are questions of posttraumatic stress. Psychologists testify as to the significance of the plaintiff's performance on tests of intelligence, memory, neuropsychological functioning, aptitude, rehabilitation potential, marital adjustment, and personality. Psychologists may be asked to render opinions as to the future status or potential of the defendant. In some instances, psychologists are asked to testify as to the status of dead persons using techniques of psychological autopsy;[12] expert testimony about the results of psychological tests is frequently used as evidence in Social Security benefit determination; and specific test instruments are sometimes required by statute.[13]

Custody Issues

Psychologists, together with other mental health professionals, have testified in matters of child custody for decades. The issue may involve the interests of the child or the suitability of the parents. Testimony based on psychological tests frequently represents the psychologist's contribution to the proceedings. Whereas psychological tests are helpful in understanding children's developmental progress and needs, they are of unproven value in helping a judge make the Solomonic decision required in awarding custody to the most appropriate parent (Blau, 1982).

Judges traditionally call for expert testimony to aid them in making custody decisions. Despite the frequent involvement of mental health professionals in custodial cases, Lowery (1981) reports that the advice of professionals is ranked at a relatively low level by jurists who are asked what factors they use to form their opinions and make their decisions.

Developmental psychology research and a wide range of testing instruments to measure children's intellect, achievement, social adjustment, neuropsychological status, and personality are uniquely helpful in implementing the recent trend toward *joint custody*, or *shared responsibility*. Recognizing the potential trauma of marital fracture to minor children, more jurisdictions are mandating *shared responsibility* for minors as part of marriage dissolution proceedings. Although the judge may determine that the primary physical residence for the child will be with one parent, most of the child's needs are to be jointly considered by the divorced parents. These statutes often specify mediation or conciliation procedures. Here psychological testing and testimony become integral aspects of the process.[14]

STANDARDS FOR THE USE OF TESTS IN COURT

As the tradecraft of psychologists becomes more generally known to the legal profession, requests for broader application of psychological measurement to adversary issues may be exercised.

The development, standardization, and use of psychological tests are, as much as anything, characteristic of psychology's long and productive history of scientific exploration of behavior, its origins, and its consequences (Anastasi, 1981).

Since 1954, the APA has formally recognized the importance of scientific standards in the development and application of test instruments. Joining with the American Educational Research Association and the National Council on Measurement in Education in 1955, the APA published *Standards for Educational and Psychological Tests and Manuals*. As issues became more complex, the APA established the Committee on Psychological Tests to study the research and prepare a revision of the earlier work. The result appeared as *Standards for Educational and Psychological Tests* (American Education Research Association et al., 1985).

Although the 1985 edition makes no specific mention of the interpretation of psychological tests in judicial settings, the recommendations, guidelines, and constraints it contains are cogent. In essence, the standards recommend, in considerable detail, the qualifications of test users, methods of choosing tests for specific purposes, administration and scoring standards to be followed, and acceptable procedures and limitations for the interpretation of psychological tests. The latter is particularly applicable to testimony based on test results.

Psychologists who testify about the meaning of psychological test scores should realize that their opinions will be subjected to minute scrutiny by competent opposing counsel. Reports and depositions in which the psychologist renders opinions about tests and test results are likely to be reviewed by psychologists retained for the specific purpose of identifying errors, distortions, improprieties, and inaccuracies. The psychologist who testifies about psychological tests or their meanings must adhere to the highest standards in order to service his or her client properly, minimize courtroom assailability and embarrassment, and protect the good name of psychology.

The *Standards* published in 1985 is intended as a statement of technical requirements for sound professional practice. As new systems and procedures develop, additional standards can be expected. Given the current state of the art, psychologists who testify on the basis of psychological tests should consider the remainder of this chapter as the current guidelines for forensic practice.[15]

General Testing Knowledge

The psychologist who uses tests as a basis for expert testimony in court should possess the education, training, and credentials appropriate to the content of the testimony and the instruments used. The test user should have a substantial general knowledge of testing principles, the relevant literature, and the tests being used, as well as the general limitations of test interpretations.

Test Selection

The forensic psychologist must scrupulously avoid bias in test selection. A periodic review of the appropriateness of often-used tests is critical. The test user should consider more than one variable for assessment and more than one test for each variable being considered.

The test user should be able to relate the history of research and development behind the intended application of the test to justify its choice for the legal issues being considered. Characteristics of the examinee, such as age, cultural background, or handicaps, should be carefully evaluated in all test selection.

Administration and Scoring

The test user should follow standardized administration and scoring procedures described in the test manual. Desirable testing conditions should be provided to enable the examinee to do his or her best. Any modification of standard procedures must be noted and documented. When ethnic or linguistic minorities are to be tested, efforts should be made to include staff with similar background during the testing procedures. Any factors interfering with optimum performance should be documented and noted when results are reported. The test user is accountable for accuracy in scoring and recording test results.

The purpose of the testing must be clearly explained to the examinee. In criminal matters, examinees must be apprised of their rights, as mandated by *Estelle v. Smith*.[16] The examiner must ensure the defendant understands which attorney or judge has requested the examination, that the defendant has the right to have his or her attorney present, that he or she has the right to refuse to participate in the examination, and that the results may be used against the defendant in court.

Readability

Most standardized tests for adults require the ability to read the directions, the items or both. A subject whose reading skills fall below the level required by the test content will probably present an invalid picture of what the subject can or cannot do. Some tests indicate the required reading level in the standardization manual. Readability formulas are available to assess the reading level required by any test (Frye, 1968; Schinka & Borum, 1994).

Presence of Third Parties

In recent years, psychologists have been faced with an increasing number of requests (or demands) that a third party be present during the testing of a subject involved in a forensic issue. Usually, it is an attorney who wants to be present. This situation may have significant effects on the responsiveness of the subject. A third party presence changes the testing conditions in comparison with standardization procedures. Fortunately the courts have generally favored excluding third parties.[17, 18, 19, 20, 21, 22, 23, 24] In some jurisdictions, a third-party observer has been ruled permissible.[25, 26, 27, 28, 29] Request for a third-party observer during a mental examination has been denied in federal court.[30]

It appears, then, that at this time third-party observers can be excluded from the psychological examination in federal cases while at the state level, observers may be allowed by the court under specific conditions.

Interpretation of Tests

If specific cutting scores are to be used as a basis for decisions, the psychologist must be prepared to justify or explain the adopted cutoff score during direct examination or cross-examination.

Test scores should be explained or interpreted as an *estimate* of performance under a given set of circumstances and should not be interpreted or put forth as an *absolute* characteristic of the examinee. Test results should not be interpreted as permanent or generally applicable to all circumstances. It is the forensic psychologist's responsibility to ensure that attorneys and triers of fact, unsophisticated in the matter of tests and testing, be provided with careful, justifiable, generally acceptable explanations of the test results sufficient for the recipients of the interpretations to view them with clarity and understanding.

On completion of testing, the forensic psychologist should render a written report of the testing that communicates scores, interpretations, conclusions, and opinions.

When relying on computer-based test interpretations, the forensic psychologist should be familiar with the rationale and validity of the interpretations and be prepared to justify their use in the judicial matter at hand.

If test scores are interpreted in relation to normative references, the user should be prepared to demonstrate that the norms of reference are appropriate to both the examinee and the judicial matter under consideration.

The test user should always consider alternative interpretations of a specific test score. Great care must be taken when generalizing test validity from one situation to another. Value judgments involved in the use of test scores in prediction must be explicitly and rationally explained.

When tests used in a forensic assessment are challenged during deposition or trial, concerning the effect of medication on test performance, the psychologist should be prepared to respond knowledgeably and carefully. Although early studies suggest there are few or no changes in test performance as a result of psychotropic drug treatment, most studies suffer from poor research design (Baker, 1968). This is an area still awaiting definitive scientific conclusions.

In comparing clinical versus statistical interpretations of psychological tests, psychologists must be candid and accurate regarding current research and be more supportive of statistically derived interpretations. If nonstatistically based interpretations are given, the test user should be prepared to justify interpretations in a manner consistent with admissibility constraints.

The guidelines discussed here must be enhanced by the psychologist's continuing efforts to be aware of new developments in tests and testing, current research regarding the testing instruments and procedures being used, and current standards for ethical and appropriate use of tests and test results.

NOTES

1. *Frye v. United States*, 293 F. 1013 (D.C. Cir. 1923).
2. 29 Stan. L. Rev. 969, 1017 (1977).
3. *Robinsdale Amusement Co. v. Warner Bros. Pictures Distributing Corp. et al.*, Civil #4584 (4th Division, Minneapolis).
4. *Fire Fighters Institute v. City of St. Louis, Mo*, 588 F.2d 235 (1978).
5. C. McCormick, *Law of Evidence* §13 (1954).
6. *Duskey v. United States*, 362 U.S. 402 (1960).
7. FRP 601.
8. M'Naghten's Case, 10 C.&F. 200, 8 Eng. Rep. 718 (H.L. 1843).
9. Model Penal Code §4.01(1) (1961).
10. *People v. Wright*, 648 P.2d 665 (Colo. 1982).
11. *Hendershott v. People*, 653 P.2d. 385 (Colo. 1982).
12. *Diagnosing the Dead*, 18 Am. Crim. L. Rev. 617 (1982).
13. 6 *Mental Disability L. Rep.* 438 (1982).
14. Fla. Stat. §61.13 (1982).
15. These recommended standards rely heavily on the 1985 *Standards*.
16. *Estelle v. Smith*, 451 U.S. 454, 101 S. Ct. 1866, 68 L. Ed. 2d 359 (1981).
17. *Pedro v. Glenn*, 8 Ariz. App. 332, 446 P.2d 31.
18. *Edwards v. Superior Ct.*, 16 Cal. 3d 905, 549 P.2d 846, 130 Cal. Rptr.14.
19. *Hayes v. District Ct.*, 854 P.2d 1240 (1993).
20. *Hess v. Henry*, 183 W. Va. 28, 393 S.E.2d 666.
21. *Whanger v. Amer. Family Mutual*, 58 Wis. 2d 461, 207 N.W.2d 74.
22. *Cline et al. v. Firestone*, 118 F.R.D. 588.
23. *Tom Lin v. Holecek*, 150 F.R.D. 628.
24. *Stoughton v. B.P.O.E.*, #251 281 N.J. Super. 605, 658 A.2d 1335.
25. *Rochen v. Huang*, 558 A.2d 1108.
26. *Robin v. Associated Indemnity*, 297 So. 2d 427.
27. *Mohr v. District Court of the 4th Jud. Dist.*, 202 Mont. 423, 660 P.2d 88.
28. *State ex rel. Staton v. Common Pleas Ct.*, 4 Ohio App. 2d 10, 211 N.E.2d 63.
29. *Tietjen v. Dept. of Labor*, 13 Wash. App. 86, 534 P.2d 151.
30. *Ragge v. MCA/Universal Studios*, 165 F.R.D. 605.

═ 7 ═══════════

Competency to Stand Trial, to Testify, and to Make Decisions

As noted previously and as explored extensively in Chapter 8, the insanity defense rarely appears in criminal trials. However, the question of competency occurs with some frequency in the early stages of arraignment if there is any reason to suspect that the defendant lacks *mens rea*. If the judge, the prosecutor, or the attorney for the defense suspects that the defendant is not able to perceive his or her situation realistically, expert opinion is usually sought to determine whether the defendant is competent to stand trial. If the judge decides that the preponderance of evidence suggests such incompetency, no trial is scheduled. This tends to abort many pleas of innocent by reason of insanity. Frequently, by the time the defendant is found to be competent to stand trial, some arrangement to deal with the charges has been negotiated. Thus the issue of competence to stand trial should precede any plea of innocent by reason of insanity.

THE LAW

Constitutional Issues

The Sixth Amendment to the U.S. Constitution, handed down in 1791, states:

> In all criminal prosecutions, the accused shall enjoy the right to a speedy and public trial, by an impartial jury of the state and district wherein the crime shall have been committed, which district shall have previously been ascertained by law, and to be informed of the nature and cause of the accusation; to be confronted with the witnesses against him; to have compulsory process for obtaining witnesses in his favor, and to have the Assistance of Counsel for his defense.[1]

Thus the defendant has the absolute right to know the nature of the charges, know the kind of evidence or allegations that led to the charges, be allowed to confront and challenge witnesses, demand that witnesses or evidence be introduced in an effort to demonstrate innocence, and participate with a knowledgeable officer of the court in constructing the best possible defense against the charges. These rights form a keystone of the American system of jurisprudence. If for any reason the defendant is not able to exercise these constitutional rights, a proper legal proceeding cannot take place. To take an extreme case, if the defendant were in a coma, the trial could not proceed. Having no ability to exercise receptive or expressive communication deprives a comatose defendant of constitutional rights to a fair trial. Such a defendant would be considered incompetent to stand trial.

Federal Rules

Specific issues of mental or psychological incompetency before trial are addressed in the U.S. code. In part, it states:

> Whenever after arrest and prior to the imposition of sentence or prior to the expiration of any period of probation the United States Attorney has reasonable cause to believe that a person charged with an offense against the United States may be presently insane or otherwise so mentally incompetent as to be unable to understand the proceedings against him or properly to assist in his own defense, he shall file a motion for a judicial determination of such mental competency of the accused, setting forth the ground for such belief with the trial court in which proceedings are pending.[2]

A motion for judicial order for examination may be made by the prosecution or the defense on behalf of the accused. Receiving such a motion, the judge, after evaluating the facts on which the request is based, has the discretion of ordering an examination of the defendant to determine whether he or she is competent to stand trial. Should the report of the examination indicate to the satisfaction of the presiding judge that the accused is incompetent, the judge may then order the defendant to a treatment facility until such time as subsequent examination or examinations indicate that the accused is competent to stand trial. The examination's sole purpose is to guide the judge in the issue of whether the trial should be postponed.[3]

The federal standard of competence to stand trial is the accused's ability to understand the charges against him or her and whether the defendant has sufficient mental capacity to consult with attorneys with a reasonable degree of rational understanding. Furthermore, the defendant must have a rational as well as factual understanding of the proceedings against him or her.[4] The landmark decision in this issue was *Duskey v. United States;* the Supreme Court held:

[I]t is not enough for the district judge to find that "the defendant is oriented to time and place and has some recollection of events" but that the test must be whether he has sufficient present ability to consult with his lawyer with a reasonable degree of rational understanding—and whether he has a rational as well as factual understanding of the proceedings against him.[5]

To be adjudicated as mentally incompetent to stand trial, in federal jurisdictions, the defendant must be shown by the preponderance of evidence to have a mental defect, illness, or condition that would result in some loss of the right to a fair trial. The federal statutes are clear that incompetency to stand trial is not defined in terms of mental illness. A defendant may be competent to stand trial while mentally ill, but a defendant may be incompetent to stand trial without being mentally ill. Conditions of "synthetic incompetence" as a result of using prescribed drugs are not grounds for a finding of incompetency to stand trial.[6] Examinations by mental health experts serve only as recommendations to the court. The judge always makes the final determination of competence to stand trial.[7,8]

State Courts

Although a state court cannot use any statute that would deprive a defendant of his or her constitutional rights, each state develops specific definitions and procedures regarding the issue of competency to stand trial.[9] The rules, examination procedures, and statutory language differ considerably from state to state. In Florida, for example, details concerning the examination and report in the matter of competence to stand trial are quite elaborate:

(a) Examination by Experts. Upon appointment by the court, the experts shall examine the defendant with respect to the issue of competence to proceed, as specified by the court in its order appointing the experts to evaluate the defendant, and shall evaluate the defendant as ordered.

   (1) The experts shall first consider factors related to the issue of whether the defendant meets the criteria for competence to proceed; that is, whether the defendant has sufficient present ability to consult with counsel with a reasonable degree of rational understanding and whether the defendant has a rational, as well as factual, understanding of the pending proceedings.

   (2) In considering the issue of competence to proceed, the examining experts shall consider and include in their report:

   (A) The defendant's capacity to:

      (i) Appreciate the charges or allegations against the defendant;

      (ii) Appreciate the range and nature of possible penalties, if applicable, that may be imposed in the proceedings against the defendant;

      (iii) Understand the adversary nature of the legal process;

      (iv) Disclose to counsel facts pertinent to the proceedings at issue;

      (v) Manifest appropriate courtroom behavior;

      (vi) Testify relevantly; and

    (B) Any other factors deemed relevant by the experts.

(b) Factors to Be Evaluated. If the experts should find that the defendant is incompetent to proceed, the experts shall report on any recommended treatment for the defendant to attain competence to proceed. In considering the issues relating to treatment, the examining experts shall report on:

    (1) The mental illness or mental retardation causing the incompetence;

    (2) The treatment or treatments appropriate for the mental illness or mental retardation of the defendant and an explanation of each of the possible treatment alternatives in order of choices;

    (3) The availability of acceptable treatment. If treatment is available in the community, the expert shall so state in the report; and

    (4) The likelihood of the defendant attaining competence under the treatment recommended, an assessment of the probable duration of the treatment required to restore competence, and the probability that the defendant will attain competence to proceed in the foreseeable future.

(c) Insanity. If a notice of intent to rely on the defense of insanity has been filed prior to trial or a hearing on a violation of the probation or community control, and when so ordered by the court, the experts shall report on the issue of the defendant's sanity at the time of the offense.

(d) Written Findings of Experts. Any written report submitted by the experts shall:

    (1) Identify the specific matters referred for evaluation;

    (2) Describe the evaluative procedures, techniques, and tests used in the examination and the purpose or purposes for each;

    (3) State the expert's clinical observations, findings, and opinions on each issue referred for evaluation by the court, and indicate specifically those issues, if any, on which the expert could not give an opinion; and

    (4) Identify the sources of information used by the expert and present the factual basis for the expert's clinical findings and opinions.[10]

In addition to an awareness of the proceedings and the capacity to cooperate with the defense attorney, the defendant must be able to present a psychological presence in the courtroom. This is stated explicitly in some states, such as California:

> . . . giving the accused the right to appear and defend in person and requiring him to be personally present at trial for felony, the accused must be

both physically and mentally present at every stage of a felony prosecution, and mere physical presence is insufficient.[11]

Again, the psychologist should understand that state statutes vary.

THE EXAMINATION FOR COMPETENCY TO STAND TRIAL

When the defendant's ability to participate in the trial process seems questionable, the presiding judge may order an examination by a mental health expert to aid the court. The decision of competency rests with the judge, and the mental health expert's report is only one factor considered in the decision process. The competency evaluation, in general, should address the issues of whether the defendant is capable of understanding and perceiving the nature of the judicial process to a reasonable degree (note that it is not the expert's role to define *reasonable*). The accused must understand how and why he or she is being charged, the pretrial and trial procedures that will occur, what will happen if convicted, and the accused's constitutional rights and privileges to participate in the process. In addition, the expert must determine whether the defendant has any mental defects or conditions that would prevent a reasonable degree of cooperation with the attorney in pursuing a good representation and a fair trial. Finally, the expert should be prepared to address the issue of whether the accused has any mental defect or disease that would preclude making a reasonable self-presentation, in his or her own best interests, during the trial proceedings.

As in many criminal issues, the psychologist as expert follows to the witness stand a long tradition established by medicine and psychiatry in matters of competency to stand trial. Traditional psychiatric examination tends to relate issues of competency to psychiatric symptomatology and diagnoses. There is no data to support such assumptions, and the reliability and validity of psychiatric opinion in the competency issue are in doubt. The presiding judge will frequently remand the accused to a restrictive psychiatric institution where a stay of as much as 60 days is necessary before an opinion as to competency is forthcoming. There is no evidence that lengthy institutional evaluations are necessary in determining the accused's mental fitness to stand trial. Evaluating a defendant's competency to stand trial in a sheltered, restraining institutional setting may have no validity in respect to the mental state of the accused in the courtroom setting. Evaluations done in the community, at the time of the trial, with reference to the statutory definitions of incompetence are likely to be more realistic (Roesch, 1979).

Psychological Procedures

Whereas some psychologists may imitate their psychiatric colleagues in conducting competency evaluations emphasizing the Mental Status Exam, results of such examinations are rarely followed in the courts' final decision (Roesch & Golding, 1978). Legal definitions of competency are not directly addressed by traditional mental health nosology or classification (Shah, 1963).

A request for a psychological evaluation of a defendant's competence to stand trial may come from the prosecutor, the defense attorney, or the court. The psychologist is asked to render an expert opinion as to the mental condition of the accused. If the defendant is mentally incompetent to stand trial, it is the psychologist's responsibility to identify, delineate, and report the incompetence in terms consonant with current standards for psychological services and ethical constraints. The report must, however, in every reasonable way, relate to the questions being asked relative to the legal definitions of incompetency to stand trial. Assessment of the accused's cognitive, affective, and behavioral capabilities and deficits should form the basis for the report. Although the referral for examination for competency to stand trial frequently includes a request for evaluation of sanity at the time of the felony, the evaluation and report of competency to stand trial must be an entirely separate, segmented issue. The psychological evaluation for issues of insanity is much more complex and is discussed in depth in Chapter 8. The psychological examination for competency to stand trial should include the following elements.

History and Interview.   The psychologist should determine how the defendant views his or her present situation. Direct questions should include:

1. Why is the defendant in jail?
2. What are the charges against the accused?
3. What are the procedures faced by the defendant?
4. Who represents the defendant, and how well are they relating?
5. What will happen if the defendant is found guilty?

Should the initial interview indicate clearly that the defendant is competent to stand trial in respect to the statutes of the jurisdiction in which the trial will take place, the psychologist may conclude the examination at this point. This is more likely to be the exception rather than the rule since few intact, stable defendants are referred for competency evaluation.

In an effort to formalize the competency evaluation, Lipsitt et al. (1971) from the Harvard Medical School developed a screening instrument to evaluate competency for trial. Consisting of 22 incomplete sentences, the instrument requires that the defendant finish the sentence stems with the best answer he or she can. The sentence stems focus on courtroom procedure and defendants. Figure 7.1 presents the items of the *Competency Screening Test.*

The responses are scored according to a 3-point scale (0, 1, or 2). Poor responses receive a score of 0, responses that are borderline but not clearly appropriate receive a score of 1, and clearly appropriate responses are

1. The lawyer told Bill that _____
2. When I go to court, the lawyer will _____
3. Jack felt that the judge _____
4. When Phil was accused of the crime, he _____
5. When I prepare to go to court with my lawyer _____
6. If the jury finds me guilty, I _____
7. The way a court trial is decided _____
8. When the evidence in George's case was presented to the jury _____
9. When the lawyer questioned his client in court, the client said _____
10. If Jack had to try his own case, he _____
11. Each time the D.A. asked me a question, I _____
12. While listening to the witnesses testify against me, I _____
13. When the witness testifying against Harry gave incorrect evidence, he _____
14. When Bob disagreed with his lawyer on his defense, he _____
15. When I was formally accused of the crime, I thought to myself _____
16. If Ed's lawyer suggests that he plead guilty, he _____
17. What concerns Fred most about his lawyer _____
18. When they say a man is innocent until proven guilty _____
19. When I think of being sent to prison, I _____
20. When Phil thinks of what he is accused of, he _____
21. When the jury hears my case, they will _____
22. If I had a chance to speak to the judge, I _____

FIGURE 7.1.   The Competency Screening Test. (*Source:* Reprinted with permission from Paul D. Lipsitt, *Competency Screening Test* [Boston: Competency to Stand Trial and Mental Illness Project, 1970]. Copyright 1970 Paul D. Lipsitt and David Lelos.)

scored 2. Scoring standards are provided; Figure 7.2 presents several examples from the scoring handbook (Lipsitt, 1970).

The original standardization of this screening instrument was based on a comparison of the test with the psychiatric and psychological evaluation of 380 people accused of felonies. These defendants were sent to a state institution to be evaluated for competency to stand trial, and 43 of the sample were found to suffer serious mental pathology. Comparing their performance with five other groups (students, nonadjudicated patients, defendants not suspected of mental disorder, civilly committed patients, and a noninstitutional group), the screening instrument appeared to be relatively efficient and successful in identifying those likely to be found not competent to stand trial.

In a cross-validation of the Competency Screening Test (CST), Nottingham and Mattson (1981) used the performance of 50 male residents of a state forensic unit to predict competency to stand trial. The criterion against which CST scores were compared was the full forensic staff decision as to whether the defendant was competent to stand trial. The CST did not predict any false negatives (competent) but did predict nine false positives (incompetent). Further cross-validation has been reported by Nicholson and his colleagues (Nicholson, Robertson, Johnson, & Jensen,

1. The lawyer told Bill that
   (a) Legal criteria: ability to cooperate in own defense, communicate, relate.
   (b) Psychological criteria: ability to relate or trust.
   Score 2:   includes obtaining and/or accepting advice or guidance
   Examples: "he should plead not guilty"
   "he was free"
   "he should plead nolo"
   "he should plead guilty"
   "he would take his case"
   "he would need to know all the facts concerning the case"
   "he should turn himself in"
   "the outlook was good"
   "he will try to help him"

   Score 1:
   Examples: "he is innocent"
   "everything is all right"
   "be truthful"
   "he will be going to court soon"
   "he is competent to stand trial"
   "it will be filed"
   Score 0:   includes regarding lawyer as accusing or judgmental
   Examples: "he was wrong in doing what he did"
   "he is guilty"
   "he is going to be put away"
   "no comment"

2. When I go to court the lawyer will
   (a) Legal criteria: ability to cooperate in own defense, communicate, relate.
   (b) Psychological criteria: ability to relate or trust.
   Score 2:
   Examples: "defend me"
   "be there to help me"
   "do his best to get me off with a light sentence"
   "represent me"
   "present my case

   Score 1:
   Examples: "be there"
   "ask for a postponement"
   "ask me to take the stand"

   Score 0:
   Examples: "put me away"
   "keep his mouth shut"
   "prosecute me"

FIGURE 7.2.   Examples of scoring standards for the Competency Screening Test. (*Source:* Reprinted with permission from Paul D. Lipsitt, *Competency Screening Test* [Boston: Competency to Stand Trial and Mental Illness Project, 1970]. Copyright © 1970 by Paul D. Lipsitt and David Lelos.)

1986). Further studies support the usefulness of the CST (Nicholson, Briggs, & Robertson, 1988). Ustad and her fellow researchers have provided further validation of these instruments for restoration of competency (Ustad, Rogers, Sewell, & Guarnaccia, 1996).

Although at the present time there is no competency screening test that can substitute for a full psychological evaluation, the development of specific instruments is a worthy objective, and it is anticipated that further research will increase the use of such instruments.

The extensiveness of the psychological assessment battery will depend on a number of style and situational factors. Should the psychologist, after examining all records and conducting a clinical interview with the defendant, believe that there is no question about the accused's competence, this may be reported to the court without further evaluation. Any sign of mental defect or disturbance, either observed or reported, requires that a full evaluation be conducted. Assuming the psychologist proceeds beyond a history and clinical interview with the defendant, the procedures used should provide information about the following:

- The defendant's intellectual capacities and deficiencies.
- The defendant's neuropsychological status.
- The defendant's personality.
- The validity of the examination.

Currently, there is no standard or prescribed series of examination procedures. Some traditions and precedents are being developed based simply on the experience of psychologists in both institutional and independent settings who have been called on to evaluate defendants' competency to stand trial. Variability is common in selection of test instruments and other procedures. The psychological expert should keep in mind that any procedure selected should stand the *Frye v. United States* and *Daubert v. Dow Chemical* tests in order to be acceptable to the court,[12] as well as other constraints regarding admissibility described in Chapter 5. Figure 7.3 presents a form that can be used by the expert to formulate his or her opinion regarding a criminal defendant's competency to stand trial.

The Interview.   There is, at present, no standard interview for matters of competency although questions concerning the defendant's current perception of his or her status with the criminal system are mandatory. Most psychologists who work as experts in the forensic field prefer to take a full background history since most examinations require the psychologist to render opinions not only about competency to stand trial but also about issues of insanity, mitigating circumstances, treatment potential, qualification of the defendant as a mentally disordered sex offender, and so forth. In respect to competency to stand trial, the expert should explore the following areas during the interview:

- The defendant's perception of why he or she is in the adjudication situation.
- The defendant's opinion of his or her attorney and what they will be doing together.
- The role of judge and jury in the anticipated court proceedings.
- The defendant's understanding of the concept of plea bargaining.
- The defendant's awareness of the consequences should a verdict of guilty be rendered by the judge or the jury.

Competency Evaluation Conclusions

Resident/Number _____ Date _____

1. *Appreciation of the charges or allegations.* Assessment of the accused's understanding or literal knowledge of the charges or allegations. It is important that he *understands* he is being accused, the consequences of which may be detrimental to him.

    ____ Unacceptable ____ Questionable ____ Acceptable ____ Not Applicable

2. *Appreciation of the range and nature of possible penalties, if applicable, which may be imposed in the proceedings against him.* Assessment of the accused's concrete understanding and appreciation of the conditions and restrictions which could be imposed on him and how long these may endure.

    ____ Unacceptable ____ Questionable ____ Acceptable ____ Not Applicable

3. *Understanding of the adversary nature of the legal process.* Does the accused understand that (a) the responsibility of his attorney is to assist him, (b) the State Attorney's responsibility is to prove his guilt, (c) the Judge is impartial and protects his rights as well as those of the State, and (d) the jury is impartial.

    ____ Unacceptable ____ Questionable ____ Acceptable ____ Not Applicable

4. *Capacity to disclose to his attorney facts pertinent to the proceedings at issue.* Assessment of the accused's capacity to give a consistent, rational, and relevant account of the facts surrounding his alleged offense or the accusations against him. Intelligence, perceptual capacity, memory, and validity of any claimed amnesia should be assessed. Consideration should be given to potential disparity between what he may disclose to a clinician and what he may share with his attorney.

    ____ Unacceptable ____ Questionable ____ Acceptable ____ Not Applicable

5. *Ability to manifest appropriate courtroom behavior.* Assessment of his current behavior and probable behavior when exposed to the stress of courtroom proceedings. Evaluate his beliefs and attitude toward the judicial system.

    ____ Unacceptable ____ Questionable ____ Acceptable ____ Not Applicable

6. *Capacity to testify relevantly.* Assessment of the accused's ability to testify with coherence, relevance, and independence of judgment including both cognitive and affective factors that may impact his ability to communicate.

    ____ Unacceptable ____ Questionable ____ Acceptable ____ Not Applicable

Conclusions:

FIGURE 7.3. A form for summarizing the expert's opinion concerning a criminal defendant's competency to stand trial.

- The defendant's status and adjustment to jail if he or she is not out on bond.
- The defendant's perception of his or her probable response to a prison term should this be an outcome of the court proceedings.

Much of the preceding will be validated to a degree by the defendant's responses on a competency screening instrument should such a device be used during the evaluation.

Most experts prefer to avoid asking defendants whether they are innocent or guilty. This is a very difficult matter when the expert must render an opinion regarding insanity. The defendant's description of what happened is vital in determining mental status at the time a crime was committed. Should the defendant discuss his or her involvement in a criminal act, it raises serious procedural questions regarding the defendant's Fifth Amendment rights to protection against self-incrimination. The privilege against self-incrimination is one that may not be violated. Some courts have ruled, however, that certain practices, including history taking by qualified experts, are securing "real" evidence (such as X rays, blood tests, and observation of behavior), as opposed to "testimonial" evidence (such as the defendant's statements about himself or herself). In the classic *Murphy v. Waterfront Commission*, the Supreme Court emphasized the importance of the privilege against self-incrimination:

> [O]ur unwillingness to subject those suspected of crime to the cruel trilemma of self-accusation, contempt, or perjury; our preference for an accusatorial rather than an inquisitorial system of criminal justice; our fear that self-incriminating statements will be elicited by inhuman treatment and abuses; our sense of fair play which dictates "a fair state-individual balance . . . by requiring the government in its contest with the individual to shoulder the entire load . . ."; our respect for the inviolability of the human personality and of the right of each individual "to a private enclave where he may lead a private life," *United States v. Grunewald*, 233 F.2d. 556, 581–582 (2nd Cir. 1956) (Frank dissenting); our distrust of self-deprecatory statements; and our realization that the privilege, while sometimes "a shelter to the guilty," is often a "protection to the innocent."[13]

While tests, including projective techniques, are midway between real and testimonial evidence,[14] the interview can represent a significant threat to Fifth Amendment values, requiring the psychologist to apprise the defendant of his or her rights before conducting any interview or history taking.[15] Procedures for ensuring the qualification and acceptability of an interview are described in detail in Chapter 4.

The psychologist is well advised *not* to probe innocence or guilt during history taking. Needless to say, very accurate note taking is required during an interview. Recording the interview is permissible if the defendant is informed and agrees. The recordings, as well as all handwritten materials, may be subpoenaed by opposing counsel. Whether material obtained during an interview by mental health experts should be admissible as part of an expert's opinion which is detrimental to the defendant's case is still a matter of judicial concern and discussion.[16] In most instances, such material as notes and test forms or profiles is "discoverable," or subject to inspection by opposing counsel during deposition (see Chapter 13). When a psychologist has any question concerning the propriety of an examination procedure, a call to the attorney or judge who requested the evaluation is indicated.

Intellectual Deficiencies and Capabilities. The instruments available to psychologists to evaluate intelligence are many, with varying degrees of validity and reliability. Different tests measure different factors. Most psychologists today depend on the Wechsler scales—for the broadest view of intellectual functioning. Other procedures or revisions of current tests are expected in the future and will probably be more effective than current instrumentation. At this writing, the age-appropriate Wechsler scale (either the Wechsler Adult Intelligence Scale-III, or WAIS-III, or Wechsler Intelligence Scale for Children-III, or WISC-III) is most frequently chosen by forensic clinical psychologists for the evaluation of a broad spectrum of intellectual function.

The law is not clearly instructive as to the issue of intellectual competence. In issues of credibility of witnesses, the courts generally consider children below 7 years as of questionable credibility although some courts have accredited younger witnesses; children between 7 and 14 years are usually considered potentially credible, subject to *voir dire* (questioning) by the court preliminary to testimony; and those over 14 years of age are usually considered credible. This is a very rough guideline for psychologists, and results of intellectual evaluations should include the appropriate calculated mental age of the defendant to aid the court in determining competence. Further exploration of the issue of juvenile competence will be found at the end of this chapter.

The following is abstracted from a psychological report of a defendant who was later found incompetent to stand trial.

INTELLECTUAL FACTORS

Objective results of the Wechsler Adult Intelligence Scale-Revised (11 subtests) were as follows:

Factor	Deviation IQ	Percentile (Ages 25–34)
Verbal scale	46	< 1st
Performance scale	63	1st
Full scale	52	< 1st

The above results suggest that Mr. A falls in the Moderate range of mental retardation. None of his subscale scores exceeded the first percentile for his age group. Mr. A's ability to understand, comprehend, and respond is equal to a child of approximately six years of age or less. Some of Mr. A's intellectual capacities fell below the scoring standards, so these results should be considered somewhat of an *over*estimate for his functional intellectual skills.

The results of the Peabody Picture Vocabulary Test (Form M) indicated a mental age of 4 years and 3 months for Mr. A. This would place him below the first percentile for adults and suggests his retardation is Moderate to Severe. In practical terms this means that Mr. A cannot comprehend most adult language where more than three sequential words are involved. He cannot add two single-digit numbers. He cannot repeat a two-digit number. In short, Mr. A is not able to cooperate, participate, or even be realistically responsive to any but the simplest interactional activities.

Although a complete evaluation was done in this case, the preceding was sufficient to convince the judge that Mr. A was not competent to stand trial. This was a very clear-cut case, without areas of variable intellectual capability to cloud the issue. If considerable variability in the Wechsler subscales occurs, the issue is more complex. The following portion of a report illustrates a situation in which a psychologist's report of intellectual functioning included a normal full-scale intelligence quotient but resulted in a finding of incompetent to stand trial by the court. Subscale scores as well as summative scores must be evaluated in rendering information as to whether an individual is competent to stand trial.

INTELLECTUAL FACTORS

Objective results of the Wechsler Adult Intelligence Scale-Revised (11 subtests) were as follows:

Factor	Deviation IQ	Percentile (Ages 55–64)
Verbal scale	100	50th
Performance scale	86	18th
Full scale	93	32nd

The above results suggest that Mr. B functions in the Low-Average range of intellectual ability. Examination of subscale variability, as follows, suggests otherwise:

WAIS-R Subscale	Percentile (Ages 55–64)
Information	95th
Digit Span	< 1st
Vocabulary	91st
Arithmetic	2nd
Comprehension	63rd
Similarities	75th
Picture Completion	37th
Picture Arrangement	< 1st
Block Design	2nd
Object Assembly	84th
Digit Symbol	2nd

The above suggests that Mr. B is intellectually disabled to a very severe degree. Significantly lowered subscale scores indicate severe distractibility, difficulties in concentration, social ineptness, impulsivity, great difficulties in accurately attributing causation to his own behavior and that of others, and poor social judgment. These results are consistent with severe neuropsychological deficit.

Later segments of the report detail the neuropsychological deficits underlying the scattered intellectual capacity noted in the subscales, as well as the effects on personality. These results of a massive stroke involving the middle cerebral artery rendered the defendant psychologically dysfunctional in several areas, and the court ruled that Mr. B was incompetent to stand trial. The psychologist reports to the court whether a defendant is intellectually competent. The expert may render opinions as to the quality of a defendant's intellectual processes, which may result in the judge's deciding that the defendant should not stand trial. The report should not contain a legal opinion (a response to the ultimate question) unless requested by the judge or the statutes.

Neuropsychological Status.   Whenever there are indications of neurological incidents or neuropathic behavior in the background history or crime report, a neuropsychological evaluation is indicated. Neuropsychological testing is also important if the defendant reports persistent or debilitating difficulties with speech, hearing, vision, memory, or other modalities commonly associated with neurological dysfunction. If the results of the intellectual evaluation suggest the presence of neuropsychological deficit, a full neuropsychological evaluation is indicated.

Most psychologists include a neuropsychological screening test with most or all of their assessment batteries. Some prefer individual visual-motor screening instruments, such as the Benton, the Bender Visual-Motor Gestalt Test, the Graham-Kendall Memory for Designs, the Wechsler Memory Scale, the Reitan-Indiana Screening Short Form (cards numbers 1, 2, 3, and 27 of the Halstead-Reitan Aphasia Screening Booklet), or other relatively simple tests that, together with the subscale pattern of the Wechsler scales, may suggest the defendant suffers neuropsychological deficit.

Even mild to moderate signs of deficit warrant a full neuropsychological battery. The preferred instruments at this writing are the Halstead-Reitan Test Battery or the Luria-Nebraska Neuropsychological Battery. The latter has the advantage of being available in several forms in the event retesting is necessary with a short intertest time interval. This is sometimes necessary for adversary purposes (both the prosecution and defense may request separate examinations). Also, alternate forms allow the psychologist to explore questions of competency under the influence of drugs; one administration of the test serves as a baseline under nontoxic conditions, whereas the other reflects function while influenced by the drug. Occasionally, two administrations of a test may be indicated to clarify questions of malingering or "faking bad." Neuropsychological batteries with alternate forms are useful in forensic practice.

The following illustrates the neuropsychological section of a psychological report that influenced a judge to declare the defendant incompetent to stand trial.

NEUROPSYCHOLOGICAL FACTORS

Variability in WAIS-R subtests suggests that Mr. C may suffer neuropsychological deficit.

The history section of this report indicates that while awaiting adjudication, Mr. C dropped a barbell on himself while exercising. A frontal contusion was treated, with minimal apparent aftereffects. This occurred approximately three weeks before this examination. Since that time Mr. C's behavior has been "strange" as noted in the Referral section of this report.

Neuropsychological screening using the Reitan-Indiana Short Form (square, cross, triangle, key) indicates moderate impairment, probably in the left hemisphere.

As a result of this, the Luria-Nebraska Neuropsychological Battery— Form A—was administered to Mr. C.

Scales which exceeded Mr. C's critical level included Expressive Speech, Motor, Receptive Speech, Intellectual Processes, and the Pathognomonic Scale. These results suggest that the primary sources of the deficits are likely to be in the left frontal and right frontal lobes. This is supported by significant elevations on the Right Frontal and Left Frontal Scales of the Brain Lesion Localization Scales.

Mr. C shows his greatest deficits in his inability to grasp verbal relationships and what the verbal relationships mean for tasks of a practical nature. He has considerable trouble comprehending even simple logical grammatical relations. He has trouble remembering and repeating both simple and complex words. Concentration and attention to auditory material are very poor. Memory is exceedingly deficient.

These deficits are characteristic of the type of injury Mr. C has suffered and are likely to interfere significantly with his ability to understand, to remember, and to cooperate.

These neuropsychological deficits were extensive enough for the court to send Mr. C to a treatment facility until such time as his neurological deficits subsided sufficiently for him to be considered competent to stand trial.

Personality Evaluation. The sequence from screening to full battery can provide an efficient approach to personality testing in issues of competency to stand trial. Where severe disturbance is suggested by police reports, interviews, or attorney's observations of behavior characteristic of well-known personality dysfunctions, a full battery of personality tests may not be indicated. If screening is the appropriate choice, most clinical psychologists prefer the Minnesota Multiphasic Personality Inventory (MMPI) although, recently, forensic reports are beginning to include the 16 PF (16 Personality Factors), the Clinical Analysis Questionnaire, and the Millon Clinical Multiaxial Inventory (Millon, 1982). The value of these types of instruments lies in the substantial body of research available to support opinions based on their results (Ziskin, 1981). Forensic clinical psychologists would be wise to include a screening test for reading comprehension to ensure that the defendant has sufficient reading skill to make a valid representation on the tests that require functional reading. Should the defendant read below the 5.5 grade level, it would probably be wise to have the items of the personality test read and the defendant's oral responses recorded.

Once the forensic psychologist decides on the administration of a full battery of personality tests (more likely with the insanity pleading), there are no hard-and-fast rules. As long as the tests applied are usual and customary to the profession and the expert is willing and able to explain the development, standardization, utilization, and validity of conclusions based on the instrument, a wide range of test instruments have been found admissible. Testimony based solely on such seldom taught or used projective techniques as the Michigan Picture Story Test and the Szondi Test has been admitted.[17]

The report of a personality evaluation that did not result in the judge's ruling that the defendant was incompetent to stand trial follows.

PERSONALITY FACTORS

Mr. D was able to complete the MMPI and the Rorschach Examination. He was unwilling to complete the Thematic Apperception Test or any of the projective drawing tasks. He refused to do the Sentence Completion Test.

The MMPI profile was characterized by extremely high elevations on the 6 and 8 (Paranoia, Schizophrenia) scales. Both exceeded T-scores of 80. This profile suggests a serious thinking disorder and strong paranoid mentation. Mr. D is generally nervous, anxious, and depressed. His reaction to any stress will be pervasively hostile and suspicious. Mr. D suffers a severe thinking disorder characterized by bizarre ideas, disorganization, and suspicion. It is the profile of a deeply disturbed psychotic person.

The Rorschach was a disturbing experience for Mr. D. He rejected Cards IV, VI, and IX. He claimed to have seen "things too dangerous to talk about." His responses to the remaining seven cards were characterized by disorganization, original responses, contaminations, and confabulations. Some truly creative original responses were spoiled by extended, confabulated ideas. Many responses indicated explosiveness.

Mr. D suffers a severe and debilitating psychosis and should be receiving intensive inpatient treatment at this time.

The Validity of the Examination.   From the defendant's point of view, it is generally preferable to be found incompetent to stand trial (or innocent by reason of insanity) than to undergo a trial that ends in conviction and sentencing. This can be a life-or-death issue for a defendant charged with a capital offense. All experts in matters of competency to stand trial, the insanity pleading, mitigating circumstances, penalty phase trials, and evaluation for classification of mentally disordered sex offenders must be aware of the potential for malingering, or faking bad.

Although clinically based statements as to the validity of the testing circumstances and the response of the accused are considered of some value by judges, more objective measures of factitious potential in defendants are likely to be given greater credibility.

The F-K ratio of the MMPI has long been considered one indicator of an individual's tendency to "fake bad" (Anthony, 1971). Other scales of malingering have been developed using the MMPI (Cofer, Chance, & Judson, 1949; Dahlstrom, Welsh, & Dahlstrom, 1975).

A simple test which has shown merit in identifying those seeking a self-serving goal through poor performance is the 15-item test, developed by

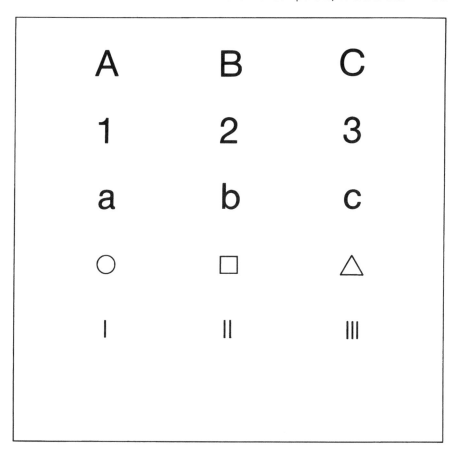

FIGURE 7.4.   The 15-Items Test.

Rey (1941). The subject is shown a card (Figure 7.4) with 15 figures illustrated. It will be noted that although there are 15 figures, they are arranged in five sets of three figures, systematically related to each other. Because of the grouping, only a profoundly brain-disordered person or orthopedically dysfunctional person could not reproduce these figures with only a brief exposure to the stimulus card.

The subject is told he or she will be asked to perform a difficult task involving the memorization of 15 different figures, with an emphasis on *difficult* and *different*. The stimulus card is then exposed for 10 seconds. The card is removed, and the subject is told to draw as many of the 15 figures as he or she can recall. Unless there is significant dysfunction in the neuropsychological or peripheral systems, adult subjects of normal intelligence should be able to reproduce at least three of the five sets accurately (Lezak, 1976).

A more detailed review of current research on deceit, malingering and, faking bad is presented in Chapter 12.

REPORT OF FINDINGS

The style of the report submitted will vary among jurisdictions, depending on the requirements of the statutes. In some jurisdictions, a simple three-part report containing the referral data, current mental status, and legal opinion is acceptable (Petrella & Poythress, 1983). In other jurisdictions, an elaborate set of statements relating the psychological test findings and interviews to specific criteria may be required.

A report of psychological evaluation of competence to stand trial may be as simple as a letter to the judge stating the psychologist's opinion. More often, the question of competence to stand trial is part of a series of questions posed by the referring attorney or judge. The following case illustrates this point.

PSYCHOLOGICAL REPORT

July 29, 1991

NAME: Jones, David Charles   DATE OF EXAMINATION: 6/26, 6/30, 7/8, 7/16/91 (9 hours total)

ADDRESS: Central Booking—County Jail   TELEPHONE: 000-0000

BIRTHDATE: 4/17/60   AGE: 31–2   OCCUPATION: Unemployed

EDUCATION: 10

Referral

Joseph Smith, refers Mr. Jones for evaluation. Mr. Smith has been appointed as a public defender for Mr. Jones who is charged with several counts of armed robbery. Mr. Smith would like Mr. Jones evaluated for competency to stand trial, capacity to waive his rights, current emotional status and their implications, and an estimate of Mr. Jones's sanity at the time of the offense.

History for Mr. Jones

Mr. Jones is charged with armed robbery and armed burglary. He feels that the maximum penalty he may receive for this is life imprisonment. He states that he is pleased that Mr. Smith is his attorney. Mr. Jones states that he has been arrested before for possession of drugs, drunkenness, and escape from a police station. Four robberies are involved in this series of charges. He states that he was sitting in a bar drinking, and some men started talking, and the first time it happened he simply "went along for the ride." After that, they came to his house and sought him out for participation. He states that at the time of the interview he felt mixed up and depressed. He has little hope that anything good will happen to him. His only wish is to get back to his first wife.

He was asked about his confession, and he indicated that he doesn't remember a good part of this. He drank a lot of alcohol the day before and had been drinking every day. In the prison situation, he has withdrawn from alcohol, and although this was difficult at first, he now feels somewhat better.

He states that he was born in Hoopers Island, Maryland. His mother is living, but he doesn't know whether or not she is well. She is a housewife. She is in her 60s. The father is living and well, 66, and retired. He has had odd jobs, but he hasn't talked to the father in several years. There is a brother, 27, and sisters, 25 and 23. He grew up in Cambridge, Maryland. He quit high school in the 10th grade at the age of 17. At that point he enlisted in the Army (RA123456789). His course in the military included basic training at Fort Bragg, and advanced training at Fort McClelland, Alabama. MOS-11 Bravo. He went to Fort Benning and attended Jump School and graduated. At Fort Dix he was given orders for the 101st Division. He was shipped to Vietnam where he became a replacement in the First Infantry Division. He spent 45 days short of two years in Vietnam, signing up for a second tour of duty. His first year he served as an infantryman and during the second year as a door gunner on a helicopter. He had several R and Rs. His basic weapons included the M-16 and M-60. He was wounded with shrapnel in his leg. His decorations included his Jump Wings, CIB, Bronze Star, and various theater ribbons. The Bronze Star was with V. He rose as high as E-5, but was "busted." He states this was because he fell asleep. He tried to get stationed somewhere near his home and couldn't. He went AWOL. He turned himself in as sick.

During the service, he took a great many drugs in Vietnam. He also drank heavily. He received a discharge in 1970 at Fort Meade, Maryland, which he claims was a medical discharge. He states that he saw psychiatrists there and feels that perhaps he had a nervous breakdown.

He had an automobile accident with unconsciousness at age 20. He had a barbiturate overdose at age 20. He was unconscious for five days as a result of his accident. He has never been in a VA hospital. He has been in the state hospital and has attended with various psychiatrists.

In talking about his military career, he is bland and flat. When asked what his job was in the military in Vietnam, he said, "My essential job was to kill people." There was a great deal of drinking, and use of marijuana and other drugs. He undertook a second tour in Vietnam because he was promised that he could get out of his enlistment several months early if he finished the second tour with less than 150 days of duty left. By the end of his tour he just wanted to get out under any circumstances.

Following his discharge, he thought about Vietnam for a while. He had bad dreams, and his first wife told him he would wake up screaming and shaking. Now he sometimes talks about it when he is drinking. He feels that he would do it again if he had to. He dislikes discussing it when sober.

He married at age 20 while he was still in the service. The wife was 17 at the time. She still lives in Maryland. She is a housewife on welfare. There are daughters, 9 and 7 years of age. He talks to her whenever he can now. She says she would like to have him back. They were divorced in 1974 because of his drinking and doing drugs.

Background Information

Mr. Smith provided police records of the offense, deposition of codefendant Morgan, summary of treatments at the Eastern Shore State Hospital, Cambridge, Maryland, therapy notes from Doctor Smithers, and military records from Jones's enlistment through his discharge.

From these records, it was learned that Mr. Jones did not live with his parents until he was five or six, being raised by his grandmother. The father was a heavy drinker. The mother and the father were generally in conflict and argumentative. The mother was running around with other men. The mother and sister have had grand mal seizures. Mr. Jones has been suspected of this, and at one time he was on rather heavy anticonvulsant medication. Mr. Jones has had some suicidal attempts. He has been deeply depressed. He has been drinking heavily for a good part of his adult life. He considered suicide when he returned from the service. He had much difficulty in the Army, and was eventually discharged after court martial. He waived his rights at the time of this court martial. He enlisted at the time when the military was taking people of questionable emotional and intellectual status. His tests indicate that he was of Low Average intellect at the time he was enlisted. In spite of this, he did his duty in a satisfactory manner. In an evaluation dated September 12, 1970, an Army psychiatrist, Dr. Rheingold, certified that Mr. Jones is "severely depressed and in need of psychiatric treatment." In spite of this, he was not given a psychiatric discharge, nor recommended for veterans' benefits. This is certainly a very poor recommendation of the military of that era and their treatment of those who served honorably in combat theaters.

Following his discharge, his emotional condition apparently worsened, and he received a variety of psychiatric treatments in Maryland, both inpatient and outpatient. He was diagnosed as having Alcohol Addiction, a Depressive Neurosis, and an Explosive Personality Disorder (Eastern Shore State Hospital, January 7, 1971).

The history is that of an individual who was raised under very poor family conditions, who did very poorly academically, left school, joined the service, received a considerable amount of combat training, performed well under extremely stressful combat circumstances, but began to "crack" while in the service. Drugs, and various emotional reactions, including getting into difficulty with the authorities, allowed him to complete his term in the military, but not before he became acutely disturbed and was discharged. He was not given proper treatment by the military or the Veterans Administration. He continued to drift and became worse. He became addicted to alcohol, continued to have considerable family and interpersonal problems, and continued downward until he has reached his present circumstance.

Examination Procedures

Wechsler Adult Intelligence Scale-Revised, Wechsler Memory Scale, Torque Test, Indiana-Reitan Neuropsychological Short Form, Competency Evaluation, Luria-Nebraska Neuropsychological Investigation, Thematic Apperception Test, Minnesota Multiphasic Personality Inventory, House-Tree Test, FIRO-B, History, Observation, and Interview. (All examinations took place at Central Booking, except the Luria-Nebraska Neuropsychological Examination which was conducted at 213 East Davis Boulevard, Tampa, Fla.)

Response to Evaluation

Mr. Jones is a short, brown-haired man with a touch of gray. He has long eyelashes. He wears a mustache. His speech is crackly and deep. He speaks low with moderate verbal skills. Motor behavior is controlled, and hearing seems within normal limits.

Clinical Observations

Mr. Jones shows little emotional affect. He listens intensely and concentrates sometimes well and sometimes poorly. In general he is somber.

Results of Examination

A. *Intellectual Factors*

Objective results of 10 subscales of the WAIS-R were as follows:

Factor	Deviation IQ	Percentile
Verbal scale	88	21st
Performance scale	96	40th
Full scale	90	25th

The above scores represent Low Average intellectual capacity. No unusual scatter is noted, and it certainly confirms the estimate made based on Army records.

B. Neuropsychological Factors

No evidence of mixed cerebral dominance is found. The Wechsler Memory Scale, Form 1, resulted in a Memory Quotient of 92 which correlates with his intelligence quotient as expected. The Indiana-Reitan Neuropsychological Short Form suggests the presence of minimal signs of cerebral disturbance, the quality of which is primarily in the left hemisphere. A complete Luria-Nebraska Neuropsychological Battery resulted in the Rhythm Scale exceeding the critical level, with the Pathognomonic Scale fairly low. This suggests that there is some mild pathology of long-standing. The primary location of his difficulties would be in the left frontal area and in the right sensory motor strip.

Analysis of the Deficit Scale indicates that Mr. Jones is brain-disordered in such a manner that he will have special difficulty in translating verbal relationship into action. The pattern is that which would be associated with anterior damage, most probably in the frontal lobes.

C. Competence to Stand Trial

Mr. Jones in general knew that he was in a difficult situation, and that he could receive a long jail sentence. He was depressed and discouraged. At the time he was given the Lipsitt Competence Screening Test, he scored a total of 25 points, which would be called "borderline competent." This means that at times he would be competent to understand the charges against him and to assist his attorney. At other times he might not. The results of the neuropsychological examinations certainly suggest that at times he understands the implications of verbal instructions, and explanations, and at other times he does not.

D. Personality Factors

(1) *Interpersonal Activity.*   This is a man who is a "loner." A dependent, concrete-thinking person, he is often unable to understand the nature of situations and the implications of his behavior. He is very dependent. He thinks simplistically. He has episodes in which he is disorganized, confused, and suffers bizarre thought processes. At times, his behavior is totally unpredictable. In general, he tends to be nervous, anxious, and depressed. At other times, he is quite apathetic and listless. He has great difficulty in concentrating, or formulating any reasonable kinds of plans or goals. Socially he is a shy, inhibited person whose behavior is quite unpredictable. His decision making is inappropriate.

(2) *Early Identifications.*   The personality tests suggest that this man had extremely poor modeling from both the mother and the father. There are indications that the parents were not available. The picture of the mother is that of a disturbed, depressed, volatile person, while the father is seen as a rigid, harsh, stubborn, inadequate model.

(3) *Anxiety Structure.*   Life to Mr. Jones is confusion. The expression of emotion is a grave danger, and he tends to avoid it. He is unable to deal with stress or conflict. His coping mechanisms are almost nil. He suffers a severe dominance/submission conflict, and he never really knows when to act, when to withdraw, when to stand up for himself, and when to comply with others. His perception of life is confused, alternating with terror and hopelessness.

(4) *Defense Mechanisms and Coping Capability.*   Mr. Jones suffers a serious thinking disorder. He could be properly classified as suffering from paranoid schizophrenia. His intellectual defenses are limited to being hostile, suspicious, keeping people at a distance, moodiness, dependent gullibility, and a tendency to be drawn to aggressive male leadership. His less intellectual defenses include turning rage inward and suffering considerable depression, the release of anxiety through the excessive use of alcohol and drugs, and the explosion of inappropriate behavior while drinking. He is unable to be efficient in vocational activity. His defense mechanisms are very poor, and this is a man who simply cannot govern his own behavior. Although he has periods of clarity, he is frequently in a psychotic state.

Summary and Conclusions

Psychological evaluation of Mr. David Jones finds him to be a man of Low Average intellectual capacity, probably suffering from a variety of brain disorders both in terms of electrical disturbance and damaged brain tissue. The personality structure is that of an individual unable to accommodate himself to life. He experiences frequent psychotic episodes, and there are times when he explodes with no control or appropriateness in the behavior. He is drawn to drinking and to drugs to relieve his terror and anxiety, but these in turn lead to acting out aggressive impulses. He adjusted poorly in his childhood, had a short period of adjustment during training in the service, but began to break down during combat. At the end of his service career, he was experiencing very severe psychiatric symptoms, and although these were identified, they weren't treated. He was discharged, faced the stress of civilian life and marital difficulties, and moved deeper into psychotic behavior. He was treated rather poorly in several psychiatric sessions, and became worse. He suffers a post-Vietnam stress syndrome, which is a special form of Posttraumatic Stress Disorder, Delayed and Chronic (309.81). Because of the organic personality disorders, he must be considered as suffering an Organic Syndrome (310.10), in addition to the above.

In the past several years, we have seen the emergence of stress disorders among Vietnam veterans (Figley, 1978). A common characteristic of the trauma of combat in this particular setting is the delayed onset of symptoms either in their development or their recognition (DeFazio, 1975). In this situation, individuals avoid psychosis or severe depression by "psychically closing off" (Krystal, 1968). People such as Mr. Jones have been found to become lower in coping abilities, particularly if they had early stressful parental relationships and had a tendency to use alcohol and drugs (Struen & Solberg, 1972). Such veterans show severe adjustment problems including disorientation, violent acting out, hopelessness, and apathy (Strayer & Ellenhorn, 1975). Such cases often show a severe depression 8 to 12 months after returning from Vietnam (Helzer, Robins, & Davis, 1974). About 35 percent of those who served in combat were found to have clinically depressed personalities on return to the United States (Beck, 1967). A large proportion of these broke down in the service and received fairly severe discipline and even court martials when they returned from Vietnam (Beck). Researchers generally agree that the Vietnam-related experiences tend to result in numerous psychiatric problems, but the emergence of these severe problems tends to be delayed until after removal from the combat setting and until the time the person returns to the United States or joins the civilian environment (Lifton, 1973; Solomon, Zarcone, Yoerg, Scott, & Maurer, 1971). It is common to find moral crises, readjustment problems, drug and alcohol addiction, and unemployment among such veterans. One of the syndromes that is often found has been called the "numbed guilt" reaction. This includes psychic numbing, depression, anxiety, nightmares, insomnia, denial, suppression, confusion, disillusionment, uncontrollable hostility, wanton violence, drug and alcohol addiction, unemployment, lack of goal-oriented motivation, and inability to adapt to civilian life (Bourne, 1969; Fox, 1972). Hostile impulses, angry episodes, alienation, interpersonal conflict, and tyrannical behavior can be expected. Fully one-third of Vietnam veterans use some kind of illicit drug, as well as alcohol.

There is no question that those who had family problems before they entered the service were much more likely to suffer the most severe kinds of reactions (Worthington, 1976). One can conclude from the above that Mr. Jones certainly has followed the pathways noted above. At the time of our examination, it is questionable whether he is competent to stand trial most of the time, although he tends to be "in and out." He is certainly very disturbed, experiences fragmented psychotic episodes, and within reasonable psychological probability, while using drugs or alcohol, based on the settled condition he suffers, is unable to understand the nature of his acts or their consequences. He, especially during such times of stress and alcohol or drug abuse, is unable to form intent. Mr. Jones is desperately in need of long-range psychiatric custody and treatment.

References

Beck, A. T. (1967). *Depression*. New York: Harper & Row.

Bourne, P. G. (Ed.). (1969). *The psychology and physiology of stress*. New York: Academic Press.

DeFazio, V. J. (1975). The Vietnam era veteran. *Journal of Contemporary Psychotherapy, 7*(1), 9–15.

Figley, C. R. (Ed.). (1978). *Stress disorders among Vietnam veterans*. New York: Brunner/Mazel.

Fox, R. P. (1972). Post-combat adaptational problems. *Comprehensive Psychiatry, 13*, 435–443.

Heltzer, J. E., Robins, L. N., & Davis, D. H. (1974). *Depressive disorders in Vietnam returnees*. Unpublished manuscript, Washington University.

Krystal, H. (Ed.). (1968). *Massive psychic trauma*. New York: International Universities Press.

Lifton, R. J. (1973). *Home from the war*. New York: Simon & Schuster.

Solomon, G. F., Zarcone, V. P., Yoerg, R., Scott, N. R., & Maurer, R. G. (1971). Three psychiatric casualties from Vietnam. *Archives of General Psychiatry, 25*, 522–524.

Strayer, R., & Ellenhorn, L. (1975). Vietnam veterans: A study exploring adjustment patterns and attitudes. *Journal of Social Issues, 31*, 81–94.

Struen, M. R., & Solberg, K. B. (1972). The Vietnam veteran: Characteristics and needs. In L. J. Sherman & E. M. Caffey (Eds.), *The Vietnam veteran in contemporary society*. Washington, DC: Veterans' Administration.

Worthington, E. R. (1976). The Vietnam era veteran. *Military Medicine, 141*, 169–170.

The U.S. Supreme Court has recently emphasized the critical importance of competency evaluation.[18]

To determine competence, not only of testamentary ability but for the individual to make such decisions as the refusal of medical procedures, the psychological expert should consider a battery of neuropsychological tests. The neuropsychological domains related to competency functions as described by Alexander (1988) are as follows:

Attention	Expressive Language
Verbal Memory	Receptive Language
Abstraction	Executive Function
Visuospatial Function	Judgment

Many neuropsyhcological instruments are available to determine the presence or absence of these cognitive factors relating to an individual's competence. Both flexible and standardized batteries of neuropsychological tests are used (Sweet, Moberg, & Westergaard, 1996).

COMPETENCE OF THE CHILD WITNESS

More and more children seem to become involved in the legal system each year. The child may be a defendant in a criminal matter or a witness in criminal or civil litigation. Cases are often decided on the basis of the credibility or the competence of the child to testify. Recently, considerable research has been generated aimed at evaluating children's credibility and competence (Ceci & Bruck, 1995). At issue are such questions as whether the child is capable of understanding and taking the judicial oath, the accuracy of the child's cognition, the reliability of the child's memory, the relationship between factual recall and fantasy, the child's vulnerability to manipulation, and the potential trauma to the child of legal proceedings (Blau & Blau, 1988; Gordon, Jens, Hollings, & Watson, 1994).

A growing area of interest and concern regarding juvenile competence has emerged in the issue of minors' competence to consent to abortion. Research in this area is still sparse, but there are no indications that a minor's decision-making capabilities in this emotionally charged area should be held incompetent unless specific psychological evidence so indicates (C. Lewis, 1987).

Juvenile Competence to Stand Trial

Most jurisdictions apply the standards used for adults in determining competence to stand trial (Grisso, Miller, & Sayles, 1987). The Supreme Court's ruling *Duskey v. United States*[19] generally applies to juveniles. Thus the child or adolescent defendant is competent to stand trial if he or she has sufficient present ability to consult with his or her attorney with a reasonable degree of rational understanding and if the adolescent has a rational as well as factual understanding of the proceedings against him or her. Some courts have questioned the applicability of the adult standard to juveniles.[20]

Savitzky and Karras (1984) found that juveniles 15 years of age and younger scored significantly lower on the Harvard Competency Screening Test than adults. Cowden and McKee (1995) found that age, severity of diagnosis, and history of remedial education were correlated with determination of incompetence to stand trial.

Although more research on this important question is required, the psychologist has a plethora of testing instruments that can answer the court's questions as to whether a juvenile has the requisite cognitive, intellectual, and personality attributes to be considered competent to stand trial.

TESTAMENTARY COMPETENCE

Although the frequency and importance of competence issues in the matter of wills is unchallenged, the doctrine underlying the law's requirement that the person (testator) making the will be competent has received little clinical, research, or judicial attention during the past 100 years or so (Spaulding, 1985).

The psychologist may be called on to render opinions to aid the court in determining whether a person long dead was competent to dispose of his or her worldly goods in the testamentary document commonly called a *will*.

The traditional rules of testamentary competence require that the willmaker:

1. Know he or she is making a will.
2. Knows the extent of the property involved.

3. Understands how the will distributes the property.
4. Knows to whom the willmaker would naturally feel generous (the natural objects of his or her bounty).

Testimony by mental health professionals concerning these requirements will require the expert witness to review all available medical, psychological, educational, and vocational records associated with the time when the will was made. Depositions of friends, neighbors, supervisors, co-workers and relatives can be helpful in terms of consistency of the behavior of the testator as described by those who supposedly knew the willmaker at the time the will was executed and whose observations are reliable.

This is an area of expert testimony where the psychologist must be extremely careful to maintain objectivity and be very willing to opine "I don't know" where appropriate.

Becoming an expert witness in the matter of competence to stand trial requires diagnostic skill and experience, a knowledge of the statutory criteria and expectancies in the jurisdiction of record in the case, and the ability to communicate clearly to the points at issue.

NOTES

1. U.S. Const. Amend. VI.
2. 18 U.S.C. 4244.
3. *United States v. Davis*, 481 F.2d 425 (4th Cir. 1973).
4. *Riccardi v. United States*, 428 F. Supp. 1059 (D.C. N.Y. 1977), *aff'd* 573 F.2d 1294 (2nd Cir. 1977).
5. *Duskey v. United States*, 362 U.S. 402 (1960).
6. Ibid.
7. *United States v. Zooluck*, 425 F. Supp. 719 (D.C. N.Y. 1977).
8. *United States v. Horowitz*, 360 F. Supp. 772 (D.C. Pa. 1973).
9. *Fed. R. Evid.* 601.
10. Fla. R. Crim. P. 3.211 (1997).
11. *People v. Williams*, 15 Cal. Rptr. 191, 194 Cal. App. 2d 523 (1961).
12. *Frye v. United States*, 293 F. 1013 (D.C. Cir. 1923) & *Daubert v. Merrell Dow*, 113 S. Ct. 2786 (1993).
13. *Murphy v. Waterfront Comm'n*, 378 U.S. 52, 55 (1963).
14. 5 Mental Disability L. Rep. 269 (1981).
15. *Estelle v. Smith*, 101 S. Ct. 1866 (1981).
16. *United States v. Byers*, No. 78–1451 (D.C. Cir. 1980).
17. *Jenkins v. United States*, 307 F.2d 637 (D.C. Cir. 1962). (See Appendix A for details.)
18. *Cooper v. Oklahoma*, 116 S. Ct. 1373 (1996).
19. *Duskey v. United States*, 362 U.S. 402 (1960).
20. Ibid.

8

The Insanity Defense

In the eyes of the law, it is insufficient to be guilty of an act of criminality, or *actus rea*. The defendant must also be found to have the capacity to understand the wrongness of the act and to choose behavior other than the criminal act. This concept of *mens rea* means knowing what one does is wrong or impermissible. As Glueck (1925) wrote: "The *mens rea* of criminal behavior includes the volitional-inhibitory as well as cognitive modes of mental life and a disease of either of these constitutes one of the legally recognized factors of the guilty mind that is the *sine qua non* to responsibility." For almost 2000 years, civilized societies have codified exculpability, or blamelessness, for those whose mental condition renders them without the ability to know right from wrong (Howell, 1982). Historically referring to "moral blameworthiness," in the 20th-century mens rea has come to refer to the specific state of mind, including intent and malice, required for conviction of particular criminal offenses (ABA Standing Committee, 1983).

The purpose of the plea of "not guilty by reason of insanity" is to allow triers of fact to consider excusing criminal behavior in those they find to be without mens rea, without awareness or cognition that their act is illegal, unacceptable, forbidden, or subject to society's judgment and punishment. The insanity defense has an entrenched place in Anglo-Saxon law and morality. The acts of deranged persons are not to be judged in the same way as the acts of rational persons (Finkel, 1988; Leo, 1982a; Slovenko, 1973).

Public concern and consequent legislative action tend to occur in dramatic instances where the insanity defense becomes a matter of public debate. In 1843, Daniel M'Naghten, in attempting to shoot Robert Peel, the prime minister of England, killed Peel's secretary. At the trial, defense counsel convinced the jury that M'Naghten was laboring under such a defect of reason resulting from a disease of the mind that he did not know the nature and quality of the act he was doing and did not know that what he did was wrong. The jury found the defendant innocent by reason of insanity. A public hue and outcry followed. A royal commission was appointed to study the issue. After much deliberation, and considerable dependence on early

19th-century psychiatric thinking, the commission established what has been since that time known as the *M'Naghten Rule*.[1]

Sometimes designated the "all-or-none rule," the M'Naghten Rule is based on an archaic and unsubstantiated psychiatric concept that an "insane" person suffers a disease rendering the cognition and volition of the individual clearly defective. This should not be surprising considering what was known and more importantly what was not known about human personality 150 years ago when the M'Naghten Rule was developed and accepted. The M'Naghten test states:

> To establish a defense on the ground of insanity, it must be clearly proved that, at the time of the committing of the act, the party accused was laboring under such a defect of reason, from disease of the mind, as not to know the nature and quality of the act he was doing; or if he did know it, that he did not know what he was doing was wrong.

This represented a narrow, cognitive definition of insanity based on the limited and often incorrect assumption in the early nineteenth century as to the nature and cause of psychiatric conditions.

In 1961, a new definition of insanity was adopted as part of the Model Penal Code of the American Law Institute (ALI):

> A person is not responsible for criminal conduct if at the time of such conduct as a result of mental disease or defect he lacks substantial capacity either to appreciate the criminality of his conduct or to conform his conduct to the requirements of the law.[2]

The ALI insanity definition broadened the M'Naghten concept by asking whether defendants understood the criminal nature of their act and whether they were able to conform their conduct to what was required by law.

Two alternatives to the insanity defense have been proposed in order to do away with the concept that a mentally disturbed person is in some way exculpated from usual standards of guilt. The first, often referred to as "guilty but mentally ill," is a standard first legislated in Michigan in the mid-1970s. "Guilty but mentally ill" allows a jury to find that although the defendant is not insane, and as a result is guilty of the offense of which he or she is charged, the mental illness demonstrated during the trial must be taken into consideration. Procedure requires that the judge sentence the defendant to a prison where meaningful mental health care is available. An opportunity to find a defendant guilty but mentally ill allows a jury an alternative to acquitting a defendant by reason of insanity.[3]

While 26 states use the M'Naghten Rule, 21 states use a version of the ALI Model Code definition of insanity. Three states—Utah, Idaho, and Montana—have eliminated the plea of innocent by reason of insanity. Although eliminating the insanity pleading, such legislation does allow

State	Test Used	Locus of Burden of Proof	Standard of Proof	GBMI	No Reforms
Alabama	ALI	D	Prep.		x
Alaska	M'N	D	Prep.	x	
Arizona	M'N	D	Prep.		
Arkansas	ALI	D	Prep.		
California	M'N	D	Prep.		
Colorado	M'N	S	BYRD		
Connecticut	ALIm	D	Prep.		
Delaware	M'N	D	Prep.	x	
District of Columbia	ALI	D	Prep.		x
Florida	M'N	S	BYRD		
Georgia	M'N	D	Prep.	x	
Hawaii	ALI	D	Prep.		
Idaho	n/a*	D	C&C		
Illinois	ALI	D	Prep.	x	
Indiana	M'N	D	Prep.	x	
Iowa	M'N	D	Prep.		
Kansas	M'N	S	BYRD		x
Kentucky	ALI	D	Prep.	x	
Louisiana	M'N	D	Prep.		x
Maine	ALI	D	Prep.		x
Maryland	ALI	D	Prep.		
Massachusetts	ALI	S	BYRD		x
Michigan	ALI	S	BYRD	x	x
Minnesota	M'N	D	Prep.		
Mississippi	M'N	S	BYRD		x
Missouri	ALIm	D	Prep.		
Montana	n/a*	D	Prep.	x	
Nebraska	M'N	D	Prep.		
Nevada	M'N	D	Prep.		x
New Hampshire	Dur.	D	Prep.		
New Jersey	M'N	D	Prep.		x
New Mexico	M'N+	S	BYRD	x	
New York	M'Nm	D	Prep.		
North Carolina	M'N	D	Prep.		
North Dakota	ALIm	S	BYRD		
Ohio	ALI	D	Prep.		
Oklahoma	M'N	S	BYRD		
Oregon	ALI	D	Prep.		
Pennsylvania	M'N	D	Prep.	x	
Rhode Island	ALI	D	Prep.		

FIGURE 8.1. Insanity defense update.

State	Test Used	Locus of Burden of Proof	Standard of Proof	GBMI	No Reforms
South Carolina	M'N	D	Prep.	x	
South Dakota	M'N	S	BYRD	x	
Tennessee	ALI	S	BYRD		
Texas	M'N	D	Prep.		
Utah	n/a*	S	BYRD	x	
Vermont	ALI	D	Prep.		
Virginia	M'N+	D	Prep.		x
Washington	M'N	D	Prep.		x
Wisconsin	ALI	D	Other		x
Wyoming	ALI	D	Prep.		

* Question of sanity relates to *mens rea* at the time of the crime.
Key:
ALI = American Law Institute   M'N = M'Naughten
Dur. = Durham   D = defense
S = state   Prep. = preponderance of the evidence
BYRD = beyond a reasonable doubt   C&C = clear and convincing evidence
m = modified

Source: Reprinted with permission. *11 Mental and Physical Disability Law Reporter* (1987).

FIGURE 8.1. *(Continued)*

expert testimony on the issue of mens rea or any state of mind that is an element of the crime in question. Such testimony is not admissible if it focuses on "insanity" or "diminished responsibility." The testimony on mental disability must strictly focus on mens rea. How broadly the courts will interpret mens rea, as defined by evidence of mental disability, is yet to be seen. Figure 8.1 presents current tests for insanity, by state and for federal jurisdictions.[4]

TRIAL STRATEGY

The insanity pleading is invoked in less than 1 in every 1,000 criminal cases. Only 4% to 5% of such pleadings result in a finding of innocent by reason of insanity. Thus only 1 in 25,000 criminal cases ends with a verdict of innocent by reason of insanity (Howell, 1982). In determining trial strategy, an attorney must weigh the possible advantage of the insanity defense against losing all the options available when pleading "not guilty." By notifying the court of intent to plead the defendant innocent by reason of insanity, so that the court may order the necessary mental examinations prescribed by statute, the attorney, in essence, pleads the defendant guilty of the crime but claims excusal on the basis of insanity. Many attorneys are reluctant to use the insanity defense because there is no going back to a plea of "not guilty" and all its consequent options. Boenhert (1989) found that 80% of successful insanity acquittees had previously been found incompetent to stand trial compared with 33% of those who plead insanity but were found guilty.

BURDEN OF PROOF

The initial burden of proof for the insanity defense falls on the defendant. The attorneys who intend to use the insanity defense must go forward and introduce some evidence that counters the assumption that the defendant is sane. Once this evidence is placed before the court, the burden of proof may fall on the prosecution or the defense. In approximately one-half of the states, the defense must prove, by *a preponderance of the evidence*, that the defendant was legally insane at the time the offense was committed. In the other half of the states and in the federal jurisdiction, the prosecution must prove *beyond reasonable doubt* that the defendant was legally sane at the time the crime was committed. Thus the defendant's rights are protected by requiring the lowest burden of proof when the defense must convince a jury that the defendant was insane. In those jurisdictions where the burden of proof falls on the prosecution, the defendant must be proved sane at the highest weight of evidence. To accomplish the latter, the prosecution must present evidence and witnesses to demonstrate unequivocally that the defendant was without disease or defect of mind at the time the crime was committed.

To this end, the judge's instructions charge the jury with the responsibility of deciding the issue. The following pattern jury instruction is currently used by judges in federal courts:

> There is an issue in this case concerning the sanity of the defendant at the time of the acts or events alleged in the indictment.
>
> The sanity of the defendant at the time of an alleged offense must be established by the government beyond a reasonable doubt because willful intent, as you have been instructed, is an essential element of the offense charged, and a person who is insane is not capable of forming such intent.
>
> A person is insane within the meaning of these instructions and is not responsible for criminal conduct if, at the time of such conduct, as a result of mental disease or defect, he lacks substantial capacity either to appreciate the wrongfulness of his conduct or to conform his conduct to the requirements of the law.
>
> The term "mental disease or defect" does not include an abnormality manifested only by repeated criminal or otherwise antisocial conduct.
>
> If, after consideration of all the evidence in the case, you have a reasonable doubt as to whether the defendant was sane at the time of the alleged offense, you must find him not guilty.

Responsive to the considerable scholarly, legislative, and public interest in the insanity defense, the American Bar Association (ABA) has proposed new standards of nonresponsibility for crime. The proposed new test of insanity identifies the defendant's appreciation of the wrongfulness of his or her conduct alone as a basis of exculpation and rejects the volitional element of the ALI Penal Code test for insanity. The ABA further opposes the enactment of statutes that supplant or supplement a verdict of not guilty by reason of insanity with a verdict of guilty but mentally ill. The proposed standard (7-6.1) states:

(a) A person is not responsible for criminal conduct if, at the time of such conduct, and as a result of mental disease or defect, that person was unable to appreciate the wrongfulness of such conduct.

(b) When used as a legal term in this standard, "mental disease or defect" refers to either:

  (i) Impairments of mind, whether enduring or transitory; or

  (ii) Mental retardation, which substantially affected the mental or emotional processes of the defendant at the time of the alleged offense. (ABA Standing Committee on Association Standards for Criminal Justice, 1983)

It is anticipated that these proposed standards will influence legislative modifications of the insanity defense in the foreseeable future.

TESTIMONY OF EXPERTS QUESTIONED

Experts are sharply divided on the issue of whether the existing statutes are fair or practical in respect to the testimony of experts. In the aftermath of the attempted assassination of President Ronald Reagan by John Hinckley in 1982, the defendant was found innocent by reason of insanity. Wide media coverage indicated that the jury was in considerable conflict about its decision (Isaacson, 1982). Various experts debated the issues. At one extreme, it was suggested that in the future psychiatrists and psychologists must confine their testimony to experimental findings and statistical facts, devoid of opinions and theoretical notions (Robinson, 1982). Some experts have long advocated the legislative banishment of all psychological and psychiatric testimony, making such statements as, "There is absolutely no scientific or medical criteria for determining the presence or absence of mental capacities" (CSPA, 1981). At the other extreme, some noted psychiatrists believed that the abolition of the existing system would lead to unfairness and danger to the mentally ill (Bockman, 1982).

In 1983, the American Psychiatric Association urged a tightening up of standards and procedures to protect the public against premature release of potentially dangerous individuals but recommended that the insanity defense be retained. The association opposed any form of the plea "guilty but mentally ill." The position expressed by the American

State	Statutory Compilation	NGRI Citation	GBMI Citation
Alabama	Ala. Code	§15-16-2	
Alaska	Alas. Stat.	§12.47.010	§12.47.030
Arizona	Ariz. Rev. Stat. Ann.	§13-502A; §13-502B	
Arkansas	Ark. Stat. Ann.	§41-601	
California[1]	Cal. Evidence Code	§522	
Colorado	Colo. Rev. Stat.	§16-8-101(1); §16-8-104; §16-8-105(2)	
Connecticut	Conn. Gen. Stat.	§53a-12; §53a-13	
Delaware	Del. Code Ann.	11 §304a; 11 §401	11 §401(b)
District of Columbia	D.C. Code Ann.	§24-301	
Florida	Fla. R.Cr. Proc.	§3.217	
Georgia	Ga. Code Ann.	§26-702; §26-703; §27-1503	§26-702; §26-703; §27-1503
Hawaii	Hawaii Rev. Stat.	§704-402; §704-408	
Idaho	Idaho Code	§18-207	
Illinois	Ill. Ann. Stat.	§6-2; §6-2(e)	§6-2(c)(d)
Indiana	Ind. Code Ann.	§35-41-3-6; §35-41-4-1(b)	§35-36-2-3(4)
Iowa	Iowa Code Ann.	§701-4	
Kansas[2]	Kan. Stat. Ann.		
Kentucky	Ky. Rev. Stat. Ann.	§504.020; §500.070	§504.130
Louisiana	La. Rev. Stat. Ann.	R.S. 14:14; Art. 652	
Maine	Me. Rev. Stat. Ann.	17-A §39	
Maryland	Md. Ann. Code	§12-108; §12-109	
Massachusetts[3]			
Michigan[4]	Mich. Comp. Laws Ann.	§768.21(a)	§330.1400a
Minnesota	Minn. Stat. Ann.	§611.026	
Mississippi[5]			
Missouri	Mo. Ann. Stat.	§552.030	
Montana[6]	Mont. Code Ann.	§46-14-201	§46-14-311
Nebraska[7]	Neb. Rev. Stat.	§29-2203	
Nevada[8]	Nev. Rev. Stat.		
New Hampshire[9]	N.H. Rev. Stat. Ann.	§628.2 (II)	
New Jersey	N.J. Stat. Ann.	§2C: 4–2	
New Mexico[10]	N.M. Uniform Jury Instructions	§41.01	§31-9-3
New York	N.Y. Penal Law	§40.15	
North Carolina[11]			
North Dakota	N.D. Cent. Code	§12.1-04-03; §12.1-01-03(2)	
Ohio[12]	Ohio Rev. Code Ann.	§2943.03; §2901.05	
Oklahoma[13]	Okla. Stat. Ann.	21 §152	
Oregon	Or. Rev. Stat.	§161.305; §161.055	

FIGURE 8.2. Statutory and case law citations.

State	Statutory Compilation	NGRI Citation	GBMI Citation
Pennsylvania	Pa. C.S.A. (Purdon)	18 §315; 18 §315(b)	18 §314
Rhode Island[14]			
South Carolina	S.C. Code	§17-24-10	§17-24-20
South Dakota[15]	S.D. Codified Laws Ann.		§25A-25-13
Tennessee[16]			
Texas	Tex. Code Crim. Proc.	§2.04; §8.01	
Utah[17]	Utah Code Ann.	§76-2-305	§64-7-2-8; §77-35-21.5
Vermont	Vt. Stat. Ann.	13 §4801	
Virginia[18]			
Washington	Wash. Rev. Code Ann.	§10.77.030(2)	
West Virginia[19]			
Wisconsin	Wis. Stat. Ann.	§971.15; §971.175	
Wyoming	Wyo. Stat.	§7-11-305	

1. *People v. Drew*, 149 Cal. Rep. 275; 583 P.2d 1318 (Cal. 1978).

2. *State v. Granerholz*, 654 P.2d 395 (Kan. 1982); *State v. Roaderbaugh*, 673 P.2d 1166 (Kan. 1982).

3. *Commonwealth v. Brown*, 434 N.E.2d 973 (Mass. 1982); *Commonwealth v. Nassar*, 406 N.E.2d 1286 (Mass. 1980).

4. NGRI, *People v. Savoie*, 349 N.W.2d 139 (Mich. 1984); GBMI, *Michigan v. John*, 341 N.W.2d 861 (Mich. Ct. App. 1983).

5. *Herron v. State*, 287 So.2d 759 (Miss. 1974).

6. *State v. Doney*, 636 P.2d 1384 (Mont. 1981).

7. *State v. Lamb*, 330 N.W.2d 462 (Neb. 1983).

8. *Poole v. State*, 625 P.2d 1163 (Nev. 1981); *State v. Behiter*, 29 P.2d 100 (Nev. 1934).

9. *State v. Plummer*, 374 A.2d 431 (N.H. 1977).

10. *State v. Wilson*, 514 P.2d 603 (N.M. 1973).

11. *State v. Wickers*, 291 S.E.2d 599 (N.C. 1982).

12. *State v. Staten*, 267 N.E.2d 122 (Ohio 1971).

13. *Munn v. State*, 658 P.2d 482 (Okla. 1983).

14. *State v. Johnson*, 399 A.2d 469 (R.I. 1979).

15. *State v. Kost*, 290 N.W.2d 482 (S.D. 1980).

16. *State v. Clayton*, 656 S.W.2d 344 (Tenn. 1983); *Stacy v. Love*, 679 F.2d 1209 (6th Cir. 1982).

17. *State v. Baer*, 638 P.2d 517 (Utah 1981).

18. *Davis v. Commonwealth*, 204 S.E.2d 272 (Va. 1974); *Price v. Commonwealth*, 323 S.E.2d 106 (Va. 1984).

19. *State v. Rhodes*, 274 S.E.2d 920 (W.Va. 1981); *State v. Bias*, 301 S.E.2d 776 (W.Va. 1983).

Source: Reprinted with permission. *11 Mental and Physical Disability Law Reporter* (1987).

FIGURE 8.2. *(Continued)*

Psychiatric Association is that there is a lack of clear, objective methods of ascertaining mental states with a high degree of accuracy (Boffey, 1983). Both the American Bar Association and the American Psychiatric Association Committee on Legal Issues have recommended reforms (Melton, 1983).

After the *Hinckley* case, the insanity defense became one of the most hotly debated and controversial issues in mental health law (Callahan, Mayer, & Steadman, 1987). Many states have instituted insanity defense reforms in such areas as the legal definition of insanity (referred to as "The Test"), whether the burden of proof lies with the prosecution and the evidentiary standard of proof as shown in Figure 8.1. Since *Hinckley*, many states have reconsidered and reformed commitment and release of dangerous insanity acquitees. Figure 8.2 presents the statutory and case law citations reflecting these reforms.

In 1984, the Congress of the United States developed a statutory formulation of the federal insanity defense by passing the Insanity Defense Reform Act[5] (IDRA). The IDRA states:

> It is an affirmative defense to a prosecution under any Federal statute that, at the time of the time of the commission of the acts constituting the offense, the defendant, as a result of a severe mental disease or defect, was unable to appreciate the nature and quality or the wrongfulness of his acts. Mental disease or defect does not otherwise constitute a defense.

In this act, Congress deleted the "volitional" element of the insanity defense found in the Model Penal Code and focused exclusively on the "cognitive" element of the M'Naghten Decision (see Appendix A). In this, the emphasis is on the accused's ability to appreciate (understand) the nature and quality or the wrongfulness of his or her actions.

It is again worthwhile to encourage the expert witness to become current as to the insanity standards in the jurisdiction in which he or she intends to testify. Judicial decisions and legislative actions constantly modify standards.

CURRENT ROLE OF EXPERTS

The courts are guided by statutory provisions in the matter of expert testimony. Judges will generally follow the *Federal Rules of Evidence,* which advises:

> If scientific, technical, or other specialized knowledge will assist the trier of fact to understand the evidence or to determine a fact in issue, a witness qualified as an expert by knowledge, skill, experience, training or education may testify thereto in the form of an opinion or otherwise.[6]

In the matter of insanity, the court may allow a variety of professional and lay witnesses. Traditionally, physicians—most frequently, psychiatrists—have testified as to the defendant's mental state at the time of the felony. More recently, psychologists have testified in the matter of insanity.

The role of the expert is to provide the judge and jury with information and opinions that the average jury member could not deduce from the evidence. These opinions are to be based on the special skill, knowledge, and experience the expert uses when examining the facts of the case and the defendant. The decision as to whether a defendant is innocent by reason of insanity lies with the triers of fact. *The expert is not brought to court to render an opinion as to whether the defendant is innocent.*

The behavioral scientist as an expert witness in a case involving the insanity defense is in a difficult position. The court is seeking information concerning the defendant's capacity to exercise free will, while the behavioral scientist is supposed to be a nonjudgmental professional. Testimony as to the defendant's background, personality, intellect, reality contact, or cognitive skills is only of importance if it leads to an opinion on the part of the expert as to the defendant's ability to understand the criminal nature of his or her act at the time it occurred or, in those jurisdictions following the ALI Model Code, if the defendant had substantial capacity to understand the wrongfulness of an act or to conform his or her behavior to the requirements of the law.

Whereas a psychiatrist generally depends on the facts of the case and a psychiatric examination of the defendant as the basis for the opinion that will be rendered in court, psychologists more often focus their testimony on the results of psychological tests. Although the testimony of mental health experts remains a critical aspect in virtually all criminal trials involving the insanity defense, psychiatric and psychological experts have been criticized in specific ways. Diagnoses are frequently a part of the expert's opinion yet reliability of most diagnostic labels has been shown to be poor. Further criticism has focused on intentional or unintentional bias as well as lack of standardized methods and procedures for making decisions related to the legal concept of insanity. These factors were studied by Beckham and her group (Beckham, Annis, & Gustafson, 1989). They selected 180 mental health professionals who agreed to evaluate a hypothetical case in terms of the insanity pleading. All subjects (psychiatrists and psychologists) were listed as forensic evaluators by the circuit courts of the state. Each was provided with extensive historical data, arrest reports, defendant's statements, mental status examinations and a wide variety of psychological tests. The subjects were divided into three groups: One group was told ɩhat they were nominated by a prosecutor; the second experimental group was told they had been referred by a circuit judge; while the third group was instructed that their names had been put forth by a defense attorney. About one-third of the experts rated the defendant as "guilty" while almost two-thirds opined the hypothetical perpetrator was "not guilty by reason of insanity." A small number (5%) offered no decision. Those who concluded that the defendant was guilty believed the record showed less schizophrenia at the time of the offense but more chronic mental illness; that the behavior at the time of the offense was less a product of the mental illness; that collateral reports from relatives, observers, police officers, and jailers were most important; and the interview and some of the psychological tests were less important. Those who decided on "guilty" reported more forensic training.

As might be expected, psychiatrists placed less importance on test findings.

PSYCHOLOGICAL EXAMINATION OF DEFENDANTS

In preparing to examine a defendant who has filed a plea of innocent by reason of insanity, the psychologist should consider what factors may indicate or suggest an absence of criminal intent or an inability to conform to the expectancies of the law. No psychological test is standardized adequately for this specific purpose. Tests and other materials serve as aids in helping the psychologist, as an expert in human behavior, to form an opinion based on *reasonable psychological probability* (more likely to be so than not) as to the state of mind of the defendant at the time of the felony.

The issue is convoluted. There are many instances where the psychologists may find insufficient information on which to base an opinion. Behavior of the defendant on psychological examination is only rarely sufficient for the expert to render an opinion concerning a previous event. A substantial approach to the psychological evaluation of a defendant who has pleaded innocent by reason of insanity requires the following elements.

1. *Events and Observations Concerning the Crime.* The psychologist has a responsibility to collect a complete dossier on the facts of the crime. This includes the police and witness reports. The psychologist must be careful not to use any statements or reports from unsworn witnesses, since such material may be ruled hearsay and could result in the psychologist's testimony being excluded during the trial. From all the material available, the psychologist must construct as objective a picture as possible of what actually happened. No exploration of the mens rea can occur until there is an accurate picture of the actus rea.

2. *The Defendant's Recall.* There should be available to the psychologist a transcript of the defendant's description of the events leading up to the crime, the act itself, and the defendant's behavior following the act, usually in the form of police reports or statements. The facts of the crime as the defendant relates them should also be part of the history taken by the psychologist. The way in which the defendant perceives and recalls his or her involvement in the crime will be an important element of the psychologist's formulation of an opinion as to whether the defendant possessed mens rea at the time the crime was committed. In some instances, the defendant will claim total or partial amnesia for the events that occurred before, during, or after the crime. This could be significant in the appraisal of the probability of the presence of a mental disease or defect at the time of the criminal act.

3. *Ancillary Sources.* In most instances, it is possible to obtain information from witnesses and bystanders about events immediately preceding the crime, the crime itself, and the behavior of the defendant immediately following the crime. In order to be able to assess the mental state of the defendant at a time and place where no direct observation was made by the psychologist, the use of techniques developed in psychological autopsy may be necessary (Shneidman, 1976). It may even be possible to retrieve information of value concerning the victim or victims of the crime to determine what influence this may have had on the behavior and cognition of the defendant. Such evidence has been ruled admissible in some jurisdictions

(Lichter, 1981). It is important that the psychologist make known during the initial contact with the attorney who requested consultation that these materials will be required. They are best obtained by the attorney's investigative staff.

4. *Psychological Evaluation.*   It is recommended that a standard, complete, psychological evaluation be the keystone of every consultation involving the insanity defense. Since questions concerning a defendant's mental status include competence to stand trial, the evaluation should include the instruments and procedures necessary to answer questions relating to both sanity and competence to stand trial. The psychological test battery should include:

a. *A History from the Defendant.*   This should include background, previous treatment experience, and recall of circumstances surrounding the crime.

b. *A History from the Family of the Defendant.*

c. *Intellectual Evaluation.*   The psychologist should use a multiscale, well-standardized battery of intelligence tests that assesses verbal and nonverbal factors.

d. *Neuropsychological Factors.*   Even if no neuropsychological deficit is suspected from either history or behavior, a screening evaluation should be done. Any anomalies of significance found on the screening test will require proceeding to a full neuropsychological evaluation. Martell (1992) has reviewed the important role neuropsychological evaluation can play in issues of criminal responsibility.

e. *Competency Evaluation.*   An evaluation of the defendant's competency to stand trial should be included, as noted previously. Procedures and instruments are reviewed in Chapter 7.

f. *Reading Skills.*   A well-standardized test of reading skills is necessary to ensure that the defendant can be given test materials requiring a variety of reading capabilities (vocabulary, comprehension, speed). This is particularly important should there be questions regarding the defendant's intellectual capacity, reality contact, confusion, or bilingualism. This may be considered and evaluated when the psychologist is called on to render opinions based on the defendant's test performance.

g. *Personality.*   Although the other areas of assessment will contribute to the psychologist's final opinion as to mens rea, it is the personality evaluation that is likely to define the defendant's perception of the world, cognitive style, response capabilities, and limitations. The choice of tests, projective and objective, must be made with a view to the psychologist's ability to justify and defend these instruments as reliable and valid. Psychologists with extensive background and experience rarely have difficulty in explaining and justifying projective techniques. Some have suggested using only a single, standardized, objective personality test as a strategic move to avoid challenge of projective methods by opposing counsel (Ziskin, 1981). In choosing personality-measuring procedures, the psychologist would be well advised to conform to the expectancies of *Frye v. United States* as well as *Daubert v. Dow Chemical*, which were addressed in detail in Chapter 5.

h. *Measures of Faking or Malingering.*   Although current methods leave much to be desired, every effort should be made to measure the presence or absence of these factors. Chapter 12 explores this thorny issue.

5. *The Report of Findings and Opinion.*   In all cases, the psychologist should prepare a report that integrates all the information, material, and examination findings noted above. The report should include the following areas or subsections:

a. The process by which the psychologist was retained.

b. The facts of the case and their sources.

c. The defendant's recollection of events surrounding the crime.

d. Observations of the defendant's behavior by friends, relatives, witnesses, and enforcement personnel.

e. Family history and events of significance in the defendant's life.

f. Tests and procedures used. Dates and time spent with the defendant.

g. Clinical observations during testing. A statement as to competence at this time is appropriate here.

h. Test results.

i. A summary statement of the defendant's psychological state at the time of the examination, including any diagnosis or categorization of this state that may be appropriate. Comments concerning the validity of the procedures and/or indications that the defendant attempted to fake bad should appear here.

j. An evaluation of the degree of "fit" or absence of such concordance of the facts of the case with the history, observations of behavior, and the defendant's psychological state and recollections.

k. A statement of the psychologist's opinion as to effect on the defendant's mens rea of any mental defect or disease and whether the events described in the facts of the case suggest, within reasonable psychological probability, that the defendant was unable to understand the acts he or she committed were unlawful or wrong. If there is reasonable evidence to support an opinion that the defendant may be capable of understanding the act was wrong but, because of a defect or disease influencing the defendant at the time of the crime, was unable to conform his or her behavior to those standards, it should appear as an opinion. This is best done in the written report, as answers to a series of questions originally posed by the retaining attorney.

Figure 8.3 presents a checklist that can be useful to the expert in ensuring that the evaluation in respect to an insanity defense has been thorough.

There are frequent instances in which the psychologist may finish an extensive evaluation and be unable to state an opinion with certainty, in respect to the statutory definition of insanity in the jurisdiction where the defendant is being tried. When this happens, it must be stated straightforwardly to the attorney retaining the psychologist at the earliest time possible. Every expert should realize that his or her opinion is a part of the retaining attorney's trial strategy and the earliest notification of the expert's findings and opinion is not only proper professional courtesy but essential to the attorney's representation of the case.

Mental health experts with much experience in examining for purposes of testifying regarding insanity find that a small number of defendants who claim this defense easily meet the legal criteria of being without mens rea, a modest number clearly had mens rea, and the largest number consists of complex, difficult cases where opinions are likely to be equivocal and varied. Some of this reflects the inexactness of all the behavioral sciences. Much of the difficulty arises, however, in attempting to reconcile the analysis of an individual by a mental health professional using classification systems derived from medicine, Aristotelian logic, and the empirical data and norms of behavioral science with the requirement of jurisprudence that a moral judgment must be made. The reconciliation is possible, but the route is tortuous and fraught with opportunities for the psychologist to slip into the role of trier of fact, rather than the proper stance as an expert presenting opinions based on material from the expert's field of science.

In a study using mock jurors, it was found that when given unequivocally clear information about the degree of control and cognitive dysfunction of the defendant, jurors relied heavily on this information in voting acquittal based on insanity (Bailis, Darley, Waxman, & Robinson, 1995).

Case Style _____ Date Referred _____

Records Review
____ Police reports   ____ Defendant's school records   ____ Pre-event mental health records
____ EMS/autopsy   ____ Defendant's military records   ____ Post-event mental health records
____ Defendant's post-event statements   ____ Collateral witness statements
____ Pre-event collateral informant interviews   ____ Incarceration records

Legal Records Review
____ Appropriate state/federal statutes   ____ Affidavits and motions
____ Indictment

Evaluation
____ Interview(s)   ____ Observation   ____ Intellectual factors
____ Cognitive factors   ____ Reading level   ____ Personality factors
____ Validity evaluations   ____ Check all scoring   ____ Recheck all scoring
____ Time and administration/scoring initials on each test and record

Report
____ Oral report to judge/retaining attorney   ____ Written report—rough
____ Check all reported scores and percentiles   ____ Cite appropriate references to support opinion

FIGURE 8.3.   Insanity defense evaluation.

The psychologist as expert in an insanity pleading would be well advised to avoid exotic or complex analyses of data. In all probability, a defendant likely to be found innocent by reason of insanity will suffer from one of the following diseases or defects which are known to affect mens rea:

1. *Mental Deficiency.*   A severely or profoundly retarded individual may simply lack the cognitive capacity to understand his or her participation in an illegal act. The exculpation of young children also falls in this category. A person with a mental age of 3 or 4 years is unlikely to be held to have mens rea, whether the individual is 3 or 33 years of age chronologically. Intelligence tests provide clear support for an expert opinion of "not able to understand the nature of the act." The issue becomes hazier as the mental age of the individual passes 5 years and will depend on factors and circumstances in addition to the limited intellectual capacity.

2. *Neuropsychological Dysfunction or Defect.*   The rapid development of neuropsychological research and of sophisticated neuropsychological examination techniques over the past decade have provided the instrumentation and the database to enable psychologists to render opinions as to defects in cognition, awareness, and judgment based on clearly defined and generally accepted neuropsychological deficits. Individuals suffering focal conditions, such as temporal and frontal lobe lesions, and more diffuse tissue disturbance or convulsive pathology are known to have periods in which judgment, planning, or awareness disappear or are seriously diminished. Such objective findings lend significant weight to the opinion of a neuropsychologist testifying that under the conditions surrounding the defendant's crime, it was probable that the defendant was not in possession of the capacity to control or understand his or her own behavior.

A decision by the Colorado Supreme Court sustained the use by a psychologist of neuropsychological assessment to support expert testimony that a defendant in a murder trial suffered minimal brain dysfunction and thus had poor impulse control. The defendant was acquitted of the charge of murder, by reason of insanity.[7] This suggests that, as Wigmore predicted, "the courts are ready for psychology when psychology is ready for the courts" (Louisell, 1955).

3. *Emotional Disturbance.*   Although in common parlance severe emotional disturbance (or psychosis) is viewed as synonymous with insanity, this equivalence is not accepted by the courts. No matter how severe the emotional disturbance, it is irrelevant to the issue of insanity unless the condition results in such a state of mind that the individuals are without an understanding of the criminality of their act or, as a result of their condition, are unable to exert their will to conform to the expectancies of society and the law.

The analysis of all the data available, including personality tests, may indicate that the defendant is the product of a very inadequate developmental experience, has suffered numerous psychiatric hospitalizations, and is subject to episodes of psychosis. Such findings indicate deep emotional disturbance but are insufficient for a jury to find such an individual innocent by reason of insanity. Expert testimony is likely to be seen as credible in this setting only if the psychologist can demonstrate that the emotional disturbance is such that the defendant's mens rea is cast in doubt for the time the crime was committed.

In evaluating the emotional status of a defendant pleading innocent by reason of insanity, the psychologist should be able to clearly relate the defendant's current test results and descriptive diagnosis to the events and observation concerning the crime, the defendant's recall of the events and his or her perceptions, and the data concerning the defendant's behavior from ancillary sources. Unless a clear, logical, and consistent pattern of behavior indicates that the defendant's emotional disturbance was responsible for an absence of awareness and/or will, the psychological expert has nothing to say that will be viewed by the triers of fact as salient to the issue of insanity.

The psychologist is placed under a considerable judgmental burden in testifying about the mental state of a person at a point in time often far removed from the time the psychological evaluation is conducted. At the time of the examination, the defendant's emotional or neuropsychological condition may be in remission. By the same token, the patient may be in worse condition during the psychological examination than at the time of the crime. The psychologist must never ignore the possibility that the defendant may attempt to present a factitious disorder since the secondary gains that could accrue from convincing an expert that he or she is crazy are considerable.

Being an expert witness in an issue involving the insanity pleading often places the psychologist in a difficult and vulnerable position. The expert will be pressed to make moral rather than scientific judgments, and the issues and data are so variable that a gaggle of opposing witnesses is more the rule than the exception. Modifying one's values as a behavioral scientist or practitioner in order to function competently as an expert is difficult. Attorneys often seek experts to validate "syndromes" that they propose will excuse criminal behavior. As Morse (1995) puts it:

> Mental disorders may give people crazy reasons for doing what they do, but virtually never negates the defendant's intention, knowledge, conscious awareness of the risk, and other required mental states.

It is important that the psychologist make as early a determination as possible as to whether the facts of the case warrant the thorough, expensive, and time-consuming procedures necessary for competent psychological opinion on the issue of insanity. In respect to expert mental health testimony, the First Circuit Court of Appeals opined in *U.S. v. Schneider*,[8] "testimony proferred as pertinent to defendant's state of mind was substantially outweighed by capacity to mislead jury into thinking that evidence mitigated the offense." It is usually best to be able to opine "I don't know" early on, instead of pursuing an extensive exploration where there are few indications that the defendant lacked mens rea.

The case illustration that follows presents a psychological examination conducted in an effort to determine whether a defendant was insane at the time he planned and executed a bank robbery. The case was being retried after the defendant had already been convicted and was serving a sentence in prison. The issue of insanity had not been raised by the defendant's counsel during the original trial even though the defendant was ruled legally incompetent before the time of the trial.

While the defendant was in prison, it became apparent to the prison's psychological counselor that the defendant had not been properly represented by counsel during the trial. A writ of habeas corpus was filed on behalf of the defendant, and a new trial was mandated by the courts. New counsel was appointed, and in preparation for the trial, a psychologist was retained to evaluate the defendant as part of a defense of innocent by reason of insanity. In the report, which follows, the psychologist addresses specific questions posed by the attorneys for the defendant in an effort to determine whether there was any possibility that the defendant was insane at the time of the bank robbery. The case jurisdiction was in federal court, so it was the defense counsel's responsibility to raise the issue of insanity. The prosecution would then bear the burden of proof to demonstrate beyond reasonable doubt that Browne was sane at the time of the robbery.

PSYCHOLOGICAL REPORT

August 8, 1983

NAME: Browne, Albert S.

DATE OF EXAMINATION: 8/3/83, 8/4/83, 8/6/83

ADDRESS: 106 Evergreen Street, Winter Haven, Florida 30000

TELEPHONE: 000-0000

BIRTHDATE: 2/12/46   AGE: 37–6

OCCUPATION: Disabled

EDUCATION: Grade 6 + GED

Referral

Mr. Browne was convicted of bank robbery in 1977. He has been in prison until recently. A writ of habeas corpus was filed on his behalf, indicating that his lawyer during his original trial did not make the insanity pleading even though Mr. Browne was at that time legally incompetent.

The courts have overturned his original conviction and have mandated a new trial. The courts have appointed Messrs. Gregg Thomas and Michael Piscitelli of the firm of Holland and Knight as his attorneys.

Attorneys Thomas and Piscitelli request psychological evaluation to determine answers to the following questions:

1. Does Mr. Browne suffer mental disease or defect?
2. Is it likely that he suffered a mental disease or defect at the time that he committed the bank robbery in 1977?
3. If indeed he does suffer a mental defect, is it one that results in a lack of substantial capacity to appreciate the wrongfulness of his conduct?
4. If Mr. Browne suffers a mental disease or defect, is it such that it results in periods of time when he is unable to conform his conduct to the requirements of the law?
5. If indeed he suffers a mental disease or defect, is it an abnormality manifested only by repeated criminal behavior or antisocial conduct?
6. If Mr. Browne suffers and has suffered a mental disease or defect, and it is your opinion that he suffered it at the time of the bank robbery, is it your opinion that he was either unable to appreciate the wrongfulness of his conduct or unable to conform his conduct to the requirements of the law at that time?

Interview with Mr. Browne

Mr. Browne was seen for psychological evaluation on August 3, August 4, and August 6, 1983. Interviews and tests covered a total of seven and three-quarter hours of time. On August 6, an extensive history was taken from Mr. Browne. Mr. Browne was first informed of the purpose of the examination and that the material would be provided to his attorneys. He agreed to all aspects of the examination. He states that Messrs. Thomas and Piscitelli were appointed as his attorneys in 1982. Mr. Browne states that he was in the Avon Park Correctional Institution, convicted of bank robbery. The bank robbery took place on September 13, 1976. It took place at the Barnett Bank in Cypress Gardens. He and his partner, Jimmy Roberts, pulled up to the back of the bank as the manager was transferring night deposits. Mr. Browne was armed with a pistol. He does not remember what kind. He was apprehended after this act because of a cigarette lighter he left, with his CB "handle" on it. They traced the name to him.

His attorney at that time was Jim T. Crowley. Mr. Browne tried to get Mr. Crowley to use the defense of insanity. He states that Mr. Crowley knew that he had been declared insane. Mr. Browne says that he was having visions and talking with his dead father.

Mr. Browne feels he is now competent to stand trial. He likes his attorneys and understands what they are trying to do for him. He has no hallucinations at the present time. He states that things seem more crystal clear to him than he ever remembers in his entire life. He states that while in prison he was a "loner" and "did my own time." He states that during the last couple of years in prison he got involved with the church and studied the Bible. He feels it took "root" in him, and is helping him to work out things in himself which were wrong. He goes to church two or three times a week.

Mr. Browne says that he was born in Myrtle Beach, South Carolina, where he lived until 18 years of age. His mother, living, 60 years of age, still is in Myrtle Beach. She is a housewife. He describes her as a person who "survives." His recollections of her are that of a cruel person who seemed to be more cruel to him than the other children. The father, who died in 1974, was 58 years of age at the time. Cause of death was a stroke with complications. He had been a farmer. He was a person who "was a terror to be around." He never gave Mr. Browne any love or affection. He drank and became violent. He beat Mr. Browne unconscious on several occasions when Mr. Browne was a child.

There are six brothers and five sisters. Two brothers have been in mental institutions. Several of his siblings are ambidextrous, and can write with both hands.

He recalls his grandmother trying to drown him in the ocean when he was small. His brothers also tried to kill him in a similar way. The family thought he was "slow." He remembers that at age 10 or 11 his brothers tied him to a tree and forced him to have oral sex with them and with some of their friends. Mr. Browne remembers trying to tell his mother and father about this, but they "slapped me down." They accused him of lying. He ran away from home on a number of occasions, living in the woods, until the family would find him and bring him home. It would then start all over. He feels his family tried to get rid of him.

He attended Myrtle Beach Elementary School through the sixth grade. He left at age 12, running away from home. In addition to living in the woods, he lived in the streets and in the alleys and sheds of the community. He was always terrified of his family. He hid from them. He stayed with friends occasionally but also slept in alleys and in boxes and in sheds. Between 14 and 15, he was picked up by the police and sent to reform school for petty larceny. They tried to get him to work on a farm. He was forced to drive a tractor against his wishes, and he cut down 12 acres of corn. They put him into seclusion, where he stayed until he was almost 16. He was picked up at school by his mother and his brothers. The same thing happened—his father became drunk and violent. Mr. Browne was picked up by the police for stealing saws from a construction job. He spent 18 months on the chain gang for that. He went in at 17 and came out when he was about 19. At about this time, he married. He decided he could not stand Myrtle Beach and came to Florida in 1966. His cousin got him a job, but he could not keep the job. He drank, and when he was not drinking, he would just walk off in a daze or a trance. He felt people were following him, and he tried to run them over. They were all imaginary. He tried to shoot them with a gun, and the sheriff picked him up and put him in jail. His wife and his cousin asked for a doctor to examine him. He was committed to Arcadia in 1967. He was there 6 to 8 months and his wife signed him out. He attended Hillsborough County Guidance Center on an outpatient basis after that. He was taking heavy medication. He went back to the county hospital about 1968. He was in and out of the county hospital because he was not taking his medicine as he was supposed to. Some truck drivers gave him some pills, and he also drank whiskey, and he just "ran around like crazy." In 1970, he was picked up for Breaking and Entering and charged with Grand Larceny. They found him insane and committed him to Chattahoochee. He was there 3 months and then was released to the courts. They sent him on an outpatient basis to the Hillsborough County Guidance Center. He stayed there until August or September 1971. He got into bad shape with drinking, and he began to scare everyone, accusing his wife of all sorts of things. He heard someone calling him. He left Hillsborough County, left his family, and went to Winter Haven. He did not know anyone. He met a woman and eventually married her.

She is now his wife. He took her to Georgia in order to get married. He was still married and told her nothing about this. She found out he was married and forced him to get a divorce, and then later they remarried, in 1973. He went off his medication, was drinking, and had lots of problems in 1973. He did not tell his wife anything about his background. He covered up his whole life. In May 1974, their house burned down. He thought he saw figures standing in the fire. People tried to calm him down. They tried to give him liquor to calm him, and this made him worse. He called home to tell them that his house burned down, and shortly after that his father had a stroke from which he never recovered. (At this point, Mr. Browne cried softly.) He says he did not know how he got to the hospital. He got a call from his baby brother, "Daddy is dead." He walked out, left his wife, and headed for South Carolina. He does not know how he got there.

He states he loved his father, but never had a relationship with him. After Mr. Browne married his second wife, he feels his father started to like him. He remembers standing at the grave of his father saying, "I won't let you die." His father replied to him, "I am not dead—I'm within you." Mr. Browne says he talked to his father a lot. The father told him that he wanted a farm. (Mr. Browne cries volubly at this point.) He says that the father told him he loved him and that Mr. Browne should go out and get a farm. He started stealing things and selling them and collecting the money. The burglaries got larger and larger. He would see people carrying money or cashing checks, and he would just go and take it. He says that his father would pat him on the back and say, "Everything will be okay, son." He says that the voice of his father told him he loved him very much.

He is not clear about all aspects of the bank robbery. The purpose of the robbery was to continue to get money for the farm. He says that he wanted his father to love him. He feels that his father finally did start to love him. He then died. When asked his memory about the bank robbery, he says that he remembers getting up in the morning, and that his father put his arm around him and talked to him and told him to wake Jimmy up and "Go get the money." He says that his father's voice said, "Go get the money—tell that man to give us the money." When asked how he knew about the bank manager taking the money out of the bank, he says that he thinks that a week or a month or so before that, he saw the transaction at the bank—with the bank manager walking across the parking lot with the bank bag. When asked how he convinced Jimmy to go along with him, he does not recall convincing Jimmy of anything—it just happened. They went back home, and he was still talking with his father. He put the money in a jar and buried it with the other money. The police found them out. He got an attorney—Jim T. Crowley. He told his story to Mr. Crowley. Mr. Browne says that Mr. Crowley told him to go and get the money and bring it to him. They dug up the money and gave him all of the money. It was in excess of $40,000.

He says that the authorities never believed him when he told them that. Mr. Crowley denied receiving it. He has only one receipt for $1,500. Mr. Browne says that he remembers piling the money on the lawyer's desk.

Mr. Browne did not testify at his own trial even though he wanted to. He was not allowed to take the stand. He was convicted and sentenced to 10 years in prison.

The writ of habeas corpus resulted from a filing by a fellow prisoner who worked in the library. He also feels that he was helped by a psychological counselor, Norman Payne, who took an interest in him. When Mr. Payne found out that Mr. Browne was 100 percent disabled and still registered as insane and legally incompetent since 1970, he helped with the writ. Mr. Browne served 5 years, 6 months, and 21 days in prison. Two cases were involved. While he was out on bond in the first bank robbery, awaiting appeal, the same lawyer told him to "listen to your father and get more money—and buy the farm." Mr. Browne was picked up on another robbery, a store down the road from his own place, where people knew him. They sent him to Doctor Darbey in Polk County in December 1978. He was still talking to his father. They put him on three or four different medications. Over several months, he seemed to improve. He has been in jail between 1977 and the present time when he was released.

Mr. Browne is under the medical care of Arturo Perez, M.D. He receives counseling from Roy Mercer, a psychologist at the Winter Haven Hospital Mental Health Clinic. Mr. Browne takes Stelazine, 2 milligrams, twice a day, and Elavil, 5 milligrams, at bedtime for sleep.

He remembers no severe accident. His only unconsciousness remembered is when his father beat him several times. Mr. Browne chews tobacco, but uses no alcohol. His activity includes shooting pool with his wife one night a week, cutting yards, landscaping yards, doing some woodwork, and jogging. He is beginning a citrus nursery and hopes that this will lead to something permanent.

He first married at age 21 to a woman who was 11 years his senior. There was one son to that union, who is now 12 years of age. Mr. Browne began to write to him when he was in prison, and he sees him occasionally. The current marriage to Judith still exists. The wife is 42 years of age, a secretary. There are two stepchildren of her former marriage, and Mr. Browne says, "I've become their daddy."

Records Reviewed

Order Adjudging Mr. Browne Incompetent, dated June 27, 1967, signed by Judge Brooker, indicating that Mr. Browne suffered a Schizophrenic Reaction, Paranoid Type. He was said to have Homicidal and Suicidal Ideas, Threatening and Uncontrolled Behavior, Potential Violence, Inappropriate Mood with Flattened Affect, Persecutory Feelings, Emotional Lability, and Low Frustration Tolerance. *Order Adjudging Restoration,* dated September 26, 1967, indicating competency was restored. *A Committee Finding of Incompetency,* dated June 26, 1967. *A Commitment to State Hospital, Hospital,* dated August 10, 1970. After a charge of Breaking and Entering to commit a felony, it was stated in this order that Mr. Browne "is deranged at the present time, did not know right from wrong." He was sent to the State Mental Institution in Chattahoochee. *Report,* signed by G. W. Barnard, M.D., and Gustave Newman, M.D., stating that Mr. Browne was incompetent, unable to stand trial, and insane. Evaluation, dated July 16, 1970. *Report* of Charles DeMinico, M.D. *Psychiatric evaluation,* dated August 31, 1971, diagnosing Mr. Browne as Schizophrenia—Paranoid Type, Chronic, Active. *Note* indicating that Mr. Browne was seen by Doctors R. H. Coffer and A. Gonzalez, Psychiatrists. They agreed on a diagnosis of Schizophrenic Reaction, Paranoid Type. *Report of A. DenBreeijen, M.D., Psychiatrist,* dated April 13, 1973. Diagnosis: Schizophrenic Reaction, Paranoid Type. Delusions, hallucinations, fears. It was found that Mr. Browne could not deal effectively with others. Prognosis poor. *Report* of J. R. Price, Ed.D., Psychologist at Community Mental Health Center, indicating a diagnosis of Schizophrenia, Chronic, Undifferentiated Type. *Report* of November 18, 1982, by Peter Holden, M.D., Psychiatrist at the Federal Correctional Institute, Camp Butner, North Carolina. Paranoid Schizophrenia, In Remission. Axis II Anti-Social Personality Disorder. Axis III Mild Hypertension. One hundred percent disability pension. *Report* by William P. Reevy, Ph.D., Psychologist at the Butner Federal Correction Institution, dated October 13, 1982. I Schizophrenia, Paranoid Type, In Remission. II Anti-Social Personality. *Deposition* by Mr. U. Richardville, dated

March 19, 1982. Mr. Richardville states he has been a neighbor of Mr. Browne for eight years. He reports Mr. Browne discharging firearms on many occasions, with no apparent purpose. He was beaten up by Mr. Browne. He described Mr. Browne as "schizo." A person given to sudden emotional outbursts. At times, Mr. Browne would shoot his weapon at cattle several miles away. *Deposition* of Judith Browne, dated March 19, 1982. She describes her husband's odd, impulsive behavior from time to time since they were married. At one time, she asked him to try some mashed potatoes, shortly after they were married, and he left, and drove off in the car, leaving her. Sometime after they were married, he suddenly pulled out some pictures at a social gathering and began showing his child and his ex-wife to her friends. Mrs. Browne claimed that the bizarre behavior was interspersed with kind and loving behavior. He would sometimes pull a gun and threaten her life. He pursued a voice that he heard on the CB. He would suddenly decide to drive 600 miles to go to visit his father's grave. He would sometimes insist that Mrs. Browne go with him while he talked to his dead father. She reports many incidents of bizarre, changeable, psychotic behavior. He would suddenly shift from awareness and good reality contact to bizarre, driven, unaware behavior that showed obvious lack of reality contact. This behavior was typical of a schizophrenic, with paranoid and delusional systems, hallucinations, and sudden dangerous behavior. *The testimony and proceedings before Honorable William B. Hand,* District Judge, in the matter of the United States of America versus Albert Browne on May 30, 1977. Mr. Jim T. Crowley for the defendant and Honorable Anthony J. LaSpada, Assistant U.S. Attorney for the United States.

Summary and Analysis of Records

The records show that Mr. Browne has a long-standing psychotic condition, which has been generally labeled Schizophrenia, Paranoid Type. This very severe mental disease and its consequent and resulting defects are well in keeping with the history reported by Mr. Browne relating to his family and his treatment therein. There is no question that at times he is actively psychotic, experiencing persecutory feelings, hallucinations, and delusions. There is no question that at times his conduct has been such that he cannot appreciate the wrongfulness of such conduct, nor can he conform his conduct to the requirements of the law or of society. He was found legally incompetent in June 1967. In 1970, he was found to be insane and committed to a state mental institution on this basis. There is little or no disagreement among the various professional persons who have examined him in the past as to his severe mental condition. It is a mental disease or defect that is sometimes subject to the ameliorating effects of medication, and sometimes appears to be in remission. Thus, the person can at times appear to be perfectly rational, with substantial capacity to deal reasonably in a seemingly normal manner, as long as there are no stressful conditions in the environment, both internal and external.

Examination Procedures

Wechsler Adult Intelligence Scale-Revised, Luria-Nebraska Neuropsychological Battery, Gates-MacGinitie Reading Tests—Survey D—Form 1, Thematic Apperception Test, Minnesota Multiphasic Personality Inventory, Draw-a-Person Series, House-Tree Test, History, Interview, and Clinical Observations.

Response to Evaluation

Mr. Browne is a man of somewhat above middle height, with dark-brown hair and dark-brown eyes. He wears a moustache. He states that he has high blood pressure and is taking medication for it. He speaks in a deep, soft, intense manner. He is very serious. Motor behavior is controlled. He cooperates well and seems to have good confidence. He talks a great deal about his poor background, his time in prison, and his tendency to be several different people at different times.

He claims that prison has given him a new perspective on life. He talks of enjoying history and expresses pride in the heritage of America. He claims descendancy from American Indians. He has tried to share his problems and experiences with other people who have problems, but he is frustrated in finding "they don't understand." He feels himself to be a changed person today. He is fearful of the label "chronic" because he wants to feel that he can change.

Results of Examination

A. Intellectual Factors

Ten subtests of the Wechsler Adult Intelligence Scale-Revised were administered with the following results:

Factor	Deviation IQ	Percentile
Verbal scale	99	47th
Performance scale	93	33rd
Full scale	96	40th

The above results place Mr. Browne in the Average range of intellectual capacity. No significant scatter. These results are in keeping with previous estimates of intellectual capacity.

B. Neuropsychological Factors

The results of the Luria-Nebraska Neuropsychological Battery indicate no signs of central nervous system dysfunction.

C.   Reading Skills

The results of the Gates-MacGinitie Reading Test—Survey D—indicate that Mr. Browne is a functional reader and has very good vocabulary and comprehension. His responses to the written tests can be considered entirely valid.

D.   Personality Factors

1. *Interpersonal Activity.*   The profile presented by Mr. Browne is that of a serious thinking disorder. About 2% of males in psychiatric populations show this profile. His thinking and behavior is frequently marked by confusion and misunderstanding. Thinking is markedly unconventional. His thoughts tend to be fragmented and tangential. He will be seen as frequently making impulsive, unrealistic decisions that show emotional unpredictability. His behavior is often hostile and suspicious, showing the Distress Syndrome (nervousness, anxiety, and depression). His ideas tend to be scattered, confused, and contaminated. His associations are often autistic and bizarre. People who know him will report sudden outbursts of unfriendliness and anger for no apparent reason. His choices and decisions are disorganized and represent behavior regression. The pattern is entirely in keeping with the history reported by the patient and the behavior reported by those who have seen him in his daily life.

2. *Early Identifications.*   His projective techniques, interviews, and personality tests suggest that the parental models were vague, disturbed, and without real substance. The mother and father were apparently frequently in conflict. Although the mother was the primary figure in his life, Mr. Browne has always been fearful of losing her love. She was apparently quite rejecting. The father was an unknown, frightening figure who became a "monster" when he drank. Mr. Browne fantasizes some sort of integration with the father figure into his life, in a delusional way.

3. *Anxiety Structure.*   Mr. Browne has no real feeling about the integrity of his body or his mind. He has no inner identity. He feels no ties to the past. He has very severe mixed feelings of repulsion and attraction in respect to his father. He experiences terror when he feels he will lose female support. He has no idea of the appropriate sexual role he should play in terms of capacity, skill, responsibility, or acceptability. His sexual identification is superficial and fragmented.

4. *Outlets and Defenses.*   Intellectual defenses abound but are of extremely poor quality. His ego is seldom of any strength. He behaves in an antisocial manner, megalomaniacal, sometimes sadistic and punishing. He can be extremely self-righteous without any realistic basis for it. He deals with new situations with suspicion, without any relation to reality. He is ruminative and overideational.

He suffers a severe psychosis. His defenses are quite deteriorated, and when there is any kind of stress or lack of chemical control, his basic schizophrenic personality structure will emerge. It is characterized by paranoia and delusional systems. He can be suicidal, and in the future, there is a potential for homicidal behavior.

Summary and Conclusions

Analysis of the records of Mr. Albert Browne, his previous professional evaluations, his history, and the current psychological evaluation indicates that he is a man of average intellectual capacity, suffering a very severe mental illness with concomitant social disorders. Although at the time of our evaluation, Mr. Browne was under control and not experiencing florid psychotic behavior, the psychosis was clearly found to be present. In answer to the questions posed at the beginning of this assessment, the following can be said on the basis of all the previously noted material:

1. Mr. Browne suffers a fixed, long-term mental disease with concomitant defects. It is agreed among all professionals who have examined him that this defect is Schizophrenia, Paranoid Type (*DSM* 295.3x).
2. Mr. Browne has suffered this condition for most, if not all, of his adult life.
3. There are times, during the florid aspects of this condition, where Mr. Browne lacks substantial capacity to appreciate the wrongfulness of his conduct (marrying a woman while he was still married to a first woman, stealing money to fulfill the wishes and demands of a dead father with whom he has consulted in his hallucinations, threatening his wife with imminent death).
4. During florid episodes of his psychosis, Mr. Browne has been unable to conform his conduct to the requirements of the law (note the above, plus driving at reckless rates of speed for 600 miles to speak with his dead father at the grave, as a result of his delusional system, attempting to "run over" or to shoot delusional figures that he thought were after him, and so forth).
5. Although Mr. Browne has acted in an antisocial manner, this has been a minute part of the manifestation of his condition.

Mr. Browne seems to do well when under medication and under little stress. His potential for dangerousness to himself and to others is quite high without proper supervision and treatment.

In the psychological report, no effort was made to determine whether Browne was insane or sane at the time of the bank robbery. The psychologist was prepared to testify, as an expert in such matters, that Browne suffered a well-known mental disease with consequent mental defects most of his adult life. Furthermore, the psychologist was prepared to testify that Browne, as a result of defects of perception and volition, was subject to florid psychotic episodes and that during such episodes Browne was more likely to be driven or governed by his delusions and hallucinations than by rational thought, usual societal controls, and legal standards. Browne's claim that he was finally winning his dead father's love and approval by stealing money to buy the farm that his father wanted was in keeping with Browne's circumscribed delusions about communicating with the dead father.

Whether Mr. Browne was sane, beyond reasonable doubt, at the time he robbed the bank is a decision to be reached by the jurors. The psychologist's role, as expert, in matters of insanity, is *not* to testify as to the ultimate issue but is to provide the jury with an opinion as to the defendant's psychological condition and potential for episodes of behavior that meet the legal criteria of insanity.

NOTES

1. M'Naghten's Rule, 10 C. & F. 200, 8 Eng. Rep. 718 (H.L. 1843).
2. Model Penal Code, §4.01 (1961).
3. 6 Mental Disability L. Rep. 363 (1982).
4. 11 Mental & Physical Disability L. Rep. 54 (1987).
5. Pub. L. No. 98-473, Title II, §402(a), 98 Stat. 2057, §20, recodified at 18 U.S.C. §17 ("IDRA"), 1984.
6. *Fed. R. Evid.* 702.
7. *People v. Wright,* 648 P.2d 665 (Colo. 1982).
8. *U.S. v. Schneider,* 1997 WL 176584 (1st Cir. R.I.).

9

Addiction and the Law

The nature, effects, and consequences of *addiction* are areas of human behavior about which psychologists may be called on to give testimony. As with many behavioral concepts, the public perception of addiction is widely varied. In criminal, civil, and family trials, the judicial decisions sometimes hinge on the presence or absence of addiction in plaintiffs, petitioners, defendants, and even witnesses. The expert witness may be asked to render an opinion about any of the following:

- Is the individual addicted?
- What are the effects of the addiction on the individual's past, present, or future behavior?
- What are the treatment options and/or the prognosis for this individual's condition?

The concept of *addiction* is subject to many interpretations. The psychologist should be thoroughly familiar with not only the scientific and professional literature but the specific areas of the law where expert opinion may be sought.

THE NATURE AND GENESIS OF THE ADDICTION CONCEPT

Historical Precedent

The word "addict" itself is derived from the Latin *addictus,* the past participle of *addere,* which means to devote, or to deliver over. There are no clear indications that the meaning was associated with drug or alcohol intake as it is today. Certainly the effects of alcohol, in particular, are noted throughout history from pre-Biblical times to the present.

A preliminary version of this chapter was delivered as the R. G. Myers Memorial Lecture at the Monash Medical School, Melbourne, Australia, on May 7, 1996.

131

An early description of addiction appears in Shakespeare's *Othello*: A herald enters with a proclamation announcing the winning of the war against the Turks and urging "every man put himself into triumph; some to dance, some to make bonfires, each man to what sport and revels his addiction leads." The reference here defines addiction as a personal celebratory or pleasure-seeking behavior (Shakespeare, 1604).

Most references to addiction or intoxication from literature focus on the effects of alcohol. In Alexander Pope's *An Essay on Criticism*, published at the end of the 17th century, he states, "A little learning is a dangerous thing; drink deep or taste not the Pierian Spring; there shallow draughts intoxicate the brain and drinking largely sobers us again" (Bartlett, 1968). In applying a metaphor about intoxication to learning, Pope reverses the usual course of events for persons drinking alcohol by claiming that the less one drinks the more one becomes intoxicated.

In 1798, Von Schiller poetically associates the intoxication of love with that of alcohol, "When the wine goes in, strange things come out. Oh tender yearning, sweet hoping! The golden time of first love! The eyes see the open heaven, the heart is intoxicated with bliss." Again, the metaphor indicates that both love and wine result in hallucinatory, pleasurable excitement.

In 1881, Henry James attributes excitement and reinforcement to the addiction of artistry in *The Portrait of a Lady*: "To see deep difficulty braved is at anytime, for the really addictive artist to feel almost even as a bang the beautiful incentive and to feel it verily in such sort as to wish the danger intensified." The description may even demonstrate an awareness by James that addictive behavior involves risk taking.

TWENTIETH-CENTURY CONCEPTUALIZATIONS

The Public Perception

The conventional concept of addiction, accepted by the media, by popular audiences, and even by some researchers (the reports of whose work does little to support a clear conceptualization of addiction) derives more from magic than science. The center of this concept is that a complicated set of feelings and behaviors is the unique result of one biological process called "addiction" (Peele, 1985).

In recent years, the concept has come to mean any habit, personal taste, or repetitive behavior. Habits that are pleasurable but illegal or unhealthy are now often called an addiction. The excessive appetite for food is considered addictive (Kayloe, 1993). Television has been described as a legal addiction (Lindley, 1990). Everett Koop, former Surgeon General of the United States, caused a considerable stir in 1982 when he described video-game playing by children as an addiction (Worsnop, 1982). Many are convinced that gambling is a "true addiction" (Grassie, 1990; Peirce, 1989).

Adding to the general public acceptance that opiate drugs, cocaine, barbiturates, alcohol, nicotine, and a variety of licit and illicit drugs are addictive, addiction to soap operas on the television has been described (Parachini, 1988). Researchers have labeled coffee drinking as addictive (Olekains & Bardsley, 1995), and eating New Mexico's hot chile peppers has been described as causing cravings and withdrawal symptoms when a user is deprived of a "chile fix" (Robbins, 1987). Even love has been labeled addictive (Peele, 1975). Computer addiction has been observed (Vranizan, 1995).

Professional Practice

The treatment of addictions as a disease entity has developed into a major industry during the 20th century (Isbell, 1958). What had previously been regarded as a moral, spiritual, or emotional failure has become medicalized. Although the vast majority of those who use licit and illicit drugs stop using such substances entirely on their own, the current treatment view is that once an individual begins using such substances—particularly opiates or cocaine—the person is "lost." Contemporary thinking has held that only treatment intervention can "save" users (Peele, 1985).

Since diagnosis should precede treatment, the confusion about this issue is demonstrated by the efforts to clarify the concept of addiction during the latter half of the 20th century. In 1964, the World Health Organization Expert Committee on Addiction Producing Drugs recommended a substitution of the term *drug dependent* for both the terms *drug addiction* and *drug habituation.* It seemed clear that in practice as well as in science, it was unsound, in view of the evidence, to maintain a single definition for all forms of drug addiction and/or habituation (Halbach, Isbell, & Seevers, 1965).

As this diagnostic issue was further explored, it became clear that attempts to classify drug addicts required acknowledgment of at least three main groups: psychiatric classifications, psychosocial classifications, and classifications by patterns of use (Cohen, 1984).

The *Diagnostic and Statistical Manual of Mental Disorders* of the American Psychiatric Association as well as the *International Classification of Diseases* has incorporated much broader definitions of chemical dependency with the issuance of each revised classification system. Currently, these systems no longer require the presence of tolerance and withdrawal, placing greater emphasis on compulsive usage. There is confusion whether it is more useful in classification to highlight similarities among chemical dependencies and other behavioral syndromes or to maintain their distinctions. The nonspecific definition may obscure important differences (Miele, Tilly, Furst, & Frances, 1990).

The effort to define a singular concept of addiction for diagnostic purposes has essentially failed. The greatest diagnostic concordance was observed for serious cases of addiction to sedatives/hypnotics, opiates, and alcohol. The poorest concordance was found for amphetamines, cocaine, and PCP (Lagenbucher, Morgenstern, Labouvie, & Nathan, 1994b).

In the 1994 *International Classification of Diseases, 9th Revision, 5th Edition,* the U.S. Department of Health and Human Services does not classify "addiction." The diagnostic system describes dependency syndromes that include issues of detoxification and withdrawal delirium, psychosis, and other signs. Drug dependence is defined as:

> [A] state, psychic and sometimes also physical, resulting from taking a drug, characterized by behavior and other responses that always include a compulsion to take a drug on a continuous or periodic basis in order to experience its psychotropic effects and sometimes to avoid the discomfort of its absence; tolerance may or may not be present.

In this volume, efforts are made to include the use of tobacco, but because it didn't quite fit with drug dependence, it is given a separate designation as a tobacco use disorder.

Insofar as practice is concerned, a variety of efforts have been made to develop specific treatment programs for those seeking to change. Inevitably, these tend to fail. Most professional practitioners, whether they approach addiction as a disease process or a social/personal inadequacy eventually end up referring patients to a 12-step program to support or enhance whatever treatment is being administered (Freiberg, 1995). The original Twelve-Steps of Alcoholics Anonymous have been adapted by many self-help groups—Overeaters Anonymous, Gay Men's Overeaters Anonymous, Sexaholics Anonymous, Co-dependence Anonymous, Batterers Anonymous, Gamblers Anonymous, Debtors Anonymous, Neurotics Anonymous, Women Who Love Too Much, Women Who Love Too Much–Lesbian Chapter, and Emotions Anonymous (Levine, 1990).

There is considerable literature on the treatment of failures in self-regulation (O'Brien, 1996). A great deal of research effort has been directed toward developing treatment programs for those who smoke and say that they "cannot quit" (Antonuccio, 1994). Obesity treatment programs also abound. These various programs demonstrate some partial or temporary success, but generally result in a failure rate of over 90% 18 months post-treatment. There is no replicated research to demonstrate that any particular treatment approach for those with self-regulatory problems is highly effective. Where people are successful in terminating habits that they decide are not in their best interests, such factors as "emotional maturity," and self-efficacy have been the most consistent predictors of success (Antonuccio, 1994; Gulliver, Hughes, Solomon, & Achintya, 1995; Kayloe, 1993). For the expert testifying as to treatment potential, this speaks for extreme caution in predicting treatment outcome.

Science

In applied behavioral science, scientific exploration seldom precedes professional practice. So it is in the area of habits and addiction. This was recognized early in this century when, in addressing opium use, researchers found that there were many contradictory theories as to how the addiction comes about and what remedial procedures might be effective. This confusion was based on disagreement as to the actual nature of the problem (Terry & Pellens, 1928).

Definitional problems have not been solved to date. Early efforts to include coffee, tea, and tobacco as addictions required a modification of definitions so that those substances, according to self-reports, which became habitual and seemed almost necessary for a person's comfort and well-being could be described as addictions (King, 1934). Self-description as being "sick" by users of drugs added to the impetus in the latter half of the 20th century for researchers to pursue a disease model for addiction (Eiser & Gossop, 1979). Despite extensive efforts to determine the etiology of these behaviors, scientists have been willing to admit that comparatively little is known about the precursors of addiction, other than those people who are described as addicts are said to display poor performance in major life roles (Falk, 1983; Milkman & Shaffer, 1985; Nathan, 1980; Nelson, Pearson, Sayers, & Glynn, 1982; Nurco, 1981).

Extensive efforts have been made to identify brain receptor sites, physiological processes, and endocrinological factors that would explain the concept of addiction in reliable and valid scientific terms (O'Brien, 1996). As the end of the 20th century approaches, there has been an increasing acceptance of the hypothesis that reinforcing effects of abused substances are related to their ability to enhance neuronal activity of the brain rewards systems. Particular emphasis has focused on the endorphins and the stimulation of endogenous opioids to explain the reinforcing effects of various substances including nicotine. This was a primary focus of the 1988 United States Surgeon General's Report (U.S. Dept. of Health and Human Services, 1988). Since that time, newer research has dispelled the notion that this is the scientific basis on which addiction is explained. It has become clear that there is no compelling support for noradrenergic, dopaminergic, or cholinergic theories (Butschky, Bailey, Henningfield, & Pickworth, 1995; Jaffe & Jaffe, 1989; Kauffman, Shaffer, & Burglass, 1984; Koelega, 1993; Kornetsky & Bain, 1995; Sutherland, Stapleton, Russell, & Feyerabend, 1995). It is becoming increasingly more common in the scientific literature to find that researchers who previously reported enthusiastically about the addictive nature of some substance later publish research contradicting their earlier opinions (Henningfield, Cohen, & Slade, 1991; Wewers, Tejwani, & Anderson, 1994). Continuing brain research on the generation of dopamine and the enzymes that break down this pleasure-related chemical show some promise in helping to explain why and how humans choose to ingest certain chemicals or to perform certain acts. As yet, such hypotheses are preliminary and speculative (Fowler et al., 1996).

With efforts to include more and more substances and behaviors under the general rubric of addiction, definitional changes were required. For a period of time, and to some extent to this date, the concept of *euphoria* has been used as a possible criterion of addictive behavior. It has been proposed that pleasurable response to a substance indicates or confirms "addiction" or "abuse liability" (U.S. Dept. of Health and Human Services, 1988). The difficulty in defining addiction has created a strong following for the concept that addictive substances are *reinforcing* or rewarding. This has been descriptively interesting but has not been consistently supported experimentally (J. Jaffe, 1990).

The more that scientists explore this issue, the more complicated it seems to become. Researchers have found that much of the data relating to the use of opiate drugs, sympathomimetics, caffeine, alcohol, and tobacco may be faulty or misinterpreted. There is a growing body of evidence that whatever is being measured in an individual insofar as the intake of substances or the performance of certain acts is concerned may have very important sequential connections with whatever has happened previously in the individual's life (Barrett, 1995; Swanson, Lee, & Hopp, 1984). Thus a study may demonstrate certain characteristics of opiate users, smokers, or alcohol users without taking into account previous drug experience. An example of these effects is increased use of caffeine during experimental periods where nicotine intake is manipulated.

To further complicate the scientific issue, it has been found that repetitive stories given by human subjects in research about use of substances or about their dependence agreed in essentials only about half of the time (Lagenbucher et al., 1994b). The attitudes of those who conduct the research and provide the treatment are of some influence in the classification of addictions. A study of treatment providers indicated that some providers believe that there is a metaphysical power that influences personal experience. Those with such beliefs in turn strongly support the disease model of addiction. Other treatment providers disagree and believe in a free-will model (Schaler, 1993).

Unexplained, except in descriptive terms, is the well-known phenomenon of *spontaneous remission* whereby users of alcohol, hard drugs, tobacco, coffee, as well as gamblers, and overeaters suddenly quit and do so very successfully with no help whatsoever from professionals or treatment programs (Hall & Havassy, 1986; Stall & Biernacki, 1986; Stockton, Jason, & McMahon, 1995). Efforts to explain the phenomenon through description of various personality characteristics have been interesting, but have never been successfully confirmed scientifically (Goodman, 1991; Mitchell, 1992; Narayanan, Mennon, & Levine, 1995).

Although several generations of extensive study have been applied to this area, researchers and practitioners attempting to clarify the concept of addiction do not share a unitary set of rules or standards for understanding or treating the condition (Milkman & Shaffer, 1985). Various definitions of addiction have been subject to change and modification, but not to verification. "Addict" remains a nebulous term (Nelson et al., 1982). Drug-related research is often inconclusive and frequently contradictory. Almost everyone in the field has his or her own set of beliefs about drug use or abuse and usually holds these beliefs firmly despite clear bias (Pomazal, 1985). In this area of research, scientific standards are too rarely met (Roache & Griffith, 1989).

About all that science can tell us at the present time is that the label "addiction" reliably involves intoxication at some point, and serious disruption of the individual's life (Bradley, Gossop, Brewin, Phillips, & Green, 1992; Griffith, Brady, & Bigelow, 1981; J. Jaffe, 1985; Kozlowski et al., 1989; Morgenstern, Lagenbucher, & Labouvie, 1994; Schaler, 1995). This realistic constraint excludes many substances and behaviors popularly labeled as addictions.

Public Policy

Definitions, the awarding of research grants, and public policy can be influenced by legislating morality and punishing deviance. This raises conflictual issues in respect to constitutional principles of individual rights and personal freedom (Sutker & Allain, 1988).

It has been suggested that five moral models of drug addiction are used in establishing public policy (Siegler & Osmond, 1968). These include the *retributive model* wherein the addict is a convicted criminal who got that way because of moral failure. The *deterrent model* suggests that the addict is a bad person and the condition arises from a lack of deterrence. The *restitutive model* proposes that the addict is a debtor (there is no acknowledgment of any importance of etiology). The fourth model, the *preventive model,* describes the addict as a failure in moral education. The etiology here is said to be a lack of moral instruction. The final model is the *restorative* or *rehabilitative model.* Here the addict is labeled a wrongdoer as a result of a moral failure caused by the human condition. One can see these models in many of the public policy positions that have occurred in the past and that are currently operant.

The media has influenced public policy regarding the control of substances. Strong pro and con positions are taken regarding the use of tobacco, alcohol, and drugs (Hilts, 1994). The media has accepted the labeling of substances as addictive determined by consensus decisions rather than replicated scientific research. Public policy can ignore, distort, or misrepresent scientific findings or the absence of such findings for political convenience

(Heath, 1988). Legislative policy makers may ignore contrary evidence suggesting that social policy or remedial programs are ineffective.

Consensus does not make science (Sommers, 1995). In an effort to help the law understand addictions, a medical perspective has been proposed to the bar and the bench (Talbott, 1989). It is suggested that there should be seven criteria for a diagnosis of the disease of addiction. These seven, of which it is suggested that the first four are primary, include *addictive compulsion, adverse or lethal consequences to an individual's physical life, adverse or lethal consequences to an individual's emotional or psychological life, adverse consequences to an individual's job, community, church, or family* (which are classified as the social-spiritual-cultural life). The three subcriteria are *changing abnormal tolerance,* wherein there is a rapid increase in tolerance with a sudden abrupt fall; *true withdrawal symptoms,* as opposed to hangovers; and *true drug amnesia* or blackouts, as compared with passing out from drug overdose or toxicity. These criteria would exclude such things as smoking, coffee drinking, gambling, love, video-game playing, and television watching from being classified as addictive.

There is a growing public controversy about punishment for the use of addictive substances. Various issues involve the criminalization or control of drug manufacture, distribution and use; the regulation of alcohol manufacture, distribution, purchase, and effects; the regulation of gambling; and more current efforts to regulate the manufacture, distribution, and use of tobacco products. There are those who propose that efforts to constrict have more tragic results than the use of the substances or the behaviors themselves (Ajzenstadt & Burtch, 1990; Glasser, 1989; A. Lewis, 1996).

Insofar as the effort to utilize scientific findings to help public policy, it's fairly clear that current concepts and reported conclusions may tend to reduce precision in the interest of getting on the right side of the war on drugs or the establishment of a smokefree society (Akers, 1991).

ADDICTION AND HISTORICAL LEGAL PRECEDENCE

There have been three great crime waves in the United States. The first followed the Civil War and began about 1870. Ex-soldiers from both the Confederate and Union sides of the war formed gangs that began to pillage and rob in a manner never known before in America. Train and stagecoach robberies, bank robberies, murder, and robbery of wealthy citizens became daily occurrences. This crime wave was of relatively short duration, and by 1890 most of the gangs had been apprehended and effective law enforcement deterred further organized criminal activity.

The second great American crime wave began after World War I. A surge of morality swept the country and the Volstead Act was passed as a constitutional amendment in 1919 forbidding the manufacture and sale of alcoholic beverages. An illicit industry arose to manufacture, import, distribute, and sell such beverages. The public supported these criminal ventures, which generated enormous profits. This particular escalation of crime resulted in the activation and implementation of federal law enforcement to deal with this out-of-hand epidemic. The repeal of the Volstead Act in 1933 ended this surge of lawlessness. The second great crime wave, like the first, was of relatively short duration.

The third great American crime wave began about 1960. This somewhat resembled the situation of the 1920s and 1930s except that it concerned the acquisition, importation, distribution, and use of illicit drugs rather than alcohol. Previous crime waves lasted for less than 20 years while the surge of drug-related crime continues to this day (Blau, 1994).

Definitions and Early Precedent within the Law

In jurisprudence, *addictive drugs* are described as "any drug, natural or synthetic which causes periodic or chronic intoxication by its repeated consumption" (Black, 1979). The concept of intoxication is primary in the law's definition.

An *addict* is described as any individual who habitually uses any narcotic drug so as to endanger the public morals, health, safety, or welfare or who is or has been so far addicted to the use of such narcotic drugs as to have lost the power of self-control with reference to his addiction.[1,2]

Within the law, a *habit* is considered a disposition or condition of the body or mind acquired by custom or a usual repetition of the same act or function. It is the customary conduct that one has acquired a tendency to pursue from previous repetition of the same acts.[3] Evidence of a specific habit may be admissible to show specific conduct or acts within the sphere of the developed habit.[4]

Where the issue of *will* occurs, the law views this as a wish; desire; pleasure; inclination; choice; the faculty of conscious and especially of deliberate action. *Compulsion* is defined as constraint; objective necessity; duress; forcible inducement to the commission of an act; the act of compelling or the state of being compelled; the act of driving or urging by force or by physical or moral constraint; subjection to force. A compulsion that will excuse a criminal act must be present, imminent, and impending and of such a nature as to induce a well-grounded appreciation of death or serious bodily harm (Black, 1979). All of these definitions may come into play at one point or another in judicial issues.[5]

In law, the term *intoxication* indicates a situation where, by reason of ingesting intoxicants, an individual does not have the normal use of physical or mental faculties, thus rendering him or her incapable of acting in a manner in which an ordinarily prudent and cautioned person, in full possession of faculties, using reasonable care, would act under like conditions.[6] Further, intoxication is defined as a disturbance of mental and physical capacities resulting from the introduction of substances into the body.

Even in early Biblical times, the priests in the Temple were forbidden to drink wine immediately before they performed their service. The Book of Leviticus says:

> And the Lord spoke unto Aaron saying: "Drink no wine nor strong drink, then, nor thy sons with thee, when ye go into the tent of meeting, that ye die not: it shall be a statute forever throughout your generations. And that ye may put difference between the holy and the common, and between the unclean and the clean; and that ye may teach the children of Israel all the statutes which the Lord has spoken unto him by the hands of Moses."[7]

The effects of alcohol intoxication are described by the Prophet Isaiah while speaking of drunken orgies:

> But these also reel through wine,
> And stagger through strong drink:
> The priest and the prophet reel through strong drink,
> They are confused because of wine,
> They stagger because of strong drink,
> They reel in vision, they totter in judgment.
> For all tables are full of filthy vomit,
> And no place is clean.[8]

Talmudic law ruled that a teacher who drinks even a small quantity of wine must not give decisions in Jewish law because he lacks the clarity of mind required for a balanced judgment.[9] So, it appears that five thousand years ago, as now, the critical legal issue in the matter of addiction is intoxication and its effects on cognitive functioning.

ADDICTION IN LEGAL PRACTICE

Criminal Issues

Issues of addiction and intoxication appear in both criminal and civil practice. In most instances, the state of mind of an individual is the issue addressed. The law is concerned with the effect of intoxication—voluntary or unintentional—as to whether it is extreme enough for the accused, the plaintiff, the defendant, or the petitioner to *lack volition* or *the requisite intention* or *knowledge*.

Self-Induced Intoxication. Evidence of self-induced intoxication may negate the mental elements of an offense such as intention, knowledge, foresight, or voluntariness and may be used to deny either basic or specific intent. *Basic intent,* or *general intent* as it is also known, is the intent to engage in a prohibited act. Basic intention crimes include manslaughter, assault, and unlawful wounding. *Specific intent* requires a desire for a particular result or purpose from the prohibited act. Murder, aggravated assault, and rape are all specific intent offenses.

Other specific intent crimes such as battery, kidnapping, and robbery may entertain a defense of lack of volition due to self-induced intoxication.

Self-induced intoxication is not a defense to criminal responsibility. The theory is that a person who voluntarily undertakes to become intoxicated generally assumes the responsibility for any wrongdoing he or she may commit as a result of intoxication. One test of the viability of the intoxication defense is whether the defendant is able to devise a plan, operate equipment, instruct behavior of others, or carry out acts requiring physical skills (Burk, 1986).

In the United States the absence of specific intent due to self-induced intoxication was applied in kidnapping.[10]

Homicide.   Murder is a specific intent crime. Voluntary intoxication of an accused may be considered as a challenge to specific intent (Callahan, 1988). Such intoxication may have prevented the accused from forming the requisite intent.[11] This also applies to kidnapping. Larceny has been determined to be a specific intent crime as indicated in *Schwab v. United States.*[12] In cases of homicide where voluntary intoxication negates the required specific intent element, the result is usually not an acquittal but rather a conviction of a lesser offense that does not require specific intent.[13]

An interesting variation of this concept is where a defendant expresses the necessary intent prior to the intoxication or becomes intoxicated merely to gain "courage" to commit the offense. When this occurs, evidence of the intoxication may not be introduced to negate intent.[14]

Involuntary Intoxication or Unintentional Intoxication.   In the United States, involuntary intoxication may be a complete defense for felonies of specific and general intent. Involuntary intoxication is defined as a result of a lack of independent judgment and volition on the part of the accused in taking intoxicating material. This usually applies to medications or externally administered substances. The involuntarily intoxicated individual does not choose to become intoxicated and is therefore considered blameless. This particular defense has not fared very well and there have been few acquittals.[15] In *Minneapolis v. Altimus,*[16] the court held that involuntary intoxication is a complete defense only when the accused, at the time of the offense, is temporarily insane as a result of the drug use.

Mental Illness/Insanity Defense.   In United States law, drug addiction is not considered a disease constituting mental illness under a criminal responsibility statute. Expert testimony to the effect that a robbery defendant was compelled to commit offenses by this disease has properly been excluded from evidence.[17]

Drug addiction and intoxication may also be elements of the *insanity defense.* Conviction for all criminal offenses requires two elements: a wrongful deed (*actus reus*) and a guilty mind or a criminal intent (*mens rea*). If a chronic alcoholic or drug addict lacks the requisite mens rea for an offense, he or she has legally not committed the crime. The classical statement of this principle is found in M'Naghten's[18] case (see Appendix A). In that case, the House of Lords in 1843 confirmed that to establish a defense of insanity the accused, at the time of committing the act, must be laboring under such a defect of reason from disease of the mind, as not to know the nature and quality of the act he was doing or, if he did know, that he did not know what he was doing was wrong.

Insofar as drug addiction itself being characterized as a mental disease or defect within the meaning of insanity, courts have held generally that it is not.[19] By and large, despite medical findings that may speak to the contrary, the courts continue to treat both alcoholism and drug addiction as voluntary intoxication.

Motor Vehicle Offenses.   This is perhaps the area of greatest attention by the law to issues of addiction and intoxication. Where alcohol is concerned, specific indicators and cutoff points have been developed to signify that driving has taken place "under the influence" of alcohol or drugs.[20] Blood alcohol levels that constitute proof of intoxication or a presumption that the driver is intoxicated may vary from state to state, and are subject to legislative change.[21]

In the United States, the courts do not punish chronic alcoholics for being alcoholics ("status") but rather for being drunk in public. Although a binding decision has not been made as to whether or not alcoholism is involuntary intoxication, the Supreme Court of the United States has opined that in the present state of medical knowledge there is no support for a conclusion that chronic alcoholics are compelled to drink.[22] In the United States, it appears that intoxication, no matter how extreme, is still viewed as voluntary by most jurisdictions.[23]

Where ingestion of alcohol or drugs does not excuse a defendant's criminal action, an accused's intoxication may be considered in determining whether there was intent necessary for conviction of a particular offense. Thus, vehicular homicide by a drunken driver may be considered involuntary manslaughter.

The law focuses attention on a number of areas such as the age at which an individual may purchase alcohol, the age at which an individual may publicly drink alcohol, and where either the owner of a dram shop (tavern, bar, or other commercial dispenser) or a social host may be held liable for damages caused by an individual intoxicated at the bar or at the host's home. This may vary from state to state in the United States. Even police officers can be held liable if they do not take direct action to protect the public welfare when they apprehend a person who is intoxicated under the influence of drugs or alcohol. In this case, the courts have found that the police officer has an affirmative duty to act. As yet there have been mixed reviews on the constitutionality of the police erecting roadblocks to conduct sobriety checks. In most states, the refusal of a driver to submit to a blood-alcohol test at the request of police is not supported by constitutional safeguards. In most states, revocation of driver's license can come about automatically if the apprehended party refuses to submit to a blood-alcohol test.[24]

Thus it appears that in driving offenses, whether misdemeanors or felonies, voluntary intoxication may only have relevance in terms of questions regarding specific intent. In most instances, the ingestion of intoxicating material tends to be considered voluntary.

Penalties for the Use of Addictive Substances. The issue of criminalization of narcotic and alcohol addictions has had a long and varied history. Punishment for the possession of substances has been ruled constitutional in the United States.[25]

There is a strong movement to decriminalize the use of some addictive substances. In the United States, it is pointed out that the state and federal prison populations numbered 200,000 in 1973 and reached 600,000 by 1989. It is anticipated that if the current statutes maintain, there will be more than 1,000,000 incarcerated Americans by the turn of the century. Much of this is a result of the public policy in the United States of criminalizing the use and the possession of addictive substances under a variety of circumstances.[26] The Supreme Court of the United States has held that state laws making the status of narcotic addiction a criminal offense was cruel and unusual punishment, violating the 14th Amendment.[27] The prevailing view is that the alcoholic's first drink and the narcotic addict's first voluntary ingestion of a drug represents blameworthiness for actions that result from a continued use of the substance.[28] Conviction of narcotics addicts for possession of narcotics, unlike a status offense, does not constitute cruel and unusual punishment.[29]

Trafficking in addictive substances carries very heavy penalties. In United States federal law, maximum sentences for traffic in opiates for first adult offense, is up to 15 years and/or $25,000 fine. For traffic in controlled substances other than narcotics/opiates, adult first offense can bring a sentence of 5 years' imprisonment and/or $15,000 fine. For simple possession of controlled substances, an individual may receive up to 1 year of imprisonment and/or $5,000 in fines (Schweber, 1981).

Although there has been much interest in classifying all the addictions as diseases, this concept has not fared very well in the courts. The mayor of the District of Columbia in his effort to be exculpated from charges of perjury and drug possession stated, "That was the disease talking. . . I was a victim." He claimed addiction to alcohol, Valium, and Xanax. This popular defense was also used in a criminal action by the famous baseball player Pete Rose, who claimed he was suffering from a gambling disease when he was charged with illegal behavior. Television evangelist Jimmy

Swaggart, when faced with charges of lewd and lascivious behavior, stated that he "lost control" because he was "addicted to the chemical release in his brain from orgasm." The position is taken by some that the labeling of miscreant behavior as "free will" is cruel. The Supreme Court of the United States conversely has upheld the right of the U.S. Veterans Administration to define alcoholism to be the result of willful misconduct (Schaler, 1991).

Insofar as being penalized for being an addict, it has been ruled that a defendant's history of drug addiction can be considered when making pretrial detention determinations. In one instance, the court opined that the addictive person can be unreliable and have a decrease in moral responsibility.[30]

Competence to Plead and Confess.   Attempts have been made to use addiction as a basis for nullifying a confession or a pleading. In a 1994 decision, a Louisiana appeals court declared that a second-degree murder defendant knowingly and intelligently waived his rights when he made his confession. The defense argued that his use of alcohol and drugs could impair his judgment. The appeals court opined that the waiver of the defendant's constitutional rights in making a confession or self-incriminatory statements does not require a higher level of mental capacity than to enter a plea of guilty, to assist counsel at trial, to waive his right to an attorney, or to waive other constitutional rights.[31]

The U.S. District Court for the Southern District of Texas laid down a decision opining that an appellant's bare allegation of a history of drug addiction was insufficient to raise an issue of his lack of mental competency at the time he pled guilty.[32] In a more recent decision, a circuit court of the United States rejected a pleading by a defendant, moving to vacate a guilty plea on the ground that his taking a prescribed depression medication affected his judgment. The court stated that there was nothing on the record to show that the defendant was not completely in command of his faculties as would be required to vitiate a plea based on drug use.[33]

Thus it appears that claiming addiction as a basis for being declared incompetent to plead has not been substantiated.

Competence to Testify.   A number of cases address the issue of whether addiction is a basis for claiming incompetence to testify at trial. In a federal hearing, it was stated that if a defendant responds to direct and cross- examination clearly and lucidly with no indication of incompetence, addiction to narcotic drugs is not a basis for a plea of incompetence to stand trial.[34] The U.S. District Court for the Southern District of Florida denied a motion to vacate a sentence because the defendant was a drug addict. The court of appeals held that the defendant clearly and lucidly responded to direct and cross examination at his trial and that there was no indication or suggestion before, during, or after the trial that the defendant was incompetent due to addiction to narcotic drugs.[35]

An interesting test of the concept that drug addiction could result in an individual's incompetence to testify occurred in the state of Florida. A defendant was convicted in the circuit court of aggravated battery with a deadly weapon. The defendant appealed for review on the basis that one of the witnesses was a prior drug user, therefore was an addict, therefore had diminished testimonial ability. The court held that evidence that the witness had taken drugs other than at the time of the trial or at the event described is not admissible to impeach the witness absent an express showing of other relevant evidence that the witness's prior drug use affects ability to observe, remember, and recount.[36]

Sentencing.   The National Addict Rehabilitation Act, 28 U.S.C. Sections 2901–2906 enacted by the United States Congress in 1966 provides that certain narcotics addicts may request civil commitment instead of penal incarceration. An addict is eligible for civil commitment if he or she is charged with a federal offense; is not charged with a crime of violence, is not charged with trafficking in narcotics, does not have a prior charge of a felony pending against him or her, and/or has not been convicted of two or more felony offenses. There is no requirement that the addict be under the influence of narcotics at the time of the commission of the offense.

When the preceding guidelines are followed, downward sentencing has been generally upheld in the courts. Where efforts to plead for downward sentencing involve felons who have had previous felony convictions, the Courts of Appeals have opined that the defendant was not entitled to rehabilitative sentencing under the Narcotics Addiction Rehabilitation Act.[37] The issue of previous felonies eventually was heard by the Supreme Court of the United States. The Court opined that addicts with two or more prior felony convictions are not denied due process or equal protection by being excluded from consideration for rehabilitative commitment in lieu of penal incarceration.[38] Without further citation, it seems clear that downward sentencing is available to those who can indicate clearly that their addiction is a personal experience and not a part of felonious activity.

Ineffective Counsel.   In a number of instances, appellate claims that the defendant was not properly represented because either addiction or intoxication was not raised at the original trial have been supported. In a Supreme Court decision involving a guilty plea, the Court of Appeals held that the defendant who claimed that he was unrepresented by counsel at the time of his guilty plea was entitled to evidentiary hearing on his verified petition and affidavit that he had not waived counsel and was incapable of understanding his rights due to illiteracy, emotional upset, and narcotics addiction.[39] Such a pleading, in the face of a defendant's clear ability to communicate, has seldom if ever been supported.[40]

A defendant appealed for vacating his sentence alleging ineffective assistance of counsel proposing that the attorney's drug addiction caused incompetent representation. The courts opined that the attorney's trial strategy was not so unreasonable that no competent attorney would have chosen it.[41]

In criminal proceedings, it seems fairly clear that the courts have generally taken a conservative stance when addiction is claimed as a basis for exculpation. Although the citations previously noted are not totally encompassing, the view of American jurisprudence appears to be that the burden of proving the importance of addiction and/or intoxication in excusing felonious behavior falls very heavily on the defense.

Addiction in Civil Issues

In civil jurisprudence, addiction is viewed either as a disease, or as a moral, spiritual, or emotional failure. Where addiction makes its appearance in civil litigation, the individual who is labeled addicted may be viewed as morally inadequate, reckless, dangerous to self or others, and liable for damages he or she may perpetrate. Some representative civil litigation follows.

Civil Competence.   Within this category of civil litigation, addiction is viewed as a disease as well as a mark of moral failure. The addict is seen as incompetent or dangerous. The courts have ruled that an addict who is committed for treatment cannot be forced to undergo such treatment against his or her will. When committed addicts refuse treatment, they should be discharged for that reason.[42] Even though the Supreme Court of the United States has recognized drug addiction as a disease,[43] involuntary treatment or incarceration is not acceptable.

Under certain circumstances, the addict can be committed involuntarily, but the state must present clear and convincing evidence that dangerous behavior or unacceptable behavior is a result of the addiction.[44] The courts have opined that an addict can sue a medical center for false imprisonment if it involuntarily detains the addict in a general mental health treatment unit that is not specifically designed for the treatment of chemical dependency and substance abuse.[45]

Where friends or relatives seek to have the court establish a plenary guardianship with the claim that the addict suffers impaired judgment and cannot manage home or finances, or places himself or herself in danger, the courts have required clear and convincing evidence to show that the addict is likely to be harmed because of an inability to provide for himself or herself and did not adequately understand or appreciate the nature and consequences of that inability.[46]

It is clear that civil liberties are prized highly by the courts. The South Dakota Supreme Court decided that a juvenile court judge who ordered the supposedly addicted parent of a child undergoing juvenile delinquency proceedings to enter an inpatient alcohol treatment program exceeded his authority.[47]

Liability for Intoxication.   Those intoxicated with either alcohol or some other drug of abuse are held liable for damages in most instances. Their behavior is considered careless or reckless. They are not excused by reason of the behavior being associated with the addiction. The law goes a step further and allows for recovery in civil cases against dram shops by those injured as a result of accidents caused by an intoxicated patron. In these cases, the issue revolves around whether the patron was addicted to the substance and whether the employees of the bar or tavern knew of the patron's addiction.[48] In some instances, the courts have ruled that the dramshop owner is not liable unless the provider had received written notice of the drunkard's addiction.[49]

Claims against druggists have not fared as well as claims against taverns and bars. When an individual claimed that a druggist did not warn him against the addictive properties of Quaaludes, an appellate court dismissed the complaint on the basis that the prescription for these drugs had been made by a knowledgeable physician and the pharmacist's failure to warn was not a failure to exercise due care.[50]

A social host may be held liable for civil damages because he or she provided intoxicating substances to an individual who later caused or had an accident (Mahon, 1986).

Divorce, Custody, and Parental Fitness.   The issue of addiction appears even in divorce litigation. In one case, the court rejected the proposal that the husband's alcoholic addictions during the marriage permanently affected the wife's emotional or physical ability to earn, or that such misconduct depleted marital assets.[51] Another court found that a wife was entitled to an equitable share of all marital assets including those dissipated by the husband's addictions.[52]

In matters of custody and parental rights, courts have placed a good deal of emphasis on the moral character of each parent in deciding custodial awards. In a study by Lowery (1981), it was found that of 20 significant factors considered by judges in awarding custody, *mental stability* of each parent was the number one consideration while *moral character* was fourth (professional advice ranked rather poorly as 12th). In one case, a mother claimed that her addictions to drugs and alcohol resulted from factors beyond her control, but the courts rejected this stating that her failure to comply with terms of performance agreements was not statutorily excusable.[53] In another illustrative case, a grandmother whose deceased daughter was the children's mother, was awarded custody and permission to take her grandchildren to her home in England because the natural father had been addicted to alcohol. (A new hearing was granted a year later after the father had voluntarily entered a hospital for rehabilitation and was released greatly improved.)[54] Determination of parental rights because of addiction is more likely to take place where a child needs special care, and the custodial parent's addiction prevents this care from being rendered.[55]

Professional Practice and Licensure.   Attorneys who become addicted to narcotics and even those convicted of narcotic-related felonies, are generally not disbarred. In a Florida case, the courts opined that automatic disbarment upon an attorney's conviction of a felony is inappropriate and that conviction of felonies based on the use of illicit drugs due to addictions warrants a suspension from the practice of law for a period of three years rather than disbarment.[56] Where an attorney misused clients' funds without intent during short periods of emotional instability in part due to drug and alcohol addictions, the offense warranted suspension from the practice of law for two years rather than disbarment.[57] One attorney attempted to claim "addiction" to challenge a disciplinary suspension of 60 days for drug abuse in violation of probation. The suspension was imposed after a previous finding of drug addiction. The courts rendered an opinion that addiction is not an excuse for repeated misconduct.[58] One court found that an attorney's drug addiction is insufficient to establish a ruling of ineffective assistance of counsel. They ruled that addiction by itself is not a basis to determine intellectual incompetence.[59] A physician whose license was revoked for chemical dependency problems appealed, claiming a disability because of addiction. The courts ruled that even though the Americans with Disabilities Act, under some circumstances, identifies addiction as a disability, this would not protect the doctor from license revocation.[60]

In the United States, the American Civil Liberties Union has challenged one state's supreme court for allowing an individual who applied to the sate board of examiners for admission to the bar to be rejected because of previous addictions. The ACLU claimed that the past use of drug and alcohol should not be grounds for rejection. No resolution of this issue has yet occurred.[61]

Addiction in the Workplace.   Drug testing in the workplace has become a major national issue in the United States. It affects sports, politics, and other workplace settings. Constitutional issues continue to be debated. Although legislatures have mandated drug testing in various workplaces, these mandates may be constitutionally deficient (Sanders, 1987). The courts have ruled that addiction "in a medical sense" should be considered by an unemployment appeals committee as possibly causing misconduct.[62] The propensity for the courts to lean over backward to protect individual rights is demonstrated in a case where a district court opined that the New York City Transit Authority's refusal to employ persons who use methadone violated the Equal Protection Clause of the Fourteenth Amendment. On appeal to the Supreme Court of the United States, the justices held that statistical evidence did not support the District Court's conclusion that neither the Authority's regulation prohibiting the use of narcotics nor its interpretation of that regulation to encompass users of methadone violated Title VII of the Civil Rights Act. A blanket exclusion of persons from employment who regularly use narcotic drugs did not violate equal protection clause of the Fourteenth Amendment by failing to include more precise rules for methadone users who have progressed satisfactorily with their treatment and who, when examined individually, satisfied the Authority's employment criteria for nonsensitive jobs.[63]

The United States District Court held that an individual seeking disability insurance payments because of drug addiction and mental problems was not entitled to a rehearing of a decision denying her claim.[64]

Several courts have ruled that employees who have resumed illegal drug use are not entitled to be identified as qualified individuals with a disability.[65, 66]

The courts have been quite clear that the decision was not prejudicial when an employee with considerable responsibility for dealing with dangerous material was removed for testing positive for cocaine during a random drug test. The courts opined that he intentionally took the cocaine and was not unaware of his actions.[67]

Although civil rights of individuals are protected by the courts, the courts have not been remiss in being quite firm about preventing individuals whose judgment is impaired from creating a public danger or a civil liability for employers.[68]

Smoking and Addiction.   During the past three decades of the 20th century, there has been a rapidly developing public policy effort in the United States to create a smokefree society. Among the many effects of this imperative has been the launching of personal injury litigation against tobacco companies. Individuals have claimed that tobacco caused addiction and they were unable to stop their habit, with deleterious health consequences. Plaintiffs have not fared well in this arena. In only one case was the plaintiff awarded damages. That award was overturned on appeal.[69] Political compromise efforts as well as individual and class action litigation continues.

IN SUMMATION

All of the applicable areas of the complex relationship of legal practice and addiction have not been addressed in depth, but the foregoing illustrates a significant and expanding awareness and interest about addiction by the law. At present, the definition and statutory implications of addiction vary from jurisdiction to jurisdiction. In general, the language of the law focuses on the individual's ability to observe, to remember, and to recount. The law is concerned with diminishing or distortion of cognitive ability that may result from addiction. The law is concerned as to whether an individual, as a result of addiction, is in command of his or her faculties.

When an individual, allegedly addicted, can respond to direct examination and cross-examination with clarity and lucidity, the courts have found no basis for a plea of incompetence. Intoxication or its aftereffects represent a key element in the law's definition of addiction. The law recognizes that an individual may lose power of self-control, and lack the normal use of physical or mental faculties as a result of the ingestion of certain substances.

It is important in law whether the lack of volition, intention, or knowledge that results from addiction is self-engendered. Responsibility or lack of responsibility is gauged by the question of whether an individual's brain is dysfunctional as a result of the addiction process. To date, the law appears to be very reluctant to give a blanket exculpation to individuals who become intoxicated and then addicted by their own choice. The testimony of neuropsychologists is likely to be of some importance as this issue is addressed in the future.

QUO VADIS?

Research activity aimed at clarifying the concept of addiction continues at a high rate. This interest among scientists may be in part due to the still-puzzling questions that abound (O'Brien, 1996). Some of the more compelling questions still challenging researchers are:

1. What areas of human intellect, cognition, control, performance, and judgment are affected by substances or circumstances labeled addictive?
2. What tests or measurements can be developed to indicate precisely and reliably the effects of various addictions?
3. What are the exact, demonstrable, and predictable mechanisms by which addiction acts?
4. To what degree are the individuals classified as addicts responsible for their involvement with addictive substances or activities?
5. What methods will provide predictably successful preventions for the initiation of physically or socially deleterious addictions?
6. What treatment methods will provide predictably successful long-term resolution of physically or socially deleterious addictions?

Financial support for addiction research continues to be relatively generous and will probably continue as long as addiction is considered a significant health and social problem.

Insofar as addiction is an issue in the law, little is likely to change until significant scientific developments clarify the technical definitional issues mentioned previously.

And so, science, practice, and jurisprudence continue to evolve. The current status of addiction and the law is perhaps best characterized by the great Wigmore. Written just before his death, in the last revision of his *On Evidence:*[70]

> Nevertheless, within the limitations of these special judicial rules (pertaining to partisan presentation of evidence in an adversary proceeding), judicial practice is entitled and bound to resort to all truths of human nature established by science, and to employ all methods recognized by scientists for applying those truths in the analysis of testimonial credit. . . . Both law and practice permit the calling of any expert scientist whose method is acknowledged in his science to be a sound and trustworthy one. Whenever the Psychologist is ready for the Courts, the Courts are ready for him.

Until persuasive research data provides the courts with compelling evidence otherwise, both legislatures and judges are likely to say "no" to addiction as a defense (Gibeaut, 1997).

THE ROLE OF THE EXPERT PSYCHOLOGICAL WITNESS

Despite the diversity of definition that one finds in studying addiction, the law is relatively clear about what it expects in the way of testimonial information. At issue is the state of mind, the cognitive ability or inability of an individual in both criminal and civil matters. Since clinical psychologists and neuropsychologists are those behavioral scientists who are most thoroughly trained in the understanding and the evaluation of brain-behavior interaction, psychological testimony can be of great value in resolving issues of fact.

The state of mind that may occur as a result of addiction can be studied at three levels: *at the time of the ingestion of the substance, during the withdrawal period,* and *psychological states that exist even during abstinence following withdrawal.*

The Psychological State of an Individual under the Influence of Addictive Substances

In criminal matters, it is exceedingly rare that a psychologist would have an opportunity to examine an individual close to the time of the alleged crime when the individual was under the influence of an addicting substance. That would be the ideal condition to obtain measurements that could then be used as a basis for testimony as to the mental state of the individual. In reality, the psychologist is most frequently called on months or even years after the criminal act to render an opinion as to the state of mind of the defendant. The best an expert psychologist may do in this instance is to inform the judge and the jury as to the usual and expected effects of the addictive substance. It is incumbent on the psychologist who testifies as such an expert to explain to the triers of fact that many variables are likely to influence the degree to which the mental state may be affected while ingesting addictive substances. Most prominent is the issue of *tolerance*. Some habitual users of addictive substances may show relatively minor cognitive defects during this ingestion, while those less accustomed to the use of the substance may have very major cognitive deficits. All of this should be explained to the triers of fact. Opinions based on such testimony must be very carefully constructed so as to not be speculative.

Psychological States during Withdrawal

In some instances, psychologists may have the opportunity to examine individuals during the process of withdrawal from addicting substances, although again, this is rare. The psychologist testifying as to the mental state of an individual who is charged with a felony or who is involved in a civil tort while withdrawing from an addictive substance may have a wide range of reactions. The expert psychologist must depend on his or her knowledge of the usual and customary actions of the substance, as well as collateral reports of the behavior of the individual in question during the time of withdrawal. It must be always kept in mind that the measurements or opinions involved in these matters should address the clarity or lack of clarity of cognitive functions, memory, and decision making. The law is not particularly interested in the discomfort that may occur during withdrawal, but in the state of mind of the individual and whether there is any basis to believe that the usual and customary ability to make decisions, to remember, or to understand is impaired.

Mental Condition during Abstinence

The research that has been generated in recent years suggests that even during periods of abstinence, those who have been addicted to certain drugs show measurable psychological deficits. Deficits in executive functions, memory, and general awareness have been demonstrated in users of opioids and cocaine after months of total abstinence (Hartman, 1995; Strickland, Stein, Khalsa-Denison, & Andre, 1996). In these matters, if the psychologist has the opportunity to examine the individual during this postwithdrawal period of abstinence, detailed descriptions of the individual's psychological deficits may emerge. Again, the opportunity to examine may occur long after the question of a criminal awareness has existed. In civil matters, it is more likely that the psychologist can examine the former addict who has been abstinent. This is particularly true in family matters where custodial and visitation issues are the point of concern.

Since 1996, the American Psychological Association through its College of Professional Psychology has sponsored certification in proficiency in the treatment of alcohol and other psychoactive substance use disorders. The psychologist who testifies as an expert in these disorders would be well served to acquire this credential.

The psychologist as expert witness in the area of the addictions may be called on to educate the triers of fact not only about what is known about excessive appetites but also to opine as to what is unknown or controversial in this complex area of human behavior. Continuing education, scholarship, and training are mandatory for expert witnessing in all areas of psychology but may be especially vital in an area of knowledge as diffuse and evolving as the addictions.

NOTES

 1. U.S.C.A. §4251.
 2. *People v. McKibben*, 24 Ill. App. 3d 692, 321 N.E.2d 362, 364 (1974).
 3. *Knickerbocker Life Ins. Co. v. Foley*, 105 U.S. 350, 26 L. Ed. 1055 (1882).
 4. *Fed R. Evid.* 406.
 5. *Handy v. Geary*, 105 R.I. 419, 252 A.2d 435, 441 (1969).
 6. Model Penal Code, §2.08.
 7. Leviticus 10:8–11.
 8. Isaiah 28:7–8.
 9. Ketubbot 10b.
10. *Wheatley v. United States*, 159 F.2d 599 (4th Cir. 1946).
11. *Wheatley v. United States*, 159 F.2d 11 (4th Cir. 1964).
12. *Schwab v. United States*, 327 F.2d 11 (8th Cir. 1964).
13. Am. Jur. 2d Sect. 155.
14. *United States v. Burnim*, 576 F.2d 236, 237 (9th Cir. 1978).
15. "Criminal Law: Chronic Alcoholism as a Defense to Crime," 61 *Minn. L. Rev.* 901, (1977).
16. *Minneapolis v. Altimus*, 238 N.W.2d 851 (Minn. 1976).
17. *Kentucky v. Tate*, 893 S.W.2d 368 (Ky. Sp. Crt. 1995).
18. M'Naghten's Case (1843) 10 Cl & Fin 200.
19. *Salzman v. United States*, 405 F.2d 358 (D.C. Cir. 1968).
20. Intoxication 1984 Utah L. Rev. 175.
21. WL 21 Suffolk U. L. Rev. 493.
22. *Powell v. Texas*, 392 U.S. 514 (1968).
23. Minn. L. Rev. 901, 912 n.43 (1977).
24. "Intoxication and the Law: Drunk Driving," 1985 *Ann. Surv. Am. L.* 229.
25. United States of America, Plaintiff-Appellee, 416 F.2d 914.
26. PLI/Crim 51 (1989).
27. *Robinson v. California*, 370 U.S. 660 (1962).
28. *United States v. Shuckahosee*, 609 F.2d 1351, 1355 (10th Cir. 1979), *cert. denied*, 445 U.S. 919 (1980).
29. *United States v. Moore*, 486 F.2d 1139 (D.C. Cir. 1973).
30. *United States v. Quartermaine*, 913 F.2d 910 (11th Circuit 1990).

31. *State v. Gibson*, 644 So. 2d 1093 (4th Cir. 1994).
32. *Sanchez v. United States*, 401 F.2d 771 (5th Cir. 1968).
33. *Carey v. United States*, 50 F.3d 1097 (1st Cir. 1995).
34. *Smith v. United States*, 431 F.2d. 565 (5th Cir. 1970).
35. Ibid.
36. *Edwards v. State*, 548 So. 2d. 656 (Fla. 1989).
37. *Neria v. United States*, 493 F.2d 913 (5th Cir. 1974).
38. *Marshall v. United States*, 414 U.S. 417, 94 S. Ct. 700 (1974).
39. *Lujan v. United States*, 424 F.2d 1053 (5th Cir. 1970).
40. *State v. Skelton*, 887 S.W.2d 699 (Mo. Ct. App. 1994).
41. *Kelly v. United States*, 820 F.2d 1173 (11th Cir. 1987).
42. *Ortega v. Rasor*, 291 F. Supp. 748 (S.D. Fla. 1968).
43. *Robinson v. California*, 370 U.S. 660 (1962).
44. *Oregon v. Sickler (In re Sickler)*, 133 Or. App. 50, 889 P.2d 1301 (1995).
45. *Davis v. St. Jude Medical Ctr.*, 645 So. 2d 771 (5th Cir. 1994).
46. *In re Hammons*, 625 N.Y.S.2d 408 (Sup. Ct. 1995).
47. *M.B. v. Konenkamp*, 523 N.W.2d 94 (S.D. Supp. Ct. 1994).
48. *Peoples Restaurant v. Sabo*, 591 So. 2d 907.
49. *Ellis v. N.G.N. of Tampa, Inc.*, 561 So. 2d 1209 (Fla. 2d DCA 1990), *quashed* 586 So. 2d 1042 (Fla. 1991).
50. *Pysz v. Henry's Drug Store*, 457 So. 2d 561 (Fla. 4th DCA 1984).
51. *Siegel v. Siegel*, 564 So. 2d 226.
52. *Huntley v. Huntley*, 578 So. 2d 890.
53. *In interest of R.*, 591 So. 2d 1130.
54. *Holman v. State*, 203 So. 2d 653 (Fla. 2d DCA 1967).
55. *In re Wise*, 96 Ohio App. 3d 619, 645 N.E.2d 812 (Wayne County 1994).
56. *The Florida Bar v. Jahn*, 509 So. 2d 285 (Fla. 1987).
57. *The Florida Bar v. Hartman*, 519 So. 2d 606 (Fla. 1988).
58. *The Florida Bar v. Liroff*, 582 So. 2d 1178.
59. *Kelly v. United States*, 820 F.2d 1173 (11th Cir. 1987).
60. *Colorado Board of Medical Examiners v. Davis*, No. 93Ca0911 (Colo. Ct. App. March 9, 1995).
61. *In re Petition and Questionnaire for Admission to the RI Bar*, 658 A.2d 894 (R.I. Supp. Ct. 1995).
62. *Ford v. Southeast Atlantic Corp.*, 588 So. 2d 1039.
63. *New York City Transit Authority v. Beazer*, 440 U.S. 568, 99 S. Ct. 1355 (1979).
64. *Cherry v. Heckler*, 760 F.2d 1186 (11th Cir. 1985), *superseded by statute, Passopulos v. Sullivan*, 976 F.2d 642 (11th Cir. 1992).
65. *McDaniel v. Mississippi Baptist Medical Ctr.*, 877 F. Supp. 321 (S.D. Miss. 1995).
66. *Wormley v. Arkla Inc.*, 871 F. Supp. 1079 (E.D. Ark. 1994).
67. *Brown v. Dalton*, No. 03950033 (EEOC Aug. 24, 1995).
68. *Garrity v. United Airlines*, 653 N.E.2d 173 (Mass. 1995).
69. *Cipollone v. Liggett Group Inc.*, 799 F. Supp. 466 (D.N.J. 1992).
70. J.H. Wigmore, 3 *Wigmore on Evidence* (3rd Ed. 1940), 367.

10

Domestic Issues: Marriage, Dissolution, and Custody

The right to marry and create a family is held to be fundamental in almost all societies. Very little beyond being of legal age and having the capacity to make a contract is required for a marriage (Clark, 1974). Although there may be legal matters at the time of marriage, such as prenuptial agreements, contracts, and property transfer arrangements, issues of law tend to occur after the marriage (or living arrangement of an unmarried couple) has existed for some time.

Until recently, the practice of family law has been considered to be of low status in the legal profession. Divorce mediation, wrongful birth, adoption of babies of surrogate mothers, and postdivorce disputes are now receiving increasing attention from the courts. Family issues are the most likely reason for a person in American society today to be exposed to the court system; for example, 60% of people with postdivorce problems go to court, as against 20% for accidents. The practice of family law has burgeoned into a broad and open field of practice. In the four years from 1980 to 1983, the membership in the American Bar Association's Family Law Section has grown from 6,000 to 14,500, and the growth continues. The most frequent and major issues in family law are property rights and child custody (Dullea, 1983). Divorcing is simpler than ever before with 48 of 50 states having no-fault laws. For every two marriages today, there is one divorce. This may make divorce easier for marital partners, but it places almost impossible burdens on the courts, to say nothing of the children of the broken marriages (Press, 1983).

In some jurisdictions, the same courts handle conflicts relating to marriage, divorce, juvenile misbehavior, abuse, battery, and custody; whereas in others, judges are designated as "juvenile," "domestic relations," or "family" judges. A judicial circuit is likely to have certain judges who hear all family matters. In a sense, such judges represent mergers of court structure with social services. Conflicts over jurisdiction, consistency, and the quality of social services are found in these settings. Efforts to organize and standardize family court procedures have resulted in the promulgation of standards (Institute of Judicial Administration, 1977). Some critics have expressed concern that organization of family court systems has attended too much to the efficiency of the judicial process at the expense of effectiveness and outcome for the families (Scanlon & Weingarten, 1963).

Merging the court system and its responsibility for family matters with social science has resulted in the development of assumptions about family dynamics, child growth and development, juvenile behavior, and appropriate treatment of family problems. The judiciary has a tendency to assign simplistic and frequently inappropriate causation and solutions to family conflict or dysfunction. The family court's treatment philosophy can sometimes disrupt the family system rather than provide helpful guidance or constraints. The courts have a poor record of diagnostic prediction concerning such questions as: Who should have child custody? Which children or parents may be dangerous? What are the effects of foster care? and Which parent is best able to enhance the child's development? (Mulvey, 1982). With the ever-mounting divorce rate, issues of custody and the child's adjustment to a one-parent family have risen. In 1970, the proportion of children living in one-parent families was 12%; by 1980, it had become 20%. In 1970, there were 47 divorced persons per 1,000 married persons, while in 1980, the ratio had risen to 109 per 1,000. In 1981, approximately 12.6 million children lived with one parent, according to the 1981 population survey of the Census Bureau (Strout, 1982). This trend continues.

EFFECTS OF DIVORCE ON CHILDREN

Divorce is almost certain to result in negative emotional experience for children. Hetherington, Cox, and Cox (1979) found that children of divorce demonstrated disruption in both play and social relations. Such children show high rates of dependence, help-seeking behavior, and noncompliant responses. Stolberg and Anker (1983) suggest that the psychopathology often seen in children of divorce may be directly related to environmental change and increased demands on the custodial parent.

In studying the burdens or tasks placed on the child of divorce, Wallerstein (1983) lists:

1. Acknowledging the reality of the marital rupture.
2. Disengaging from the parental conflict and distress and resuming customary pursuits.
3. Resolving loss.
4. Resolving anger and self-blame.

5. Accepting the permanence of the divorce.
6. Achieving realistic hope regarding relationships.

In her longitudinal studies of the responses of young adults who were children of divorce, Wallerstein (1985) reported that many appear to be burdened by vivid memories of the marital break, residual sadness, continuing resentment of parents, and a sense of deprivation. For themselves, they seem apprehensive about repeating their parents' involvement in an unhappy marriage and indicate an eagerness to avoid divorce for the sake of their children.

Research continues to confirm that children of contested divorces suffer long-term negative effects, although one study suggests that open discussion of conflicts can provide children with a more realistic view of their role and future and lessen separation anxiety (Wolman & Taylor, 1991). The more effective the parenting postdivorce, the better the children's social skills and involvement in prosocial activities are likely to be (Stolberg & Bush, 1985).

There have been significant changes in family law that parallel changes in family structures and interaction during the past quarter century. As a result, the expert testimony of psychologists knowledgeable in family dynamics and child development is likely to be more frequently sought (Melton & Wilcox, 1989).

CUSTODIAL ISSUES

Current Perspectives

In about 85% of all divorces or dissolutions, custody of the children is awarded to the mother without contest from the father (Weitzman & Dixon, 1979). Even when the divorce is contested, the court has usually awarded custody of the children to the mother (Freed & Foster, 1981). In recent years, the frequency of naming fathers the custodial parent has increased (Molinoff, 1977). Even unmarried fathers have been deemed to have custodial rights.[1]

The contemporary style of custodial award is joint custody (sometimes labeled "shared responsibility"). This rests on the concept that children have the right to keep alive their relationship with both parents. It allows divorced fathers to have more say in their children's everyday lives and is designed to ease the pressures of single parenthood.

Until 1839, children of divorce were automatically awarded to the father as a form of property. From the mid-19th to the mid-20th century, the awarding of children in custody matters depended heavily on the tender years doctrine. Known as a *judge's shibboleth*, or informal rule, this doctrine suggested that mothers are able to provide better and more loving, natural care than fathers. During the past four decades, this doctrine has been seriously questioned. The Uniform Marriage and Divorce Act (National Conference of Commissioners, 1971) recommends:

> The court shall determine custody in accordance with the best interests of the child. The court shall consider all relevant factors including: (1) the wishes of the child's parent or parents as to his custody; (2) the wishes of the child as to his custodian; (3) the interaction and interrelationship of the child with his parents, his siblings, and any other person who may significantly affect the child's best interests; (4) the child's adjustment to his home, school, and community; and (5) the mental and physical health of all individuals involved. The court shall not consider conduct of a proposed custodian that does not affect his relationship to the child.

Despite these recommendations, many courts continue to depend on subjective judgment and traditional concepts (Ruback, 1982).

Current research casts question on the traditional concepts of the importance of early bonding with the mother (Ainsworth, 1973; Brody, 1983). Many fathers have been found to be competent primary caretakers. Their children seem to do as well as or better than children in sole custody of the mother (Santruck & Warshak, 1979).

Joint Custody

At this writing, 28 states permit or give priority to joint custody of children following marriage dissolution. Each state has a different set of guidelines and generally spells out the details of the concept and delineates the judge's responsibilities. An example of a joint-custody law, enacted in Florida, follows:

> Be It Enacted by the Legislature of the State of Florida:
>
> Section 1. Subsection (3) and paragraph (b) of subsection (2) of section 61.13, Florida Statutes, are amended to read:
>
> 61.13 Custody and support of children, etc., power of court in making orders.
>
> The court shall determine all matters relating to custody of each minor child of the parties as a part of any proceeding under this chapter in accordance with the best interests of the child and in accordance with the Uniform Child Custody Jurisdiction Act. It is the public policy of this state to assure each minor child frequent and continuing contact with both parents after the parents have separated or dissolved their marriage and to encourage parents to share the rights and responsibilities of child-rearing. Upon considering all relevant factors, the father of the child shall be given the same consideration as the mother in determining custody regardless of the age of the child.
>
> 2. The court shall order that the parental responsibility for a minor child shall be shared by both parents unless the court finds that shared parental responsibility would be detrimental to the child. If the court determines that shared parental responsibility would be detrimental to the child, the court may order sole parental responsibility.

a. "Shared parental responsibility" means that both parents retain full parental rights and responsibilities with respect to their child, and requires both parents to confer so that major decisions affecting the welfare of the child will be determined jointly. In ordering shared parental responsibility, the court may consider the expressed desires of the parents and may grant to one party the ultimate responsibility over specific aspects of the child's welfare or the court may divide those aspects between the parties on the basis of the best interests of the child. Where it appears to the court to be in the best interests of the child, the court may order or the parties may agree how any such responsibility will be divided. Such areas of responsibility may include primary physical residence, education, medical and dental care, and any other responsibilities which the court finds unique to a particular family and/or in the best interests of the child.

b. "Sole parental responsibility" means responsibility of the minor child shall be given to one parent by the court, with or without rights of visitation to the other parent.

c. The court may award the grandparents visitation rights of a minor child if it is deemed by the court to be in the child's best interest. Grandparents shall have legal standing to seek judicial enforcement of such an award. Nothing in this section shall be construed to require that grandparents be made parties or given notice of dissolution pleadings or proceedings, nor shall such grandparents have legal standing as "contestants" as defined in §61.1306. No court shall order that a child be kept within the state or jurisdiction of the court solely for the purpose of permitting visitation by the grandparents.

3. Access to records and information pertaining to a minor child, including but not limited to medical, dental, and school records, shall not be denied to a parent because such parent is not the child's primary residential parent.

For purposes of shared parental responsibility and primary physical residence, the best interests of the child shall be determined by the court's consideration and evaluation of all factors affecting the best welfare and interests of the child, including, but not limited to:

(a) The parent who is more likely to allow the child frequent and continuing contact with the nonresidential parent.

(b) The love, affection, and other emotional ties existing between the parents and the child.

(c) The capacity and disposition of the parents to provide the child with food, clothing, medical care or other remedial care recognized and permitted under the laws of this state in lieu of medical care, and other material needs.

(d) The length of time the child has lived in a stable, satisfactory environment and the desirability of maintaining continuity.

(e) The permanence, as a family unit, of the existing or proposed custodial home.

(f) The moral fitness of the parents.

(g) The mental and physical health of the parents.

(h) The home, school, and community record of the child.

(i) The reasonable preference of the child, if the court deems the child to be of sufficient intelligence, understanding, and experience to express a preference.

(j) Any other factor considered by the court to be relevant to a particular child custody dispute.[2]

Many marriage dissolutions result in a more informal "joint custody" and never come before the court. When a court mandates joint custody, or shared responsibility, there is usually some conflict regarding custody. Some attorneys are skeptical about whether these new procedures will result in significant lessening of custodial conflict. An appellate court has stated: "But despite our belief that joint custody will be a preferred disposition in some matrimonial actions, we decline to establish a presumption in its favor or in favor of any particular custody determination."[3]

The court opined that for joint custody to be workable and in the child's best interests, the parents must show a potential for cooperation in matters of child rearing. Some judges find that joint custody eases their conflicts in the Solomonic issue of "splitting the child." The facts involved in some custodial issues are mind-boggling. The joint-custody concept relieves the judge of the responsibility of dealing with these vague, tangential, and often convoluted issues.

Early research in joint custody suggests that it is not as simple a solution as it may appear. Parents tend to find the arrangement more convenient than the children. A large proportion of the children are overburdened by the demands of being part of two families in two homes (Steinman, 1981).

Divorce can be disturbing for children. The immediate results can be disruptions of school, play, and social relationships in preschool children (Hetherington et al., 1979). There is reason to believe that the distress one sees in children two and more years following divorce is the result of parental instability, anxiety, and stress. The more relaxed and less guilty the parent, the more likely the child will be spared extreme psychological reactions to the divorce (Luepnitz, 1978).

The myth that joint custody will prevent divorce from changing children's lives should not be encouraged. The reality is that no court can order joint custody and make it work. The parents must be able to suspend their own hostility, anxiety, guilt, and personal animosity. These are often long-standing and may be what led to the breakdown of the marriage in the first place. When joint custody is ordered for a family despite obvious personal antagonisms, it is a sham (Span & Cantor, 1983). Appellate courts are beginning to recognize that an order for joint custody is inappropriate where the parents have little potential for cooperation.[4] Research on the effects of various life-cycle changes, parenting styles, and home environments on joint-custody outcomes is sorely needed (Clingempeel & Reppucci, 1982).

Sometimes, joint custody seems to work well. According to early research, factors leading to success in joint custody include commitment to the arrangement, mutual support between the divorced parents, a flexible sharing of responsibility, and agreement on the implicit rules of the sharing system. Even with these positive factors, structural impediments may diminish success or satisfaction in a joint-custody arrangement. Structural factors include lack of geographic proximity, children getting older and insisting on more control of the arrangement, children insisting on one-home continuity, and stresses caused by a parent living with a new partner, creating blended families in one or both homes (Abarbanel, 1979). Wolchick, Braver, and Sandler (1985) studied 133 children of divorce who were in joint-custody arrangements as well as maternal custody (33% and 67% respectively). They reported that children in joint custody had a somewhat greater number of positive experiences and slightly high self-ratings of esteem than children in maternal custody.

Twiford (1986) cautions that positive results of joint custody depend on whether the parents are cooperative in child-rearing activities, live in close geographic proximity, and have few postdivorce adjustment difficulties. This suggests that few divorces meet all the criteria necessary for a successful joint-custody arrangement.

There are some indications that fathers who participate in a joint-custody arrangement have a higher degree of involvement with their children than fathers who are granted visitation rights with children in sole custody of the mother (Greif, 1979). Although research about joint custody has been quite limited, with rather loose experimental designs, the consistency of a variety of reports suggests that some broken families are able to retain important bonds. About 30% of the couples who have joint-custody arrangements maintain a friendly, caring interaction, compared with 20% of a matched, single-custodian (mother) sample. Even when joint custody seems to work, it is likely that the formerly married partners are not "coparenting" but are "parallel parenting," where each parent operates as a self-contained unit (Collins, 1982).

Feiner and his colleagues (1985) studied the practices and attitudes regarding custody of 74 attorneys and 43 judges experienced in family court and custodial issues. Both groups opined in the majority that maternal custody was most often the best option in 60% of cases. Thus, legal professionals do not enthusiastically share the views of those who favor joint-custody arrangements. Marital attorneys and family court judges apparently have a pessimistic view of the ability of most divorcing couples to cooperate to the extent necessary for joint custody to be in the best interests of the child.

Parental Fitness

The court is likely to evaluate a wide range of factors in determining parental fitness. These include both the mental and the physical health of the proposed custodian.[5]

Although each state defines fitness in a variety of ways, judges are prone to consider such issues as the wishes of the child, the parents' desires, the sex of the child, adjustment to siblings, biological relationships, length of the custodial relationship, age of the child, age of the parents, school and community status, parents' moral character, financial sufficiency, and the stability of the home. Psychological testimony is appropriate for some of these matters but not for others. The psychological expert is again warned not to go beyond the boundaries of recognized competence in testifying as to parental fitness. This will be addressed in the section "The Psychologist's Roles." (Table 10.1, which appears later in this chapter, presents the factors most influential in judges' decisions concerning parental fitness.)

Change of Custody

Petitions to modify custody are seldom granted. The initial custody decision is frequently challenged, and the issue is usually heard and decided by the same judge who mandated the original custody decision. Once custody is granted, a change is warranted only if it can be shown that the child will be placed in immediate jeopardy, emotional or physical, by continuation of the custodial arrangement.[6,7] Thus to effect a change in a previously agreed-on and mandated custodial arrangement, the petitioner must demonstrate to the court's satisfaction that the child is likely to suffer a fairly immediate danger to growth and development if the existing arrangement is continued. In this instance, the best interests of the child are very narrowly defined as imminent danger to his or her physical or emotional state. This is the essential reason why a relatively small number of petitions for change of custody are granted. A noncustodial parent would be well advised to proceed cautiously in petitioning for a change of custody when the reasons do not meet the criteria of immediate danger to the child's physical or mental health.

Visitation

The courts usually mandate that the child should have reasonable and frequent contact with both parents in a joint-custody arrangement and with the noncustodial parent in sole-custody situations. Each judge is apparently guided by his or her own standards. At the 1983 annual meetings of the American Academy of Marital Attorneys, a family judge stated that "regardless of the circumstances" he insisted that the children spend two weekends per month with the noncustodial parent. A well-known judge is noted for his predilection to insist that the noncustodial parent take up residence within walking distance of the custodial parent's residence and that the children spend alternate nights in the divorced parents' separate homes. Most judges favor visitation plans that concentrate on vacations and holidays rather than on the needs of a specific child. Together with issues of monetary support, visitation conflicts are likely to be the most frequent reasons for petitions to modify custodial decisions.

Forty of the fifty states permit grandparent visitation when the child's parents divorce. When judicial intervention is properly invoked, most states provide a mechanism for a request for third-party visitation privileges with a minor child. The courts have come to acknowledge the importance of the child's relationship with third parties (Morris, 1989). The importance of children's continuing relationships with grandparents in particular has been appearing in the literature (Bartram, Kirkpatrick, Hecker, & Prebis, 1996; Ehrle & Day, 1994). Grandparents can provide a sanctuary for the child where security is enhanced and a sense of family within society is established and maintained (Blau, 1984). All grandparents are not equal and there are instances where legal procedures instituted by grandparents to gain access to a minor child have resulted in negative consequences (Thompson, Tinsley, Scalora, & Parke, 1989).

OTHER FAMILY AND CHILD ISSUES

Child Abuse

All states have a variety of regulations and procedures designed to protect children's physical and emotional health. A community agency, operating under state laws, is usually vested with responsibility for identifying instances of child abuse and bringing these to the attention of the courts. The most frequent sources of such complaints are the reports of neighbors or the resource personnel at the child's school. When a complaint is made, the child is frequently taken from the home and placed in a protective-custody situation until the issue is settled at court.

The following represents the type of petition filed in such cases.

IN THE CIRCUIT COURT OF THE THIRTEENTH JUDICIAL CIRCUIT OF THE STATE OF FLORIDA, IN AND FOR HILLSBOROUGH COUNTY
JUVENILE AND DOMESTIC RELATIONS DIVISION

CASE NO. X-137-B

In the Interest of: Jane Doe   83–6274A

_____ , *Child* _____

PETITION

To the Judge of the Juvenile and Domestic Relations Divisions: Your petitioner, ___Mary Smith, District Intake Counselor___ , respectfully represents under the Court that _____Jane Doe_____

_____

residing at ___123 Elm Street, Tampa, Florida___ of the age of 14 years, (is) (X̶X̶X̶) _a dependent child_____ within the intent and meaning of Chapter 39 of the Florida Statutes, in that, the petitioner is informed and believes, that: Jane Doe is an abused child in that her parents permitted the child to live in an environment which would likely cause physical, mental, or emotional injury to the child or cause the child's physical, mental, or emotional health to be in danger of being significantly impaired. To Wit: On March 6, 1983, James Doe threatened to strike Jane with an awl, and a belt. Further, Mr. Doe hit Jane about the body. Jane states that on numerous occasions she has been threatened with physical harm by her father and she is very fearful of him. Mrs. Doe admitted putting bruises on the child's arm when the child did not clean the bathroom as told.

Jane Doe is an emotionally neglected child in that her parents, although financially able, deprived the child of, or allowed the child to be deprived of, the necessary medical treatment or permitted the child to live in an environment when such deprivation or environment causes the child's mental and emotional health to be significantly impaired or to be in danger of being significantly impaired. To Wit: Mr. Doe admitted to emotionally neglecting and threatening the child with a belt. Mr. Doe has stated he feels his child does have serious emotional problems which he has not sought counseling for in the past.

The names of the parents or legal custodians of the child _Jane_ are: _James and Mary Doe_____

residence and address is ___123 Elm Street, Tampa, Florida___ whose relation to said child _Jane_ to that of __parents__ . Wherefore your petitioner requests that the Court take jurisdiction of the child __Jane__ and if the facts alleged are true, adjudicate the child __Jane__ to be a __dependent__ child _____ .

Date: __3.29.83__

Mary Smith
PETITIONER

STATE OF FLORIDA ⎫
Hillsborough County ⎬ SS.
⎭

___Mary Smith___ , the petitioner who subscribed __her__ name to the foregoing petition in my presence, being duly sworn, deposes and says that the allegations contained in said petition are, to the best of information and belief, true, that this petition is filed in good faith.

___J. D. Brown___

Most communities have arrangements for the investigation of such charges by caseworkers. Psychological evaluation of the child and the parents is frequently conducted by mental health professionals on the staff of local institutions or by independent professionals who are retained as experts. The parents have the right to retain their own mental health professionals to evaluate the parties in the alleged abusive situation. Judges rely heavily on the reports of social workers, psychologists, and psychiatrists in these matters.

Juvenile Misbehavior

Juvenile offenders tend to be treated with special concern and leniency by the courts. Judges tend to be much more sanguine about rehabilitating youthful offenders than adult felons.

In matters of delinquency, the juvenile, usually under 17 years of age, has traditionally been "taken over" by the court, which acts as *parens patriae*, or responsible custodian. In 1967, the Supreme Court held that juveniles have a wide range of rights.[8] In these criminal cases, judges are very responsive to social service investigations and psychological reports when deciding the disposition of the case.

The larger group of judicial proceedings involving juveniles is called "status offenses" (truancy, running away, lack of parental control, promiscuity, drinking, and so on). Judges have very wide discretion in the disposition of such cases (Glaser, 1979). Reports from social workers, caseworkers, and mental health experts are well received by most judges. For first offenders, probation or warnings and remedial recommendations are usual.

Adoption

Although very elaborate procedures have been developed by most adoption agencies, and state laws can be quite specific, the advice of professional mental health workers is rarely sought before an adoptive decision is made. Adoption procedures vary greatly: The rather casual, physician-arranged adoptions stand in contrast to the often rigid agency requirements focusing on socioeconomic status, age, community stability, and so on. Rarely are psychologists called on for an expert opinion in these matters. Occasionally, when prospective parents are questionable, a psychological evaluation may be requested to attest to their aptitude and stability in respect to parenting.

Marital Reconciliation and Mediation

Although a divorce is easier to obtain than ever before, as noted earlier in this chapter, some judges are reluctant to grant dissolution of a marriage until the couple has sought professional help in an effort to save the marriage. Where the reconciliation fails or where the couple wishes to challenge the reconciliation mandate, the psychologist may be called on to evaluate the partners and render an opinion as to the feasibility of reconciliation.

Although this is less likely to occur now than in the past, most states have passed or are considering legislation mandating that mediation to settle adversary issues be recommended before formal court litigation in a marriage dissolution takes place. The concept of mediation is well-intentioned. Mediation consists of several (usually half a dozen) sessions with the disputing marital partners and an attorney as well as a mental health professional, who may be a psychologist, a social worker, or a family specialist. The goals or benefits of this nonjudicial procedure include:

- A less stressful environment to help ease the bitterness of the marital breakup.
- A less expensive modality than the adversary system.
- Time savings for the court and the marital partners.
- Assistance in working through custody issues with fewer damaging side effects than in traditional adversary resolutions.
- Opportunity to benefit from therapeutic intervention due to non-threatening procedures and professional expertise.

Many lawyers and judges have serious questions about mediation as a realistic solution to divorce conflicts. Some lawyers feel that divorce mediation may be the unlawful or unethical practice of law. Laws concerning property are more complex today than ever before, and a matrimonial lawyer in a mediation situation may not be able to protect the rights of both parties. A single attorney in a mediation situation may become hopelessly involved in a conflict of interest in dealing with both spouses. Some states mandate that an attorney may not form any kind of partnership with a nonlawyer in matters related to the practice of law.[9] Although many matrimonial attorneys have given their time to early settlement programs, such programs differ from mediation in that no fee is charged.

It has been suggested that mediation represents a philosophical attack on the adversary system in marital dissolution. It is suggested that if two attorneys are involved, there is less of a chance that some significant aspect of the law will be missed to the detriment of one or both spouses. In mediation, one lawyer is more likely to miss such points. In favor of the adversary system, it is argued that without competent counsel the passive partner in a divorce may agree to things not in his or her best interests. In mediation, the mediators may not fully inform each participant of their rights for fear of encouraging hostility or negativism in the mediation setting. Thus many attorneys fear that mediation can result in uninformed and ill-advised settlements.

Although most matrimonial lawyers applaud the concept of mediation to enhance a positive relationship between the divorcing spouses, there is concern that such efforts may be made at the expense of a spouse's long-term legal rights. Additionally, since only about 5% of all matrimonial matters are tried as contested cases, some lawyers question the value of adding a procedure that may, in the end, increase rather than decrease court time (Executive Committee, 1983).

Some attorneys believe mediation can work despite the preceding concerns (Gourvitz, 1983). The Association of the Bar of the City of New York has set forth some safeguards in these matters:

1. The lawyer must clearly and fully advise the parties of the limitations on his or her role and, specifically, of the fact that the lawyer represents neither party and that, accordingly, they should not look to the lawyer to protect their individual interests or to keep confidences of one party from the other.
2. The lawyer must fully and clearly explain the risks of proceeding without separate legal counsel and thereafter proceed only with the consent of the parties and only if the lawyer is satisfied that the parties understand the risks and understand the significance of the fact that the lawyer represents neither party.
3. A lawyer may participate with mental health professionals in those aspects of mediation which do not require the exercise of professional legal judgment and involve the same kind of mediation activities permissible to lay mediators.
4. Lawyers may provide impartial legal advice and assist in reducing the parties' agreement to writing only where the lawyer fully explains all pertinent considerations and alternatives and the consequences to each party of choosing the resolution agreed upon.
5. The lawyer may give legal advice only to both parties in the presence of the other.
6. The lawyer must advise the parties of the advantages of seeking independent legal counsel before executing any agreement drafted by the lawyer.
7. The lawyer may not represent either of the parties in any subsequent legal proceedings relating to the divorce.[10]

Thus the law is well on its way to setting guidelines and limits in mediation style. As yet, no substantial research is available to suggest whether mediation is useful, and if so, under what conditions.

Property Agreement Challenges

On rare occasions, a contested divorce action may involve property settlement issues where one of the spouses agreed to a business matter, such as transfer of property, stock ownership, corporate voting rights, and so forth, during the course of the marriage. At the time of the dissolution, the spouse who previously gave up property or rights may indicate that he or she did so under unusual emotional strain and was not able to act in his or her own best interests.

An example of this might be the case in which a wife was an officer in her husband's corporation, holding a significant block of stock in the corporation. During a stormy period in the latter phases of the marriage, the wife discovered that the husband had become emotionally involved with a woman executive in one of their subsidiary corporations. During the course of their arguments, the husband proposed that the wife sign over all her stock rights to him, so that this issue would not interfere with their efforts to reconcile. The wife, a severely dependent person, fearing the loss of the husband, complied. Four years later, the husband filed for divorce. In evaluating the assets of the marriage prior to the final agreement, the wife's attorney discovered the circumstances of the stock transfer and filed a claim for the wife's original share of the corporation. The husband's position was that the wife willingly exchanged the stock for other considerations and was not entitled to the value of the original stock. The wife had seen two different psychologists during the stressful period of the marriage. Both were deposed by the wife's attorney to determine whether she indeed was unable to make business decisions in her own best interests at the time of the stock transfer. One had conducted an evaluation, and the other was the wife's therapist. Both were able to testify that their records showed that the wife was an inordinately dependent person, morbidly fearful of losing her husband and willing to do almost anything to placate him and keep the marriage intact.

As psychology continues to expand its research base, both in new areas and in replication studies, the range of opportunity for psychologists to serve as experts in family law is likely to broaden. An example is provided by the research of Jameson and her colleagues (1997) on the relevant factors for developing custody recommendations by psychologists. They propose that assessment should consider relational factors between the child and the parents, the developmental needs of the child, and the parenting skills and abilities of the parents.

THE PSYCHOLOGIST'S ROLES

Traditionally, psychologists have been called on for evaluation and expert testimony in a variety of matters in family court:

- Psychological status and needs of a child and the best interests of a child.
- Fitness of the mother as sole parent.
- Fitness of the father as sole parent.

- Parents' potential as joint custodians.
- Significance of grandparents in the child's life.
- Change of custody petitions.
- Current scientific thought on issues of child development and family dynamics.
- Visitation plans.
- The child's potential for dangerousness to self and others.
- Potential of parents as abusers.
- Issues of mental status at time of property agreement.

Standards already developed by the American Psychological Association for the delivery of professional services (APA, 1977), the code of ethics of psychologists (APA, 1992), and the principles for the use and interpretation of psychological tests (Chapter 6) apply to the work of psychologists in domestic relations or family court issues.

More recently, the American Psychological Association has recommended the following guidelines for child custody evaluations in divorce proceedings:

1. The primary purpose of the evaluation is to assess the best psychological interests of the child.
2. The child's interests and well-being are paramount.
3. The focus of the evaluation is on parenting capacity, the psychological and developmental needs of the child and the resulting fit.
4. The role of the psychologist is that of a professional expert who strives to maintain an objective, impartial stance.
5. The psychologist gains specialized competence.
6. The psychologist is aware of personal and societal biases and engages in nondiscriminatory practice.
7. The psychologist avoids multiple relationships.
8. The scope of the evaluation is determined by the evaluator, based on the nature of the referral question.
9. The psychologist obtains informed consent from all adult participants and, as appropriate, informs child participants.
10. The psychologist informs participants about the limits of confidentiality and the disclosure of information.
11. The psychologist uses multiple methods of data gathering.
12. The psychologist neither overinterprets nor inappropriately interprets clinical or assessment data.
13. The psychologist does not give any opinion regarding the psychological functioning of any individual who has not been personally evaluated.

14. Recommendations, if any, are based on what is in the best psychological interests of the child.

15. The psychologist clarifies financial arrangements.

16. The psychologist maintains written records.

A fuller description and details of these recommended guidelines can be found in Appendix D.

The Guidelines have not received universal acceptance, particularly in regard to psychologists who have served as psychotherapists to one or more of the family members. Saunders and his colleagues (1996) specifically suggest:

- The Guidelines address complaints and cite literature too restrictive of psychologists' potential roles.
- The Guidelines make loose and erroneous adaptations of legal terminology.
- The Guidelines have an absence of a family perspective and an imperative to preserve the children's relationship with both parents.
- The Guidelines lack reference to developmental research and perspectives.
- The Guidelines denigrate the role of psychopathology in assessments, a factor which often plays an important role in the Court's decisions.
- Verbal allusions to "objective" and "impartial" suggest that those doing child custody assessments should be detached, making the psychologist's job more difficult.

The authors suggest that the APA Guidelines can undermine the credibility of competent psychologists.

Interest in establishing methods, procedures, and psychological instruments for child custody evaluation continues. In some instances, local psychological groups have established their own recommended procedures (Braunstein & Schuman, 1996). Reviews of procedures and commonly used instruments continue to appear, adding to the experience and opinion likely to shape guidelines for practice in the future (Heinze & Grisso, 1996; Keilin & Bloom, 1986). A survey of custody evaluation practices among experienced psychologists reflects considerable diversity (Ackerman & Ackerman, 1977).

Research is growing rapidly in child development and family interaction. As forthcoming new data support some concepts and cast question on others, the psychologist who serves as an expert witness in these areas cannot afford to testify on the basis of what he or she learned in graduate school or "several years ago." The fields of family interaction and structure as well as child growth and development are dynamic, benefiting from a continuing infusion of data from research programs and demonstration projects. The work of the psychologist as an expert witness is subject to public scrutiny in the courts and should reflect excellent training, professional competence, awareness of current research, and adherence to the highest ethical and professional standards. In this chapter, examples of the work of psychologists as expert witnesses in family law are presented in some detail.

The Psychological Status of the Child and the Child's Best Interests

In the effort to administer custody decisions, the courts often seek professional advice, guidance, and even justification, and when the courts are addressing the best interests of the child, an evaluation of the child's psychological status is often helpful. Ideally, such an evaluation would include:

1. *The Facts of the Case.*   The psychologist should be provided with as objective a set of facts in the matter as possible. This may prove difficult when the expert is retained by the attorney for one parent or the other in an adversary matter. Sometimes, the psychologist must accept the attorney's presentation of the facts, which should be obtained in writing since attorneys are usually more objective when committing the facts of a case to a document. When the expert serves as *amicus curiae* in custodial issues, the judge usually presents both the facts of the case and the questions to be addressed by the expert.

2. *Background Factors.*   Ideally, the psychologist will take a history from both parties in the disputed issue. This is not always possible, and if history is taken from one parent only, the psychologist must view the parent's judgmental responses cautiously. If both parents are interviewed, discrepancies in the history should be noted and, as far as possible, omitted from the psychologist's assessment process. Interviews with the child are important. Those who do not use psychological tests may depend heavily on interviews (Gardner, 1982). Bathurst, Gottfried, and Gottfried (1997) found that mothers, fathers and even stepparents demonstrated defensive underreporting and self-favorability on the MMPI-2.

3. *School Adjustment.*   An interview with the child's teachers is often helpful in assessing the child's adjustment to the most significant segment of time in his or her life. Children spend 30 to 40 hours per week in school, and their response to this setting is an important consideration in the evaluation of the child's adjustment.

4. *Psychological Status.*   Decisions concerning custodial placement, visitation, treatment, or remedial education should be made with an objective view of the child's current status, special abilities, needs, and problems. Such an examination should generally include:

   a. A through evaluation of intellectual status and potential.

   b. An evaluation of neuropsychological factors.

c. An assessment of academic achievement.

d. A personality evaluation and measures of personal adjustment.

Specific tests and procedures will depend on the age and background of the child.

5. *Report of Findings.*   A report of the findings of the psychological evaluation must be made available to the retaining attorney. In addition to the objective findings, the psychologist should summarize the results and state, as specifically as possible, the child's current developmental status, the child's anticipated needs, and specific remedial or therapeutic recommendations. The expert should remember that the decision as to custody will be made by the court. The psychologist must avoid making that decision in the report of the evaluation of the child.

In reporting a child's current psychological status, the psychologist must be aware of current research concerning the effects of divorce on children so that findings of psychological dysfunction are not misattributed to inappropriate causalities. Much is known about the child's reaction to family conflict (Beal, 1979; Glick, 1979; Hetherington, 1979; Hetherington et al., 1979; Luepnitz, 1978; Rutter, 1971; Wallerstein & Kelly, 1975). The psychologist who acts as an expert witness in custodial matters should be aware of the contrasts between children of fractured families and children of intact families.

These suggested procedures are ideal but not always practical or possible. The extent and completeness of a psychological evaluation may be influenced by the constraints placed on participants by the attorneys in the case or by the judge. Where these constraints seriously interfere with the conduct of an adequate evaluation, the psychologist must make this known, in writing if necessary. Should the constraints continue, the psychologist may have to withdraw from the case.

The following psychological report and testimony involve a petition for change of custody. Initial contact was made by the attorney representing the father. The divorce took place when the male child was 16 months of age. Both the mother and the father had remarried. The father had maintained regular contact with his son through visitation arrangements set by the court. As the boy began to mature, the father became concerned about the youngster's emotional development and sexual identification. A petition for change of custody was filed, and the psychological examination was conducted to determine whether such a change was likely to be in the child's best interests.

Originally, both the mother and father were to be interviewed as part of the assessment. The attorneys for the mother decided that the mother should not be interviewed, so the entire history was given by the father. School records were retrieved and provided by the father. The following report resulted from the evaluation of the youngster.

PSYCHOLOGICAL REPORT

June 13, 1988

NAME: Doe, Jack

DATE OF EXAMINATION: 5/19, 6/2,
6/5, 6/14/88

ADDRESS: 123 Elm Street,
Palatka, Florida 31702

TELEPHONE: 000-0000

BIRTHDATE: 3/10/80   AGE: 7–9

OCCUPATION: Student

EDUCATION: 2.9

Referral

This youngster is referred via R. M. Roe, Esquire. Mr. Roe is attorney for Albert M. Doe, the father, who is concerned about his son's emotional adjustment. The boy has been living with his mother. The mother remarried in 1985. Mr. Doe feels that from that point on communication between himself and his child deteriorated rapidly.

The purpose of the assessment is to answer a number of questions:

1. Is there cause for concern as to how this youngster is developing psychologically?
2. What kind of custodial arrangements are likely to be best for the boy at this stage in his life?
3. Is he in a setting likely to be conducive to masculine identification and optimum opportunity to develop his potential?
4. Are there any specific recommendations that would be made in view of psychological findings?

Background Factors

The information is provided by Mr. Doe. He states that he and his ex-wife were married in 1974 while the father was in college. He feels that he married because it was the "normal thing to do." He found that their personalities did not match. They have been divorced for six and one-half years at the time of this assessment. Mr. Doe states that he is regretful that his son has had to pay a price for the divorce.

The mother, Mrs. Jane Smith, received her divorce in 1982 after seven years of marriage to her husband. Jack was 16 months of age at that time. The mother is said to be 34 years of age. She has a bachelor's degree in education. She is described as a heavy smoker and overweight.

The stepfather is Mr. Bill Smith, about 37 years of age. He is a computer salesman.

The real father, Albert M. Doe, is a 38-year-old accountant. He received his education at Yale and at Case. He is in good health. He remarried two years ago. The stepmother, Harriet, is a 29-year-old HRS Child Support Enforcement professional. She has a bachelor's degree from Georgia State University.

The custody arrangements at the present time are that Mr. Doe picks up the youngster for a weekend every two weeks. Mr. Doe also has five weeks of custodial visitation in the summer. Mr. Doe complains that his ex-wife refers to him as "Al" and doesn't encourage the boy to call him "Father" or "Dad." The mother has been describing the stepfather as "Jack's Father." Mr. Doe insists that he has never spoken to his son negatively about the boy's mother. He feels, however, that his ex-wife speaks disparagingly of him.

Jack sees the paternal grandparents on Sunday afternoons. He also sees the maternal grandmother. As far as Mr. Doe knows, they all get along well.

Jack weighed eight pounds at birth. Early growth and development are described as occurring essentially within normal limits. He has attended with a general practitioner in Tampa, according to the father. The father plans a thorough dental evaluation in the near future.

He still maintains some childhood habits. He cannot complete his own bathroom behavior and tells the father he needs wiping.

The father states that the boy hit a wall at age seven and one-half and was "unconscious" according to the youngster's reports. He sleeps fitfully and reports nightmares.

The boy had preschool at Mulberry, and the first grade at Palatka Heights. As far as the father knows, the boy is doing average work. Father visited the school three months ago. The boy seems to seek attention and is slightly disruptive.

At the father's home he has his own room. The father tries to encourage him to get outdoors. The father is concerned that he may be watching too much TV at the mother's home. The father has occasionally spanked him. The father has taken him camping. Jack enjoys boating, fishing, and swimming. He likes to look for fossils.

The father gives him a dollar every two weeks as an allowance. The father tries to associate this with instructions to mind the mother and to do what is expected. Bedtime is between eight and eight-thirty.

On occasion Mr. Doe and his ex-wife have had some altercations about Jack's visitation and how holidays might be spent.

Currently Jack suffers from constipation. He seems to be fitful in sleep. There has been a little bit of stuttering for the past year and one-half. He reports nightmares and will call out to his father two or three times a night. He is still fearful of the dark, and at home he is said to sleep with a nightlight. He is somewhat dependent, slightly shy, and tends to be moody at times.

Mr. Doe forwards a report from Jackson Epp, M.D., who reports in a brief letter to Woodworth Pell, Esquire, that Jack was evaluated on January 27, 1988, using a psychiatric interview, a Bender-Gestalt, and a Draw-a-Person Test. He states that there is no evidence of organicity or psychosis. He states that Jack appears to be adjusting well in his present situation. This cannot be considered an adequate psychological evaluation.

Examination Procedures

Wechsler Intelligence Scale for Children-Revised, Peabody Picture Vocabulary Test, Torque Test (repeated), Indiana-Reitan Neuropsychological Short Form, Metropolitan Achievement Tests, Thematic Apperception Test, Draw-a-Person Test, Child Sentence Completion Test, House-Tree Test, History, Observation, and Interview.

Response to Evaluation

Jack is a round-faced youngster with brown hair and brown eyes. He appears to be close and affectionate with his father. He looks somewhat like his father. His speech is clear with a slight scratchiness. Hearing is within normal limits. Motor behavior is controlled. He fidgets slightly, appropriate to age. He socializes in a quiet, polite manner. He enjoys playing and interacting. Cooperation is good. His confidence seems fairly good.

He has had camping experience, but he says he is not too sure he is going to enjoy it again.

Results of Examination

A. Intellectual Factors

Results of the WISC-R are as follows:

Factor	Deviation IQ	Percentile
Verbal scale	123	93rd
Performance scale	132	98th
Full scale	131	98th

The above results suggest that this youngster falls in the Superior to Very Superior range of intellectual capacity. There is a slight lowering in arithmetic reasoning and attention span, but all other factors fall in the Superior ranges. The lowering is probably an artifact of age and development.

Results of the Peabody Picture Vocabulary Test place Jack at the 96th percentile, confirming the results of the WISC-R. The youngster has a mental age of approximately 11 years at the present time.

B. Neuropsychological Factors

The Torque Test indicates that Jack is solidly right-handed and left-brained with no evidence of mixed cerebral dominance. The Indiana-Reitan Short Form indicates that central nervous system development is appropriate for age. No signs of anomalies.

C. Achievement Factors

Objective results of the Metropolitan Achievement Tests are as follows:

Factor	Grade Equivalent	Percentile (End of 2nd Grade)
Word Knowledge	3.7	86th
Word Analysis	2.6	44th
Reading Comprehension	2.9	64th
Spelling	2.7	42nd
Math Computation	4.2	94th
Math Concepts	3.4	68th
Math Problem Solving	3.7	86th

The above results indicate that this youngster is ahead of his grade placement except for Word Analysis and Spelling. He should do quite well in the third grade and probably ought to have a stimulating intellectual environment in his school.

D. Personality Factors

(1) *Interpersonal Activity.*   This is a youngster who for his age is quite cautious about expecting success. He seems fearful of thinking about good things coming to him. He enjoys physical activity most of all. His basic values and character are good.

(2) *Early Identifications.*   Primary identification is with the father. The unconscious picture of the father is that of a fairly aggressive person who is powerful. He sees the father unconsciously as an individual who tries to separate emotion from intellect. The father is seen as a person who feels pleasant with his child. Father has a poor tolerance for hostility and sees calmness and control as a primary value. Father can be quite stubborn. He controls his emotions and does not like to be too spontaneous.

The mother is the love object. She is seen unconsciously as a person who has high aspiration. She is often unable to face her own limitations, denying that they exist. She denies stress. She can be quite impetuous. She can blow up in a volatile manner. When frustrated, she becomes extrapunitive, blaming those around her. He sees her unconsciously as having a poor tolerance for frustration. She can be quite nourishing to her children. She insists that they be dependent upon her. She has a compulsion to know everything that's going on and prefers the children have no secrets. She is a relatively traditional, available mother.

(3) *Anxiety Structure.*   Jack is going through a very important emotional stage in his life. He is fearful of many things. One of the most frightening things to him is the expectancy of maturity. He fears he cannot do the large number of things he sees coming up in the future. He has a great many masculine-aggressive impulses but fears that these are unacceptable. He thinks that expressing anger is intolerable to older people.

He is unsure about the nature of the real world and tends to substitute television values. These are quite aggressive and frightening to him.

He is quite frightened of taking risks. He would like to take the initiative, but he fears this. He is developing fairly normal negative attitudes toward his mother as he prepares to move into the latency period where he will relate more to males than to females. He fears being engulfed by the mother and yet feels vulnerable about the future without her. Thus he has a dependence-independence conflict with her.

(4) *Defense Structure and Outlets.*   His intellectual defenses include a tendency to be very dependent and compliant. When he is frightened, he seeks all kinds of intellectual reasons to avoid trying new things. He gets a great deal of relief through fantasy, although this is somewhat frightening to him.

When his anxiety is not settled by intellectual defenses, and avoiding what is uncomfortable, he begins to regress to earlier levels of behavior. He gets some relief from his science-fiction fantasy. He is beginning to develop phobias in order to punish himself for his guilt feelings about his own anger. Swimming seems to give him a great deal of relief.

Summary and Recommendations

Psychological evaluation of Jack Doe indicates that he is a youngster of Very Superior intellectual capacity who seems to be growing intellectually and physiologically according to expectancy. His academic achievement indicates that he is ready for the third grade with no expectancy of difficulty. It is possible that the public school does not challenge him enough. The personality structure is that of a youngster with a mental age several years beyond his chronological age who is beginning to look to the future and wonder about his own capacity to meet expectancy. He suffers the anxiety and the dominance-submission conflicts of most youngsters who are victims of a split family. There is some evidence that his anxieties are being magnified by the amount of television that he watches. The personality structure is that of a youngster who is holding in and has been quite successful in this for some time. One can expect more rebelliousness in order to relieve the natural tension that comes with this stage of growth. The following recommendations seem appropriate:

1. He needs some additional stimulation to that which can be provided by the ordinary school setting. Special projects, visits to museums, traveling whenever possible to see educational types of presentations would be helpful. There is a gifted-child program at the University of South Florida, which operates on Saturdays, that would be helpful for him. He is eligible.

2. He ought to have summer camp and a chance to split off from the tense family situation.

3. He should be given as much encouragement as possible to experiment with new things, and both parents would do well to make an effort to give the boy less "no" and more "try."

4. He should have sex education from his father and appropriate materials will be provided.

5. Between now and his 11th year, he would profit considerably from fairly intense joint activity with his father. This should include building things, such as a tree house, going to the Go-Karts on weekends, learning fundamentals of physical activity, such as running, jumping, swimming, and so forth.

6. I believe for the next couple of years this boy should not watch any weekday television. Weekend television can be fairly unrestricted, but the presence of an adult to help him interpret complex situations, particularly aggression, would be helpful.

7. Both parents would do well to prepare to tolerate negativism and aggression. This is a natural part of a child growing up and learning about his own power in the world. He should not be forced to be a "compliant" child any more.

It is difficult to specify an exact custodial arrangement. No fractured marriage is good for children. They are going to be in conflict regardless of the custodial arrangement. At this particular time in Jack's life, the more time he spends with his father, probably the better, but this of course should not be to the exclusion of regular interactions with the mother.

When the report was given to the father in a follow-up interview, it was suggested that most judges consider a change of custody only when the child's physical or psychological well-being is threatened. Although the father was clearly aware that his petition had little chance of succeeding, he chose to go forward with the petition since he felt strongly that his son's best interests would be served by a change of custody.

Custody hearings are generally much more informal than the litigation that takes place in a courtroom. The judge will often hear petitions in a small conference-type room adjoining his or her office. Although legal protocol and language characterize the proceedings, the degree of exactness in procedural matters reflects the degree of divisiveness between the litigating parties. Where the issues are hard-fought, procedures tend to be similar to those found in open court. Where the custodial issues are fairly clear-cut and the adversary parties are on reasonably good terms, the judge is likely to encourage an easier style of information exchange. Figure 10.1 shows a typical judge's chambers where custody issues are often heard.

The psychologist is asked to appear during the evidentiary portion of the proceedings and is led through qualification and direct examination by the attorney for the petitioner. Following direct examination, the attorney for the defendant-parent is given the opportunity to cross-examine the witness. Often the psychologist's report is offered in evidence by the petitioner's attorney.

After attorneys for both the petitioning parent and the defendant-parent complete their examination of the expert witness, the judge usually has a period of questioning where he or she will attempt to clarify issues that will play a significant role in his or her custodial decision. Following the testimony by the psychologist in the case of Jack Doe, the judge chose to examine the expert as follows:

The Judge: Mr. Doe touched on one matter that I am interested in. You had this young man tested for a period of some nine hours, and you had some contact with his father at a different time. I assume your interview with him was outside the presence of Mr. Doe, the father, wasn't it?

Dr. Blau: My interview with the child? Oh, yes.

The Judge: It was private?

Dr. Blau: Those nine hours are spent only with the child. No parent is involved.

The Judge: At any time did Jack, either voluntarily or spontaneously or in response to your questions, express his feeling about the stepfather or the stepmother?

Dr. Blau: No, sir, he did not.

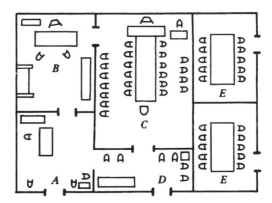

FIGURE 10.1.   A typical judge's suite, with C as the usual setting for custody hearings. A: office of the judge's secretary; B: judge's chambers; C: judge's hearing room; D: hearing room reception area; E: witness or lawyer's conference rooms.

The Judge: In neither case?

Dr. Blau: No, sir. It is my experience that children of fractured families will bend over backward to give a neutral or positive recommendation to all parties concerned. They do not want to be the cause of any difficulty—none whatsoever. As I say, I make the assumption that all four natural and surrogate parents are first-rate. I saw no evidence to the contrary.

The Judge: What opinion, if any, do you have, doctor, with respect to the workability of divided custody in the case of a child of this age, under these conditions?

Dr. Blau: My only opinion is that the more complex a custody arrangement, the more complex the child's adjustment to it. It would depend entirely on the amount of stress placed on the parents because the child is going to be a reflection of the degree of personal comfort and self-satisfaction of the parents. Happy parents do tend to make happy children. Miserable parents seem to share it with the children, whether they wish to or not.

The Judge: Does either counsel have any further questions?

One can see that the judge is clarifying in his own mind that the child has nothing terrible to say about the new stepparents in Jack's two families. Also, the judge is seeking the expert's opinion as to whether sole custody is "workable" (read: "anything but disastrous for the child"). The report suggests that the best interest of Jack, at this stage of his development, would be served by his living with his father. The presiding judge's reluctance to modify a custody arrangement except under the most stringent circumstances involving the child's physical and psychological well-being is reflected in the order denying a change of custody.

ORDER DENYING CHANGE OF CUSTODY, EXTENDING VISITATION, AND INCREASING SUPPORT PAYMENTS

Both parents of the 7½-year-old child, Jack Doe, were before the court with counsel for consideration of the mother's request for an increase in support and the father's petition for change of custody. Extensive testimony was taken with particular emphasis on an evaluation of the child conducted in June 1988 by Dr. Theodore H. Blau, eminent clinical psychologist.

After considering all the testimony and evidence, including results of the child's tests and measurements and his psychological profile, skillfully presented by Dr. Blau, the results of which are not being disputed by either party, the court summarizes his finding of fact as follows:

1. Jack Doe was placed with the mother by stipulation during the divorce proceeding approximately seven years ago and has had visitation with his father every two weeks commencing Friday night and extending until Sunday.

2. Both parents have remarried, and each concedes the other to be a fit parent.

3. The evidence shows the child to be extremely bright, with a high potential for learning and achievement. It also reveals that he needs greater intellectual stimulation than he receives in public schools with large classes and that he is not performing in school to the level of his capacity. He appears to enjoy a satisfactory relationship with both his stepfather and his stepmother and is the only child in either household. While evidently reflecting some degree of emotional trauma and anxiety as an aftermath of his parents' divorce, the child is revealed as a reasonably well adjusted, normal, and bright youngster with capabilities of a child several years older. Psychologically, he is found to need the warmth and protectiveness of his mother but also is believed to need the firmer, better-disciplined guidance of his father—a paternal "bonding" process which Dr. Blau describes as essential for a male child's proper development.

4. The evidence shows that the father's financial resources have improved since the dissolution of marriage between the parties. The child's present needs are in excess of the father's current contributions, thus making it incumbent upon the stepfather to make up the deficit.

5. There is no showing that the child will be placed in any immediate jeopardy, emotionally or physically, if custody is not changed. It is clear, however, that he should be allowed to spend more time in the company of his father without maternal interference.

Applying the principles of *Hutchins v. Hutchins* (2d DCA) 220 So.2d 438 and *Collins v. Newton* (2d DCA) 362 So.2d 174 (1978) to the above facts, the court is of the opinion that a change of custody is not warranted at the present time. It is thereupon

ADJUDGED, ORDERED, AND DECREED as follows:

1. The petition for change of custody filed by Albert Doe is denied.

2. Visitation of Jack Doe with his father will be extended so as to allow his father to have the child visit with him each weekend, commencing Friday evening and ending at 2:00 P.M. on Sundays, until further order of the court, subject to the right of the parents to vary the aforesaid precise hours of visitation by mutual consent.

DONE AND ORDERED at Palatka, Florida, this 15th day of November 1989.

L. A. Coleman
Circuit Judge

Examining Parents

The issues involved in parental fitness can be very complex. Age, health, intelligence, financial stability, community involvement, and morality are but a few of the factors a judge may evaluate in deciding the fitness of a parent. If it can be clearly documented that the parent poses a potential physical, intellectual, or emotional danger to the child, the psychological expert's task is fairly easy.

The following illustrates an examination of a mother thought to be unfit to have custody of her own child. Because of the mother's Hispanic background, the court wisely mandated that the examination be conducted by a psychologist of the same cultural background as the defendant-parent. The examination was conducted in Spanish, and the following report was submitted to the court by Maria Molinar, Ph.D.

PSYCHOLOGICAL EVALUATION

NAME: Niza, Anselma   DATE SEEN: 4-6-93

C.A.:   32   REFERRED BY: HRS & Fam. Prot. Team

BIRTHDATE: 4-25-61

EDUCATION: attended thru 9th

Reason for Referral

Ms. Niza is the mother of six children. The two oldest children reside with her mother. The four younger children, aged, according to her, between 8 and 14 years, are in foster care. She is seeking the return of these four children into her care. A psychological evaluation was requested, focused on her ability to care for her four children. She was seen for two and a half hours; the evaluation was conducted in Spanish.

Background Factors

A detailed history is available elsewhere; thus only some salient factors will be repeated. Ms. Niza, who at times has insisted her last name was spelled *Nisa,* is a Mexican-American born in Texas. She recalls traveling with her family but says she did attend school in Texas. She stopped attending at the age of 14.

She believes the father of her two oldest children is dead. The father of the two youngest children is now out of the picture. For the last nine months she has been living with a man by the name of Roberto Marón. This man is apparently applying for disability payments and is said to have some visual problems. She is also getting some type of assistance. They have a house that has three beds. She understands that, should the children be returned, she must clothe them and see that they attend school regularly. She states she cannot have any more children, wishes to have her children back, and feels that she will be able to provide adequate care.

Evaluation Measures

Wechsler Adult Intelligence Scale (EIWA-Spanish version); Indiana-Reitan Neuropsychological Screening Test; informal reading evaluation in Spanish and English; Draw-a-Person Test; Thematic Apperception Test; Rorschach Psychodiagnostic Test; and clinical interview.

Observation and Test Results

Ms. Niza is a dark-complexioned woman, overweight, who looks her stated age. She was cooperative and not distractible. The evaluation was conducted primarily in Spanish, but at times she seemed to understand English better than Spanish. There were some communication difficulties, partly on the basis of vocabulary but partly because Ms. Niza substitutes some sounds, omits others, and transposes yet others. At times she had difficulty understanding instructions, and even once she understood them, she had difficulty remembering instructions. That is, they had to be repeated for each item within a subtest rather than just being given at the beginning and for one or two items. When she did not know the answer to a question, she was quite likely to give some kind of answer as if by doing so she would not be pressured to respond further. This tendency may also be in part cultural; that is, it would not be polite not to answer. If one does not know the answer, one attempts to give some kind of answer. Affect was not inappropriate as much as flat. She was very passive, not physically restless. She said she was not on any medication related to any emotional problems. Hearing and vision were grossly normal. She is left-handed.

Ms. Niza was not well oriented. She had much difficulty, could not give the year different things had occurred, had even difficulty in giving how many years she had lived, for example, with the father of the last two children she had. She has lived, she states, at the present address for eight or nine months but cannot give the address. When asked if she had been told the wrong date for the evaluation (since she had gone strawberry picking the morning she was to be picked up), she pointed out that a neighbor had told her that the appointment was the next day.

The Spanish version of the Wechsler Adult Intelligence Scale (EIWA) was administered. The present psychologist had seen Ms. Niza in the fall of 1987 when, at that time, question had been raised as to the advisability of returning her four younger children to her care. Thus it had been five and a half years since the prior evaluation, and there was negligible practice effect. She had had another evaluation using much of the material from the Performance scale in 1989, but using United States norms rather than Hispanic norms against which to evaluate her functioning. Enough time has elapsed to ignore the practice effect. On the EIWA she earned a Verbal scale IQ of 63, which falls within the mildly mentally retarded range; a Performance scale IQ of 88, which falls within the low normal range, and a Full scale IQ of 74, which falls within the borderline deficient range. These results are practically identical to those reported in 1987.

The norms used against which to evaluate the performance of an individual on a test are of utmost importance. The Spanish version of the Wechsler has unfortunately not been revised since 1968 and was normed on a Puerto Rican population. If one takes the three subtests from the EIWA, which are identical or practically so to the same subtests on the Wechsler Adult Intelligence Scale-Revised, which is normed on a carefully chosen sample from the United States (testing done 1986–1990), then it becomes clear that in comparison to the general population in the United States she is functioning at a mildly retarded level, estimated IQ of 65. These test results are significantly higher than those reported on the Wechsler Adult Intelligence Scale in 1987 and 1989 (48, 43) when her functioning level was evaluated in comparison to a United States population. It has been found that the EIWA tends to overestimate the functioning level of adults when compared to expectancy in the United States.

However, even taking into account the many difficulties there are in evaluating a person from a deprived environment and, in addition, a bilingual person, Ms. Niza did not give evidence during the interview of functioning anywhere near the level one would predict on the basis of overall mild mental retardation. She cannot write except to print her name and does not do this either consistently or correctly. Secondly, while she can name some letters of the alphabet, she cannot read in Spanish at all and can only read a very few words at a first-grade level in English. Her number concepts are extremely limited, below expectancy for a beginning first-grader. One would predict that the typical individual who is functioning at a mildly retarded level would acquire the basic reading and number skills of at least third grade.

She was asked to complete the Indiana-Reitan Neuropsychological Screening Test. Her functioning on this suggests the presence of moderate intracranial pathology. She does not report any seizures, loss of consciousness, or dizziness. This is most likely to be a chronic situation. The likelihood of some organic factors being present and helping to account for some of her difficulties was suggested a few years ago.

Ms. Niza's difficulty in coping with, in earlier years, the school situation and, at present, in coping with adult responsibilities is not primarily due to her lack of intellectual ability. Her underlying emotional disturbance became quite evident in her responses to the personality tests. These represented for her unstructured and stressful situations. Her thinking became quite confused, her logic autistic. Her reality contact was obviously disrupted. Certainly she views the world as a dangerous place but the outstanding characteristic of her responses is not depression, as reported earlier, but rather serious distortion of thought processes, very poor reality contact. Ms. Niza is not at this time overtly psychotic but is suffering from a Schizophrenic Disorder, Residual Type, 295.6. This is in line with the diagnosis made in November 1987.

Summary and Recommendations

Ms. Niza's functioning on formal tests is within the mildly mentally retarded range. However, this is not the primary reason for her difficulty to function independently and care for her children. Rather the primary factor interfering with her ability to function is a chronic schizophrenic reaction. Her emotional problems, not her intellectual limitations, interfere with her ability to cope adequately with her environment. She is able to remain outside an institutional setting as long as she can live within a relatively simple and supportive environment wherein other adults provide an informal network of care. Despite the fact that she expresses love for her children, she is unable to provide minimally adequate care for herself, much less for four children.

During the judicial hearing, after the expert witness presented her report in the direct examination, the court examined her as follows:

The Court: Thank you, Doctor Molinar. Did you conduct your examination entirely in Spanish?

Dr. Molinar: Yes, your Honor, for the most part.

The Court: Do you feel that Mrs. Niza understood what you required of her and was able to do her best on your interviews and examinations?

Dr. Molinar: Yes, your Honor.

The Court: Thank you for your excellent report, Doctor.

Dr. Molinar: Thank you, your Honor.

Following the close of the hearings, and after due deliberation, the judge ordered the children to remain in a foster home and the mother in a community halfway house, with ancillary treatment opportunities.

The psychological expert must be exceedingly cautious about making absolute pronouncements or adhering to a rigid value system in issues of parental competency. Except where issues are as clear-cut as noted in the preceding example, evaluations and decisions must be conservative, cautious, and made with a thorough awareness of wisdom and constraints based on current research in parenting roles and behaviors.

Most litigation concerned with parental fitness is more complex than the previous example. In the absence of clear-cut, measurable psychological deficiencies associated with an inability to perform usual parental duties, mental health professionals should be extremely cautious in agreeing to serve as experts unless there is a very specific question concerning the parent. Most custodial battles have more to do with the intense feeling between former spouses than with the best interests of the child. At this writing, there is no body of research that suggests a psychological profile of the fit or unfit parent. Such decisions are moral determinations to be made by the court. The best that can be done by a behavioral scientist is to present a psychological assessment to the court. Judges differ considerably in their psychological sophistication and philosophical views of the family. The way in which a general psychological evaluation of a parent will be used by the court in determining fitness is likely to reflect the judge's values, with the psychological report interpreted, misinterpreted, accepted, or rejected accordingly.

Some judges request psychological evaluation of parents preliminary to a custodial decision as part of a broad process of attempting to serve the child's best interests while protecting the parents' rights. The judge does not ask for an evaluation of fitness but a general evaluation to help know better the parties who will be affected by the judicial decisions. Such reports may be helpful, depending on the way the judge uses them.

Child Maltreatment

Most requests for evaluation of parents relate to specific accusations of unfitness, and in a sense, the psychologist is being asked to examine the parent and tell the judge whether the parent has a propensity for child neglect or child abuse. Except in the extreme cases noted previously, such determinations are of very questionable validity. In adversary hearings, mental health experts are usually brought in by the attorneys for both sides and the court is treated to a battle of the experts.

Despite the lack of research data to support pronouncements by experts about parental fitness, this continues to be an area of considerable activity for psychiatrists, social workers, marriage and family counselors, and psychologists who work in family courts. Courts in larger jurisdictions often have access to agencies that specialize in evaluating the fitness of parents disputing the custody of a child or the accusation of abusive actions by parents toward their children. Evaluations, often quite cursory, are done regularly and submitted to the court couched in language similar to laboratory reports, implying a validity and reliability of the findings not warranted by the evaluative procedures. Using personal observation and interviews of family members as the bases for pronouncing on the fitness of parents, some mental health experts see themselves as "impartial observers" (Gardner, 1982, 1987). Such gratuitous self-evaluations perpetuate the participation of experts in court matters beyond their genuine scope or skill.

Allegations of child sexual abuse have emerged with increasing frequency during custody litigation. This and domestic violence have begun to appear more frequently in the courts' decisions regarding custody and visitation. Forty-four states and the District of Columbia now have statutory guidance for custodial determination involving domestic violence and the best interests of the child. Although judges are generally reluctant to allow visitation where domestic violence or child sexual abuse is suspected, they are bound by the U. S. Supreme Court decision in *Santosky v. Kramer*[11] "to encourage" a continuing relationship between the child and both parents unless parental rights are terminated (Lehrman, 1996).

Although a good deal of attention and opinion has emerged as a result of the increase in child sexual abuse allegations in custody and divorce disputes (Sheridan, 1990; Wakefield & Underwager, 1996) the actual incidence of sexual abuse allegations in divorce litigation appears to be less than 1% in all divorce actions and about 2% in contested cases. When physical abuse allegations are added, the figures rise to 3% in all cases and 8% in contested actions (McIntosh & Prinz, 1993).

Accusations of child sexual abuse within the context of divorce or custody litigation or under any circumstances must be viewed as a serious problem. Psychologists have been involved in such issues but the reliability and validity of expert psychological opinion has been subject to serious question (Brooks & Milchman, 1991; Hall & Crowther, 1991; Melton & Limber, 1989). Much as psychological testimony may be sought by the bar and the bench in these issues, the general applicability of psychological research and assessment techniques in identifying participants and effects of child maltreatment leaves much to be desired.

If the psychologist believes that an evaluation of a parent will aid the court in the complexities of the Solomonic decision, the expert should scrupulously avoid predicting positive or negative behavior on the part of the evaluated parent. There is no research to substantiate the accuracy of such moral decision making, and to do so would be to make unethical use of psychological procedures, laying the expert open to charges of unprofessional behavior. All references in reports to the court should be made in terms of substantive findings, based on reliable and valid techniques. The moral evaluation and prediction must remain with the court.

In the past, mental health experts have testified in these matters, giving wide-ranging opinions about the character and potential of parents. Judges and attorneys are becoming much more aware of the limits of the reliability and validity of human behavior data in the areas of personality and character. Experts in the mental health professions can expect vigorous challenges to opinion not substantiated by data and/or generally accepted in the expert's special field. An example follows.

In a recent custodial matter, the father of the children was accused by the wife of being an amoral, hard-drinking person whose values were questionable. The ex-wife was requesting the end of visitation privileges for the father. A psychologist examined both parents and wrote reports, favorable for the mother and unfavorable for the father. He recommended that the father's visitation privileges be revoked since the psychological evaluation showed the father to have "a confirmed character disorder with psychopathic tendencies." The psychological examination consisted of a Wechsler Adult Intelligence Scale-Revised, an MMPI, a Rorschach examination, and an interview (a very limited but not an unusual battery for such cases). On the basis of a history of enjoying skydiving and scuba diving, a 4-9 profile on the MMPI, the Performance scale exceeding the Verbal scale on the WAIS-R, and two unstructured color responses on the Rorschach, the psychologist opined that the father was an unfit parent for his two children, ages eight and six. During the custodial hearing, in the judge's chambers, the following cross-examination of the psychologist, Dr. Elfred Gordon, was conducted by Mr. Robert Harper, attorney for the father:

Mr. Harper: I found your testimony very interesting, doctor.

Dr. Gordon: Thank you, counselor.

Mr. Harper: As I understand it, because the father has what you call a "4-9" profile, you have decided he is unstable—is that correct?

Dr. Gordon: That is correct. Those who have the 4-9 profile tend to be aggressive, with little conscience, and likely to engage in asocial and antisocial acts.

Mr. Harper: I see—and so you believe that because the father's MMPI profile is a 4-9, he ought not to see his children.

Dr. Gordon: Yes—such people usually live on the fringe of society and are much more likely to get into trouble than the average citizen.

Mr. Harper: Are we to understand then that all men with 4-9 MMPI profiles ought not to be fathers?

Dr. Gordon: Well, I'm not sure I'd put it that way—

Mr. Harper: Are men with 4-9 MMPI profiles *ever* good fathers?

Dr. Gordon: Well—I don't know if *all* wouldn't be good.

Mr. Harper: So it is *possible* that a man with a 4-9 profile could be a good father?

Dr. Gordon: I suppose it's *possible.*

Mr. Harper: Are you familiar with MMPI 4-9 research in general?

Dr. Gordon: Yes, in general.

Mr. Harper: Would you be so kind as to tell the court the MMPI coding of successful police officers in the Los Angeles Police Department selection studies?

Dr. Gordon: Well, they had 4-9 profiles but . . .

Mr. Harper: Are you aware that replication studies of the Atlanta Police Department resulted in similar findings?

Dr. Gordon: Well yes, but . . .

Mr. Harper: Are you aware that these two police departments are considered among the finest in the country?

Dr. Gordon: Well, no . . . but . . .

Mr. Harper: Doctor, would you have us believe that none of the thousands of successful, effective, policemen in Los Angeles, California, and Atlanta, Georgia, are unfit to be fathers?

Dr. Gordon: Well, I couldn't say that.

Mr. Harper: And by the same token I submit that you couldn't and *shouldn't* say that about the father who you have condemned based on his performance on your MMPI!

Certainly Dr. Gordon was entitled to discuss the *probable* behavioral responses of a man with an MMPI 4-9 profile. His error occurred in moving from description to prediction in his report and making a prediction about a person's future moral behavior and fitness as a father without substantiating it by any significant research at this point in time. Few courts will give credence to personalistic, unsubstantiated, or unspecific statements by experts directed at depriving a parent of the right of access to his or her children.

Summing up, psychologists who intend to give testimony about the fitness of parents are well advised to conduct a careful, standard evaluation; report results in a cautious, supportable style; and avoid addressing issues of fitness until such time as substantial evaluative research appears that would support such predictions.

Evaluating Child-Rearing Settings

Psychologists are not infrequently asked to give opinions as to the quality of home settings and developmental environment provided by custodial or noncustodial parents. Being an expert in this area requires extensive education, training, and experience possessed by few psychologists. It is an error for a psychologist to believe his or her specific psychological training and experience are sufficient for the evaluation of environmental assets and liabilities. Social workers, public health nurses, caseworkers, and other professionals who understand the complexities of environmental safety, opportunity, stimulation, and support should conduct such evaluations. The most competent expert knows his or her limitations and does not exceed these regardless of pressures to do so by bar or bench.

Evaluating Marital Partners

Aside from child custody and parental fitness issues, psychological experts are sometimes called on to testify as to the state of mind or the psychological adjustment of one partner or the other at some time during the marriage or in respect to the dissolution procedures. Most frequently, the focus of the controversy is financial. In some way, the mental state of one of the partners is considered to be of crucial importance in an equitable division of jointly held assets. The psychologist is advised to consider the following questions before entering into an agreement to be an expert in this or other areas where the psychological factors are tangential to the adversary issue:

1. Are the questions to be answered by the expert within the usual and ordinary framework of the science and profession of psychology and the psychologist's training, knowledge, and experience?
2. Would other highly skilled and respected colleagues use similar evaluation procedures and come to similar conclusions?

3. Can the expert present his or her findings in a conservative manner with appropriate disclaimers and alternate possibilities?

4. Is the expert prepared to define the limits of his or her expert opinion and resist any manipulation by attorneys or judges to extend testimony or opinion beyond reasonable limits?

These are the acid tests of whether a psychologist can serve as an expert in an ethical and professional manner.

Examples of psychological evaluations of marital partners may be helpful. In the first, a psychologist was consulted by the attorney representing a man seeking extensive alimony payments from his wealthy wife in conjunction with the dissolution of the marriage. The husband claimed that his wife's excessive demands and domination ruined his artistic potential, causing him such distress that he could not produce salable art during their marriage. The attorney sought a psychological evaluation to assess the degree to which the husband's artistic productivity was negated by the wife's behavior and influence. The psychologist properly refused to accept the role as expert in this case. The questions asked of the psychologist clearly failed at least two of the four acid tests of an acceptable adversary issue with which an expert can become associated. In another marital dissolution conflict, initially discussed in the section "Property Agreement Challenges," the attorney representing the wife approached a psychologist with a request to serve as an expert in determining the wife's mental condition and state of mind at a time years previous to the dissolution proceedings. At issue was a block of stock in the husband's company signed over to him by the wife some eight years previously. The wife contended that the husband manipulated her dependency on him to force her to sign the stock over. The husband contended that the wife "willingly and knowingly" made the transfer and was entitled to no part of that stock in the dissolution agreement.

The wife had consulted with the psychologist just previous to the stock transfer in question. He had conducted an extensive psychological evaluation of the wife at that time in response to her request for help. She was confused, deeply depressed, and almost nonfunctional. The psychological evaluation, consisting of several hours of history and interviews, complete intellectual, neuropsychological, interest, marital, and personality assessment, revealed her to be a woman of superior intellectual endowment, of emotionally impoverished family background, deeply and pathologically dependent on her brutally manipulative husband, who was similar in character to her own father. During the assessment, the issue of signing over the stock arose. The psychologist advised the woman to consult an attorney and to begin psychotherapy. The wife was able to start therapy with a skillful female therapist but was too fearful to oppose her husband's domination by seeking legal counsel. She shortly thereafter stopped therapy and signed over her stock when her husband threatened to leave her if she did not do both. The husband made his demands known not only to his wife but to the psychologist and the wife's therapist.

The attorney representing the wife requested a copy of the psychologist's original report and a letter stating his opinion as to whether the wife's decision to sign over her stock was made under any degree of mental duress. The psychologist forwarded the following response:

> Pursuant to your letter of November 7, I contacted your client, Ms. Gladys Rumfree, and received her permission to send a copy of my psychological report dated April 7, 1976, and this letter responding to your questions. Ms. Rumfree has reviewed both the report and this letter before granting her permission to release them. I saw Ms. Rumfree on six occasions previous to my writing the enclosed report. Our initial consultation was arranged by her husband with the referral comment "she needs straightening out."
>
> Ms. Rumfree herself expressed the wish to understand herself better and gain some degree of independence. Psychological evaluation indicated that though she was of superior intellectual endowment and possessed many skills and talents, she was pathologically dependent and unable to resist the demands and manipulations of her family. The enclosed report provides details of procedures and findings regarding this.
>
> During the course of the assessment Ms. Rumfree reported that she was deeply distressed by her husband's suddenly demanding that she sign over to him her stock rights in a closely held family company. She didn't want to do this, but the husband threatened to leave her if she didn't comply.
>
> Ms. Rumfree was advised to consult an attorney regarding the legal aspects of her situation and was referred to an experienced female psychotherapist, Dr. Mary Isch, to deal with the emotional pressures she faced.
>
> Although Ms. Rumfree finished her psychological evaluation, received the results, and began her psychotherapeutic program, she was unable to consult an attorney for fear it would offend her husband. She stopped her therapy very shortly after she began for the same reason. Several telephone calls received from Mr. Rumfree (noted in my report) conveyed his feelings to me that this psychological work was "putting bad ideas" in his wife's head.
>
> It is my opinion that, at the time I examined Ms. Rumfree, she was a deeply distressed, dependent person, unable to act in her own best interests in any issue opposed by her husband. Although not incompetent to manage ordinary affairs of life, she was exceedingly vulnerable to threats and manipulations at that time.

After contacting Dr. Isch, Mr. Jones, the attorney representing Ms. Rumfree, arranged for depositions from both psychologists who had seen Ms. Rumfree. After qualification and preliminary questions, the following direct examination of Dr. Isch was conducted by Mr. Jones:

Mr. Jones: As I understand it, Dr. Isch, Ms. Rumfree stopped seeing you after 10 sessions of psychotherapy.

Dr. Isch: That is correct.

Mr. Jones: Had she finished or did you dismiss her?

Dr. Isch: No. She had just begun her therapy.

Mr. Jones: Why did she stop?

Dr. Isch: She told me that her husband had demanded she sign over her stock to him and discontinue the therapy.

Mr. Jones: Did Ms. Rumfree want to do this?

Dr. Isch: No, she did not. She was deeply disturbed during our last session, indicating that she would prefer to continue in psychotherapy.

Mr. Jones: Why did she not continue?

Dr. Isch: She said that her husband threatened to leave her, and she was so fearful of being without him that she was going to sign her stock over to him and stop her psychotherapy to comply with his wishes.

Mr. Jones: Did you believe that Mr. Rumfree made such demands on her?

Dr. Isch: Yes, I did. During the time she was in psychotherapy, I received several telephone calls and a visit from her husband. At first, he demanded to know what we discussed in his wife's sessions. When I told him I couldn't discuss that, he told me that this was "nonsense" and he knew more about what was good for his wife than anyone. He told me that he would have her stop the therapy and put her total faith in him.

Mr. Jones: Did you report his comments to your patient?

Dr. Isch: Of course.

Mr. Jones: Thank you very much, Doctor.

Psychotherapists are generally reluctant to serve as expert witnesses since their work is conducted with due concern for confidentiality. Once a patient uses his or her psychological status as a basis for litigation, however, he or she is no longer entitled to claim privileged communication. This poses a variety of ethical and professional issues for psychotherapists, and these will be addressed in detail in Chapter 15.

Guiding the Court

The psychological expert will find that in family or domestic courts the degree to which judges are knowledgeable or sophisticated in matters of child development, marital relationships, and parenting varies considerably. Few judges are formally trained to discharge their awesome responsibilities with an awareness of what psychological research suggests in these specialized areas. Some judges develop personalistic and even bizarre ideas of what constitutes good parenting or the best interests of the child. Many judges are aware of the imbalance between their power to influence a family and their knowledge of family structure and dynamics. Well-founded information is usually welcomed by such judges.

Psychologists are uniquely qualified by education and training to be helpful in complex family decisions. As part of the expert witness's role, the provision of current psychological theory and research can be extremely helpful.

If the court is dealing with decisions that should include information from the behavioral sciences, the psychological expert should provide such information, which may be requested by the court or by attorneys for either party in an adversary action. Certain guidelines are desirable in providing such recommendations or evaluations to the court, including the following:

1. The topic or subject must be within the expert's area of training, education, and experience.
2. Opinions proffered by the expert should be supported by appropriate research references.
3. The report should be conservatively written and in keeping with usual standards of objectivity.
4. Advocacy should be avoided.

Several examples of learned treatises that have been presented to courts by psychologists follow.

Visitation Plans. In virtually all marital dissolutions that involve minor children, the judge will lay down a set of visitation rules to ensure reasonable contact between the children and the noncustodial parent. The issue of visitation, together with custody and financial sharing, constitutes essentially all the conflict one finds surrounding dissolution of marriage. Whereas change of custody is rarely granted, judges are more willing to modify visitation plans in order to ensure equality between parents and reasonable contact between the child and the noncustodial parent.

The first report presents a psychological visitation plan concerning the problem of a father living in a state quite distant from the residence of the mother-custodian and the child. One of the mother's concerns is that visits with the father should not be traumatic for the child. The mother is also of the opinion that the child should not have caretakers other than the mother. The following report was submitted to the court, after first being reviewed by attorneys for both the mother and the father.

A RECOMMENDED VISITATION PLAN

in re

Jones v. Smith

Referral

Jonothan Doe, Esquire, requested consultation in this matter on July 15, 1981. Mr. Doe represents Mr. Smith, natural father of William Smith, age

22 months, for whom the mother, Jane Jones, seeks sole custody. Mr. Doe states that his client, Mr. Smith, seeks reasonable visitation privileges with his son. Mr. Smith and Mr. Jones state they would like to have a visitation plan devised which would allow Mr. Smith to have frequent and continuing contact with his son while fully supporting the welfare and best interests of the child.

The parents are divorced. Ms. Jones lives in Florida, while Mr. Smith's primary domicile is in Ohio.

The purpose of this proposal is to recommend a visitation plan that would be fair and equitable to the parents while supporting the best interests of the child and ensuring maximum opportunities for optimum growth and development.

Psychological Factors

Classically and scientifically, the first year of life has been considered the critical parental attachment phase of growth and development. There is considerable controversy as to whether attachment responses of infants represent emotional bonding (Waters, 1980). At the end of the first and beginning of the second year of life, flexibility, rather than dependency, is the hallmark of the typical infant-adult relationship. Distress and disorganization based on separation from the primary caretaker are of developmental significance before one year of age. Simplistic concepts of mother bonding and separation anxiety are not borne out by infant studies (Ainsworth, 1973). During the past decade it has become clearer that the *quality* of the child-parent bond, as opposed to the *strength* of the attachment bond, is of greater significance to development. Discrete behavior indices or reports of attachment are not reliable. As bonding and attachment increase beyond the 12-month level, such behavior becomes incompatible with exploratory behavior. Thus early separation from the mother may be deleterious, while later separation can be developmentally helpful (Joffe & Vaughn, 1982). Fathers tend to spend more and varied interactional time with firstborn male children (Clarke-Stewart, 1978). No developmental time period beyond the very early months has been found to have unique and irreversible importance (Sroufe, 1979).

During the past decade, considerable research on language acquisition suggests that the early interaction between the mother and the child is crucial to language development. This begins early in infancy. This special communicative interaction is called "motherese." The important stages for this interaction appear to be between a few days after birth and about two years of age (Molfese, Molfese, & Carrell, 1981).

Ages two to three represent exploratory opportunities, which include socialization, communication, problem solving, skill development, and social training. If infant day care is a significant part of the child's development between 3 and 29 months of age, there are no significant developmental differences between children who were at a well-run, nurturing, responsible group-care center and a matched group raised at home. Only in concept formation did the children raised at home appear to be superior to those in a day-care center. These findings only apply to responsibly and conscientiously implemented day-care centers defined as follows:

> A conscientious and nurturing caretaker in a group setting is keenly aware of the psychological diversity among the children in the setting as well as the differences in the values between each parent and herself. As a result, the caretaker is unlikely to hold rigid standards of behavior for each child regarding talkativeness, cooperativeness, cleanliness, aggression, quality of play, or the age when particular developmental milestones should appear. The caretaker, being less profoundly identified with the children in her care, is likely to be more relaxed about these standards than the parents. It is neither a source of deep pleasure if one of her children is slightly precocious in learning to drink from a cup nor a source of anxiety if a motorically retarded child spills his or her milk every day. This tolerant attitude toward diversity in growth patterns leads the caretaker to give each child considerable license to behave in accord with his or her temperamental disposition and relative level of maturity. As a result, with the exception of extremely destructive or regressed children, the caretaker does not impose constraints on the children when they seem occupied and happy. As a result, the average child does not generate serious uncertainties about the caretaker's actions when he or she is exploring the environment.

For purposes of the research previously reported, the typical mother is "identified and emotionally involved with her young child. She has a set of discrete standards for the child's behavior, and she vigilantly watches for deviations from those standards."

Thus, *assuming certain characteristics,* day care probably does not interfere with children's development (Kagan, Kearsley, & Zelazo, 1977).

Joint, cooperative parenting that involves issues of interstate custody often requires extensive mediation and when joint-custodial parents are separated by great distances, frequent consultation is difficult and misunderstandings can be magnified (Bodenheimer, 1981).

Legal Considerations and Expectancies

Conciliation efforts are being required by many courts (Orlando, 1978). Rights of fathers have received increasing attention, including the rights of unmarried fathers (Bedwell, 1979).[12] More and more the focus has been directed to the best interests of the child when the courts must decide on custody and visitation (Goldstein, Freud, & Solnit, 1973). In almost 90% of cases, custody has been awarded to the mother without contest by the father (Weitzman & Dixon, 1979). The classical *tender years* doctrine for custodial award to the mother has come into question in the past decade.

About 40 states, including Florida, have rejected this doctrine. The Uniform Marriage and Divorce Act (National Conference of Commissioners, 1971) recommends:

> The court shall determine custody in accordance with the best interests of the child. The court shall consider all relevant factors including: (1) the wishes of the child's parent or parents as to his custody; (2) the wishes of the child as to his custodian; (3) the interaction and interrelationship of the child with his parents, his siblings, and any other person who may significantly affect the child's best interests; (4) the child's adjustment to his home, school, and community; and (5) the mental and physical health of all individuals involved. The court shall not consider conduct of a proposed custodian that does not affect his relationship to the child.

Judges continue to depend on subjective judgment as to the child's best interests (Ruback, 1982). More recently, the advice of mental health professionals has received favorable reception by the Bench (Litwak, Gerber, & Fenster, 1980; Woody, 1977). The recent trend toward joint custody seeks to preserve and protect the child's relationship with both parents, ensure easy access to both parents, and allow opportunities for both parents to be supportive of each other's parenting efforts (Weiss, 1979).

On July 1, 1982, Florida Statutes required shared responsibility by parents at the discretion of the court and establish family mediation or conciliation services to assist parties in resolving controversy.[13] The statute proposes as public policy that:

1. Each minor child be assured frequent and continuing contact with both parents.
2. Parents share the rights and responsibilities of child-rearing where the Court so decides.
3. Both parents retain full parental rights and responsibilities.
4. Parents confer on major decisions affecting the welfare of the child.

Final decisions in all these matters reside with the court.

Visitation Plan

For Ages 24 Months through 60 Months

The following visitation proposal is made in respect to the following considerations and assumptions:

1. No visitation plan can replace a warm, accepting dual-parent environment.
2. The most propitious developmental opportunities and expectancies for a child between 24 months and 60 months of age are clarified and understood.

3. Both parents are willing and able to participate in shared responsibility, mutual support in the child's interest, and mediation when irresolvable conflicts arise.
4. Both parents are willing to preserve the child's attachments to the opposite parent.
5. Both parents are willing that the child have frequent and continuing contact with both natural parents.
6. The proposal meets with expectancies and requirements of Florida Statutes.

The plan is divided into four age-developmental stage-related segments. These segments correspond to important developmental milestones and are designed to help the parents achieve all the considerations noted above. Both parents must be willing to view these proposals as somewhat flexible in respect to realistic stresses that may occur in their own environments.

1. *24–30 Months of Age.*   During this stage of development, William is likely to extend his language development, curiosity, and exploration. Almost constant motor activity can be expected. Although still very dependent on a familiar environment, the child will welcome all sights, sounds, and pleasant sensations. The child's capacity to interact with more than two or three adults continues to grow. Recommended visitation frequency and style for the father would include one or two visits a month, of one week each. Although the visitation plan which is herein recommended requires a great deal of inconvenience for the father, the gradual development of familiarity is deemed very important for the child. Each visit might follow a sequence of familiarity as follows:

   a. *1st Day.* Father arrives and spends one hour at child-care center with William.
   b. *2nd Day.* Father will pick up William at mother's home and spend one hour at child-care center.
   c. *3rd Day.* Father will pick up William at home, spend two hours at child-care center with him and return child to mother's home at the end of the day.
   d. *4th and 5th Days.* Father will pick up the child from mother's home, spend the entire day with William, and return William to the mother's home.
   e. *6th and 7th Days.* Father will pick up William, keep him overnight, and return him to mother's home at end of seventh day, saying "good-bye" until the next visit.

2. *31–36 Months of Age.*   During this phase fairly complete transfer from motherese to communicative speech should be taking place. Early identification can begin here, and the father as a unique, safe parent becomes known. "Daddy" becomes a pleasant and meaningful concept.

Games and play with father become more motoric and complex. Six to twelve visits during this phase would again be desirable, depending on father's availability. The sequence of events during visits that is recommended for the father is:

  a. *1st Day.* Father should spend two hours at the child-care center with William.

  b. *2nd Day.* Father should pick William up at home, take him to the child-care center, and spend two hours there. The rest of the day should be spent with father, and then William should be returned to the mother's home.

  c. *3rd Day.* Father should pick up William at home and spend all day with him. Father should return William to the mother's home after supper.

  d. *4th–7th Days.* Father should pick up William at home, keep him three nights and days, and return William to the mother's home the final evening before supper.

3. *37–48 Months of Age.*   Language should be well developed during this phase. William should be now be capable of short telephone conversations. He should have pictures of his father and himself framed in his room. He should receive occasional letters from his father that should be read to him and kept in his room. By now William should be sleeping in a single bed of his own, have a toy chest in which he keeps all toys, and be fully toilet trained. Communication, exploration, development of new motor skills, game playing, and limit testing will be part of his daily life. He should now know "Daddy" by picture, by voice on the telephone, and by sight. Visitation during this phase can be once every two months for a two-week period at the father's residence. The sequence should include:

  a. Anticipatory explanation of forthcoming trip by both parents.

  b. *1st Day.* William should meet father in the morning and spend the day with him. He should return to the mother's home that night.

  c. *2nd Day.* William should be picked up by father in the morning and they should fly to the father's home.

  d. *3rd–13th Days.* William will reside with father at the father's home. Father should ensure that William feels secure and comfortable. To this end the father should:
  (1) Arrange William's room to be as much like his room at home in color, content, furniture, and decor as possible.
  (2) Follow the same times for meals, bed, naps, and bathing as at home.
  (3) Introduce new family members singly or in pairs quite gradually.
  (4) Arrange daily telephone contact between William and his mother.

(5) Avoid sudden, unexpected, or intense stimuli experiences (Disney World, amusement parks, large parties, and so forth).

(6) Arrange play-school-like activities with other children Monday through Friday.

e. *13th Day.* Father and William should fly back to Florida, and William should be taken to the mother's home by father.

f. *14th Day.* Father should pick William up at home in the morning, take him to day care or play school, and say "good-bye," ending the visit with promises of telephone calls and the next visit. William should have a Polaroid snapshot of himself and his father taken during the visit.

4. *49–60 Months of Age.* During this stage of development, William will probably be in nursery school or prekindergarten. He will probably follow a regular routine during the school year. He should be able to spend summers and vacation time with his father, who by this time will be well known and a part of William's affective attachments and identifications. William should now be ready for many varied and stimulating experiences. The summer period might be split, one month with father, two weeks at midsummer with mother, then a month with father.

Beyond the fifth year, psychological assessment would be a helpful adjunct in making visitation recommendations, as testing could address in detail William's current intellectual, social, and emotional development and needs (Goldstein et al., 1973; Litwak et al., 1980; Sroufe, 1979; Woody, 1977). Such an evaluation could be a milestone assessment to help the parents understand how William is developing, how well they are doing as parents, and what opportunities lie ahead for continuing to share the responsibility for William's growth and development.

Auditing

No visitation plan can be followed with exactness. Variations and modifications should be made with a view toward abiding by the positive spirit of shared responsibility. If conflicts between parents become irresolvable or intense, a moderating influence in the child's best interests should be invoked in the form of a professional mediator. Such a person should be selected and agreed to by both parents before issues arise, so that conflicts may be early considered and resolved.

References

Ainsworth, M. (1973). The development of infant-mother attachment. In B. Caldwell & H. Riccioti (Eds.), *Review of child development research* (Vol. 3). Chicago: University of Chicago Press.

Bedwell, M. A. (1979). The rights of fathers of non-marital children to custody, visitation, and to consent to adoption. *University of California, Davis Law Review, 12*, 412–451.

Bodenheimer, B. M. (1981). Interstate custody: Initial jurisdiction and continuing jurisdiction under the UCCJA. *Family Law Quarterly, 13*, 203–227.

Brodsky, J. G., & Alford, J. G. (1977). Sharpening Solomon's sword: Current considerations in child custody cases. *Dickinson Law Review, 81*, 683–731.

Clarke-Stewart, K. A. (1978). And daddy makes three: The father's impact on mother and young child. *Child Development, 49*, 466–478.

Goldstein, J., Freud, A., & Solnit, A. J. (1979). *Before the best interests of the child.* New York: Free Press.

Joffe, L. W., & Vaughn, B. E. (1982). Infant-mother attachment: Theory, assessment, and implications for development. In B. Wolman (Ed.), *Handbook of developmental psychology.* Englewood Cliffs, NJ: Prentice-Hall.

Kagan, J., Kearsley, R. B., & Zelazo, P. R. (1977). The effects of infant day care on psychological development. *Evaluation Quarterly, 1*(1), 109–142.

Litwak, T. R., Gerber, G. L., & Fenster, C. A. (1980). The proper role of psychology in child custody disputes. *Journal of Family Law, 18*, 269–300.

Molfese, D. L., Molfese, V. J., & Carrell, P. L. (1981). Early language development. In B. Wolman (Ed.), *Handbook of developmental psychology.* Englewood Cliffs, NJ: Prentice-Hall.

National Conference of Commissioners on Uniform State Laws. (1971). Uniform marriage and divorce act. *Family Law Quarterly, 5*, 205–251.

Orlando, F. A. (1978). Conciliation programs. *Florida Bar Journal, 52*, 218–221.

Ruback, R. B. (1982). Issues in family law. In J. C. Hanson & L. Abade (Eds.), *Values, ethics, legalities and the family therapist.* London: Aspen Systems.

Sroufe, L. A. (1979). The coherence of individual development: Early care, attachment and subsequent developmental issues. *American Psychologist, 34*, 834–841.

Waters, E. (1980). Traits, relationships and behavioral systems: The attachment construct. In K. Immelman et al. (Eds.), *Development of behavior.* New York: Cambridge University Press.

Weiss, R. S. (1979). Issues in the adjudication of custody when parents separate. In G. Levinger & O. C. Moles (Eds.), *Divorce and separation.* New York: Basic Books.

Weitzman, L. J., & Dixon, R. B. (1979). Child custody awards: Legal standards and empirical patterns for child custody, support, and visitation after divorce. *University of California, Davis Law Review, 12*, 473–521.

Woody, R. H. (1977). Psychologists in child custody. In B. D. Sales (Ed.), *Psychology in the legal process.* New York: Spectrum.

Sometimes the expert witness is called on to express an opinion on a fairly unusual or bizarre visitation situation. In the following example, a father of record was found not to be the child's biological father. The biological mother divorced the father of record and then married the biological father. This couple sought exclusive custody of the child. The former father of record sought visitation rights. The attorney representing the biological parents requested an evaluative study of the likely psychological effects of forced visitation.

The following report was prepared for submission to the court after an evaluation of the facts in this convoluted case and a review of what appeared to be pertinent research associated with the question at issue: Should a child be forced to participate in a visitation plan involving a non-biological parent with psychological attachments to the child?

EVALUATION STUDY, FORCED VISITATION, AND THE BEST INTERESTS OF THE CHILD

Introduction

This evaluative study was undertaken at the request of Richard Roe, Esquire. The purpose of the study is to explore the potential psychological effects of a variety of visitation decisions on the best interests of Mary White, a minor female child of approximately five years of age.

Background Factors

Mr. Roe is attorney for Mr. and Mrs. B. Brown who filed suit seeking a determination that Mr. Brown is the biological father of Mary White. The suit further seeks a termination of Mr. White's rights of parenthood to Mary and that he be enjoined from contacting or visiting Mary. Mr. Roe has alleged the following:

1. Jane White, now known as Jane Brown, married Tom White on January 18, 1975.
2. Jane White gave birth to a daughter, Mary, on March 2, 1977 while married to Mr. White.
3. Jane Brown and Bob Brown claim that Mr. Brown is the biological father of Mary.
4. Mr. White claims he is the biological father of Mary.
5. In August 1978, Mr. Brown separated from his wife at that time, Susan Brown, and in January or February of 1980, their marriage was dissolved by final judgment.
6. Jane White separated from Tom White, and she together with the daughter Mary commenced living with Mr. Bob Brown.
7. On October 3, 1980, Jane and Tom White signed a marital settlement agreement granting custody of Mary to Jane. Mr. White was to pay $400 per month for child support and have visitation rights. On January 20, 1981, the marriage was dissolved by final judgment.
8. On July 18, 1981, Jane White married Mr. Bob Brown.
9. In January or February 1982, Jane Brown told Mr. White for the first time that he was not the biological father of Mary, but that Mr. Brown was.

10. Jane White (now known as Jane Brown) was with Mr. Brown on a frequent basis from May 1977 until they commenced living together in 1980.
11. After Mary's birth, the child was with her mother during the majority of the times her mother met Mr. Brown.
12. Since the divorce, Mr. White has had visitation with Mary.
13. An examination attested to by Dr. J. Jorgens, dated May 26, 1982, states that the probability is 99.85% that Mr. Brown is the biological father of Mary.
14. Since the filing of the suit for termination of Mr. White's rights of parenthood, no further child support has been accepted by the mother.

Questions to be Answered

In response to Mr. Roe's consultation request, a search of the pertinent behavioral science literature was made in pursuit of data to clarify the following questions:

1. What are the general conclusions in the psychological literature about the best interests of a child, under six years of age, who is the product of a fractured marriage?
2. What is the likely psychological effect on a child, under six years of age, of forced visitations to a former psychological father outside the home in respect to a biological and psychological father in the primary custodial and caretaking residence?

The Best Interests of the Child

Divorce is a legal device designed to be a social remedy for terminating an unsatisfactory marital union. The emotional and developmental problems of children of broken unions represent one of the potentially most unhappy sequelae of divorce. Family disruption through divorce triggers regression, fretfulness, cognitive bewilderment, heightened aggression, and neediness in the preschool child just following the family split. The symptoms are usually temporary if continuity of physical and emotional care and love is restored and maintained by the parent and/or a competent substitute caretaker. The child's view of dependability and predictability is usually threatened, and his or her sense of order regarding the world is disrupted. In children with no prior history of psychological problems, about one-half show some psychological development problems one year following the marital fracture.

Where there is a diminution in the quality of the mother-child relationship following divorce, a deterioration in the psychological condition of the child is more likely to occur (Wallerstein & Kelly, 1975). Most researchers agree that the parents' personal and emotional response to the divorce and the quality of the child's relationship with parents immediately after divorce have a substantial effect on the child's coping and adjustment. Conflict between immature, poorly adjusted parents tends to nullify any positive effect of frequent contact with both parents. The positive influence of frequent visitations with a noncustodial father, especially with male children, is found if there is no father in the custodial home and the divorced parents are friendly and supportive (Hetherington, 1979).

Some broken families are able to retain many bonds, including new parents and the former spouse of the caretaking parent. Friendly relationships are maintained in about 30% of couples who have joint custody and about 20% of couples where the mother has custody. In a study of the child-sharing behavior of divorced couples, one year and two years following the divorce, it was found that some couples are sufficiently friendly and cooperative so as to decrease the negative effects of custody-visitation conflicts in the children of the divorce (Collins, 1982). Success or failure in multiple caretaking seems to be based on the quality of the relationship between estranged former marital partners. If feelings are warm and positive among the adults involved, there is a higher likelihood that the child will be less negatively affected by multiple parenting (Santruck & Warshak, 1979).

If parents or caretakers are in conflict, the interaction between them is likely to be transferred to the children of divorce through the mechanism of *child-focus*. The family members tend to deal with their interactional stress by focusing their anxiety, often unwittingly, on the child (Beal, 1979).

To date, what constitutes a child's best interests remains a controversial legal and clinical question. The simplest position in this matter has been taken by Goldstein, Freud, and Solnit (1973, 1979) who, in their book *Beyond the Best Interests of the Child,* suggest that the key to positive child development is day-to-day interactions with the *psychological parents* (those living in the child's present home). They urge that the custodial parent decide all conditions under which the child should be raised. They proposed that a noncustodial parent should have no legally enforceable right to visits which the custodial parent feels are not in the best interests of the child. It is suggested that the shifting and disruption in a child's life that occurs in visitation situations is likely to be deleterious to principles of healthy psychological development.

For any kind of custodial sharing to be effective, it is necessary that the adults involved be emotionally committed to mutual support, flexible sharing, and agreement on the implicit rules and share relatively unambivalent acceptance of the arrangement. Frequent moving back and forth is usually unsettling. Some children are of a nature as to need one home base rather than two. As children mature, they tend to exert pressure on a multihome visitation system. Some shared custody and visitation systems work out well for children, but it is more likely to be the exception than the rule (Abarbanel, 1979).

Parents often, with the best of overt intentions, try to make visitation work. Despite such good intentions, where a genuine hostility or resentment exists between the parents, it will emerge in such ways as "forgetting" the time the child is to be ready or to be returned, unconsciously disrupting a visit or a return, creating conflict through incautious remarks, being too rigidly conscientious regarding visitation times, and in other human, natural but disruptive behavior (Gardner, 1982).

In visitation arrangements, the *schedule* has been found to be a primary source of conflict between parents and, as a result, for the child. During discussions of scheduling, conflicts regarding time, consistency, money, causes of the divorce, and personal character often arise (Keshet & Rosenthal, 1978).

The absence of the father in a child's life has been studied extensively. Only about 10% of children live in single-parent homes with their fathers. The difficulties associated with an absent father are strongest for young male children. Father-surrogates work well to give children a balanced parental modeling framework. Females are less affected developmentally by the absence of a father (Biller, 1981); however, the complete absence of a father figure in a female's developmental years can disrupt discipline, social attitudes, and personality (Biller & Weiss, 1970). Some research suggests that "it takes a mature man, one who has found an unneurotic solution to his own oedipal conflict and has achieved a satisfying marriage relationship, to be able to offer his daughter desexualized affection at the crucial stages of her development" (Leonard, 1966).

General Conclusions about Conditions Following Divorce That Are Positive for the Child's Psychological Growth and Development

1. The mother or father is not overburdened by being a solo parent.
2. The child is fixed and stable in a consistent household with caring, warm, available, and stable mother and father figures.
3. The child is sheltered from exposure to conflict that may exist between the partners of the dissolved family.
4. Milestones and opportunities at expected ages and stages of the child's development are not disrupted by custodial or visitation mandates.
5. There is an absolute minimum of the compensatory mechanism of child-focus by former spouses in conflict with each other.
6. Female children develop best when living under the influence of a father who has achieved a satisfactory marital relationship, without

neurotic oedipal problems (too great a need to be attached to a mother or daughter).

The Probable Psychological Effect of Forced Visitations

Given both the available research and questions still unanswered as to how children cope with conflict, the following is more likely to occur than not if interpersonal conflict and tension remain between the parents in a visitation situation unacceptable to one or more of the involved parental figures:

1. Child-focus conflicts.
2. Impossible loyalty choices for the child.
3. Disruption of the parenting by the psychological and biological father.
4. Disruption of the routine and schedule of the child's home and peer environment.
5. Increased awareness of the original spousal conflict for the child.
6. Consequent symptoms of social, academic, and personal maladjustment.

References

Abarbanel, A. (1979). Shared parenting after separation and divorce: A study of joint custody. *American Journal of Orthospsychiatry, 50*, 320–329.

Beal, E. W. (1979). Children of divorce: A family systems perspective. *Journal of Social Issues, 35*(4), 140–154.

Biller, H. B. (1981). Father absence, divorce, and personality development. In M. E. Lamb (Ed.), *The role of father in child development.* New York: Wiley.

Biller, H. B., & Weiss, S. D. (1970). The father-daughter relationship and the personality development of the female. *Journal of Genetic Psychology, 116*, 79–93.

Collins, G. (1982, December 20). Some broken families retain many bonds. *New York Times*, p. 17.

Gardner, R. A. (1982). *Family evaluation in child custody litigation.* Creekskill, NJ: Creative Therapeutics.

Goldstein, J., Freud, A., & Solnit, A. J. (1979). *Before the best interests of the child.* New York: Free Press.

Hetherington, E. M. (1979). Divorce: A child's perspective. *American Psychologist, 34*, 851–858.

Keshet, H. F., & Rosenthal, K. M. (1978, January). Fathering after marital separation. *Social Work*, pp. 11–18.

Leonard, M. R. (1966). Fathers and daughters. *International Journal of Psychoanalysis, 47*, 325–333.

Santruck, J. W., & Warshak, R. A. (1979). Father custody and social development in boys and girls. *Journal of Social Issues, 35*(4), 112–125.

Wallerstein, J. S., & Kelly, J. B. (1975). The effects of parental divorce: Experiences of the pre-school child. *Journal of the American Academy of Child Psychiatry, 14*, 600–616.

Tender Years Doctrine.   Although most states have fairly recent statutes casting some question on the traditional concept that the child of young and tender years belongs with the mother, judges are reluctant in many instances to give up this shibboleth. In the following example, attorneys for a father, seeking custody of his sons, requested a learned treatise on the current psychological thought regarding the parenting needs of younger children and the quality of fathers as custodial parents.

THE TENDER YEARS DOCTRINE: CURRENT PERSPECTIVES

Traditionally, the court has awarded custody of most children of dissolved marriages to the mother under the shibboleth that "the child of young and tender years belongs with the mother." Judicial interpretation of "young and tender years" has varied considerably.

With the advent of greater sophistication in matters of child development among jurists, the focus has shifted to the "best interests of the child" and beyond (Goldstein et al., 1973, 1979). More fathers began to be named custodial parents (Molinoff, 1977), and more recently, joint custody, or shared responsibility, has become the decision of choice with growing frequency. The Florida statute mandates:

> *It is the public policy of this state to assure each minor child frequent and continuing contact with both parents after the parents have separated or dissolved their marriage and to encourage parents to share the rights and responsibilities of child-rearing.* Upon considering all relevant factors, the father of the child shall be given the same consideration as the mother in determining custody *regardless of the age of the child* [italics added].[14]

This idealistic approach is unlikely to be effective or helpful to the child in all cases, and the statutes frequently provide for mediation of disputes before sole custody is granted. Significant numbers of divorced parents are unable to work equitably and effectively in the child's best interests, once again burdening the court with the Solomonic decision.

In most divorces (85%), custody is awarded to the mother without contest by the father (Weitzman & Dixon, 1979). Until the middle of the 19th century, it was believed that fathers were better able to care for children (Weiss, 1979). From the 1850s until the 1950s, custody was routinely awarded to the mother unless she was judged unfit. Once the children passed the "tender years," it was assumed that the father would be given custody of the boys, while the mother would retain custody of the girls, although the courts have always been reluctant to separate siblings (Krause, 1977). More recent research suggests that fathers are quite capable of being competent custodial parents (Orthner & Lewis, 1979). Since the early 1970s, the tender years doctrine has been rejected by legislative act or court decision in 40 states (Freed & Foster, 1981).

Children's needs during the growing years have been extensively studied, and an understanding of developmental needs and how they may be met is readily available to all parents. Experts agree that divorce is harmful to all children. They also agree that it is desirable for the children to stay with one of the parents and to be helped, sometimes by a professional, to maintain a good relationship with the absent parent through regular and sensible visiting plans (Granger, 1978). Between ages 3 and 6, children require sensible, knowledgeable, and consistent parental supervision, particularly as the child develops toward school entrance, beginning with nursery school (Hymes, 1976).

The nature of the infant-mother relationship has been extensively studied over the years. Research does not support the concept of a tie between the infant and the mother as a specific parent. The so-called mother-infant bond has been found to exist with any close figure in the infant's development, including soft, warm inanimate objects. Although human infants are predisposed toward becoming attached to some person, if given the opportunity, it is *not* predetermined to whom they will become attached. These attachments become increasingly complex through the 24th month of life and develop into a *secure base* from which the child can learn and grow through exploration. An attachment figure is important but need not be a "mother" per se.

The child is considered to have developed secure relationships with an attachment figure when he or she greets the parent positively, actively attempts to reestablish proximity or interaction after separation, and does not display strongly negative behaviors during reunion episodes in a strange situation. Sustained early separations (birth to 12 months) from attachment figures may inhibit or prevent attachment.

Children who are securely attached by 18 months of age tend at 4 to 5 years of age to be described as highly resilient (resourceful in initiating activities, curious, exploring, self-reliant, and confident). Children who have not formed attachments by 18 months are described by teachers at 4 to 5 years as restricted (inhibited, disengaged under stress, anxious when the environment is unpredictable). The basic attachments, good or bad, tend to occur with the primary caregiver from birth through the 18th month of life (Joffe & Vaughn, 1982).

Specific studies of father-infant interaction indicate that the mother as primary caretaker is a stereotype of society and not specifically necessary and reinforcing for the infant. Fathers are potential equals where the role of primary caretaker is concerned. Over a wide age range throughout infancy, fathers, when placed in one-on-one relationships with their babies, interact as well as mothers, as demonstrated by a variety of studies. Fathers may operate somewhat differently with infants than do mothers (more playful, more physical than verbal, and more task oriented) but are equally competent as primary caretakers. Boys show a clear preference for fathers over mothers by the end of the second year of life (Hodapp & Mueller, 1982).

Warshak (1983) summarizes research regarding the positive values of fathers as custodial parents. There seems to be some consistent evidence that male children, in particular, are less adjusted when the mother is the custodial parent and more adjusted when custody resides with the father.

Where mother-child attachment is concerned, Bowlby (1969) states: "Although the growth of attachment behavior during the first year of life is reasonably well-chronicled, the course it takes during subsequent years is not." The ideal early developmental interaction involves the mother-child-father triad. After the first year of life, the father's role becomes increasingly important (Clarke-Stewart, 1978).

Research in respect to the child of young and tender years doctrine suggests:

1. Joint-parental custody is the more desirable situation when both parents are stable, competent, available, and cooperative.
2. Whatever exclusive mother-child bonding may exist is probably most significant during the first year of life.
3. During the 12th to 30th months, mother-child-father influences are most important.
4. After 30 months, there is no research to suggest that children develop better in a single-parent custodial situation with the mother than with the father.
5. If a single-parent custodial situation is necessary, male children, in particular, seem to show better long-term adjustment when such custody resides with the father.

References

Bowlby, J. (1969). *Attachment and loss.* New York: Basic Books.

Clarke-Stewart, K. A. (1978). And daddy makes three: The father's impact on mother and young child. *Child Development, 49,* 466–478.

Freed, D. J., & Foster, H. H., Jr. (1981). Divorce in the fifty states: An overview. *Family Law Quarterly, 14,* 229–284.

Goldstein, J., Freud, A., & Solnit, A. J. (1973). *Beyond the best interests of the child.* New York: Free Press.

Goldstein, J., Freud, A., & Solnit, A. J. (1979). *Before the best interests of the child.* New York: Free Press.

Granger, R. H. (1978). *Your child from one to six* (HEW Publication No. OHDS 78-30026). Washington, DC: U.S. Government Printing Office.

Hodapp, R. M., & Mueller, E. (1982). Early social development. In B. Wolman (Ed.), *Handbook of developmental psychology.* Englewood Cliffs, NJ: Prentice-Hall.

Hymes, J. L. (1976). *Three to six: Your child starts school* (Public Affairs Pamphlet No. 163). New York: Public Affairs Committee.

Joffe, L. W., & Vaughn, B. E. (1982). Infant-mother attachment: Theory, assessment, and implications for development. In B. Wolman (Ed.), *Handbook of developmental psychology.* Englewood Cliffs, NJ: Prentice-Hall.

Krause, H. D. (1977). *Family law in a nutshell.* St. Paul, MN: West.

Molinoff, D. (1977, May 22). Life with father. *New York Times Magazine.*

Orthner, D. K., & Lewis, K. (1979). Evidence of single father competence in child-rearing. *Family Law Quarterly, 13,* 27–47.

Warshak, R. A. (1983). *Custody disposition and children's psychosocial development.* Unpublished manuscript.

Weiss, R. S. (1979). Issues in the adjudication of custody when parents separate. In G. Levinger & O. C. Moles (Eds.), *Divorce and separation.* New York: Basic Books.

Weitzman, L. J., & Dixon, R. B. (1979). Child custody awards: Legal standards and empirical patterns for child custody, support, and visitation after divorce. *University of California, Davis Law Review, 12,* 473–521.

In writing such reports, the expert should maintain a working knowledge of current research to ensure that recommendations to the court represent the best available research findings.

THE COURT'S RESPONSE TO PSYCHOLOGICAL EXPERTS

Most family court judges welcome the opinions and testimony of mental health professionals in family issues (Litwak et al., 1980). Although some judges deem themselves competent authorities in family matters, most are sensible enough to recognize their limitations in technical aspects of child growth and development, personality, and family systems. Judges tend to be most positively inclined toward experts who attempt to be objective (Kazen, 1977). Some jurisdictions employ staff psychologists to conduct child custody investigations and provide information to the judge. These psychologists serve as *amicus curiae,* and their reports are available to the lawyers of both parties in the adversary issue (Gozansky, 1976).

Although judges frequently laud the contributions of experts in family matters, what they say may not represent what they do. Carol Lowery (1981) studied 70% of the 85 available state circuit court judges and 32 commissioners in the state of Kentucky in respect to the factors they considered important in deciding custody in a divorce. Using an 11-point rating scale for each of 20 items, the judges and commissioners ranked the importance of each variable in deciding custody issues. The items, in rank order of importance, are presented in Table 10.1.

One must assume that judges vary considerably, among themselves and in response to various case situations. Although professional advice is almost always welcomed, it may, in the final analysis, have modest impact on the judge's final decision.

Judges appointed or elected to serve judicial roles in family matters now enter their jobs with broader backgrounds in psychology as a result of the increasing likelihood that attorneys today will be exposed to psychology as part of their undergraduate courses. It is probable that psychologists will be called on by family judges to serve more frequently and in a greater variety of roles than in the past. As curriculum builders in law schools become more aware of and more responsive to the emerging partnership of psychology and the law, an increase in both quantity and quality of psychological involvement in family legal issues can be expected.

Because, in effect, courts have understood little of the complexities of child growth and development and family dynamics, experts from a wide range of the behavioral sciences have been deemed acceptable as expert witnesses. With the growing sophistication of attorneys and judges in family practice, experts will no longer be able to testify in vague generalities, personalistic notions, or outdated concepts. Such "experts" are likely to be discouraged by the learned treatise attacks of knowledgeable attorneys or the rejection of their opinions by judges who know that a body of

TABLE 10.1.   RANK ORDER OF FACTORS CONSIDERED BY JUDGES IN AWARDING CUSTODY

Rank	Item
1	Mental stability of each parent.
2	Each parent's sense of responsibility.
3	Biological relationship to the child (when one parent is a stepparent).
4	Each parent's moral character.
5	Each parent's ability to provide stable community involvement.
6	Each parent's affection for the child.
7	Keeping the child with siblings.
8	Each parent's ability to provide access to schools.
9	Keeping a young child with the mother.
10	Physical health of each parent.
11	The wishes of the parents.
12	Professional advice.
13	Biological relationship to the child (when one parent is an adoptive parent).
14	Each parent's financial sufficiency.
15	The child's wishes.
16	Length of time each parent has had custody.
17	Each parent's ability to provide contact with the child's other relatives.
18	Each parent's ability to provide access to other children of about the same age.
19	Each parent's ability or intention to provide a two-parent home.
20	Placing a child with the parent of the same sex.

Source: Lowery (1981).

research exists and who expect responses concordant with the concept of expert witness.

Until continuing research results in better assessment procedures and instruments, psychologists who undertake child custody evaluations should do so with due regard to their limitations as experts (Morris, 1997).

NOTES

1. *Rothstein v. Lutheran Social Services,* 59 Wis. 2d 1, 207 N.W.2d 826 (1973).
2. Fla. Stat. §61.13 (1982).
3. *Beck v. Beck,* 86 N.J. 480 (1981).
4. *Mastropole v. Mastropole,* 181 N.J. Super. 130 (App. Div. 1981).
5. *Atwood v. Atwood,* 550 S.W.2d 465 (Ky. 1976).
6. *Hutchins v. Hutchins,* 220 So. 2d 438 (Fla. App. 1969).
7. *Collins v. Newton,* 362 So. 2d 174 (Fla. App. 1978).
8. *In Re Gault,* 387 U.S. 1, 87 S. Ct. 1428, 18 L.Ed. 2d 527 (1967).
9. Disciplinary Rule 2-103, New Jersey Bar.
10. N.Y.C. B.A. Comm. on Professional & Judicial Ethics No. 80-23 (Feb. 27, 1981).
11. *Santosky v. Kramer,* 455 U.S. 745, 760 (1982).
12. *Rothstein v. Lutheran Social Services,* 59 Wis. 2d 1, 207 N.W.2d 826 (1973).
13. Fla. Stat. §§61.13, 61.21 (1982).
14. Fla. Stat. §61.13 (1982).

11

The Expert Witness and Personal Injury Litigation

A personal injury lawsuit takes place when an individual feels that he or she has suffered an injury or a loss and seeks advice or assistance from an attorney in an attempt to obtain remedy. Personal injury litigation may be simple or complex. There are many grounds for legal recovery that may support a claim for personal injuries. The most common categories include the following:

1. *Negligence (Simple or Gross)*. This usually involves a duty owed to the plaintiff by the defendant. That duty has been breached by the defendant's act or omission, creating an unreasonable risk of harm (in some cases, such as health-care delivery, a deviation from a reasonable standard of care). As a result of the defendant's breach of responsibility, an injury or damage is claimed. If the negligence case is against a professional, the legal standard of care is usually determined by reference to the activities of similar professional practitioners. The legal definition of a causal relationship between a defendant's breach of responsibility and a plaintiff's damages varies considerably from state to state. In such matters, there are often derivative actions, which are secondary injuries to a person related to the plaintiff, such as a spouse filing an action for loss of consortium (ordinary benefits expected in a marital relationship) or parents filing an action for medical expenses for an injured child.

2. *Willful or Wanton Misconduct*. A person's attorney may file for damages (usually punitive) if there has been a willful or wanton misconduct on the part of an individual who was to deliver services or provide in some way for the plaintiff.

3. *Nuisance*. An individual or a group may seek damages from a defendant who has created a public nuisance or a private nuisance. This covers a wide range of behaviors of commission or omission.

4. *Breach of Warranty*. In this type of personal injury action, the plaintiff may seek an attorney to file suit against the defendant who has expressly

avoided fulfilling a warranty or a guarantee. This can include such things as merchantability of goods, usefulness of materials or objects, or habitability of buildings or dwellings.

5. *Strict Liability.*   This refers generally to product liability or ultrahazardous or abnormal activities. In product liability, action may be instituted against those who own or manufacture a product because of direct damage that has been done, or because of a failure of some type of warranty. Ultrahazardous or unusual activities involving water, fire, electricity, gas, pesticides, nuclear waste, or nuclear explosions can result in claims that the defendant did not do the right thing in regard to the products or activities. Strict liability also applies to unacceptable behavior of animals, to accidents or misconduct at sea, and to responsibilities of individuals or organizations as defined by statute.

6. *Defamation.*   Seeking personal injury recovery because of libel or slander is a complex issue, generally requiring that the plaintiff prove that the defendant had an avowed intention to defame the plaintiff.

7. *Fraud, Deceit, and Misrepresentation.*   Personal injury that results from these actions is usually associated with a claim of intentional efforts on the part of the defendant to deceive or defraud the plaintiff. Negligent misrepresentation is also included in this category. Even if an individual who perpetrates a fraud, a deceit, or a misrepresentation is found criminally innocent, a personal injury suit may be filed against him or her.

8. *Intentional Acts.*   Personal injury that results from assault and battery, false arrest and imprisonment, malicious prosecution, abusive process, alienation of affection, criminal conversation, invasion of privacy, intentional or reckless infliction of mental suffering, trespass, outrage, or bad faith is considered an intentional act for which recovery is possible by personal injury litigation.

9. *Breach of Contract.*   Wherever a contract exists that is not fulfilled in the eyes of one party, such party may seek remedy by filing a personal injury lawsuit.

10. *The Effect of a Statute, Regulation, or Ordinance.*   Personal injury lawsuits may be filed against a variety of individuals or agencies where the defendant's duty has not been carried out and has resulted in some kind of injury to the plaintiff. Such personal injury lawsuits can involve wrongful death statutes, survival statutes, the Workers' Compensation Act, Death on the High Seas Act, the Federal Employees' Compensation Act, the Federal Employees' Liability Act, and a wide range of other statutes involving safety and consumer protection.

Some attorneys and indeed some statutes categorize personal injury actions according to the basic facts of the situation. The 12 most common patterns of fact in personal injury litigation are:

1. Personal injury resulting from the activity of vehicles or transportation situations.
2. Injuries occurring on premises.
3. Contractor and construction cases.
4. Personal injury occurring from the function or malfunction of manufactured products.
5. Malpractice.
6. Aviation accidents.
7. Admiralty actions.
8. Sports and athletic suits.
9. Toxic torts involving exposure to and injury by pollutants, chemicals, or radiation sources.
10. Personal injury suits involving government bodies as the defendant.
11. Personal injury cases involving family responsibilities and actions.
12. Special personal injury actions, including prenatal injuries, preconception cases involving harmful or mutigenic substances, actions for wrongful life, bereavement, and wrongful discharge of employees.

The preceding list suggests that personal injury litigation is one of the broadest areas of civil law. The procedures are long and complex (Norton, 1981).

Personal injury litigation falls under the *law of torts* (French for "wrong"). The purpose of the tort is to arrange corrective justice, to ensure that there are principles whereby a plaintiff can achieve a fair compensation from a liable defendant. Under these statutes, injured parties are entitled to compensation under a wide variety of conditions. In essence, all of the preceding can be summarized in three main theories of tort law. In the first, a plaintiff is entitled to recovery for harms *intentionally inflicted* by a defendant on a plaintiff. In the second instance, an opportunity is provided for recovery for harms that are *inflicted negligently* through the lack of reasonable or ordinary care. The third general area entitles a plaintiff to recover under the concept of *strict liability,* by which the harm may be inflicted on the plaintiff *without intention or negligence* on the part of the defendant. These theories, of course, encompass many variations (Gregory, Kalven, & Epstein, 1977).

THE ROLE OF THE PSYCHOLOGICAL EXPERT IN TORT LITIGATIONS

Psychologists and other experts may be called on to provide expert opinion in a number of evidentiary aspects of personal injury litigation. The expert may be used to provide technical or professional opinions in almost any aspect of the litigation where the triers of fact require special aid in deciding on the cause, outcome, or consequences of alleged injuries or losses. Experts may be called on to provide information and opinion as to:

1. *The Existence of an Injury.*   The plaintiff's attorney must convince the triers of fact that a loss has been suffered. The loss may relate to decreased intellectual capacity in a brain-injured accident victim or the bereavement of the survivors of a tragic and wrongful death. A corporation may claim a loss of business as a result of trademark infringement. Experts are called as witnesses to define, in terms understandable to the average juror, the nature and extent of the loss that is alleged by the plaintiff to have occurred.

2. *The Cause of an Injury.*   In addition to rendering opinions as to whether the plaintiff has suffered an injury, and the extent of that injury, experts are usually asked for an opinion as to the probable source or causal factors leading to the plaintiff's injuries or loss. Before a jury can assign liability, a causal connection between the plaintiff's loss and the defendant's accountability must be demonstrated.

3. *Permanence, Replacement, or Remediation.*   To aid the triers of fact in making decisions about just and fair remedies, experts are asked to render opinions as to the degree of which an injured person will recover, the plaintiff's future capacity to function, and estimates as to his or her rehabilitation potential and requirements. An expert may be asked to estimate the gap between an individual's likely or eventual quality of life in work, family relationships, health, or recreation as a result of the injuries suffered in comparison with an estimated quality of life had the injury not occurred.

When a person is injured in an automobile accident or is hurt in any of the many kinds of accidents that injure millions of persons each year, personal injury litigation frequently follows the event. Whether it involves a child profoundly brain damaged after being hit by an automobile or a person suffering a very limited orthopedic strain as a result of being bumped by a cart in a hotel, personal injury litigation may result. A psychologist may be called by the plaintiff's attorney to evaluate the psychological deficits and consequences of the injury, and the psychologist's testimony would be part of the attorney's efforts to convince the jury that the plaintiff has suffered and deserved compensation. A psychologist may be retained by the defense attorney to provide expert testimony to demonstrate to the jury that the psychological effects of the injury are minimal. Personal injury litigation is sometimes referred to as "the battle of the experts," since the effects and future outcomes of personal injury can be evaluated and perceived in different ways by different experts. In almost every community, there are experts in various health professions who are known as *plaintiff's experts* or *defense experts*. This may mean that the expert has specialized in some aspect of his or her profession that lends itself uniquely to the goals or tasks pursued by the attorney for the plaintiff or the attorney for the defense. More frequently, such a label suggests that the expert has a bias for one side or the other and is willing to expand subjective opinions to meet the competitive adversary requirements of the attorney who retains the expert. Such a stance is to be scrupulously avoided by psychologists who function as experts in the courts.

A considerable variety of situations occur in tort litigation where psychological experts have been called on to testify. This chapter presents a number of usual and unusual litigations to illustrate such situations, as well as the procedures that psychologists should follow to perform competently as expert witnesses.

Accidental Injury

This is the tort litigation in which a psychologist, especially the neuropsychologist, is most likely to be called as an expert witness. When the attorney (representing a person injured in an automobile accident, a malfunctioning elevator, a fall over an object, or any of thousands of tort litigation situations) calls a psychologist, it may be assumed that the attorney has reason to believe that the psychological expert can be a helpful witness. The attorney for the plaintiff anticipates testimony supporting claims of loss or deficit, while the attorney for the defendant seeks expert testimony to raise questions about such claims. The psychologist must remain as neutral as possible in the case; for no matter how encouraging, suggestive, flattering, or manipulative the lawyer, it is the expert's job to render an honest, complete, conservative opinion well within the ethical and contextual framework of his or her science and profession.

Intake Interview. During the initial interview with the retaining attorney (usually by telephone), the psychologist should consider the following before agreeing to accept the case:

1. *The Facts of the Case.* Attorneys are usually willing to give the expert a concise summary of the facts of the case and the attorney's position as plaintiff or defense counsel. The expert must know what happened, when it happened, and the apparent results.

2. *Anticipated Court Date.* It takes a month or more to prepare adequately to be an expert in an accident case. Pressure from attorneys to examine an injured patient and be prepared to testify next week should be politely but firmly rejected. If the attorney has a court date that conflicts with the expert's availability, this should be clear at the outset.

3. *Hypothetical Questions.* During the initial interview, the psychologist should find out the probable hypothetical questions that will be asked by the attorney. This ensures that the attorney's expectancies are within the technical, scientific, or professional expertise of the psychologist. It is important that the psychologist make clear the boundaries or limits of psychology in respect to the facts of the case and the anticipated hypotheticals.

4. *The Condition and Availability of the Plaintiff.*   During the initial conference, the psychologist should find out whether any limitations or constraints exist that might prevent a thorough evaluation. In some cases, the judge may have limited the number of hours that the plaintiff is available for evaluation. If the constraints are so stringent as to prevent a thorough and competent professional evaluation, the consultation should be refused.

5. *Retrieval of Records.*   Since the expert will be asked questions concerning the plaintiff's current level of psychological functioning in comparison with the level that existed before the accident, every possible source of objective data concerning psychological status previous to the accident should be obtained. As an officer of the court, the attorney is able to obtain such records more efficiently than the expert, and his or her willingness to do so should be ensured at the outset. School records, with a specific request for test scores and counselor reports, should be sought. Work, military, and treatment records are all potentially important since they may provide objective evidence of premorbid levels of function. The psychologist should also ask the attorney to forward all hospital and posthospital treatment records. It is most important to have the attorney find out whether other psychologists have examined the plaintiff and, if so, the dates of such examinations. This will ensure that tests are administered with sufficient time lapse to avoid test-retest effects.

6. *Fee Arrangements.*   During the initial interview, the expert should ensure that the retaining attorney understands and agrees to financial arrangements and responsibilities required by the psychologist. It is suggested that the expert cover the following during the initial interview:

    a. *Fee Structure.*   The expert should inform the retaining attorney of the hourly rate charged by the expert for all direct work in the case accomplished by the psychologist. This should ordinarily be the psychologist's usual hourly fee for professional services.

    b. *Approximate Cost.*   Since the attorney is frequently accountable to his or her clients for consultative fees, the psychologist should be able to tell the attorney the approximate costs for the anticipated professional work.

7. *The Psychologist's Product.*   During the initial interview the psychologist should inform the retaining attorney about procedures that are likely to be conducted, the scope of preliminary work, and the type of evaluative procedures tentatively planned. The psychologist should indicate what areas of exploration will be pursued and the kind of report that can be expected. It is always appropriate to indicate at this early stage that other evaluative directions may seem appropriate as information is collected. The psychologist should tell the attorney that should additional assessment or exploration be necessary, the psychologist will discuss this with the attorney before proceeding. The psychologist should inform the attorney that an interim or formative report will be made by phone as soon as the psychologist has enough information to form an opinion.

8. *Scheduling.* Scheduling should be done through the attorney's office in order that some responsibility for the client's keeping appointments can be shared by the attorney. Missed or forgotten appointments can seriously interfere with an orderly and timely collection of the data necessary for decision making by the psychologist. Coordinating appointments through the attorney's office can be important when the plaintiff must be examined by a variety of experts.

The Assessment Process. The number of assessment tests and procedures available to psychologists for use in personal injury issues is considerable (Buros, 1933–1978). New tests and assessment instruments are continually being developed and marketed (Conoley & Impara, 1995; Conoley & Kramer, 1989; Kramer & Conoley, 1992; Mitchell, 1985). The choice of tests or procedures to be used is a matter of professional judgment, based on well-defined principles. The psychologist needs always to keep in mind that the assessment procedures selected in any case must be appropriate for the hypothetical questions in the case at hand, appropriate for the individual who is being evaluated, and recognized and accepted within the profession (see Chapter 6).

The psychologist should conduct the assessment under the best standardized conditions possible. Plaintiffs may be quite uncomfortable about being interviewed and tested, so the psychologist must make every effort to ensure that the testing atmosphere is comfortable and conducive to the plaintiff's asserting his or her best efforts.

Before beginning the assessment, it is important that the psychologist identify himself or herself, indicate the name of the attorney retaining the expert, and specify that a report of the assessment will be forwarded to that attorney. If the psychologist is retained by the attorney adversary to the examinee's case, the examinee should be reassured that the report will be available to the examinee's attorney.

Before scheduling and conducting an assessment, the psychologist should be familiar with all background materials and records about the examinee so that pertinent facts associated with the issues and questions in the case can be taken into consideration in selecting and administering the assessment procedures. It is important to keep in mind that the plaintiff may be examined by several psychologists, thus raising the issue of test-retest effects.

Reporting Findings. Once the psychologist has reviewed all records relating to the facts of the case, has conducted the evaluation, has checked all scoring and profiling, and is satisfied that the assessment is complete, the report should be constructed in first draft and the psychologist should list findings, conclusions, and opinions (responses to the hypothetical questions). Before writing the formal report, the psychologist should telephone the retaining attorney and report briefly as to what was done, what was found, and the expert's opinions. At this point, the attorney may pose additional questions for the psychologist to answer on the basis of the findings. If the results add nothing to the case, the attorney may terminate the consultation at this point and ask the psychologist to submit a final bill. In most cases, the attorney requests that the psychologist submit the final report.

There is no one style of psychological report, and throughout this book there are examples of different styles. As long as the report is complete, is within the ethics and standards required of the profession, and is understandable, there is considerable leeway permissible in style. Very careful copy reading is important since the written report is the document from which the psychologist will render expert testimony at deposition or at court.

The following psychological report was submitted in an accident case.

PSYCHOLOGICAL REPORT

October 8, 1991

NAME: Mullen, Ruth   DATE OF EXAMINATION: 10/7, 10/8/91

ADDRESS: P.O. Box 721, Oxford, Florida   TELEPHONE: 000-0000

BIRTHDATE: 9/22/71   AGE: 19-11   OCCUPATION: None

EDUCATION: 10th

Referral

James East, Esquire, made a telephone request on the eighth of September for psychological consultation concerning the case of *Mullen v. Bently Corp. et al.* He states that the plaintiff, Ms. Mullen, was attending a promotional festival in Hilton County when a polesitter giving an exhibition landed on her. The result of this interaction was a head injury which was first treated at Lundeen General Hospital and then at the Murtry Regional Medical Center. There she was found to be bilaterally decerebrated. Jack Lott, M.D., performed a left posterior parietal craniotomy, with evacuation of left epidural hematoma.

Ms. Mullen did fairly well according to history. She was subsequently examined twice by Bill Surt, Ph.D., and once by Pearl Flack, Ed.D. Mr. East requests a review of the background records, and psychological evaluation of Ms. Mullen.

Background Factors

This young woman was born on September 22, 1971. The information following was given by her mother, Jane Potts, on October 8, 1991. Ms. Potts says that she is 41 years old and is not working at the present time. She was a fruit packer. Before that she did factory work. She received an 11th-grade education at Grove, Michigan. She quit in the 11th grade. She is in good health. She is currently beginning to work selling Amway products.

She was married to Arthur Mullen, who is the father of Ruth. They divorced on May 8, 1984. At that time Ruth was 12, according to the mother. The real father does not work. He used to be a semi-truck driver. He quit school in the eleventh grade. She and her brother saw the father last in 1988.

Since June 1979 Mrs. Potts has remarried, and Ruth lives with her and with the stepfather. There is a brother, Jack, age 21, who is with the U.S. Navy and who "puts bombs on airplanes."

In giving the history, it is noted that Mrs. Potts has a remarkably similar speech distortion to her daughter, Ruth. She speaks in a very nasal, twangy manner. The mother is unable to remember dates and facts and must refer to a series of sheets of paper which she keeps in her purse concerning all important dates. During the interview, it became obvious that the mother has a very poor memory.

She gives the history that Ruth weighed four pounds and four ounces at birth. Ruth was born a month early, and they "didn't expect her to live." Ruth spent a month in the incubator. The mother states that Ruth was born with weak eye muscles. She received her first eye operation in June 1976 and another one in July 1977. The mother states that for all practical purposes Ruth is blind in her left eye. "There is not enough that it would be noticed for her to see." Ruth wears glasses for her weak right eye. Ruth was also born with a hip problem. She had to wear a brace on her shoes and between 1 year and 1½ years of age had to sleep with a brace.

She has been under the care of Dr. Storr of Williston. She had her first menstrual cycle at age 17. The mother claims that Ruth has been irregular since the accident. Early medical problems are denied.

Ruth started kindergarten at the Olney Elementary School at the age of six. Mrs. Potts says this was because of her birthday. She then went from the first through the third grade in the Olney Elementary School, and then the family moved to Waycross, Georgia, during the third grade, and then four months later they moved to Williston, Florida. Ruth failed this grade, and the mother says that this was because of the move. During the history, the mother indicates that Ruth was nine years of age at that time, but it may be that she was really 10 since the mother was very confused about ages and miscalculated several times.

The third grade was repeated in Williston, where she completed the fourth, fifth, and sixth grades. Mrs. Potts insists that Ruth's work was "average" and that she was "an average student." (The school records do not support this.)

Ruth, according to her mother, entered the seventh grade in the Maple Junior High School and did average work through the eighth grade. In the ninth grade, she entered the South Maple High School and did "pretty good." In the 10th grade, she didn't do well, but Mrs. Potts said that this was because "she got mixed up with a bunch of kids and let her grades drop but still she passed." When asked how old she was when Ruth finished the 10th grade, at first Mrs. Potts said "seventeen" but by looking at records, it turns out that Ruth was 18 at that time. Mrs. Potts said, "I don't really remember her failing another year."

Mrs. Potts says that Ruth makes friends very easily. Ruth has her own room at home but will not sleep there, preferring to take cushions from the couch and put them by her mother's bed and sleep there. The mother doesn't seem to mind this, and although they have made efforts to get Ruth to sleep in her own room, these have been unsuccessful. The mother states that Ruth is now going to a psychiatrist and has been for the past four weeks. The psychiatrist says that "we should not try to force her—he will get her back into her own bed." The psychiatrist is Thomas Berd, M.D. He has been giving her some medication "for her nerves." This consists of two yellow capsules two hours before bed.

The mother says that Ruth never joined the Girl Scouts, and the only activity that she can remember was in the fifth grade when Ruth twirled the baton. Ruth has always liked dolls and has collected quite a few. She had a boyfriend before the accident, but he was getting too serious so she dropped him because she wasn't ready to settle down. Ruth gets no allowance, but the mother and the stepfather give her money when they think she needs it.

She helps her mother around the house all the time. She is a fanatic about cleaning, according to the mother, and keeps their house very well. Ruth collects aluminum. Since July when the mother began working with Amway, Ruth has been helping her. The mother states that Ruth does most of the selling. She says that Ruth has a good style and people like her. The mother says, "I don't let her drive that much alone, but she does most of the selling. She writes up the orders on her own. She has been doing better since she got started at this. It wasn't very good for her to be laying around at home."

Ruth is very insecure. If the mother and stepfather forget to tell her at least once a day that they love her, she comes to them and says, "You don't love me anymore," until they very pointedly tell her that they love her.

The mother gives the facts of the accident. She was present. She states that she, Ruth, the brother, and a neighbor friend were standing by a building in the shade. A loudspeaker announced that there would be a polesitting exhibition and anyone who wished to see it should go to the field. Ruth ran toward the field. The mother then noticed that the son was screaming, "I think it's Ruth." The mother says that the polesitter swooped down and tried to "catch" Ruth. Instead he hit her and dragged her. He was holding onto her and then apparently dropped her. When he did, her head hit on the blacktop of the road. This is the mother's version of the accident.

When asked what changes have occurred, she indicates that since the accident Ruth has cried more, has difficulty talking as well as she did before, has nightmares, wakes up screaming, gets tired more easily, and has dizzy spells. These come sometimes once a day and sometimes not for a week. Her balance is not as good as it was, and she tends to stagger. The mother feels that Ruth gets upset easily. The mother feels that Ruth's memory is real bad. The mother feels that Ruth wants to say something but doesn't know the words to use. Ruth is very sensitive and feels that the parents criticize her too much. The difficulty in sleeping alone since the accident has been noted previously.

Medical Records

The accident took place on May 19, 1990. After Ruth was hit by the polesitter and dragged, she was given some first aid. She was then brought to the Lundeen General Hospital. She was apparently comatose at that time. Blood was coming from her left ear. She was immediately transferred to the Murtry Regional Medical Center, where she was found to be bilaterally decerebrated. Examination by Dr. Jack Lott (neurosurgeon), including an emergency CT scan, suggested left posterior parietal epidural hematoma and a small left temporal epidural hematoma. The patient was taken to the operating room, and Dr. Lott performed a left posterior parietal craniotomy and evacuation of left epidural hematoma. The preoperative diagnosis of left acute epidural hematoma was confirmed.

The patient did fairly well and was followed by Dr. Lott. Subsequently she received two psychological examinations from Bill Surt, Ph.D. (assisted by Karl Coller in the first evaluation and Edward Moody, Ph.D.). Dr. Surt found neuropsychological dysfunctions but in particular noted a strong negative emotional response that he attributes to the accident. Ms. Mullen was also seen by Pearl R. Flack, Ed.D., a counselor.

Dr. Lott's records consist of admission notes beginning on June 19, 1990. There is a description of the operative procedure (left posterior parietal craniotomy with evacuation of left epidural hematoma). It was stated that the patient tolerated the operation well and returned to consciousness. She was discharged on July 6, 1990 and was placed on Dilantin to prevent the occurrence of seizures.

A postoperative follow-up on July 27, 1990 notes that this patient had "roving eyes since birth." The doctor increased the Dilantin to 400 mg per day.

A postoperative note of August 21, 1990 indicates that the neurological examination was "very good." The doctor notes, "The patient has not sustained permanent physical injury." He further states that it is too early to find out about her mental condition.

In a postoperative note dated January 18, 1991, Dr. Lott says that the neurological examination is entirely normal but that this patient has suffered mental impairment. He recommends additional psychometrics to follow Dr. Surt's evaluation in the fall of 1990. He notes that the family is having financial problems and that this is affecting the patient.

In a postoperative follow-up note of June 17, 1991, he notes that the patient suffers headaches, which are probably from tension. The neurological evaluation is again normal. The doctor states that the "economical situation" is a significant factor in the situation.

Dr. Lott notes that this patient is extremely thin and notes her weight to be 80 pounds. This is unusual and one would wonder whether there is the possibility of anorexia.

The first psychological examination reported by Dr. Surt is apparently a standard psychological evaluation. Dr. Surt indicates that the patient was 19 at the time of the examination, with 11 years of education. There are no indications that this is true, since we have records showing that she finished schooling in the tenth grade. He notes that the girl is right-handed. She was referred by an attorney by the name of Yurtey. The examination occurred four months after the accident, and it could be expected to show the maximum deficit since it was so close to the time of the accident.

Ms. Mullen was tested for six hours in a one-day session. This may have been pretty tiring to her. The examination consisted of some standard administrations and partial administration of the Halstead-Reitan Neuropsychological Battery.

The Wechsler scores were as follows:

Verbal scale—95
Performance scale—83
Full scale—89

The above scores included Comprehension with a weighted score of 12 and Similarities with a weighted score of 11.

Dr. Surt found poor memory, better performance on tactile tasks with the left hand than the right, better tapping with the right hand than the left (30 in 10 seconds as opposed to 27 in 10 seconds). He found her to be at the twentieth percentile on the Controlled Word Association Test, although no normative reference is given.

The Wide Range Achievement Test indicated the following:

Factor	Grade Equivalent	Percentile (No Norms Given)
Reading	6.6	18th
Spelling	6.7	19th
Arithmetic	5.3	12th

The personality was referenced to the MMPI, which showed "a troubled and anxious individual." No notation is made of the effects that poor reading may have on the MMPI. The report refers to changes that are reported by either the patient or the parents.

Dr. Surt apparently examined Ms. Mullen in August of 1991. A letter to Dr. Lott indicated that an examination took place on the 14th of July, 1991, at the offices of Dr. Edward Moody in Garville.

Dr. Surt expressed a great deal of alarm about Ms. Mullen's emotional condition and suggested immediate intervention. No details of his examination were enclosed. Although this letter came approximately six weeks after the examination, Dr. Surt apologized for the press of time preventing him from giving a more detailed report. He did indicate that a more detailed report would follow. Dr. Flack apparently did some kind of rehabilitation evaluation. The tests administered were simply the Bender, the Wide Range Achievement Test, and the WAIS-R.

Results of the WAIS-R were as follows:

Factor	Deviation IQ
Verbal scale	84
Performance scale	84
Full scale	82

His report indicates that the patient received a weighted score of 4 in Information and Picture Completion, a score of 6 in Vocabulary, Arithmetic, and Object Assembly, a score of 9 in Digit Span and Digit Symbol, and a score of 11 in Picture Arrangement.

The results of the WRAT were as follows:

Factor	Grade Equivalent
Word Recognition	6.8
Spelling	6.9
Arithmetic	6.6

School Records

It is unclear what school district produced these records. Some of the records are clear, and some of them are quite unclear. They cover the years 1979 to 1987 for six grades of school. Absences of as long as 30 or 36 days were noted in some of the school grades. In some cases, they were attributed to illness, and in some cases there were question marks for the cause. She was given a conditional promotion from Grade 2 to 3 and a social promotion from Grade 3 to 4. She was absent 16 days in the seventh grade. She was absent 34 days in the eighth grade. For junior high school she received Cs and Ds in all subjects except a B in home economics and a B in vocational courses.

Her Metropolitan Achievement Test total achievement scores were as follows:

Year	Grade Equivalent
1980	1.9
1981	2.3
1982	2.9
1983	3.5
1984	4.3

She took Grade 9 between 1988 and 1989, and she received three Fs (basic science, general math, and civics). She received four Ds (English, general math, world geography, health) and two Cs (physical education, drivers' education). She received one B (physical education) in the second term.

In Grade 10, which was taken between 1989 and 1990, she received two Ds (general science and fundamentals of business), three Cs (agriculture, general math, physical education), three Bs (basic English, agricultural occupations, and general science). This is the last record noted. Apparently she had completed the tenth grade when she was 18½ years of age.

Metropolitan Achievement scores for the intermediate and junior high school years were as follows:

Age	Grade	Date	Tot Reading	Tot Language	Tot Arith	Tot Battery
13–6	5	4/85	4.7	5.5	5.4	5.2
14–5	6	3/86	5.0	5.7	5.2	5.1
15–5	7	3/87	6.1	5.7	6.9	6.4
16–6	8	4/88	5.1	4.7	6.6	5.5
17–5	9	3/89	7.0	5.7	—	—

The above results indicate that this young woman has had a very difficult time in school. She has never achieved above the elementary school level. She was 17½ years of age when she finished the ninth grade. There are no recorded indications of where she failed in school. She apparently began school in 1979, but she may have been seven and a half years of age at that time if the birthdate of October 1971 indeed represents her birthdate. Even so, there is evidence that she must have failed at some grade levels.

The particular school system she attended gave some intelligence tests called the SFTAA. These results were as follows:

Chronological Age	Language IQ	Nonlanguage IQ	Total IQ
13–6	78	88	82
15–5	85	85	84
16–6	74	80	75

In a letter received on October 26, 1991, Bill Surt, Ph.D., enclosed a copy of his second examination and report, which he dated October 3, 1991. He essentially administered the same examinations that were given in October of 1990. He reports a WAIS VIQ of 89, a PIQ of 97, and a Full Scale of 92.

In his summary, he states that some recovery has occurred for selective higher mentative functions but that other cognitive abilities, especially those associated with the left hemisphere, have not improved. He again emphasizes that the patient's reaction to these losses has intensified emotional problems. Timely therapeutic intervention at this critical juncture in her life is strongly recommended.

It is instructive to look at a basic measure of the patient's functional skills-intelligence. The following table presents the highest level of intellectual function as measured by the Short-Form Test of Academic Aptitude in comparison with three measures of intelligence given during three psychological examinations since the accident:

SFTAA and Wechsler Results

Factor	School Records SFTAA 3/87	Surt #1 10/24/90 WAIS	Flack 1/20/91 WAIS-R	Surt #2 7/14/91 WAIS
Verbal scale IQ	85	95	84	89
Performance scale IQ	85	83	84	97
Full scale IQ	84	89	82	92

The above measures suggest on objective evaluation that at the time of the last intellectual assessment, Ruth Mullen's Verbal Scale Intelligence, Performance Scale Intelligence, and Full Scale Intelligence exceeded the best intellectual performance that she demonstrated between the ages of 13 and 16 while in school. Thus, her postaccident results are not reflective of lower intellectual functioning since the accident.

Examinations Given during Current Evaluation

Peabody Picture Vocabulary Test, Form M; Flanagan Aptitude Classification Tests (Inspection, Coding, Memory, Precision, Mechanics, Assembly, Scales, Coordination, Judgment and Comprehension, Arithmetic, Patterns, Components, Tables, Expression); Gates-MacGinitie Reading Test—Form 1; Metropolitan Achievement Test—Advanced 1, Form JS, Reading and Mathematics; Wechsler Memory Scale, Form I; Luria-Nebraska Neuropsychological Battery; Draw-a-Person series; Sentence Completion Test; House-Tree Test; Millon Clinical Multiaxial Inventory (items read to patient); History Taking, Interview, and Follow-up Interview.

Response to Evaluation

Ms. Mullen is a young woman with brown hair and brown eyes who is quite small and thin. Her mother also has a very tiny body image. She wears glasses. Her voice is clear and light. She speaks in a somewhat nasal manner. Hearing is within normal limits. She is slow and deliberate in writing and drawing. She forms fancy letters. She is polite, friendly, shows good manners, and is very "sweet." She cooperates well and seems to have good confidence. She works quite slowly, and this results in some lower scores, since she does not attempt a number of the items. The air conditioning was not functioning properly and it was quite warm in the test room. This made everyone somewhat uncomfortable during the testing session on October 7.

Ruth herself was interviewed; she and her mother both were told the purpose of the examination and by whom the psychologist was retained. Ruth talked very positively about her family. She states that her mother remarried when she was about 15, and that Ruth likes her stepfather. For recreation, she likes most to go to the game room uptown. She likes to help her mother out. She enjoys watching TV three or four hours a day. She has been selling Amway for months and goes all over with her mother.

Since the accident Ruth feels that she forgets more, but when she is reminded she will remember. She feels her math and English are worse, and she notices this since she is studying in a GED book to try to prepare for this examination. She feels that "things" in general bother her more.

Results of Examination

A. *Intellectual Factors*

The intellectual evaluation consisted of the examination of previous results, and since Doctor Surt conducted a WAIS examination in July, it was felt that a reexamination at this time would confuse the issue with practice effect. A review of the intellectual test results is presented on Page Eight of this report.

Ruth was given the Peabody Picture Vocabulary Test and she fell at the second percentile in this test. She had a relatively narrow range of response with a basal score at 99 and ceiling at 132. Her raw score was 118, which resulted in a mental age equivalent of 11 years and 10 months. This would suggest that she has the mental facility to do sixth- to seventh-grade work.

B. *Neuropsychological Factors*

On the Wechsler Memory Scale, the total scale resulted in a Memory Quotient of 90. This compares favorably with the various Intelligence

Quotient results noted previously. Her performance would be considered Low Average.

On the Luria-Nebraska Neuropsychological Battery, Ms. Mullen exceeded the Critical Level in 6 of the 14 scales (Rhythm, Receptive Speech, Writing, Reading, Arithmetic, and Intellectual Processes). This would place her in the brain-disordered range of performance.

Primary areas of difficulty are apparently in the left parieto-occipital area and the right temporal areas.

Specific neuropsychological skill deficits demonstrated on this test include the reading of simple material, motor writing skill, logical grammatical relations, concept recognition, relational concepts, arithmetic calculations, complex verbal arithmetic, and simple phonetic reading. She has some mild difficulty with kinesthesis-based movement.

These results show that Ms. Mullen is a person of somewhat deficient neuropsychological function. Her difficulties are likely to show up in any academic area or in any situation that requires applied intelligence. She will show some modest discrepancies in rhythmic motor movements, she will misunderstand directions in some cases, she will show difficulty in writing and reading as well as in arithmetic. In general, her intellectual processes show limitations.

The Pathognomonic scale is moderate, indicating that at the present time there is no highly active disease process affecting the neuropsychological systems.

C.   Achievement Factors

The Metropolitan Achievement Tests—Advanced Form 1 indicate that general reading is at the 3.5 grade level when given a speed test, while mathematics falls at the 6.3 grade level.

The reading was further investigated using the Gates-MacGinitie, and the following results were obtained:

Factor	Grade Equivalent
Reading Speed	3.5
Reading Accuracy	3.3
Vocabulary	5.8
Comprehension	3.9

Viable independent reading starts at the 3.5 grade level. These results show that Ms. Mullen is penalized by time and does rather poorly under any kind of time pressure for reading. Her vocabulary is at about the fifth-grade level, and her comprehension at about the fourth-grade level. This is somewhat lower than previous testings have indicated, but the Gates-MacGinitie and the Metropolitan are somewhat more demanding tests.

D. *Aptitudes*

Results of the Flanagan Aptitude Classification Tests were as follows:

Factor	Percentile (Compared with High School Graduates about to Enter Trade School)
Inspection	2nd
Coding	8th
Memory	8th
Precision	8th
Assembly	17th
Scales	17th
Coordination	17th
Judgment and Comprehension	8th
Arithmetic	8th
Patterns	2nd
Components	2nd
Mechanics	50th
Expression	2nd

The above results indicate that Ms. Mullen has poor skills to prepare her for any kind of trade training.

Doing an Aptitude Classification Analysis, her highest prediction for trade training would be in the area of agriculture and farming. Here she falls at approximately the seventeenth percentile in predicting success from such training.

E. *Personality Factors*

The projective techniques performed by Ms. Mullen are at a preteen to early teen level. She tends to see the world in fairly simplistic ways. Her values and her interests are that of a 12- to 13-year-old teenager. She would appear to be extremely dependent, particularly on the mother.

Problems are approached quite simplistically. She has a fairly active fantasy life. She shows a great deal of anxiety about new situations and independence. She enjoys being sociable and thrives on approval and praise.

The results of the Millon Clinical Multiaxial Inventory show this young woman to be a fairly dependent and submissive person who suffers a moderate amount of anxiety. There are indications that she has "ups and downs." She fears abandonment, and this leads her to seek nurturance by acting in an overly compliant and obliging way. She can act gregarious and pleasant. She often dramatizes her own behavior. She has a naive attitude about interpersonal problems, and her thinking is unreflective and somewhat scattered. When faced with tension, she will make an effort to maintain an air of pleasantness and deny that things are bothering her. To maintain dependence, she will tend to admire and accommodate to and be responsive to the needs of other people. She prefers to play an inferior role to accomplish this, and she often looks for situations to feel useful, sympathetic, strong, and competent. She actively solicits praise. Harmony with others is very important to her even at the expense of deeper values or beliefs. She is quite unassertive. She has little sense of her own identity because she spends most of her time trying to please others and gain their approval. She values herself in terms of the persons to whom she is attached. She feels most comfortable when she feels that the bonds with others are unshakable. She seems quite sensitive to hostility from others and does everything she can to minimize the danger of their disapproval. When faced with responsibility; she feels helpless. She becomes depressed when she is afraid of the loss of dependency. She will display guilt, illness, anxiety, and depression to deflect criticism and to transform threats of disapproval into support.

Clinically she may show distressing phobias, indecisiveness about tiny matters, acute physical discomfort, insomnia, muscular tightness, headaches, tremors, and cold sweating. She can feel pessimistic about the future.

She would probably be seen as a *Generalized Anxiety Disorder* (300.02) with a possible secondary diagnosis of *Dysthymic Disorder* (300.40).

She has probably long had a dependent personality disorder.

The major personality features herein described reflect long-term or chronic traits that are likely to resist resolution. Therapeutically, Ms. Mullen will welcome the opportunity to form rapid therapeutic identification. This will create the impression of rapid progress. It will be extremely difficult for the therapist to terminate the relationship. Developing independence will be very difficult.

Summary

Psychological evaluation of Ms. Ruth Mullen, her background, her history, and previous professional reports indicates that she is a young woman of limited intellectual endowment and current function. She falls at the Borderline level, although this seems to vary to some extent. She demonstrates neuropsychological deficit in a variety of areas. She has limited academic achievement as well as limited academic potential. She shows poor aptitude for trade training. She has had some modest success in domestic activities and in service-sales. She suffers moderate emotional distress and a fairly severe dependency state.

Possible Causes or Contributing Factors to the Current Conditions

1. There are indications that Ms. Mullen had difficulties at birth that could well have led to neuropsychological dysfunction.

2. Her academic progress has been at best borderline, and could well reflect the difficulties noted in Item 1 or perhaps Item 3.

3. Ms. Mullen may have some inherent genetic limitations. Neither of her parents demonstrated very extensive educational or intellectual attainments. Her speech patterns, which are characteristic of mild articulation disorder, are very similar to her mother's.

4. Ms. Mullen sustained a brain injury at age 18 which required neurosurgery. Some of her current condition might be attributable to this.

5. There is no way that her current condition can be solely attributed to her recent accident. The consistency of intellectual performance over a period of years, as well as the obvious difficulty in matters involving reading, arithmetic functions, and other academic ventures, suggests that there has always been some neuropsychological deficit. To attribute her current condition to the recent accident would require a very marked difference in her state and status before and after the examination. Such a difference is only suggested in terms of her emotional response and some limited neuropsychological dysfunctions. There is evidence that the personality is such that many of the symptoms would emerge to demonstrate and enhance the very strong dependency needs that were found.

Recommendations

1. I believe that Ms. Mullen would profit from supportive psychological and psychiatric care.

2. Anything that can be done to prepare Ms. Mullen through training for a service-sales occupation at a rather basic level with strong support and supervision would probably be helpful. She might consider domestic service, since she has demonstrated interest and skill in this area.

3. She would probably profit from simple, straightforward social skills training.

This report clearly indicates the importance of retrieving early records where estimates of psychological deficit must be made following an accident. In this instance, both Drs. Surt and Flack assumed Ms. Mullen had at least average intellectual capacity before the accident. Close examination of school records indicated that the assumptions made by Drs. Surt and Flack were inaccurate, rendering their findings questionable.

The courts have had and continue to have mixed responses to the limits of admissibility of psychological testimony. This is particularly true where the expert is testifying about neuropsychological test data. For example, in Florida and a number of other states, appellate courts have ruled that the neuropsychological expert may testify as to the presence of brain deficit but the psychologist's opinion as to the proximate cause of the damage as well as the long-range consequences is inadmissible (Schwartz, 1987). In other jurisdictions the courts allow more leeway and jurisdictional choice in allowing broader opinions by psychological experts.

Recently a state court judge in Washington, in the course of a personal injury trial, opined that the results obtained from a fixed neuropsychological battery (Halstead-Reitan) were more scientifically objective under the *Daubert* rules (see Chapter 5) than opinions based on a flexible battery.[1] This decision emphasizes the importance of expert witnesses maintaining rigorous scientific standards in presenting their opinions in the legal arena (Landsman, 1995; J. Reed, 1996).

Expert opinions by qualified neuropsychologists will play an increasingly prominent role in the evidentiary phases of personal injury litigation not only because brain injury and consequent behavioral dysfunction are key issues in so much of personal injury litigation but because instrumentation and scientifically sound research in neuropsychology are developing rapidly. To cite some examples, neuropsychologists have studied the delayed neurobehavioral sequelae of traumatic brain injury, reporting that traumatic brain injury increases the risk of late occurring effects by factors of 5 or 10 for depression, 2 to 5 for psychotic disorders, and 4 to 5 for seizures (Gualtieri & Cox, 1991). Paniak and his colleagues (Paniak, Shore, & Rourke, 1989) have reported on the recovery of memory after severe closed head injury. Brooks and his research associates (Brooks, McKinlay, Symington, Beattie, & Campsie, 1987) have studied return to work within the first 7 years following severe head injury. They found that employment role had dropped from 86% before injury to 29% years later. Such research findings from well-designed studies and especially when replicated (Wehman et al., 1989) supply the expert witnesses with substantial support for their opinions.

Attorneys are more than ever before aware that expert neuropsychological testimony can aid juries in understanding the subtle as well as obvious behavioral effects of brain damage (Schutte & Howell, 1997). Neuropsychologists can be very effective experts in explaining the neuropsychological abilities and deficits of children who are plaintiffs in personal injury cases (Dennis, 1989).

Bereavement and Wrongful Death

The survivors or the estate of an individual who dies as a result of the negligent or wrongful activities of a person or corporation may seek remedy as the injured party or plaintiffs in civil litigation. In addition to the usual approaches of determining the monetary value of what the deceased may have earned in his or her lifetime, the statutes make provision for recovery or compensation for pain, suffering, bereavement, and loss of *consortium* (the benefits of the deceased person's company) experienced by surviving members of the deceased's family. Psychologists may be called on to testify as to the intellectual, academic, or achievement potential of the deceased. This testimony would be based primarily on an examination of school and other records. In issues of bereavement, evaluation of the significant survivors is also part of the assessment by the psychologist in order that an opinion may be rendered as to bereavement effects.

Bereavement effects can be measured by applying well-known, standardized psychological assessment procedures. Shneidman (1978) had reported that the effects of a tragic death can be extensive, even devastating, on survivors; others report similar findings (Fulconer, 1942; Glick, Weiss, & Parkes, 1974). These effects can be long-term (Lehman, Wortman, & Williams, 1987).

Intake Interview.   During the initial interview with the attorney seeking expert consultation, the psychologist should ask for the facts of the case and other basic information, very much as indicated in the accidental-injury type of case presented at the beginning of this chapter. The intake sheet (Chapter 4) would be completed in the usual way.

Of special importance in a bereavement case is a complete list of all family members who are likely to have suffered, or will suffer in the future, as a result of the tragic death. At this point, the psychologist should indicate to the attorney the number of evaluations that are likely to be necessary to identify the extent of bereavement among the surviving family members. Since this can mean an extensive set of evaluations and considerable expense, practical issues of time, availability of family, and likely cost should be discussed during the initial conference. It is important to recommend at this time that all significant family members receive complete physical examinations since the survivors of a tragic death seem much more at risk for development of a serious medical condition than they might be without the stress of the tragic loss (Holmes & Masuda, 1973; Petrich & Holmes, 1977; Rahe, 1972).

The Assessment Process.   After all records and other background information have been evaluated, the psychologist should plan a complete assessment of each significant family member likely to be affected by the tragic loss. The assessment will ordinarily be a basic psychological evaluation, consisting of history, interview, assessment of intellect, neuropsychological screening, and personality assessment. The procedures should all be conducted within the guidelines for assessment detailed in Chapters 4 and 6.

Reporting Findings.   Preliminary results and opinions should be reported to the attorney by telephone, as suggested previously. At this point, the results may suggest additional assessment (neurological or medical evaluation, vocational assessment for a surviving spouse, and so on). After all evaluations are complete, the report is written and forwarded to the retaining attorney. The following bereavement report illustrates some of the procedures described in this section.

BEREAVEMENT EVALUATION

January 3, 1989

NAME: Murtrey (Mr. George, Mrs. Rae, Ms. Alice)

DATE OF EXAMINATION: 1/3/89

ADDRESS: 2314 Oak St., Ocala, Florida   TELEPHONE: 000-0000

BIRTHDATE:	AGE:	EDUCATION:	OCCUPATION:
H—4/10/48	40-10	12	Electrician
W—11/12/48	39-2	12+	Housewife
D—12/17/71	17	11	Student

Referral

John B. Grandly, Esquire, of this city, refers the Murtrey Family. On the 14th of July, 1988, a pickup truck in which Colleen Murtrey and Alice Murtrey, daughters of Mr. and Mrs. Murtrey, were riding was struck by a train. Colleen, 15, was killed at that time, while Alice was injured as was the driver of the vehicle, the maternal grandmother, Mrs. Harcourt. The purpose of this evaluation is to determine whether there is any psychological evidence of residual bereavement as a result of the tragic death.

Evaluation Procedures

Family Interviews, Interviews with each member of the family separately, Minnesota Multiphasic Personality Inventory, Thematic Apperception Test, Draw-a-Person Series, Sentence Completion, Wechsler Adult Intelligence Scale-Revised Subtests, Wechsler Memory Scale, Observation, Family History.

Initial Family Contact

An entire day was set aside for the bereavement evaluation. Mr. and Mrs. Murtrey and Alice Murtrey were brought to our clinic at 8:00 A.M., January 3, by James Cowley, Esquire, and introduced. The initial hour was spent in determining how comfortable the family would be and trying to make them as comfortable as possible for the evaluation. The time of the accident was discussed briefly and the conditions under which the two girls were visiting their grandparents at that time. The week previous to the tragic incident was reviewed with the family. Discussion of the family patterns; eating habits, religious preference, leisure-time activities, and general style of life was developed during this initial interview. All members of the family were found to be cooperative. The remainder of the day was spent in alternately examining individual members of the family and conducting subsequent individual interviews. A final family interview was completed, and this constituted the evaluation. Each member of the family was given approximately seven hours of psychological evaluation.

Interviews

MR. GEORGE MURTREY

This is the first tragic death experience for Mr. Murtrey. He himself was born and raised in Krelltown, Tennessee, and his parents are both living and well. He was one of six children. He works as an electrician, and the family income he brings in is about $26,000 a year. They are buying their own home. He has no hobbies but enjoys family things. He reads the newspapers and watches TV. Most of his leisure activity is focused on camping and fishing. Since Colleen's death, they have not done any camping.

He is under the care of Doctor Chalmers. His last physical examination was in August, and he is in good health. No illness since the tragic death.

He smoked until two years ago, and he drinks beer. He sleeps well. He had early dreams about Colleen, but they stopped after about six months. After the accident he thought of her every day, but recently his thoughts are on Colleen only two or three times a week. The family talks occasionally about her.

The effect on him of this tragic death, in his opinion, includes the idea of death itself, missing Colleen as part of the family, and feeling that the closeness has been disrupted. He is not sure how his life has really changed as a result of Colleen's death, but feels it's something that could happen to anyone. He feels that his wife is the person most affected by the tragic death.

MRS. RAE MURTREY

Mrs. Murtrey was born in Krelltown, Tennessee. Both of her parents are still living. She has experienced no tragic death previously. She feels her mother, who was driving the truck that was hit by the train, was severely affected by the death. Her mother is seeing a psychiatrist in Tampa.

Mrs. Murtrey has been studying genealogy, enjoys music, and at one time liked camping. The family can't seem to do it since Colleen died. She doesn't want to repeat those activities where they were all together.

The family are regular churchgoers, and they attend the Baptist Church in Krelltown. All go on Sunday, and the women go on Wednesday night.

Mrs. Murtrey has always worked with children, but after Colleen's death she had to stop working with younger children, because she simply couldn't go camping. It reminded her of her time with Colleen.

Sometimes she gets close to accepting Colleen's death but feels that other times that she can't. Since Colleen's death she has had an odd eating pattern where she will avoid eating and then go on eating binges. She has gained 80 pounds since Colleen died. She has found that she has been unable to cook supper after Colleen's death, since Colleen used to "bounce in" to the home at 4:30 very hungry and mother would cook something for her. The family used to have a definite pattern of eating, with supper at the kitchen table. No one eats at the kitchen table now because it reminds the mother of Colleen. They tried to change Colleen's bedroom furniture two weeks after her death, but any furniture that the mother associates with Colleen is disturbing.

Mrs. Murtrey has found herself seriously withdrawn sexually from her husband since the death of Colleen. She will cry suddenly. She feels she has not been happy since Colleen died. She feels that a lower section of her heart has been ripped out and can identify this as the lower left quadrant of her heart. She says she is searching for someone who can tell her why she has this very specific response.

She is not aware of being depressed, although the doctor has told her she is. She feels she is fine until people bring up Colleen, and then she cries. She cries when she is in the house. Christmas has been particularly difficult, because they did not hang up a stocking for Colleen.

Since Colleen's death, Mrs. Murtrey has been under the care of Doctor Kane and Doctor Chalmers. They found she had thyroid problems. She was in the hospital last month. She had a biopsy for a mass in the breast, but it was benign. She is out of balance in her thyroid, and she is anemic. She has had urinary infections. Her cervix will be cauterized soon. The anemia and infections have all occurred since Colleen's death. She has never had this sort of trouble before.

She takes thyroid medication and vitamins. She has had only two dreams of her daughter, and she doesn't dream now. She believes there are meanings to her dreams.

Ms. Alice Murtrey

Born in Krelltown, Alice is in high school and says that she likes it quite a bit. She is a member of the French and Latin Club. She loves to play the piano and do crafts. She collects miniature figures. She states that she doesn't like to read. She likes physical activities, such as rollerskating, swimming, volleyball, fishing, tennis, and paddle ball. She has a boyfriend, but they don't really date.

She is under the care of Doctor Frank Lane. He is concerned about her weight, but she has always been thin. She has had occasional dreams about

Colleen. She feels they were very close, and they always did things to-gether. She is lonely without her sister. She has become "sort of quiet" since her sister's death.

She finds that she is bothered when going over a railroad track. She finds herself overly cautious and watchful. She finds she is very responsive when other people are depressed or hurt. She denies being upset emotionally about her sister's death at the present time. She states that it helped her rather than bothered her. She feels it brought her closer to God. It hurts her that her sister is not around, but she is willing to accept it as the way it is and feels that she cannot change things. She has been praying more since Colleen's death and attends church regularly. She denies that the death bothers her at the present time. She still thinks of Colleen once or twice a week, the things they did, and the good times they had together. She be-lieves the mother is having the hardest time accepting Colleen's death.

Summary of Interviews

The Murtreys look very much like bereaved families. They all superficially accept Colleen's death and are trying to make adjustments. There are some permanent residual difficulties even though it has been almost 18 months since the death. They avoid their family activity—camping—because it re-minds them of Colleen. From the clinical point of view, it seems that Mrs. Murtrey is suffering the most severe bereavement reaction and is able to show some of it. The next most severe reaction is being suffered by Alice, although this is almost entirely repressed and could become a dangerous situation in the future. Mr. Murtrey seems to be tolerating the tragic death the best of the three family members.

Results of Psychological Evaluation

MR. GEORGE MURTREY

A. *Response to Evaluation*

Mr. Murtrey is a man of average height and weight with dark hair. He shows little emotional expression. He speaks in a clear, rapid voice. Hear-ing is within normal limits, and motor behavior is controlled. He jokes oc-casionally as he becomes comfortable. He seems to avoid spontaneity. He was cooperative throughout.

B. *Personality Structure*

1. *Interpersonal Activity.*   Mr. Murtrey is a person who focuses his life on his home and his children. His interests in child rearing and home life are greater than the average male. He is seen by others as ambitious and persevering. He is known for having common sense. He is rather quiet and

passive, although he attempts to be helpful when he can. His basic values are simple and rather rigid. He likes children. He can be quite stubborn. He is what would be called a fairly traditional person who is intolerant of unconventional beliefs.

2. *Sources of Anxiety.* In general, Mr. Murtrey is most anxious about matters that require decisions. He is fearful of risks and prefers an orderly life. He has a great deal of difficulty exposing his feelings. He likes things to be "the way they usually are" and is uncomfortable with new things. He realizes that he is rather passive, and he worries about it sometimes. He has a hard time doing things just for himself.

In respect to the tragic death, he is very anxious about revealing bitterness. He tries to hide this. He feels that perhaps in some vague way he was not a good enough father, which may have in some way been associated with the occurrence of the tragic death. He doesn't necessarily feel at a deep level that he caused it, but perhaps it is a punishment for not having done all he could have for his family.

3. *Outlets for Anxiety.* Intellectual outlets in dealing with anxiety include the need to appear controlled, passivity, subtle criticalness, usually in a joking form, and suppression of a lot of feeling. He relieves a lot of anxiety by being dependent on his wife and children. His work occupies much of his tension and relieves stress. He achieves much satisfaction and balance through family ties. When anxious, he usually blames himself first. Strong emotional feelings are denied. He deals with the tragic death through these defenses as well as a tendency to externalize and see death as inevitable.

C. Adjustment to the Tragic Death

1. *External.* Mr. Murtrey accepts the death as having happened, denies emotional response, avoids interaction about it when possible, but passively goes along when it appears.

2. *Internal.* Mr. Murtrey uses the mechanisms of denial, in turning his bitterness inward, as well as "accepting the inevitable." He has some guilt feelings which vaguely connect him with his daughter's death, thinking he was in some way not "good enough."

3. *Quality of the Bereavement Response.* Mr. Murtrey would be ranked as 1 on a scale of 0 to 4 for current response to the tragic death. He has not completely recovered, without residuals, but has recovered considerably with only a sporadic bereavement reaction. He is functional in the usual everyday responses of living.

4. *Prediction.* At the present time, Mr. Murtrey seems to be doing fairly well. His eventual adjustment is going to be highly dependent on the reactions of his wife and his surviving daughter in the future, since he is so thoroughly dependent on his family for his own adjustment.

MRS. RAE MURTREY

A. Response to Evaluation

Mrs. Murtrey is a tall, obese, cheerful woman with gray/brown hair. Her speech is clear and hearing is within normal limits. Motor behavior is controlled. She socializes in an open but subtly angry and tense manner. Cooperation is good. She apparently has a very strong need to ventilate.

B. Personality Factors

1. *Interpersonal Activity.*   Mrs. Murtrey suffers a chronic and intense anger that she is unable to express openly. In dealing with people she is sociable and has a strong need to be the center of attention and to be appreciated. She has strong emotions and can be volatile. The family is important, and she expects it to represent her, particularly her children. Although she is seen as a conformist, her ideas are quite different from the average person. She tends to be watchful and dominant. She is controlling her impulses but having great difficulty with this. Her deep and bitter feelings tend to emerge in sudden spurts. She is desperately busy doing many different things.

2. *Anxiety Structure.*   Mrs. Murtrey internally is full of anxiety and explosiveness. She is very fearful of being wrong, being rejected, or being guilty of anything. The daughter's death has instigated an enormous amount of anxiety about her own worth. Her defense against her loss is to be angry and enraged. She is terribly fearful of anger and rage and therefore represses it. She has great fear of losing control and being destructive. She had an intense dependency interaction with her youngest child, and this loss has devastated her. Since she is terribly concerned with how she appears to others, she hides these deep anxieties.

3. *Outlets.*   Intellectual defenses are beginning to deteriorate. She uses mechanisms of denial, holding in, suppression, and compulsive concern about tiny details to hold in anxiety. She leads a life of busy desperation trying to hold down her real feelings. She swallows her anger and her resentment. Her expressions of anger are passive, indirect, or humorous. She is a severely overcontrolled person. She may experience brief efforts of anger or explosiveness, but to date they are fairly mild. She is growing much pickier and much more suspicious than she has ever been in her life.

Her primary mechanism of dealing with her deep anxieties is repression. She is not even aware of how violently angry and resentful she is. She has turned much of her stress and anxiety into overeating, and she has an obesity syndrome where she has somatized her anxiety. Additional ways of dealing with anxiety include sexual dysfunction and a tendency to distort the world.

As her defenses fail, one can expect suicide potential to be activated, and one can expect acting out through fugue episodes, dissociation, violence, or psychotic episodes. Although Mrs. Murtrey seems pretty well compensated on the surface, she is a deeply disturbed person.

C. Adjustment to the Tragic Death

1. *External.* Externally Mrs. Murtrey is the family leader, energetic, concerned with church work and other projects. She is severely overcontrolled. She has occasional expressions of sudden lability.

2. *Internal.* Mrs. Murtrey is severely disturbed, with anxiety and resentment growing and opportunities for expression decreasing. Her rage is both suppressed and repressed. She is becoming more dangerously explosive. Her guilt is becoming intolerable. She has somatized much of this and has moved into an obesity syndrome. Her adjustment is extremely precarious, and her external defenses are just barely controlling the internal explosiveness.

3. *Quality of Adjustment.* I would rate Mrs. Murtrey 4 on a scale of 0 to 4 with 0 being complete recovery from the effects of the tragic death with no dysfunction and 4 being where she would be considered debilitated, dysfunctional, continuing in the bereavement reaction, and in danger of more severe reactions.

4. *Prediction.* Unless Mrs. Murtrey is given immediate and extensive treatment, and a great deal of support, as well as opportunity to externalize the guilt and resentment, we can expect some explosive episode which might take the form of a dissociation or a fugue. Violence either internalized or externalized, possibly in connection with a psychotic episode, should be considered a real possibility.

Ms. Alice Murtrey

A. Response to Evaluation

Ms. Murtrey is a tall young woman of about 5 feet 6 inches in height. She weighs about 100 pounds. She has green eyes and brown/auburn hair. She chews gum intensely. She speaks in a clear manner and is quite loquacious. Hearing seems within normal limits, although occasionally she misunderstands directions. She is fidgety, socializes pleasantly, and is quite cooperative.

She talks about going to nursing school after high school. She hopes to marry and have children. Her primary interest is in helping others in the future.

B. Personality Factors

1. *Interpersonal Activity.* The external picture of Ms. Murtrey's personality is that of a youngster who tries to be too perfect and do the right

things all the time. She tends to be idealistic, seems mature to others, and tends to be popular. People see her as honest, peaceable, and persevering. Her values are traditional and rather rigid. Most people see her as a serious person, conscientious, who always tries to put on a good face. She can be somewhat Pollyannaish.

2. *Anxiety Structure.*   Ms. Murtrey has the usual anxieties about the future, her role as a woman, and others' expectations for her. Her greatest fear is that of committing herself to a particular course in the future. On the one hand she would like to be independent, seek a career, and "do good in the world." On the other hand she has a mutual dependency interaction with her mother that has been made very strong and intense by the loss of her sister. She feels her mother needs her and that she may be useful to the mother. By maintaining this close interaction with the mother, her own dependency needs are met, and it is unnecessary for her to make decisions.

She is very frightened of expressing feelings. She is fearful of asking questions and clarifying her own anxieties. She has great trouble competing with other females. She feels the expression of any kind of anger is forbidden, and she is frightened of her own anger.

3. *Outlets.*   Some of her intellectual defenses include doing her best to appear well adjusted and helpful in every situation. She truly believes how you look is more important than the way you feel. She focuses a great deal on religion to relieve tension. She is very close and dependent on the mother. She withdraws from pressure or risks. Some of her anxieties are expressed in hyperactivity. She tends to be drawn to dependent males because she feels useful. She denies her fear of anger, and rationalizes, seeing almost everything as "God's will" or "That's the way it is." She tries to keep busy and work at many different things in order to relieve anxiety. Her prime focus is helping others.

Less intellectual defenses include a very rich fantasy life about which she feels somewhat guilty, a proneness to anniversary reactions of depression, an inwardly gloomy picture about the future, occasional subtle cries for help, and the avoidance of really close relationships. Both repression and denial are primary mechanisms of defense against anger.

She is likely to make a choice soon between marriage, which will give her a strong defense of dependency, and a career, which will allow a defense of "doing for others." She will probably give up the career idea in order to be close to the mother if the mother needs her. This suggests that one of her choices will be an early marriage to someone in her "home town" in order to maintain dependency and closeness to the mother.

C. *Adjustment to the Tragic Death*

1. *External.*   The primary reaction to her sister's death by Alice is denial. She sees it as over and done with, and she has pushed it away.

2. *Internal.*   Her dependency on her mother has tightened, and her degree of adjustment is quite dependent on the degree to which the mother needs her. She does feel guilty and anxious about her sister's death, but this is well hidden. If her mother adjusts well, her internal reaction will be seeking a career to help others.

3. *Quality of Adjustment.*   I would consider Ms. Murtrey to be adjusted at a level of 2 on a scale of 0 to 4, where 2 would represent recovery from extreme reaction to the death and functional performance at the present time. She experiences regular bereavement reactions on an internal basis, with a tendency for these to be periodic and based on anniversaries. I would consider her partially recovered but still experiencing stress.

4. *Prediction.*   The quality of the continued adjustment to her sister's death is going to be heavily dependent on the mother's adjustment. If the mother resolves her enormous tension, it is likely that Alice will go on to balance her deeper anxieties by seeking a career and denying her anger by doing things for others. If the mother continues to be deeply distressed, it is likely that Alice will give up her career, seek an early marriage, and remain near home in order to be of help.

Summary and Recommendations

Bereavement evaluation of Mr. George Murtrey, Mrs. Rae Murtrey, and Ms. Alice Murtrey indicates that indeed the entire family has suffered from the tragic death of Colleen Murtrey which occurred almost a year and a half ago. The most severe reaction is taking place internally for Mrs. Rae Murtrey. Both Mr. George Murtrey and Ms. Alice Murtrey have accommodated to the death, and their bereavement is sporadic and does not interfere with their ability to be functional. They are, however, both intensely dependent on Mrs. Murtrey, and if her precarious adjustment fails, both of them will likely be thrown into a very intense anxiety reaction and will become dysfunctional. The following recommendations seem appropriate:

1. The first order of business is immediate, intense support and crisis intervention for Mrs. Murtrey. Competent mental health professionals who are experienced with bereavement reactions should be contacted, and early appointments scheduled. It is likely that there will be a need for intensive work for a period of 6 months to a year.
2. Family sessions with Mrs. Murtrey, Mr. Murtrey, and Alice should be scheduled on a once-a-month basis for the next six months. The degree to which these are successful will be to some extent dependent on the success of Mrs. Murtrey in individual therapy.
3. Alice Murtrey should have some individual vocational/personal counseling sessions to help her work through the painful dependent/independent pressures that are going to develop in the next year.

4. All members of the family should have regular physical examinations every 6 months for the next 18 months. The research suggests that in 70% of families where there has been a tragic death, another member dies within an 18-month to 2-year period following the tragedy. Mrs. Murtrey seems the most probable candidate for this danger at the present time, and medical supervision is urgent.

Prognosis is guarded. A lot depends on the success of the intervention with Mrs. Murtrey. I would consider that this family is suffering a moderate to severe bereavement reaction on the basis of the tragic death they have experienced in their family. The effects are likely to continue for several years. Final outcomes will be very dependent on the success of treatment and the avoidance of further tragedy, particularly in respect to Mrs. Murtrey.

References

Abraham, K. (1927). *Selected papers of K. Abraham*. London: Hogarth Press.

Becker, H. (1933). The sorrow of bereavement. *Journal of Abnormal and Social Psychology, 27,* 391–410.

Britchnell, J. (1970). Early parent death and mental illness. *British Journal of Psychiatry, 116,* 307.

Doyle, N. (1972). *The dying person and the family* (Public Affairs Pamphlet No. 485). New York: Public Affairs Committee.

Eliot, T. B. (1932). The bereaved family. *Annals of the American Academy of Political and Social Sciences, 160,* 184–190.

Fulconer, D. M. (1942). *The adjustive behavior of some recently bereaved spouses*. Doctoral dissertation, Northwestern University.

Glick, I. O., Weiss, R. S., & Parkes, C. M. (1974). *The first year of bereavement*. New York: Wiley.

Grollman, E. A. (1967). *Explaining death to children*. Boston: Beacon Press.

Hagin, R. A., & Corwin, C. G. (1974). Bereaved children. *Journal of Clinical Psychology, 3(2),* 39–40.

Hilgard, J. R., et al. (1959). Strength of adult ego following childhood bereavement. *American Journal of Psychiatry, 30,* 788–798.

Lindemann, E. (1944). The symptomatology and management of acute grief. *American Journal of Psychiatry, 101,* 141–148.

Marris, P. (1958). *Widows and their families*. London: Routledge & Kegan Paul.

Maurer, A. (1966). Maturation of concepts of death. *British Journal of Medical Psychology, 39,* 35–41.

Ogg, E. (1976). *A death in the family* (Public Affairs Pamphlet No. 542). New York: Public Affairs Committee.

Shneidman, E. S. (1978). *Voices of death*. New York: Bantam Books.

The inclusion of appropriate references is sometimes helpful in a report which is out of the ordinary experience of the referring attorney. Many attorneys who practice tort litigation want to become more familiar with the available research associated with the case at hand and such references are usually appreciated.

Malpractice

When the services of a professional person in some way cause pain, loss, embarrassment, or other conditions considered to be a result of negligence, fraud, deceit, misrepresentation, or willful misconduct, the aggrieved party may institute litigation to recover damages. Sometimes psychologists are called on to testify as experts in usual and acceptable standards of care or ethics in psychological procedures or services.

The psychological expert is also likely to be called on to evaluate the psychological effects of an alleged malpractice. Specific examples would be cases where someone allegedly suffers brain damage as a result of improper or insufficient intubation procedures by an anesthesiologist during surgery or claimed loss of intellect as a result of seizures caused by improper medication. In such cases, psychologists are generally asked to examine a plaintiff and indicate whether psychological deficits are found, to what degree they are found, and whether such findings can be ascribed to the alleged malpractice.

In recent years, litigants have begun to claim damages for psychological distress or posttraumatic stress syndromes based on alleged professional misconduct. The claim may be the result of situations where the plaintiff was forgotten, left untreated, or subjected to an operation later found to be unnecessary or to other conditions representing malpractice.

Charges of sexual misconduct by a professional person are being filed more frequently than ever before by plaintiffs who claim injury and loss as a result of the professional's alleged improper attention. In such cases, "psychic trauma" or consequent psychological anguish and disturbance are commonly cited as the effects for which compensation is sought. Psychologists, together with other mental health professionals, are frequently sought as experts to define the presence and extent of the claimed deficits.

Intake Interview.   In ascertaining the purpose of the psychological consultation during the initial interview with the attorney, the psychologist should try to get the attorney to be as specific as possible as to the effects claimed by the plaintiff as a result of the alleged malpractice. Whether the attorney who contacts the psychologist represents the plaintiff (the party claiming injury) or the defendant (usually the accused professional's insurance company), the psychologist can expect a fairly strong, possibly biased account of what supposedly happened and the residual effects of that happening. Such statements as "He was psychologically devastated by the experience" or "We think she's faking" are not uncommon. The psychologist should do everything possible to clarify, in measurable terms, what kind of deficits are being claimed by the plaintiff.

Assessment. The nature of the assessment in a malpractice case will depend on the nature of the alleged injury and the effects of the malpractice. The most frequent type of referral received by psychologists is for evaluation of a plaintiff who claims loss of function as a result of improper treatment or care. In such cases, the assessment is similar to accident cases for which the attorney seeks an opinion as to the nature and extent of psychological deficit to be found in the plaintiff and the extent to which the deficit may be considered a result, direct or indirect, of the alleged malpractice. Assessment procedures, instruments, and focus are similar to those cases described previously.

In some malpractice cases, the psychologist is asked to serve as an expert in "usual standards of care." The psychologist may be called on to render an opinion as to proper assessment procedures, the accepted standards for psychotherapy practice, issues involving duty to warn, and so on. In such cases, the assessment may require interviews with the accused professional, as well as examination of records and depositions. Before accepting such a consultation, the psychologist should be sure he or she possesses the experience and resources for information necessary to judge the behavior and performance of a coprofessional. A thorough familiarity with state licensing requirements, state and national codes of ethics, standards for delivery of professional services, and appropriate state and federal statutes, which may be involved in the issues at hand, is mandatory.

Reporting Findings. Guidelines for reporting that have been outlined in previous sections are applicable here. The psychologist should avoid making any value judgments concerning guilt, innocence, or liability in malpractice suits. Answering hypothetical questions as clearly, accurately, and succinctly as possible is the expert's job.

Where the psychologist functions as an expert in professional standards and ethics, the written report should be directed to the referring attorney (or, in some cases, a judge or an administrative master). The report should address the questions at issue, and copies of pertinent statutes, codes of ethics, and recommended professional standards should be appended to the report.

It is becoming less rare that a psychologist will be called to testify on standards of care in a malpractice suit. It is more likely that an assessment of the effects of the alleged malpractice will be the focus of the psychologist's assessment. The following report presents psychological findings in a medical malpractice suit in which the survivor's grief and bereavement was one aspect of the injuries claimed.

PSYCHOLOGICAL REPORT

September 9, 1978

NAME: Raul Perdida   DATE OF EXAMINATION: 8/21, 8/22/78

ADDRESS: 324 Mare St., Apt. 11,
          Cedar Grove, FL 33178

                                    TELEPHONE: 000-0000

BIRTHDATE: 3/11/49   AGE: 29-6   OCCUPATION: Broker

EDUCATION: 13

Referral

Mr. Perdida is referred by Edwin R. Won, Esquire. A psychological evaluation for the purpose of determining the impact upon his life caused by the untimely death of his wife is requested.

At the time Mr. Perdida and his wife, Maria, were married for approximately one year, she entered the Cedars Hospital in March 1977 for what was projected to be a normal delivery of their first child. During the delivery, it was decided that a cesarean section was necessary. This procedure was accomplished the following day, at which time Mrs. Perdida suffered severe hypoxia. The infant which was born, a female, suffered from brain damage due to hypoxia in the mother. On the day of the cesarean section, Mrs. Perdida went into coma (this was the day of their first wedding anniversary). Seven days later, after repeated negative brain scans, the life support system on Mrs. Perdida was disconnected by the County Medical Examiner, and she was pronounced dead. Mr. Perdida continues to grieve regularly as a result of these events.

Mr. Perdida was examined on August 21 for approximately three and one-half hours and on August 22 for approximately six hours. At that time, he stated that he sees his daughter every day. She lives with his parents. It is a painful experience for him. He always remembers the plans that he and his wife had. It's his worst time. Whenever he sees other families with their children being happy, he becomes deeply depressed. He is very bitter, wondering, "Why did this happen to me?" When he is home alone, he has a lot of memories. Anything that his wife gave him, such as a present or a piece of clothing or some music, when noticed, will ruin his day. He is very depressed. He is irritated. He is aggressive with people when it isn't their fault.

In the last few months, it has eased somewhat in the sense that it doesn't happen daily, but when it does happen, it is just as strong. He cried a great deal at the beginning, but he is crying less now.

He married his wife on April 29, 1976. He had known her for five and one-half years. He met her after he was in the service. He was 26 at the time of the marriage. The daughter, 16 months of age, is named Maria Elana after her mother. Mr. Perdida fulfills his obligation as a father, but each day is extremely painful to him.

Background Factors

Born in Havana, Mr. Perdida came to the United States when he was 11 years of age. His mother, 54, living and well, is a housewife. His father, 59, living and well, works at a gas station. Mr. Perdida attended Latimer School, and then Cedar Senior High School where he graduated. He spent some time at Cedar Junior College. He entered the U.S. Army at the age of 20 and spent two years as a clerk personnel specialist. He was discharged E-5. He spent four years in the Reserve.

Presently he works as a loan broker—specializing in commercial loans—at the Springs National Bank in Maitland.

Although he goes to movies and attends club meetings and eats out in restaurants, his social life is minimal. He prefers to read and listen to music. He tried to get out and do some boating as a result of some recommendations by a psychiatrist, but he stopped this.

He is trying to date and to see someone regularly, but he is not serious. He can't seem to form a relationship with anyone. He is continually comparing her with his dead wife. He is trying hard, but it has been difficult. He still has pictures of his wife in the house, and he will talk about her "perhaps too much."

He saw a psychiatrist for about a year, Doctor Alvarez. It was helpful to a certain point, and he did everything he could. At that time Mr. Perdida claimed strong suicidal tendencies, and he feels Doctor Alvarez helped him.

The sleep pattern is typical of deep grief reaction. There were many problems the first 9 to 12 months. He started taking some pills for sleep but felt this was bad for him, and he quit this. He usually goes to sleep sometime after 11:30 and wakes up about 7:30. Sometimes he wakes up in the middle of the night. He has many dreams about his wife and the life they would have had. He often dreams that she is not dead. He sometimes dreams that he found someone exactly like her. His dreams are repetitive.

The course of events in his life has given him a reality basis for an anniversary depression. In the March-April time sequence he has his own wedding anniversary, his father's birthday, his dead wife's birthday, his child's birthday, his wife's death, and the occurrence of a trauma causing a knee injury that prevented him from playing professional football anymore (this was his original career choice).

Examination Procedures

Wechsler Adult Intelligence Scale, Ammons Full Range Picture Vocabulary Test, Wonderlic Personnel Test, Vocational Guidance Summary, Wechsler

Memory Scale, Indiana-Reitan Neuropsychological Short Form, Depression Calendar, Hand Dynamometer Test, Rey 15 Symbols, Thematic Apperception Test, Quality of Life, Minnesota Multiphasic Personality Inventory, Draw-a-Person Test, Sentence Completion Test, Edwards Personal Preference Schedule, House-Tree Test, FIRO-B, History, Observation, and Interview.

Response to Evaluation

Mr. Perdida is a tall, well-built man with black hair. He dresses very well. He wears a mustache. He speaks in a soft voice, with Hispanic accent. His hearing is within normal limits. Motor behavior is controlled, and he is right-handed. He socializes in a polite, comfortable manner. He seems flat and depressed. He cooperates well. Confidence varies: He reports that he still often thinks in Spanish, making it difficult for him to take some tests where the directions are complex and in English.

Results of Examination

A. Intellectual Factors

Despite language barriers, Mr. Perdida falls within the High Average range of intellectual capacity. In comparison with his own normative group of high school graduates he falls at the 76th percentile. His best intellectual trait is verbal comprehension. He has significant lowering in attention span and ability to concentrate. Memory is significantly lowered also. These factors are associated with stress.

B. Neuropsychological Factors

Mr. Perdida's performance is within normal limits and is shown to be contraindicative of any central nervous system difficulty. The Rey Test 15-Item is performed within normal limits indicating no effort to "falsify bad."

C. Personality Factors

1. *Interpersonal Activity.*   At the first level of interpersonal activity, Raul Perdida showed a number of Need-Drives (above the 75th percentile for adult men) and Need-Avoidances (below the 25th percentile for the same group) as follows:

Need-Drives	Need-Avoidances
Exhibition	Orderliness
Intraception	Abasement
Heterosexuality	Change
Consistency	Endurance

The preceding pattern is characteristic of people who are strongly drawn to saying witty and clever things, talking about personal adventures, being the center of attention, having others notice and comment on appearance, and talking about personal achievements.

He prefers situations that require analyzing one's motives and feelings, observing others, trying to understand why people do what they do rather than simply what they do, putting oneself in another person's place, attempting to analyze the behavior of others, and predicting how they will act.

He favors being with members of the opposite sex, engaging in social activities with the opposite sex, being in love, participating in sexual activity, being regarded as physically attractive by the opposite sex, reading books about sex, and being sexually excited.

He prefers being consistent in the expression of needs.

People who show this pattern are most comfortable when they avoid having written work neat and organized, seldom making plans before starting out, have trouble keeping things neat and orderly, and rarely keep letters and files according to a system.

He dislikes feeling guilty when something goes wrong, accepting blame when things do not go right, feeling personal pain and misery beyond the point where it does any good, being drawn to punishment for wrongdoing, feeling better when punishment is given, preferring to give in rather than fight, tending to feel depressed by inability to handle situations, and feeling timid in the presence of superiors.

He is not comfortable doing new and different things, traveling, meeting people, breaking the daily routine, going to different places, participating in fads.

He does not like keeping at a job until it's finished, completing jobs undertaken, working at a task even though progress is slow, but excluding other extraneous demands until the job is finished, sticking to problems, and being interrupted while at work.

In dyadic interactions, Mr. Perdida is a very energetic and dynamic person. He is drawn to those who have a very strong need to exchange their inner ideas with him and to tolerate his expressing his inner thoughts. In the area of Control, he is drawn to a strong person who can guide and direct him. In the area of Affection he has a strong need to both give and to receive affection. It is a profile of overreaction and withheld feeling that is characteristic of bereavement profiles.

On the surface, Mr. Perdida attempts to express himself as "doing okay." He has a Quality of Life Index of 390. This is quite unusual in depressed persons, but the matter clarifies as we look at his Minnesota Multiphasic Personality Profile and we find that he has suppressed the depression, in favor of an agitation and stress reactions. He literally "keeps busy" to avoid and deny the deep feelings of bereavement and depression.

At a deeper interpersonal level, people see Mr. Perdida as a person who is loyal, is honest, has good manners, and is conscious of his status. He tends to be dependent and inwardly pessimistic. A cautious person, he is nevertheless desperate for friendship. He tends to be bitter about life and what it has dealt him.

2. *Early Identification.*   No distortions are noted here. Primary identification is with the father, who is seen as a quiet, industrious person very dependent on the wife. A person quite talented in practical matters. Admired. A sacrificing person who was not too much involved in raising children.

The mother is the love object. She is seen as a concerned, available person somewhat cautious and unsure of her own intellect. She is seen as having been a person who held in a lot of emotional feeling. Quite nourishing.

3. *Anxiety Structure.*   The deepest source of anxiety is the combination of guilt regarding his wife's death and the fear of risking future interactions. He feels that he caused his wife's death. At a deep and unconscious level he feels it should have been he that died. He has unconscious rage toward his child, feeling that the child should not have survived but rather that his wife should have survived.

Alone now, he fears that there will be no mate figure who could guide and direct him. He fears making any kind of attachment, expecting that he might be deserted again. He is still severely traumatized by the death of his wife.

His anxiety is stirred by feelings of loneliness and the inability to make close relationships in one-to-one interactions. A deep and abiding bereavement reaction has been found in the anxiety structure.

4. *Defense Structure.*   Intellectual defenses include a tendency to internalize his feeling, rigid attempts to control his life and show nothing of his real feelings, overcontrolled responses to his feelings of vengeance about his loss, and an intense attempt to "work" out his stress. All of this increases his stress. He tries to protect himself by expecting the worst in life, seeking strong supervisors to depend on, and trying to "make the best" out of anything that comes along.

His deep resentment of the surviving child is likely to come out very shortly. He is beginning to suffer an agitated depression where instead of seeming sad and withdrawn, he will not tolerate his excessive energies. He is beginning to somatize and is exceedingly prone to illness and accidents at the present time. The data on bereavement suggest that there is a strong chance that surviving members of a family in which there has been a tragic death may themselves die or become seriously ill within 18 to 24 months after the tragic death (Fulconer, 1942; Ogg, 1976; Shneidman, 1978).

He arranges to have nothing but superficial relationships with females in order to avoid the risk of potential involvement in further trauma in life.

Mr. Raul Perdida suffers a very severe grief reaction in response to his wife's death, and a consequent agitated depression.

Summary

Psychological evaluation of Mr. Raul Perdida indicates that he is a man of above-average intellectual capacity who has suffered a traumatic loss, and a consequent intense, acute, and chronic grief reaction. The following seem to be the direct results of the bereavement experience:

1. Mr. Perdida now has the personality structure that is liable to set him up for anniversary depressions of increasing severity.
2. His grief follows a pattern of severe bereavement, and under the best circumstances, he still is likely to experience one to three years of intense grieving.
3. There is evidence of lowered attention and memory as a result of the agitated depression.
4. There is a real and present danger that Mr. Perdida may suffer severe illness or even accidental death as a result of his grief reaction to his wife's tragic death.
5. He is beginning to somatize distress that has developed since the death of his wife, and this stress seems to be increasing. The rigid internalization is likely to lead to further agitation.
6. Because he is fearful of making relationships that will disappoint him, his basic dependency needs are not being met, increasing the probability that the grief will continue.
7. His experience of grief is intensified by self-blaming and resentment, much of which is hidden.

Recommendations

I believe that Mr. Perdida is in clear danger of suffering any one of a number of aftereffects of a severe bereavement response, including his own illness or death. The following recommendations seem urgent:

1. He must have a very complete physical evaluation immediately. This should be followed by physical evaluations at six-month intervals for the next three years.
2. He must immediately have some professional help to deal with the growing depression. This would include:
   a. Concentration on his feelings of self-blame.
   b. Evaluation of his inner feelings of blame toward his child.
   c. Fearfulness of trusting new dependency relationships.
   d. Agitation that comes from not having his dependency needs met.

    e. Importance of settling the grief work before marrying again.

    f. Medication where appropriate.

Mr. Perdida puts on a "good front." From a mental health point of view he is in very dangerous straits. Immediate help is needed and will be required for some time.

References

Becker, H. (1933). The sorrow of bereavement. *Journal of Abnormal and Social Psychology, 27,* 391–410.

Doyle, N. (1972). *The dying person and the family* (Public Affairs Pamphlet No. 485). New York: Public Affairs Committee.

Eliot, T. B. (1932). The bereaved family. *Annals of the American Academy of Political and Social Sciences, 160,* 184–190.

Fulconer, D. M. (1942). *The adjustive behavior of some recently bereaved spouses.* Doctoral dissertation, Northwestern University.

Glick, I. O., Weiss, R. S., & Parkes, C. M. (1974). *The first year of bereavement.* New York: Wiley.

Lindemann, E. (1944). The symptomatology and management of acute grief. *American Journal of Psychiatry, 101,* 141–148.

Marris, P. (1958). *Widows and their families.* London: Routledge & Kegan Paul.

Ogg, E. (1976). *A death in the family* (Public Affairs Pamphlet No. 542). New York: Public Affairs Committee.

Shneidman, E. S. (1978). *Voices of death.* New York: Bantam Books.

After completing the assessment, Mr. Won, the referring attorney, was called and a preliminary report rendered. Mr. Won was incredulous about the suggestion that Mr. Perdida might suffer physical manifestations of his grief. He pointed out to the psychologist that Mr. Perdida had been a professional football player, was only 29 years of age, and looked to be a "perfect physical specimen." The psychologist reviewed the grief and bereavement research with the attorney and urged him to arrange a complete physical examination for his client.

    A week later Mr. Won called and stated that the physician who examined Mr. Perdida found his blood pressure to be 185 over 120 and had begun treatment for hypertension. The psychological evaluation aided not only in a satisfactory legal settlement but in early identification of a potentially life-threatening illness.

Product Liability and Negligence

The psychologist is most likely to be called as an expert if a plaintiff claims a loss or disability of some kind that allegedly results from use of or exposure to the effects of a substance or piece of equipment causing loss, pain, or suffering. In this respect, most opinions sought from psychologists are concerned with psychological deficit. These cases differ little from those where a person is injured or affected by an accident or malpractice.

In other instances, a psychologist may be called on to render an opinion based on current scientific thinking, which in some way relates to the issue at hand. The issue may involve a product or service.

Intake Interview.   During the first interview with the referring attorney, the psychologist, as in all other cases, should ascertain very clearly what questions, in measurable behavioral terms, are going to be addressed by the psychologist's opinion. The hypothetical "Was this plaintiff caused any psychological injury, distress, or deficit as a result of the accident caused by the explosion of the defective gasoline tank in his car?" is quite clear and lends itself to psychological procedures, conclusions, and opinion. The question "Did this child become unsocialized and dangerous to herself and others because of her exposure to unrestrained violence presented on evening television?" is a much more vague, diffuse, and perhaps impossibly difficult question for a psychologist to address competently at our current stage of scientific understanding. A clear understanding of expectancies during the initial interview with the attorney is especially desirable in product liability cases.

Assessment.   If the product liability case involves alleged psychological effects on a plaintiff, the assessment procedures are similar to those used with an accident victim. The selection of tests and procedures is based on the nature of the questions concerning psychological deficit.

Should the psychologist be retained to render an opinion as to the nature and effect of a product, the approach follows procedures more identified with evaluation science than with professional clinical practice. Evaluation is the assessment of merit. Standards and procedures have been developed to guide evaluation studies (Rossi, 1982). Such evaluation reports are usually rendered by psychologists with a strong scientific background and evaluation resources and skills. Serious, in-depth literature review is often the primary assessment tool of such evaluations.

Reporting Findings.   If the case consultation involves a traditional assessment of psychological deficit, the report procedures differ little from accident cases. If evaluation of scientific issues is concerned, the product of the psychologist's work is an evaluation report that attempts to answer the referral question.

An evaluative report may review the literature and render an opinion as to the quality or effects of a product or a service. An example of this might be an experimental study of the sound characteristics of a particular siren and the range of human response to the warning device where this is a product liability issue. In issues that involve professional negligence (malpractice), the courts expect the professional to maintain a minimal standard of care. As an example, in a malpractice suit involving a patient's suicide, a lower court found a hospital and treating doctors not negligent in *Speer v. State*,[2] the appellate court of Connecticut reversed this decision finding that the intake history was inadequate to discover suicidal tendencies. They also found that the professional staff should have known of the patient's proclivity for suicide thus finding the defendants negligent, or guilty of malpractice for failure in standards of care. Although the law requires specific guidelines in matters such as the standards of care in suicide prevention, such standards are hard to come by. Berman and Cohen-Sandler (1983) surveyed 156 psychologists, psychiatrists, and social workers as to suicidal outcomes and standards of care and found considerable variance in what they accepted as adequate standards.

The following report was conducted in response to a request by attorneys for the estate of a plaintiff who committed suicide while awaiting professional help at a crisis center.

EVALUATION REPORT

In re: *Prentiss v. Armedia Health Centers*

Referral

This case is referred by Jack C. Smith, Esquire, of Smith, Baine and Wilson of Armedia. Mr. Smith states that Mr. Prentiss, while on his way from Atlanta to San Francisco, was removed from an airplane for inebriation. According to a police officer's report, Mr. Prentiss was brought from the airport to Central Intake, where he attempted to put a razor to his throat. Central Intake personnel transported Mr. Prentiss to Crisis Center at Armedia Hospital for psychiatric evaluation. There Mr. Prentiss was registered as a "volunteer patient." Apparently, he spoke briefly with the psychiatric resident and was told to wait. At that point, Mr. Prentiss apparently left the building, went outside, and hung himself with his belt.

Mr. Smith would like an evaluation of all records, and an opinion based on current and customary practice as well as research as to the appropriate professional responsibilities in the above situation.

Materials Provided

1. *Armedia Hospital Emergency Department Treatment Record*

Dated June 18, 1982, 10:30 P.M. Handwritten note. Signed by B. Carstair, M.D. States that Dr. Carstair asked the patient to sit in the lobby. About 10 minutes later, the staff were asked to find the patient and the staff looked around and did not find Mr. Prentiss in the immediate area. The staff went outside to look for the patient. The patient was found hanging from a tree outside in the parking lot, with a belt around his neck. Appropriate emergency medical procedures were instituted. Beneath Doctor Carstair's signature is the notation, "Reviewed by Doctor Farber, June 20, 1982."

2. Offense—Incident Report—Public Safety Department, Armedia County

A police report signed by Officer M. Browne (Badge No. 4267). Listed as Case No. 2376-B, Attempted Suicide. This report dated June 18, 1982 at 9:40 P.M. was in response to a call regarding a man who had hung himself with his own belt. The subject's name was listed as James Prentiss, with a birthdate of November 15, 1935. The officer reported that he responded to a 4-55 signal at the Crisis Center. The officer found a large crowd in the parking lot attempting to revive the subject Prentiss. Witness No. 1, Bill Kerr, an Armedia Hospital Security employee, stated that at approximately 9:45, an unknown female approached him at the Crisis Center stating that "a man is hanging in the tree out there." Kerr went to the man and found him kneeling. He felt for vital signs and finding none, he contacted PSD.

Witness No. 2, Mary Jones, employed at Crisis Intervention, stated that at approximately 9:45 P.M. an unknown patient came into the Crisis Center screaming, "There's a man hanging in the tree out there." Ms. Jones states that she and other staff members ran out of the Crisis Center and discovered subject Prentiss hanging from a branch of the tree with his knees on the ground and a belt around his neck. They observed Kerr standing over the subject. When they approached, Kerr said, "Don't touch him, I think he's dead, leave him for the police." Ms. Jones stated that she pushed Kerr aside and she and a nurse cut the belt from the subject's neck and gave CPR.

Witness Bill Font confirmed the above.

Witness Leroy Elvin confirmed the above, and states that he saw Jones and Font removing the belt from Prentiss's neck and he assisted them with CPR.

Sylvester Giff arrived after the belt was removed and gave mouth-to-mouth resuscitation.

Albert Goff, a medical student, arrived after CPR had begun, and he assisted in attempting to revive the subject.

Dr. Jane Brady arrived when Prentiss was on a stretcher under the tree. There was no blood pressure or pulse and Prentiss had dilated pupils. After some time, Brady was able to revive the victim, who was transported to the emergency room. Brady diagnosed considerable brain damage and possibly a broken neck. It was learned from Crisis's staff that the subject was brought from Armedia Airport to Central Intake because he appeared too drunk to continue his flight.

According to the Crisis staff, while at Central Intake the subject was found with a razor blade at his throat. Fearing for his safety, Intake personnel transported the subject to Crisis for a psychiatric evaluation. Crisis advised that the subject was clocked in as a voluntary patient but that he had not spoken with a psychiatrist.

3. Deposition—Ben Carstair, M.D.

Taken November 29, 1983. Dr. Carstair states that he is a psychiatrist at Armedia Hospital, Psychiatric Institute. He also has a private practice. Dr. Carstair states that in June 1980 he was in his second year of residency. He states, "He was never my patient—the only thing I did, I started intake." He indicated that he saw Mr. Prentiss on June 18, 1982. He states that he was intoxicated with alcohol. He was brought from Central Intake to the Crisis emergency room, and the person who brought him said that the patient, while at the airport, tried to cut his neck with a pocket knife. He states that the people from Central Intake wanted to know what the patient had to say. He does not remember a lot of the details.

Dr. Carstair says that the person in charge was Dr. Albert Rez. Part of the transcript is blurred, and it is impossible to read page 8. Dr. Carstair states that there was a man from Central Intake with them when they spoke originally. He says that the patient denied the situation and said, "I don't know what I did." There is some discrepancy in his report as to whether the man said, "I don't know what I did," or "I don't know why I did." Dr. Carstair states that he explained to the patient that he would have to be treated for a night to be able to continue his trip. The patient said that he was living in Atlanta, was married, with his wife in Atlanta. He states that 10 minutes later the patient disappeared from the area. He sent for him, and he was found hanging from a tree with a belt around his neck. When asked what he did after he first spoke to Mr. Prentiss, he says that he returned to his other patient and told Prentiss to wait to be seen later on. When asked if Mr. Prentiss was under observation by anybody else, he stated that he was a voluntary patient, so there was no reason to have anyone looking at him. He denies recalling whether he instructed any other staff member to keep an eye on Mr. Prentiss. He states that even though he was a resident, there was not another doctor supervising him at that moment.

Dr. Carstair says that the case was discussed with the staff, with Dr. Farber supervising. This was a mortality mobility meeting.

Dr. Carstair contradicts himself about what he heard from Mr. Prentiss in terms of his inebriation.

4. Deposition—Mary L. Jones

November 19, 1983. Taken by attorneys for the plaintiff in the presence of the attorney for the defendant. Ms. Jones states that she is employed at the

Armedia Hospital and has been there for 18½ years. She functions as a unit secretary. Her job is to do hospital records.

She does not remember a lot of details. Mr. Prentiss came to the psychiatric room. She does not recall how. She states that in 1982 the whole area was "voluntary." If a person walks in, they have a triage area. A person up front greets the individual with the question, "Why do you want to see the doctor?" They would then ask the person to have a seat, and someone else would come to get information about background and financial status. She states that there was no security area at that time; it was open. Her recall is relatively poor. She states that Central Intake is an alcohol detoxification place. She states that they receive patients from Central Intake regularly. She states that the Central Intake people bring a form with them when they turn over a patient.

Suicide Research

The importance of suicide in America today is measured by the large numbers of citizens, young and old, who take their own lives every day.

1.   *Characteristics of Those Who Commit Suicide*

Three-quarters of those who commit suicide had previously threatened or attempted to take their lives. All efforts or gestures toward suicide must be considered serious by those faced with such behavior. Suicidal behavior is most serious when it follows some sort of emotional crisis. The availability of professional psychiatric, psychological, and social work specialists for the treatment of a potentially suicidal person may mean the difference between life and death (Shneidman & Farberow, 1957).

Patients who have made suicide attempts and are entered into treatment have the highest suicide rate of any patient group (Shneidman, 1976).

Those who actually commit suicide generally do so during an acute suicidal crisis. This period is usually a matter of hours or days at most, and the individual is either helped, cools off, or dies. Eight out of 10 who kill themselves have given definite warnings of their suicidal intentions. To intervene and prevent a suicide, hospitals and crisis centers must provide good rapport, contact the patient's family, give emotional support, and focus on the reduction of lethality during the period of the suicidal crisis (Shneidman, 1973).

2.   *Dealing with Potentially Suicidal Patients*

It is a misjudgment professionally to classify a first act of self-injury as a purely manipulative gesture. This constitutes a warning and must not be ignored by mental health professionals. Any act of deliberately inflicted self-damage that looks like a suicide attempt, or serious efforts in this direction, ought to be regarded and treated as a serious venture (Worden, 1976).

Suicide risk is considerably increased when an individual is under the influence of alcohol. Professionals must be acutely tuned to inebriated patients who are overwhelmed by feelings of despair, fear, and uncertainty. As Kiev (1976) states:

> Many people, by virtue of their social class membership or life situation have ready-made explanations for their distress and as such, may not seek appropriate help and for this reason be considered at high risk. One such group is the patients who attempt suicide, are evaluated as non-serious and summarily discharged from emergency rooms.

Kiev goes on to state that the potentially suicidal patient may turn to excessive alcohol use to relieve despair. Professionals must recognize the emotional disturbance that underlies such behavior and be aware of the potential for suicidal behavior. Some individuals demonstrate their deep disturbance preceding suicidal behavior by being unable to adequately express ideas or by misunderstanding the ideas of others. In weighing the gravity of suicidal attempts, the professional should evaluate:

- The dangerousness of the attempt.
- Efforts to prevent assistance.
- Precipitating stresses.
- The use of alcohol.
- The patient's tendency to be impulsive.

Patients with the highest degree of impulsivity tend to be the most dangerous or lethal.

Good treatment consists of appropriate medication and a meaningful patient-therapist relationship. What counts most is warmth, sympathy, understanding, and orientation to reality. Crisis intervention is vital.

A patient who is obviously disturbed and shows defects in reasoning and deductive fallacies requires treatment that includes protecting the patient from his or her own impulses. Such a patient is the least predictable (Shneidman, 1960).

Many hospitals have specific, written, known security measures. An example from a California hospital follows:

SUICIDE PRECAUTIONS*

When a patient drops clues such as "life is no longer worth living, I caused the problems," alert yourself to observe patient further. Make your report

---

* Reprinted with permission from D. K. Reynolds and N. L. Farberow, *Suicide Inside and Out* (Berkeley: University of California Press, 1976).

to the nurse. If patient's doctor feels patient is contemplating suicide, he may write an order placing patient on Suicidal Status.

Your responsibility then would be:

1. To make the environment safe. Remove articles that could be harmful such as glass vase, ceramic ash tray, cords, etc. Replace with articles that are less harmful. Be alert to solutions kept in housekeeping cupboards; check equipment left out in treatment room; check bathroom and shower room. Use common sense. Remember, you could take everything away, and if a patient wanted to, he could still harm himself. Be alert to your window screens, that they are locked at all times.

2. To be alert to use of utensils in the dining room. Allow patient to use knife, fork, spoon, china plate, glass, etc., but observe his handling of them. If his actions indicate misuse, step forward and quietly put it back in place. Allow your patient to be as other patients. Don't leave suggestion that you expect him to harm himself. Most patients are ambivalent; they want to live and they want to die. Try to give them more reason to want to live.

3. To be alert to use of tools at activities, especially O.T. If patient is using sharp tools, sit next to him working on some object yourself. Do not become so preoccupied with your work that you forget the patient. If you notice his behavior indicates possible misuse, reach over and place the tool in its proper place. Talk with the patient and others at the table. When occupied with group, patient is less likely to think of attempting suicide. Check that tools are replaced before leaving the clinic.

4. When escorting outside, be alert to roadways and walkways. Do not allow your patient to be the first one standing on the curb. Keep him more in the middle of the group. If escorting alone, time your stride so you arrive at the curb after cars have passed. When walking on sidewalks that have walls on one side, keep patient to the opposite side. Sometimes the wall tempts the patient and he jumps over the wall, falling to the ground below. Seldom have our patients who attempted this actually killed themselves, but they have sustained injuries such as broken ankles, heels, shoulders, and arms.

5. Supervise the use of sharps on the ward. Example: Patient asks to use the scissors. Ask what he plans to do with them. If you feel he can handle the scissors, then let him have them, but follow and observe his use of them. Chat with him. If you feel he is too impulsive, then go with him and tactfully use the scissors yourself. Sharps would be scissors, nail file, toenail clippers, can opener, bottle opener, needle. These articles are kept in the Nursing Office in a locked cabinet.

6. Observe what patient picks up when you are escorting him. Patients see many things you and I would miss. Feel free to ask him what he has and take those things that qualify as contraband. Example: Sometimes a patient stops and picks up something from the ground. You step up and say, "What did you find?" Patient shows you a rusty razor blade. "Oh, that would cut someone's foot, it's good you saw it. We'll put it in a can so it can be safely discarded." What you say and how you say it is very important. If you notice patients are finding syringes and needles on the grounds, report this immediately to your nurse.

7. To be alert to patient when he is in the bathroom. Some patients plan to drown themselves in the lavatory. This means they will have to plug the sink. Drowning is difficult, so many patients plan to hit their heads against the faucet, hoping to become unconscious and face fall in the water. If patient's behavior indicates this type of thought, unplug sink and suggest they clean the sink. You are not expected to enter the individual closed commode area when such is present, but you observe the patient's feet which are showing. Example: Metal door is usually cut off about 2½ feet from the floor. As long as patient's toes are facing you, or his heels, he's probably using the commode for the intended purpose; but if the sole of his shoe is showing, then investigate for the possibility that he may be trying to drown himself in the commode.

8. To be alert to your patient at medication time to see if he's saving medication. Example: Station yourself ahead of the patient if he's in a medication line. As he leaves line, observe movements of his arms as he walks away from you. If elbow bends and arm comes up, there is a possibility he may be spitting the medication out to save. When you make your report to Nurse, state you *suspect* the patient is not taking his medication. Role playing is used to demonstrate the approaches for effective use of safety precautions. Class is asked to suggest others not mentioned so far.

9. Close observation. Be aware of your patient—where he is, what he is doing. Try to keep him involved in activities or in area where others are present. Involve patient in your ward duties when possible. If you have been assigned to a special patient on suicidal status, he is your responsibility. Follow through on your safety precautions.

   You do not need to breathe down his neck or hold on to him, but you need to be aware of where he is and what he is doing. If you have to leave the area, ask someone else to assume your specialing. Verbal and written reports of your observations and patient clues are very important to the doctor and the nurse. Display a genuine interest in your patient as a person.

Problem Solving: You have been assigned to *special* an actively suicidal patient on status. Describe three additional safety precautions you would use.

Remember—Suicide is most likely to occur when the depression begins to lift.

Conclusions

Suicidal behavior is a frequent, tragic event in American life. It ranks as a major health problem. The conditions under which suicide occur have been extensively studied and are well known. Professionals in the mental health field are generally trained in identifying and dealing with a variety of suicidal phenomena. Suicidal emergencies require immediate professional attention of a warm, supportive, personal nature; the institutionalization of suicide precautions that include close observation of the patient, contact, and enlistment of significant others; and maintenance of these treatments through the crisis period. Previous suicidal ventures, excessive use of alcohol, mental disturbance, and impulsivity are the most dangerous signs of an imminent lethal effort.

Given the information regarding James Prentiss and his treatment at Armedia Hospital on June 18, 1982, the following evaluative comments seem appropriate:

1. The Crisis Center was apparently established to deal with patients experiencing mental crises, including suicidal thoughts and behavior.
2. The staff should have been trained in identifying and treating suicidal crises.
3. Mr. Prentiss was delivered from another treatment setting specifically for psychiatric treatment.
4. The ranking staff member:
   a. Communicated with Mr. Prentiss.
   b. Was aware he was being transferred from another treatment facility.
   c. Was aware Mr. Prentiss was inebriated.
   d. Was aware Mr. Prentiss acted in a peculiar or unusual manner at the airport.
   e. Was informed that Mr. Prentiss had engaged in self-dangerous behavior before coming to the Crisis Center.
   f. Was not able to elicit a coherent or sensible story from Mr. Prentiss.
   g. Told Mr. Prentiss to "wait."
   h. Did not consult with a superior despite the above and despite the physician's status as a second-year psychiatric resident.

Usual and customary professional procedure for the circumstances in which Mr. Prentiss came to the Crisis Center would include:

1. Immediate efforts to determine in detail the circumstances preceding Mr. Prentiss's being brought to the Crisis Center.
2. Assignment of a staff person to establish rapport with the patient and ensure that impulsive behavior would not occur.
3. Evaluation of the patient's current emotional status and potential dangerousness.
4. Consultation with a senior staff person if there is any doubt as to appropriate procedures, medications, or staff involvement in the patient's best interests.

As soon as a staff member establishes rapport with the patient, efforts should be directed to:

1. Identifying the precipitating incident for the crisis.
2. The lethality of the patient's suicidal ideation.
3. The degree of emotional disturbance being suffered by the patient.
4. Significant other persons who might level support to see the patient through the crisis.
5. Engaging the patient in making stable, realistic plans to ease tension and resolve conflicts.
6. Reassuring the patient of the availability of help and support.
7. Where necessary, arranging for the involvement of other staff or facilities to ensure that the patient survives the crisis.
8. Keeping the patient under observation at all times.

There appears to be a considerable discrepancy between the usual and customary procedure to be followed in treating a suicidal crisis and the treatment received by Mr. Prentiss on June 18, 1982.

References

Kiev, A. (1976). Crisis intervention and suicide prevention. In E. S. Shneidman (Ed.), *Suicidology: Contemporary development*. New York: Grune & Stratton.

Litman, R. E. (1957). Some aspects of the treatment of the potentially suicidal patient. In E. S. Shneidman & N. L. Farberow (Eds.), *Clues to suicide*. New York: McGraw-Hill.

Reynolds, D. K., & Farberow, N. L. (1976). *Suicide inside and out*. Berkeley: University of California Press.

Shneidman, E. S., & Farberow, N. L. (Eds.). (1957). *Clues to suicide*. New York: McGraw-Hill.

Shneidman, E. S. (1960). The logical environment of suicide. *California's Health, 17*(22), 193–196.

Shneidman, E. S. (1973). Suicide. In *Encyclopedia Brittanica* (14th Ed.) (Vol. 21, pp. 383–385).

Shneidman, E. S. (Ed.). (1976). *Suicidology: Contemporary developments.* New York: Grune & Stratton.

Worden, J. W. (1976). Lethality factors and the suicide attempt. In E. S. Shneidman (Ed.), *Suicidology: Contemporary developments.* New York: Grune & Stratton.

In this instance, the psychologist was used as a rebuttal witness (discussed in Chapter 13).

The assessment of dangerousness and the *duty to warn* is an area of mental health law that poses complex issues for psychologists who testify as experts (American Psychological Association, 1994). Since the *Tarasoff*[3] decision, many jurisdictions impose on mental health professionals a duty to warn an intended victim where the professional knows or should know that a patient presents a serious threat of violence to any third party. Although many states follow the California ruling in *Tarasoff*, others are reluctant to hold psychiatrists, psychologists, and social workers responsible for the prediction of dangerousness as in *Boynton v. Burglass*[4] where an appellate court found that a psychiatrist had no duty to warn even though the patient committed a murder after issuing threats to harm the eventual victim. In this decision, the Court specifically noted "because psychiatry is, at best, an inexact science, courts should be reluctant to impose liability." This echoed the findings in *Ake v. Oklahoma*[5] regarding the difficulty in predicting future dangerousness. Psychologists who expect to testify as to standard of care and prediction of dangerousness should become very familiar with both the scientific and legal literature relating to these areas. In most situations, the false positive rate of future violence prediction exceeds 40%, lending support in most cases to the defense in malpractice litigation (Cope, 1989; Klassen & O'Connor, 1989; Leesfield, 1987; Monahan, 1988). As can be seen from these few examples of the use of psychological testimony or opinion in personal injury litigation, this area of litigation probably offers the broadest opportunity as well as challenges for the use of psychological scientists and practitioners in the courtroom.

NOTES

1. *Chapple v. Ganger*, 851 F. Supp. 1481 (E. D. Wash., 1994).
2. *Speer v. State*, 495 A.2d 733 (Conn. App. 1985).
3. *Tarasoff v. Regents of University of California*, 17 Cal. 3d 425, 131 Cal. Rptr. 14, 551 P.2d 334 (1976).
4. *Boynton v. Burglass*, 590 So. 2d. 446 (Fla. App. 3 Dist. 1991).
5. *Ake v. Oklahoma*, 470 U.S. 68, 81, 105 S. Ct. 1087, 1095, 84 L. Ed 2d.

12

Malingering, Deceit, and Exaggeration

In recent years, behavioral experts such as psychologists and psychiatrists have been expected by the courts to render opinions as to *malingering*. The meaning of the concept is not always clear but in general, it is defined as something close or equivalent to *lying*. In mental health practice, malingering or lying may be of little professional concern or issue (as during psychotherapy). In the forensic setting, especially during the evidentiary phase of litigation, truth is paramount.

THE PSYCHIATRIC VIEW

The psychiatric view of malingering is simplistic in that it is defined in the *Diagnostic and Statistical Manual of Mental Disorders, Fourth Edition (DSM-IV;* American Psychiatric Association, 1994). The *DSM-IV* is the official mental illness classification system currently recommended by the American Psychiatric Association. *Malingering* is not graced with a formal diagnostic label but is included in a section of the *DSM-IV* entitled "Other Conditions That May Be a Focus of Clinical Attention." Herein, the essential feature of the behavior is defined as "the intentional production of false or grossly exaggerated physical or psychological symptoms motivated by external incentives such as avoiding military duty, avoiding work, obtaining financial compensation, evading criminal prosecution or obtaining drugs" (p. 683). The psychiatric definition is only a slight expansion of a standard dictionary definition "To pretend to be ill or injured in order to avoid duty or work" (Berube, 1982).

The *DSM-IV* recommends that malingering should be strongly suspected if any combination of four conditions is found:

1. The person is referred by an attorney.
2. There is a marked discrepancy between the person's claimed stress or disability and the objective findings.

3. Lack of cooperation.
4. The presence of an antisocial personality disorder.

Although a strong suspicion may be a useful start in making a differential diagnosis in a medical setting, it is too speculative to be of much use in forensic situations. In the medical setting, accurate diagnosis is necessary as a foundation for effective therapeutic management (Overholser, 1990). Triers of fact in judicial venues are more interested in veracity or truth-telling at a point in time (in such issues as sanity, competence, specific intent, and credibility).

Current studies suggest that diagnostic interviews alone are without sufficient reliability to differentiate genuine from malingered mental deficiency, psychosis, or neurological impairment. Credible expert testimony regarding the probability that these conditions are being faked or malingered requires the support of psychological test data (Schretlen, 1988).

THE PSYCHOLOGICAL VIEW

Reflecting their awareness of individual differences and a long tradition of scientific inquiry, psychologists approach the issue of malingering as a complex social/personality phenomenon with clinical, physiological, legal, moral, and motivational aspects. This complexity is illustrated by the variety of descriptions currently found: lying, lack of optimal effort, malingering, distortion, faking, dissimulation, in validity, exaggeration, and so forth.

The majority of research in this area has been done and continues to be produced by psychologists. A thorough review is beyond the scope of this volume but references herein provided are sufficient to guide the interested reader further (Rogers, 1997; Rogers, Harrell, & Liff, 1993).

Rogers, Sewell, and Goldstein (1994) have proposed a three-factor model of malingering. The *pathogenic factor* applies to persons motivated primarily by underlying psychopathology. The *criminological factor* suggests an antisocial and oppositional motivation for malingering to obtain unearned or undeserved rewards. The third model, called *adaptational*, refers to malingering by a person who believes that this is a constructive attempt to succeed in a highly adversarial situation. All these factors follow a generic model of malingering as "lying to win."

THE LEGAL VIEW

In both civil and criminal issues, the judiciary is interested in truth, lying, deception, and malingering. Usually, the decision as to the role and significance of these issues is left to the judge and the jury. The classic definition of malingering within legal circles is:

> To feign sickness or any physical disablement or mental lapse or derangement, especially for the purpose of escaping the performance of a task, duty, or work. A person who consciously feigns or simulates mental or physical illness for gain. (Black, 1979, p. 864)

Here the law does away with testimony about "unconscious malingering" as an issue of volitional distortion. This narrows the task of the expert witness to issues of lying, distortion, faking, deception, or dissimulation as a choice of the subject.

For a mental health professional to testify as to the truthfulness or credibility of a subject, issues of admissibility are of paramount importance. Courts have generally held that expert psychiatric or psychological testimony as to the *genuineness* of an alleged mental disorder is admissible. Evidence as to the *credibility* of a subject has generally been ruled inadmissible (Ogloff, 1990).

THE ASSESSMENT OF DECEPTION, MALINGERING, DISSIMULATION, OR FAKING

Psychologists have produced instruments and procedures to measure or identify deceptive behavior. A number of approaches have been reported, and the major directions in these efforts are reviewed in this chapter. A forensic example of such methods also is presented.

Physiological Indicators

Aside from interview and speculation, the earliest efforts at detecting deception were based on physiological responses to questioning. The development of instrumentation during the 20th century led to the concept of the polygraph, which measures multiple physiological responses such as skin resistance, heart rate, and breathing. The apparatus has come to be called "the lie detector." Especially favored by law enforcement agencies, the validity and reliability of these techniques have come under considerable negative review by scientists, legislators, and the courts (Brooks, 1985; Katkin, 1985; Lykken, 1979; Saxe, Dougherty, & Cross, 1985).

Very few psychologists do polygraph testing and most states have limited the use of these instruments. Most courts have continued to restrict these tests as evidence.

Some interest has developed in applying physiological measures and computer technology to identify stress in a subject's voice as an index of lying. Appellate courts have ruled testimony based on this procedure inadmissible.[1]

Observational Techniques

Many believe they can identify deception by close observation of a subject's behavior. This is almost a maxim among trained law enforcement personnel, attorneys, gamblers, and many laypersons. Ekman, Friesen, and O'Sullivan (1988) studied forms of smiling during active deception and found no difference in smiling between truthful and deceptive subjects.

Ekman and O'Sullivan pursued their interest in lying behavior and reported their study of 509 subjects who viewed a videotape of 10 people either lying or telling the truth in describing their feelings. The subjects included U.S. Secret Service agents, members of the Central Intelligence Agency, agents of the Federal Bureau of Investigation, National Security Agency, and the Drug Enforcement Agency, California police officers, psychiatrists, judges, college students, and working adults. Only the Secret Service Agents performed better than chance. Those who tended to identify liars and truth-tellers more accurately tended to use nonverbal clues (e.g., "voice strained," "avoids eye contact," "phony smile") and speech clues (e.g., "answers too slowly," "evasive," "talks too much") to make their decisions. The "hit" rate of professional lie-catchers was not impressive.

A special case of detection of deception that is of interest in forensic work is the genuine versus simulated amnesia. Claims of amnesia are relatively common among defendants accused of committing violent crimes. In general, there is, outside of "feeling of knowing ratings," little evidence that genuine and simulated amnesia can be distinguished in criminal cases (Schacter, 1986a, 1986b). *Feeling of knowing* refers to an amnestic person's belief that an unrecalled event could be recalled or recognized if more powerful clues or hints were given. In some experiments, deceivers consistently expressed less confidence that further clues would facilitate recall (Schacter, 1986c). Wiggins and Brandt (1988) point out that many true amnesiacs can learn new material whereas naive amnesia malingerers appear to be deficient and probably are unaware that in cases of true amnesia, immediate memory skills are retained. This suggests a psychometric approach to detection of deception in faked amnesia. In their studies of simulated amnesia, Wiggins and Brandt found that amnesia simulators demonstrated almost no memory for biographical data while their small sample of neurologically damaged true amnesiacs had little difficulty remembering personal data such as name, age, birthdate, telephone number, address, mother's first and maiden name, etc. The authors suggest that laypersons frequently have inaccurate beliefs about the cognitive effects of amnesia and tend to exaggerate poor memory. They caution, however, that individuals can learn or be coached to demonstrate behavioral deficits characteristic of true neurological damage. They suggest that administration of multiple test batteries are more likely than single tests to catch out amnesia fakers.

Objective Interview Measures

Where a subject is a criminal defendant or a civil plaintiff, the emotional effects of litigation procedures can distort the presence and degree of disability. Weissman (1990) proposed that these conditions can promote conscious and unconscious symptom production or exaggeration for secondary gain. Although interview and historical data are useful in determining the validity of reported symptoms and conditions, Weissman suggests the value of a multiple approach, adding personality testing to interview and history data.

The most widely used and researched interview instrument is the SIRS (Structured Interview of Reported Symptoms). Developed by Rogers, Bagby, and Dickens (1992), this instrument reliably differentiates *reliable response style* (honest and self-disclosing) from *irrelevant response style* (inconsistent responses), *defensiveness* (minimizers), and *malingering*. Scoring of the SIRS provides eight primary scales (Rare Symptoms, Symptom Combinations, Improbable and Absurd Symptoms, Subtle Symptoms, Selectivity of Symptoms, Severity of Symptoms, and Reported vs. Observed Symptoms). There are five supplementary scales. Requiring 30 to 45 minutes to administer, the SIRS results in respectable hit rates for Honest Responders and Probable Feigners.

Although the SIRS was first developed for use with subjects involved in civil litigation, subsequent research indicates that this instrument has a 97% hit rate in identifying malingering in competency-to-stand-trial evaluations (Gothard, Viglone, Meloy, & Sherman, 1995).

Cornell and Hawk (1989) demonstrated that experienced forensic psychologists are able to differentiate malingerers from psychotics in the criminal justice system with fair accuracy using clinical presentation variables such as general presentation, affective symptoms, hallucinations, delusions, and formal thought disorders. Accurate classification was reported to be 89%.

Magnitude of Error Testing

Also referred to as Symptom Validity Testing (Denney, 1996), these instruments in essence are relatively simple tasks presented to the subject as difficult or at least somewhat difficult. The subject is provided with an easy opportunity to fake bad by purposely giving incorrect responses or performing very badly.

A frequently used and studied form of magnitude of error testing presents the subject with a simple cognitive test that all but the most profoundly deficient individuals should be able to accomplish by chance at least half the time. The Digit Memory Test (Hiscock & Hiscock, 1989) and the Portland Digit Recognition Test (Binder, 1993) are currently popular forms of this approach. In the latest revision of the Digit Memory Test (Guilmette, Hart, Guiliano, & Leinenger, 1994), the subject is shown a card with a series of five random digits and asked to read them aloud. The subject is told to remember the numbers. After this the stimulus card is removed. The examiner waits five seconds and then exposes a card with a pair of 5 random numbers, one of which is the same as the stimulus card. The subject is asked to choose the correct number (by pointing). After the first 12 cards, the next 12 are each followed by a delay of 10 seconds, followed by a final series of 12 cards with a 15 second delay between the stimulus card and the response card. Figure 12.1 shows a simple scoring sheet and suggests cutoff scores for brain damaged, faking bad, and psychiatric subjects. The validity of the Digit Memory Test as an identifier of malingering of neuropsychological deficits was recently confirmed in studies reported by Prigatano and his group (Prigatano, Smason, Lamb, & Bortz, 1997).

Name: _____ Date: _____

5″

L ___ 1	R ___ 9	L ___ 17	15″	L ___ 25	L ___ 33
R ___ 2	L ___ 10	L ___ 18		R ___ 26	L ___ 34
R ___ 3	L ___ 11	R ___ 19		L ___ 27	R ___ 35
L ___ 4	R ___ 12	R ___ 20		R ___ 28	R ___ 36
L ___ 5 10″	R ___ 13	L ___ 21		R ___ 29	
R ___ 6	L ___ 14	R ___ 22		L ___ 30	
L ___ 7	R ___ 15	R ___ 23		R ___ 31	Total
R ___ 8	L ___ 16	L ___ 24		L ___ 32	Score: ___

Distribution of Scores on the Revised Hiscock for All Groups

Items Correct	Brain Disordered	Normal Subjects Faking Bad	Psychiatric Patients
36	15	2	15
35	3	0	3
34	2	1	1
33	0	0	0
Cutoff—90% Correct			
32	0	0	1
31–27	0	2	0
26–22	0	3	0
21–17	0	6	0
≤ 16	0	6	0

Source: Guilmette, Hart, Guiliano, and Leinenger (1994). Detecting simulated memory impairment: *The Clinical Neuropsychologist, 8*(3), 283–294.

FIGURE 12.1. Scoring sheet and cut-off scores for the Hiscock Forced Choice Test.

A variety of similar instruments and procedures are available (Lezak, 1995). Many, if not most, have been developed for use where separating real from feigned brain damage is the issue (Martin, Franzen, & Orey, 1996). More subtle and sophisticated neuropsychologically oriented measures of deception, distortion, or faking will be considered next.

The magnitude of error strategy has been applied to a variety of cognitive test instruments. Most are focused on immediate memory functions whereas others identify subscale discrepancies on tests of cognitive skills. The oldest of these tests, generally called the *15-Item Test* was developed over 50 years ago in France (Rey, 1941). This test was illustrated in Chapter 7. It is the precursor of all the more recent instruments that invite a subject to fake bad by presenting what is supposedly a very difficult array of 15 items. Exposed for only 10 seconds, the subject is asked to reproduce all 15 figures. Only the most severely deficient subjects are unable to reproduce most of these simple and familiar stimulus items. Scores of nine or less suggests efforts to feign cognitive impairment (DiCarlo, Gfeller, & Drury, 1997; Lee, Loring, & Martin, 1992; Lezak, 1995).

Magnitude of Error with Standard Cognitive Tests

Martin et al. (1996) have demonstrated that the magnitude of error strategy can be applied to the results of standardized neuropsychological tests. Several examples of this rapidly emerging research thrust follow.

Mittenberg, Azrin, Milsaps, and Heilbronner (1993) compared head-injured outpatients with age-matched subjects instructed to malinger on the Wechsler Memory Scale-Revised (WMS-R). They found that the discrepancies between the Index Scores for General Memory and Attention/Concentration were able to accurately classify 91% of the nonlitigating brain injured subjects and 83% of the simulators. Figure 12.2 presents a scoring sheet for converting WMS-R subscales into probabilities of malingering

This malingering index was cross-validated by Iverson, Slick, and Franzen (1997) who reported a large sample study lending support for the validity of the difference score between General Memory and Attention/Concentration Indexes as a marker for nonoptimal effort. Further utilization of the WMS-R as a vehicle for discriminating between simulated malingering and closed head injury has been reported by Bernard, McGrath, and Houston (1993). They found that malingerers showed significantly poorer performance on Visual Reproduction I and Visual Memory Span together with better performance on Visual Paired Associates I and Digit Span. This study also confirmed the Mittenberg et al. (1993) findings that malingering simulators performed excessively poorly on the Attention/Concentration subtest.

Pursuing their interests in identifying malingered head injury, Mittenberg, Theroux-Fichera, Zielenski, and Heilbronner (1995) compared nonlitigating head-injured patients with a control group matched for age,

Name: _____ Date: _____

General Memory – Attention/Concentration = Difference Score

(Index Scores) _____ – _____ = _____

Probability of Malingering = _____

Probability of Malingering Classification

General Memory-Attention/Concentration Score	Probability of Malingering
35	.99
34	.98
—	.97
33	.96
32	.95
—	.94
31	.93
30	.92
29	.91
—	.90
25	.85
22	.80
19	.75
15	.70
12	.65
9	.60
5	.55
2	.50

Source: W. Mittenberg, R. Azrin, C. Milsaps, and R. Heilbronner (1993). Identification of malingered head injury on the Wechsler Memory Scale-Revised. *Psychological Assessment, 5*(1), 34–40.

G. Iverson, D. Slick, and M. Franzen (1996, October & November). Evaluation of a WMS-R malingering index in a non-litigating clinical sample. *Archives of Clinical Neuropsychology, 12*, 341.

FIGURE 12.2. Scoring sheet for a malingering index for the Wechsler Memory Scale-Revised.

intelligence, and occupation who were structured to malinger head injury while taking the Wechsler Adult Intelligence Scale-Revised (WAIS-R). They found that Vocabulary minus Digit Span age-corrected subscale scores accurately discriminated 79% of the head-injured and 71% of the malingering simulators. Figure 12.3 illustrates a worksheet for calculating the probability of malingering according to this research.

Neuropsychologists continue to produce most of the current research on malingering, focusing on standard neuropsychological test performance by normal, psychiatric, and coached simulator subjects. Mittenberg, Rothole, Russell, and Heilbronner (1996) developed a formula for the identification

Name: _____ Date: _____

WAIS-R

Age-Corrected Scale Scores

Vocabulary – Digit Span = Difference Score

_____ – _____ = _____

Probability of Malingering Classification

Vocabulary-Digit Span Difference Score	Probability of Malingering
10	.99
9	.95
8	.90
—	.85
7	.80
6	.75
5	.70
4	.65
3	.60
2	.55
—	.50
1	.45
0	.40
−1	.35
−2	.30
−3	.25
−4	.20
—	.15
−5	.10
−6	.05
−7	.01

Source: W. Mittenberg, S. Theroux-Fichera, R. Zielenski, and R. Heilbronner (1995). Identification of malingered head injury on the Wechsler Adult Intelligence Scale-Revised. *Professional Psychology: Research and Practice, 26,* 491.

FIGURE 12.3. Scoring sheet for the identification of malingered head injury on the Wechsler Adult Intelligence Scale-Revised.

of malingered head trauma using the Halstead-Reitan Battery. In this study, the researchers found an overall hit rate of more than 88% with 16% false positives and 6% false negatives. Further research in an effort to cross-validate the complex formula developed by Mittenberg and his colleagues partially supported the original work; although the approach appeared promising, further research was indicated (McKinzey & Russell, 1997).

Research with the Luria-Nebraska Neuropsychological Battery by McKinzey, Dodd, Krebbiel, Mensch, and Trombka (1997) resulted in a formula to detect malingering on this battery. The formula was derived from an item analysis of the tests of malingerers compared with motivated patients matched on education, age, and severity of the profile. The derived formula was then cross-validated on 51 simulators and 202 medical patients. The formula produced a respectable hit rate of 88% with 23% false negatives and 9% false positives. Where normal and profound impaired profiles were eliminated, the overall hit rate was 91% with false negatives of 17% and false positives of 7%. Figure 12.4 shows a scoring sheet useful in applying this formula.

Pursuing the issue of using Halstead-Reitan tests to identify malingerers, Tenhula and Sweet (1996) found that experimental malingerers averaged 2½ and 5 errors respectively on subtests 1 and 2 of the Booklet Category Test while both brain-injured patients and normal controls demonstrated no errors on these easy subtests. Figure 12.5 presents a scoring sheet using this research-developed and cross-validated formula.

In keeping with the growing trend to develop research-based indices of malingering, deceit, or invalidity on standard neuropsychological tests, many new studies have emerged. Hasker and his group (1997) report the use of a computerized priming test to detect malingering simulators. Ray

Name: _____ Date: _____

Formula: Items A Scores > Items B Scores = Likely Malingering

A Scores		B Scores	
Item	Score	Item	Score
3 (×2)	_____	132	_____
4	_____	170	_____
44	_____	173	_____
48	_____	174	_____
64	_____	187	_____
66	_____	192	_____
67	_____	199	_____
69	_____	217	_____
71	_____	221	_____
101	_____	223	_____
112	_____	225	_____
160	_____	239	_____
261	_____	241	_____
Total A	_____	Total B	_____

_____ A < B   _____ A > B (Likely Malingering)

Source: R. McKinzey, M. Dodd, M. Krebbiel, A. Mensch, and C. Trombka (1997). Detection of malingering on the Luria-Nebraska Neuropsychological Battery: An initial and cross-validation. *Archives of Clinical Neuropsychology, 12,* 505–512.

FIGURE 12.4. Scoring sheet for detection of malingering on the Luria-Nebraska Neuropsychological Battery.

Name: _____ Date: _____

Number of Errors

Subtest I	_____
Subtest II	_____

Normative Scores (Number of Errors)

	Malingerers	Brain Injured	Controls
	M (SD)	M (SD)	M (SD)
Subtest I	2.4 (2.5)	0.0 (0.2)	0.0 (0.0)
Subtest II	5.1 (4.7)	0.4 (0.5)	0.1 (0.3)

Hit rate for the above is 92.2%. False Positives = 0% False Negatives = 27%.

Source: W. Tenhula and J. Sweet (1996). Double cross-validation of the Booklet Category Test in detecting malingered traumatic brain injury. *The Clinical Neuropsychologist,* *10,* 104–116.

FIGURE 12.5. Scoring sheet for detecting malingering on the Booklet Category Test.

and his colleagues (1997) conducted a study using the Cognitive Behavioral Driver's Inventory to distinguish brain-damaged patients from malingering simulators. Hasker, King, Bloodworth, Spring, and Klebe (1997) successfully demonstrated the utility of a computerized category classification test in differentiating among normal students, malingering simulators, and amnestic patients. Reitan and Wolfson (1997) administered the WAIS or WAIS-R and the Halstead-Reitan Battery to 20 head-injured subjects involved in litigation and 20 head-injured subjects not involved in litigation. All subjects were retested on the same tests about 12 months later. They found that the litigating group earned lower mean scores, while the nonlitigating group earned higher mean scores on all tests with the second testing. Using the difference scores, the researchers developed a *Retest Consistency Index* that correctly identified 90% of the litigants. It is suggested that this approach might be useful in identifying malingering. Cross-validation would be required to make these results useful in practice.

Other researchers report studies of pediatric malingering (Faust, Hart, & Guilmette, 1988) and malingering by substance abusers (Arnett & Franzen, 1997). Computerized versions of symptom validity tests have begun to appear on the market (Cool Spring Software, 1998).

Addressing the issue of the symptom-exaggerator who seeks monetary compensation for a feigned injury, Price (1990) developed the Dallas Area Money Malingering Intelligence Test (DAMMIT). Price observed that personal injury litigants—both the truly injured and the fakers—often do badly on the Arithmetic subtest of the Wechsler Adult Intelligence Scale-Revised

(WAIS-R) or the third edition of this scale WAIS-III. In the DAMMIT, the subject is given the WAIS-R or the WAIS-III in the usual and customary manner. Later in the examination process, the patient is told:

> This next test is *very* important. We use this test to determine your ability to manage money in your own best interest. So, do your best or someone else, such as a family member, may be required to be in charge of any money you have or any checks that you have coming to you. You may have heard some of these exact problems or some very similar before, so be very careful when you answer.

The subject is then given the Arithmetic subtest of the Wechsler Adult Intelligence Scale (WAIS). Comparing the age-corrected Scaled Scores, if the second Arithmetic subtest exceeds the first by three or more points, malingering is suggested.

Detection of Malingering or Motivational Deficits on Personality Tests

Traditionally, within the mental health professions, malingering has been considered a symptom of character pathology. It makes its appearance in classifications of personality disorders (*DSM-IV*, 1994). Personality tests have a long history of attention to such factors as *dissimulation, consistency, symptom validity,* and *motivation.* Most of the standardized self-report (paper and pencil) personality tests have one or more scorable indices to measure these factors. Most are tangential to the issue of lying, faking, or malingering and generally focus on descriptors such as "Validity of the personality profile." Hopes or expectations that projective techniques would offer opportunity for the detection of malingering have not been consistently supported by research (Kahn, Fox, & Rhode, 1988).

The most extensive studies of malingering, faking ("good" and "bad") have been conducted with the most popular of self-report personality inventories—the MMPI and its successor, the MMPI-2. Pope et al. (1993) reviewed the three forms of the MMPI and their application in the forensic setting. In general, dissimulation or invalidity is indicated, according to the authors, by exaggerated profiles and exaggerated symptomatology.

More recent research with the MMPI-2 has provided data which allows more definitive differentiation and estimation of the probability of malingering, faking, deception, or inattention to the testing materials. Most of the research depends on group comparisons without providing usable cutoff scores for the identification of individuals who are malingering (Bagby, Rogers, & Buis, 1994; Iverson, Franzen, & Hammond, 1995; Lim & Butcher, 1996; Walters, White, & Greene, 1988; Wasyliw, Grossman, Haywood, & Cavanaugh, 1988; Youngjohn, Davis, & Wolf, 1997). Most of these studies support the concept that elevations on *F, F-K* Index,

Ds Scale, the *O-S* Scale, the *Fb* Scale, and the new *S* Scale all may be useful in differentiating motivated, forthcoming, honest test-takers from deceivers and distorters. Specific formulas for use in an individual forensic case are rare.

The *F-K* Index has a relatively long history of research to support the concept that a high number of unusual responses coupled with low defensiveness (willingness to reveal weakness or illness) can indicate faking bad." There are differences of opinion as to what cutoff point indicates faking bad (Lees-Haley, 1989; Rothke et al., 1994). There also remains the question as to whether the research on the *F-K* Index on MMPI-2 has equivalent discrimination power to that demonstrated by original MMPI research. To further complicate the direct interpretation of a plus *F-K* Index as simply exaggerations of symptoms or faking bad, alternate interpretations have been proposed (a "cry for help," self-denigration, lack of emotional resources, random response, etc.).

An MMPI-2 scale developed empirically to identify personal injury malingerers was reported by Lees-Haley, English, and Glenn (1991). This Fake Bad Scale (*FbS*) with an item raw score range of 0–43 successfully discriminated those malingering neurological injuries from genuine injury and from psychiatric patients. In this initial study of the *FbS*, a cutoff score of 20 correctly classified 96% of the malingerers and 90% of the nonmalingerers. In a subsequent study of the *Fb* Scale comparing malingering litigants with patients suffering posttraumatic stress disorder (PTSD), Lees-Haley (1992) reported that a cutoff score of 24 for males and 26 for females correctly classified about 75% of the pseudo-PTSD patients and over 90% of the control patients. Figure 12.6 presents a simplified scoring sheet for the *Fb* Scale.

As with all current scales of malingering, faking bad, deception, and exaggeration, further research is necessary to validate the usefulness of these scales and to provide increased accuracy. With continuing research, it is likely that several forms of malingering will be identified (Greiffenstein, Baker, & Gola, 1996).

THE EXPERT WITNESS AND THE ISSUE OF MALINGERING

It is clear that psychologists are likely to examine patients who voluntarily produce symptoms or amplify physical or emotional disorders (Adams, 1993). The psychologist as expert witness is likely to be expected to render an opinion as to the validity of emotional or neuropsychological deficits claimed in criminal and civil issues. Forensic examiners must be aware that some subjects may be coached to perform badly, although some research suggests that memory deficits are more likely to be successfully faked than other characteristics (Franzen & Martin, 1996; Thompson et al., 1997). Wetter and Corrigan (1995) suggest that attorneys or examiners telling subjects

Patient's Name: _____ Date: _____

True (Check if item answered true.)

11 ____ , 18 ____ , 28 ____ , 30 ____ , 31 ____ , 39 ____ , 40 ____ , 44 ____ , 59 ____ , 111 ____ ,
252 ____ , 274 ____ , 325 ____ , 339 ____ , 464 ____ , 469 ____ , 505 ____ , 506 ____

Total: _____

False (Check if item answered false.)

12 ____ , 41 ____ , 57 ____ , 58 ____ , 81 ____ , 110 ____ , 117 ____ , 152 ____ , 164 ____ ,
176 ____ , 224 ____ , 227 ____ , 248 ____ , 249 ____ , 250 ____ , 255 ____ , 264 ____ , 284 ____ ,
362 ____ , 373 ____ , 374 ____ , 419 ____ , 433 ____ , 496 ____ , 561 ____

Total: _____

Total of Checked True and False Responses: _____

Source: P. Lees-Haley (1992). Efficacy of MMPI-2 validity scales and MCMI-II modifier scales for detecting spurious PTSD claims: F, F-k, fake bad scale, ego strength, subtle-obvious subscales, DIS, and DEB. *Journal of Clinical Psychology, 48*(5), 681–689.

• Males: Cutoff is ≥ 24, 75% pseudo PTSD and 96% controls correctly classified. Females: Cutoff is ≥ 26, 74% pseudo PTSD and 92% controls correctly classified.

P. Lees-Haley, L. English, and W. Glenn (1991). A fake bad scale on the MMPI-2 for personal injury claimants. *Psychological Reports, 68*, 203–210.

• Cutoff of 20, 96% hit rate for malingerers.

FIGURE 12.6.   A simplified scoring sheet for the Lees-Haley Fake Bad Scale (FbS) for the MMPI-2.

that psychological tests contain validity measures may facilitate biased responses and deception.

Until further research produces highly reliable indices of malingering, no single test or formula is sufficient to support an expert witness's conclusion that a subject is malingering or exaggerating. Mossman and Hart (1996) have suggested a Bayesian mathematical approach to the interpretation of psychological test indices of invalidity. This approach has scientific merit but may be very difficult to apply and present in the courtroom setting. So—how should the expert witness go about doing a credible job of evaluating and reporting issues of validity and veracity of subject responses? Figure 12.7 presents some practical Rules of the Road.

To illustrate the application of these Rules of the Road, a case follows.

Mr. X was charged in a federal jurisdiction with multiple counts of mail fraud, tax evasion, and other felony offenses in connection with a scheme to double investors' money in a six-month period. The offenses were incontrovertible but the defense pleaded diminished capacity and lack of specific intent based on a psychiatrist's diagnoses of Bipolar Disorder plus memory defect residuals of an early mild concussive disorder following a motor vehicle accident.

Psychological evaluation included a full intellectual, neuropsychological, and personality evaluation using standardized test instruments. The

Rules of the Road

- Never conclude that a subject is faking or malingering from records provided by the attorneys.
- Avoid speculation as to the subject's motivation from observational clues.
- Assume the subject is approaching the examination prepared to do his or her best.
- Conduct the examinations in the appropriate standardized manner.
- Be sure that multiple tests or indices of faking, malingering, or exaggeration are given during the evaluation.
- Render an opinion on what the majority of these measures indicate.
- Consider and report all reasonable alternative interpretations of discrepant or critical findings.
- Render an expert opinion in a conservative manner.

FIGURE 12.7.   Maximizing accuracy and fairness in the evaluation of the presence or absence of subject distortion on psychological tests.

results showed mild neuropsychological deficits particularly in memory items, and very extensive emotional disturbance. Neither of these were noted during observation of the subject outside the test room.

Validity indices were as follows:

a. MMPI-2, f-k = 17
b. MMPI-2, FbS Scale = 29
c. Mittenberg WMS-R, Memory – Concentration = 32
d. Mittenberg WAIS-R, Vocabulary – Digit Span = 8
e. Rey 15 – Item Test = 9
f. Luria-Nebraska Malingering Index—A = 18, B = 4
g. Booklet Category Test—Subtest I = 3, II = 6

These findings were presented by the psychologist as part of her report as follows.

PSYCHOLOGICAL REPORT

Validity Evaluation

As a usual and customary part of Mr. X's examination procedures, a number of research-derived tests and test indices were evaluated to determine if Mr. X's participation in the evaluation process was straightforward and forthcoming. Of the seven tests or indices, Mr. X's performance fell well within the scores of experimental normal subjects who were coached to appear emotionally disturbed or neuropsychologically deficient on six of these and "Borderline" on the seventh.

These results suggest that Mr. X's responses to psychological testing were probably invalid, representing a propensity to malinger, fake bad, or exaggerate symptoms. Although his performance on any one or two of these tests might represent confusion or inattention, the consistency of the results suggests the probability of the first interpretation. The test results should be considered as not representative of Mr. X's true neuropsychological or emotional status.

After the psychologist's report was made available to all parties, the defense accepted a plea bargain with the prosecution.

In a similar case, with similar findings, the expert witness presented his findings at trial during direct examination (see Chapter 13) and was cross-examined by opposing counsel as follows:

Opposing Counsel: Doctor, you're a psychologist—is that correct?

Expert Witness: Yes.

Opposing Counsel: You're not a mind reader are you?

Expert Witness: No, Sir.

Opposing Counsel: You're not even a graduate of an accredited medical school are you?

Expert Witness: That's true.

Opposing Counsel: Yet, you are willing to say bad things about my client based on a bunch of tests?

Retaining Counsel: Object your honor—mischaracterization.

Opposing Counsel: Withdraw the question—Now Doctor, your tests are not 100% accurate are they?

Expert Witness: No, sir.

Opposing Counsel: There can be errors of interpretation—what you call "false positives"?

Expert Witness: Yes, sir.

Opposing Counsel: So it's possible that your opinions about my client could be wrong.

Expert Witness: Just about anything is possible.

The opposing counsel's job is to discredit or neutralize the expert's opinion. The expert must not rise to the challenge and debate opposing counsel. It is the retaining counsel's role to clarify issues with his or her expert witness during the re-direct examination (see Chapter 13). In this case, the re-direct examination included the following:

Retaining Counsel: My learned opponent mentioned "accredited medical schools," are psychologists required *anywhere* to be a graduate of such a school?

Expert Witness: Psychologists take their doctorate in accredited graduate schools of psychology.

Retaining Counsel: Is it not true, however, that psychologists are *professors,* teaching medical students and residents in every accredited medical school in the United States?

Expert Witness: Yes, sir, that's true.

Retaining Counsel: Now, Doctor, your opinion that Mr. X was probably not honest and forthcoming on his psychological tests is a probability, is it not?

Expert Witness: Yes, sir.

Retaining Counsel: Thank you, Doctor—no further questions.

When on the witness stand, the expert witness represents all of psychology. Following the Rules of the Road will help the expert represent his or her colleagues properly.

NOTE

1. *Barrel of Fun, Inc. v. State Farm,* 739 F.2d 1028 (1984).

13

Your Day in Court

The chances that you will prepare for the role of expert witness and then step into the courtroom to give testimony are slim. Most civil and criminal trials are settled by negotiation or plea bargaining. For every 15 or 20 cases the expert witness prepares, he or she is likely to give testimony in only 1, which is disconcerting to some psychologists, who experience a sense of incompletion.

In reality, justice and the promotion of human welfare are probably better served when the expert's work results in a conclusion before a trial commences. Magnificent as the American system of jurisprudence is in comparison with other systems, overcrowded dockets continually jeopardize the essential constitutional right to a speedy trial. Anything that aids in the resolution of adversary issues represents a major social contribution. Expert testimony, available to both the plaintiff and defense attorneys in civil matters and the prosecution and defense in criminal matters, often provides information that contributes to pretrial settlements (Fuchsberg, 1991).

The findings of the expert become known to the attorney who retains the expert (or to the judge for whom the expert is *amicus curiae*) when the report of findings is submitted. At that point, the retaining attorney may decide that the results are not useful for his or her trial strategy, and the expert is thanked, paid, and not listed as a witness; under these circumstances, the work of the expert is privileged and may not be revealed to anyone without the explicit permission of the attorney who had retained the expert.

THE DEPOSITION

Once the retaining attorney places the expert on the witness list, the opposing counsel has the right to know the essential content of the expected testimony by the expert. During what is known as the *discovery phase* before the trial, attorneys for both sides have the right to subpoena (demand) all records related to the expert witness's role in the proceedings. Sometimes the opposing counsel is satisfied to receive a copy of the expert's report. More usually, the opposing counsel obtains a court order called *subpoena duces tecum,* which, in effect, sets a date and hour when the witness is to produce all records connected with his or her role in the case and be prepared to answer questions posed by the opposing counsel.

Usual procedure is for the attorney's secretary to call the psychologist's office and ask for an hour or so of time when the opposing counsel can come to the expert's office and conduct the *deposition.* This formal procedure more frequently takes two hours, and the expert should block out this time accordingly. The psychologist should provide a place where five or six people can sit and work comfortably, since the deposition is a court-like procedure involving the attorney who retained the expert, opposing counsel, a court reporter (complete with stenotype machine and tape recorder), and frequently one or two neophyte lawyers brought along by each attorney. It is during the deposition process that young lawyers learn their tradecraft much as do interns and residents during rounds in a medical setting.

Ordinarily, the attorney who retains the expert witness will call and ask to see the expert a half-hour or so before the deposition. During this time, the attorney prepares the expert for the expected questions and reviews the psychologist's file to remove any materials that constitute *work product.* This legal term refers to materials that may relate to the attorney's trial strategy or plan and are *not discoverable* (available to opposing counsel during the discovery process).

It is the wise or experienced expert who, after agreeing to a deposition time, contacts the retaining attorney's secretary or assistant to ensure that they are aware of the date and time the deposition will take place and to further ensure a predeposition conference, so that the attorney prepares his or her expert and is aware of the content and limits of the psychologist's material.

Some attorneys encourage their experts to prepare no report before the trial. The purpose of this legal maneuver is to reveal as little as possible to opposing counsel regarding the expert's findings and position. What might constitute clever case strategy for an attorney can be potentially unethical or professionally unacceptable behavior for a psychologist. Within the clear limits imposed by law, the psychologist as expert must conduct scientific and professional activities as expected by the ethics and standards of psychology; the expert witness must always do exactly that and not be an advocate in the case at hand (Wirthlin, 1987).

The deposition is conducted in a relatively formal manner, depending on the jurisdiction in which it occurs and the style of the attorneys involved. It usually proceeds as follows:

1. Swearing in.
2. Qualifications.

3. Direct examination.
4. Cross-examination (rare).
5. Re-direct examination (rare).
6. Re-cross-examination (rare).
7. Records access.
8. Certification of the deposition.

Because a deposition is a matter of legal record, the court reporter will ask the expert witness to stand and "swear (or affirm) to tell the truth, the whole truth, and nothing but the truth—so help you God?" This makes the proceedings official. At that point, the attorney who scheduled the deposition begins the proceedings with *qualifications*. This introduces the expert witness and proffers his or her credentials as a basis for the forthcoming testimony. Questions include name, office address, number of years in the community, definition of professional role, education, training, accomplishments, experience, honors, and special credentials. During the course of this recital, the retaining attorney may proffer the witness's curriculum vitae or resume to save time. The expert should anticipate this request and have a copy of his or her curriculum vitae available. This becomes an *exhibit* as part of the deposition materials.

Unless the opposing counsel objects to the qualifications of the expert as sufficient for testimony, at some point, he or she may "stipulate to the doctor's credentials as an expert," meaning that the expert is acceptable. At this point, the direct examination begins. It is here that the expert witness "tells the story." Some attorneys ask the expert to tell how he or she was retained, what was done, and what conclusions were reached in very broad questions, allowing the expert to testify according to his or her own style—usually following the expert's report format. Other attorneys conduct direct examination point by point either in respect to the expert's written report or according to an internal format unique to the attorney. (In court, where direct examination is conducted by the retaining attorney, it usually follows a plan agreed on by the attorney and the expert. In the deposition, the format of direct examination is controlled by the opposing counsel.) When the direct examination becomes picky, tangential, or hostile, the retaining attorney will usually "object for the record" and suggest that his or her colleague be more reasonable, patient, to the point, and so on, or "give the witness a chance to explain in his [her] own way."

Once the attorney who conducts the direct examination has finished questioning the expert, retaining counsel may conduct a cross-examination on anything brought out during direct examination. During depositions, the cross-examination (usually conducted by the attorney who hired the expert) is ordinarily rare or quite brief, designed to clarify any misunderstandings but not to increase opposing counsel's knowledge of the expert's opinions.

Following cross-examination, the attorney who conducted the direct examination may choose to ask a few more questions. This is rarely done, but if he or she does, the retaining counsel is entitled to conduct a re-cross-examination. Charts and illustrations are ordinarily not presented during depositions, since this would require that the psychologist provide copies to be marked as exhibits and retained by the court reporter.

When these procedures are completed, the attorney who scheduled the deposition will usually ask for copies of reports, interviews, notes, test forms, and profiles in the expert's case folder. The expert may provide these using his or her own staff and equipment or may provide the entire file to the court reporter, who will reproduce it and later return the file to the expert. Some experienced witnesses simply reproduce everything in the file and have it ready for the deposition. Raw test data should not be provided to the attorney or the court reporter. This professional material may be provided to a qualified psychologist named by the attorney. If a judge's court order demands that raw data be turned over to the attorney directly, the expert must comply, with a cover letter explaining his or her reluctance.

When all attorneys present agree that the deposition is finished, one of them or the court reporter will ask, "Will the witness waive reading and signing?" This means that the deposition can be typed and forwarded to the attorneys without the witness reading the transcription and attesting to its accuracy by signing it. Most lawyers recommend "waiving" as a convenience to the court reporter and as a time-saver for themselves. *The expert should never waive reading and signing of the transcript.* The materials are complex, and even the best court reporter makes mistakes, such as "percentage" for "percentile," "chemical psychologist" for "clinical psychologist," ".10 level of confidence," for ".01 level of confidence," and so on. The transcript is the official, sworn statement of the expert and can in most cases be introduced during the trial during cross-examination. Errors should be identified and corrected in the interests of the expert and the clients served by the expert's testimony.

Of even greater importance is the opportunity for the expert to reproduce a copy of the deposition for the case file. In major cases, the expert may appear in court months after the deposition was taken. If the expert does not have a copy to review what he or she has told opposing counsel during the deposition, the psychologist may find that his or her responses to specific questions posed months ago are all but forgotten. An *ad lib* response without access to the original transcript may put the psychologist in the embarrassing and precarious position of giving an answer on the witness stand that appears to be different from an answer given during the deposition. This could result in opposing counsel's claiming that the expert witness's credibility is *impeached* by the expert's own confusion. *Do not waive the reading and signing of depositions.* Correct the transcript when received from the court reporter, make a copy for the case file, and review the transcript the day before the trial.

THE TRIAL

Should the case not be settled or plea-bargained, the trial will commence. The date of trial is set in a procedure sometimes called *docket sounding*, in which the judge, with the various attorneys, apportions a certain number of days per trial or a certain number of trials per week during the court's calendar. Such dates are approximate. The expert witness is likely to receive a letter from the retaining attorney stating:

> The *Smith v. Jones* case is set on the docket for the week of February 16th. Please note this on your calendar and contact this office if for any reason you cannot be available for testimony during that week. This office will be in touch with you just before the trial to schedule your testimony in this matter.

Experienced experts understand that court dockets are flexible and that some cases take longer to try than anticipated. Some are settled "on the courthouse steps," freeing court time for the next case or for the calendar to be moved up. The expert should specify preferred times to appear during the week of the trial but remain somewhat flexible in respect to the uncertainties of trial procedures.

The expert witness has a relatively small, albeit usually important, part in the trial proceedings. Civil and criminal trials proceed in slightly different ways. The court has discretion in changing the order of trial proceedings, but in general both criminal and civil trials follow a format that includes:

1. Filing of motions by attorneys.
2. Voir dire (jury selection).
3. Instructions to jury (judge).
4. Opening statements:
   a. Prosecutor or plaintiff's attorney.
   b. Defendant's attorney.
5. Presentation of evidence—direct:
   a. Plaintiff or prosecutor's case.
   b. Defendant's case.
6. Presentation of evidence—rebuttal:
   a. Plaintiff's attorney or prosecutor's rebuttal.
   b. Defendant's rebuttal.
7. Opening final argument:
   a. Plaintiff's attorney or prosecutor.
   b. Defendant's attorney.

8. Closing arguments:
   a. Plaintiff's attorney or prosecutor.
   b. Defendant's attorney.
9. Instructions to jury.
10. Decision:
    a. Settlement for civil cases.
    b. Guilt or acquittal in criminal cases.

The expert witness appears during the presentation of direct evidence (item 5 in preceding list), proffered by the attorney for the plaintiff, the prosecutor (the state), or the defendant. Occasionally, the expert witness may be called during rebuttal (item 6). On very rare occasions, the expert witness may appear as *amicus curiae,* or "friend of the court," called by the judge. *Amicus curiae* is more usual in juvenile court procedures or very rarely in appellate reviews (appeals).

PRETRIAL PREPARATION

Scheduling and Conferences

The expert witness should request that the attorney schedule his or her appearance as the first witness in the morning or afternoon court session. Whereas some expert witnesses prefer to be on call and leave their offices 15 to 20 minutes before they are required, testify, and return to their waiting patients, it is unusual for psychologists to qualify and testify so briefly as to allow this. It is wiser to block out an entire morning or afternoon and ask to be the first witness called when court reconvenes at 9:00 A.M. or for the afternoon session. Most attorneys will try to arrange this if it doesn't interfere with the order of evidence they've planned.

The afternoon before the expert is scheduled to testify, a call to the attorney's assistant will ensure that the trial is continuing and that there is no change in the expected time of testimony. It is disconcerting to arrive at the courthouse and discover that the trial was settled or postponed the previous day. These procedural matters are complex, and sometimes witnesses are not informed of changes in plans.

It is of cardinal importance that the psychologist arrange a final conference with the retaining attorney before the court appearance. All the following should be clearly determined between the retaining attorney and the expert witness before the witness is called to the stand:

1. Questions to be used in qualification.
2. The sequence of questions and the expert's responses in the direct examination.

3. Hypothetical questions the attorney is likely to pose to the witness following direct examination.
4. The limits of the psychologist's findings.
5. Probable approaches to be used by opposing counsel during cross-examination.
6. Something about the demographics of the jury members.
7. The presiding judge's style and special expectancies.
8. Any special limitations the physical environment of the courtroom may pose for presentation of charts or other visual materials.

Some attorneys assume that the psychologist will give brief, generalized opinions, followed by answers "within reasonable medical certainty" to hypothetical questions posed by the attorney. During pretrial conferences, the psychologist should be sure that the retaining attorney understands that psychological testimony generally involves an extensive presentation concerning what psychology is as a science and profession, the nature of probability, the nature of science, the purposes of psychological examinations, the qualitative and quantitative output of such examinations, and the limitations of findings and conclusions. The attorney must be helped to understand that all hypothetical questions he or she asks during direct or redirect examination should be addressed "within reasonable psychological probability." It is clearly better to resolve all these matters before the psychologist takes the stand.

Some expert witnesses find that a checklist of pretrial tasks is helpful to ensure that all preparatory steps have been taken in getting ready for court day. Figure 4.9 in Chapter 4 presents such a checklist.

Charts and Illustrations

Sometimes a particular aspect of psychological testimony is best presented through a chart, a table, or an illustration. The decision to use visual aids should be governed by the opportunities and limitations of the physical environment of the courtroom, as well as the judge's patience. Visual aids that lend little to the expert's verbal explanations are poorly received by most judges and are sometimes rejected or excluded. Charts that are complex, difficult to see, or overly bulky disrupt the flow of testimony and lessen the witness's effectiveness. Easels, chalkboards, and projection screens are usually provided for chart display. Psychologists are advised to be extremely cautious about treating the judge and jury as undergraduates who must tolerate the professor's tangential or indistinct chalkboard illustrations or scribbled formulas. Charts should be clear at a distance of 25 feet, since both judge and jury must view the material at the same time. Videotape and slide presentations tend to disrupt the smooth flow of a witness's testimony. Using a small number of charts to illustrate key data or conclusions in the expert's report probably represents the most reasonable approach to this matter. Figure 13.1 is a simple but powerful example of the kind of chart that serves as a useful adjunct to an expert witness's testimony. This chart illustrates total scores on the Holmes Stress scale for the plaintiff who claimed that the stress level resulting from the tragic death of his wife and daughter in a railway accident contributed to the subsequent decline in his health.

Cue Book

Opposing counsel's job is to win for his or her client. Part of a winning trial strategy is to cast doubt on the credibility or standing of expert witnesses presented by an opponent. During cross-examination, an opposing attorney may ask a wide range of tangential or esoteric questions in an effort to fluster the expert. Such questions as "What is the standard error of measurement?" or "Please tell the jury the standard deviation for Full-scale Wechsler Adult Intelligence Scale-Revised for people between the ages of 55 and 64," or "What do psychologists mean by 'validity'?" are typical. Although retaining counsel may, on occasion, object to such questions as immaterial, irrelevant, or incompetent, in general, experts are expected to field such probes. Should the expert answer well, opposing counsel will be placed in the undesirable position of having demonstrated the quality and credibility of the opponent's expert.

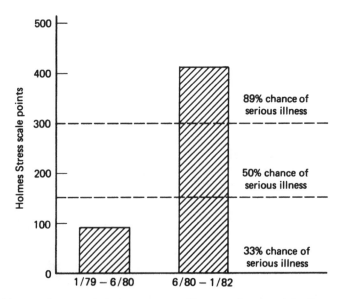

FIGURE 13.1.   A chart used during court to illustrate the stressful effects of a tragic death. A comparison of stress levels for Mr. J. Doe for a period of 18 months previous to the tragic death of his wife and daughter and the 18 months following this event; also, the probable results of these stress levels on illness—vulnerability.

The expert witness may wish to respond to all questions *ad lib,* but it is quite permissible to refer to materials and references. A *cue book* is a collection of materials that may be useful to support direct testimony or as reference in responding to questions during cross-examination. Taking a cue book to court ensures the availability of authoritative reference material should this be required. Figure 13.2 illustrates a table of contents of such a cue book. It will be noted in Figure 13.2 that some items in the cue

---

CUE BOOK CONTENTS

FIGURE 13.2.   A sample table of contents of a cue book.

book are quite basic, or general, while others are specific, directed to particular test instruments or issues in the case. Building a cue book in a large, three-ring notebook will allow the expert to arrange it differently for each trial appearance.

Since the majority of cases are settled without a court appearance, preparation of charts, illustrations, and cue book materials should take place the day before the expert expects to testify.

Dress and Decor

Courtrooms are formal settings and they operate with a great deal of ritual. No matter what a witness may personally feel about the usefulness of such formality, experts who want to be effective in court will dress and conduct themselves accordingly. Dark suits and conservative, even muted, accessories are recommended. The expert witness is expected to be a serious, concerned, dedicated professional person whose grasp of information and ability to communicate stand out. Nothing in the expert's dress or demeanor should detract from the essential roles.

To transport case file, cue book, test materials, and other paraphernalia to court, the expert should consider obtaining a large briefcase or sample case specifically for court work. Since legal files tend to be quite bulky, such a case is a convenience as well as a part of the expert witness's self-presentation as a conservative person, serious and professional. The same is true of chart folders or chart cases, obtainable at either stationery supply houses or artists' supply stores. Black is the preferred color for these occasions, in keeping with the conservative theme.

Getting to the Courtroom

The expert should know where the courtroom is located, how to get there, and what parking facilities exist. Arriving late can have serious consequences for the retaining attorney's planned trial strategy and characterizes a thoughtless and unprofessional expert. Arriving somewhat early is advisable.

If the retaining attorney does not meet the expert at the courthouse, the expert should announce his or her presence to either the judge's secretary or to a bailiff in the corridor near the courtroom where the trial takes place. The judge's office is usually very close to the courtroom and is clearly identified. Bailiffs are men and women, usually in uniform, wearing a badge. They are available in the corridors and courtrooms whenever a trial is in progress. The witness should indicate who he or she is and ask that the retaining attorney be informed that the witness is present and ready. The judge's secretary or the bailiff may ask the witness to wait or may put the expert in a witness room. There is usually a separate witness room for each side in the case. Under no circumstances should the expert converse in any way with persons associated with the opposing side in the case. This could result in the judge declaring a mistrial.

The witness must be especially careful not to enter the courtroom while the trial is in progress until called to give testimony. Judicial rules require that no witness in an adversary matter be exposed or have interaction with the presentation of trial evidence other than that to be given by the expert witness.[1] This procedure of keeping witnesses uncontaminated by the trial proceedings until their turn comes is called *invoking the rule*. Should an expert witness arrive early, sit in the courtroom during the trial, and then later be sworn in as a witness, the judge, on being informed of this, usually by opposing counsel or a bailiff, may declare a mistrial or even hold the expert in contempt of court, subjecting the witness to a fine (or even some time in the local jail if the judge is so inclined). In some jurisdictions, the judge does not invoke the rule on occasion, and the witnesses may sit in the courtroom and hear each other's testimony. A witness should always ask the retaining attorney if the judge invokes the rule.

Sometimes it is necessary to wait in the witness room while some aspect of trial business takes place: Motions are filed, issues are discussed in the judge's chambers, the judge may declare a recess, or previous testimony may take longer than was anticipated. The well-advised expert will bring along some reading or busy work *not associated with the case at hand*. Going over reports or case materials while waiting to be called to the witness stand will only serve to make the expert more tense and probably less effective.

THE COURTROOM DRAMA

The expert witness may appear in a number of courtroom settings. Some of these settings may be moderately informal, such as the judge's chambers for custody hearings or a hearing room for disability determinations. Most settings and all procedures in which the expert witness will participate are quite formal. Figure 3.1 in Chapter 3 illustrates the state and federal court systems of the United States.

Experts are unlikely to be called to testify in municipal or lower district courts at the state levels or at magistrate courts in the federal system. Minor offenses and arraignments take place in these courts. Trials take place in the circuit courts at the state level and in federal district courts. Rarely are witnesses called during appeals at any level since most appellate courts review the records in issues being addressed.

Most courtrooms follow the same general architectural plan. A raised portion, called the *bench*, is the domain of the judge. Surrounded by flags and shields, the judge reigns supreme in this setting, sitting in a large swivel chair, surveying all and everything. To the judge's right (or sometimes left) is the jury box, also raised (but not as high as the judge's bench).

As many as 15 to 30 chairs or seats will be found here, since potential jurors are sometimes examined during the *voir dire* (jury selection phase of the trial). A table for the plaintiff or prosecution and one for the defendant, a table for the court reporter, a podium for the attorneys' presentations, chairs for the bailiffs, and a spectators section complete the usual court-room environment. The expert witness sits in the witness-box, usually to the judge's right (in some courtrooms, if the jury box is to the judge's left, so is the witness-box). Figure 13.3 illustrates a typical courtroom setting.

When called from the witness room or corridor, the expert is generally ushered in by a bailiff. At this point, the trial is in full swing. The jury has heard opening statements from both sides and a fair amount of evidence before the expert appears. Most expert witnesses are called toward the end of the evidence portion of the trial. The jury is ready to hear something that is not in their everyday experience and to learn and weigh the value of what the expert says in the matter at hand before facing the responsibility of rendering a fair verdict. The expert enters the courtroom after the judge has said to the attorney at the podium, "You may proceed,

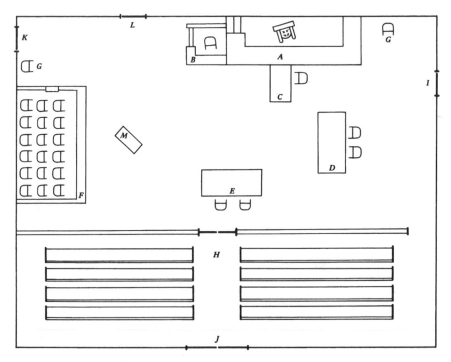

FIGURE 13.3.   A typical courtroom. *A:* judge's bench; *B:* witness box; *C:* court reporter; *D:* defense table; *E:* prosecution or plaintiff table; *F:* jury box; *G:* bailiff's chairs; *H:* spectators, observers, and reporters; *I:* witness entrance; *J:* public entrance; *K:* jury entrance; *L:* judge's entrance; *M:* attorney's podium.

counselor." At this point, the attorney who retains the expert usually says, "I call Dr. _____ ."

Some bailiffs will explain what is expected of the witness, while others leave the witness to her or his own devices. When ushered into the courtroom (*J* in Figure 13.3), the witness should stop and evaluate the setting. Nothing will happen until the witness is properly seated. First, the witness should identify the location of the witness-box (*B* in Figure 13.3). Occasionally, a courtroom will have *two* witness-boxes, one on each side of the judge's bench. The proper one for the witness is the witness-box being faced by the court reporter seated at *C* in Figure 13.3. The witness should walk directly to the corner of the witness-box and say *nothing* to anyone in the courtroom but nod to the judge as the bench is passed. Reaching the corner of the witness-box, *B*, the witness should turn, face the man or woman seated at *C* (the court clerk or reporter), and raise the right arm. Do not wait to be instructed. Do not hesitate. Nothing can be done until the witness is sworn. Following these procedures without hesitation announces to all present that this expert understands courtroom procedure and is, indeed, an expert.

At this point, the court clerk will stand and raise his or her hand and say: "Do you swear (or affirm) to tell the truth, the whole truth, and nothing but the truth so help you God?"

There may be a slight modification of this in some jurisdictions, but this is the essential procedure. Occasionally, the court clerk will approach the witness with a Bible, asking that the left hand be placed on the Bible and the right hand raised. This is a rare procedure today.

After the witness says "I do" or "I shall," the court clerk usually says, "Take the stand" or "Be seated." The status and significance of witnesses is illustrated by the fact that the witness-box is usually raised one step—equal to the jury but lower than the judge.

Once sworn, the witness should step up into the witness-box. There are usually a swivel armchair and a shelf on the front rail of the witness-box that can serve as a desk for the expert's materials. On being seated, the witness should turn to the judge, only two or three feet away, smile, and quietly say, "Good morning (or good afternoon), your Honor." This acknowledgment of the judge is good manners and helps to establish the witness's credibility with the bench. Briefcase and chart case should be opened but left on the floor of the witness-box, readily available when materials are to be retrieved.

THE EVIDENTIARY PROCESS

The expert has been called by one side or the other to be a part of the presentation of evidence to the judge and jury. The process may vary in content, but the structure is fairly rigid and predictable. It is a process of taking turns between two attorneys representing adversary positions in the matter at hand. Unless the witness serves as amicus curiae, he or she will be called during the evidentiary portion of the trial assigned to the attorney who retained the witness (see the section "The Trial"). Once the witness is called and sworn, the following process occurs for the purpose of entering the expert's statements and conclusions in the minds of the judge and jury and in the record of the trial.

The expert witness is usually called toward the end of the retaining attorney's presentation. The judge and jury have heard presentations from the attorneys and various witnesses. Most of the jurors and probably the judge have formed a framework for the evidence. They have been hearing other evidence and may even have reached some preliminary conclusion as to the decisions they will render in the case. The testimony of the expert may solidify or modify a series of conclusions that are, to some degree, already formed. The expert will be identified to the jury as such by the attorney, with the approval of the judge. The jury will have been instructed by the judge that all decisions are theirs. They will be told that they are to weigh the opinions of experts as they weigh other evidence. They may accept, reject, or question expert opinion. The expert witness serves as a *source of influence* on the *targets of influence* (see Figure 13.4). The retaining attorney has a right to expect that the expert will do everything possible to make the presentation thorough, defensible, scientifically reliable, and valid within reasonable psychological probability in a manner logical and understandable to the judge and jury. Attorneys have studied and written about the effective presentation of the expert witness (Bernstein, 1994; Lubet, 1993). The expert can expect the retaining attorney to advise and suggest during the pretrial conference regarding the expert's responses during direct and cross-examination.

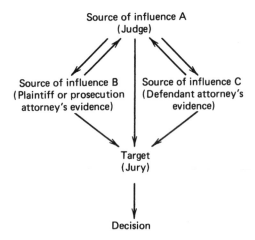

FIGURE 13.4.   A model of social influence in the courtroom.

The expert witness is not required and should not attempt to advocate for one side or the other, shade the data in favor of one adversary or the other, omit pertinent facts or expand inconsequential elements of a presentation. It is the expert's responsibility to resist and discourage such maneuvers. The expert should be neither surprised nor offended by any efforts by attorneys to expand or aggrandize evidence in favor of their client—that is their job. The expert is an element of the adversary process but not an advocate. Anything the expert can do to avoid thinking in terms of "our side," "our case," "winning," or "beating them" will be helpful in maintaining perspective and appropriate behavior as an expert witness.

Qualification of the Witness

The witness is called by an attorney to provide information that, because of its uniqueness in relation to some science, profession, training, or experience, is unlikely to be common knowledge or in the experience of the average juror. The first step in the process is to demonstrate the expert's specialness or right to claim expert status. If opposing counsel and the judge accept the witness as qualified, the evidence may be presented. If opposing counsel objects to the expert's qualifications and the judge agrees with the objections or if the judge determines that the "expert" is not qualified, the judge will say, "You may step down," thus dismissing the proffered expert before testimony is given. The following is a representative sequence of questions and answers that may be used to qualify an expert in clinical psychology:

Mr. Jones *(Retaining Attorney):*   Please state your name.

Dr. Doe: John Doe.

Mr. Jones: Would you tell the Judge and jury your profession.

Dr. Doe: I am a clinical psychologist.

Mr. Jones: Where do you practice, Doctor?

Dr. Doe: I am staff psychologist at the Kaufman Mental Health Center.

Mr. Jones: Is that here in Okachobee?

Dr. Doe: Yes, at 121 Main Street.

Mr. Jones: How long have you been staff psychologist there?

Dr. Doe: For the past 14 years.

Mr. Jones: Please tell the Judge and jury what a clinical psychologist is in terms of education, training, and function.

Dr. Doe: A clinical psychologist is a person who has received a bachelor's degree in psychology and has then gone on to receive the doctorate in psychology, these degrees taking between 8 and 10 years to complete. During this time, studies are taken in basic science, behavioral science, human development, learning, emotions, adjustment, normal and abnormal human behavior, and research in psychology. The individual learns techniques of diagnosis, therapy, and other helping interventions in supervised training and internship centers. Following the award of the doctor's degree, the psychologist must acquire a minimum of one year's postdoctoral supervised training in order to be eligible for licensing examination administered by the state. Licensed clinical psychologists diagnose and treat a wide range of mental disorders, emotional disturbances, family and marital problems, and difficulties associated with child development, adolescence, problems of aging, and so on. A clinical psychologist is an expert in the practice of the science of human behavior.

Mr. Jones: Are you licensed in this state?

Dr. Doe: Yes, sir.

Mr. Jones: Are you an expert in neuropsychology?

Dr. Doe: Yes, sir.

Mr. Jones: In your work as a neuropsychologist, do you have occasion to examine patients and determine whether they have brain injury or brain disorder?

Dr. Doe: Yes, sir.

Mr. Smith *(Opposing Counsel):*   I object, Your Honor. There are no indications that this witness is a graduate of an accredited medical school.

This rarely occurs during qualification nowadays, but on occasion, where the lawyers are not familiar with the background of psychologists, this type of objection might be made. This can be handled in several ways. Mr. Jones, the retaining attorney, may ask, "May we approach the bench, your Honor?" for the purpose of discussing the psychologist's qualification and citing legal decisions or precedent qualifying psychologists in these matters. The counsel who retained the psychologist may debate the issue directly, before the jury, without asking to approach the bench:

Mr. Jones: Your Honor, I submit that psychologists have testified as experts in matters of brain injury, brain disorder, mental disease, and mental illness for many years. I submit that, according to the laws of the state, and federal procedure, Dr. Doe is fully qualified in this matter, and I would be happy to have him voir dired as to his specific qualifications.

The preceding statement refers to the attorney's response to opposing counsel's challenge, indicating that he is more than happy to show the jury how eminently qualified Dr. Doe is as an expert. At this point, the judge may allow such questioning or may ask the bailiff to take the jury out so that the judge can conduct some questioning of the witness in order to determine that the witness is qualified to give testimony as an expert in the matters being considered.

As noted, it is rare that psychologists of good qualification are challenged in any court of the land. This is far different from the situation several decades ago. Ordinarily, the procedure is more likely as follows:

Mr. Smith: *(standing)* Your Honor, we wish to stipulate as to the qualifications of the witness.

This means that Mr. Smith, the opposing attorney, does not want the jury to hear any more about the qualifications of Dr. Doe. At this point, the retaining attorney may simply accept this. On the other hand, it may be of interest to him to have more of the qualifications presented to the jury. The judge is unlikely to allow the retaining attorney to "aggrandize" the witness. It is up to the retaining attorney to demonstrate the necessity of presenting the qualifications. This is sometimes done as follows:

Mr. Jones: Your Honor, I would like to continue with the qualification, since in this case, the issue of addiction and the use of alcohol is of considerable significance. Dr. Doe has certain special qualifications that I believe are important as part of the qualification.

The Court: You may proceed in your qualification, but I want you to be sure that you focus only on the pertinent background.

Mr. Jones: Thank you, Your Honor. And now, Dr. Doe, have you had any special background or training in the treatment of alcohol or other drug-related conditions?

Dr. Doe: Yes, sir, I have.

Mr. Jones: Would you please tell the Judge and jury what special background you have in these areas?

Dr. Doe: Following the receipt of my doctor's degree, I spent two years, first as a postdoctoral trainee and then as a staff psychologist, at the Alcoholic Rehabilitation Center at Camp Butner, North Carolina. During that time, my duties were entirely involved with alcohol abuse, its diagnosis, its treatment, and rehabilitation. We also had a drug rehabilitation center attached to our unit, and I spent considerable time there both in training and in practice.

Mr. Jones: Your Honor, I submit that Dr. Doe is qualified in this matter.

The Court: You may proceed, Mr. Jones.

The preceding statement by the judge means that Dr. Doe has been qualified to proceed with his testimony.

Direct Examination

The direct examination is conducted by the attorney who calls the expert witness. The purpose of the direct examination is to present as clearly and strongly as possible information supportive of the retaining attorney's case. Evidence presented by an expert witness is usually considered very seriously by the judge and jury. The attorney who retains the expert will usually conduct the direct examination in such a way that the findings and opinions of the expert are presented to the judge and jury in a smooth, logical, and understandable sequence of questions and answers. Some attorneys prepare their expert witnesses with one or more pretrial conferences, whereas other attorneys prefer their experts to testify "spontaneously" as to their findings. The psychologist who expects to be a credible and effective witness in the direct examination would be well advised to arrange a pretrial preparation of the direct examination. Agreement between the attorney and the expert as to the sequence of questions, length, style, and content of answers, use of charts or illustrations, and the form in which hypothetical questions are to be presented will help ensure a smooth, professional direct examination.

Because of the complexities and technicalities of psychological matters, much attention must be paid to the issue of carefully educating the judge and jury to these matters as the testimony unfolds. In some ways, the expert must function as a teacher, explaining procedures and methods, before the results of an assessment or an opinion concerning an occurrence are presented to the judge and jury. The expert witness and the presenting attorney must strike a rather difficult balance in the direct examination, neither boring nor confusing the judge and jury with too much or too little information. Two or three experiences on the witness stand or even the reading of the court transcripts of direct examination of expert witnesses will probably be sufficient to convince most neophyte expert witnesses of the wisdom of the pretrial conference.

A traditional approach for a clear and effective presentation requires a series of simple questions by the attorney and relatively short answers by the expert, gradually bringing out both the scientific bases of the testimony and the findings and opinions of the expert. This approach is effective but puts great demands on the expert to be precise and concise at the same time. This particular communication skill, in a sense, defines the *expert* witness. No matter what credentials and technical knowledge the expert witness possesses, the effectiveness with which the expert conveys information is the paramount issue in court.

All direct examinations have unique features, but a general format may be expected. The presenting attorney will first ask questions concerning how the expert became involved in the matter at hand. The expert will be asked what he or she did and the significance of the procedures. This will be followed by questions concerned with results and interpretations. The final questions will be *hypothetical questions* designed to summarize the expert's testimony, clearly but simply state the expert's opinions in the matter, and relate the testimony to the attorney's key premises and positions in the case.

The following illustrates how the direct examination begins in a case involving a 34-year-old woman who was the victim in an automobile accident that occurred 2½ years before the trial. She was a passenger in a car that was struck head-on by a truck; was unconscious for 10 days following the initial trauma; and underwent surgery for the removal of a subdural hematoma in the left parieto-occipital area of the brain shortly after admission to the hospital. Residual complaints include right-sided weakness, headaches, memory deficits, nervousness, clumsiness, double vision, and impulsive acts. Arithmetic skills are said by the patient to be lowered since the accident. The direct examination is by Mr. Albee, the retaining attorney, who represents the plaintiff, Mrs. Alberts; the psychologist-expert witness is Dr. White; and opposing counsel, representing the defendants (the driver of the truck and his insurance company) is Mr. McCracken:

Mr. Albee: When did you first become involved in this case, Doctor?

Dr. White: I received a call from you on September 18, 1982, requesting me to examine Mrs. Alberts.

Mr. Albee: What was the purpose of the examination, Doctor?

Dr. White: You asked that I conduct a psychological examination to determine whether Mrs. Alberts was at that time suffering brain disorder, what the quality of her current psychological functions were, and whether any abnormal findings were related to Mrs. Alberts' accident in June of 1980.

Mr. Albee: Were you provided with any background material or records?

Dr. White: Yes, sir.

Mr. Albee: Please tell the court and the jury what materials you reviewed previous to your examinations of Mrs. Alberts.

Dr. White: I reviewed the emergency room records dated June 21, 1980, from the Kaufman Memorial Hospital; the operating room notes and summary report of Dr. Barclay, the neurosurgeon who operated on Mrs. Alberts; various progress and treatment notes associated with her hospitalization; and the discharge summary written by Dr. Barclay. I have reviewed Dr. Barclay's follow-up reports dated August 15 and November 12, 1980, as well as his notes dated February 6 and June 20, 1981. I've read Dr. Barclay's neurological evaluation, with enclosed CAT scan and EEG reports dated August 14, 1982. I've reviewed the rehabilitation reports covering the period January 1981 to the present from the Coleman Rehabilitation Center. I've reviewed the psychological report and test materials of Dr. Harkey, who examined Mrs. Alberts in August of 1981. I believe that covers it.

Depending on the complexity of the case and the style of the attorney, the interrogatory might continue into details as to the weight and meanings of the background material. Sometimes, this section of the direct examination is for purposes of assuring the jury that the expert witness was thoroughly familiar with the circumstances surrounding the plaintiff's injury.

Following the initial interrogatory, the lawyer will usually lead the expert witness into the presentation of information concerning the types and purposes of the examinations and procedures conducted by the expert:

Mr. Albee: When did you examine Mrs. Alberts, Dr. White?

Dr. White: I saw Mrs. Alberts initially for a clinical history on October 6, 1982. Subsequently, Mrs. Alberts was examined on October 12, 13, 16, and 18, 1982. She was seen for a total of 14 hours of interviews and psychological examinations.

Mr. Albee: Did you conduct all the examinations yourself?

Dr. White: All the interviews and examinations were conducted by me or under my direction and supervision by Mr. Bunter, my psychological assistant.

Mr. Albee: Approximately how many hours did you spend with Mrs. Alberts during this time?

Dr. White: I spent a total of five and one-half hours examining Mrs. Alberts, and the remaining eight and one-half hours of the examination took place in my test room with Mr. Bunter administering various psychological tests under my direction.

Mr. Albee: Is this usual and standard procedure for psychological examinations?

Dr. White: Yes, it is.

Mr. Albee: Please tell the court the types of examinations administered and the purpose or purposes of each.

Dr. White: Mrs. Alberts was given a rather complete battery of psychological tests and procedures to determine her psychological status and condition. A clinical history was taken to establish the nature of Mrs. Alberts' background, development, family, education, and life experiences. The history also identified Mrs. Alberts' view of the difficulties she experienced since the accident.

Mr. Albee: Would you please summarize the problems Mrs. Alberts associated with her accident.

Dr. White: During the clinical history, Mrs. Alberts stated that since the accident, she is "different." She stated that she has difficulty in remembering recent events, that she is much more nervous and irritable than ever before in her life, and much more impatient with her husband and her two children. She states that she is unable to lift things with her right hand and that her handwriting has become poor since the accident. She can no longer type effectively. Her arithmetic calculations are inaccurate since the accident. She suffers many more headaches than before the accident. She states that since the accident she suffers double vision frequently. She indicates that her diminished social judgment, such as being critical, laughing too much or too loudly, and interrupting people without meaning to, has become a source of embarrassment since the accident.

Mr. Albee: Do these symptoms mean anything to you, Doctor?

Mr. McCracken: Objection, Your Honor. No premise has been laid to allow the doctor to speculate. The hypothetical is too vague.

The Judge: Objection sustained.

Mr. Albee: Let me back up a bit, Doctor. Were these responses a result of standard, acceptable interview procedures?

Dr. White: Yes, sir.

Mr. Albee: And did you evaluate Mrs. Alberts' statements according to known and generally accepted methods?

Dr. White: Yes, sir.

Mr. Albee: And in your field, Doctor, is there a standard interpretation or conclusion that psychologists would reach from such signs and symptoms?

Dr. White: Yes.

Mr. Albee: Would you tell the court your opinion as to the meaning of such symptoms reported by a person who had been in an automobile accident and suffered unconsciousness for 10 days following the accident?

Dr. White: The experiences described by Mrs. Alberts are considered consistent with the sequelae, or aftereffects, of a severe closed-head injury.

The attorney has neatly brought out that the defendant's difficulties, associated with the accident, are characteristic of persons who have been brain injured. The objection raised by Mr. McCracken represents the proper response of a skilled attorney who has caught his opponent rushing things and seizes the opportunity to disrupt the smooth flow of the direct examination. Strategically, such disruptions serve the purpose of suggesting to the jury that the presenting attorney is less than perfect in his tradecraft. Mr. Albee takes this in stride and continues the direct examination, taking no issue with the objection, and hoping that the jury will view Mr. McCracken's objection as petty and unnecessary.

In the presentation of information about the use and interpretation of psychological tests, accuracy is of signal importance. Chapter 6 presents in detail the technical and ethical guidelines within which test data should be presented. During the direct examination, the test data should be presented in a sequence that is logical and understandable in respect to the issues being considered by the jury:

Mr. Albee: After the clinical interview, what procedures did you then follow, Doctor?

Dr. White: I then began the formal psychological testing.

Mr. Albee: What was your purpose in giving Mrs. Alberts psychological tests?

Dr. White: The battery of tests given Mrs. Alberts consisted of standard psychological test instruments to help me determine if Mrs. Alberts suffered any psychological problems or deficiencies and, if so, what these might be.

Mr. Albee: Would you tell the judge and the jury what type of tests were administered?

Dr. White: Mrs. Alberts was given a series of tests of intellectual capacity, neuropsychological functioning, reading ability, skills, aptitudes, rehabilitation potential, and personality.

Mr. Albee: Would this be considered a standard and proper test battery, in your profession, for a person in Mrs. Alberts' circumstances?

Dr. White: Yes, it would.

Mr. Albee: I would like, Doctor, for you to go through your examination and explain what you did, what you found, and what it meant. What tests were given first?

Dr. White: Mrs. Alberts was first given the Wechsler Adult Intelligence Scale-Revised.

Mr. Albee: What does this test measure?

Dr. White: The Wechsler Adult Intelligence Scale is made up of 11 subtests measuring a variety of skills, abilities, and response capacities that can be generally grouped together and called "intelligence."

Mr. Albee: Is this what we used to call "IQ" tests?

Dr. White: Yes sir, although the IQ is a fairly out-of-date concept. We can be much more accurate in describing intelligence today than we could 40 years ago when the concept of "IQ tests" was current.

Mr. Albee: Then, Doctor, just what do these 11 subtests of the Wechsler measure?

Dr. White: The Wechsler scales are the most generally accepted and most used tests of intellectual ability in psychological practice today. Developed and revised over the past 50 years, they measure an individual's ability to acquire information, organize ideas, use memory, perform logical operations—both verbal and nonverbal—and solve problems that are both simple and complex, verbal and mechanical. In short, human intelligence is a variety of abilities to process information, communicate, solve problems, and use materials appropriately to perform a wide range of tasks. High intelligence represents efficiency, speed, and skill in these abilities, while low intelligence represents lesser or deficient skill and ability.

Mr. Albee: Are there scores that a person makes on these tests?

Dr. White: Yes. Scores on the 11 Wechsler scales are summarized into Verbal Scores, representing the tests that measure the general information a person has collected, ability to comprehend verbal material, attention span, memory for numbers, problem solving, vocabulary, and reasoning. A Performance Score represents such skills as eye-hand coordination, picking out key ideas, ability to manipulate objects skillfully and to put together various kinds of puzzles with speed and accuracy.

Mr. Albee: How do you determine the quality or the goodness of a person's test performance?

Dr. White: If a person's scores on various tests result in an Intelligent Quotient of 100, the performance is considered "Average." Psychologists prefer to use the concept of "percentile" in order to be more accurate about what test scores mean. A percentile is a person-to-person ranking that tells exactly how well a person performed when compared with a group of people in a specific population—such as men, women, high school graduates, and so on. An IQ of 100 would be the 50th percentile. This would mean that a person getting total scores which place them at the 50th percentile on the Wechsler Adult Intelligence Scale-Revised is able to perform equal to or better than 50 out of 100 people of their own age range in the general population. It also means that about 50 percent of the people in that group or population are likely to perform better than the person who achieves an IQ of 100 and falls at the 50th percentile. A person whose scores result in an intelligence quotient of 120 on the Wechsler scales falls at the 90th percentile. Such performance is considered Superior and equals or exceeds the scores of 90 out of 100 who have taken these tests. A person whose test scores result in an intelligence quotient of 80 on the Wechsler scales falls at the 10th percentile. This performance is considered Borderline. Ninety percent of those in the same age category as the person with the IQ of 80 perform better on the tests.

Mr. Albee: You administered the Wechsler Adult Intelligence Scale-Revised to Mrs. Alberts?

Dr. White: Yes, I did.

Mr. Albee: Please tell the Judge and jury the scores on Mrs. Alberts' intelligence tests.

Dr. White: Mrs. Alberts had a Verbal IQ of 104, which placed her at the 56th percentile; a Performance IQ of 70, placing her at the second percentile for these tests, and her Full scale IQ was 83, or the 14th percentiie.

Mr. Albee: In practical, everyday terms, Doctor, what does this mean?

Dr. White: These results suggest that at the time I evaluated Mrs. Alberts, she was able to perform intellectual tasks with a strong verbal component, that is, involving communication—hearing, analyzing, speaking, calculating—at an average level. That would be as good as about one-half of the people her age in the general population. By the same token, about one-half of the people in her age bracket in the general population are able to do these tasks more efficiently or better than Mrs. Alberts.

   In Performance, or nonverbal tasks that require picking out key ideas, using social intelligence, eye-hand coordination, the ability to put things together, and new learning, Mrs. Alberts does as well as only 2 out of 100 in her age bracket; 98 out of 100 are likely to do better than she.

   In short, Mrs. Alberts is able to do an average job in using intelligence that involves basic communication, but in practical areas of life she is severely limited.

Mr. Albee: Is this pattern of response something that Mrs. Alberts has always had?

Dr. White: Not likely. Mrs. Alberts is a college graduate. She had worked successfully for seven years before her accident as a marine biologist. It is unlikely that a person with the measured skills I've described could either graduate from college or work successfully or safely in the usual work setting of a marine biologist. At the time of her accident, she was assistant chief of her research section with the U.S. Coast and Geodetic Survey.

Mr. Albee: Then if I understand you correctly, Doctor, your test results suggest that Mrs. Alberts is now less capable than she was at one time, such as during the years she acquired her education and during her professional career.

Dr. White: That is correct.

The attorney for the plaintiff has neatly led his witness through a presentation designed to demonstrate clearly to the triers of fact (judge and jury) that Mrs. Alberts has been carefully examined and found to have intellectual deficits. The attorney has also led the expert to an opinion that says that the plaintiff has suffered this loss after demonstrating intellectual capacity of a fairly high quality through education and work performance.

The attorney conducting the direct examination would probably continue his questioning of Dr. White to bring before the judge and the jury all aspects of Dr. White's psychological examination and the opinions formulated by Dr. White about Mrs. Alberts' deficiencies, losses, problems, rehabilitation efforts, and potentials. The interaction will tend to be smooth and comfortable for all parties if a pretrial conference between the expert witness and the attorney covered all aspects of the attorney's expectations and the expert's conclusions. In the style previously illustrated, the attorney conducting the *direct examination* will bring out the essence of the expert's examinations and conclusions. Following the presentation of the intellectual evaluation, the expert might then be asked similar questions concerning the neuropsychological evaluation, the aptitude assessment, and the personality examination. The effectiveness of the direct examination in terms of conveying the expert's opinion to the judge and the jury will largely depend on the competence of the expert, the experience and style of the attorney, and the amount of preparation they have put into the case, both separately and together.

After the presenting attorney has led the expert through examinations conducted and conclusions reached, the expert is likely to be presented with the key questions of the direct examination: the hypothetical questions.

Hypothetical questions bring together the salient issues of the case. The response by the expert witness is to focus attention on what the attorney wants the judge and the jury to understand and believe. It is critically important that the attorney and the witness are quite clear as to what will be asked and how the expert plans to respond before the expert goes to court. The earlier in the case the expert knows what hypothetical questions are liable to be asked, the more clearly he or she can tell the lawyer what answers can be given. It is disruptive and unprofessional to discover at the eleventh hour that expert and attorney have different ideas as to what hypotheticals will be asked and what answers will be forthcoming.

The following represents the hypothetical questions that might be asked after the direct examination in the case previously illustrated:

Mr. Albee: Now that you have explained your examination and your results to the jury, Doctor, I should like to pose a question to you: Assume that Mrs. Alberts is a successful college graduate, and further assume that before her accident of July 6, 1981, Mrs. Alberts worked professionally and efficiently as a marine biologist. Given your examination of the hospital records made available to you, given the results of your extensive psychological and neuropsychological examinations, given your broad experience and skill as an expert, is it your opinion that Mrs. Alberts now suffers measurable and significant brain disorder?

Dr. White: Yes, sir. That is my opinion.

Mr. Albee: Now, Doctor: Assuming all the above and that Mrs. Alberts functioned well up until July 6, 1981, further assume that since the time of her accident on that date, there has been no further injury or illness affecting Mrs. Alberts' brain. Is it your opinion, within reasonable psychological probability, that the aforesaid accident is the cause of Mrs. Alberts' present psychological and neuropsychological deficits?

Dr. White: Yes. That is my opinion.

Mr. Albee: No further questions, Your Honor.

The attorney has focused the attention of the jury on two conclusions: There is significant deficit in brain function and the most probable cause is the accident of 1981 for which the attorney is seeking damages and remedy for his client.

Recess

In keeping with the tradition of taking turns in the adversary process, it is time for opposing counsel to question the witness. Before this takes place, the presiding judge, aware that the witness has been under questioning for an hour or more, is likely to interrupt the interrogatory by striking his or her gavel and saying, "We shall have a 10-minute recess." At this point, the judge gets up—a signal for *all* to rise—and leaves the courtroom.

Because lawyers spend much of their time in the courtroom, they may not be aware that judicial procedures are foreign to their witnesses who may be in the courtroom for the first time. The expert witness, when thus left standing in the witness-box after the judge has left, should assess his or her own situation. If there is a need to use the restroom, get a drink of water, or simply walk around, the proper procedure is to find a bailiff in the courtroom and indicate one's needs. It is important that one doesn't simply go out and find the nearest restroom that may be available. This might put the witness in contact with opposing counsel, witnesses for the opposition, or witnesses who are yet to be called. This could violate the *sequestration* rules that are established against interaction between witnesses. The bailiff is the person to ensure that this does not happen.

In less formal courtroom settings, the judge may invite the witness to chambers to have a cup of coffee and to "chat." This is not likely to be a usual process, but the expert should be prepared for this, particularly if the judge has been favorably inclined toward the expert's testimony.

The expert should not be concerned if the attorney who retained the expert does not immediately come to the witness stand and congratulate the witness on a sterling performance. This is one small part of the attorney's presentation, and many matters are likely to take the attorney's attention at this point. The witness should not be disturbed if the two opposing counsels, almost bitter in their interaction during court, seem quite friendly and sociable during recess. They may be momentary antagonists, but they are professional colleagues.

The expert witness would be well advised to utilize the recess, after consulting with the bailiff, by walking around, getting a drink of water, and using the restroom facilities. Psychological testimony tends to take time, and it is very inconvenient to the process for an expert to ask for a recess in the middle of some part of the trial. It is best to follow the judge's lead and use the recesses that are made available.

Should the judge declare a lunch recess or an overnight recess at the end of a portion of the expert's testimony, the expert should immediately approach the attorney who retained the expert and ask for directions and instructions. In the event it is a lunch recess, the retaining attorney may take the witness to lunch in order to discuss the testimony that has occurred up to that time. In a situation where the expert is still not finished with testimony at the end of the day and the judge recesses court until the following morning, it is likely that the judge will admonish the witness not to discuss the testimony or the anticipated presentation with anyone. With careful planning, this type of split testimony is likely to be rare.

Cross-Examination

The cross-examination is conducted by the attorney opposing the attorney who called the expert witness. The purpose of the cross-examination is to cast some doubt or question on the quality of the witness as an expert, on the thoroughness of the material presented, or on the credibility of the opinion that has been rendered by the expert. During the direct examination the expert may notice that opposing counsel has been taking notes and, in some cases, looking up references in various books on the counsel's table. This is in preparation to conduct the cross-examination.

It is unlikely that the expert witness will find the cross-examination similar to what is shown on television or in motion pictures about courtroom scenes. Each attorney has a particular style, and very few of them emulate fictional characters. It is important that the attorney impress and influence the jury, and few attorneys believe that they can do this by imitating familiar media characters (Perdue, 1993).

Most attorneys begin cross-examination in a very gentle and persuasive manner. They are likely to be polite and even complimentary about the expert's testimony. Nevertheless, their hope and expectation is to leave the jury with the impression that the expert witness's testimony is to be given very little weight and credibility.

The most effective kind of cross-examination involves a process by which the opposing attorney can arrange for the expert witness to *impeach* himself or herself. The process of impeachment requires that the attorney ask questions that result in the witness making contradictory statements. If the lawyer can bring the witness to face and admit that he or she has said two different things about the same issue, the attorney will have succeeded in impeaching the witness and can then suggest that the entire testimony of the expert be disregarded.

It cannot be overemphasized that careful professional work by the expert and extensive preparation for the trial between the retaining attorney and the expert will limit the effectiveness of opposing counsel's maneuvers to cast significant doubt on the expert's opinion during cross-examination. Poor professional preparation and lack of sufficient communication between the expert and the retaining attorney are likely to open many doors for successful cross-examination.

If the psychologist has "followed all the rules," it is unlikely that opposing counsel will do much during the cross-examination to lessen the credibility of the witness in the eyes of the judge and jury. Opposing counsel must take her or his turn, however, and Dr. White of the previous direct examination will be subject to something like the following cross-examination by Mr. McCracken, opposing counsel:

Mr. McCracken: That was very interesting, Miss White.

Mr. Albee: Objection, your Honor. Counsel is baiting the witness.

The Court: You will address the witness properly, Counselor.

Mr. McCracken: I'm sorry, your Honor—I apologize, *Dr.* White, but it is true that you are not a medical doctor, is that not so?

Dr. White: That is correct.

Mr. McCracken: You are, in fact, only a doctor of philosophy?

Mr. Albee: Objection. Counsel's remarks are immaterial and provocative. Dr. White's credentials have been ascertained and stipulated.

The Court: Sustained. I shan't warn you again, Counselor. Confine your questions to the issue.

Mr. McCracken: I'm sorry, Your Honor, if it pleases the court, I shall continue.

The Court: You may proceed.

Although not a rule of thumb, some attorneys prefer to begin the cross-examination with a smoke screen of pseudochallenge to lay some doubt before the jury as to the credentials of the witness, knowing full well that the witness has been qualified and the questions will be ruled out of order by the judge. Some judges tolerate this type of trial strategy, while others may warn opposing counsel sharply. Hostile tactics have been shown to incur disapproval (Gibbs, Sigal, Adams, & Grossman, 1989). The witness may *not* enter in with rebuttal, counterquestions, or explanations outside of the direct question. Any such attempt by the expert will be immediately quashed by the judge. If the witness is unfamiliar with these procedures, the following might occur:

Mr. McCracken: That was very interesting, Miss White.

Dr. White: I'm afraid you've forgotten that I'm a doctor and that—

The Court: *(interrupting)* The witness will confine her responses to direct questions only. Do you understand, Dr. White?

Dr. White: But, Your Honor, I—

The Court: *(interrupting)* Although you are designated as an expert witness, you must respond as I've just told you. Do you understand that?

Dr. White: Yes, Your Honor.

No matter how unfair the attorney conducting the cross-examination may be, the witness may not complain, correct, or advocate. Either the opposing counsel or the judge may interrupt to prevent abuse of the witness, but the witness may respond only to the questions asked.

The tone of cross-examination of a well-qualified witness is more likely to be as follows:

Mr. McCracken: Dr. White—please explain to the jury what psychologists mean by "standard deviation."

Dr. White: Standard deviation is a statistical term. It is a measure of dispersion. By that, we mean the degree to which a test score may vary by chance alone. It is one measure of the stability of a test score.

Mr. McCracken: And what is the standard deviation of the Wechsler Adult Intelligence Scale-Revised?

Dr. White: Fifteen IQ points on the Full scale intelligence score represents one standard deviation.

Mr. McCracken: That means, does it not, that any single IQ score is not an absolute, sure, certain, valid, reliable representation of what the person's "real" IQ is?

Dr. White: Well, in a sense, I . . .

Mr. McCracken: Please answer my question, Doctor—yes or no?

Dr. White: Well, yes . . .

Mr. McCracken: Then the IQ scores you gave for Mrs. Alberts are really not "true" or "accurate" or "stable" scores, are they?

Dr. White: Well, I wouldn't really . . .

Mr. McCracken: If the Court pleases, could the good doctor be directed to be more responsive?

The Court: Doctor, please answer Counsel's questions directly.

Dr. White: Yes.

Opposing counsel has cleverly led the expert into a cul-de-sac using a basic statistical question to cast doubt on the quality, stability, or significance of the expert's conclusions offered during the direct examination.

The expert is not totally helpless in these matters. When opposing counsel uses a clever focus to cast question on the expert's conclusions, the attorney who retained the witness may raise issues of fairness or procedure to protect the expert. Most attorneys are somewhat reluctant to do this since it takes the jurors' attention away from the expert's testimony. It is much better for the expert to be capable of dealing with these issues without help. One very effective technique, which should be used sparingly, is the *qualification*. This enables the witness to explain why the opposing counsel's innuendo or implication is only *partially* correct. The witness makes this request *after* answering one of the opposing counsel's "clever" questions. Thus, in the case being considered, it might go as follows:

Mr. McCracken: When it comes right down to it, Doctor, all the tests you gave and the results you reported on Mrs. Alberts really amount to little more than guesses, or "probabilities," as you call them—is this not so?

Dr. White: Well, in a sense, yes . . . but—

Mr. McCracken: And when you tell us that Mrs. Alberts has a lower IQ than what she probably had before the accident, this is nothing more than a guess, or "probability," and *not* a fact—is this not so?

Dr. White: Yes *(quickly turning to face the Judge)*. Your Honor, may I qualify?

It is critical for the expert to be prepared to move quickly. Should the witness hesitate, the opposing counsel will go right on to the next question, leaving the impression with the jury that Dr. White's testimony was of little import. By quickly and politely appealing to the court, the witness requests permission to present her view fairly:

The Court: Yes, Doctor, you may qualify.

Dr. White: As an expert, I can only give my best and most carefully developed opinions. These are based on tests and other data that indeed are estimates of behavior and must be viewed in light of their inherent stability as measuring instruments. When I stated the difference between Mrs. Alberts' Full scale intelligence after her accident in comparison with her Full scale IQ before the accident, the probabilities are 95 out of 100 chances that the figures I gave are the "true" figures. Thus my conclusions are based on probabilities, but the chances that these conclusions are based on incorrect figures are less than 5 in 100.

The witness has shown Mr. McCracken's intimations of gross guessing and inaccuracy to be unfounded. The witness has clarified the issue in a simple, dignified professional style. Mr. McCracken's trial strategy has probably failed.

Under *no* circumstances should the witness ask opposing counsel if he or she may qualify. If that happens, the following is likely to occur:

Mr. McCracken: And when you tell us that Mrs. Alberts has a lower IQ than she probably had before the accident, this is nothing more than a guess, or "probability," and not a fact—is this not so?

Dr. White: Yes, may I qualify?

Mr. McCracken: No, your answer seems perfectly clear to me, and I'm sure that it is to the jury.

At this point, Mr. McCracken will probably turn his back on the witness and walk away, offering no opportunity at all to qualify. It is in the best interests of his case to do everything possible to place in the minds of the jury a question as to the competency, accuracy, and quality of the opposing expert's testimony.

Most successful trial attorneys attend workshops and seminars, often given by highly qualified psychologists, on how to deal with the expert witness in psychology. However, the matter is not completely simple for opposing counsel. If the lawyer attempts a gambit of trial strategy and the expert responds in a competent manner, the jury clearly sees that the opposing counsel is "tilting at windmills" and begins to develop sympathy for the expert witness. This is certainly not desirable for the opposing counsel. Thus after failing to discredit the witness after one or two attempts, the intelligent attorney will cease his or her efforts, since, in effect, the questions may actually enhance the expert's presentation to the jury.

Some attorneys attempt to discredit the expert witness by asking statistical questions, to imply that the expert is not really an expert:

Mr. McCracken: In discussing these tests, Doctor, I assume that you have some knowledge of them and their construction?

Dr. White: Yes, sir, I believe so.

Mr. McCracken: Would you explain to the judge and to the jury the meaning of the term *validity?*

Dr. White: Validity refers to the extent to which an instrument, such as a test, measures what it is supposed to measure. There are four main types of validity. Would
you like me to outline each?

Mr. McCracken: Well, Doctor, I . . .

Dr. White: There is content validity, predictive validity, construct validity, and concurrent validity. These are statistical terms that are used in the validation of tests
that are—

Mr. McCracken: Thank you very much, Doctor, I'm sure that's very instructive, but
I would like to move on now.

Mr. McCracken's hope that Dr. White would stumble around and be unable to answer the question has not been fulfilled. To the contrary,
Dr. White was prepared and demonstrated to judge and jury that she is indeed an expert. This is contrary to Mr. McCracken's plans, and he wants to
leave the discussion as quickly as possible. If the retaining counsel is sufficiently attentive, he may further enhance the expert's credibility by ob-
jecting to the quasi-harassment being perpetrated by opposing counsel:

Mr. Albee: Your Honor, I object. My worthy opponent first asks Dr. White a question and then does not allow her to finish. I suggest that Mr. McCracken is merely
baiting the witness in an effort to discredit her testimony. If it pleases the Court,
the witness should be allowed to complete her answer.

The Court: Mr. McCracken, you will please allow the witness to complete her answer.

Mr. McCracken: Yes, Your Honor. You may proceed, Doctor.

Dr. White: Thank you. As I was saying, there are four main types of validity, and
each one is a method of ensuring that a test is an instrument that measures what
it is supposed to measure and the degree to which it actually does this. I could
go into a long technical description of these matters if this is your desire.

Mr. McCracken: No thank you, Doctor, that's quite enough.

No expert can have at his or her fingertips all figures, definitions, and descriptions. This is the primary purpose of the cue book. When opposing
counsel asks a question about which the expert is not quite sure, it is perfectly permissible to ask permission to make reference to the cue book.
Again, this request is addressed to the court and not to opposing counsel.
Opposing counsel may make a fuss about the expert referring to the cue
book, but this can be dealt with readily, as follows:

Mr. McCracken: Please tell us, Doctor, if indeed you are an expert, the meaning of
the term *standard error of measurement.*

Dr. White: Certainly *(turning to the Judge, who after all is only about two and one-
half feet to her immediate left),* may I refer to some of my materials, Your Honor?

The Court: Yes, Doctor.

Dr. White: *(turning to the appropriate page in her cue book)* The standard error of
measurement is one way in which the reliability of a test may be expressed. It provides an estimate of the range of variation in a set of repeated measurements of

the same thing. I'll illustrate this: Repeated administration of a test instrument will yield a frequency distribution of scores. That means that the scores may differ to some extent on repetition. The mean of these scores represents what we call the *true score* and yields a standard deviation that indicates the extent of variation of the scores. This standard deviation is the deviation of the errors of measurement, and this is called the *standard error of measurement*. It gives us an estimate of how frequently errors of a given size may be expected to occur when the test is used. A low standard error of measurement is an indication of a test's reliability.

Mr. McCracken: Thank you, Doctor, but what is that book you are reading from?

Dr. White: This is a book of materials that I refer to when I wish to be very accurate about a definition or a statistical conversion.

Mr. McCracken: That means you don't really know the definition, is that not right?

Dr. White: That means I would like to answer your questions as accurately as I possibly can.

Mr. McCracken is fighting a losing battle. Dr. White has demonstrated a quiet, direct, unthreatened response to Mr. McCracken's machinations. It is quite unlikely that he will go as far as we have indicated in the preceding interrogatories. He would have to be a very incompetent attorney not to realize that Dr. White is responding extremely well, creating a very favorable impression before the jury, and having her testimony enhanced by this cross-examination. By the same token, opposing counsel has begun to look like a nitpicker and is creating a relatively negative impression about himself before the jury. It is more than likely that one or two appropriate answers by the witness will cause opposing counsel to be very, very careful about continuing to ask potentially difficult or embarrassing questions.

The expert witness must be prepared to give up materials brought to court if these are used in any way by the witness during direct or cross-examination. It is wise to bring copies that can be handed over should opposing counsel request that such materials be marked and entered as an exhibit. The attorney may ask for tests, test materials, books, reprints, charts, or illustrations. In most cases, this request serves no immediate purpose. Opposing counsel may be ensuring that the material being referred to is available for later examination and reference during the trial. The attorney may be "making a record" in the event the material might be helpful should the case be appealed. The opposing attorney may only be attempting to annoy the expert.

Should the attorney request something the expert is not prepared to give up, the expert must depend on the good offices of the presiding judge to protect the witness's property:

Mr. McCracken: You referred to a group of percentiles in relating to the jury Mrs. Alberts' so-called intellectual deficits, did you not, Doctor?

Dr. White: Yes, I did.

Mr. McCracken: Is that something you worked out yourself?

Dr. White: No, they are the percentiles developed from the normative sample used in the standardization of the Wechsler Adult Intelligence Scale.

Mr. McCracken: Where does one find such percentiles?

Dr. White: In the manual for the WAIS-R, the Wechsler Adult Intelligence Scale-Revised, published by Harcourt, Brace and Jovanovich in 1981.

Mr. McCracken: Is that the manual that you are referring to—that booklet with the black cover?

Dr. White: Yes, sir.

Mr. McCracken: May I see it please?

Dr. White: The table to which I referred for the percentiles is in Appendix D. It is labeled *Table 22.*

Mr. McCracken: All right. Yes—I see that. Your Honor, I should like to enter this booklet as plaintiff's exhibit—let's see—number 43.

Once the material is stamped and entered, the witness will probably never see it again. This is an excellent reason to have a photocopy of any material to be cited or demonstrated available to be turned over to opposing counsel should such a request be made. If, indeed, the opposing counsel tries to take the expert's tools or equipment, rather than expendable copies, the witness should appeal to the judge. Following the attorney's request for permission to mark the material as an exhibit, the witness should turn to the judge and say:

Dr. White: Your Honor, if it pleases the Court, that booklet is used daily in my practice and is my only copy. May I reproduce the page in question and forward it to the court reporter?

The Court: I think that we will let the Doctor keep her materials. If the bailiff will take the material to my office and have my secretary make a copy of the pages designated by Dr. White, we will mark those as exhibit number 43. Is that satisfactory, Mr. McCracken?

Mr. McCracken: Yes, Your Honor.

Dr. White: Thank you, Your Honor.

The Court: Please proceed, Counselor.

Few judges allow an attorney to interfere with the personal property or professional tools used by the expert witness.

In concluding the cross-examination of an expert witness who has responded efficiently and has maintained credibility with the jury, opposing counsel may use a series of questions designed to convince the jury that the opinions of the expert should be disregarded or, at best, considered lightly:

Mr. McCracken: And so, to sum it all up, Doctor, you're a psychologist, not a doctor, who has been hired to give Mrs. Alberts some tests and give your opinion. This opinion is based on "probabilities," as you call them, and not on hard absolute facts. Is this so, Doctor?

Dr. White: Yes, sir.

Mr. McCracken: No further questions, Your Honor.

Even though these questions and innuendoes have appeared before, and Dr. White has responded effectively, opposing counsel wishes to have the last word in the cross-examination. The expert should not rise to the negative tone of the cross-examination. This is part of the courtroom drama and the adversary system. If the expert is on shaky ground or is not much of an expert, opposing counsel has the right and the duty to bring this out during cross-examination and to negate the effect of the witness against his or her client's case. The jury understands this, having experienced a number of exchanges between opposing attorneys before the expert has testified. The effective expert witness should rely on his or her knowledge, communication skills, and emotional control. There are any number of gambits and strategies opposing attorneys may use to upset a witness. A sensible dignity on the part of the expert will usually be perceived by jury members in a positive way.

Occasionally an opposing counsel may focus on the expert's fee during cross-examination, insinuating that the witness is "bought" or is a "hired gun." The following is an overdone but plausible cross-examination made up of dialogue from court transcripts. Mr. Mandell, a particularly hostile opposing counsel, questions the expert witness, Dr. Lawrence, who is experienced, calm, and unflappable.

Mr. Mandell: Your testimony has been very interesting, Doctor; I imagine that you testify in courts quite frequently.

Dr. Lawrence: I have testified before.

Mr. Mandell: Please tell the jury how much you were paid to testify here today.

Dr. Lawrence: I was paid nothing to testify.

Mr. Mandell: Nothing?

Dr. Lawrence: No, sir. My testimony cannot be bought. I was paid at my usual professional rates for my time, spent in evaluating and giving my opinion here today.

Mr. Mandell has attempted a standard ploy used in cross-examination to cast some doubts on the expert's motivation and objectivity as a witness. Another such ploy is as follows:

Mr. Mandell: As an expert, your name is quite well known. Haven't I seen it in some professional journals?

Dr. Lawrence: That is possible. I've published several . . .

Mr. Mandell: Oh yes! Haven't I seen an advertisement in some law journals where you offer yourself to anyone as an expert?

Dr. Lawrence: Certainly not! I've never. . .

Mr. Mandell: It's not that important, Doctor. I'm sure the jury understands.

This represents a strategy of desperation and is rare. When it does happen, it usually suggests that the opposing counsel is unprepared and willing to risk his or her client's case on a very long and very cheap shot. Few jury members are likely to be impressed by such nonsense. It behooves the expert to realize that such behavior will tend to damage the reputation of opposing counsel and not that of the expert witness.

Each attorney develops his or her own approach to cross-examination. An expert should be prepared for a variety of strategies, ranging from smooth, efficient probing to gross, tangential hacking. An attorney's behavior during deposition is sometimes a fair prediction of the style of cross-examination that can be expected in the courtroom.

Some attorneys scour the expert's deposition to find an opportunity to discredit the expert by getting the expert to impeach himself or herself. If the attorney can arrange for a witness to give different answers to the same question, the witness is *impeached*, casting grave doubts on the competence and veracity of the expert testimony. This is the primary reason for not "waiving the reading and signing" of the deposition when it is originally taken. To insist on reading and signing means the witness can make a copy of the deposition and review his or her pretrial testimony before getting on the witness stand. The following, taken from the record of a trial in federal court, illustrates what may happen if the expert has not reviewed the deposition. In this case, the federal prosecutor, Mr. Horwitz, has a copy of Dr. Blau's deposition taken 6 months previous to the trial. Dr. Blau waived reading and signing on the advice of the attorney who retained him. The deposition was taken at a place far distant from the witness's office, and to expedite the trial process, the retaining attorney requested the waiving, assuring Dr. Blau that a copy of his deposition would be made available before the trial. Six months passed, and somehow the attorney forgot. The following occurred during cross-examination:

Mr. Horwitz: Now, Doctor, you've testified that you conducted all of your examinations of the defendant at the Green County Jail. Is that correct?

Dr. Blau: That is correct.

Mr. Horwitz: And all of your examinations were completed on April 22, the one day you spent with the defendant?

Dr. Blau: Yes, sir.

Mr. Horwitz: And you've based all of your conclusions on your observations, tests, and recall of that day.

Dr. Blau: To a large extent, yes.

Mr. Horwitz: How many hours did you spend that day testing the defendant?

Dr. Blau: According to my records, I spent just over five hours with the defendant.

Mr. Horwitz: What time did you start your examinations?

Dr. Blau: About 10 in the morning. I drove to Deland from Tampa that morning. I arrived about 9:30 A.M. By the time an examination room was available and the defendant brought to me, it was about 10 or 10:30.

Mr. Horwitz: Were testing conditions good?

Dr. Blau: I've never examined anyone in a jail where testing conditions were "good." They were adequate in my opinion.

Mr. Horwitz: What did you do about lunch?

Dr. Blau: I beg your pardon?

Mr. Horwitz: You began your examination at 10 or 10:30. You examined the defendant for a period of about five hours. You were in an institution, a jail. What did you do to ensure the defendant would not miss lunch?

Dr. Blau: Well, ordinarily, when testing in an institutional setting, we tell the guards to let the person being tested eat at the usual time or bring a tray, and testing can be delayed while the person eats in the testing room.

Mr. Horwitz: What did you do in this case?

Dr. Blau: I believe the defendant went to lunch at his usual time—about 11:30—and returned shortly thereafter to continue testing.

Mr. Horwitz: So you began testing at 10 A.M. or so, worked until about 11:30, allowed the defendant to go to lunch, resumed testing after lunch, and finished during the afternoon. Is that about right?

Dr. Blau: Yes, sir.

Mr. Horwitz: So I take it, in following good testing procedure, you worked with the defendant giving tests and so forth, and then broke for lunch, and then continued until you were finished. Is that about right?

Dr. Blau: Yes, that seems about right.

Mr. Horwitz: *(taking a blue-backed deposition from a pile of documents on the prosecution table)* Dr. Blau, I'm going to show you a deposition taken from you on the 14th of May, and I would like you to look at it.

Dr. Blau: Yes.

Mr. Horwitz: Is this the transcript of a deposition I took from you at that time?

Dr. Blau: It certainly looks like it.

Mr. Horwitz: I have marked page 37 of this deposition, and I would like you to begin reading from the deposition where the red arrow is pointing *(handing the deposition to Dr. Blau)*.

Dr. Blau: *Mr. Horwitz:* You did the entire examination at the jail? *Dr. Blau:* Yes, I did. *Mr. Horwitz:* You started at about 10 in the morning? *Dr. Blau:* Yes, that's about right. *Mr. Horwitz:* What did you do about lunch? *Dr. Blau:* Because the testing time that was available was quite limited, the defendant agreed that he would be willing to work right straight through lunch. The guards said that they would feed him after he was finished. We took several "bathroom breaks," and the guards allowed us to have some cold drinks, but we skipped lunch and worked right straight through.

Mr. Horwitz: *(taking the deposition from Dr. Blau)* That certainly doesn't sound like what you just said a few moments ago, Doctor.

Dr. Blau: Well, that was taken a long time ago and I . . .

Mr. Horwitz: So what you told us a few minutes ago is diametrically opposed to what you had just read from the deposition. Now, either you were wrong a few moments ago or you were wrong on the deposition. Which was it?

Dr. Blau: My recollection . . .

Mr. Horwitz: Would you please answer the question directly, Dr. Blau?

Dr. Blau: I was in error in my testimony before reading the deposition. Now that I have read the deposition, I realize that we did skip lunch in order to complete the testing.

Mr. Horwitz: So you do make errors in your testimony. Is that not correct?

Dr. Blau: Well, I suppose . . .

Mr. Horwitz: Either you do or you don't—which is it?

Dr. Blau: I certainly made an error in that case.

Mr. Horwitz: I submit, Dr. Blau, that this error may represent a whole class of errors that you may have made in your testimony—no further questions.

To the casual observer, the preceding dialogue may seem to be inconsequential, and in point of fact it might be so, in terms of the quality of the witness's testimony. To the jury, however, Dr. Blau's credibility, his sharpness, and his ability to handle detail are called into question. This was a very clever and very effective ploy by the prosecuting attorney. This underscores the importance of *never* waiving the signing and the reading of the deposition. The expert witness should have in his or her possession a copy of every deposition given in the case about which he or she is going to testify. There should be no surprises.

In another criminal case, it is obvious that the expert witness has learned his lesson. In this case, a deposition was taken approximately five months before the trial. The expert did not waive the reading and the signing and obtained a copy of the deposition. The following dialogue took place between Mr. Golden, the prosecuting attorney, and Dr. Blau, the expert witness:

Mr. Golden: Now, Doctor, you've testified in direct examination that the defendant is "psychotic." Is that correct?

Dr. Blau: No, sir.

Mr. Golden: He is not psychotic?

Dr. Blau: I said that my examination indicated that the defendant has a very disturbed and fragmented personality and that he experiences episodes of psychotic thinking and behavior.

Mr. Golden: Then are you saying that the defendant was or was not insane at the time of the homicide of which he is accused?

Dr. Blau: Neither. Insanity is a legal concept, and the decision as to insanity lies with the judge and jury, not with me as a psychologist.

Mr. Golden: Then you don't say he was insane at the time of the homicide.

Dr. Blau: I've not been asked that.

Mr. Golden: Was the defendant insane at the time of the homicide of which he is accused?

Dr. Blau: I don't know.

Mr. Golden: *(opening a deposition folder)* Dr. Blau—I have here a certified copy of a deposition given by you and certified by you in this matter. Please read this to the Judge and jury, beginning at the place I've marked with a red X.

Dr. Blau: *(reading) Mr. Golden:* Would you say he was insane? *Dr. Blau:* No, sir, I would not.

Mr. Golden: *(taking transcript)* So when I took your deposition you said he wasn't insane and now you say you don't know—is that it?

Dr. Blau: No, sir, it is not so.

Mr. Golden: What do you mean "No, sir"—in the deposition you said you wouldn't say the defendant was insane, now you say, here in open court, sworn to tell the truth, that you "don't know."

Dr. Blau: If you will read the previous page in the deposition, I believe you will find that you asked me if I were a member of a jury, and if I were convinced that the defendant understood that he was doing wrong at the time of the homicide, and if I were convinced he deliberately took the life of the victim, would I consider the defendant "insane." To that I answered, "No sir, I would not." The question was totally different, *not* addressed to me as an expert.

Mr. Golden: Let me go on now to the next point, Doctor.

The value of not waiving the reading and signing of depositions so as to be sure to have a copy of one's deposition is obvious. Hostile or abrasive cross-examinations happen more frequently in movies or television drama than in the courtroom. Most experienced attorneys know that harshness, anger without real purpose, and abuse of expert witnesses is distasteful to most jurors and will result in a lessening of the attorney's esteem by jurors who might ordinarily be positively inclined toward the attorney's presentation.

Experienced opposing attorneys prefer that an expert discredit himself or herself on cross-examinations. In a first-degree murder trial, Dr. Artfield has testified that the defendant was insane at the time he shot and killed his former supervisor. Mr. Carnella conducts the cross-examination as follows:

Mr. Carnella: I found your testimony most interesting, as I often do when I hear you on the stand.

Dr. Artfield: *(unruffled)* Thank you, Counselor!

Mr. Carnella: I particularly note the calm, easy, absolute assurance with which you give your opinion that the defendant was insane when he shot and killed his former supervisor who had fired the defendant for repeated incompetence.

Dr. Artfield: He was insane.

Mr. Carnella: You have no doubt, no question, no slight unsureness?

Dr. Artfield: Certainly not!

Mr. Carnella: No possibility that you could be mistaken? be guilty of a slight error of professional judgment?

Dr. Artfield: *(becoming heated)* I told you—certainly not!

Mr. Carnella: As a professional, Dr. Artfield, don't you think it's unusual for a well-qualified expert to claim absolutely no room for error? Doesn't the psychiatric profession have a label or a diagnosis for folks who think they are never wrong?

Dr. Artfield: Damn it! I said the man was insane! He was crazy as a bedbug! Is that not clear enough for you?

The Court: *(banging gavel sharply)* The witness will control himself. Answer the questions directly, Doctor.

Mr. Carnella: No further questions, Your Honor.

Dr. Artfield has shown himself to be easily annoyed, overemotional, and unprofessional. The jury, when later polled, indicated that almost to a member, they had disregarded his testimony because of his poor emotional control. Mr. Carnella very cleverly arranged for this expert to spoil his own testimony.

The cross-examination is the part of the procedure where the incompetent or poorly prepared witness may receive deserved comeuppance for poor preparation. In the following personal injury case, Dr. Pintz has testified that the plaintiff, Mr. Reading, suffers a brain dysfunction as indicated by poor performance on various psychological tests. Further, Dr. Pintz, in his response to hypothetical questions in the direct examination, has indicated that the disability results from an automobile accident that occurred in August 1981. At this time, Mr. Reading was riding as a passenger in a vehicle that was hit from behind. The cross-examination proceeds as follows, with opposing attorney, Mr. Richard Bear, cross-examining Dr. Pintz, Mr. Siegal's witness:

Mr. Bear: So, Doctor, it is your opinion that Mr. Reading's neuropsychological problems are a result of a rear-end collision between automobiles, with Mr. Reading being a passenger in the forward vehicle.

Dr. Pintz: Yes—that is my opinion.

Mr. Bear: Is it your opinion that the neuropsychological damage occurred in the accident of August 1981?

Dr. Pintz: That is my opinion.

Mr. Bear: If the accident had happened in January 1981 or in December 1981, would that significantly change what you found in your psychological studies?

Dr. Pintz: I'm not sure I understand.

Mr. Bear: I'm asking if your results would be substantially the same if the accident occurred, say, four years ago or two years ago, rather than specifically three years ago?

Dr. Pintz: No—that would not be the significant factor. Our findings show that there is deficit, and the history identifies the trauma of the rear-end collision as the source of the deficit.

Mr. Bear: If there had been two, or three, or four rear-end collisions in which Mr. Reading was a passenger in the forward car during the past four or five years, would your tests or procedures have the capacity to identify which accident caused the damage?

Dr. Pintz: No, we couldn't tell that.

Mr. Bear: To your knowledge, has Mr. Reading been involved in any rear-end collisions other than the one at issue, which occurred in August 1981?

Dr. Pintz: Not to my knowledge.

Mr. Bear: If there *had* been other such rear-end collisions, would that change your opinion that the damage definitely, unquestionably be the result of the collision which occurred in August 1981?

Dr. Pintz: Of course!

Mr. Bear: Did Mr. Reading tell you whether he had any previous accidents?

Dr. Pintz: No, he didn't.

Mr. Bear: I have here, a deposition, taken from Mr. Reading on October 15, 1982. I should like to enter this into evidence, Your Honor.

The Court: *(to the court reporter)* You may mark that defendant's exhibit number . . . 22. You may proceed, Mr. Bear.

Mr. Bear: Dr. Pintz. I should like for you to read the material in this deposition beginning with the point marked with a red X.

Dr. Pintz: *(taking the deposition from opposing counsel)* Let's see—oh—okay. *Mr. Bear:* Now, Mr. Reading, have you ever had any accidents in any way similar to the accident of August 1981. *Mr. Reading:* Do you mean just like it? *Mr. Bear:* Any accidents at all? *Mr. Reading:* Well, not so serious. *Mr. Bear:* Have you had *any* accidents other than the August 1981 accident? *Mr. Reading:* Well, on Christmas Eve of 1980 I was riding home from a party. My wife was driving, and we were hit from behind while we were stopped for a red light. The other driver was charged. *Mr. Bear:* Were you hurt? *Mr. Reading:* Well—not much. I might have been knocked out for a minute or two. *Mr. Bear:* Did you see a doctor? *Mr. Reading:* Well, we were taken to the hospital, and they gave me some X rays. I got over it pretty quickly. I had some headaches for a while, but they weren't as bad as after the accident in 1981. *Mr. Bear:* But you *did* have a head injury following a rear-end collision in 1980—almost a year before the accident of 1981? *Mr. Reading:* I suppose you could say that.

Mr. Bear: Thank you, Dr. Pintz *(taking the deposition from the witness and giving it to the court reporter).* Is this information a surprise to you, Doctor?

Dr. Pintz: Well, it, well I . . .

Mr. Bear: During your evaluation of Mr. Reading did he reveal this incident to you on his own?

Dr. Pintz: No, I don't believe he did, I really don't . . .

Mr. Bear: Did you *ask* Mr. Reading, as part of your history, whether he had experienced any accidents or traumas other than the accident of August 1981 that might account for your findings of neuropsychological deficit?

Dr. Pintz: No . . . I assumed that I'd been provided with all the pertinent medical records so I . . .

Mr. Bear: If you *had* asked Mr. Reading about head traumas *other* than the accident of August 1981, he *might* have told you about his head trauma in a similar accident, which, in fact, did occur in December 1980, might he not?

Mr. Siegal: I object, your Honor. Counsel is leading the witness.

The Court: Objection overruled. Dr. Pintz—please answer the question.

Dr. Pintz: *(uncomfortable and compromised)* I suppose he might have told me about the previous accident if I had . . .

Mr. Bear: So, Doctor, you might say that you wish you had asked this question and obtained this additional information.

Dr. Pintz: Well, yes . . .

Mr. Bear: Had you known that Mr. Reading had *two* quite similar auto accidents with head trauma, you might not be so sure that your findings of neuropsychological deficit are attributable *only* to the accident of August 1981. Is this not a reasonable conclusion?

Dr. Pintz: Yes—I suppose.

Mr. Bear: Please, sir, do not suppose. Would this new information cast doubt on the August 1981 accident as the only possible source of your neuropsychological findings?

Dr. Pintz: *(resigned and chagrined)* Yes, it would.

The expert witness has good reason to be chagrined. Opposing counsel has used his discovery of an omission in Dr. Pintz's evaluation which casts serious doubt on the expert's opinion as to the cause of the plaintiff's deficit that is critical to the defendant's claim for damages. It has been neatly demonstrated to the jury that Dr. Pintz is fallible and that his opinions must be doubted.

The expert witness who conducts his or her professional work properly, prepares a careful report, participates in a proper pretrial conference, follows the rules, and maintains decor and emotional control is unlikely to be discredited or embarrassed during cross-examination.

Re-Direct Examination

In keeping with the process of taking turns during the trial, the attorney who retained the expert follows the cross-examination with an opportunity to emphasize the strengths of the expert witness and to repair any damage that may have been inflicted to the expert's testimony by the cross-examination. No new material can be brought out. The attorney conducting the cross-examination may only refer to matters brought forth in the direct examination or raised in the cross-examination. If opposing counsel has muddied the waters during cross-examination by suggesting the expert or the expert's opinion is fallible, the attorney retaining the witness will ordinarily attempt to reestablish the witness' credibility.

During cross-examination by opposing counsel, the attorney who retains the expert usually takes careful note of any issue that might give members of the jury concern about the credibility of the expert witness. While not annoying or antagonizing the jury with too many details unrelated to the issue at hand, the lawyer will do what can reasonably be done to convince the members of the jury that none of the issues raised in cross-examination is of significance and can be dismissed in the interest of justice. Re-direct examination may focus on substantial or peripheral challenges to the testimony of the expert witness. The following re-direct examination might occur in response to the earlier cross-examination of Dr. White on a peripheral issue concerning opposing counsel's attack on Dr. White's credentials:

The Court: Do you wish to conduct re-direct examination, Mr. Albee?

Mr. Albee: Yes—with the Court's permission—just a few more questions for the good doctor. Now, Dr. White, my esteemed colleague asked you a few minutes ago if you were a "medical doctor." You are, in fact, a psychologist, are you not?

Dr. White: That is correct.

Mr. Albee: And I understand that you are licensed to practice psychology in this state?

Dr. White: Yes, sir.

Mr. Albee: Am I correct that medical doctors are *not* licensed as psychologists?

Dr. White: That is right.

Mr. Albee: Of what help would a medical degree be for a psychologist, Dr. White?

Dr. White: None, in my opinion.

Mr. Albee: Am I to understand that you have taught at a medical school?

Dr. White: Yes, sir, I have. At the Medical School of the State University.

Mr. Albee: So—you have *taught* medical students, have you not?

Dr. White: Yes, I have.

The attorney who retained Dr. White is pointing out to the members of the jury that opposing counsel, Mr. McCracken, has tried to cloud the real issues. Mr. Albee hopes that his polite, low-key questioning of Dr. White will convince jury members that his opponent will do almost anything to keep the *real* facts from the jury. This point-counterpoint of courtroom drama is all part of the adversary process.

Some attorneys will conduct very little re-direct examination on the assumption that their cause will *not* be served by focusing on peripheral issues raised in the cross-examination. Re-direct examination based on that trial strategy might proceed as follows:

The Court: Do you wish to conduct re-direct examination, Mr. Albee?

Mr. Albee: With the Court's permission—just a question or two for Dr. White. Forgetting the side issues raised by Mr. McCracken, you *did* conduct a thorough and complete psychological evaluation of Mrs. Alberts, did you not?

Dr. White: I did.

Mr. Albee: And you have analyzed all the medical records, accident records, rehabilitation reports, and so on?

Dr. White: I have.

Mr. Albee: Given all of this lengthy, extensive, and thorough professional evaluation, it *is* your opinion, is it not, that Mrs. Alberts suffers a variety of psychological deficits about which you testified in detail?

Dr. White: That is true.

Mr. Albee: Would you say that she is not the woman she was before her accident and has suffered significant losses in intelligence, skill, coping ability, working skills, and quality of life?

Dr. White: I would say so.

Mr. Albee: No further questions, Your Honor.

Briefly, clearly, and sharply, counsel has focused on the main reasons for the expert's presence. The expert is advising the triers of fact that the plaintiff, Mrs. Alberts, has been seriously affected by her accident. Later, the attorney will present other experts to support and justify the *remedy* he proposes to the jury, such as money for rehabilitation, pain, lost earnings, loss of consortium (emotional or sexual deprivation), or even punitive damages where gross negligence contributed to the plaintiff's condition. The expert witness forms one part of the attorney's effort to convince the jury and the judge of what happened, what results have occurred, and what remedy is appropriate.

Re-Cross-Examination

Opposing counsel has the last chance at the expert witness, but no new material or approaches may be raised during re-cross-examination. Focus must be on what was brought out in direct examination or what was explored in the cross-examination. It is opposing counsel's last opportunity to cast doubt on the quality of the expert witness's testimony or to dilute the impact of this testimony on the developing decision-making process of the jurors. The expert can expect to experience a variety of styles of re-cross-examination, since the focus and intensity of questioning, as in cross-examination, depends on the opposing attorney's trial strategy, personal style, and perception of the most vulnerable portions of the expert's presentation. If the expert has done his or her job thoroughly, little can be done to weaken the expert's opinion. If the expert has made mistakes or prepared poorly, a strong closing can be expected from opposing counsel on re-cross-examination. An example follows:

The Court: Do you wish to re-cross-examine, Mr. Bear?

Mr. Bear: Just a few questions for Dr. Pintz. Reviewing what we've said during the cross-examination, I believe you said that the fact that Mr. Reading "forgot" about an automobile accident, which occurred before the accident we are considering in this case, could modify your opinion regarding the cause of his psychological deficit, is that not so?

Dr. Pintz: Well, yes, it could.

Mr. Bear: So, Doctor, would it be fair to say that the opinions you gave concerning Mr. Reading's psychological deficits and their origins must be reexamined—by you and the jury—in light of the information you have received during this trial?

Dr. Pintz: Yes—I suppose . . .

Mr. Bear: Might I say that if you had a chance to rewrite your report, with this new information—that report would be *different?*

Dr. Pintz: Well—yes.

Mr. Bear: Thank you, Doctor—no further questions.

Opposing counsel, Mr. Bear, has underscored the fragmentation of Dr. Pintz's opinion which occurred during cross-examination. He has shown the jury that Dr. Pintz's original report and his conclusions are in error and that the expert's testimony must be given revised and more limited credibility.

Few attorneys will give up their "turn" at re-cross-examination even though the expert witness has been outstanding. A final effort to lessen the impact of such testimony might proceed as follows:

The Court: Will you proceed with the re-cross-examination, Counselor?

Mr. McCracken: Yes, your Honor. I'd like to ask Dr. White, as an expert witness retained by the plaintiff, whether she believes that psychology is an "exact" science?

Dr. White: I'm not sure what you mean by *exact.*

Mr. McCracken: Do you, and other psychologists, believe or claim that psychology as a science can make the statements and predictions with the accuracy and predictability of, say, chemistry and physics?

Dr. White: No, as yet . . .

Mr. McCracken: A simple no is quite clear. Am I correct that as a psychologist, you would agree that all the opinions you expressed here today are based on probabilities rather than absolute facts?

Dr. White: That is correct.

Mr. McCracken: No further questions, Your Honor.

Opposing counsel's purpose is to make every legitimate effort to dilute the impact of an opposing counsel's witness on the thinking of the triers of fact.

At this point, when re-cross-examination is completed, the expert witness is finished, except in rare circumstances. The judge may ask questions, offer the jury an opportunity to ask questions of the witness, or even ask the expert witness to come to the judge's chambers. Ordinarily, however, the procedure is as follows:

The Court: Well . . . all right. If there is nothing further, you may step down. Thank you for your testimony, Doctor.

Witness: Thank you, Your Honor.

The witness is now excused. All files and papers should be packed. Do not hurry. When ready, the expert should stand in the witness-box, turn and nod another "thank you" to the judge, step down, nod to the jury, and move toward the door through which the expert entered the courtroom.

The expert witness who expects to improve the quality of his or her testimony should stop briefly at the court reporter's desk, drop a business card there, and whisper, "Please make me a copy of my testimony and bill me for it." Given these instructions, the court reporter will transcribe the expert's testimony, usually within a week, and mail it to the expert. Charges range from $2 to $5 per page. Though expensive, it allows the expert to review the details of the testimony, identify discrepancies, inadequacies, and undesirable responses and to improve on skills as an expert witness. The testimony will ordinarily not otherwise be transcribed by the attorneys or the court unless the case is appealed.

Occasionally, the judge will call the witness to chambers. The purpose is usually to tell the expert that the judge was pleased with the quality of the testimony. The judge may wish to ask the expert's opinion as to the defendant's rehabilitation potential in a criminal case. Judges have considerable leeway in the matter of questioning experts in chambers. Ordinarily, the expert will be told that the judge wishes to speak with the expert privately by a bailiff who will conduct the witness to the chambers. Here the judge is likely to be out of his or her robes, offer the witness coffee, and chat informally.

When finally dismissed by the judge, the expert should return to his or her office and make a note of the proceedings for the clinical file. Charges should be calculated, portal to portal, and a final invoice sent to the attorney who retained the witness. Unless specifically noted by the judge or one of the attorneys, "the rule" remains in force: The witness should not return to the courtroom as a spectator.

Rebuttal

On very rare occasions, one attorney or the other may call a rebuttal witness or witnesses. This would occur after all the regular witnesses have testified and before summation and final arguments. The purpose is usually to focus on an issue important in judging the quality of the evidence. Experts called during rebuttal may have little or no personal contact with the plaintiff or the defendant in the case. The rebuttal witness is called to deal with a specific issue. The following presents the testimony of a rebuttal witness called by the defense in the sentencing phase of a criminal proceeding.

Witnesses for the prosecution have testified that their examinations have shown that the defendant is dangerous and is likely to be homicidal in the future. The state has asked for the death penalty. Defense counsel has presented no witnesses for direct examination. Instead, his trial strategy is to call a rebuttal witness to discuss dangerousness as a scientific concept:

Mr. Spurrier: If it pleases the Court, we should like to call a rebuttal witness.

The Court: You may proceed.

Mr. Spurrier: The defense calls Dr. Richard Jaeger. *(Witness is sworn and seated.)* Please state your name.

Dr. Jaeger: Richard Jaeger.

Mr. Spurrier: Where do you reside, Doctor?

Dr. Jaeger: Greensboro, North Carolina.

Mr. Spurrier: What is your profession, sir?

Dr. Jaeger: I am Professor of Statistics and Evaluation Science at the University of North Carolina.

Mr. Spurrier: Would you please explain to the Judge and the jury the nature of statistics and of evaluation science?

Dr. Jaeger: Certainly *(whereupon the witness proceeds to succinctly explain his science and profession).*

The witness is qualified in the manner demonstrated earlier in this chapter. His credentials are stipulated to by opposing counsel, and the judge accepts the witness as an expert:

The Court: You may proceed, Mr. Spurrier.

Mr. Spurrier: Thank you, your Honor. Dr. Jaeger, have you ever "examined" the defendant?

Dr. Jaeger: I have not.

Mr. Spurrier: Have you heard the testimony of the State's witnesses during this trial?

Dr. Jaeger: I have.

Mr. Spurrier: Are you familiar with the issue of "dangerousness" and its prediction?

Dr. Jaeger: I am.

Mr. Spurrier: Have you, yourself, conducted and published research on the prediction of such traits as dangerousness?

Dr. Jaeger: I have.

Mr. Spurrier: Doctor, would you please explain to the court the nature and quality of the research on dangerousness.

Dr. Jaeger: Research on dangerousness is a part of behavioral science research on what we call *infrequent events.* This is as opposed to research on such things as *learning* where the behavior is frequent, regular, and of such a nature that laboratory experiments can be designed to measure and understand the behavior. With human responses, such as dangerousness, the events occur quite infrequently so that scientific measurement and study is much more difficult.

Mr. Spurrier: Then it is harder to study dangerousness, for instance, than to study how a child learns to read?

Dr. Jaeger: Yes, sir.

Mr. Spurrier: Has dangerousness been studied very extensively?

Dr. Jaeger: Yes, it has.

Mr. Spurrier: Please tell the court what the science of evaluation has contributed to this.

Dr. Jaeger: Evaluation studies of dangerousness indicate that it is not so much a trait of an individual but a phenomenon or occurrence that happens when certain conditions occur in almost any environment.

Mr. Spurrier: Please tell the Judge and jury about these "conditions."

Dr. Jaeger: Violence or dangerousness tends to occur when there are conflict and provocation, few alternative solutions to the conflict, physical proximity between opponents, the means and the opportunity to be violent and, frequently, significant quantities of alcohol having been taken recently by one or both opponents.

Mr. Spurrier: Are you saying that almost anyone could be dangerous, given the circumstances and conditions you've described?

Dr. Jaeger: The research does so indicate.

Mr. Spurrier: You have heard that the defendant has been described by various experts in psychiatry and psychology, retained by the State, as "potentially dangerous." Have you any information on the reliability of such statements?

Dr. Jaeger: Yes, sir, I have.

Mr. Spurrier: Would you please tell the court the source of this material.

Dr. Jaeger: Studies in dangerousness or violence have been based on a wide range of populations. Prisoners represent one of the largest populations that have been studied. In many judicial settings, predictions of dangerousness or violence have been made, and then the individuals in the study have been followed very carefully for years. In this way, the effectiveness of predictions of dangerousness can be checked or evaluated.

Mr. Spurrier: If a person is predicted to be dangerous, what is the likelihood that this prediction will actually come about?

Dr. Jaeger: Given the considerable number of studies, it is my opinion that a professional prediction of dangerousness based on psychiatric examination and/or psychological tests is likely to be correct no more than one-third of the time.

Mr. Spurrier: Do you mean to tell us that if an expert predicts that 100 criminals he has examined are likely to be dangerous in the future, that only 34 out of a 100 will turn out to be dangerous?

Dr. Jaeger: Yes, sir, that is true. The prediction of dangerousness tends to have about 66 percent "false-positive" rate. This means that the vast majority of people who are predicted to be potentially dangerous do not, according to a current research, actually turn out to get into additional trouble and appear again in the criminal justice system.

Mr. Spurrier: Then according to the information you provided us, Dr. Jaeger, when an expert makes a prediction of dangerousness, his chances are about twice as great of being wrong than of being right, is that not so?

Dr. Jaeger: That is approximately correct, sir.

Mr. Spurrier: Do you understand the concept of beyond a reasonable doubt?

Dr. Jaeger: I believe so.

Mr. Spurrier: In the law, *beyond a reasonable doubt* means that the probability of a thing occurring is extremely high, probably well beyond 9 chances out of 10. Is that the way you understand it?

Rules of the Road

- *Do* base opinion on multiple data sources.
- *Do* be prepared to cite reviews, studies, or other corroboration of techniques used in assessment.
- *Do* have citations from references to support choice of instruments.
- *Do* answer "I don't know" when this is the truest answer.
- *Do* avoid answering the ultimate question whenever possible.
- *Do* include contrarian views when explaining data on test results.
- *Do* be mindful of the implications of *Frye v. U.S.* and *Daubert v. Dow Pharmaceuticals* when formulating an opinion.
- *Do* expect opposing counsel to do his/her homework and to challenge expert opinion.
- *Do* expect retaining counsel to obtain all appropriate records that would be helpful to the expert.
- *Do* give a lecture if opposing counsel asks a general question in an area where you are knowledgeable.
- *Do* ask for more details when opposing counsel poses a hypothetical question that is not absolutely clear to the expert.
- *Do not* formulate an opinion clearly at odds with reliable factual behavioral observations.
- *Do not* lose your temper when challenged—in court or at deposition.
- *Do not* attempt to guess or estimate what an attorney is asking; ask for clarification before answering.
- *Do not* be humorous when giving sworn testimony.
- *Do not* be pompous or patronizing when giving sworn testimony.
- *Do not* be complicated or steeped in professional or scientific jargon when giving sworn testimony.
- *Never* speculate or guess when giving sworn testimony.
- *Do not* cite your clinical experience as a sole basis of an opinion.
- *Do not* speak rapidly.
- *Try not to* be threatened by attorneys implying that the absence of definitive research is evidence.
- *Do not* testify outside your own expertise, qualifications, or experience.
- *Do not* advise lawyers on trial strategy.
- *Do not* advocate with opposing counsel.
- *Never* disregard a judge's instructions or questions.
- *Never* be late for court.
- *Always* stand when the judge stands.
- *Do not* believe that jurors are dumb.
- *Do not* dress unattractively or inappropriately when testifying.
- *Do not* sit in the courtroom before or after testifying without the permission of retaining counsel.
- *Never* talk with witnesses, attorneys, or litigants on the opposing side without the retaining attorney's permission and presence.

FIGURE 13.5.   The expert witness at trial.

Dr. Jaeger: Yes, sir.

Mr. Spurrier: In your professional opinion, as an evaluation scientist, does the research on dangerousness justify a prediction of dangerousness on any individual beyond a reasonable doubt?

Dr. Jaeger: No, sir, not by a long shot.

The rebuttal witness has cast scientific doubt on fairly absolute statements made by the previous experts.

Figure 13.5 presents a summary of the "Do's" and "Don'ts" expert witnesses would be wise to follow in deposition or trial. These Rules of the Road will help to ensure competence and effectiveness of expert testimony.

NOTE

1. Rule of Sequestration. Fla. Rules of Crim. Procedure 3.131 B-3.

14

Emerging Applications and Issues

The opportunities for psychologists to serve as expert witnesses have increased significantly during the past three decades. New directions are emerging constantly. Although not long ago psychologists as experts in the court served roles similar to those of the psychiatric witness (Blau, 1959), today new opportunities appear regularly.

To show the diverse applications of psychology as a science and profession in American jurisprudence, some examples are presented in this chapter.

EYEWITNESS TESTIMONY

Although it still has a limited area of application, the concept of psychology's potential contribution to this important aspect of evidentiary testimony is quite old, having been proposed in Munsterberg's original treatise, *On the Witness Stand* (1908). In the half-century subsequent to Munsterberg's serious questions concerning the reliability of eyewitness identification, experimental psychologists have demonstrated that the testimony of witnesses based on what they believe they saw is not as consistent and accurate as the courts have traditionally assumed (Loftus, 1981).

The courts have not been unmindful of such findings. In 1967, the U.S. Supreme Court attempted to define some limits on eyewitness testimony of questionable reliability.[1] The safeguards provided a defendant with an attorney during pretrial eyewitness identification procedures.

Since judges and jurors must ultimately decide on the reliability of eyewitness testimony, most attention and concern has been focused on them. Tentative efforts to ensure that jurors are aware of some of the inaccuracies

330 Emerging Applications and Issues

and discrepancies possible in eyewitness testimony are found in recommendations for instructions by judges to jurors.[2] Such instructions caution jurors to consider the credibility of eyewitness testimony in respect to who renders such testimony and the conditions under which the event was witnessed. These concerns mainly deal with the dangers of solidifying vague eyewitness testimony by having witnesses identify a potential defendant in a police or investigative setting under conditions that imply or suggest guilt. This tends to encourage positive identification. Many factors can influence the fairness of a police identification lineup (Wells, Leippe, & Ostrom, 1979). The Supreme Court has ruled that eyewitness identification that may have been reinforced by exposure of the defendant's photograph to the eyewitness by police anxious to have a positive identification is inadmissible.[3]

More recently, efforts have been made to decrease jurors' unrealistic reliance on eyewitness testimony by using psychologists as experts in the courtroom. In such instances, efforts are made to qualify a psychologist as expert in the reliability and validity of eyewitness accounts. The psychologist gives direct testimony as to those factors that affect the reliability and validity of recall. A number of courts have ruled that the experimental findings regarding eyewitness identification are not a fit subject for expert testimony. Some courts have opined that the average juror has sufficient knowledge as to those factors that contribute to unreliable eyewitness identification.[4,5] An appellate decision ruled that the testimony of a psychologist regarding the reliability of eyewitness identification was not admissible since it might take from the jury their own determination as to what weight to give the evidence of the eyewitness.[6]

A more recent state appellate court opined:

> The State asserts that the facts affecting the reliability of an eyewitness identification are within the ordinary experience of jurors, that the conclusions to be drawn from the facts affecting the reliability of an eyewitness should be left to the jury, and that expert opinion should be excluded where the facts testified to are of a nature as not to require any special knowledge or experience to form a conclusion.[7]

This decision seems explicit, yet it states that "where the facts testified to are of a nature as not to require any special knowledge or experience." Some attorneys believe that further appellate review will eventually define areas of special knowledge where expert psychological testimony will be admitted at trial. To this end, attorneys may request that a psychologist prepare testimony that will be proffered or submitted as an offer of proof to a trial judge, requesting that the psychologist be allowed to testify as to the reliability of eyewitness testimony. The following report illustrates such an offer of proof.

OFFER OF PROOF
Proffered Deposition

The Psychologist as Expert
in Witness Credibility

Prepared for Mr. Jones
of the Public Defender's Office
13th Judicial District
State of Florida

Qualification

A. Is the Field of Witness Credibility a Scientific Field within Psychology?

The hundredth anniversary of psychology was recently celebrated in America. Perhaps 10 years before this founding in 1881, the first psychological laboratory was established by Wundt in Leipzig. All of the early experiments in psychology had to do with learning, memory, recollection, and accuracy of observation. The capability of human beings to observe and identify things in the environment has always been a major element of the study of psychology.

The question of how people see things, retain things, remember things, and make identifications of people and objects is a major subject of scientific study in psychology. The first studies of the testimony of witnesses in courts of law occurred in 1895 in Europe. Munsterberg's book in 1908 was the first to summarize research in this area. Since that time, the areas of psychology associated with accuracy of witnesses' reports, such as perception, memory, observation, recall, and so forth, have been elementary to the study of psychology.

The American Psychological Association publishes more than 20 scientific journals. Studies of memory, perception, and learning can be found in almost all of these journals as a regular part of the scientific reporting system. Hundreds of thousands of experiments have been conducted to determine basic principles in these fields. It is certainly to be considered a field of scientific exploration and study.

B. Is It Likely That the Average Person Who Might Appear on a Voters' Registration List Would Understand the Basic Principles of Memory, Cognition, Learning, and Recall?

Many principles that have been developed in psychology are known to the general public, such as *reinforcement* (that which is rewarded will tend to be repeated). Other principles are not well known, such as the inability to identify and remember colors under low illumination. In the question of witness credibility, memory, and learning, there are many findings in the scientific field of psychology that are simply not known to laypersons or, for that matter, to many psychologists who are not specialists in this field. One example might be whether witnesses who state what they remember with great certainty actually remember events better than those who express more doubt. Numerous experiments have been done in which subjects are asked to identify the degree of assuredness of their memory with a variety of true and false memories being tested.

The results consistently show that the intensity with which a witness reports the sureness of his or her recall has nothing to do with the accuracy of the recollection. In a study reported by Loftus in 1980, over 500 registered voters in the state of Washington were given a series of witness-report situations and asked what they knew about the accuracy of different kinds of observations under a variety of conditions. The results indicated widespread misunderstanding of the principles of memory. It is clear that the average venireman knows something about memory from his or her own experience but very little about the scientific data that has been developed over the past 100 years concerning the complex phenomena of remembering.

C. What Would Be the Qualifications of an Expert Witness Who Could Inform a Jury about Memory and Witness Credibility?

Certainly the doctorate in psychology is the basic and fundamental requirement for such expertness. The holder of the degree should have conducted at least a dissertation for the doctorate and perhaps even a thesis for the master's degree associated with the phenomena of learning and remembering. Those who have taught basic psychology with its emphasis on perception, cognition, and memory are in a better position to instruct the jury than a person who has done some research in this area or has simply read about it. It is helpful if the witness has conducted research in the area of memory, cognition, perception, learning, and recalling.

D. Would You Please State the Background Qualifications You Possess?

I received the bachelor of science, master of science, and Ph.D. in psychology. My courses of study included a great many which emphasized memory, perception, cognition, learning, and recall. My professors of experimental psychology included William Lepley, noted for the Lepley Hypothesis in Learning and Memory; Joseph DeCamp, experimental psychologist; W. Ray Carpenter, professor of social psychology; Joseph Grosslight, professor of experimental psychology and others.

My master's thesis was a study of learning and memory as it was associated with physiological phenomena. I measured the pulse rate and blood volume of over 100 subjects while they were presented with "interesting" learning material and "not interesting" learning material to attempt to identify those physiological factors that might be associated with material which is better-remembered. As one might expect by "common sense," interesting material tends to be remembered for a longer period of time than "not interesting." It was found that this is associated with increases in systolic blood pressure. That study indicated, as have others, that memory is quite imperfect, and people will forget critical details and add details which are simply not there.

For my doctoral dissertation, I conducted studies as a research fellow for the Aero-Medical Research Unit of the United States Air Force studying the effects of high intensity noise on the intellectual performance and memory of Air Force personnel. That was the time when jet planes were initially being acquired for our Air Force, and discrepancies in learning behavior and in memory were being noted. My studies found that under conditions of noise, people remember about 9% better in terms of quantity than when people are learning and observing in quiet conditions. An analysis of what they remembered, however, indicated that all 9% of the increase in quantity was in the form of "errors." This suggested that under stress, memory may seem to be increased, but the increase is almost entirely inaccurate.

From 1964 until 1971, I was closely associated with the National Society for Programmed Instruction and conducted many studies of the effect of various kinds of perception and learning on immediate and long-range recall. I studied normal people, retarded children, college students, and many others. Based on our findings, we built an automated learning center that utilized the most salient principles of high-performance learning. This learning center was eventually donated to U.S. International University, where it is used for training.

In 1974, I became a consultant to the Office of Education and then later to the National Institutes of Education. My prime role was to evaluate laboratories and centers that were doing work in developing material to increase the learning capacity and the effectiveness of instructional materials for children. At about that time, I began to consult with the United States Army in a variety of settings, establishing research programs and conducting evaluations of training and learning procedures where memory, cognition, perception, and recall were intrinsic parts of all of the work that we did. All of these studies were published by the United States Army, and most of them are classified. In 1976, I published one released study, "Automated Educational Systems and Instructional Devices."

In 1979, I wrote a chapter for the book *Minimum Competency Testing*, which addressed learning and memory in public school children.

I have taught memory, cognition, and perception in a variety of settings. I taught for the Department of Behavioral Science at the University of South Florida (Introductory Psychology, Introduction to Human Behavior,

Introduction to Behavior Modification), as well as for the Department of Psychology when that department was formulated at the university.

I have also taught at U.S. International University.

As a researcher, my skills have been sought by a number of journals where I have been asked to review and evaluate the quality of scientific psychological research. I have reviewed for such journals as the *American Psychologist*, the *Journal of Abnormal and Social Psychology*, the *Journal of Selected Documents in Psychology*, *Contemporary Psychology*, *Professional Psychology*, *Science*, and the *Journal of Perceptual and Motor Skills*. I have presented a number of papers and symposia at scientific meetings and to Bar meetings in the area of the use of psychology in the courtroom. My academic rank has been Full Professor at the University of South Florida, the Medical School of the University of South Florida, and U.S. International University. I have been Visiting Professor at St. Louis University, the University of Maryland Medical School, the University of Oregon Medical School, California School of Professional Psychology, and the Illinois School of Professional Psychology. I am a member of the American Psychological Association, the primary scientific/professional organization of psychologists in the United States. At present, there are more than 85,000 qualified psychologists who are members of this organization.

Witness Interrogatory

A.   What in General Has Psychological Science Learned about the Memory Process and the Recollection of Events?

Human memory is part of the study of perception, cognition, and learning. The average person believes he or she knows a great deal about these things, but the gap between the average person's knowledge and the psychologist's understanding, based on scientific research, of human memory is quite extensive (Saks & Hastie, 1978). The superiority of the scientific approach to the study of memory lies in its systematic character. Stringent standards of proof are required before generalizations are accepted.

Psychologists are generally agreed that there are three stages of memory: *acquisition*, *retention*, and *retrieval*. In the first stage, information is encoded, enters into the subject's memory system, and becomes part of the neural network. During the retention stage, we have a period of time that passes between acquisition and utilization of the stored memory material. The third stage is the retrieval stage, or the utilization stage, in which stored information is recalled or activated.

In psychological studies of human memory, an attempt is made to account for the failure of people to retrieve or utilize information. There are many causes of retrieval failure, which can occur at any stage of the process. A person who sees an accident or witnesses a crime and is then asked to describe what he or she saw cannot call up an "instant replay."

The person must depend on memory, with all its limitations. These limitations may be of minor import in ordinary daily activities. If the memory is unreliable and the truth is slightly altered, it is ordinarily not significant. When a person must act as a witness, however, inaccuracy can escalate in importance (Buckhout, 1974). Perception and memory are not "copying" processes but decision-making processes affected by all of a person's abilities, background, attitudes, motives, and beliefs. The environment in which things occur has an important influence on quality of memory. Retrieval of memory occurs when the individual evaluates fragments of recalled information and then reconstructs them.

B.   What Factors Have Been Found to Affect Memory during the Acquisition Stage?

Before an event can be recalled, it must be *perceived* in such a way that it can be stored in the brain (encoded in the memory). The event must be within a witness's perceptual range (loud enough, close enough, sufficiently well-lit—in other words, available to the senses). Certain elements of the acquisition stage have been carefully studied by psychologists. They include:

1. **Exposure Time.**   It is consistently true that the longer an individual has to look at something, the better he or she will remember it. By the same token, when things are observed in a "fleeting moment," they are less likely to be remembered accurately or at all (Buckhout, 1974; Loftus, 1979).

2. **Observation Conditions.**   This relates to the perceptual range of the observer. A fast-moving, threatening, or chaotic flow of events, such as a crime in progress, often conflicts with the perceptual capabilities of the human observer (Saks & Hastie, 1978).

3. **Violence of the Event.**   A person's observation about a violent incident during the acquisition stage will be less accurate than when observing an equivalent nonviolent situation (Clifford & Scott, 1978).

4. **Stress.**   During any kind of stress the heart rate will increase, adrenaline will flow, blood pressure will rise, and as a result of these physiological conditions, incidents will be more poorly remembered than when stress is mild. As stress increases, the accuracy of memory decreases (Buckhout, 1974; Loftus, 1980).

5. **Distorted Perceptions.**   People can acquire only a limited amount of information from their environment at one time. What they acquire consists of fragmented bits and pieces, and many of these will be distorted. When events are rapid, mistakes will be made and things will be omitted on recall simply because they were not acquired (Buckhout, 1974; Gardner, 1933; Munsterberg, 1908).

6. **Depth of Processing.**   Different stimuli in the environment are processed at various levels of depth during the acquisition stage,

depending on the amount of time the person is exposed to it and the importance of the item to the person. The deeper the processing, the more accurate the later recall (Bower & Karlin, 1974).

7. **Social Expectation.**   As Whipple pointed out as long ago as 1909, "Observation is peculiarly influenced by expectation so that errors amounting to distinct illusions or hallucinations may arise from this source. . . . We tend to see and hear what we expect to see and hear." This is unfortunately illustrated each and every year when hundreds of hunters are killed and wounded by their friends who "expect" any moving object to be a deer, and it unfortunately turns out to be one of their fellow hunters. Expectancy errors are quite common and were clearly illustrated by Allport and Postman in 1945.

8. **Personal Needs, Biases, and Emotions.**   "Honest" mistakes occur when witnesses, in strong emotional states, express absolute recall about events that were fragmentedly acquired. They remember because they "want" or "need" to remember.

9. **Weapon-Focus Phenomena.**   Where a crime victim is faced with an assailant brandishing a weapon, the weapon captures a good deal of the victim's attention, frequently resulting in a reduced ability to recall other details from the environment. Thus fragmented peripheral impressions may be either forgotten or distorted (Loftus, 1980).

C.   Can You Tell Us What Scientific Psychology Has Found Out about the Retention Stage of Memory?

The retention stage is all that an individual has to work with when the time comes to retrieve information. There are a number of factors which determine the degree to which the retention will be complete and undistorted. Some of these are:

1. **The Motivational, or Emotional, State of the Witness.**   Retention is affected by the feelings of the witness at the time of the event. Alteration of the shape and content of the information occurs as a result of those factors (Marshall, 1969). Strong emotional states improve retention up to a point, but after that retention is interfered with (Hilgard, Atkinson, & Atkinson, 1975). This is called the Yerkes-Dodson Law.

2. **The Kinds of Questions That People Are Asked Will Influence Their Recall.**   Any hint by the kind of question or the form of the question that there was something in the situation (that really wasn't there) can have the influence of creating a perception of memory (Loftus & Palmer, 1974). The kind of words that are used influence the richness and quality of the rememberer's response. In experiments where the same material is presented to groups of witnesses, one group was

asked to recall without influence, and the other was asked specific questions. Where specific questions were asked, the influence on retention is strong and often biasing.

3. **Decay over Time.**   The longer the time delay between the original acquisition and the retrieval (retention time), the poorer the memory.

4. **Filling Gaps.**   Memory is a process of active construction. Descriptions and details become more complete over time and often include details that were not originally encoded during the acquisition stage. Thus, during the retention stage, the mind is active, "putting things together." A person will create and fill in concepts and add details to eliminate inconsistencies in memory (I. Bem, 1967).

5. **Postevent Information.**   Any new information that occurs after the original acquisition may be absorbed and distort the original memory. Discussion and exchange of ideas may increase agreement among witnesses. Nonexistent objects can be introduced into the memory when such objects are mentioned during discussions.

6. **Peripheral Activity.**   Where there has been a strong focus of attention, the actions, people, or things that were in the periphery are either more poorly retained or more distorted than central details.

D.   *What Has Psychological Science Found Out about the Retrieval Aspects of Memory?*

As noted previously, memory is not an instant replay. When an individual retrieves a memory, he or she has a series of fragments that are "filled in." The degree of accuracy with which a person fills in varies considerably. The original event may be distorted. Some of the influential factors are as follows:

1. **Individual Differences.**   The accuracy of retrieval of events depends on personal and social factors. Marshall (1969) showed a 42-second film to a large group of subjects who had various degrees of education. Out of 15 possible memories, law students remembered on an average of 14, police trainees remembered 10.3, while low-income adults remembered 5.3. Subjects "remembered" things which didn't exist in the film.

2. **Age.**   Schaie and Gribbon (1975) found that free recall tends to deteriorate after age 40 and more so after 50 and even more after 60 years of age. Older people are poorer at dividing their attention (Loftus, 1980). As a result of this, poor retrieval can occur. Retrieval tends to decline with age (Farrimond, 1968). People in their 60s recall about 60% of what people in their 30s recall.

3. **Introduction of False Items.**   When, in the recounting of an event, an individual unknowingly introduces a detail into his account that

did not actually exist, his perception of the false item will be that of "absolute memory" and in the future will be included in his description of the event (F. C. Bartlett, 1957).

4. **Conformity.**   People tend to make reports from their fragmented memory conform with all kinds of expectations—personal as well as social. Two witnesses can and will agree on an *error* as well as on accurate observations. One will influence the other, particularly if the first opinion is strongly given. Buckhout and his students (1974) at the University of California presented an assault scene to 141 witnesses. Sworn statements taken from the witnesses shortly after viewing the scene showed details that were quite inaccurate in terms of the appearance, the dress, and the actions of the people in the assault scene. Witnesses reinforced each other's statements. It was estimated that only 25% of the details were correct.

5. **The Need to Reduce Uncertainty.**   There is a natural human tendency to avoid uncertainty. As a result, during the retrieval stage, witnesses will form opinions with great sureness and later find out that the facts are simply not so.

6. **Specific Questioning.**   Questions that are asked as a witness reports an incident can lead to more inaccuracy than if the witness is allowed to give a completely open narrative report.

7. **Relation of a Surety to Facts.**   The research shows clearly that the degree to which the subject is "sure" about details bears no relationship to whether the fact is accurate or not.

8. **Consistency of Errors.**   Ever since Whipple's original observations (1909), it has been found over and over again that even competent observers, making observations under favorable conditions, frequently make errors of observations. They will attest that the observations are correct but this does not guarantee accuracy. Repeating testimony will tend to fix the details.

In 1976, Lord Devlin undertook a review of the issue of eyewitness testimony for the courts of England. In his report to the House of Commons that year, he stated that "it is only in exceptional cases that identification evidence is by itself sufficiently reliable to exclude a reasonable doubt about guilt."

References

Allport, G., & Postman, L. (1945). *The basic psychology of rumor* (Series II). New York: Academy of Sciences.

Bartlett, F. C. (1957). *Remembering*. Cambridge, England: Cambridge University Press.

Bem, D. (1966). Introducing belief in false confessions. *Journal of Personality and Social Psychology, 3*, 707.

Bem, I. (1967, June). When seeing is believing. *Psychology Today*, p. 21.

Bower, G. H., & Karlin, M. B. (1974). Depth of processing pictures of faces and recognition memory. *Journal of Experimental Psychology, 103*, 751–757.

Buckhout, R. (1974). Eyewitness testimony. *Scientific American, 231*(6), 23–31.

Clifford, B. R., & Scott, J. (1978). Individual differences and situational factors in eye-witness testimony. *Journal of Applied Psychology, 63*, 352–359.

Farrimond, T. (1968). Retention and recall: Incidental learning of visual and auditory material. *Journal of Genetic Psychology, 113*, 155–165.

Gardner, D. S. (1933). The perception and memory of witnesses. *Cornell Law Quarterly, 18,* 391–409.

Hilgard, E. R., Atkinson, R. C., & Atkinson, R. L. (1975). *Introduction to psychology.* New York: Harcourt Brace Jovanovich.

Lindsay, R. C. L., Wells, G. L., & Rumpel, C. M. (1981). Can people detect eyewitness-identification accuracy within and across situations? *Journal of Applied Psychology.*

Loftus, E. F. (1979). *Eyewitness testimony.* Cambridge, MA: Harvard University Press.

Loftus, E. F. (1980). *Memory.* Reading, MA: Addison-Wesley.

Loftus, E. F., & Palmer, J. P. (1974). Reconstruction of automobile destruction. *Journal of Verbal Learning and Verbal Behavior, 13*, 585–589.

Marshall, J. (1969). *Law and psychology in conflict.* New York: Doubleday Anchor.

Saks, M. J., & Hastie, R. (1978). *Social psychology in court.* New York: Van Nostrand-Reinhold.

Schaie, K. W., & Gribbon, K. (1975). Adult development and aging. *American Review of Psychology, 26*, 65–96.

Whipple, G. M. (1909). The observer as reporter: A survey of the psychology of testimony. *Psychological Bulletin, 6*, 153–170.

Woocher, F. D. (1977). Did your eyes deceive you? Expert psychological testimony on the unreliability of eyewitness identification. *Stanford Law Review, 29*, 969–1030.

The following two affidavits illustrate the kind of controversy and varied expert opinions that often occur in cases where one side or another wishes to present an expert to instruct the triers of fact about research. Presented to the presiding judge, one suggests the importance and validity of presenting the research while the second affidavit casts question on the reliability and relevance of the first.

AFFIDAVIT

State of Illiana
County of Melbrook

I, Edward V. Smith do swear and affirm the following to be true to the best of my knowledge:

1. I am an Illiana licensed clinical psychologist. My address is 727 Wayside St., Stuart, Illiana 25976. My educational background includes a doctorate in clinical psychology, an internship in medical psychology at

the Illiana University School of Medicine, and a two-year postdoctoral research fellowship at Keystone University.

2. Psychological research has demonstrated that jurors overbelieve eyewitnesses and place undue weight on witnesses' confidence as an indicator of witness accuracy (Penrod & Cutler, 1995; Wells, 1993). Research has demonstrated that witnesses' confidence is influenced by numerous factors unrelated to the accuracy of identification, such as repeated questioning, briefings in anticipation of cross-examination, social influences, and inferences based on information unrelated to the identification. For example, a witness who makes a tentative identification and then learns that the identified individual is the actual suspect is likely to experience inflated confidence, unrelated to the actual accuracy of the original identification. Indeed, eyewitness confidence has been demonstrated to be a dubious indicator of eyewitness accuracy, even when confidence is measured immediately at the time an identification is made.

3. I have been asked by defense counsel for Walter Jenks to render an expert opinion concerning factors identified by psychological research that may bear on the reliability of an identification by Mary Jones regarding Mr. Jenks as her assailant in a sexual assault and beating on July 22, 1982.

4. For the purposes of forming an opinion I have accepted defense counsels description of the sequence of events by which Ms. Jones made the identification of Mr. Jenks and other related facts.

5. A well-demonstrated source of distortion in human recollection is the presence of external information which becomes unconsciously and inextricably incorporated into the individual's "memory."

Other persons may provide external information which becomes unwittingly incorporated into a "guessing" process when actual memory fails. This external information is then falsely incorporated into mind as if it were an actual memory. Such mechanisms operate in normal persons and are a factor in the accuracy of unimpaired eyewitnesses. The effects of this mechanism would be magnified by brain injury. When a brain-injured person cannot recall, he or she frequently relies on others to explain what has transpired. These hearsay accounts and other external stimuli then become incorporated into the patient's mind and come to be experienced as the patient's own memories or are accepted as the truth because the patient lacks independent recollection.

Indeed, Ms. Jones's testimony contains numerous instances in which she reports the statements of others as facts. For example, in describing her interview with Detective Brown at the hospital, she reports:

Jones: . . . when I first came from unconscious—when I came to, my mother said there was a police officer there to take my statement. She took it from there because I was in the hospital for a few weeks. And then I was—uh—I was at a mental place for a while, because they thought I would have some problems. They say I gave a statement right after I came to. I don't remember that.

Despite her lack of memory, later she reports with certainty that she made a statement:

Jones: . . . I'm sure they took a statement. That's what my mother told me.

Attorney: Do you remember it?

Jones: No, I don't. For a couple of weeks I really wasn't myself. Uh—they thought I had brain damage or something, because he asked my mother if I was retarded. I was awake before I was really aware of who I was or what I was.

6. Yuille and Tollestrup (1990) studied the effect of alcohol intoxication (average blood level of 0.10) on eyewitness memory in a controlled study which compared intoxicated subjects to sober controls who viewed the same events. Of particular relevance to the present case is their finding that when a perpetrator's photo was *not* present in a photospread, alcohol intoxication at the time of witnessing increased the rate of false identifications.

This research may be relevant to the present case because in her hospital statement, Ms. Jones makes repeated references to drinking gin at the time of her assault. For example:

. . . he started telling us that he was going to get us a drink and stuff. And he made us start drinking.

He made me drink it.

And he made me drink a lot of it, and it tasted pucky. I told him I hated it.

Notes from her hospital admission on July 22, 1982 were reported to indicate a blood alcohol level of 0.35 which would indicate extreme intoxication. Intoxication at this level is substantially above that described in Yuille and Tollestrup study and carries significant additional risk of complete amnesia due to the potential for alcoholic blackout (an acute poisoning of structures in the area of the brain known as the hippocampus which are essential to the formation and consolidation of memories).

Furthermore, any negative effect of alcohol on ability to form accurate memories would be compounded by the effects of likely brain injury as will be described.

7. Evidence of severe brain injury at the time of the assault lends credibility to the hypothesis that Ms. Jones may never have formed an accurate memory trace of her assailant. Evidence related to brain injury is present

in Ms. Jones' hospital records, in both the form and content of her statement to Detective Brown and in her testimony at Jenks's trial.

Several pieces of evidence converge in support of a conclusion that Ms. Jones suffered a significant brain injury at the time of her assault. The brain, of course is the organ of memory, judgment, and self-awareness whose intact functioning is essential to tasks such as identifying an individual and being aware of uncertainty. Ms. Jones's testimony describes severe injuries from a beating with an object such as a tire iron or jack. Notes from Community Hospital records describe a cerebral contusion (bruising of the brain), left parietal and basilar skull fractures, ecchymosis of the right orbit, contusion of the nose, bleeding from the left ear, contusions of the neck, a scalp laceration, abrasions of the ankles and arms, and a 2-inches wide "lashmark" on the back. At the time of hospital admission on July 22, 1982 she attempted to communicate, but her words were unrecognizable, incoherent, and not meaningful and she required physical restraints of all extremities. Notes describing Ms. Jones's mental status indicated that she was irrational, disoriented, restless, and uncooperative. University Hospital admission records indicate she was unconscious for two days and then semiconscious for an unspecified period thereafter.

Duration of amnesia following a brain injury is a good indicator of the severity of injury. It is also a useful predictor of outcome and of the likelihood of continuing impairments after the period of acute injury has passed (Taylor & Price, 1994). A duration measured in days would indicate a very significant brain injury. The presence of such severe amnestic symptoms raises serious doubt about whether Ms. Jones would have been able to consolidate any accurate memories of her assailant, even though by her account she may have been in the presence of her assailant for more than a brief period of time.

A brain-injured individual may be especially susceptible to the formation of inaccurate or false memories. To some extent, this may simply represent an amplification of the factors that may influence the memory of any person. One major mechanism by which false memories are formed is specific to brain injury and is known as "confabulation." Brain-injured persons are often unaware of their memory impairments. For this reason, they may be unable to distinguish an imagined idea or mental association from a true memory. The process of confabulation compensates for the memory impairment by filling in unconscious gaps in the patient's recollection with false "memories." A confabulated memory feels absolutely real to the patient and may be communicated to others with apparently great, albeit utterly erroneous conviction. For example, in a recent consultation with a colleague I encountered a case of a man who had shot himself in a suicide attempt injuring the frontal lobe of his brain. Subsequently, he insisted vigorously that the wound was the result of an assault despite unequivocal forensic evidence that it was self-inflicted. University Hospital progress notes indicate that Ms. Jones appeared to have a good memory for events occurring in the hospital. This is relevant to the issue of earlier confabulation to the extent that a person who has recovered from a brain injury and whose contemporaneous memory functions have improved often will not appreciate how impaired they were at the time of the injury. This, in turn, can lead to excess confidence in the accuracy of recollected confabulations, which are relabeled as "memories."

8. Ms. Jones testified that her assailant threatened her with a sawed-off shotgun. She indicated that while raping her he held the gun on her belly between them. There is some evidence that individuals confronted with a weapon may be distracted by it and as a result, their identification of the person holding the weapon may suffer. At best, this effect is small (Steblay, 1992) and probably is most relevant to situations where the contact between the witness and perpetrator is brief. In my opinion weapon focus is not likely a significant source of distortion in the present case.

9. Ms. Jones's assault was undoubtedly an extremely stressful traumatic event. Statements made in her hospital interview indicated continued fear of her assailant with an expectation that he knew where she lived and would come and harm her again in the future.

Some psychological literature suggests that extreme stress leads to impairment in eyewitness accuracy. While this may be true in individual cases, on the whole, group studies show that this belief is overly simplistic (Christianson, 1992) and overall, research findings on this hypothesis are best described as equivocal (Egeth, 1993).

However, because Ms. Jones harbored the frightful expectation that her assailant represented a continuing danger to herself, it would be reasonable for her to experience psychological pressure to identify *someone*. Having someone identified and incarcerated would reduce the anxiety associated with uncertainty and would tend to provide greater sense of personal safety.

10. Ms. Jones is Caucasian. Mr. Jenks is African American. Compared with identifications when both persons are members of the same racial group, "cross-racial identification" is known to involve greater risk of identification error. Anthony, Copper, and Mullen (1992) conducted a meta-analysis of 15 studies of this situation comprising a total of 1,725 subjects. Results supported a significant tendency for increased accuracy in recognizing face of in-group members compared with out-group members. The risk of inaccuracy was greater among Whites and, paradoxically, was noted

to increase rather than decrease as a function of duration of exposure for Whites but not for Blacks.

FURTHER THE AFFIANT SAIETH NOT

Edward V. Smith

References

Anthony, T., Copper, C., & Mullen, B. (1992). Cross-racial facial identification: A social cognitive integration. *Personality and Social Psychology Bulletin, 18*(3), 269–301.

Christianson, S. A. (1992). Emotional stress and eyewitness memory: A critical review. *Psychological Bulletin, 11*(2), 284–309.

Egeth, H. (1993). What do we *not* know about eyewitness identification? *American Psychologist, 48*(5), 577–580.

Ellison, K. W., & Buckhout, R. (1981). *Psychology and criminal justice* (pp. 313–317). New York: Harper & Row.

Loftus, E. F. (1996). Memory distortion and false memory creation. *Bulletin of the American Academy of Psychiatry and the Law, 24*(3), 281–295.

Loftus, E. F., & Pickrell, J. E. (1995). The formation of false memories. *Psychiatric Annals, 25*(12), 720–725.

Penrod, S., & Cutler, B. (1995). Witness confidence and witness accuracy: Assessing their forensic relation. *Psychology, Public Policy and Law, 1*(4), 817–845.

Steblay, N. M. (1992). A meta-analytic review of the weapon-focus effect. *Law and Human Behavior, 16*, 413–424.

Taylor, C. A., & Price, T. R. P. (1994). Neuropsychiatric assessment. In Silver, Tudofsky, & Hales (Eds.), *Neuropsychiatry of traumatic brain injury* (p. 90). Washington, DC: American Psychiatric Press.

Wells, G. L. (1993). What do we know about eyewitness identification? *American Psychologist, 48*(5), 553–571.

Yuille, J. C., & Tollestrup, P. A. (1990). Some effects of alcohol on eyewitness memory. *Journal of Applied Psychology, 75*(3), 268–273.

AFFIDAVIT

State of Illiana
County of Milbrook

I, Jacob C. Werthbreimen do swear and affirm the following to be true to the best of my knowledge:

1. I am a licensed and board-certified clinical psychologist. My mailing address is 122 Elm St., Milltown, Illiana, 83921. I have received the Bachelor of Science, the Master of Science and Doctor of Philosophy, all

in psychology. I am professor of psychology at the University of Illiana. I teach courses in memory, cognition, intelligence, and brain-behavior relationships.

2. I have reviewed the Affidavit presented by Dr. Edward V. Smith regarding his opinion of eyewitness identification research and the application of this research to the testimony of Ms. Mary Jones as witness and victim in the case of *State v. Walter Jenks.* He indicates that he has been asked by the defense counsel for Mr. Jenks to render an expert opinion concerning psychological research that might bear on the reliability and eyewitness identification by Mary Jones of Mr. Jenks as her assailant in a sexual assault and beating on July 22, 1982. After receiving information from defense counsel as well as records of various sorts, Dr. Smith raises issues of preexisting emotional disturbance with history of false reporting for Ms. Jones, the likely presence of brain injury that would influence her accuracy of testimony, and then opines based on psychological research that he has cited as well as his professional opinion, as to the effects of conditions in this case that might have distorted Ms. Jones's testimony. In his affidavit, he reports some research on such factors as cross-racial identification, that her assault was an extremely stressful traumatic event, fear of continuing danger to herself, the issue of weapons-focus and the effects of anterograde amnesia on memory. The sum total of his Affidavit suggests that Ms. Jones might be an unreliable reporter because of both her own emotional and cortical integrity status as well as certain conditions that might have operated during the course of the events during her assault.

3. After reviewing all of the above, as well as current research in the area of eyewitness testimony, the following conclusions and opinions seem substantially warranted:

    a. In his affidavit, Dr. Smith's opinions about Ms. Jones's reliability as a witness are speculative rather than based on examinations of Ms. Jones and reliable research to support the opinions.

    b. Dr. Smith's opinions regarding eyewitness testimony exclude portions of the studies he cites as well as the findings of other scientific studies which contradict his opinions. To give only one example, in his affidavit he cites the opinion of Dr. J. C. Yuille as supporting his opinion. He does not point out that in a 1993 article in the *American Psychologist,* Dr. Yuille states, "Although the quality and quantity of research on eyewitness identification is impressive it has one basic flaw: Almost none of the research has been conducted with forensic eyewitnesses, that is, with witnesses of actual crime enmeshed in the criminal justice system."

    c. Although the presentation to the courts of psychological opinion as to eyewitness credibility goes back over a hundred years, the admissibility of such testimony is still an issue of controversy among psychologists as well as the courts (Blackburn, 1996; Yuille, 1993).

d. In the past ten years, considerable research has focused upon a variety of areas in the credibility of eyewitness identification (Wells, 1993). Specifically, a number of areas of concern have been addressed: A meta-analysis of *weapon focus* evaluated 19 tests of the hypothesis that when a weapon is displayed it detracts from the quality of eyewitness identification. The results indicated that six showed significant effects of the focus on the weapon reducing identification accuracy for faces. Thirteen showed no effect (Steblay, 1992).

e. Some research suggests that identification of perpetrators improves when arousal is higher in the situation while other research shows that accuracy deteriorates (Burke, Heuer, & Reisberg, 1992).

f. One of the more complex issues that psychological research has addressed is *cross-race identification.* In cross-race identification, it is suggested that Blacks are better able to identify Black faces while Whites are better able to identify White faces. The research has indicated that there are other patterns than the obvious: In *incomplete crossover*, Black faces are recognized equally well by either race or White faces are recognized better by Whites than by Blacks. In *one-way crossover* Black witnesses do equally well with Black and White faces while Whites do better with White faces than with Black faces. However a number of studies show no interaction whatsoever (Egeth, 1993).

g. Almost all of the psychological research studies are based on a single brief exposure of a so-called "culprit" to the eyewitnesses, usually students (Bekerian, 1993; Egeth, 1993; Wells, 1993). This leads to one of the most consistent criticisms of information about psychological research on eyewitness identification and jury deliberation. All of this research lacks *ecological validity* (Yuille, 1993). This means that studies are done in situations and circumstances other than where real eyewitness identification takes place. As reported in one criminal case, a juror who heard testimony from an expert about *unconscious transference* said after the trial:

> We believe that an unconscious transference can sometimes take place and yet we feel that the experience of a subject in a psychologist's experiment and the experience of a person with a knife at his throat . . . they just aren't the same. (Loftus & Monahan, 1980)

h. Despite all the research that has been done, there are still questions as to the generalization and applicability of the research that is available regarding eyewitness identification quality. Further research might clarify these issues and in the future provide the basis for reliable and relevant expert testimony.

FURTHER THE AFFIANT SAIETH NOT

Jacob C. Werthbreimen

References

Bekerian, D. (1993). In search of the typical witness. *American Psychologist, 48*(5), 574.

Blackburn, R. (1996). What is forensic psychology? *Legal and Criminological Psychology, 1*(1), 3.

Burke, A., Heuer, F., & Reisberg, D. (1992). Remembering emotional events. *Memory and Cognition, 20*, 277–290.

Egeth, H. (1993). What do we *not* know about eyewitness identification? *American Psychologist, 48*(5), 577–580.

Loftus, E. F. (1976). Unconscious transference in eyewitness identification. *Law and Psychology Review, 2*, 93.

Loftus, E. F., & Monahan, J. (1990). Trial by data: Psychological research as legal evidence. *American Psychologist, 35*(3), 270.

Steblay, N. M. (1992). A meta-analytic review of the weapon-focus effect. *Law and Human Behavior, 16*, 413–424.

Wells, G. L. (1993). What do we know about eyewitness identification? *American Psychologist, 48*(5), 553–571.

Yuille, J. (1993). We must study forensic eyewitnesses to know about them. *American Psychologist, 48*(5), 572.

Such documents may eventually result in a more thorough appellate review of the issue of allowing experts to testify concerning eyewitness testimony.

PSYCHOLOGICAL AUTOPSY

Can psychological procedures or methods provide reliable information concerning the premorbid psychological state of an individual after that person is deceased? Forensic pathologists commonly testify about conditions that existed prior to death, frequently in respect to the cause of death. In recent years, psychologists have developed methods to construct a psychological portrait of the deceased, which has come to be known as the *psychological autopsy* (Shneidman, 1967). Originally a tool that was developed to determine whether a death was the result of natural causes or of suicide, a psychological picture of the deceased would be constructed by an investigation team based on history; interviews with relatives, friends, and fellow workers; personal communication; and reported premorbid behaviors. Since then, the technique has been extended to the investigation of aircraft accidents (Jones, 1977) and the relation of a death by suicide to family dynamics (Rudestam, 1977). The psychological autopsy has been used to aid bereaved family members (Sanborn & Sanborn, 1976).

Although the techniques are relatively new, psychological and psychiatric autopsies have been admitted in court. Used in both civil and criminal cases, admissibility is determined by the judge in each case (Lichter, 1981). A Florida appellate court in 1989 opined that psychological autopsies are admissible.[8]

The following example of a psychological autopsy was presented in a civil case. The plaintiff, Mrs. Horner, wife of Karl Horner, deceased, claimed that the conditions of her husband's new employment contributed to his untimely death and sought remedy in the form of both an immediate award and extended payments in lieu of the deceased husband's earning potential. Evidence was needed that the conditions of Mr. Horner's new work placed him in a more vulnerable status for a heart attack than his previous job. There also needed to be some objective evidence that the new job was more stressful than Mr. Horner's previous employment. The following report was the result of the psychological autopsy on Mr. Horner.

FORENSIC PSYCHOLOGY EVALUATION REPORT

December 15, 1980

In re: *Horner v. Brand and Sills Communications*

A.   Purpose of Evaluation

A request for forensic psychological consultation was received from James West, Esquire, of West, Lowery and Ilt on December 2, 1980. Mr. West requires expert consultation regarding effects of job activity and conditions on vulnerability to cardiac disease. Mr. West represents the estate of Karl B. Horner, the plaintiff in this issue.

B.   Sources of Information

Deposition of Ron Sacker, vice president, Brand and Sills Communications. Examination of work records and medical records. Interview with Mr. Horner's widow.

An interview with Mrs. Mary Horner, widow of Karl Horner, was held on December 12, 1980. The couple had been married for 20 years. There were five children. Mr. Horner had worked for AT&S for nine and one-half years before moving to the job at Brand and Sills. He worked 40 hours per week while at AT&S. After three and one-half years in crafts, he moved to management. He took regular vacations, as required by AT&S. His social life revolved around his wife and children, although he and his wife also played cards and went out with friends. Mr. Horner swam regularly in the family pool. His family income was $23,000 per year.

When he moved to Brand and Sills, his income increased to $40,000 per year. There were major changes in his living, working, and recreational activities. He worked long hours, evenings, and weekends. He gave up bowling. He no longer swam regularly. His interaction with the family on a regular basis ceased. His eating and sleeping habits became erratic. He lost over 40 pounds between January 1, 1979, and the time of his heart attack on May 13, 1979. He received a speeding ticket while driving the company truck in Ohio. His life and lifestyle changed considerably and rapidly after January 1, 1979.

C.   *Summary of the Facts in This Case*

Karl B. Horner, age 44, a high school graduate and father of five children, married 20 years, died on May 30, 1979. Between January 1, 1979, and the time of his death five months later he was employed by the Brand and Sills company. Previous to his move to Brand and Sills, Mr. Horner was employed for almost 10 years by AT&S. In that company he started in crafts and moved to management approximately three and one-half years after starting with AT&S.

Beginning on January 1, 1979, Mr. Horner worked for Brand and Sills under Mr. Ron J. Sacker, vice president of Data Basics, a subsidiary of Brand and Sills. In his deposition, Mr. Sacker describes their work as follows: "We supply manpower and overload-type manpower systems for just about every telephone company going." He further states his work is "strictly an overload-bodyshop-type operation." Mr. Horner was initially employed as a project manager (Engineering) for Brand and Sills. (The intent was not to leave him with Field Projects but to bring him into management.) During the five months he worked for Brand and Sills, Mr. Horner worked on projects in Arabia, Ohio, Georgia, Texas, Michigan, Oklahoma, Massachusetts, and New York.

He was "on the move" approximately three days per week and sometimes on weekends. He lived in hotels, a company apartment, and his employer, Mr. Sacker's, house. He traveled extensively. He was working 60–80 hours per week. He worked many nights until midnight. His wife flew to various cities to meet him approximately three times. He visited home in Tampa rarely. He worked against stringent deadlines. When Mr. Horner died, Mr. Sacker hired three people to replace him. The project was minimally staffed for maximum work effort. It was the beginning phase of long-range plans, and Mr. Horner was required to put forth excessive effort to accomplish his missions.

The day of his first heart attack, on May 13, 1979 (Sunday), he was in New Orleans at Mr. Sacker's house. He arose early to catch a plane to Albany, NY, to work on a project. He had worked all day Saturday. The early departure on Sunday was for the purpose of stopping in Dayton, Ohio, to evaluate a project there while on his way to Albany, NY. All of this intensive activity, according to Mr. Sacker, was to "prove something to the corporate people in order to get this company off the ground." The volume of work from January 1 to May 13, 1979, increased steadily.

Mr. Horner entered the hospital on May 13, 1979. According to his wife he suffered a myocardial infarction. One day later, he was said to have suffered complications in the form of pericardial inflammation. Three and one-half days following the initial attack he suffered a CVA, left hemisphere, with paralysis and aphasia. He died on May 30 of a second M.I.

D.   Significant Factors

Occupational factors are very significant in development of stress disorders (Freese, 1976). Certain people are particularly prone to certain types of coronary disease when exposed to highly stressful, demanding vocational situations (Glass, Contrada, & Snow, 1980). Changes in residence, occupation, and sociocultural environment produce "social discontinuity" and increase coronary risk (Karassi, 1979). Feelings of work overload (demands of job greater than can be handled given the available time, resources, and abilities) are associated with elevated coronary risk. Deadlines are a frequent source of overload (Gentry & Williams, 1975). In a study of 299 men in a wide variety of white-collar and blue-collar jobs, House (1972) found a composite measure of overload, responsibility, and role conflict was associated with greater risk for heart disease in the entire range of occupations studied.

Russek (1965, 1967) compared 100 young coronary patients with an equal number of controls. Prolonged emotional strain associated with job responsibilities preceded the heart attacks of 91% of the patients, while strain was evident in only 20% of the control group. Miles (1954) found that 50% of heart disease patients worked long hours with few vacations prior to their attacks, while only 12% of the control group did. The risk for coronary heart disease is 45/1,000 in laborers and 90/1,000 for professionals (Russek, 1975).

Rapid change in occupational environment predisposes men to heart disease. "Complexification," the rate at which things change or become increasingly complex in the occupational environment, is a form of overload. People whose work involves occupational and geographic mobility experience a greater incidence of heart disease, as do men whose occupational status is higher than their educational status (Gentry & Williams, 1975). Contact with a variety of occupational environments increases heart disease risk (Caplan, 1971). Emotional stress emanating from increased job responsibility is seen by some as more significant in the etiology of coronary disease than heredity, high-fat diet, obesity, body build, tobacco consumption, or exercise patterns (Russek, 1967). Some myocardial infarction victims may feel increased pressures to achieve goals that become threatened by a reduced life expectancy. Those who die of recurrent myocardial infarction have higher stress-prone scores. In comparison with other occupational levels, managers and forepersons are highest on stress scales of "job involvement" and "hard-driving" in terms of vulnerability for coronary incidents (Dembroski, Weiss, Shields, Haynes, & Feinlieb, 1970). Higher rates of coronary heart disease occur among persons experiencing various types of life change and mobility (National Institutes of Health [NIH], 1979).

Where a job requires crossing time zones, body time zones become imbalanced and create stress. "Relax and recovery" time must be allotted to such individuals by top management (Boggiano, 1966).

Table A, abstracted from *Vital Statistics* (U.S. Health, Education and Welfare [USHEW], 1963) indicates that risk for cardiac disease in general and coronary heart disease in particular is significantly higher in the manager/official occupational category than in the professional/technical category. At AT&S, Mr. Horner was in the professional/technical occupational category (11% risk above base rate for coronary heart disease at his age). When he moved to Brand and Sills, his work placed him in the manager/official category (50% risk above base rate for coronary heart disease).

E.   Psychological Analysis of Karl B. Horner's Response to Vocational Expectancies: 1978 and 1979

From information taken from the deposition of Mr. Ron Sacker and clinical interview with Mrs. Mary Horner, a picture is obtained of the environmental/vocational expectancies and conditions in Mr. Horner's life in 1978 and 1979. Mr. Horner is depicted as a conscientious, competent telephone-system

TABLE A.   BASE RATE DATA (VITAL STATISTICS, VOL. 53, NO. 3, 1963. MORTALITY BY OCCUPATION AND CAUSE OF DEATH. GURALNICK U.S. HEW)

Deaths from all causes—all occupations	327,271
Deaths from all causes—all occupations—ages 35–44	44,534
Deaths from *cardiac*—all occupations—ages 35–44	15,161
Deaths from *coronary*—all occupations—ages 35–44	8,044

Base rate for ages 35–44—all occupations—*cardiac*	40%
Base rate for ages 35–44—all occupations—*coronary*	18%

Percentage of Total Deaths—Ages 35–44 (1950)

Occupational Category

	Clerical	Professional/Technical	Managers/Officials
All *cardiac*	38%	35%	42%
Coronary	18%	20%	27%
	(At base rate)	(11% above base rate)	(50% above base rate)

project planner and expediter. He is further described as extremely reliable. Although hard-driving and time-urgent, he was not described as competitive and aggressive, suggesting that his personality only partially fits the Type A pattern.

The information available suggests that Mr. Horner's job with Brand and Sills Engineering produced or required the following:

1. Geographic mobility and frequent time-zone crossings without adaptation time.
2. Changes in residence.
3. A position superior to Mr. Horner's educational background.
4. A great increase in working hours per week.

TABLE B.   HOLMES STRESS SCALE ITEMS FOR MR. KARL B. HORNER (JANUARY 1, 1978–DECEMBER 31, 1978, COMPARED WITH JANUARY 1, 1979–MAY 14, 1979)

Stress Scale Items and Their Values			
Jan. 1, 1978–Dec. 31, 1978	Value	January 1, 1979–May 14, 1979	Value
14. Gain of new family member	(39)	14. Same	(39)
30. Trouble with the boss	(23)	16. Change in Financial State	(38)
41. Vacation	(13)	18. Change to a different line of work	(36)
42. Christmas	(12)	22. Change in responsibilities at work	(29)
		25. Outstanding personal achievement (work)	(28)
		28. Change in living conditions	(25)
		29. Revision of personal habits	(24)
		30. Major change in working hours or conditions	(20)
		31. Change in residence	(20)
		34. Change in recreation	(19)
		36. Change in social activity	(18)
		38. Change in sleep habits	(16)
		39. Change in family gatherings	(15)
		40. Change in eating habits	(15)
		43. Minor violation of law	(11)
Total	87	Total	373

5. Elimination of vacation time.
6. Highly stressful, demanding project requirements and time limits (overload).
7. A change in sociocultural environment.
8. A considerable increase in responsibility.
9. Prolonged absences from home and family.
10. Rapid changes in the occupational environment.
11. Pressures to achieve goals far beyond his previous occupational setting.
12. Higher expectancies to be job-involved and hard-driving than his previous vocational environment.
13. A major change in recreation and social activity.
14. Many different social and cultural settings.

The research is clear in associating all of the preceding factors with increased coronary disease vulnerability. In order to make an objective analysis of Mr. Horner's vulnerability to illness before and after coming to work with Brand and Sills, the information available was subjected to the Holmes SRE Stress Scale (Holmes & Rahe, 1967; Petrich & Holmes, 1977). This 43-item scale evaluates the stress impact of life changes on disease-proneness. Many of the items refer to the stress impact of vocational changes and expectancies. Table B shows a comparison of life-change events for 1978, the year before Mr. Horner began work for

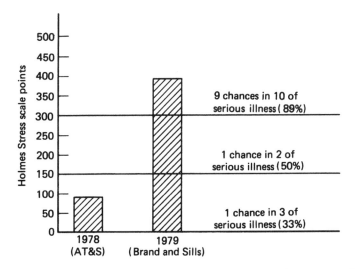

ILLUSTRATION A.   A comparison of stress levels for Mr. Karl Horner for January 1–December 31, 1978, while employed by AT&S and January 1–May 14, 1979, while employed by Brand and Sills.

Brand and Sills, and 1979, the first four and one-half months of which he was in their employ before his death. Illustration A presents a visual comparison of Mr. Horner's stress levels before and after his job change.

F. Conclusions

Within reasonable psychological probability, the extraordinary stress conditions required by Mr. Horner's job with Brand and Sills and the relatively short period of time over which these changes were required raised his vulnerability and potential for severe illness to very significant levels, forming a stress basis for his coronary heart disease.

References

Boggiano, W. (1966, January). Time zone woes: Potential hazard to decision-making ability. *Business Travel*, pp. 10–11.

Caplan, R. (1971). *Organizational stress and individual strain: A social-psychological study of risk factors in coronary heart disease among administrators, engineers, and scientists.* Unpublished doctoral dissertation, University of Michigan.

Dembroski, T., Weiss, S., Shields, J., Haynes, S., & Feinlieb, M. (1970). *Coronary-prone behavior.* New York: Springer-Verlag.

Freese, A. S. (1976). *Understanding stress* (Public Affairs Pamphlet No. 538). New York: Public Affairs Committee.

Gentry, W. D., & Williams, R. B. (1975). *Psychological aspects of myocardial infarction and coronary care* (p. 29). St. Louis: Mosby.

Glass, D. C., Contrada, R., & Snow, B. (1980). Type A behavior and coronary disease. *Weekly Psychology Update, 1*, pp. 1–6.

Holmes, T. H., & Rahe, R. H. (1967). Social readjustment scale. *Journal of Psychosomatic Research, 11*, 213–218.

House, J. S. (1972). *The relationship of intrinsic and extrinsic work motivations to occupational stress and coronary heart disease risk.* Unpublished doctoral dissertation, University of Michigan.

Karassi, A. (1979). *Acute myocardial infarction* (p. 74). New York: McGraw-Hill.

Miles, H. H. W. (1954). Psychosomatic study of 46 young men with coronary artery disease. *Psychosomatic Medicine, 16*, 455.

National Institutes of Health. (1979). *Working group on heart disease epidemiology* (NIH Publication No. 79-1667, p. 7). Washington, DC: Author.

Petrich, J., & Holmes, T. H. (1977). Life changes and onset of illness. *Medical Clinics of North America, 61*(4), 825–838.

Russek, H. I. (1965). Stress, tobacco and coronary heart disease in North American professional groups. *Journal of the American Medical Association, 192*, 189.

Russek, H. I. (1967). Role of emotional stress in the etiology of clinical coronary heart disease. *Diseases of the Chest, 52*(1), 1–9.

Russek, H. I. (1975). *New horizons in cardiovascular practice* (p. 131). Baltimore: University Park Press.

U.S. Health, Education and Welfare. (1963). Mortality by occupation and cause of death: Men 20–64. *Vital Statistics–1950, Special Reports, 53*(3), 95–195.

Zyzanski, S. J. (1978). Coronary-prone behavior pattern and coronary heart disease. In T. M. Dembroski, S. M. Weiss, J. L. Shields, S. G. Haynes, & M. Feinleib (Eds.), *Coronary prone behavior* (pp. 29–39). New York: Springer-Verlag.

After reviewing the report, the judge in this case allowed the psychologist to testify. The tables and the figure were admitted into evidence as plaintiff's exhibits.

GRAND JURY TESTIMONY

The Fifth Amendment to the U.S. Constitution provides: "No person shall be held to answer for a capital, or otherwise infamous crime, unless on a presentment or indictment of a Grand Jury." This is generally interpreted to mean that no person can be charged with a major crime unless he or she is indicted by a grand jury. In every jurisdiction there are usually one or more grand juries sitting at any one time. A grand jury is usually impaneled for several months, is constituted with powers similar to those of regular juries, and consists, usually, of 12 to 23 members, panelists, or veniremen chosen from current voters' registration lists. Aside from regularly scheduled grand juries, the court can summon additional or special grand juries "at such times as the public interest requires."

Grand jury hearings differ from open court in that only the witness, the grand jurors, the government attorneys, and a court stenographer may be present inside the grand jury room. There is no judge present in the grand jury room. Only the grand jurors may be present when deliberating or voting on an indictment. An indictment, or "true bill," can be returned only if 12 or more jurors vote for such an indictment in federal grand juries. In some state jurisdictions, the grand jury consists of 12 members, and a vote of 8 is necessary for an indictment. Deliberations in the grand jury room are secret and may not be discussed outside the grand jury room by the prosecutor or the jurors. Witnesses may afterward discuss whatever was asked of them and whatever their responses were, although some prosecuting attorneys may suggest or imply otherwise.[9] If the grand jury votes an indictment, it is returned to a judge in open court.

There are few statutory provisions governing the procedures by which witnesses are called and questioned. Rights and privileges are covered by common-law case law. Thus, without a judge presiding, few of the formalities and safeguards found in open court apply during grand jury testimony. The district attorney, state attorney, or federal attorney directs the activity, calls witnesses, and conducts both direct examination and cross-examination.

The grand jury can subpoena any witness without having to give a reason. Fourth Amendment constraints against stopping, searching, or seizure without probable cause do not apply to a subpoena requiring a person to appear and testify before the grand jury.[10] The grand jury does not have to reveal the nature of the investigation being conducted, and witnesses cannot challenge the relevance of questions.[11]

The witness appearing before a grand jury generally has no right to counsel during the grand jury hearings inside the grand jury hearing room. A witness can be excused to consult with counsel outside the grand jury room after any question is asked.

During a witness's appearance before the grand jury, jurors, as well as the prosecution attorney, may ask the witness questions. The witness may not, in turn, ask jurors questions.

It is most important for the psychologist who is called to testify before a grand jury to know the following:

1. There is no presiding judge.
2. The prosecuting attorney will generally guide or dominate the proceedings.
3. Any consultation with an attorney must be requested by the witness after a question is asked. The attorney must be outside the grand jury room. The witness is responsible for making notes about the question so that when the attorney is consulted outside the grand jury hearing room, the witness can be reasonably sure of the details of the question. Note taking by witnesses is allowed.
4. If a prosecuting attorney seems to be leading, distorting, or segmenting the witness's testimony, it is the witness's responsibility to redirect the jury's attention to the focus of his or her testimony.

As can be seen from the preceding list, an understanding of how the grand jury process operates is necessary if a witness is to be comfortable and effective in this setting (Grand Jury Defense Office, 1982).

In the following example of expert testimony before a grand jury, the issue involved the use of deadly force by a police officer. When a police officer discharges his or her weapon in the line of duty, a departmental hearing is convened to determine whether the action was warranted and occurred within police department guidelines for the discharge of weapons and/or the use of deadly force. At the same time, particularly if someone has been injured or killed, the state attorney's office reviews the circumstances surrounding the use of deadly force. The state attorney's office may conclude that no charges are warranted, or the state attorney may file a charge, ranging from first-degree murder down to involuntary manslaughter if a death has occurred, or may refer the case to the grand jury. In the latter instance, the grand jury must hear evidence and then decide whether to issue an indictment, or a true bill, specifying the charges to be placed against the officer. If the grand jury finds insufficient evidence to issue a true bill, there is no indictment, and the officer is exculpated of any criminal blame (however, a civil suit can, and often is, filed by the survivors of the deceased).

In the following case, the psychologist, Dr. Smith, was retained by Richard Baker, Esquire, attorney for Sgt. Charles White of the Narcotics Division, State Police. Sgt. White had discharged his weapon during a narcotics raid, killing one of the suspects. Although a departmental hearing cleared Sgt. White of wrongdoing, the state's attorney for that region considered placing the case before the grand jury to determine whether Sgt. White should be charged with some degree of homicide.

Mr. Baker requested psychological evaluation as part of his efforts to clarify the situation with the state attorney's office and settle questions that office might have concerning Sgt. White and thus negate the necessity of going to the grand jury. The following is the report prepared for Mr. Baker.

PSYCHOLOGICAL REPORT—DEADLY FORCE EVALUATION

NAME: White, Charles   DATE OF EXAMINATION: 5/19/83

ADDRESS: Narcotics, State Police,   TELEPHONE: 000-0000
Division 5, Nohoma, Illiana

BIRTHDATE: 3/15/42   AGE: 41-2   OCCUPATION: Police Officer
EDUCATION: Grade 12   (Sergeant)

Referral

Richard Baker, Esquire, refers this case. By telephone, he states that Sgt. White, a police officer, while on duty on February 5, 1983, in a drug raid in which 10,000 units of LSD and drugs were seized, shot and killed Jack Gardner. The facts of the case have been such that Prosecuting Attorney is considering Grand Jury review. Sgt. White is cloudy about his thinking following the time he killed Mr. Gardner with his service revolver.

Questions for evaluation include:

1. Did Sgt. White have intent to kill at time of incident?
2. Was Sgt. White's response self-protective, reasonable, and responsive to the situation?
3. Is any psychological instability noted in Sgt. White that would suggest defective judgment?

At the time of the incident, the deceased had concentrations of opiates in his blood in the range associated with overdose and which could be toxic.

He was known to be a mentally disturbed person. Mr. Baker wonders whether these circumstances could explain the deceased's disobedience of the police officers' orders which led to the homicide.

Procedures

Review of all pertinent records regarding the shooting during the narcotics arrest, pertinent events previous to and subsequent to this, laboratory reports, reports of witnesses, criminal records of defendants, and other material. History and interview with Sgt. White. Review of Sgt. White's records. Minnesota Multiphasic Personality Inventory, Holmes Stress Scale. Review of pertinent research relating to deadly force and its use by police officers. Review of dangerousness and violence research.

Essential Facts of the Case

On February 5, 1983, Sgt. White led a team of agents of the State Police to accomplish the arrest of a number of suspected drug dealers. During the course of the procedures, Sgt. White became concerned for the safety of his undercover men who were inside the house preparing to make the initial arrests. He led a team of officers through a locked, wrought-iron gate and through a door in order to assist the officers inside the house. Upon entering the front door of the house, the agent immediately preceding Sgt. White found one of the suspects disobeying a police officer's orders to stay against the wall. He pushed this suspect (Gardner) against the wall and instructed him to remain there. As Sgt. White came through the door, he noticed that this subject was not obeying the officer's commands, again. As he moved toward this suspect to ensure safety of himself and his men, the suspect suddenly turned to Sgt. White and moved himself quickly toward him. Sgt. White, in a position of readiness, was taken quite aback and assumed a proper defense posture. Before the move by the suspect, Sgt. White had his weapon at a 45-degree angle from his body, which was usual for such circumstances. As the suspect came at him, both surprising and threatening Sgt. White, Sgt. White attempted to move backward, in the limited space available, while at the same time, his partially raised weapon began to arc downward into a usable, protective position, as would be natural under such circumstances. At that point, Sgt. White discharged his weapon. The shot killed the suspect. Sgt. White reports a somewhat fragmented perception of events from that point until he made the telephone call requesting the proper personnel to deal with the death that had occurred during this police action.

Sgt. White's Perception of the Events

On interview, Sgt. White states that when he entered the door of the house he saw Officer Chavez put the suspect to the wall. He saw the suspect start off the wall. Suddenly, the suspect was "on top of me." Sgt. White says, "I was moving toward him with my gun at 'ready.' This would be about a 45-degree angle. He scared me. My heart was in my throat. I stopped and started to pull back, and pulled the trigger instinctively. I didn't `see' this. Suddenly, there was something there. I didn't know what he was doing. After the shot he suddenly disappeared. I said to myself, `Where did he go?' For an instant it surprised me. Then it dawned that I had shot my gun. I looked down and there he was. I thought to myself, 'We've got a shooting.' I remember going to the counter and starting to unload my gun. I realized they would need it for evidence. I called and advised the office of the shooting. I didn't even tell them who had been shot. I then called Lt. Fleming and told him."

Sgt. White remembers the officer who preceded him through the door shoving Mr. Gardner against the wall. He remembers feeling "I better get him under control" when he saw Gardner come off the wall. It was later noted that this man was wearing a hat. Sgt. White does not remember the hat. He states he never saw the suspect's hands. Suddenly, he had the feeling of this man's "presence" upon him. He does not remember any physical contact, but he does remember that he did not know what was "going on" (the defendant's intent in moving off the wall) and he reacted instinctively (automatically taking a defensive-protective action). When asked about his memory, Sgt. White stated that for at least 30 minutes after this he was in a "daze," in a state of shock. He remembers going out of the front door and seeing the people with the bolt cutters opening the wrought-iron door. He cannot remember saying anything from the time he shot the suspect until the time he used the phone. He says that some of his fellow officers said that he had said some things.

In discussing the events leading up to this, Sgt. White noted that one to two weeks previous to the event described above, in another case, he was in a similar situation where surveillance contact was lost. He had deep concerns for the safety of the officers who were involved in an arrest that was going on. He became extremely tense. Because of the communication problems, his two agents had to make the arrests by themselves. Although nothing serious happened, he was extremely upset by this, being fully aware of the grave dangers that occur during the very initial phases of narcotics arrests. He is acutely aware that this was the time that an officer is likely to be injured or killed by a perpetrator facing arrest. In the current incident, he states that the radio reports that he was monitoring upset him considerably. Hearing what he heard, he said to himself, "These guys are in trouble." His actions after that point were based on the concept that it was his responsibility to ensure that this police action would not result in injury or death to any of his agents.

Background Factors

Sgt. Charles White, 41-year-old police officer with 17½ years of experience in the Illiana State Police, was born in California but raised in Oklahoma.

His mother and father are both living and well. His parents divorced when he was very young, and his mother remarried in about 1945. He himself was raised by his grandmother on the mother's side as well as his father's mother and a great aunt. The great aunt was particularly important in his early life. He was raised in a very religious home with strong traditional standards. He has three brothers and a sister. He always considered his stepfather as his father, and they got along well. The stepfather died a year and a half to two years ago.

Graduating from high school in Oklahoma, Sgt. White worked at a number of jobs including the Safeway stores, the oil fields, as a carpenter, and as a worker in a baking company. He entered State Police training at the age of 23. After nine weeks of recruit training, he was assigned to Las Cruces station and remained a trooper until 1979. He served in a variety of locations. Twelve years of his service have been in the Narcotics Division, on and off in uniform. He entered Narcotics after six years on the force.

He had training in hand-to-hand combat and the use of firearms on the basis of one hour per day for nine weeks in his early training. Since that time, he has had to qualify in the use of arms on a regular basis as is the policy of the Illiana State Police. He had special training as a first aid instructor, in search and seizure at the FBI School, and in a three-week course leading to a Certificate of Competency from the U.S. Department of Justice, Bureau of Narcotics and Dangerous Drugs in the enforcement of narcotics and dangerous drugs. He has been to management school and a variety of State Police in-service training schools, including electronic intelligence.

Sgt. White is in good health. He has no physical condition of untoward nature at the present time. He has taken a total of ten days of sick leave while on the State Police Force. He uses tobacco, smoking about a pack a day. He rarely uses alcohol, confining himself to an occasional beer. He is in relatively good physical condition.

His work is very demanding, and he has relatively little time for himself. There is a good deal of pressure on him and his family. He enjoys being around the home. At one time he fished, but he does not have the time or the availability of facilities. He owns a motorcycle and enjoys doing his own mechanical work. He and his wife like to ride the cycle, attend movies, go to town, and go to the Flea Market. He enjoys working in the yard.

His first marriage occurred when he was 18 years of age, and he stayed in this for 15 years. There are two sons and two daughters to this union. His second marriage occurred when he was 34 years of age. His wife at the present time had been formerly married. She has two children from the former marriage, whom he considers his own and whom he has raised as his own. They see him as their father.

He has discharged his weapon a total of six times in his 17½ years in police work. There have been many incidents where he restrained himself from discharging his weapon in spite of the fact that the situation was dangerous.

Psychological Evaluation

The history of Sgt. White is not unusual in any way. Early family problems are frequently found in the histories of successful police officers and other persons who enter dangerous social service occupations. His focus on his strong early religious upbringing again is a factor often found in the family history of successful police officers.

Analysis of the Minnesota Multiphasic Personality Inventory indicates that Sgt. White falls completely within the normal personality range. No eccentricities, evidence of instability, poor judgment, inappropriate behavior, or other disturbance is noted.

A description of Sgt. White's personality would indicate that he has a tendency to overlook faults in himself, his family, and his circumstances, although this defensiveness would be considered quite mild. His cautious personality is standard for police personnel. Impulsive and grossly inappropriate expression of feelings would not be expected in this man. He can expect to be energetic, active, and, in general, an overworker. His highest scale on the MMPI is that scale generally found to be highest among successful police officers.

When faced with stress, Sgt. White is the kind of a person who will tend to internalize it rather than to express it. He may tend to suffer fatigue, aches and pains, and other somatic or depressed feelings rather than express his tension. He tends to be a controller of tension.

The personality is that of an individual who expresses strong conformist, traditional attitudes but who will tend to enter an occupation where he is required to deal with people who are marginal or dangerous. The personality pattern is that which we find in successful police officers and combat commanders. It is interesting to note that the personality research suggests that such individuals tend to have more dissociative phenomena than those persons who do not have this profile. This personality profile is that of individuals who tend to be aggressive and extrapunitive in their reaction to stress and frustration. There is no psychiatric diagnosis or disorder for such persons, and they are considered to be completely normal.

The Holmes Stress Scale was administered to Sgt. White. This scale evaluates the significant life changes that occur in an individual in order to determine the degree of stress under which he or she ordinarily operates. Stress is a measure of the changes in a person's life that intensify his or her pace of living and lead the person into situations where he or she is likely to experience more illness and more overreaction than the average individual. An analysis of Sgt. White's activities in life in the past 18 months results in a stress index that would be rated at 326 conservatively and 411 when including items that are somewhat equivocal. The research shows that individuals whose stress index falls below 120 suffer very little stress and are generally able to function in a wide range of situations without any type of overreaction or propensity to suffer illness as a result of the stress. Between 120 and 300, a 50-50 chance of overreaction or stress reaction can be expected. When a scale exceeds 300, the chances are 89 or more out of 100 that the person will have stress reactions. Certainly, Sgt. White can be considered to be under considerable stress at the present time, excluding the incident under consideration. This in itself is not unusual, since people in his type of dangerous work, which requires rapid, aggressive decisions, are generally found to suffer high levels of stress. This accounts for the significant and unexpected occurrence of hypertension and other somatic diseases in police officers at relatively early ages. It also probably helps account for the high rate of suicide that occurs among police officers.

The psychological evaluation indicates that Sgt. White is a man of normal personality, ideally suited for his job as a police officer operating in stressful and dangerous situations, conscientious, and concerned about those serving under him. He is a man who is likely to act in what he considers to be the best interests of those he is responsible for. Under pressure, he has a higher propensity for mild, brief dissociative reactions than the average.

Deadly Force and Dangerousness Research

There is a large body of research concerning the use of deadly force on police officers and by police officers. An average of 102 police officers a year are killed by civilians, and approximately 275 legal interventions by police officers result in a civilian death.

In pursuit of their mandate to preserve life and keep the peace, police do kill or maim suspected lawbreakers. One of the most important indicators of whether such events will occur in a police force has been found to be the social or community propensity of the city's armed criminal suspects to act with assaultiveness and aggressiveness toward police. This differs from one town to another.

The research indicates that the better the police force in terms of training and selection, the higher will be the fatality rate from police-discharged weapons. For example, the Los Angeles Police Department, considered the most carefully selected and best-trained police department in the United States, has a fatality rate of 37% for weapons discharged other than in training. The "hit" rate for officers' weapons discharged is 62%. By contrast, in Chicago, where selection and training procedures are considered to be extremely lax and where the police department has suffered a great deal of criticism, the hit rate has been 18%.

Police officers are aware of the dangers of their profession. Three law enforcement officers are murdered annually for every 10,000 officers in the United States. Since there are 21,000 police departments in the United States, there are certainly a great many dangerous events that police officers are aware may confront them in the line of duty.

The research shows that although police officers become much more cautious and concerned when they are aware that suspects may have a weapon, this is not particularly helpful in protecting themselves. In the research, it was found that 71% of officer victims knew or had good reason to believe that the suspects were armed before any shooting started. This indicates that although officers may be forewarned by their perception of the dangerousness of a situation, they remain at very high risk. The research shows that officers in tactical units are seven to nine times more likely than patrol officers to become involved either as shooters or as victims.

The largest study of the use of deadly force concludes, "The use of deadly force by the police is concentrated within an environment of community violence in general." Thus it is a community's culture of violence, or the neighborhood of the community in which the police officer is operating, that determines the likelihood of a police officer's shooting or being shot.

There is a general myth, mostly believed by civilians, that most police officers are shot by "unstable" individuals. The research indicates that this indeed is a myth. A police officer is in greatest danger from and most likely to be killed by a rational criminal who is attempting to flee the scene of the crime. The criminal's intention is secondary to his attempts to protect himself from capture. Thus the strongest signal to a police officer that he is in danger is a suspect indicating that he is about to make an effort to escape (Geller, 1982).

Dangerousness and violent people have been carefully studied during the past 25 years. The number-one fact emerging from all of this research is that dangerousness cannot be accurately predicted. Those people who are most dangerous are those who have a history of being dangerous, those who associate with individuals having a history of being dangerous, and those who live, work, or recreate in settings that have been known to be places where dangerous, violent behavior occurs. Violence is a basic human propensity. It is ordinarily used as a defensive measure, but in modern society we see many cases where violence and dangerousness are used for political purposes, personal gain, vengeance, and so forth.

Law enforcement officers must evaluate and gauge individuals in terms of their propensity to be violent and dangerous. Persons who become violent become activated by closeness of dangerous other persons. In social/psychological research, the concept of "buffer zone" has emerged. The probability of a violent act occurring increases geometrically with the decrease in distance between two potentially dangerous subjects. This is true for dangerous criminals, and it is true for law enforcement personnel in dangerous settings. In police training, this is referred to as the "critical defense zone." Dangerousness is defined as the capacity to use deadly force. This is part of the training and part of the requirements of all law enforcement officers on active duty. It is inconceivable that a law enforcement officer who would be hesitant to use deadly force in an appropriate situation could function or be trusted by the personnel working with him or her. If one cannot accept the concept that law enforcement personnel must have the capacity to be violent in appropriate situations, one must reject the entire concept of law enforcement.

The buffer zone is considered to be 24 to 48 inches. In dangerous situations, violence is likeliest to be activated as the distance between the stimulus individual and the response individual decreases. Given a police officer with a capacity to be violent in appropriate situations, this violence is likeliest to be activated when a dangerous stimulus moves physically closer to such a police officer, particularly as the distance decreases from 48 inches downward (Hays, Roberts, & Solway, 1981).

Summary and Conclusions

Psychological evaluation of the circumstances surrounding the incident noted previously, the personality and the background history of Sgt. Charles White, and the research appropriate to the use of deadly force, dangerousness, and violence indicates the following:

1. Sgt. White shows no psychological pathology.
2. Sgt. White's personality is that which is expected and found among successful police officers.
3. Sgt. White works in a unit of law enforcement that is considered among the most dangerous.
4. In the narcotics trade, it is rare that weapons are not present where drugs are transferred or sold.
5. In the incident noted here, Sgt. White was in charge of the situation and responsible for his men.
6. In addition to the ordinary anticipation of danger to himself and to his men, Sgt. White had a recent experience where he was concerned for the safety of his men because of communication difficulty.
7. In the current situation, a similar miscommunication occurred, and he heard information over his radio that led him to believe that his men might be in difficulty.
8. Sgt. White's record, his history, and his previous performance indicate that his actions were concurrent with a law enforcement supervisor taking the responsibility of protecting the men of his unit on a dangerous assignment.
9. Psychologically, his state of mind at the time of the above occurrences was that of an individual under a great deal of stress, taking appropriate action under time-stressful circumstances with his men's lives at stake.
10. On entering the scene as previously noted, Sgt. White was aware that one of the suspects was disobeying the orders of one of Sgt. White's officers.

11. Sgt. White moved in, properly, to neutralize the suspect who again disobeyed police orders.

12. The suspect suddenly made sharp movements threatening Sgt. White's defense zone, and Sgt. White reacted in a proper, instinctive, trained manner as any law enforcement officer would be likely to do under similar circumstances.

13. Sgt. White's reaction immediately following the incident, in which he does not remember details of what he may have said to other officers or in their presence, is well in keeping with a minor, not unexpected dissociative response. "A sudden temporary alteration in the normal integration functions of consciousness. A sudden inability to remember important personal information. A localized amnesia following a severe psychosocial stress. The termination of the amnesia tends to be abrupt and to end in less than an hour" (American Psychiatric Association, 1981).

Nothing in our psychological evaluation indicates that Sgt. White has ever had a propensity to unusual violence, malicious intent, or propensity to overstep his professional mandates. The evaluation suggests that an experienced officer dealing with a known dangerous situation had his buffer safety zone suddenly and intensely violated and reacted accordingly with a defense-of-life shooting.

References

American Psychiatric Association. (1981). *Diagnostic and statistical manual of mental disorders* (3rd ed.). Washington, DC: Author.

Geller, W. A. (1982). Deadly force: What we know. *Journal of Police Science and Administration, 10*, 2.

Hays, J. R., Roberts, T. K., & Solway, K. S. (Eds.). (1981). *Violence and the violent individual.* New York: S. P. Medical and Scientific Books.

After consultation with Mr. Baker, Richard Bennett, state's attorney, decided he would place this issue before the grand jury without recommendations. Dr. Smith was called to testify before the grand jury after it had reviewed all the evidence and heard testimony from police officers who were on the raid, from defendants, and from Sgt. White. Dr. Smith's testimony is reconstructed from his notes, taken during his grand jury appearance and completed immediately after he finished his testimony. The proceedings of grand juries are sealed records:

Mr. Bennett: Would you please take a seat here, Doctor?

Dr. Smith: Thank you.

Mr. Bennett: Would you please state your name for the grand jury?

Dr. Smith: Rupert Bob Smith.

Mr. Bennett: And what is your occupation, Dr. Smith?

Dr. Smith: I am a clinical and consulting psychologist.

Mr. Bennett: Would you please tell the grand jury something about your background and training as a psychologist?

Dr. Smith: I have received the bachelor of science, the master of science, and the doctor of philosophy in psychology. My specialty at Penn State was clinical psychology. Following my doctorate I spent two years in postdoctoral training with the United States Veterans Administration. My training has been in hospitals and clinics, involving children, adolescents, and adults. I have been trained in a complete range of human behavior from the normal to the abnormal. I specialize in assessment, evaluation, and treatment of human behavioral problems.

Mr. Bennett: The issue before the grand jury concerns the use of deadly force. Have you any special background or training that would qualify you to testify in this matter?

Dr. Smith: Aside from the fact that I was asked to make a psychological evaluation of mental status of the police officer in question, I have had a number of consultations involving the use of deadly force.

Mr. Bennett: Would you describe these to the grand jury?

Dr. Smith: For the past 12 years, I have been consultant to the United States Army, and to the United States Department of State. In the course of these consultations, I have been called upon to evaluate training systems and the effectiveness of such systems where deadly force was a key issue. In many of these the deadly-force issue was related to combat situations. In other consultations deadly-force concerns involved the activity as well as expected constraints in special military forces. I have been associated with the training and evaluation of special personnel associated with antiterrorist activity and counterintelligence activity.

Mr. Bennett: I believe that we can accept and stipulate to your qualifications as an expert . . .

Dr. Smith: There are other . . .

Mr. Bennett: I think we can go on. Did you have an opportunity to examine Sgt. Charles White?

Dr. Smith: Yes, sir, I did.

Mr. Bennett: How did this come about?

Dr. Smith: I was retained by Mr. Richard Baker, attorney for Sgt. White, as well as the legal staff of the State Police. I was asked to conduct a psychological evaluation of Sgt. White to understand his motivation at the time he killed a suspect during a buy/bust drug raid that occurred on February 5, 1983.

Mr. Bennett: Did you examine Sgt. White?

Dr. Smith: Yes, sir, I did.

Mr. Bennett: Would you tell the grand jury about your findings?

Dr. Smith: I'll go through my procedures and my report so that you can understand what I did and how I came to my findings.

Mr. Bennett: That's not necessary, simply give us your conclusions.

Dr. Smith: Some of them may pose some questions to the jury, without knowing the reasons why we conducted certain examinations and how we came to certain results.

Mr. Bennett: We'll get to that if we have to. Please tell us what your conclusions were.

Dr. Smith: Well, as a result of my evaluation of the circumstances surrounding the incident in which Sgt. White shot and killed a suspect, together with my taking of a history from Sgt. White and examining all of his State Police records, I compared Sgt. White, the circumstances, and the outcome with the research on deadly force that is available and with the research on dangerousness. My conclusions are as follows: Sgt. White shows no psychological difficulties or pathology. His personality is that which would be found among successful police officers. Sgt. White has worked in a unit of police enforcement that has a 7 to 10 times higher risk of danger than patrol work. He is in a situation where weapons are generally used by suspects. Sgt. White was in charge of the detail making the buy/bust. Sgt. White had a recent experience of miscommunication that almost resulted in disaster. A similar miscommunication occurred during the current buy/bust when Mr. Gardner was killed. Sgt. White's record, his history, and his previous performance indicate that he was doing exactly what a good supervisor should do on a dangerous assignment. Certainly, Sgt. White was under a great deal of stress at the time. Sgt. White, during the drug buy/bust, was aware that one of the suspects was disobeying the orders of one of the police officers. Sgt. White moved in to control the suspect. He acted properly. The suspect made sudden sharp movements threatening Sgt. White's defense zone, or buffer zone. Sgt. White reacted in the proper, trained manner as would any person properly trained in dealing with deadly force. Sgt. White's reaction immediately following the incident, where details were vague, was not unexpected and would be associated with a fairly common reaction called a "dissociative" response. This is defined as "a sudden temporary alteration in the normal integration functions of consciousness, a sudden inability to remember important personal information, a localized amnesia following a severe psychosocial stress. The termination of the amnesia tends to be abrupt and to end in less than an hour." In short, nothing in our psychological evaluation indicates that Sgt. White has ever had a propensity to unusual violence, malicious intent, or a need to overstep his professional mandates. The evaluation suggests that an experienced police officer dealing with a known dangerous situation had his defense safety zone suddenly and intensely violated and reacted accordingly with a defense-of-life shooting.

Mr. Bennett: Thank you, Doctor, and now I would like to show you this sketch of the crime scene *(demonstrating)*. Do you recognize this?

Dr. Smith: Yes, sir, I have seen this.

Mr. Bennett: Would you step over here where we have chalked out the details of the room in which the shooting took place?

Dr. Smith: Yes, sir *(getting up and moving with Mr. Bennett)*.

Mr. Bennett: Now I want you to stand in this place marked doorway while I stand against the wall with my hands on the wall. You are in the position that Sgt. White was in when he entered the crime scene. I'm standing in the position that Mr. Gardner was in. Does this fit the facts as you know them?

Dr. Smith: Yes, sir, I believe so.

Mr. Bennett: Now I will turn, as apparently Mr. Gardner did, into you *(demonstrating)*. Now what would your reaction be?

Dr. Smith: Are you asking me to put myself in Sgt. White's mind?

Mr. Bennett: I'm just asking you to act as anyone might act in such circumstances.

Dr. Smith: Considering that I have had defense-of-life training, and if I were in such circumstances, I would instinctively defend myself.

Mr. Bennett: Do you think that will be absolutely necessary? Couldn't you use some sort of special karate?

Dr. Smith: I think you are suggesting that in these split-second circumstances, a person might have a chance to review options and make a selection. I don't think that is what happens in such circumstances.

Mr. Bennett: So you actually really don't know what Sgt. White was thinking at the time?

Dr. Smith: No, sir, other than what I have already testified to. Sgt. White said that he acted instinctively, and I believe that that is a reliable report of what happened.

Mr. Bennett: You may return to the witness stand.

Dr. Smith: Thank you.

Mr. Bennett: Now your experience has been entirely in the military, so this would be a different situation. Is that not true?

Dr. Smith: You didn't let me finish my description of my background, so at this point I can tell you no. My experience included two and a half years of work with prison riot personnel and police personnel and issues of deadly force and when to use it. My work also includes antiterrorist training, where the decision to use deadly force is a key issue for evaluation.

Mr. Bennett: But in this situation, we have a man discharging a deadly firearm in a home with civilian persons. This is quite different from your experience. Is it not?

Dr. Smith: I believe you're suggesting that decisions regarding innocent civilians must be made by a police officer and that this is a special case.

Mr. Bennett: Exactly.

Dr. Smith: I would point out to you that a sky marshal, trained in antiterrorist activity, must make that decision, for instance, when an aircraft is skyjacked. Hundreds of innocent civilians are involved, and the sky marshal or the antiterrorist personnel involved must always calculate the risk to innocent bystanders. This is work in which we have evaluated the effectiveness of the training and the realities involved in the use of deadly force.

Mr. Bennett: I believe I have no further questions. Perhaps some members of the grand jury would like to ask some questions of Dr. Smith.

Grand Juror A: I believe I would like to ask Dr. Smith a question. Do you think that Sgt. White had any alternative other than to shoot the suspect?

Dr. Smith: There are always alternatives. One of which might be to hold off and to receive a knife or gunshot wound if the defendant were armed. That is an extremely difficult decision to make, and under the stressful circumstances, it was probably made with respect to Sgt. White's concern for the safety of his entire group.

Grand Juror A: Thank you, Doctor.

Grand Juror B: Doctor, I want to ask you a straightforward question—wasn't there a tragedy here?

Dr. Smith: Of course. Any death is a tragedy. Regardless of the circumstances, a human being perished. Approximately 270 people are killed each year as a result of the discharge of firearms by police officers. I certainly believe that this represents 270 tragedies. On the other hand approximately 120 police officers each year are killed by perpetrators attempting to escape the scene of a crime. This represents 120 additional tragedies. Violence is almost always a tragedy, and I think all of us work and hope for a lessening of violence as a way of resolving conflicts of all sorts.

Mr. Bennett: No one else seems to have any further questions, so we will excuse you now, Doctor. Thank you very much for coming to testify.

Dr. Smith: Thank you and thank you all.

As can be seen above, the usual courtroom procedures, governed by a judge, do not apply. The district attorney is in charge of the proceedings. In this case, he cut off the witness on a number of occasions before the witness could complete a statement. The district attorney can be very powerful in establishing the focus and direction of the expert's testimony.

The witness has certain rights and responsibilities under these circumstances. The witness can interrupt the district attorney. The witness can suggest that the district attorney is withholding or manipulating information. The witness can push onward even though the district attorney says that he is satisfied with the answer.

The greatest difficulty for the expert witness in grand jury appearances is that there is no retaining attorney to carry the psychologist through a direct examination. Direct examination by the retaining attorney is the point at which the psychologist as an expert is helped to tell a coherent and concise story about his or her role in the proceedings. In effect, the psychological expert at a grand jury hearing must conduct his or her own direct examination. Although such appearances are relatively rare at the present time, as the value of psychological testimony becomes more apparent to lawyers and judges, psychologists can expect to be called more frequently to testify at grand jury hearings.

THE PSYCHOTHERAPIST AS EXPERT WITNESS

Psychotherapists are rarely called to testify as experts. Where a psychotherapist is subpoenaed, it is usually as a "treating doctor" or one who may have information as to some aspect of the case at hand. An attorney may call on a psychotherapist during the discovery phase of any litigation, criminal or civil. The attorney seeks evidence that will support or enhance the position of the attorney's client.

The psychotherapist is rarely a willing expert. The essence of the psychotherapeutic relationship is considered by many as the seal of confidentiality on all matters discussed between psychotherapist and client. All communications are considered privileged. Few psychotherapists are familiar with the limits and constraints that exist for privileged communication (Chapter 15).

Some attorneys will approach a psychotherapist during the discovery phase of a trial, complete with a *subpoena duces tecum* and insist on examining all the psychotherapist's records. The attorney may schedule a deposition during which the psychotherapist will be subjected to probing questions concerning the client's character, past, and personal revelations. Psychotherapists can be overwhelmed by such an authoritarian approach and reveal information about their client that the therapist is actually under no legal compulsion to reveal. In such cases, the psychotherapist may be guilty of breach of privilege and subject to various criminal, civil, or ethical charges. Lawyers have begun to challenge the admissibility of psychotherapists as experts testifying about their clients (S. Reed, 1997). Some courts have rules that the expert opinion of a psychotherapist is too subjective to carry weight as evidence.[12]

Although the psychologist's code of ethics states principles of confidentiality in general terms, each state may have specific guidelines, constraints, and exceptions for the psychotherapist as expert witness. Furthermore, such legal guidelines and exceptions are continually subject to legislative modification, rendering the position of the psychotherapist quite difficult in deciding what can and cannot be revealed about a client. When faced with a subpoena duces tecum for the records of a client, the psychotherapist should do the following:

1. *Contact the Client.* The psychotherapist's first duty is to inform the client that a subpoena has been issued and that an attorney will be questioning the therapist. The psychotherapist should obtain the name of the client's lawyer. The psychotherapist should suggest that the client contact his or her attorney. The psychotherapist should request permission to call the attorney to discuss the subpoena and the anticipated deposition. The psychotherapist should ask what restrictions the client wishes to place on the psychotherapist for the deposition. Regardless of whether the client tells the therapist to "use your own judgment," "say nothing," or "tell about anything that isn't personal," the psychotherapist should ask the client to provide a written document that includes permissions or constraints expressed by the client.

2. *Contact the Client's Attorney.* After the psychotherapist receives the client's permission to contact the client's attorney, the psychotherapist should make this call. The attorney should be informed of the contents of the subpoena duces tecum (the name of the attorney, the dates, the material requested) and should ask the client's attorney for advice and guidelines.

The attorney should be asked to forward a copy of the most current statutes on privileged communication for psychotherapists.

3. *Review the Record.* The psychotherapist should conduct a thorough review of the client's record in psychotherapy to determine whether there is information that could be deleterious to the client, should it be revealed during an adversary deposition. The psychotherapist should discuss this review with the client and the client's attorney, preferably in a joint session if the client agrees.

4. *Review Current Statutes.* Before complying with the subpoena, giving up records, or testifying at a deposition or court hearing, the psychotherapist should review current statutes regarding privileged communication for the clients of psychotherapists. These are sometimes quite complex. If statutes are unclear, the psychotherapist should consult the client's attorney or the psychotherapist's own legal counsel for clarification. The psychotherapist must be prepared to refuse to answer questions that impinge on the client's rights to privileged communication. There are frequently exceptions to the rules of privileged communication, and these are addressed in greater detail in Chapter 15.

Where a psychotherapist has seen more than one member of a family, especially in conjoint therapy, the issue can be extremely difficult. This most frequently occurs in cases of marital dissolution, child-custody litigation, and other family-involved adversary proceedings. In such cases, the psychotherapist may find that the privilege is owned by both parties in an adversary proceeding. One party may seek certain testimony to further his or her case, and the other party seeks to suppress such testimony. Both can claim privilege. Where one party waives privilege, the psychotherapist is usually *not* free to testify, since the privilege held by the opposing party still applies. The psychotherapist must understand this and refuse to testify unless ordered to do so directly by a sitting judge who holds jurisdiction in the matter at hand. Before doing so, the psychotherapist should clearly indicate to the judge which client has *not* granted the psychotherapist permission to reveal privileged material (G. White, 1990).

Should the therapist's notes reveal information of an embarrassing or private matter, unassociated with the legal issues at hand, there is a way for the psychotherapist to protect this information. Where such a situation exists, the psychotherapist should contact the client's attorney and request a hearing with the presiding judge for purposes of sealing the record. These procedures may be termed *motion for a protective order* or *motion to certify questions.* In such a procedure, which takes place in the judge's chambers, the psychotherapist will be asked to specify what portions of the record are, in the psychotherapist's opinion, of a privileged and confidential nature but not significantly related to the adversary issues of the case. If the judge, after hearing the psychotherapist's description of the information, agrees, he or she will order the record sealed for the material specified.

After this procedure, the psychotherapist may refuse to testify about any of the matters under the seal of the court. The witness may request such a motion even during a deposition.

When a psychotherapist is called on to testify as an expert witness in any issue, it is always helpful to consult with a colleague who has more experience in the forensic area for suggestions and guidance.

LEGISLATIVE TESTIMONY

When the U.S. Congress develops new legislation, the Senate or House Committee responsible for the bill as it will appear for vote in each respective house (the *final markup*) frequently holds hearings on the proposed wording of the legislative act. During these hearings, those individuals and organizations with vested interests in supporting or opposing the legislation are invited to present testimony. Experts are scheduled to appear, usually in groups of two to five witnesses, to make a brief, oral presentation of their views and opinions. Longer, more detailed reports are accepted "for the record" before the witness testifies, to be published in the record of the hearings after all testimony is complete. After making the oral presentation, the various senators or representatives on the committee that hears the testimony may cross-examine the witness. Figure 14.1 shows the typical congressional hearing chambers where such testimony takes place.

Those who are sponsoring the witness's appearance will usually ensure that several weeks before the hearing the witness submits a copy of the testimony to be given. This should be camera-ready, double-spaced manuscript copy. The sponsoring organization will usually submit as many as 50 copies of the anticipated testimony to the congressional staff, so that the expert's opinion can be reviewed by all interested parties on the subcommittee before the witness testifies.

On the day the witness is to testify, the sponsor has usually contacted congressional assistants on the subcommittee to determine the order of witnesses. Experts are usually assembled outside the hearing room just before the hearings begin (usually 9:30 A.M. or 2:00 P.M.). When the hearing-room doors are opened, the witnesses and their sponsors usually take seats at the front of the gallery. The witness is ordinarily introduced to other witnesses in the panel who will be called. When the chairperson of the subcommittee takes his or her seat at the center of the raised bench where the subcommittee sits and announces, "These hearings are now in session," the hearings have begun. The chair may make several announcements, issue a statement, joke with the press, or comment about people in the gallery. Procedures and protocol range from very formal to very informal.

Although the language and interaction is very similar to that which an expert witness has heard in courtrooms and depositions, the interchange

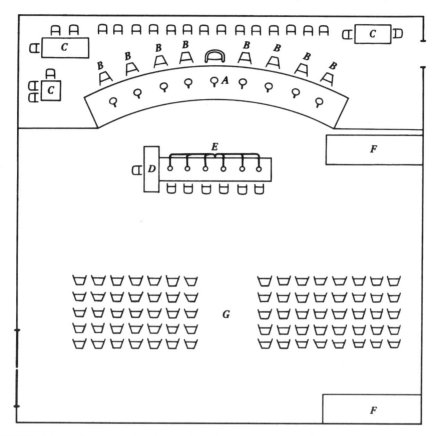

FIGURE 14.1.   A congressional committee hearing room. *A:* chairperson of subcommittee holding hearings; *B:* members of subcommittee; *C:* subcommittee staff and assistants; *D:* committee legal stenographer; *E:* witness table; *F:* television and sound podiums; *G:* spectator, witness, and lobbyist gallery.

between and among members of congress may range from the serious to the humorous.

After the preliminaries, the chair will usually read the names of the witnesses scheduled for that session and invite them to take seats at the witness table. The expert will usually find paper cups and several pitchers of water, as well as a number of microphones, on the witness table. In most congressional hearings, a staff assistant will have placed a name card on the witness table for each expert. This helps the members of congress in identifying the witness to whom they later direct their questions.

The witnesses at the table are usually called to testify in a predetermined order, agreed on before the hearings begin. Questions are usually not asked by the subcommittee members until all testimony has been presented, although this is not a hard-and-fast rule. The chair may interrupt a witness to suggest that the testimony be summarized, since the congressional staff have distributed copies of the expert's proposed testimony before the hearings. The witness should always courteously acknowledge the importance of the subcommittee members' time, promise to be as brief as possible, and then go on to give as much or as little of the planned presentation as the expert feels is necessary to convey the opinion properly.

After the experts have finished making their presentations, the Chair invites the subcommittee members to question the presenters. The Chair may begin the cross-examination or may defer to subcommittee members. Each subcommittee member is usually allotted a specific amount of time to question the panel—usually about five minutes. Sometimes the subcommittee member may use this allotted time to make a statement as to his or her opinion about the matter at hand and will ask no questions of the witnesses.

DANGEROUSNESS AND VIOLENCE

Psychological evaluations of dangerousness may constitute the largest single category of evaluation and opinion called for from psychologists by the criminal justice system. Mental health professionals are asked to determine the propensity for future violence of thousands of people each year who are under control of the courts and the criminal justice institutions in America. The reports of mental health professionals are used by the courts and the criminal justice system for a considerable variety of decisions (Shah, 1978). These include:

- To hold without bail, grant bail, or release on personal recognizance.
- To move juveniles to adult courts to be tried for serious crimes.
- To grant a lesser sentence or probation after conviction of a criminal offense.
- To grant work-release status to offenders in prison.
- To parole or conditionally release offenders.
- To commit, mandate treatment, or release sexually dangerous persons, delinquents, and so forth.
- To determine whether felons found incompetent to stand trial are also dangerous.
- To determine which felons are too dangerous for ordinary prison routine and require special incarceration.
- To determine whether drug addicts should be committed because of a propensity for violence.
- To commit mentally disturbed persons involuntarily because they constitute a danger to themselves or others.
- To decide whether to release involuntarily confined mental patients conditionally or unconditionally.

- To hospitalize defendants acquitted by reason of insanity.
- To transfer a mental patient to a high-security ward or special hospital for violent patients.
- To invoke special sentencing options for habitual or violent offenders.
- To recommend the death penalty for those convicted of capital crimes because of a likelihood of continued dangerousness.

Although the final decision in all these matters is made by a judge or a responsible administrator, the information supporting such decisions often comes from the report or testimony of a mental health professional (Monahan, 1981; Robitscher, 1980).

There are three basic types of dangerousness predictions (Morris & Miller, 1987):

1. Statistical predictions (actuarial).
2. Anamnestic predictions (based on repetitive behavior).
3. Clinical predictions.

With regard to mentally ill patients, actuarial predictions based on past history have been shown to be more accurate than clinical predictions (Gardner, Lidz, Mulvey, & Shaw, 1996; Slovic & Monahan, 1995). Heilbrun (1997) has proposed that in considering violence risk, not only violence risk should be considered but also efforts at anger management should be an important aspect of the clinical contact since this should lead to risk-reduction.

Court decisions require mental health professionals to breach professional ethics and privileged communication to predict that a patient or client is about to act in a violent manner.[13] The professional then has a duty to warn endangered parties.

The mental health professional rarely appears at court to explain or defend the basis of a prediction of dangerousness or violence. On those rare occasions when the mental health professional does appear in open court to present findings, it is rare that the witness is appropriately cross-examined as to the reliability and validity of his or her opinion.

Too few mental health professionals include caveats, cautions, or concerns regarding the accuracy of their predictions of dangerousness. The courts and the administrators of the criminal justice system are in dire need of expert opinion to aid them in making decisions concerning potential dangerousness. This need has influenced the production of opinions viewed as reliable and valid but poorly supported by substantial research or professional agreement.

Predictions of dangerousness and potential violent behavior are to a large degree inaccurate. Predictions of dangerousness or violence that does not come about (false positives) are reported to range from 54% to

99% (Monahan, 1975). The courts are concerned with both a public protectionist philosophy, in which the public is protected from dangerous persons, and the civil libertarian view, in which individual rights are protected. Whereas false-positive predictions of dangerousness may protect the general public, this protection is achieved at great cost to the civil liberties of those restrained as a result of false-positive predictions (Steadman & Morrissey, 1981).

Although the general public has always linked mental disturbance to dangerousness and violence, there is little evidence that emotional disturbance is a primary component of a propensity to harm the self or others (Walters, 1981). The courts have begun to recognize that mental disturbance is not inevitably linked with dangerousness.[14]

Despite all evidence to the contrary, courts and clinicians continue to interact in the matter of predicting dangerousness. In most instances, the clinicians view their task as one of using the best clinical judgment to arrive at a difficult decision (Schoenfeld & Lehmann, 1981). Monahan (1981) proposes a series of questions that the mental health professional should ask and attempt to answer when assessing potential for dangerousness. The following is an abstract of these questions:

1. Am I really being asked to predict future violence or dangerousness?
2. Am I competent as a professional to estimate future violence?
3. What events led to questioning the defendant's propensity for violence?
4. What are the defendant's demographic characteristics relevant to the issue of predicting dangerousness or violence?
5. What is the defendant's history of violent behavior?
6. What are the base rates for dangerous or violent behavior for individuals of similar background to the defendant?
7. What are the stress factors in the defendant's environment?
8. What psychological factors indicate that the defendant may be predisposed to cope with stress by behaving violently?
9. Are there indications that the defendant can cope with stress in a nonviolent manner?
10. If there has been violence in the past, how similar are the contexts in which the dangerous behavior occurred to the contexts in which the defendant will function in the future?
11. Who might be the likely victims of the defendant's violent behavior in the future, and how available will such persons be to the defendant?
12. What means will the defendant have to be dangerous or violent in the future?

13. What ethical constraints exist to prevent the reporting of a prediction regarding future violence?

14. Regardless of the expectancies of the referral source, is this an appropriate case about which to offer a prediction?

Dix (1977) offered a series of pragmatic suggestions for mental health professionals who wish to conduct careful evaluations and submit realistic, ethical reports of their findings with respect to a prediction of dangerousness. Schoenfeld and Lehmann (1981) summarize these as follows:

1. As part of qualifying as an expert witness, a mental health professional should demonstrate reasonable acquaintance with the developing literature on prediction of behavior.

2. Testimony should be given only if it can be based on all four of the following:
   a. A complete and consistent diagnostic framework, with broad professional support.
   b. An extensive personal clinical examination of the subject.
   c. An exhaustive history, not limited to information obtained from the subject himself.
   d. The result of psychological tests.

3. A mental health professional should not express an opinion as to whether a subject will engage in certain behavior unless the professional has a complete understanding of the legal standard involved, including:
   a. The acts that, if committed, would meet the standard.
   b. The likelihood of those acts that the standard requires being committed.
   c. The time frame of the question (i.e., how far in the future does the standard cover).
   d. The circumstances which are to be involved, i.e., does the standard ask about the likelihood of given acts if the subject is imprisoned, or if the subject is simply released to society without rehabilitative efforts.

4. No expert opinion should be expressed unless the subject has actually engaged in dangerous behavior, and an analysis of that behavior should be a major factor in the conclusion of the expert.

5. Any opinion should be expressed only in terms of comparative group probability.

6. The testimony should include a complete statement and explanation of the basis or grounds for any opinion expressed, including:

    a. Any statements made by the subject that are relied on as accurate statements of fact.

    b. Clinical observations made during the expert's examination of the subject.

    c. Prior behavior of the subject, and the source of the information concerning that behavior.

    d. Past mental history, such as prior hospitalization, diagnosis, and the like.

7. The opinion should include an objective statement of the empirical basis for the witnesses' classification of the subject and the predictive value of that classification.

Stringent as these criteria may be, they help meet some of the most serious objections to the use by the criminal justice system of evaluations of dangerousness by mental health professionals.

Few psychological evaluations of dangerousness or potential violence are so carefully done as to meet all the recommended criteria. The time, professional skill, arid cost required for such proper assessments exceed the number of competent professionals and funds available in respect to the number of requests for evaluation of dangerousness generated by courts and criminal justice agencies (Webster, Harris, Rice, Cormier, & Quinsey, 1994).

The following two reports contrast a psychological evaluation performed in a busy forensic psychology unit in a state prison with a report of examination by a psychologist in independent practice in a community where the courts are known to value careful psychological evaluation and consultation.

The first report is characteristic of a professional setting where 8 to 10 examinations are conducted each week by the forensic psychologist in a western state prison.

PSYCHOLOGICAL EVALUATION

Forensic Unit
ABC State Hospital   Ronald, Reggie
January 16, 1980   MSH# 19,919

Referral

This 21-year-old male patient was referred by Dr. Will Jones, Director, Forensic Treatment Center, to assist in differential diagnosis and evaluation of dangerousness.

Tests Administered

Revised Beta Examination, Wechsler Adult Intelligence Scale, Sixteen Personality Factors Questionnaire, Minnesota Multiphasic Personality Inventory, and Thematic Apperception Test.

Behavioral Observations

Reggie appeared tense on the Revised Beta. His hands shook when he tried to draw the objects on subtest 5. He complained that subtest 4 was beyond his comprehension and refused to attempt it after spending five minutes on the practice section.

On the WAIS subtest Comprehension, Reggie asked that the statements be repeated several times. Arithmetic subtest showed that Reggie uses his fingers to add and subtract. Reggie smoked excessively, especially when he responded that he didn't know a particular answer. On the Digit Symbol subtest, Reggie tapped his feet, wrung his hands several times, and appeared to be breathing hard. Reggie's hands shook very hard on the Block Design subtest.

Reggie's feet were rocking and tapping back and forth while answering the MMPI.

Test Results

The Revised Beta Examination indicated that Reggie was functioning in the "Below Average" range of the population equivalent of the Wechsler's "Dull Normal" (16.1% bottom range of the population). The Revised Beta Examination IQ was 83.

Wechsler Adult Intelligence Scale Full Scale IQ was 76—"Borderline" (6.7% bottom range of the population); Verbal Score IQ was 72; Performance Score IQ was 83.

The discrepancy between the Revised Beta and the WAIS indicates educationally that Reggie is not very fluent in the English language. His performance scores and the Revised Beta, which is a nonverbal instrument, seem to more clearly indicate the level of his intellectual functioning.

The personality tests revealed that Reggie was aggressive, suspicious, and likely to act impulsively.

The MMPI indicated that Reggie was suffering from a psychotic depression manifested in schizophrenic tendencies. The MMPI further indicated that Reggie is unsociable, unstable, and inadequate in his relationships with others. The MMPI indicated a high degree of impulsiveness and selfishness resulting in his inability to relate to others. Reggie seems dangerous inasmuch as he is prone to act out his anger against others.

The Thematic Apperception Protocols were short sketches about the present situation in each picture. Low affect appeared present inasmuch as

Reggie wasn't interested in developing a story line. No father figures in any of the Protocols.

Diagnostic Impression.   Schizophrenia, paranoid type (295.3).

The next report was done by a psychologist in a medium-sized California community where funds are provided by the courts for consultation by mental health professionals.

REPORT OF PSYCHOLOGICAL EXAMINATION

NAME: Wayne, Alan   BIRTHDATE: 5/12/62   AGE: 16   EDUCATION: 12.7

Referral

Mr. Wayne is charged with rape and first degree murder. While "hanging out" with some of his friends at the beach, Mr. Wayne took a 15-year-old girl into a van, forced her to have intercourse with him, and then bludgeoned her to death with a tire iron. Mr. Wayne was being held at Juvenile Hall at the time of this evaluation. The judge will later decide whether Mr. Wayne will be dealt with as a juvenile or charged as an adult.

Background History

The family history is provided by the mother, Mrs. Blanche Wayne. The mother is 51 years old and employed in a school cafeteria. She completed the eleventh grade and has had some technical training in electronics. She describes her health as being "good until this happened." She states that now she has headaches, trouble with her nerves, trouble sleeping, and nightmares. She describes her personality as "a homebody." She used to drink for a period of about 10 years but denies drinking now. However, she does admit to being drunk at times. The mother describes Mr. Wayne's father, George, as being 60 years old and presently working for Alcoholics Anonymous. He had worked previously as a contractor. She thinks that he completed the tenth grade. She saw him last approximately seven years ago. Asked to describe his personality, her response was: "If you do, you're wrong; if you don't, you're wrong."

Mrs. Wayne indicates that she and the father were married in 1948 and separated in 1966. At that time Alan was 4 years old. She stated that the marriage started out "pretty good," and she describes Mr. Wayne as drinking "a little" at the beginning of the marriage but that the drinking became more and more frequent, to the point that the last few years of the marriage he was drinking all of the time. Several years before the marriage ended,

Mrs. Wayne stated that she got a job so that she could pay the bills for the family. She described Mr. Wayne as being mean and fighting with her when he was drunk. Asked to describe what she meant by fighting, she indicated that he yelled and used physical force. She indicated that she has several scars from injuries she sustained from his aggression and stated that "the law was called a lot." She indicated that he threatened her with both a gun and knives but actually only used as a weapon a baseball bat. She indicated a scar on her head as a result of having been hit by him with a baseball bat. She indicated that the children, including Alan, were around the house and observed Mr. Wayne's behavior. Asked what Alan would do when this physical fighting was occurring, she indicated that he would crawl back in a corner and cry. She indicated that Mr. Wayne was not as violent with the children as he was with her but would yell at them a lot. Asked if Mr. Wayne ever became physically violent with Alan, Mrs. Wayne replied that she really did not know because she was out working so much of the time when Alan was home alone or with the other children and the father.

Mrs. Wayne stated that her pregnancy with Alan was "bad." She indicated that she did not have the proper food and that she had no prenatal care at all. She indicated that her own mother died one month before Alan was born, so she was quite emotionally upset during this time shortly before his birth. She indicated that Mr. Wayne beat her up an unknown number of times while she was carrying Alan and, at least one time while she was carrying him, pushed her down the steps from one floor to the next. She indicated that Mr. Wayne served one year in jail for this abuse to her and her unborn infant.

Mrs. Wayne states that her son was full-term and that his birth was natural. She states that Alan was bottle-fed but that there was no money to buy milk for him a lot of the time. Asked what she would use for a substitute during this time, she stated sweetened water or weak tea. She indicated that he had no feeding problems as far as she could recall and described him as being weaned very early but was unable to remember exactly when. She stated that she began toilet training Alan at about 9 months and that he was completely potty trained by the time he was 1year old.

Asked what she remembered about Alan from the time he was born until he was 1 year old, she stated that he was "just terribly thin and absolutely white." She described him as being so white that at birth his blood was checked to see whether he was an albino. She described his second through fifth years as being a time when he was a good child, but if they had company he would try to show off. She indicated that "he had nothing to do with his dad." She stated that he was taken care of by his four older siblings during the time that she worked. Mrs. Wayne indicates that the family physician is Dr. Featherington but that Alan has not seen him for several years. She indicated that he has not had his tonsils or adenoids removed and has had no other surgeries. She stated that he had a broken finger about three years ago and a cracked foot about four years ago. She also indicated that Alan had the mumps when he was about 8 or 9 and that he had the chicken pox when he was about 14. The mother indicates that his immunizations are current and that he has had regular complaints about not seeing too well the last three or four years. The mother indicates that Alan began puberty at about 11 or 12 and seemed to develop quite fast. Asked who gave Alan his sexual education, the mother replied that she didn't know if anyone had. She thought maybe he had gotten some sexual education at school or from his older brothers but denied that he had ever asked her any questions about sexual matters. She stated that she had talked to him only once, when a film about venereal disease was shown at school, and she describes Alan as thinking that it was a film about railroads.

Mrs. Wayne indicates that there was one incident when Alan was about 5 or 6 years old when he was seen at a physician's office in Fontana (she could not recall the physician's name) when he became unconscious for five to ten minutes after being given a shot in the physician's office. She indicated that he was put on a respirator and cold towels were used. She also indicated that whenever he got the flu or other kinds of illnesses he always became sicker than her other children and would run high fevers in excess of 104 degrees. She could not recall any periods of dizziness not connected with illness but stated that he often got headaches, especially from the hot sun. She denied periods of poor sleep.

Mrs. Wayne indicated that Alan went to Head Start. She indicated that there were no problems while he attended kindergarten and first grade and described his grades as okay. The mother states that in the second and third grades Alan was absent a lot for what she described as "financial purposes." Asked what she meant by this, Mrs. Wayne stated that she did not have money to buy clothes for Alan that he could wear to school. She stated that this situation occurred quite frequently and that by the time he reached fourth grade, he was "a little behind in his group" and had to be placed in a special class. She indicated that this appeared to be when Alan began to really like school and indicated the reason that he liked school seemed to be that he helped with the school lunches in the cafeteria. He held this job through the sixth grade. She stated that in fourth, fifth, and sixth grades, Alan did "pretty good" in school with grades of C's and D's and presented no behavior problems.

The mother indicated that when Alan left the sixth grade, he did not go to school "for a year or so." The mother was unclear as to whether he was out of school two years or two terms, but she did indicate that Alan said he did not want to go to school, and so he just stayed home.

The mother stated that it was during this time period—when Alan was not going to school—that he took an overdose of phenobarbital. She estimates his age at about 12 or 13 at the time. She stated that she did not know how many he took but that he was treated at Riverside General Hospital and kept there for several days. She cannot remember whether counseling was recommended or not, but he received no counseling following this overdose and hospitalization, and the only interventive step that was taken was that Alan went to live with his older brother Jim for "a couple of months."

When Alan finally entered seventh grade, the mother indicates that he hated school and his grades were low. She stated that there were behavior problems and, asked what those were, indicated that "they didn't allow him to smoke." The mother also indicated that the eighth grade was "a bad year" for Alan. She indicated that when he entered high school, things began to get better for him in the ninth grade because he had football and wrestling. She stated, however, that "as soon as wrestling was over it got bad again." She stated that the tenth grade was essentially the same as the ninth, with things going along pretty well during football and wrestling season and deteriorating when wrestling was over. During the eleventh-grade year, Alan went to Oklahoma for approximately one month, and when he returned he entered continuation school.

At home, before Alan was arrested, he shared a room with his brother. The mother states that for the most part he kept it very neat and clean. She describes his recreational interests as fishing, weight lifting, having his friends over, and playing a lot of loud music. She indicates that she believes he got along well with his brothers and sisters but described Bill (the second-oldest child) as helping her discipline Alan when she had trouble doing this. Asked what brother Bill usually did to discipline, she stated that he usually talked to Alan. Asked if he ever hit him, the mother seemed unsure but thought he might have hit him a time or two. She denied ever spanking him even when he was very young.

Asked about Alan's dating behavior, the mother seemed to have essentially no information at all. She indicated that maybe he started to date in about the tenth grade and that there was one girl he would pick up and take to the football game and then take home afterward. She states that she could recall one time when Alan went to the wrestling match with this girl, but this was the extent of the information she had about Alan's dating behavior. She indicates that he receives no allowance nor has he ever been to summer camp. She described his bedtime as being about 9:30 P.M. during weeknights and between 11:00 and 11:30 P.M. during weekends. She indicated that his chores were to keep his own room clean, do the yard work, and sometimes share doing dishes and emptying the trash.

Mrs. Wayne describes her son's behavior as very moody with variable and unpredictable emotions, becoming irritable without cause and being impulsive. She was unsure as to whether he was stubborn but described him as quite independent. She was also unsure whether he was able to learn from experience but stated that he had difficulty in completing projects and following directions, believing that he could do neither very well.

Mrs. Wayne indicates that Alan sucked his thumb from the age of about 1 to 3 and that he has been a nail biter from infancy to the present time. She indicates that about the time the parents separated, Alan began to have verbal problems in sometimes saying words and phrases backward. She also indicates that at about this time he began to show temper-tantrum behavior whenever company would visit. She indicated this latter behavior continued until he was approximately 8½ years old. She describes Alan as always having excess energy, always being jealous, and always being a dependent child. She indicates that he began to lie at about the age of 12 and that at about the age of 6 he began to present a picture of lacking self-confidence and being overly sensitive. She describes mood swings as beginning when Alan was approximately 13 years old and continuing to the present time.

Asked to describe her son's biggest problems, she indicated the following three: (1) not going to school, (2) the friends he picked, and (3) his smoking of marijuana. The mother denied that Alan used any other drugs but then added "except Benzedrine." Asked to describe how her son appeared when he smoked marijuana, she indicated "different ways." She stated that he seemed "happy, giggly, stupid—saying silly things." Asked how he behaved when she observed him to be drunk, she indicated that he seemed happy and would spend most of his time apologizing, coming up and putting his arm around her and kissing her. She indicated that she had seen him pass out from drinking approximately an hour after he had been observed by her as being drunk.

Near the end of the interview, when asked if there was anything else that was important to know about Alan, the mother indicated that when he was about 12 years old she caught him and one of his friends sniffing gasoline and they stated that they had done it several times. She also added that she feels she had a closer personal relationship with Alan than either Bill or Jim.

Interview with Alan Wayne

Mr. Wayne was seen at the Juvenile Hall. He stated his mother is Blanche, who lives in Escondido and works in a cafeteria for the school district. Mr. Wayne states that his parents separated when he was about 8 years old and that the family never really talked about the parents' separation, and he remembers little about it. He states that his father is in San Francisco, and he remembers very little about his father, indicating that he does not keep in touch with the family.

Mr. Wayne says he is the sixth of eight children. He states that his oldest brother, Jim, is about 30 or 31 years old and works as a detective. He describes his brother Bill as being 28 or 29 years old, living in Pomona near his family and managing a gas station. He states that his sister Maria, age 26 or 27, lives in Baker and works at clean-up tasks with a construction company. He describes his sister Jane, age 24 or 25, as living in Pomona and working as a substitute teacher, though he states that she never went to college. He indicates that his brother Jack is 19 years old, a senior in high school, and lives at home with his mother. His younger sister, Vivien, is 15 and lives with his sister Maria. Finally, he indicates that his youngest brother is about 13 years old. (There are discrepancies between his history and statements of the mother.)

Asked how he got along with his mother, Mr. Wayne states that he and his mother always had an agreement. He indicated that she put very few limits on him as long as he let her know what he was doing. Even when he would exceed limits, for example, coming in after curfew, the mother was not particularly strict in enforcing consequences. He stated that the one stipulation which his mother seemed quite firm about was that she did not want him having girls in the house while he was alone, particularly if they went to his room and closed the door. He describes his mother as a nice person and caring for the children a lot. He also indicates that she worries a lot.

Evaluation Procedures

Culture Fair Intelligence Test, Peabody Picture Vocabulary Test, Wide Range Achievement Test, Brief-Reitan Short Form, Memory for Designs, Torque Test: A Measure of Cerebral Dominance, Sentence Completion, Sixteen Personality Factor Questionnaire—Form E, Clinical Analysis Questionnaire—Part II, Motivation Analysis Test, Chromatic and Achromatic House-Tree-Person, Draw-a-Person, Draw-a-Family, Self-Portrait, Thematic Apperception Test—Cards 1, 2, 3BM, 4, 6BM, 7BM, 8BM, 13MF, 18BM, 15, 14, 13G, and 13B, Observation, and Interview.

Response to Evaluation

Mr. Wayne was evaluated in Juvenile Hall for three and one-half hours on April 3, two and one-half hours on April 4, and one and three-quarter hours on April 6. Total evaluation time was seven and three-quarter hours. Mr. Wayne was cooperative and seemed adequately motivated to perform all tasks requested of him. He worked hard and was persistent even when he seemed to become a bit tired. He seemed honest in answering all questions even though, initially, he was somewhat guarded and cautious in his responses.

Results of Evaluation

A.   Intellectual Factors

A nonlanguage measure of intelligence, the Culture Fair Intelligence Test, Scale 2, was administered to Mr. Wayne inasmuch as verbal intelligence measures frequently give inaccurate assessment to delinquent populations. On this measure, Mr. Wayne obtained an intelligence score of 99, which can best be described as being in the Average range of intellectual capacity.

The Peabody Picture Vocabulary Test was given, and Mr. Wayne achieved a Mental Age of 12 years and 9 months. This would place him in the eleventh percentile, with a Calculated IQ of 80. This suggests that he has unusually poor ability to use or conceptually understand verbal material.

The discrepancy between nonverbal and verbal intellectual measures suggests that Mr. Wayne is within the Average range of intellectual potential with nonverbal information but functions at the lowest end of the Low-Average range of intellectual functioning when language skills are required.

B. Neuropsychological Factors

The Memory for Designs resulted in a raw score of 1, which, in terms of both raw score and difference score, places him within the Normal range. This score is contraindicative of brain disorder.

The Brief-Reitan was performed with slight distortions. The distortions were not significant and would not suggest brain dysfunction. Results of the Torque test indicate severe mixed cerebral dominance. This result has a possible genetic source inasmuch as Mr. Wayne is left-handed, as is his sister.

C. Achievement Factors

Results of the Wide Range Achievement Test were as follows:

Factor	Grade Equivalent	Percentile Rank
Reading	7.1	27th
Spelling	2.4	34th
Arithmetic	5.9	16th

The preceding results, compared with Mr. Wayne's present grade placement of 12, indicate that he is significantly below grade expectancy in all of his achievement scores. These scores reinforce the intelligence testing, and together indicate that academic and verbal tasks will be extremely difficult for Mr. Wayne.

D. Personality Factors

(1) *Interpersonal Activity.*   Mr. Wayne is likely to be somewhat tactless in dealing with people, though he will usually be perceived as honest and candid. He will get along best in settings where occasionally saying the wrong thing is not a serious matter and where his frankness is appreciated. He is likely to have difficulty when diplomacy and tactfulness are important.

Mr. Wayne is likely to be more of a follower than a leader, but he is also likely to want things his own way. He is not comfortable around people, and when situations require that he relate with any degree of depth, he is likely to become emotionally detached, suspicious, threatened, and hostile.

He tries to base his decisions and judgments on rational consideration of facts, a "hard-nosed" approach to problems. The resulting insensitivity to both his own and others' feelings leads him to ignore human values in considering issues. Most sensitive people may find themselves uncomfortable relating with him.

(2) *Early Identification and Parental Influences.*   Considerable anxiety and conflict exists for Mr. Wayne in this area. Superficially, as described in the interview section, Mr. Wayne indicates that his mother is essentially easy to get along with and that he has a good relationship with her. However, the unconscious picture of the mother is filled with fear, futility, and feelings of being overwhelmed. Superficially, Mr. Wayne perceives the mother as appearing strong and available to him, but he also sees her as really overwhelming and at the same time weak. At a deeper level, he perceives her as emotionally closed and unnurturing, empty and unavailable to him. The mother figure is seen as demanding, manipulative, and easily threatened. She is certainly the most significant figure in Mr. Wayne's life, but she is an individual who needs to know everything that is going on and likely has made the subject feel spied upon, invaded, and with little privacy. There is a great deal of depression surrounding the mother, and Mr. Wayne perceives that the mother is so weak and emotionally shaky that at any time she will collapse, and her collapse will come down and crush him. Testing shows strong overambitious striving to try to make emotional contact with the mother, but underneath there is futility and hopelessness that this striving will ever be effective. Test results indicate that Mr. Wayne is frightened of his mother and that she is a person who promises but does not keep her promises to him. Much of his relationship and contact with the mother figure is accomplished through excessive and strong fantasy.

Mr. Wayne perceives fathers as getting drunk and as sinners. He sees them as enjoying strength but also feels that while they make overtures of being available, they really are inept, weak, and unavailable. There is considerable disdain and anger for the father figure, but there is also a sense that the father views the son with hostility and depreciation. Mr. Wayne indicates a strong sense of striving for contact with a father figure but essentially feels that this striving brings no satisfaction, and he shows a sense of futility that real contact with a father figure will ever be successful. He does not know what to say to his father or father figures.

Mr. Wayne essentially is overwhelmed and crushed by the mother figure and abandoned by the father figure. Projective testing indicates that on the one hand he is afraid of losing his parental contact, while on the other hand he feels that this parental contact has already died or been lost to him.

(3) *Sources of Conflict and Anxiety Structure.*   There is considerable anxiety reflected in the test results of both a general and specific nature.

Generalized anxiety is at a percentile level of 95 with specific areas including parental relationships, personal identity, hostility, comfort, security and fear, love and sex, and becoming psychotic.

The parental relationships with both mother and father are a deep source of anxiety for Mr. Wayne. He feels unfathered and yet disdainful toward the father, and he feels overwhelmed and at risk of being crushed by the mother.

Mr. Wayne shows a severe retardation in his emotional development. His whole sense of emotional and psychological identity ranges between that of a very young child of perhaps two or three to a preadolescent of 11 or 12. He feels helpless before the body drives which frequently overwhelm him, and he feels helpless and futile that his strong overinvested attempts at "being somebody" are ineffective. Despite his superficial appearance of looking somewhat "together," his personal sense of self-worth is so low that 98% of adolescents his age feel more self-worth than he does.

Mr. Wayne strives for victory over those he perceives as opponents or enemies; violence and destructiveness are implied, although they may be repressed through legal and socially acceptable channels much of the time. Habitual, focused, aggressive behavior is less part of the pattern than is deeply felt hostility and a compulsion to compete and win. The hostility is likely to emerge unchanneled and uncontrolled under slight provocation and in moderately stressful situations.

Mr. Wayne enjoys personal comfort and ease, although habits of lesser self-indulgence are also present. Thus moderate self-denial can be expected in situations that demand and support such unselfishness, but a strong drive to avoid discomfort is likely to appear in less structured situations. In these kinds of situations, Mr. Wayne is likely to go to any length in an impulsive effort to reduce feelings of discomfort.

Mr. Wayne actively seeks security. He is deeply afraid, and while he fears realistic threats, such as illness, accident, and financial loss, there is also a strong underlying feeling of being easily threatened even to an irrational degree. This means that he is likely to perceive as frightening and even terrifying small things which many other people would not perceive as threats at all.

Alan shows a strong response to sexual and romantic stimulation. Test indications are that he invests a substantial commitment of time and energy to this area, but there are also indications that he tries through sexual activity to obtain the love and emotional closeness which he wants even more than sexual involvement. There is severe frustration and anxiety noted in the area of emotional closeness, and Alan generally tries to meet this closeness through sexual behavior. Test results indicate that his attempts are not effective in making him feel more emotionally close, and extreme deprivation is noted in this area.

A final area of anxiety for Alan is a deep sense of unworthiness and self-hate. The depression shown in the test results is so strong as to suggest that he becomes confused to the point of psychosis. There is clear paranoid ideation with severe schizoid thought patterns and his tendency to distort reality is unconscious and generalized and not something which is available to Mr. Wayne's conscious awareness.

(4) *Behavior Controls and Defense Structure.*   Alan's behavior controls are so low that more than 98% of adolescents are better able to control their impulses and conform their behavior within expected rules and regulations.

His defense structure is one which oscillates primarily between strong fantasy and acting-out behavior. Much of Alan's need satisfaction is obtained essentially through fantasy. He acts out his impulses at a level greater than 96% of other adolescents his age.

Much of the time he is not able, either through fantasy or acting-out behavior, to control the anxiety involved with his urges and impulses, and during these times he is likely to have breaks with reality contact to the point of becoming actually psychotic. Alan shows deep feelings of self-hatred and disgust, weariness and inability to cope with life, and obsessive ideas and impulses with generalized fears. The high level of anxiety appears to be a by-product of depression rather than a primary symptom; however, there are numerous specific areas that generate and contribute to both the depression and anxiety. Danger to the self is indicated, and there is some tendency toward suicide. While the tendency is not extreme and the actual likelihood of a suicidal attempt is small, it is not so small that it can be safely ignored. Suicide precautions should be taken. Distorted thinking and perception are rather clearly indicated, and some kind of antipsychotic medication may be helpful in controlling the symptoms. Elements of chronicity and long duration suggest a guarded prognosis with any kind of treatment.

Summary and Recommendations

In summary, Mr. Wayne can be described as a person who is probably within the Average range of intelligence when verbal and language skills are not required but functions with a significant handicap when verbal performance is required. He shows severe mixed cerebral dominance and probably suffers from some developmental lag because of this. His achievement scores are all significantly below grade expectancy and reinforce his difficulty with academic and verbal skill requirements. The personality is the area of most serious concern. While Alan is likely to be considered frank and honest in some situations, he is also tactless with people. He is more of a follower than a leader, and he is not comfortable around people. He is insensitive to both his own and others' feelings and generally relates in a "hard-nosed," factual approach to interpersonal relationships as well as to problems. There is significant conflict regarding both parents. He sees the mother as overwhelming and crushing to him as well as empty and unnourishing. This is in spite of the fact that consciously he describes himself as having a close relationship with the mother figure. Alan perceives fathers, and men in general, as enjoying strength but as really being inept and weak, and looks on them with significant disdain. There is much anxiety both of a general and a specific nature. Areas producing anxiety and conflict include the parental relationship, primitive emotional development, very strong repressed hostility, a high unmet need for comfort, severe fear and insecurity, strong needs for love and emotional closeness that he attempts to fulfill through a strong sex drive but that continue to go deprived, and deep feelings of unworthiness and self-hate. The degree of emotional disturbance is to such an extreme that depression becomes psychotic in degree, there is clear paranoid ideation with severe schizoid thought patterns, and there are high indications that reality is misperceived and distorted. The behavior controls are low to the point of often being nonexistent, and the high unmet needs and conflicts show a pattern of impulsivity so great that Alan is likely to behave in ways to fulfill these needs and impulses through almost any means.

Considering the results of the psychological evaluation, the following recommendations seem in order:

1. Whatever the outcome of Mr. Wayne's trial, he needs to be in a treatment program that will focus on and specifically address the following treatment needs:

    a. The underlying psychotic process must be addressed and attended to at all times, most likely including medication management that will counteract symptoms during active and acute episodes.

    b. The deep feelings of self-hatred and disgust that become extreme to the point of rendering Mr. Wayne a danger to himself.

    c. The antisocial feelings need to find expression through safe, legal channels that can provide a needed safety valve, and these should be encouraged.

    d. Desensitization and other therapeutic techniques specifically for dealing with specific fears and obsessions.

    e. The conflicted parental relationships and deep sense of having been unparented, at least in an emotional and psychological way.

    f. Effective ways of both defusing and channeling the strong repressed hostility.

    g. Appropriate means for meeting the needs for comfort that will neither repress the need nor give in to selfish disregard for other people's needs.

    h. Specific therapeutic work that will include attention to sexual education, sexual identity, and role characteristics and education and support in learning how to build reciprocally warm relationships with women.

2. Because Mr. Wayne is a moderate danger to himself, and therefore a suicide risk, attention should be paid to his behavior in this respect. When environmental stress factors are minimal, this danger may not exist at that particular time. However, when even minimal stress or threat exists, Mr. Wayne is likely to behave in self-destructive ways. This behavior may sometimes be extreme and overt, while other times it may be more indirect, such as taking drugs to the point of an accidental overdose.

3. Mr. Wayne needs opportunities to experience real situations that provide even moderate success in small endeavors. He superficially presents a self-confident picture, but beneath this exterior is a human being so devoid of self-worth that he feels himself to be of practically no value at all.

4. Encouragement and structured education and exploration in values clarification, particularly as it relates to moral and ethical issues, should be part of any planning program for Mr. Wayne from this point on. He needs both individual help and reinforcement for his attempts in this respect.

5. In whatever situations that he is in, he needs detailed plans and structures for carrying them out and specific feedback so that he perceives benefit to himself from that behavior and may more specifically learn the consequences of his actions and thus increase self-discipline and personal effectiveness.

Any treatment program for Mr. Wayne should include both individual and group psychotherapy specifically to deal with the treatment needs outlined in no. 1, as well as treatment conditions spelled out in recommendations 2 through 5. Any performance-oriented program produces a special counseling need for Mr. Wayne because he feels confused and unable to cope with reality and, in fact, distorts reality so significantly that at times he can be deemed psychotic. Extra explanation and counseling support with patience and yet firmness will be needed if a treatment program is effective.

Because of some elements of chronicity, prognosis for improvement with any treatment program is guarded. However, it is felt that unless a treatment program which incorporates *all* of these needs can be provided for Mr. Wayne, he is at serious risk of continuing to disregard the needs and feelings of both himself and other people because of his overwhelming impulsivity, poor behavior controls, and extreme psychopathology.

Although these reports illustrate a wide range of content, detail, and focus, neither included a disclaimer section clearly stating that opinions concerning future dangerousness and potential for violence are based on clinical judgment and that the research literature suggests that such predictions most frequently err in the direction of false positives.

On a more pragmatic note; both defendants described in the two reports were sentenced to long terms in prison. The defendant in the second report has had no reported incidents of violence during the past three years; the defendant in the first report has since murdered four people while in prison.

Research continues to provide important insights in the complex task faced by experts called upon to opine as to future dangerousness. "Second generation" research has begun to focus on base rates, an essential aspect of improving predictive accuracy (Otto, 1992). Increases in both interest and funding should improve the accuracy of violence prediction in the coming decades (Monahan, 1996; Monahan & Steadman, 1994).

COMPETENCY FOR EXECUTION

Over 3,000 individuals have been sentenced to death in the United States and await execution. Competency for execution is a significant part of the capital punishment process. Competency for execution implies the absence of disabilities which would render an individual unfit to perform a legal task. In the specific case of competency for execution, the question is whether the convicted party is able to understand and assist his or her attorney in legal tasks such as ongoing appeals (Heilbrun, 1987). Various states specify various standards for postponing execution. Other states specify that the prisoner be able to comprehend the nature of the proceedings against him or her or the punishment for offense charged. Severe mental retardation may be considered a basis for not carrying out the death penalty.[15]

The testimony of the expert witness on the issue of competence for execution may take place in the *penalty phase* of a trial which has resulted in a conviction of a capital offense. Such testimony may propose that the individual was mentally disturbed or mentally deficient at the time of the offense and so should not be held completely responsible (Davis, 1991; L. White, 1987). In other cases, testimony may be presented as part of a stay of execution petition. Failure to explore neuropsychological deficits during a capital trial may be deemed trial error by appellate courts.[16]

The examination which might best be used by the psychologist who expects to render an opinion as to the competency for execution should include objective measures of intellect, neuropsychological status, personality, and symptom validity. Specific instruments and approaches are discussed elsewhere in this book.

When rendering opinions as to a convicted felon's intellectual or neuropsychological test performance, it is sometimes important to make normative comparisons on standardized tests given to other felons. Such norms were developed by Selby, Airy-Eggertsen, and Laver (1998). A tabular extract from their study is presented in Appendix G.

POLITICAL ASYLUM

An increasingly larger group of foreign immigrants have sought admission to the United States seeking *political asylum*. Claiming refugee status, these individuals are rarely able in hearings before immigration judges, to provide evidence of murder, threats, death lists other than their own testimony.

Since a strong basis for granting asylum is a well-founded fear of persecution, immigration judges must be convinced that the applicant has personally suffered from the alleged persecution. A psychological evaluation that indicates a refugee has suffered post traumatic stress disorder can be a useful piece of evidence (Austerlitz, 1986). Both interviews and test instruments must be presented in language readily understood by the refugee and the examiner must comprehend the refugee's language or work with a reliable interpreter.

VIOLENT SEXUAL PREDATORS

In the 1997 term, the U.S. Supreme Court opined that states have the right to enact and enforce sexual predator laws whereby convicted sex offenders, scheduled to be released from prison, can be civilly committed if they can be shown to have a mental abnormality that makes them likely to engage in predatory acts of sexual violence (Parry, 1997).

Psychologists and psychiatrists will be called on to render opinions as to future violent sexual behavior of this group of convicted felons. Since the standard of proof is *clear and convincing evidence*, the current state of psychological research does not as yet strongly support such predictions. The strongest opinions are likely to be rendered by psychologists retained by the defense to bring to the court's attention the limitations of dangerousness predictions.

REPRESSED MEMORY SYNDROME

When a prosecutor in a criminal matter or a plaintiff in a civil issue proposes that an individual was sexually abused many years ago (usually as a child) and then in adulthood "recovers" the memory, litigation focuses on the validity of such memories. This issue has resulted in considerable controversy as to the believability of such memories (Benedict & Donaldson, 1996; Golding, Sanchez, & Sego, 1996; Golding, Sego, Sanchez, & Hassemann, 1995; Kazdin, 1996; Lindsay, Memon, Poole, & Bull, 1996; Loftus, 1996; Spar et al., 1995; Wakefield & Underwager, 1996). Strong proponents and opponents of the validity of recovered memories abound. A working group appointed by the American Psychological Association found there were many areas of disagreement about this issue (Alpert et al., 1996). It is recommended that experts would be well advised as follows:

- Psychologists who testify about repressed memory should avoid speaking to the ultimate issue.
- Therapists treating cases of repressed memory should avoid testifying as expert forensic witnesses.
- Experts should confine their testimony to their specific areas of expertise and knowledge.
- Care should be utilized in making inferences from the symptoms to the credibility of the plaintiff's report.
- When feasible, expert clinical opinions should be based on direct or videotaped observation.

The U.S. Supreme Court let stand in *Borawick v. Shaw*[17] a decision that stated, "Furthermore we are highly skeptical of the belief in the clinician's ability to 'weed out the most patently groundless claims.' " Recent legal reviews suggest that testimony in favor of repressed memory syndromes is not generally well-received (Richmond, 1996).

The applications and issues which involve psychologists with the legal system have by no means been fully cataloged in this chapter. As the relationship between psychology and the law becomes more extensive, new areas of application and further questions of appropriateness are very likely to emerge.

NOTES

1. *United States v. Wade,* 388 U.S. 218 (1967).
2. *United States v. Telfaire,* 469 F.2d 552 (D.C. Cir. 1972).
3. *United States v. Crews,* 445 U.S. 463, 100 S. Ct. 1244, 63 L. Ed. 2d 537 (1980).
4. *Dyas v. United States,* 376 A.2d 827 (D.C. 1977).
5. *Nelson v. State,* 362 So. 2d 1017 (Fla. 1978).
6. *United States v. Amaral,* 488 F.2d 1148 (9th Cir. 1973).
7. *Johnson v. State,* 393 So. 2d 1069 (Fla. 1980), *cert. denied,* 454 U.S. 882 (1981).
8. *Jackson v. State of Florida,* 553 So. 2d 719 (Fla. App. 4 Dist. 1989).
9. *In Re Minkoff,* 349 F. Supp. 154 (D.R.I. 1972).
10. *Fraser v. United States,* 452 F.2d 616, 620 (7th Cir. 1971).
11. *Hale v. Henkel,* 201 U.S. 43, 65 (1906).
12. *Tyson v. Tyson,* Wash. Sup. Ct. No. 51908-1, 10/30/86.
13. *Tarasoff v. Regents of the Univ. of Cal.,* 13 Cal. 3d 177, 529 P.2d. 553, 118 Cal. Rptr. 129 (1974).
14. *O'Connor v. Donaldson,* 420 U.S. 563 (1975).
15. *Kansas v. Hendricks,* 117 S. Ct. 2072 (U.S. Sup. Ct. 1997).
16. *Hoskins v. State of Florida.* 1997 WL 633400.
17. *Borawick v. Shaw,* 66 F.3d 597 (1995).

15

Ethics, Constraints, Concerns, and Standards

The burgeoning use of psychologists as experts in legal proceedings continues. Efforts to establish standards and guidelines are just emerging. Differences of opinion have arisen and are being debated. Practitioners must make do with current ethical constraints, legal expectations, and professional standards. During the past decade, a good many forensic psychologists have proposed and opposed various standards (Fitch, Petrella, & Wallace, 1987; Golding, 1990; Greenberg & Shuman, 1997; Guilmette & Hagen, 1997; Hess, 1987; Lees-Haley, 1997; Rogers, 1987; Stromberg, Lindberg, & Schneider, 1995).

ETHICS

The *Ethical Principles of Psychologists* (APA, 1992) provides some guidance within general ethical principles. For the first time, the APA ethical code includes some specific references to the practice of forensic psychology. The 1992 APA Ethical Principles and Code of Conduct specifically refers to the relationship of ethics and law (Standard 1.02) and compliance with laws and rules (Standard 7.06). Although generalized, the entire APA principles apply to forensic work (see Appendix H).

It became clear during the past decade that specific guidelines were necessary as forensic psychology emerged as a specialty. A joint committee of the Division of Psychology and the Law (Division 41 of the APA) and the American Academy of Forensic Psychology spent several years developing and refining such guidelines. *The Specialty Guidelines for Forensic Psychologists* were formally adopted by both the members of APA Division 41 and the American Psychology—Law Society. Focusing on such issues as responsibility, competence, relationships, confidentiality and privilege, methods and procedures, and public and professional communications, the *Specialty Guidelines* provide specific and detailed standards for the improvement and maintenance of quality of professional forensic services. Appendix F presents these guidelines.

PRIVILEGED COMMUNICATION AND CONFIDENTIALITY

Many psychologists confuse the concept of confidentiality with that of patient privilege. In certain respects, the ethical standard concerning confidentiality (the professional's obligation never to reveal information obtained in the professional relationship without specific permission from the client) is at odds with the legal concept of privileged communication (legal constraints on the psychologist not to reveal information about the client obtained in the course of professional contacts). The ethical constraint against revealing confidential information is almost absolute, allowing only the leeway of revealing a confidence in the duty to warn where dangerousness is predicted. Both the APA Code of Ethics and the law seem to agree that psychologists should be able to determine when a patient poses a serious danger of violence to others (Shah, 1977).

Privileged communication is granted by statute. Each state usually specifies in its professional codes the nature, extent, and limitations of privileged communication.

The following excerpts from the code of one state illustrate how privilege is granted and the 13 exceptions that specify the conditions under which a psychologist *cannot* refuse to testify in that state:

1009. General Provisions.

(a) Except as otherwise provided in this section, the right of any person to claim a privilege provided in Section 954 (lawyer-client privilege), 980 (privilege for confidential marital communications), 994 (physician-patient privilege), 1014 (psychotherapist-patient privilege), 1033 (privilege of penitent), or 1034 (privilege of clergyman) is waived with respect to a communication protected by such privilege if any holder of the privilege, without coercion, has disclosed a significant part of the communication or has consented to such disclosure made by anyone. Consent to disclosure is manifested by any statement or other conduct of the holder of the privilege indicating his consent to the disclosure, indicating his failure to claim the privilege in any proceedings in which he has the legal standing and opportunity to claim the privilege.

(b) Where two or more persons are joint holders of a privilege provided by Section 954 (lawyer-client privilege), 994 (physician-patient privilege), or 1014 (psychotherapist-patient privilege), a waiver of the right of a particular joint holder of the privilege to claim the privilege does not affect the right of another joint holder to claim the privilege. In the case of the privilege provided by Section 980 (privilege for confidential marital communications), a waiver of the right of one spouse to claim the privilege does not affect the right of the other spouse to claim the privilege.

(c) A disclosure that is itself privileged is not a waiver of any privilege.

(d) A disclosure in confidence of a communication that is protected by Section 954 (lawyer-client privilege), 994 (physician-patient privilege), or 1014 (psychotherapist-patient privilege), when such disclosure is reasonably necessary for the accomplishment of the purpose for which the lawyer, physician, or psychotherapist was consulted, is not a waiver of the privilege.

1010. "Psychotherapist."

As used in this article, "psychotherapist" means:

(a) A person authorized, or reasonably believed by the patient to be authorized, to practice medicine in any state or nation who devotes, or is reasonably believed by the patient to devote, a substantial portion of his time to the practice of psychiatry.

(b) A person licensed as a psychologist under Chapter 6.6 (commencing with Section 2900) of Division 2 of the Business and Professions Code.

(c) A person licensed as a clinical social worker under Article 4 (commencing with Section 9040) of Chapter 17 of Division 3 of the Business and Professions Code, when he is engaged in applied psychotherapy of a nonmedical nature.

(d) A person who is serving as a school psychologist and holds a credential authorizing such service issued by the state.

(e) A person licensed as a marriage, family and child counselor under Chapter 4 (commencing with Section 1780) of Part 3, Division 5 of the Business and Professions Code.

1011. "Patient."

As used in this article, "patient" means a person who consults a psychotherapist or submits to an examination by a psychotherapist for the purpose of securing a diagnosis or preventive, palliative, or curative treatment of his mental or emotional condition or who submits to an examination of his mental or emotional condition for the purpose of scientific research on mental or emotional problems.

1012. "Confidential Communication between Patient and Psychotherapist."

As used in this article, "confidential communication between patient and psychotherapist" means information, including information obtained by an examination of the patient, transmitted between a patient and his psychotherapist in the course of that relationship and in confidence by a means which, so far as the patient is aware, discloses the information to no third persons other than those who are present to further the interest of the patient in the consultation, or those to whom disclosure is reasonably necessary for the transmission of the information or the accomplishment of the purpose for which the psychotherapist is consulted, and includes a diagnosis made and the advice given by the psychotherapist in the course of that relationship.

1013.   "Holder of the Privilege."

As used in this article, "holder of the privilege" means:

(a) The patient when he has no guardian or conservator.

(b) The guardian or conservator of the patient when the patient has a guardian or conservator.

(c) The personal representative of the patient if the patient is dead.

1014.   Psychotherapist–Patient Privilege; Application to Individuals and Entities.

Subject to Section 912 and except as otherwise provided in this article, the patient, whether or not a party, has a privilege to refuse to disclose, and to prevent another from disclosing, a confidential communication between patient and psychotherapist if the privilege is claimed by:

(a) The holder of the privilege;

(b) A person who is authorized to claim the privilege by the holder of the privilege; or

(c) The person who was the psychotherapist at the time of the confidential communication, but such person may not claim the privilege if there is no holder of the privilege in existence or if he is otherwise instructed by a person authorized to permit disclosure.

1015.   When Psychotherapist Requires to Claim Privilege.

The psychotherapist who received or made a communication subject to the privilege under this article shall claim the privilege whenever he is present when the communication is sought to be disclosed and is authorized to claim the privilege under subdivision (c) of Section 1014.

1016.   Exception: Patient–Litigant Exception. There is no privilege under this article as to a communication relevant to an issue concerning the mental or emotional condition of the patient if such issue has been tendered by:

(a) The patient;

(b) Any party claiming through or under the patient;

(c) Any party claiming as a beneficiary of the patient through a contract to which the patient is or was a party; or

(d) The plaintiff in an action brought under Section 376 or 377 of the Code of Civil Procedure for damages for the injury or death of the patient.

1017.   Exception: Court-Appointed Psychotherapist. There is no privilege under this article if the psychotherapist is appointed by order of a court to examine the patient, but this exception does not apply where the psychotherapist is appointed by order of the court upon the request of the lawyer for the defendant in a criminal proceeding in order to provide the lawyer with information needed so that he may advise the defendant whether to enter or withdraw a plea based on insanity or to present a defense based on his mental or emotional condition.

1018.   Exception: Crime or Tort. There is no privilege under this article if the services of the psychotherapist were sought or obtained to enable or aid anyone to commit or plan to commit a crime or a tort or to escape detection or apprehension after the commission of a crime or a tort.

1019.   Exception: Parties Claiming through Deceased Patient. There is no privilege under this article as to a communication relevant to an issue between parties all of whom claim through a deceased patient, regardless of whether the claims are by testate or intestate succession or by *inter vivos* transaction.

1020.   Exception: Breach of Duty Arising out of Psychotherapist–Patient Relationship. There is no privilege under this article as to a communication relevant to an issue of breach, by the psychotherapist or by the patient, of a duty arising out of the psychotherapist-patient relationship.

1021.   Exception: Intention of Deceased Patient Concerning Writing Affecting Property Interest. There is no privilege under this article as to a communication relevant to an issue concerning the intention of a patient, now deceased, with respect to a deed of conveyance, will, or other writing, executed by the patient, purporting to affect an interest in property.

1022.   Exception: Validity of Writing Affecting Property Interest. There is no privilege under this article as to a communication relevant to an issue concerning the validity of a deed of conveyance, will, or other writing, executed by a patient, now deceased, purporting to affect an interest in property.

1023.   Exception: Proceeding to Determine Sanity of Criminal Defendant. There is no privilege under this article in a proceeding under Chapter 6 (commencing with Section 1367) of Title 10 of Part 2 of the Penal Code initiated at the request of the defendant in a criminal action to determine his sanity.

1024.   Exception: Patient Dangerous to Himself or Others. There is no privilege under this article if the psychotherapist has reasonable cause to believe that the patient is in such mental or emotional condition as to be dangerous to himself or to the person or property of another and that disclosure of the communication is necessary to prevent the threatened danger.

1025.   Exception: Proceeding to Establish Competence. There is no privilege under this article in a proceeding brought by or on behalf of the patient to establish his competence.

1026.   Exception: Required Report. There is no privilege under this article as to information that the psychotherapist or the patient is required to report to a public employee or as to information required to be recorded in a public office, if such report or record is open to public inspection.

1027.   Exception: Child under 16 Victim of Crime. There is no privilege under this article if all of the following circumstances exist:
(a) The patient is a child under the age of 16.
(b) The psychotherapist has reasonable cause to believe that the patient has been the victim of a crime and that disclosure of the communication is in the best interest of the child.

1028. Exception: Unqualified Psychotherapist. Unless the psychotherapist is a person described in subdivision (a) or (b) of Section 1010, there is no privilege under this article in a criminal proceeding.

The psychologist who serves as an expert witness should be very familiar with the applicable laws regarding privileged communication so as to be able to inform the client of both the privilege and the exceptions. In most circumstances where the client's psychological status is a part of the litigation, there is an exception to the usual privilege.

STANDARDS

American jurisprudence has developed certain standards for the expert witness. Rule 702 of the *Federal Rules of Evidence* (1975) states:

> If scientific, technical or other specialized knowledge will assist the trier of fact to understand the evidence or to determine a fact in issue, a witness qualified as an expert by knowledge, skill, experience, training, or education, may testify thereto in the form of an opinion or otherwise.

The principles regarding expert testimony were reiterated by the U.S. Court of Appeals for the Ninth Circuit in its *Amaral* decision.[1] The general principles regarding testimony by an expert witness can be summarized as follows:

1. **The Witness Must Be a Qualified Expert.** During qualification, the judge hears a recitation of the proffered expert's education, training, and experience and decides whether the testimony of the witness is to be admitted.

2. **The Testimony Must Be about a Proper Subject Matter.** To qualify, the testimony must present information beyond the knowledge and experience of the average jury panelist. Further, the testimony of the expert must not invade the jurors' province by evaluating evidence or witnesses.

3. **The Expert's Testimony Should Be in Accordance with a Generally Accepted Explanatory Theory.** The expert's testimony is expected to meet the test put forth in *Frye v. United States* that the scientific community accepts and agrees about the reliability and validity of devices or machines that are used to come to conclusions or opinions presented by the expert witness.[2] This principle is seldom applied to the testimony of medical experts or psychologists.[3] This principle may be applied more stringently in the future.

4. **The Probative Value of the Testimony Must Outweigh Its Prejudicial Effect.** Probative value refers to evidence that is important in determining culpability or liability. If the expert's testimony has

Rules of the Road

A. Quality of Work

- The psychologist should follow the principles and standards for scientific and professional conduct promulgated by the American Psychological Association and the Division of Psychology and the Law of APA (Appendixes F and H).
- All procedures utilized by the psychologist in the process of research review, assessment, research, or evaluation preliminary to an appearance as an expert witness should be carefully documented and available for discovery procedures, direct examination, and cross-examination.
- Before testifying as an expert witness, the psychologist should submit a written report of findings and opinions to the attorney or the court that has retained the psychologist.
- The quality of work done, the practices and procedures used, and the conclusions reached should follow the usual and customary standards of the profession.
- The psychologist who gives evidence as an expert witness should be sure that the opinions rendered are consonant with the appropriate current research base in the behavioral sciences.
- Opinions and conclusions rendered by the psychologist serving as an expert witness should be supported by a known and generally respected theoretical position.

B. Competence and Decorum

- The psychologist who serves as an expert witness represents psychology when appearing in court and should conduct himself or herself with such professional skill and style as to bring credit to the science and profession of psychology.
- The psychologist who represents himself or herself as an expert witness should be prepared to demonstrate education, training, and experience in the avowed area of expertise sufficient to meet the standards of psychology and the requirements of the court.
- The psychologist as expert witness should be sufficiently familiar with local, state, and federal statutes regarding the role of the expert witness in order to serve that role without confusion or errors of ignorance.
- The psychologist who serves as an expert witness should be sufficiently familiar with the case law associated with the matter at hand so that the evidence presented by the expert will be appropriate and probative.
- The psychologist who serves as an expert witness should ensure that sufficient consultation takes place before deposition or trial so that the attorney who has retained the psychologist understands the extent as well as the limits of the expert's findings and opinions.
- Where clients, patients, or defendants are involved in the matter at hand, the psychologist who is to act as an expert witness should understand, and clearly state to all parties involved, the nature and limitations of privileged communication in the case.
- When in doubt about any practice or procedure, the psychologist preparing to serve as an expert witness should consult with an attorney and/or an experienced colleague for guidance, within the constraints of professional ethics and privileged communication.
- When testifying as an expert witness, the psychologist should ensure that nothing in his or her report or testimony infringes on the responsibilities or privileges of the triers of fact by rendering opinions concerning the verdict in the litigation to which the expert testimony is directed.

(continued)

FIGURE 15.1. Competent and ethical forensic practice.

C. Financial Arrangements
- The psychologist should never accept a fee contingent on the outcome of a case.
- The fee structure and details of reimbursement should be established between the psychologist and the retaining attorney during the initial consultation. The understanding should be in writing between the two parties.
- All outstanding fees should be paid before the psychologist testifies.
- Misunderstandings or disagreements about fees should be resolved before proceeding in the case.
- Psychologists who testify regularly as expert witnesses should devote some portion of their professional time to *pro bona publica* cases.

FIGURE 15.1. *(Continued)*

no relationship to the issue of guilt or innocence or the issues of contention between two parties, it is generally not admissible. The judge must also ensure that the expert's testimony does not unduly or unrealistically prejudice the members of the jury or confuse the issue at hand.

There are those who have suggested that the *Frye* test is too stringent (Suggs, 1979), while others have proposed that psychologists should generally not be experts in the courtroom (Ziskin, 1982). Bazelon (1974), Bonnie and Slobogin (1980), and Morse (1978) have proposed that the testimony of mental health professionals is of questionable value. Poythress (1982) has responded to these critiques by pointing out that psychologists have been acting with reasonable restraint as credible experts. Poythress suggests that scientific or academic colleagues are sometimes unaware of the courtroom realities of testifying as expert witness. The *Daubert* decision (reviewed in Chapter 5 and presented in Appendix A) has begun more or less to eliminate the *Frye* standard, at least in the federal courts.

It would seem that it is time to explore possible Rules of the Road (Figure 15.1).

As psychologists gain more experience as expert witnesses in a variety of settings, it is expected that other standards will be developed and promulgated. The guidelines in Figure 15.1 are suggestions, having no special quality or status.

In 1909, Wigmore wrote that the courts were not ready for psychology. In 1937, Wigmore revised his thinking and wrote that the courts are ready for psychology when psychology is ready for the courts. Psychology is ready.

NOTES

1. *United States v. Amaral*, 488 F.2d 1148 (9th Cir. 1973).
2. *Frye v. United States*, 293 F. 1013 (D.C. Cir. 1923).
3. *Coppolino v. State*, 223 So. 2d 68 (Fla. App. 1968), *appeals dismissed*, 234 So. 2d 120 (Fla. 1969), *cert. denied*, 399 U.S. 927 (1970).

Appendix A

Landmark Cases

**Vincent E. Jenkins, Appellant,
v. United States of America,
Appellee. No. 16306. United States
Court of Appeals District of
Columbia Circuit. On Rehearing in
Banc. Reargued February 9, 1962.
Decided by Judgment Entered
April 12, 1962. Opinion Rendered
June 7, 1962.**

Defendant was convicted of house-breaking with intent to commit an assault, assault with intent to rape and assault with a dangerous weapon. The defendant relied solely upon defense of insanity. From a judgment of the United States District Court for the District of Columbia, Edward M. Curren, J., the defendant appealed. The Court of Appeals, Bazelon, Circuit Judge, held, inter alia, that the court's sua sponte exclusion of psychiatrist's testimony concerning his changed diagnosis of accused because psychiatrist did not conduct a personal re-examination constituted prejudicial error requiring reversal for new trial, and that the determination of a psychologist's competence to render an expert opinion based on his findings as to presence or absence of mental

disease or defect must depend upon nature and extent of his knowledge, and it does not depend upon his claim to title "psychologist," and that determination, after hearing, which may be conducted in presence of jury unless special circumstances warrant its exclusion, must be left in each case to traditional discretion of trial court subject to appellate review.

Reversed and remanded for new trial.

Separate concurring opinion by Fahy, Circuit Judge, with whom Edgerton and Washington, Circuit Judges, concurred.

Separate concurring opinion by Burger, Circuit Judge.

Bastian, Circuit Judge, and Miller, Chief Judge, dissented with opinion.

1. CRIMINAL LAW   741(4)

Testimony of psychiatrist, whose expert qualifications were unquestioned, that he could arrive at a valid diagnosis of accused's mental capacity on basis of earlier examination and later psychological test reports was improperly excluded since psychiatrist's ability to make revised diagnosis without conducting impersonal re-examination presented a question for jury in assessing weight of his testimony and not a question for court upon which it might

403

rest exclusion of diagnosis as a matter of law.

2. CRIMINAL LAW   486
Evidence   555
Opinion testimony based in part upon reports of others which are not in evidence but which the expert customarily relies upon in practice of his profession is admissible.

3. CRIMINAL LAW   486

Where psychiatrist testified that he considered undifferentiated psychosis a possibility when he first examined accused, and improvement in accused's I.Q. scores was inconsistent with mental defect, and induced psychiatrist to abandon that diagnosis in favor of undifferentiated psychosis which was consistent with his earlier clinical observations and later test reports, opinion so formulated was admissible, and any infirmity arising out of psychiatrist's failure to re-examine accused would go to weight and not to admissibility of his opinion.

4. CRIMINAL LAW   1170(1)

The court's sua sponte exclusion of psychiatrist's testimony concerning his changed diagnosis of accused because psychiatrist did not conduct a personal re-examination constituted prejudicial error requiring reversal for new trial.

5. CRIMINAL LAW   1038(1)

Court of Appeals would consider alleged error in instruction to disregard testimony of defense psychologist notwithstanding accused failed to object to instruction where instruction presented question which was likely to arise upon a new trial.

6. CRIMINAL LAW   479

Some psychologists are qualified to render expert testimony in the field of mental disorder.

7. CRIMINAL LAW   469
Evidence   505
The test in determining admissibility of expert testimony is whether opinion offered will be likely to aid the trier in search for truth.

8. CRIMINAL LAW   479
Evidence   474(4)
Generally, anyone who is shown to have special knowledge and skill in diagnosing and treating human ailments is qualified to testify as an expert, if his learning and training show that he is qualified to give an opinion on particular question at issue, and it is not essential that witness be a medical practitioner.

9. CRIMINAL LAW   478(1)
Evidence   536
If experience or training enables a proffered expert witness to form an opinion which would aid the jury, in absence of some countervailing consideration, his testimony will be received.

10. CRIMINAL LAW   481

The determination of a psychologist's competence to render an expert opinion based on his findings as to presence or absence of mental disease or defect must depend upon nature and extent of his knowledge, and it does not depend upon his claim to title "psychologist," and that determination, after hearing, which may be conducted in presence of jury unless special circumstances warrant its exclusion, must be left in each case to traditional discretion of trial court subject to appellate review.

11. CRIMINAL LAW   481

The qualification of particular witness to testify as an expert is largely within domain of trial judge, and particular inquiries which may be appropriate in some cases may be inappropriate in others.

12. CRIMINAL LAW   479

Although there are no statutory criteria for licensing psychologists in District of Columbia to assist trial courts, the American Psychological Association's list of approved graduate training programs provides some guidance, and when completion of such training is followed by actual experience in treatment and diagnosis of disease in association with psychiatrists or neurologists, the opinion of psychologists may properly be received in evidence.

13. CRIMINAL LAW   479

If the post-doctoral experience required for certification has included substantial experience in a hospital or clinical setting in association with psychiatrists or neurologists, clinical psychologists who are diplomates of the American Board of Examiners in Professional Psychology should ordinarily qualify as expert witnesses.

14. CRIMINAL LAW   479, 481

The lack of a medical degree, and lesser degree of responsibility for a patient care which mental hospitals usually assign to psychologists, are not automatic disqualifications of psychologists to testify as experts, but where relevant, these matters may be shown to affect the weight of their testimony, even though it be admitted in evidence, and critical factor in respect to admissibility is actual experience of witness and the probable probative value of his opinion, and trial judge should make a finding in respect to individual qualifications of each challenged expert.

15. CRIMINAL LAW   481, 741(4)

Qualifications to express an opinion on a given topic are to be decided by trial judge alone, and weight to be given any expert opinion admitted in evidence by judge is exclusively for jury, and they should be so instructed.

16. CRIMINAL LAW   432

Determination of accused's eligibility to stand trial may be established by a finding of "restored competency" or a finding that he never was incompetent, and hence assuming that a proceeding to set aside original adjudication of incompetency is required, substance of such proceeding was provided by hearing in which hospital psychiatrist testified that accused was not a mental defective and that there was no indication of organic brain injury or mental illness. D.C. Code 1951, § 24-301(b).

Mr. Gerald Golin, Washington, D.C. (appointed by the District Court) for appellant.

Mr. Anthony G. Amsterdam, Asst. U. S. Atty., with whom Messrs. David C. Acheson, U. S. Atty., Charles T. Duncan, Principal Asst. U. S. Atty., and Harry T. Alexander, Asst. U. S. Atty., at the time the brief was filed, were on the brief, for appellee. Messrs. Nathan J. Paulson and David J. McTague, Asst. U. S. Attys., also entered appearances for appellee.

Messrs. Arthur B. Hanson, Dean Farrington Cochran and Samuel J. L'Hommedieu, Jr., Washington, D. C., filed a brief on behalf of American Psychological Association, as *amicus curiae,* urging reversal.

Mr. Warren E. Magee, Washington, D. C., filed a brief on behalf of American Psychiatric Association, as *amicus curiae,* urging affirmance.

Before WILBUR K. MILLER, Chief Judge, EDGERTON, PRETTYMAN, BAZELON, FAHY, WASHINGTON, DANAHER, BASTIAN and BURGER, Circuit Judges, sitting *in banc.*

BAZELON, Circuit Judge.

Appellant relied solely upon the defense of insanity in a jury trial which culminated in his conviction for housebreaking with intent to commit an assault, assault with intent to rape, and assault with a dangerous weapon. He alleges that the District Court erred in (1) determining his competency to stand trial, (2) excluding diagnostic opinions of two defense psychiatrists on the ground that their opinions were

without "proper basis," (3) instructing the jury to disregard the testimony on three defense psychologists that appellant had a mental disease or defect on the ground that "a psychologist is not competent to give a medical opinion as to a mental disease or defect," and (4) depriving him of a fair trial by conducting a lengthy and disparaging examination of some expert witnesses.

I. The Facts

The record discloses the following pertinent information. After indictment, appellant was committed to the District General Hospital for a mental examination on September 4, 1959, to determine his competency to stand trial and his condition at the time of the alleged offense.[1] Appellant was given a series of psychological tests on October 20 and 22, 1959, by staff psychologists under the supervision of the Chief Psychologist, Dr. Bernard I. Levy. Appellant scored 63, high moron, on the I.Q. section of the tests. He was also interviewed three or four times by Dr. Richard Schaengold, Assistant Chief Psychiatrist. Appellant's test performance and his "dullness and inability to relate correctly" led Dr. Schaengold to consider and reject the possibility of undifferentiated psychosis in favor of a diagnosis of mental defect: a basic, unchanging deficiency in brain function.[2] His findings were confirmed by Dr. Mary V. McIndoo, District General's Chief Psychiatrist, on the basis of interviews on November 23, 24 and 25, and a review of appellant's history and test results. By letter of November 25, 1959, signed by Dr. Schaengold and

---

[1] See generally Winn v. United States, 106 U.S.App.D.C. 133, 270 F.2d 326 (1959).

[2] Durham v. United States, 94 U.S.App.D.C. 228, 241, 214 F.2d 862, 875, 45 A.L.R.2d 1430 (1954).

countersigned by Dr. McIndoo, the District Court was advised that appellant was "suffering from an organic brain defect resulting in mental deficiency and impaired judgment. He is, therefore, psychotic, incompetent, and incapable of participating in his own defense." Appellant was adjudicated incompetent to stand trial on the basis of this report and was committed to "Saint Elizabeths Hospital until he is mentally competent to stand trial pursuant to Title 24, Section 301, District of Columbia Code, 1951 Edition, as amended August 9, 1955."

At St. Elizabeths, Dr. Lawrence Tirnauer, a staff psychologist, administered another battery of psychological tests on February 25 and March 2, 1960, in which appellant scored 74 on the I.Q. section. Dr. Tirnauer concluded that appellant was suffering from schizophrenia. Thereafter Dr. David J. Owens of St. Elizabeths interviewed appellant several times, "probably [for] fifteen or twenty minutes," and saw him at a staff conference on October 3, 1960. Dr. Owens found no evidence of mental disease or defect. He classified appellant as "a borderline intelligence." Dr. William G. Cushard, another psychiatrist at St. Elizabeths, who saw appellant at the staff conference, reviewed the test reports and agreed with Dr. Owens' findings. Dr. Margaret Ives, Chief Psychologist at St. Elizabeths, was also present at the staff conference. Subsequently, she reviewed Dr. Tirnauer's test results and appellant's past history and administered one part of a six-part Szondi profile test. She agreed with Dr. Tirnauer that appellant "had a mental illness by name of schizophrenia."

Ten days later, the Acting Superintendent of the Hospital notified the District Court that "it has been determined that he [appellant] is, at this time, mentally competent to stand trial

and to consult with counsel and assist properly in his own defense. He is not suffering from mental disease. * * *. Although he is not suffering from mental deficiency, he has only borderline intelligence." Upon appellant's objection to this report, the court conducted a hearing on November 4, 1960, wherein appellant was found competent and ordered to stand trial.

In preparation for their testimony at trial, Drs. McIndoo and Schaengold noted the later and different diagnosis and the apparent change in appellant's I.Q. reported by the St. Elizabeths psychologists. They requested Dr. Levy of their staff to re-test appellant in order to reconsider their diagnoses that he was mentally defective on June 10, 1959, the date of the alleged offenses. This time appellant scored 90 on the I.Q. test, an improvement inconsistent with mental defect. In reporting this result, Dr. Levy, who had previously been unable to make a diagnosis, concluded that upon review of all test data appellant "is psychotic and schizophrenic." Considering this report in the light of the hospital record and "reports" from St. Elizabeths, Drs. McIndoo and Schaengold revised their previous diagnoses without seeing appellant again. Dr. McIndoo concluded that appellant was schizophrenic, and Dr. Schaengold diagnosed his condition as undifferentiated psychosis.

II.   Admissibility of the Psychiatrists' Opinions

The trial court, *sua sponte*, excluded the revised diagnoses of Drs. McIndoo and Schaengold and instructed the jury to disregard testimony of the three defense psychologists that appellant had a mental disease when he committed the crimes charged.

We discuss first the exclusion of Dr. Schaengold's testimony. After questioning him at great length about the basis of his revised opinion, the court rules: "All I will allow is that in his opinion on June 10, 1959 [the date of the alleged offenses], the defendant was mentally defective"; it excluded Dr. Schaengold's later diagnosis of mental illness because "there isn't any testimony here that is based on any proper evidence that he was suffering from a mental disease. I am not going to allow it on the basis of a report of a psychologist." The court gave no further explanation.

The Government suggests that the ruling rests on the familiar principle that an expert witness' knowledge of "basic facts" must be adequate to support his conclusion.[3] It urges that the later psychological reports could not provide Dr. Schaengold with such information," absent a personal re-examination of appellant," since thirteen months had elapsed between his personal examination of appellant and his revised diagnosis. The proposition seems to be that a psychiatric witness may not rely on psychological test reports unless he has considered them in conjunction with a contemporaneous personal examination. We are aware of no authority for such a rigid and artificial stricture.[4]

[1] Dr. Schaengold, whose expert qualifications were unquestioned, testified that he could arrive at a valid diagnosis on the basis of an earlier examination and later test reports. The court must be deemed to have rejected this statement. We find no basis for such action. We think it clear that Dr. Schaengold's ability to make the revised diagnosis without conducting a personal re-examination presents a question for the consideration of the jury, under appropriate instructions, in assessing the weight of his testimony and not a question for the court upon which it may rest exclusion of the diagnosis as a matter of law.

[2, 3] It is at least as likely, however, that the court predicated its ruling on cases which bar an expert's opinion based upon facts not in evidence unless it is derived solely from his own observations.[5] But we agree with the leading commentators[6] that the better reasoned authorities admit opinion testimony based, in part, upon reports of others which are not in evidence but which the expert customarily relies upon in the practice of his

---

[3] Toho Bussan Kaisha, Ltd. v. American Pres. Lines, Ltd., 265 F.2d 418, 76 A.L.R.2d 1344 (2d Cir. 1959); Haug v. Grimm, 251 F.2d 523 (8th Cir. 1958). The Government cites United States v. Alker, 260 F.2d 135, 155 (3d Cir. 1958), cert. denied, 359 U.S. 906, 79 S.Ct. 579, 3 L.Ed.2d 571 (1959), where the proposition appears as dictum.

The Government's reliance upon Blunt v. United States, 100 U.S.App.D.C. 266, 275, 244 F.2d 355, 364 (1957); and Carter v. United States, 102 U.S.App.D.C. 227, 236, 252 F.2d 608, 617 (1957), is misplaced since our discussion of the absence of detailed testimony concerning the underlying basis for the psychiatrists' opinions related to the weight of the testimony and not its admissibility.

[4] Cf. Williams v. United States, 104 U.S.App.D.C. 277, 278, 261, F.2d 743, 744 (1958), where we held that a new trial would be required if appellant could establish his allegations concerning newly discovered evidence of changed psychiatric opinion "without additional examination of appellant."

[5] E.G., People v. Black, 367 Ill. 209, 10 N.E.2d 801 (1937) (alternative holding); Equitable Life Assur. Soc'y v. Kazee, 257 Ky. 803, 79 S.W.2d 208 (1935) (dictum). See generally McCormick, Evidence § 15 (1955).

[6] McCormick, Evidence § 15 (1955). See 3 Wigmore, Evidence § 688 (3d ed. 1940).

profession.[7] The Wisconsin Supreme Court has forcefully stated the policy underlying the application of this rule to medical testimony:

"In order to say that a physician, who has actually used the result of * * * tests in a diagnosis * * * may not testify what that diagnosis was, the court must deliberately shut its eyes to a source of information which is relied on by mankind generally in matters that involve the health and may involve the life of their families and of themselves—a source of information that is essential that the court should possess in order that it may do justice between these parties litigant.

"This court * * * will not close the doors of the courts to the light which is given by a diagnosis which all the rest of the world accepts and acts upon, even if the diagnosis is in part based upon facts which are not established by the sworn testimony in the case to be true" [Sundquist v. Madison Ry., 197 Wis. 83, 221 N.W. 392, 393 (1928)].

The record in this case confirms the well-known practice of psychiatrists of relying upon psychologists' reports in aid of diagnosis.[8] And it shows that Dr. Schaengold's changed diagnosis did not rest solely on the later test reports which were not in evidence when he testified,[9] but also upon his own earlier

examination.[10] This diagnosis was "the type of clinical opinion he is accustomed to form and to rely upon in the practice of his profession. * * * Though [his] conclusions were not mathematically demonstrable certainties, neither were they mere conjectures, suspicions or hunches." Blunt v. United States, 100 U.S.App.D.C. 266, 275, 244 F.2d 355, 364 (1957).

[4] It follows from the foregoing that the court's *sua sponte* exclusion of Dr. Schaengold's testimony concerning his changed diagnosis was error.[11] Since the exclusion was clearly prejudicial, the conviction must be reversed for a new trial.[12]

Appellant also objects to the similar exclusion of Dr. McIndoo's revised

---

[7] Taylor v. Monongahela Ry., 155 F. Supp. 601, 604 (W.D.Pa. 1957), aff'd per curiam, 256 F.2d 751 (3d Cir. 1958); Sundquist v. Madison Ry., 197 Wis. 83, 221 N.W. 392 (1928); Schooler v. State, 175 S.W.2d 664 (Tex.Civ.App. 1943).

[8] Hidden v. Mutual Life Ins. Co., 217 F.2d 818, 821 (4th Cir. 1954); Scheflen, The Psychologist as a Witness, 32 Pa.Bar Ass'n Q. 329, 333 (1961). See McDonald, Psychiatry and the Criminal 162 (1958).

[9] Such reliance would amount to offering an opinion of another in violation of the hearsay rule. Cf. McCormick, Evidence § 15 (1955).

[10] Dr. Schaengold testified that he considered undifferentiated psychosis a possibility when he first examined appellant. The improvement in appellant's I.Q. scores was inconsistent with mental defect, and induced Dr. Schaengold to abandon that diagnosis in favor of undifferentiated psychosis which was consistent both with his earlier clinical observations and the later test reports. An opinion so formulated is admissible. Cf. Williams v. United States, supra note 4. Any infirmity arising out of Dr. Schaengold's failure to re-examine appellant would go to the weight and not to the admissibility of his opinion. Cf. Brill v. Mushinsky, 90 U.S. App.D.C. 132, 194 F.2d 158 (1952).

[11] See Hidden v. Mutual Life Ins. Co., supra note 8; Watts v. State, 223 Md. 268, 164 A.2d 334 (1960) (alternative ground).

[12] In holding Dr. Schaengold's testimony admissible, we do not intimate approval of his failure to re-examine appellant. Compare Winn v. United States, 106 U.S.App.D.C. 133, 270 F.2d 326 (1959); Carter v. United States, 102 U.S.App.D.C. 227, 236, 252 F.2d 608, 617 (1957); Blunt v. United States, 100 U.S.App.D.C. 266, 275, 244 F.2d 355, 364 (1957).

diagnosis. She testified that the later tests induced her to change her opinion. But when the court, in very extensive questioning, made clear its view barring reliance upon psychological test reports, she stated that she "did not have a medical opinion about the new diagnosis." At one point she said, "I'm strictly confused now." Later the following occurred:

THE COURT: Would you express an opinion as to a person's mental condition on the basis of a report given to you by a psychologist?

THE WITNESS: I do, Your Honor, very frequently.

THE COURT: Without even seeing the patient?

THE WITNESS: In most cases I do see the patient. This person I had seen. He was showing certain signs and symptoms. I made a wrong diagnosis. The suggested diagnosis from a psychologist explains my wrong diagnosis.

Since the new trial required by the exclusion of Dr. Schaengold's testimony will afford an opportunity for clarification of Dr. McIndoo's testimony in light of our earlier discussion, we think it unwise to engage in the speculation required to resolve the meaning of her testimony at the trial under review. Hence we refrain from deciding whether the court erred in excluding her opinion.

III. Admissibility of the Psychologists' Opinions

[5] The next assignment of error we discuss concerns the court's instruction to the jury to disregard testimony of three defense psychologists that appellant had a mental disease when he committed the crimes charged. Although appellant failed to object to this instruction, we consider it because it pre-

sents a question which is likely to arise upon a new trial.[13]

The first psychologist, Dr. Tirnauer, administered a battery of tests to appellant, studied his case history, and concluded he had been suffering from schizophrenia when he committed the crimes. In his opinion, the disease and the crimes were "related." The second psychologist, Dr. Margaret Ives, had reviewed Dr. Tirnauer's test results, had seen appellant at a staff conference, and had administered part of a Szondi profile test. She stated that appellant was suffering from schizophrenia and that his crimes were the product of the disease. The third psychologist, Dr. Levy, interpreted test results obtained by members of the District General staff in October 1959, and administered two additional tests shortly before trial. He testified that defendant had been suffering from schizophrenia on June 10, 1959, but could give no opinion concerning the relationship between the illness and the crimes. At the conclusion of the trial the court instructed the jury:

"A psychologist is not competent to give a medical opinion as to a mental disease or defect. Therefore, you will not consider any evidence to the effect that the defendant was suffering from a mental disease or a mental defect on June 10, 1959, according to the testimony given by the psychologists."

[6] The trial court apparently excluded these opinions because psychologists lack medical training. We agree with the weight of authority, however, that some psychologists are qualified to render expert testimony in the field of mental disorder.[14]

---

[13] Villaroman v. United States, 87 U.S.App.D.C. 240, 184 F.2d 261, 21 A.L.R.2d 1074 (1950).

[14] See Hidden v. Mutual Life Ins. Co., supra note 8; Watson v. State, 161 Tex. Cr.R.

We begin by placing this problem in the context of the considerations governing the reception of expert testimony:

"An observer is qualified to testify because he has firsthand knowledge which the jury does not have of the situation or transaction at issue. The expert has something different to contribute. This is a power to draw inferences from the facts which a jury would not be competent to draw. To warrant the use of expert testimony, then, two elements are required. First, the subject of the inference must be so distinctively related to some science, profession, business or occupation as to be beyond the ken of the average layman, and second, the witness must have such skill, knowledge or experience in that field or calling as to make it appear that his opinion or inference will probably aid the trier in his search for truth. The knowledge may in some fields be derived from reading alone, in some from practice alone, or as is more commonly the case, from both. [McCormick, Evidence § 13 (1954), citing authorities.]"

[7–9] The test, then, is whether the opinion offered will be likely to aid the trier in the search for truth. In light of that purpose, it is hardly surprising that courts do not exclude all but the very best kind of witness. See 2 Wigmore, Evidence § 569 (3 ed. 1940). Accord: Fightmaster v. Mode, 31 Ohio App. 273, 167 N.E. 407 (1928). Thus a general practitioner may testify concerning matters within a medical speciality if his education or experience, or both, involves demonstrable knowledge of the subject.

5, 273 S.W.2d 879 (1954), rev'd on other grounds on rehearing. People v. Hawthorne, 293 Mich. 15, 291 N.W. 205 (1940) (dictum); State v. Padilla, 66 N.M. 289, 347 P.2d 312, 78 A.L.R.2d 908 (1959) (dictum). See generally, Scheflen, supra note 8; Louisell, The Psychologist in Today's Legal World, 39 Minn.L.Rev. 235 (1955).

Sher v. DeHaven, 91 U.S.App.D.C. 257, 199 F.2d 777, 36 A.L.R.2d 937 (1952), cert. denied, 345 U.S. 936, 73 S.Ct. 797, 97 L.Ed. 1363 (1953); 2 Wigmore, op. cit. supra. Nor need a skilled witness on a medical subject be duly licensed to practice medicine. Ibid. The general rule is that "anyone who is shown to have special knowledge and skill in diagnosing and treating human ailments is qualified to testify as an expert, if his learning and training show that he is qualified to give an opinion on the particular question at issue." "It is not essential that the witness be a medical practitioner." 32 C.J.S. Evidence § 537 (1942). Thus, non-medical witnesses who have had experience in electrical work may testify to the effects of electrical shock upon the human body. Vessels v. Kansas City Light & Power Co., 219 S.W. 80 (Mo.Sup.Ct.1920); Blakeney v. Alabama Power Co., 222 Ala. 394, 133 So. 16 (1931). Optometrists, whose training includes instruction in the symptoms of certain eye diseases, may testify to the presence of cataract discovered in the course of fitting glasses, Jackson v. Waller, 126 Conn. 294, 10 A.2d 763 (1940), and to the effect of a scar upon vision. Black Starr Coal Corp. v. Reeder, 278 Ky. 532, 128 S.W.2d 905 (1939). A toxicologist has been permitted to testify to the effect of oxalic acid, a poison, upon the human eye. Reynolds v. Davis, 55 R.I. 20-6, 179 A. 613 (1935). The kinds of witnesses whose opinions courts have received, *even though they lacked medical training and would not be permitted by law to treat the conditions they described*, are legion. The principle to be distilled from the cases is plain: if experience or training enables a proffered expert witness to form an opinion which would aid the jury, in the absence of some countervailing consideration, his testimony will be received.

Suggesting the diagnostic category into which an accused's condition fits, and relating it to his past behavior require skill far in excess of that possessed by laymen. Lest the jury be misled into relying on opinions which are not based upon relevant learning and experience, we must examine the reality behind the title "psychologist." Many psychologists may not qualify to testify concerning mental disease or defect. Their training and experience may not provide an adequate basis for their testimony. Some psychologists, for example, teach and engage in theoretical research in fields unrelated to the diagnosis and treatment of mental disease. Others are employed in personnel administration, still others advise industry on problems of employee morale. See Western Personnel Institute, Opportunities for Psychologists, Psychiatrists, Psychiatric Social Workers 8–10 (1958); Daniel and Louttit, Professional Problems in Psychology 250–52, 297 (1953). Such experience does not ordinarily provide the skill essential to offer expert testimony concerning mental disorders. Cf. Albee, Mental Health Manpower Trends 116 (1959). Some psychologists, moreover, have had no post-graduate instruction. Id. at 121–22.

On the other hand, the Ph.D. in Clinical Psychology involves some—and often much—training and experience in the diagnosis and treatment of mental disorders. Typically, candidates are trained, *inter alia*, in general psychology, theory of personality and psychodynamics, psychopathology, diagnostic methods, therapeutic techniques, selected aspects of physiology and anatomy, and clinical methods. A one-year internship in a mental hospital is required for this degree.[15] After

graduation, many clinical psychologists administer and interpret diagnostic tests which elicit the patient's intellectual level, defenses, personality structure, attitudes, feelings, thought and perceptual processes. See 1 Rapaport, Diagnostic Testing 7–9 (1945). In many institutions and clinics their reports, which regularly include opinions concerning the presence or absence of mental disease or defect,[16] are important aids to psychiatrists who customarily have the final responsibility for diagnosis. Some psychologists, moreover, regularly administer psychotherapy and related non-organic therapies in the treatment of certain types of mental disorders.[17]

[10–12] The determination of a psychologist's competence to render an expert opinion based on his findings as to the presence or absence of mental disease or defect must depend upon the nature and extent of his knowledge. It does not depend upon his claim to the title "psychologist." And that determination, after hearing,[18] must be left in each case to the traditional discretion of the trial court subject to appellate review.[19] Although there are no statutory

---

certifies only those programs meeting the standards laid down in this report.

[16] Scheflen, supra note 8.

[17] See Clark, America's Psychologists 188–205 (1957). See also Joint Commission on Mental Illness and Mental Health, Action for Mental Health 244–50 (1961).

[18] The court may conduct this hearing in the presence of the jury unless special circumstances warrant its exclusion.

[19] Cf. Pollard v. Hawfield, 83 U.S.App.D.C. 174, 170 F.2d 170 (1948), cert. denied, 336 U.S. 909, 69 S.Ct. 514, 93 L.Ed. 1073 (1949). Compare State v. Padilla, 66 N.M. 289, 347 P.2d 312, 78 A.L.R.2d 908 (1959). See also McDonald, supra note 8.

The qualification of a particular witness to testify as an expert is largely within the domain of the trial judge. Particular

---

[15] See Report of the Committee on Training in Clinical Psychology of the American Psychological Association, in 2 Am. Psychol. 539, 543–58 (1947). The Association

criteria for licensing psychologists in the District of Columbia to assist trial courts,[20] the American Psychological Association's list of approved graduate training programs provides some guidance. When completion of such training is followed by actual experience in the treatment and diagnosis of disease in association with psychiatrists or neurologists, the opinion of the psychologist may properly be received in evidence.

[13] Some graduate clinical psychologists, moreover, are certified by the American Board of Examiners in Professional Psychology.[21] Certification, which indicates exceptional professional competence, is awarded upon completion of written and oral examinations in, *inter alia*, diagnosis and treatment.[22] Applicants must have four years, acceptable professional experience and must present credentials, including a sample of their work and letters of recommendation, showing sufficient professional achievement to warrant further examination.[23] The

purpose of Board certification is to identify and evaluate psychologists at an advanced professional level. If the postdoctoral experience required for certification has included substantial experience in a hospital or clinical setting in association with psychiatrists or neurologists, clinical psychologists who are diplomates of the American Board of Examiners in Professional Psychology should ordinarily qualify as expert witnesses.

[14, 15] We need not decide whether the three psychologists who testified for the defense at the trial under review were qualified to offer expert opinions since they may not be called to testify at the retrial.[24] We hold only that the lack of a medical degree, and the lesser degree of responsibility for patient care which mental hospitals usually assign to psychologists, are not automatic disqualifications. Where relevant, these matters may be shown to affect the weight of their testimony, even though it be admitted in evidence. The critical factor in respect to admissibility is the actual experience of the witness and the probable value of his opinion. The trial judge should make a finding in respect to the individual qualifications of each challenged expert. Qualifications to express an opinion on a given topic are to

---

inquiries which may be appropriate in some cases may be inappropriate in others. The majority of this court think the matter should be left to the sound judicial discretion of the trial judge, with no more specific guidance than is contained in this opinion.

[20] Such statutes are in force in several states. See, e.g., Conn. Gen. Stat. Ann. §§ 20–188 to 20–191 (1960); Md.Ann Code Art. 43 §§ 618–620, 629–636 (1957); Mich.Stat.Ann.   §§ 14.677(3)–14.677(11) (Supp. 1959), Pub. Acts 1959, No. 257.

[21] Kelley, Sanford & Clark, The Meaning of the ABEPP Diploma, 16 Am. Psychol. 132–34 (1961). Prior to 1949, the Board waived the Ph.D. or examination requirements, or both, if a candidate was judged qualified on the basis of training, professional experience and his colleagues' endorsements. Id. at 132.

[22] Id. at 134, 138.

[23] Id. at 134.

---

[24] The trial judge might have concluded that one or more of the three defense psychologists were competent to testify as experts. All are clinical psychologists; all hold doctoral degrees from institutions approved by the American Psychological Association; all are associated with psychiatrists and neurologists in a hospital setting in the diagnosis and treatment of mental illness. Two were chief psychologists at the hospitals where they were employed, and the third had diagnosed more than a hundred patients during his three years at St. Elizabeths.

be decided by the judge alone.[25] The weight to be given any expert opinion admitted in evidence by the judge is exclusively for the jury.[26] They should be so instructed.

IV. *Competency to Stand Trial*

[16]   Another ground urged for reversal is that the November 4 order adjudicating appellant competent to stand trial was not authorized by D.C.Code § 24-301(b). That section provides, in substance, that when an accused person *"is restored* to mental competency" and when the hospital superintendent so certifies, the court may enter an adjudication of competence "unless the accused or the Government objects, in which event, the court, after hearing without a jury, shall make a judicial determination of the competency of the accused to stand trial." Emphasis supplied. Here, the Superintendent did not certify that appellant's competency had been "restored" but rather that appellant "is, at this time, mentally incompetent." Upon appellant's objection, the court conducted a hearing in which Dr. David J. Owens, a hospital psychiatrist, testified that appellant was not a mental defective, and that there was no indication of organic brain injury or mental illness. His testimony clearly implied that appellant had been competent when committed. Appellant presented no evidence, and the court adjudicated him "mentally competent to stand trial."

Appellant contends that the statute applies only to cases of "restored competency" and cannot be invoked, as here, to set aside an original adjudication of incompetency. He argues that an adjudication of "restored competency" was precluded by the evidence at the hearing which showed only that appellant's condition was unchanged.

Clearly the determination of appellant's eligibility to stand trial may be established by a finding of "restored competency" or a finding that he never was incompetent. Assuming, *arguendo,* as appellant implies, that a proceeding to set aside the original adjudication of incompetency is required, we think the substance of such proceeding was provided by the hearing conducted below. Appellant does not claim that he was surprised or otherwise prejudiced by the Government's evidence that he never was incompetent.

Appellant's remaining contention concerns the conduct of the trial court in questioning certain expert witnesses. Since this issue may not arise upon the new trial, we do not consider it.

The judgment of conviction is reversed and the case is remanded to the District Court for further proceedings in accordance with this opinion.[27]

Reversed and remanded for a new trial.*

FAHY, Circuit Judge (concurring).

Having joined in the opinion issued October 26, 1961, reversing and remanding for a new trial, I join now in similar action taken by the court after

---

[25] Sher v. De Haven, 91 U.S.App.D.C. 257, 199 F.2d 777, 36 A.L.R.2d 937 (1952), cert. denied, 345 U.S. 936, 73 S.Ct. 797, 97 L.Ed. 1363 (1953).

[26] O'Donnell v. Geneva Metal Wheel Co., 183 F.2d 733 (6th Cir. 1950), cert. denied, 341 U.S. 903, 71 S.Ct. 612, 95 L.Ed. 1342 (1951).

[27] See note 19 supra.

* The retirement of Senior Circuit Judge Prettyman became effective April 16, 1962. Prior thereto he concurred in the foregoing opinion and joined in the judgment entered April 12, 1962.

rehearing en banc. I concur generally in the opinion, adding the qualifications to be stated.

While, strictly speaking, it is not necessary, as the present opinion states, to decide whether the three psychologists who testified for the defense at the trial were qualified to offer expert opinions, since they may not be called to testify at the retrial, it would be altogether appropriate to pass upon their qualifications on the record before us; for the record is here for our review of the rulings on the District Court in excluding their testimony. Upon the reasoning of both the original and the present opinions, considered with the facts, I would hold that these witnesses were qualified. A ruling to that effect now would be useful to the District Court.

The main feature of the present opinion, however, is its holding that psychologists may qualify as experts on the question of mental disease or defect under the standards set forth in the opinion. I am in entire agreement with this, which was the gist of the opinion of the division prior to the rehearing en banc.

I am authorized to say that Judges EDGERTON and WASHINGTON join in the views above expressed.

BURGER, Circuit Judge (concurring).

I concur in the remand because the court's basic holding that a psychologist is not barred as a matter of law from giving expert testimony about mental diseases makes it essential that we have a comprehensive record before us on the education and training of psychologists in general and clinical psychologists in particular. This is emphasized by recalling that appellant's entire case in this court, including his oral argument, was based on matter *outside* the record in the form of recitals of what various writers thought on the subject of whether, and to what extent, psychologists should be permitted to testify relating to mental *disease*. Similarly the majority opinion relies largely on "the literature." The literature cited and relied on by the appellant, and indeed by the majority opinion originally, was and is now a series of references selected to support one or the other point of view. They were not developed in the record by an adversary process or subjected to adversary examination. The reason we now remand is to have a record made in an orderly way and in that process authoritative texts, or parts thereof, may well be offered and received, subject, of course, to the established rules of evidence.

At the outset certain factors should be kept in mind. The issue is not now and never was whether a psychologist's testimony is admissible in litigation where "sanity" is in issue. Such testimony has long been admissible in the form of psychological tests and the analysis and explanation of such tests by a psychologist. No one doubts that such matter is admissible. The real issue in dispute is whether the clinical psychologists in this case, by which we mean persons having degrees of Doctor of Philosophy in Psychology, and also additional training as clinical psychologists, are competent in a scientific sense and hence legally qualified.

(1) to make a diagnosis of the existence and character of a mental disease, and

(2) whether there is a causal relationship between a disease and an unlawful act.

The issue can be stated also in terms of whether *medical* opinions and *medical* diagnoses can be made by and be the subject of expert testimony by a Doctor of Philosophy in Psychology with added clinical experience. For convenience I will hereafter refer to such a psychologist as a Clinical Psychologist.

While the issue is new to this court it is not new to medicine and psychiatry. In 1954 a Resolution was adopted by the American Medical Association, the Council of the American Psychiatric Association and the Executive Council of the American Psychoanalytical Association to the effect that psychologists and other related professional groups were autonomous and independent in matters where *medical* questions were *not* involved, but that where *diagnosis* and *treatment* of mental illness was involved the participation of psychologists "must be co-ordinated under medical responsibility."[1] This Resolution,

---

[1] The Resolution in full is as follows:

"For centuries the Western world has placed on the medical profession responsibility for the diagnosis and treatment of illness. Medical practice acts have been designed to protect the public from unqualified practitioners and to define the special responsibilities assumed by those who practice the healing art, for much harm may be done by unqualified persons, however good their intentions may be. To do justice to the patient requires the capacity to make a diagnosis and to prescribe appropriate treatment. Diagnosis often requires the ability to compare and contrast various diseases and disorders that have similar symptoms but different causes. Diagnosis is a continuing process, for the character of the illness changes with its treatment or with the passage of time, and that treatment which is appropriate may change accordingly.

"Recognized medical training today involves, as a minimum, graduation from an approval [sic] medical school and internship in a hospital. Most physicians today receive additional medical training, and specialization requires [sic] still further training.

"Psychiatry is the medical specialty concerned with illness that has chiefly mental symptoms. The psychiatrist is also concerned with mental causes of physical

while not controlling on the courts is plainly entitled to great weight.

---

illness, for we have come to recognize that physical symptoms may have mental causes just as mental symptoms may have physical causes. The psychiatrist, with or without consultation with other physicians, must select from the many different methods of treatment at his disposal those methods that he considers appropriate to the particular patient. His treatment may be medicinal or surgical, physical (as electroshock) or psychological. The systematic application of the methods of psychological medicine to the treatment of illness, particularly as these methods involved gaining an understanding of the emotional state of the patient and aiding him to understand himself, is called psychotherapy. This special form of medical treatment may be highly developed, *but it remains simply one of the possible methods of treatment to be selected for use according to medical criteria for use* when it is indicated. Psychotherapy is a form of medical treatment and does not form the basis for a separate profession.

"Other professional groups such as psychologists, teachers, ministers, lawyers, social workers, and vocational counselors, of course, use psychological understanding in carrying out their professional functions. Members of these professional groups are not thereby practicing medicine. *The application of psychological methods to the treatment of illness is a medical function.* Any physician may utilize the skills of others in his professional work, but he remains responsible, legally and morally, *for the diagnosis and for the treatment of his patient.*

"The medical profession fully endorses the appropriate utilization of the skills of psychologists, social workers, and other professional personnel in contributing roles in settings directly supervised by physicians. It further recognizes that these professions are entirely independent and autonomous *when medical questions are not involved;* but when members of these professions contribute *to the diagnosis* and treatment of illness, their professional contributions must be co-ordinated *under medical responsibility.*" (Emphasis added.)

My difficulty with the opinion of the majority, as distinguished from the remand for additional evidence, is that it fails to give adequate guidance as to the scope and nature of the inquiry to be conducted by the trial judge on remand. I agree that it is entirely within the discretion of the District Court whether he should conduct the hearing out of the presence of the jury. In this particular case, since this is an exploratory process, there are probably valid practical reasons to hold the hearing out of the presence of the jury although once we resolve the basic problem, that process would not be necessary in future cases.

As I see it, the hearing to be conducted in this case will be somewhat unusual because of the nature of the question and the need for a comprehensive record of testimony. The practical reason for conducting this particular hearing out of the presence of the jury is that the hearing could well take several days. It is not a question which can be resolved simply by examination of the particular psychologists whose testimony is offered. The preliminary hearing on qualifications will be enlarged if the District Judge allows, as he might well do, participation by the several amici curiae, who are highly qualified to be of aid to the court. That would be a dubious process for every future case but entirely appropriate for this case. We have said that the conduct of the hearing lies in the sound discretion of the trial judge. But it is not enough to say that it is within the sound discretion of the trial judge and at the same time fail to reflect just what we are driving at.

We must bear in mind that there is a difference between the holdings "that some psychologists are qualified to render expert testimony in the field of mental disorder" (see note 14 majority opinion) and the question of a psychologist's competence to make a diagnosis

of *mental disease*. The former proposition is, as we have noted, widely accepted; the latter is not—and it is the latter we are now exploring.

On remand I assume broad areas are to be explored and should be explored in order to give the trial judge, in the first instance, and this court if need be, an evidentiary basis and a record on which to act. As I see it, the remand hearing ought to cover among other things the following:

(a) The scope, nature and extent of the education of a Ph.D. in Psychology and in Clinical Psychology, including time spent in hospitals, with patients, and under what supervision.

  (1) What is the education, training and clinical experience of the proffered witness?

  (2) Define for the record the term "clinical experience."

(b) What, in particular, is the extent and scope of this Clinical Psychologist's clinical education in physiological and medical subjects? How does it compare with that of a psychiatrist?

(c) What is the scope of the work of Clinical Psychologists at St. Elizabeths Hospital?[2]

  (1) Do they make diagnosis of mental diseases on their own independent responsibility or only subject to the supervision of a psychiatrist? The relationship should be developed fully.

---

[2] In this connection an obviously well qualified expert, who might well be called as a witness by the court, if he is not called by any party, is the Superintendent of St. Elizabeths Hospital who has presided over a staff of psychiatrists and clinical psychologists dealing with precisely the issues of criminal responsibility.

(2) What is the scope of the work and extent of clinical responsibility of the particular Clinical Psychologist with patients *independent* of psychiatrists? That is, what work is done fully by the Clinical Psychologist alone and without regard to any supervision or overseeing by a psychiatrist?

(d) In how many specific cases has the particular Clinical Psychologist made a diagnosis of mental disease, prescribed or supervised treatment of patients without the intervention or approval of a psychiatrist?

(e) In how many cases approximately (whether at St. Elizabeths or elsewhere) has the witness made a diagnosis of the existence or nonexistence of mental disease and communicated that diagnosis directly to the patient or patient's family independent of a psychiatrist?

(f) To what extent has the witness prescribed or supervised treatment of mental patients independent of a psychiatrist?

(g) The opinions of both psychiatrists and clinical psychologists ought to be made part of the record on the following:

(1) In what kinds or categories of mental disease are the physiological and medical factors not of any consequence?

(2) In what categories does a diagnosis of mental disease involve analysis, understanding and synthesis of physical and physiological factors as well as psychological factors?

(3) If diagnosis of mental disease always involves consideration of or evaluation of physical, biological or physiological data, how does a clinical psychologist

acquire clinical experience and scientific competence to make such diagnosis?

(4) What is a differential diagnosis in the context of diagnosis of mental disease?

(5) Is the process of diagnosis of mental disease the elimination of various alternative explanations?

(6) In this process what factors must be taken into account?

(7) In the process of eliminating alternative explanations do the medical history of the patient, the physical examination and various medical tests play a part?

(8) Can any mental disease be diagnosed without taking into account pathological data? If so, what mental diseases can be diagnosed independent of and without regard to pathological data?

The cases cited by the majority concerning the optometrist, the toxicologist and other skilled specialists who are not medical doctors are not in any real sense relevant. Indeed they tend to divert us from the central issue. Of course an optometrist or the toxicologist is permitted to give *some* expert testimony within his competence just as a skilled shoemaker might be qualified to testify from long observation and experience as to the effect of wearing certain kinds of shoes, or a farrier to give expert testimony about the effect of certain types of shoeing on horses.

The heart of our problem is not whether a clinical psychologist is qualified to testify as an expert, for of course he is in some areas, but whether he is qualified to give expert testimony in the form of a diagnosis of a mental disease or illness, and to express an opinion on whether a stated mental disease "caused" the patient to commit a given unlawful act or "produced" that act. More rationally the question ought to be whether mental disease so substantially affected him that he was unable to control his conduct.

I agree with the majority that the scope of the training of the psychologist is of critical importance and that many factors other than academic degrees go to the admissibility and weight of the expert testimony. For example, if a general medical practitioner testified on the subject of mental disease, and gave a diagnosis of presence or absence of mental illness in opposition to a trained psychiatrist it would obviously be proper for the trial judge to tell the jury they could take into account the differences in training and experience in weighing the testimony of the one against the other. In the same way it would be proper, if a clinical psychologist is found qualified to testify as to the presence or absence of a mental disease and does so in opposition to a psychiatrist, to tell the jury they could take into account the difference in the education, training and experience of psychologists and psychiatrists and the absence of medical training in the former.

BASTIAN, Circuit Judge, with whom WILBUR K. MILLER, Chief Judge, joins, dissenting.

In the early morning of June 10, 1959, the complaining witness was in her apartment alone, in the process of getting ready to go to work that day, when she heard a knock at her front door and, upon partially opening it, she found herself face to face with the appellant. He showed her a card, saying something about an address. Then he suddenly burst into the apartment, knocked her to the floor, stuffed a gag into her mouth, and informed her he was going to rape her. When she began to fight back at her attacker, kicking and scratching at him as best as she could, he proceeded to punch her into unconsciousness with his fists. When she regained consciousness, she found herself lying on her apartment floor, disheveled, badly beaten, and bleeding profusely. She had been stabbed with a sharp instrument, presumably a knife, a number of times, causing severe loss of blood and necessitating subsequent surgery. As a result of this ordeal she remained hospitalized for approximately six weeks. In the District Court, a jury convicted appellant of housebreaking, assault with intent to commit rape, and assault with a dangerous weapon.

In reversing this conviction, the majority of this court, without adequately discussing the real nature and present medical understanding of mental illness, hold *inter alia* that certain psychologists can qualify to give *expert* opinion concerning the existence *vel non* of a mental disease or defect and its connective relationship, if any, to criminal behavior. We cannot agree. In our opinion it should be an absolute condition precedent to expert testimony as to a medical diagnosis that the witness be a medical doctor.

In the first place, we think it must be concluded beyond doubt that the existence of a mental disease or defect is, first and foremost, a *medical* problem. The ascertainment of such a medical illness in a given individual with reference to kind, quality, degree and influence is, except in extreme cases, a highly unverifiable process, judged by any objective standard, even when undertaken by a *medical* doctor with years of special training in the detection of medical disturbances of the mind. Time and time again, where insanity is raised as a defense at the trial of criminal cases in this jurisdiction, sincere and experienced *psychiatrists* have taken the stand and voiced diametrically opposite opinions as to whether or not the defendant had a mental disease or defect at the time he committed the crime charged against him. And even when these psychiatrists are in some agreement that the defendant had a mental disease or defect at the time of the crime, they frequently differ widely concerning its symptoms, nature, intensity, and causal influence with respect to the offense committed.

Our emphasis of this situation is not to belittle the integrity of the psychiatrists who testify at these trials, nor to disparage the integrity of the psychiatric profession, but merely to illustrate how nebulous and uncertain is the issue of mental illness even to those of the *medical* profession who are experienced and trained in its diagnosis and treatment. If the issue is so debatable among conceded professional medical experts, it is sheer folly, in our opinion, to attribute to a lay psychologist, who admittedly is not a doctor of medicine, such presumptive medical knowledge and diagnostic acuity as to entitle him to wear in a criminal courtroom the badge of an expert witness with respect to the existence of that elusive *medical* condition known as mental disease or defect.

By this we do not mean to suggest that a psychologist should never be called upon to testify in insanity cases. In proper circumstances, testimony concerning the results of psychological tests administered to a defendant should be admissible as a means of enlightening a jury with respect to the specific information contributed by the psychologist to the over-all mass of information ultimately utilized by the medically trained psychiatrist in arriving at an expert opinion concerning the medical diagnosis of mental disease or defect. But to say that a psychologist is qualified to give an expert opinion with reference to a medical diagnosis is, in effect, to say that a non-medical witness can render an expert answer to a medical question on the strength of information insufficient to resolve it.[1] Such an opinion is a conclusion by guesswork, as far as a valid and proper medical determination is concerned.

We are not alone in our views on this precise issue. The American Psychiatric Association, an organization "comprised of those twelve thousand qualified Doctors of Medicine who specialize and practice as psychiatrists," in its amicus curiae brief, urges this court not to allow psychologists to qualify as experts to express opinions. We find in the brief this pertinent observation in regard to the proper medical ascertainment of mental disease or defect:

"The diagnostic synthesis of *all data* collected is properly carried out only by an individual Doctor of Medicine with a broad training, experience, and familiarity with *all* of the areas indicated, and the diagnosis must reflect a comprehensive medical judgment in which the proper weight is given to all of the data available. Further, we know of no mental illness which does not have a biological as well as a psychological component. No facet of the data can be assumed

---

[1] It is well to remember that a psychologist's opinion in this respect is grounded basically upon his interpretation of the results of certain psychological tests administered to the defendant. As an example of the instability of such test results, we mention that in the instant case the appellant was subjected to the same I.Q. test on three separate occasions, scoring, respectively, 63 (high moron), 74 (borderline defective), and 90 (average).

to reflect the total diagnosis until viewed in the context of the total picture. A clinical psychologist, lacking *medical* training and the specialization required of the qualified psychiatrist, is not qualified to make this total *medical* diagnosis or to testify as a *medical* expert thereon." [Emphasis appears in amicus brief.]

The majority of the court ignores the above quoted wise counsel from the only undisputed experts now at work in the area of medical illness of the mind. In doing so, the court, we suggest, is bypassing all objective criteria in reaching the highly questionable and subjective conclusion that lay psychologists, whose opinions are predicated on the basis of test results, may qualify as experts on the medical question of the diagnosis of mental disease or defect, as well as experts concerning the causal relationship between a particular defendant's mental abnormality, as such may be "diagnosed" by these psychologists, and that defendant's criminal activity. In our opinion, the holding of the majority on this issue is wholly untenable. We would affirm the judgment and sentence of the District Court.

Frye v. United States. (Court of Appeals of District of Columbia. Submitted November 7, 1923. Decided December 3, 1923.) No. 3968.

1. CRIMINAL LAW   472—EXPERT TESTIMONY, EXPLAINING SYSTOLIC BLOOD PRESSURE DECEPTION TEST, INADMISSIBLE.

The systolic blood pressure deception test, based on the theory that truth

is spontaneous and comes without conscious effort, while the utterance of a falsehood requires a conscious effort, which is reflected in the blood pressure, *held* not to have such a scientific recognition among psychological and physiological authorities as would justify the courts in admitting expert testimony on defendant's behalf, deduced from experiments thus far made.

2. CRIMINAL LAW   472—PRINCIPLE MUST BE GENERALLY ACCEPTED, TO RENDER EXPERT TESTIMONY ADMISSIBLE.

While the courts will go a long way in admitting expert testimony, deduced from a well-recognized scientific principle or discovery, the thing from which the deduction is made must be sufficiently established to have gained general acceptance in the particular field in which it belongs.

Appeal from the Supreme Court of the District of Columbia.

James Alphonzo Frye was convicted of murder, and he appeals. Affirmed.

Richard V. Mattingly and Foster Wood, both of Washington, D.C., for appellant.

Peyton Gordon and J. H. Bilbrey, both of Washington, D.C., for the United States.

Before SMYTH, Chief Justice, VAN ORSDEL, Associate Justice, and MARTIN, Presiding Judge of the United States Court of Customs Appeals.

VAN ORSDEL, Associate Justice. Appellant, defendant below, was convicted of the crime of murder in the second degree, and from the judgment prosecutes this appeal.

A single assignment of error is presented for our consideration. In the course of the trial counsel for defendant offered an expert witness to testify to the result of a deception test made upon defendant. The test is described as the systolic blood pressure deception test. It is asserted that blood pressure is influenced by change in the emotions of the witness, and that the systolic blood pressure rises are brought about by nervous impulses sent to the sympathetic branch of the autonomic nervous system. Scientific experiments, it is claimed, have demonstrated that fear, rage, and pain always produce a rise of systolic blood pressure, and that conscious deception or falsehood, concealment of facts, or guilt of crime, accompanied by fear of detection when the person is under examination, raises the systolic blood pressure in a curve, which corresponds exactly to the struggle going on in the subject's mind, between fear and attempted control of that fear, as the examination touches the vital points in respect of which he is attempting to deceive the examiner.

In other words, the theory seems to be that truth is spontaneous, and comes without conscious effort, while the utterance of a falsehood requires a conscious effort, which is reflected in the blood pressure. The rise thus produced is easily detected and distinguished from the rise produced by mere fear of the examination itself. In the former instance, the pressure rises higher than in the latter, and is more pronounced as the examination proceeds, while in the latter case, if the subject is telling the truth, the pressure registers highest at the beginning of the examination, and gradually diminishes as the examination proceeds.

Prior to the trial defendant was subjected to this deception test, and counsel offered the scientist who conducted the test as an expert to testify to the results obtained. The offer was objected to by counsel for the government, and the court sustained the objection. Counsel for defendant then offered to have the proffered witness conduct a test in the presence of the jury. This also was denied.

Counsel for defendant, in their able presentation of the novel question involved, correctly state in their brief that no cases directly in point have been found. The broad ground, however, upon which they plant their case, is succinctly stated in their brief as follows:

"The rule is that the opinions of experts or skilled witnesses are admissible in evidence in those cases in which the matter of inquiry is such that inexperienced persons are unlikely to prove capable of forming a correct judgment upon it, for the reason that the subject-matter so far partakes of a science, art, or trade as to require a previous habit or experience or study in it, in order to acquire a knowledge of it. When the question involved does not lie within the range of common experience or common knowledge, but requires special experience or special knowledge, then the opinions of witnesses skilled in that particular science, art, or trade to which the question relates are admissible in evidence."

[1, 2] Numerous cases are cited in support of this rule. Just when a scientific principle or discovery crosses the line between the experimental and demonstrable stages is difficult to define. Somewhere in this twilight zone the evidential force of the principle must be recognized, and while courts will go a long way in admitting expert testimony deduced from a well-recognized scientific principle or discovery, the thing from which the deduction is made must be sufficiently established to have gained general acceptance in the particular field in which it belongs.

We think the systolic blood pressure deception test has not yet gained such standing and scientific recognition among physiological and psychological authorities as would justify the courts in admitting expert testimony deduced from the discovery, development, and experiments thus far made.

The judgment is affirmed.

W. J. Estelle, Jr., Director, Texas Department of Corrections, Petitioner, v. Ernest Benjamin Smith. No. 79-1127. Argued October 8, 1980. Decided May 18, 1981.

Texas prisoner sought federal habeas corpus relief. The United States District Court for the Northern District of Texas, Robert W. Porter, J., 445 F.Supp. 647, issued writ, and the state appealed. The Court of Appeals, 602 F.2d 694, affirmed. Certiorari was granted. The Supreme Court, Mr. Chief Justice Burger, held that: (1) where prior to in-custody court-ordered psychiatric examination to determine competency to stand trial defendant had not been warned that he had right to remain silent and that any statement made could be used against him at capital sentencing proceeding, admission at penalty phase of capital felony trial of psychiatrist's damaging testimony on crucial issue of future dangerousness violated Fifth Amendment privilege against compelled self-incrimination; because of lack of appraisal of rights and a knowing waiver thereof death sentence could not stand, and (2) Sixth Amendment right to counsel was violated as defense counsel was not notified in advance that the psychiatric examination would encompass issue of future dangerousness.

Decision of Court of Appeals affirmed.

Mr. Justice Brennan filed a concurring statement.

Mr. Justice Marshall filed a statement concurring in part.

Mr. Justice Stewart filed an opinion concurring in the judgment, in which Mr. Justice Powell joined.

Mr. Justice Rehnquist filed an opinion concurring in the judgment.

1. CRIMINAL LAW 393(1)

Fact that testimony of psychiatrist who was sua sponte appointed by the court to determine defendant's competency to stand trial was used only to determine punishment in capital felony case and not to determine guilt did not render inapplicable the Fifth Amendment privilege against compelled self-incrimination. Vernon's Ann.Tex. C.C.P. arts. 37.071, 46.02; Vernon's Ann.Tex.P.C. art. 1257(b)(2); U.S.C.A.Const. Amend. 5.

2. WITNESSES 300

Just as the Fifth Amendment prevents a criminal defendant from being made the deluded instrument of his own conviction, it protects him as well from being made the deluded instrument of his own execution; there is no basis to distinguish between guilty and penalty phases of a capital murder trial so far as protection of Fifth Amendment privilege is concerned. U.S.C.A.Const. Amend. 5.

3. CRIMINAL LAW 986.6(2)

Given gravity of decision to be made at the penalty phase of a capital murder case, the state is not relieved of the obligation to observe fundamental constitutional guarantees. Vernon's Ann. Tex.P.C. art. 1257(b)(2); Vernon's Ann.

Tex.C.C.P. art. 37.071; U.S.C.A.Const. Amend. 5.

4. CRIMINAL LAW 412(5)
Witnesses 300

Any effort by state of Texas to compel criminal defendant to testify against his will at sentencing phase of capital murder prosecution would contravene the Fifth Amendment; also state's attempt to establish future dangerousness by relying on defendant's pretrial statements to a psychiatrist appointed sua sponte by the court to determine competency to stand trial, with defendant not having been advised that he had right to remain silent and that any statement could be used against him at sentencing proceedings, similarly infringed Fifth Amendment values. Vernon's Ann.Tex. C.C.P. arts. 37.071, 46.02; Vernon's Ann.Tex.P.C. art. 1257; U.S.C.A.Const. Amend. 5.

5. WITNESSES 300

Fifth Amendment is not violated where the evidence given by a defendant is neither related to some communicative act nor used for the testimonial content of what was said. U.S.C.A.Const. Amend. 5.

6. CRIMINAL LAW 393(1)

Where court-appointed psychiatrist's prognosis of defendant's future dangerousness, as admitted at sentencing hearing of Texas capital felony prosecution, rested on statements which defendant made and remarks which he omitted in reciting details of the crime during court-initiated pretrial examination to determine competency to stand

trial the Fifth Amendment privilege was directly involved because the state used as evidence against defendant the substance of his disclosure and privilege was not inapplicable on ground that psychiatrist based his adverse diagnosis merely on observation of defendant. Vernon's Ann.Tex.C.C.P. arts. 37.071, 46.02; Vernon's Ann.Tex.P.C. art. 1257; U.S.C.A.Const. Amend. 5.

7. CRIMINAL LAW 412(5)

Fact that Texas defendant's statements were uttered in context of court-ordered pretrial psychiatric examination did not automatically remove them from reach of Fifth Amendment as regards admission, at penalty phase of capital murder trial, of psychiatrist's adverse prognosis on critical issue of dangerousness; although trial judge sua sponte ordered evaluation for limited, neutral purpose of determining competency to stand trial, results of inquiry were used for broader objective plainly adverse to defendant but if application of psychiatrist's findings had been confined to insuring that defendant understood charges and was capable of assisting counsel, no Fifth Amendment issue would have arisen. Vernon's Ann. Tex.P.C. art. 1257(b)(2); Vernon's Ann. Tex.C.C.P. arts. 37.071(b)(2), 46.02; U.S.C.A.Const. Amend. 5.

8. CRIMINAL LAW 412.2(3)

Where at capital felony murder case Texas defendant introduced no psychiatric evidence and did not indicate that he might do so and to meet its burden on crucial penalty issue of future dangerousness the state used defendant's statements to psychiatrist who had been sua sponte appointed to trial to determine competency to stand trial and defendant had not been warned of his right to remain silent and that any statement he made could be used against him at capital sentencing proceeding, the Fifth Amendment privilege was implicated. Vernon's Ann.Tex.P.C. art. 1257(b)(2); Vernon's Ann.Tex.C.C.P. arts. 37.071(b)(2), 46.02; U.S.C.A.Const. Amend. 5.

9.   CRIMINAL LAW   412.2(3)

Absent other fully effective procedures, a person in custody must receive certain warnings before any official interrogation, including that he has a right to remain silent and that anything said can and will be used against the individual in court. U.S.C.A.Const. Amends. 5, 14.

10.   WITNESSES   300

Fifth Amendment privilege is as broad as the mischief against which it seeks to guard and the privilege is fulfilled only when a criminal defendant is guaranteed the right to remain silent unless he chooses to speak in the unfettered exercise of his own will, and to suffer no penalty for such silence. U.S.C.A.Const. Amend. 5.

11.   CRIMINAL LAW   698(1)

Texas defendant did not waive his Fifth Amendment claim by failing to make a timely, specific trial objection to court-appointed psychiatrist's adverse testimony on future dangerousness issue at penalty phase of capital murder trial, specifically, claiming that Fifth Amendment was violated because prior to the in-jail examination defendant had not been warned that he had a right to remain silent and that any statement he made could be used against him at a capital sentencing proceeding and, also, state did not present the waiver argument in its petition for certiorari. U.S. Sup.Ct. Rule 40, subd. 1(d)(2), 28 U.S.C.A.; Vernon's Ann.Tex.P.C. art. 1257(b)(2); Vernon's Ann.Tex.C.C.P. arts. 37.071(b)(2), 46.02; U.S.C.A.Const. Amend. 5.

12.   CRIMINAL LAW   412(4)

A criminal defendant who neither initiates a psychiatric evaluation nor attempts to introduce any psychiatric evidence, may not be compelled to respond to a psychiatrist if his statements can be used against him at a capital sentencing proceeding. Vernon's Ann.Tex.P.C. art. 1257(b)(2); Vernon's Ann.Tex.C.C.P. arts. 37.071(b)(2), 46.02; U.S.C.A.Const. Amend. 5.

13.   CRIMINAL LAW   412.1(4),
412.2(3)

Where prior to court ordered pretrial psychiatric examination to determine competency to stand trial defendant had not been informed of his right to remain silent and possible use of his statements, the state could not rely on defendant's statements of psychiatrist for purpose of establishing future dangerousness issue at death penalty phase and since statements were made while defendant was in custody his statements to psychiatrist, who testified adversely to defendant at penalty phase, could not be said to have been given freely and voluntarily and, hence, death sentence could not stand. Vernon's Ann.Tex.P.C. art. 1257(b)(2); Vernon's Ann.Tex.C.C.P. arts. 37.071(b)(2), 46.02; U.S.C.A.Const. Amend. 5.

14. CRIMINAL LAW 641.12(1)

Where defendant had been indicted and counsel appointed before he was examined at jail by a psychiatrist sua sponte appointed to determine competency to stand trial and counsel had not been notified of the hearing, defendant's Sixth Amendment right to assistance of counsel was violated when prosecution, at penalty phase of Texas capital murder prosecution, introduced psychiatrist's adverse diagnosis regarding crucial issue of future dangerousness; interview proved to be a "critical stage" of the aggregate proceedings, and waiver was neither shown nor alleged. Vernon's Ann.Tex.P.C. art. 1257(b)(2); Vernon's Ann.Tex.P.C. arts. 37.071, 37.071(b)(2), 46.02; U.S.C.A.Const. Amends. 6, 14.

See publication Words and Phrases for other judicial constructions and definitions.

15. CRIMINAL LAW 641.4(2)

Waivers of assistance of counsel must not only be voluntary but constitute a knowing and intelligent relinquishment or abandonment of a known right or privilege, a matter which depends upon the particular facts and circumstances surrounding each case. U.S.C.A.Const. Amends. 5, 6, 14.

Syllabus*

After respondent was indicted in Texas for murder, the State announced its intention to seek the death penalty.

---

* The syllabus constitutes no part of the opinion of the Court but has been prepared by the Reporter of Decisions for the convenience of the reader. See *United States v. Detroit Lumber Co.*, 200 U.S. 321, 337, 26 S.Ct. 282, 287, 50 L.Ed. 499.

At an ensuring psychiatric examination, ordered by the trial court to determine respondent's competency to stand trial and conducted in the jail where he was being held, the examining doctor determined that respondent was competent. Thereafter, respondent was tried by a jury and convicted. A separate sentencing proceeding was then held before the same jury as required by Texas law. At such a proceeding the jury must resolve three critical issues to determine whether or not the death sentence will be imposed. One of these issues involves the future dangerousness of the defendant, *i.e.,* whether there is a probability that he would commit criminal acts of violence that would constitute a continuing threat to society. At the sentencing hearing, the doctor who had conducted the pretrial psychiatric examination was allowed to testify for the State over defense counsels' objection that his name did not appear on the list of witnesses the State planned to use at either the guilt or penalty stages of the proceedings. His testimony was based on the pretrial examination and stated in substance that respondent would be a danger to society. The jury then resolved the issue of future dangerousness, as well as the other two issues, against respondent, and thus under Texas law the death penalty was mandatory. The Texas Court of Criminal Appeals affirmed the conviction and death sentence. After unsuccessfully seeking a writ of habeas corpus in the state courts, respondent petitioned for such relief in Federal District Court. That court vacated the death sentence because it found constitutional error in admitting the doctor's testimony at the penalty phase. The United States Court of Appeals affirmed.

Held:

1. The admission of the doctor's testimony at the penalty phase violated

respondent's Fifth Amendment privilege against compelled self-incrimination, because he was not advised before the pretrial psychiatric examination that he had a right to remain silent and that any statement he made could be used against him at a capital sentencing proceeding. Pp.˙1872–1876.

(a) There is no basis for distinguishing between the guilt and penalty phases of respondent's trial so far as the protection of the Fifth Amendment privilege is concerned. The State's attempt to establish respondent's future dangerousness by relying on the unwarned statements he made to the examining doctor infringed the Fifth Amendment just as much as would have any effort to compel respondent to testify against his will at the sentencing hearing. Pp.˙1872–1873.

(b) The Fifth Amendment privilege is directly involved here because the State used as evidence against respondent the substance of his disclosures during the pretrial psychiatric examination. The fact that respondent's statements were made in the context of such an examination does not automatically remove them from the reach of that Amendment. Pp.˙1873–1875.

(c) The considerations calling for the accused to be warned prior to custodial interrogation apply with no less force to the pretrial psychiatric examination at issue here. An accused who neither initiates a psychiatric evaluation nor attempts to introduce any psychiatric evidence may not be compelled to respond to a psychiatrist if his statements can be used against him at a capital sentencing proceeding. When faced while in custody with a court-ordered psychiatric inquiry, respondent's statements to the doctor were not "given freely and voluntarily without any compelling influences" and, as such, could be used as the State did at the penalty phase only if respondent had been apprised of his rights and had knowingly decided to waive them. *Miranda v. Arizona*, 384 U.S. 436, 478, 86 S.Ct. 1602, 1630, 16 L.Ed.2d 694. Since these safeguards of the Fifth Amendment privilege were not afforded respondent, his death sentence cannot stand. Pp.˙1875–1876.

2. Respondent's Sixth Amendment right to the assistance of counsel also was violated by the State's introduction of the doctor's testimony at the penalty phase. Such right already had attached when the doctor examined respondent in jail, and that interview proved to be a "critical stage" of the aggregate proceedings against respondent. Defense counsel were not notified in advance that the psychiatric examination would encompass the issue of their client's future dangerousness, and respondent was denied the assistance of his counsel in making the significant decision of whether to submit to the examination and to what end the psychiatrist's findings could be employed. Pp.˙1876–1877.

5 Cir., 602 F.2d 694, affirmed.

Anita Ashton, Austin, Tex., for petitioner.

Joel Berger, for respondent.

Chief Justice BURGER, delivered the opinion of the Court.

We granted certiorari to consider whether the prosecution's use of psychiatric testimony at the sentencing phase of respondent's capital murder trial to establish his future dangerousness violated his constitutional rights. 445 U.S. 926, 100 S.Ct. 1311, 63 L.Ed.2d 758 (1980).

I

A

On December 28, 1973, respondent Ernest Benjamin Smith was indicted for murder arising from his participation in the armed robbery of a grocery store during which a clerk was fatally shot, not by Smith, but by his accomplice. In accordance with Art. 1257(b)(2) of the Texas Penal Code (Vernon 1973) concerning the punishment for murder with malice aforethought, the State of Texas announced its intention to seek the death penalty. Thereafter, a judge of the 195th Judicial District Court of Dallas County, Texas, informally ordered the State's attorney to arrange a psychiatric examination of Smith by Dr. James P. Grigson to determine Smith's competency to stand trial.[1] See n. 5, *infra*.

Dr. Grigson, who interviewed Smith in jail for approximately 90 minutes, concluded that he was competent to stand trial. In a letter to the trial judge, Dr. Grigson reported his findings: "[I]t is my opinion that Ernest Benjamin Smith, Jr. is aware of the difference between right and wrong and is able to aid an attorney in his defense." App. 6. This letter was filed with the court's

papers in the case. Smith was then tried by a jury and convicted of murder.

In Texas, capital cases require bifurcated proceedings—a guilt phase and a penalty phase.[2] If the defendant is found guilty, a separate proceeding before the same jury is held to fix the punishment. At the penalty phase, if the jury affirmatively answers three questions on which the State has the burden of proof beyond a reasonable doubt, the judge must impose the death sentence. See Tex.Code Crim.Proc., Art. 37.071(c) & (e) (Vernon Supp. 1980). One of the three critical issues to be resolved by the jury is "whether there is a probability that the defendant would commit criminal acts of violence that would constitute a continuing threat to society." Art. 37.071(b)(2).[3] In

---

[1] This psychiatric evaluation was ordered even though defense counsel had not put into issue Smith's competency to stand trial or his sanity at the time of the offense. The trial judge later explained: "In all cases where the State has sought the death penalty, I have ordered a mental evaluation of the defendant to determine his competency to stand trial. I have done this for my benefit because I do not intend to be a participant in a case where the defendant receives the death penalty and his mental competency remains in doubt." App. 117. See Tex.Code Crim.Proc., Art. 46.02 (Vernon 1979). No question as to the appropriateness of the trial judge's order for the examination has been raised by Smith.

[2] Article 37.071(a) of the Texas Code of Criminal Procedure (Vernon Supp. 1980) provides: "Upon a finding that the defendant is guilty of a capital offense, the court shall conduct a separate sentencing proceeding to determine whether the defendant shall be sentenced to death or life imprisonment. The proceeding shall be conducted in the trial court before the trial jury as soon as practicable. In the proceeding, evidence may be presented as to any matter that the court deems relevant to sentence. This subsection shall not be construed to authorize the introduction of any evidence secured in violation of the Constitution of the United States or of the State of Texas. The state and the defendant or his counsel shall be permitted to present argument for or against sentence of death."

[3] The other two issues are "whether the conduct of the defendant that caused the death of the deceased was committed deliberately and with the reasonable expectation that the death of the deceased or another would result" and "if raised by the evidence, whether the conduct of the defendant in killing the deceased was unreasonable in response to the provocation, if any, by the deceased." Tex.Code Crim.Proc., Art. 37.071(b)(1) & (3) (Vernon Supp. 1980).

other words, the jury must assess the defendant's future dangerousness.

At the commencement of Smith's sentencing hearing, the State rested "subject to the right to reopen." App. 11. Defense counsel called three lay witnesses: Smith's stepmother, his aunt, and the man who owned the gun Smith carried during the robbery. Smith's relatives testified as to his good reputation and character.[4] The owner of the pistol testified as to Smith's knowledge that it would not fire because of a mechanical defect. The State then called Dr. Grigson as a witness.

Defense counsel were aware from the trial court's file of the case that Dr. Grigson had submitted a psychiatric report in the form of a letter advising the court that Smith was competent to stand trial.[5] This report termed Smith "a severe sociopath," but it contained no more specific reference to his future dangerousness. *Id.*, at 6. Before trial,

---

[4] It appears from the record that Smith's only prior criminal conviction was for the possession of marijuana. See App. 64.

[5] Defense counsel discovered the letter at some time after jury selection began in the case on March 11, 1974. The trial judge later explained that Dr. Grigson was "appointed by oral communication," that "a letter of appointment was not prepared," and that "the court records do not reflect [the entry of] a written order." App. 118. The judge also stated:

"As best I recall, I informed John Simmons, the attorney for the defendant, that I had appointed Dr. Grigson to examine the defendant and that a written report was to be mailed to me." *Ibid.* However, defense counsel assert that the discovery of Dr. Grigson's letter served as their first notice that he had examined Smith. *Id.*, at 113, 116.

On March 25, 1974, the day the trial began, defense counsel requested the issuance of a subpoena for the Dallas County Sheriff's records of Dr. Grigson's "visitation to . . . Smith." *Id.*, at 8.

defense counsel had obtained an order requiring the State to disclose the witnesses it planned to use both at the guilt stage, and, if known, at the penalty stage. Subsequently, the trial court had granted a defense motion to bar the testimony during the State's case-in-chief of any witness whose name did not appear on that list. Dr. Grigson's name was not on the witness list, and defense counsel objected when he was called to the stand at the penalty phase.

In a hearing outside the presence of the jury, Dr. Grigson stated: (a) that he had not obtained permission from Smith's attorneys to examine him; (b) that he had discussed his conclusions and diagnosis with the State's attorney; and (c) that the prosecutor had requested him to testify and had told him, approximately five days before the sentencing hearing began, that his testimony probably would be needed within the week. *Id.*, at 14–16. The trial judge denied a defense motion to exclude Dr. Grigson's testimony on the ground that his name was not on the State's list of witnesses. Although no continuance was requested, the court then recessed for one hour following an acknowledgment by defense counsel that an hour was "all right." *Id.*, at 17.

After detailing his professional qualifications by way of foundation, Dr. Grigson testified before the jury on direct examination: (a) that Smith "is a very severe sociopath"; (b) that "he will continue his previous behavior"; (c) that his sociopathic condition will "only get worse"; (d) that he has no "regard for another human being's property or for their life, regardless of who it may be"; (e) that "[t]here is no treatment, no medicine . . . that in any way at all modifies or changes this behavior"; (f) that he "is going to go ahead and commit other similar or same criminal acts if given the opportunity to do so"; and (g) that he "has no remorse or sorrow for what he has done." *Id.*, at 17–26. Dr. Grigson, whose testimony was based on information derived from his 90-minute "mental status examination" of Smith (*i.e.*, the examination ordered to determine Smith's competency to stand trial), was the State's only witness at the sentencing hearing.

The jury answered the three requisite questions in the affirmative, and, thus, under Texas law the death penalty for Smith was mandatory. The Texas Court of Criminal Appeals affirmed Smith's conviction and death sentence, 540 S.W.2d 693 (Tex.Cr.App.1976), and we denied certiorari, 430 U.S. 922, 97 S.Ct. 1341, 51 L.Ed.2d 601 (1977).

B

After unsuccessfully seeking a writ of habeas corpus in the Texas state courts, Smith petitioned for such relief in the United States District Court for the Northern District of Texas pursuant to 28 U.S.C. § 2254. The District Court vacated Smith's death sentence because it found constitutional error in the admission of Dr. Grigson's testimony at the penalty phase. 445 F.Supp. 647 (1977). The court based its holding on the failure to advise Smith of his right to remain silent at the pretrial psychiatric examination and the failure to notify defense counsel in advance of the penalty phase that Dr. Grigson would testify. The court concluded that the death penalty had been imposed on Smith in violation of his Fifth and Fourteenth Amendment rights to due process and freedom from compelled self-incrimination, his Sixth Amendment right to the effective assistance of counsel, and his Eighth Amendment right to present complete evidence of mitigating circumstances. *Id.*, at 664.

The United States Court of Appeals for the Fifth Circuit affirmed. 602 F.2d

694 (1979). The court held that Smith's death sentence could not stand because the State's "surprise" use of Dr. Grigson as a witness, the consequences of which the court described as "devastating," denied Smith due process in that his attorneys were prevented from effectively challenging the psychiatric testimony. *Id.*, at 699. The court went on to hold that, under the Fifth and Sixth Amendments, "Texas may not use evidence based on a psychiatric examination of the defendant unless the defendant was warned, before the examination, that he had a right to remain silent; was allowed to terminate the examination when he wished; and was assisted by counsel in deciding whether to submit to the examination." *Id.*, at 709. Because Smith was not accorded these rights, his death sentence was set aside. While "leav[ing] to state authorities any questions that arise about the appropriate way to proceed when the state cannot legally execute a defendant whom it has sentenced to death," the court indicated that "the same testimony from Dr. Grigson based on the same examination of Smith" could not be used against Smith at any future resentencing proceeding. *Id.*, at 703, n. 13, 709, n. 20.

II

A

Of the several constitutional issues addressed by the District Court and the Court of Appeals, we turn first to whether the admission of Dr. Grigson's testimony at the penalty phase violated respondent's Fifth Amendment privilege against compelled self-incrimination because respondent was not advised before the pretrial psychiatric examination that he had a right to remain silent and that any statement he made could be used against him at a sentencing proceeding. Our initial inquiry must be whether the Fifth Amendment privilege is applicable in the circumstances of this case.

(1)

[1] The State argues that respondent was not entitled to the protection of the Fifth Amendment because Dr. Grigson's testimony was used only to determine punishment after conviction, not to establish guilt. In the State's view, "incrimination is complete once guilt has been adjudicated," and, therefore, the Fifth Amendment privilege has no relevance to the penalty phase of a capital murder trial. Brief for Petitioner 33–34. We disagree.

[2] The Fifth Amendment, made applicable to the states through the Fourteenth Amendment, commands that "[n]o person . . . shall be compelled in any criminal case to be a witness against himself." The essence of this basic constitutional principle is "the requirement that the State which proposes to convict *and punish* an individual produce the evidence against him by the independent labor of its officers, not by the simple, cruel expedient of forcing it from his own lips." *Culombe v. Connecticut,* 367 U.S. 568, 581–582, 81 S.Ct. 1860, 1867, 6 L.Ed.2d 1037 (1961) (opinion announcing the judgment) (emphasis added). See also *Murphy v. Waterfront Comm'n,* 378 U.S. 52, 55, 84 S.Ct. 1594, 1596–1597, 12 L.Ed.2d 678 (1964); E. Griswold, The Fifth Amendment Today 7 (1955).

The Court has held that "the availability of the [Fifth Amendment] privilege does not turn upon the type of proceeding in which its protection is invoked, but upon the nature of the statement or admission and the exposure which it invites." *In re Gault,* 387 U.S. 1, 49, 87 S.Ct. 1428, 1455, 18 L.Ed.2d 527

(1967). In this case, the ultimate penalty of death was a potential consequence of what respondent told the examining psychiatrist. Just as the Fifth Amendment prevents a criminal defendant from being made "'the deluded instrument of his own conviction,'" *Culombe v. Connecticut, supra,* at 581, 1867, quoting 2 Hawkins Pleas of the Crown 595 (8th ed. 1824), it protects him as well from being made the "deluded instrument" of his own execution.

[3, 4] We can discern no basis to distinguish between the guilt and penalty phases of respondent's capital murder trial so far as the protection of the Fifth Amendment privilege is concerned.[6] Given the gravity of the decision to be made at the penalty phase, the State is not relieved of the obligation to observe fundamental constitutional guarantees. See *Green v. Georgia,* 442 U.S. 95, 97, 99 S.Ct. 2150, 2152, 60 L.Ed.2d 738 (1979); *Presnell v. Georgia,* 439 U.S. 14, 16, 99 S.Ct. 235, 236, 58 L.Ed.2d 207 (1978); *Gardner v. Florida,* 430 U.S. 349, 357–358, 97 S.Ct. 1197, 1204–1205, 51 L.Ed.2d 393 (1977) (plurality opinion). Any effort by the State to compel respondent to testify against his will at the sentencing hearing clearly would contravene the Fifth

---

[6] Texas law does provide that "[n]o statement made by a defendant during the examination or hearing on his competency to stand trial may be admitted in evidence against the defendant *on the issue of guilt* in any criminal proceeding." Tex.Code Crim.Proc., Art. 46.02(3)(g) (Vernon 1979) (emphasis added). See also 18 U.S.C. § 4244; Fed.Rule Crim.Proc. 12.2(c); *United States v. Alvarez,* 519 F.2d 1036, 1042–1044 (CA3 1975); Note, Requiring a Criminal Defendant to Submit to a Government Psychiatric Examination: An Invasion of the Privilege Against Self-Incrimination, 83 Harv.L.Rev. 648, 649, and cases cited at nn. 8–9 (1970).

Amendment.[7] Yet the State's attempt to establish respondent's future dangerousness by relying on the unwarned statements he made to Dr. Grigson similarly infringes Fifth Amendment values.

as to future dangerousness rested on statements respondent made, and remarks he omitted, in reciting the details of the crime.[9] The Fifth Amendment privilege, therefore, is directly involved here because the State used as evidence against respondent

(2)

[5]   The State also urges that the Fifth Amendment privilege is inapposite here because respondent's communications to Dr. Grigson were nontestimonial in nature. The State seeks support from our cases holding that the Fifth Amendment is not violated where the evidence given by a defendant is neither related to some communicative act nor used for the testimonial content of what was said. See, *e.g.*, *United States v. Dionisio*, 410 U.S. 1, 93 S.Ct. 764, 35 L.Ed.2d 67 (1973) (voice exemplar); *Gilbert v. California*, 388 U.S. 263, 87 S.Ct. 1951, 18 L.Ed.2d 1178 (1967) (handwriting exemplar); *United States v. Wade*, 388 U.S. 218, 87 S.Ct. 1926, 18 L.Ed.2d 1149 (1967) (lineup); *Schmerber v. California*, 384 U.S. 757, 86 S.Ct. 1826, 16 L.Ed.2d 908 (1966) (blood sample).

[6]   However, Dr. Grigson's diagnosis, as detailed in his testimony, was not based simply on his observation of respondent. Rather, Dr. Grigson drew his conclusions largely from respondent's account of the crime during their interview, and he placed particular emphasis on what he considered to be respondent's lack of remorse. See App. 27–29, 33–34.[8] Dr. Grigson's prognosis

sheds no light on whether such factors alone would enable a psychiatrist to predict future dangerousness. The American Psychiatric Association suggests, however, that "absent a defendant's willingness to cooperate as to the verbal *content* of his communications, . . . a psychiatric examination in these circumstances would be meaningless." Brief for American Psychiatric Association as *Amicus Curiae* 26 (emphasis in original).

[9] On cross-examination, Dr. Grigson acknowledged that his findings were based on his "discussion" with respondent, App. 32, and he replied to the question "[w]hat . . . was the most important thing that . . . caused you to think that [respondent] is a severe sociopath" as follows:

"He told me that this man named Moon looked as though he was going to reach for a gun, and he pointed his gun toward Mr. Moon's head, pulled the trigger, and it clicked—misfired, at which time he hollered at Howie, apparently his other partner there who had a gun, 'Watch out, Howie. He's got a gun.' Or something of that sort. At which point he told me—now I don't know who shot this man, but he told me that Howie shot him, but then he walked around over this man who had been shot—didn't . . . check to see if he had a gun nor did he check to see if the man was alive or dead. Didn't call an ambulance, but simply found the gun further up underneath the counter and took the gun and the money. This is a very— sort of cold-blooded disregard for another human being's life. I think that his telling me this story and not saying, you know, 'Man I would do anything to have that man back alive. I wish I hadn't just stepped over the body.' Or you know, 'I wish I had checked to see if he was all right' would indicate a concern, guilt, or remorse. But I didn't get any of this." *Id.*, at 27–28.

---

[7] Th State conceded this at oral argument. Tr. of Oral Arg, 47, 49.

[8] Although the Court of Appeals doubted the applicability of the Fifth Amendment if Dr. Grigson's diagnosis had been founded only on respondent's mannerisms, facial expressions, attention span, or speech patterns, 602 F.2d, at 704, the record in this case

the substance of his disclosures during the pretrial psychiatric examination.

[7] The fact that respondent's statements were uttered in the context of a psychiatric examination does not automatically remove them from the reach of the Fifth Amendment. See n.6, *supra*. The state trial judge, *sua sponte*, ordered a psychiatric evaluation of respondent for the limited, neutral purpose of determining his competency to stand trial, but the results of that inquiry were used by the State for a much broader objective that was plainly adverse to respondent. Consequently, the interview with Dr. Grigson cannot be characterized as a routine competency examination restricted to ensuring that respondent understood the charges against him and was capable of assisting in his defense. Indeed, if the application of Dr. Grigson's findings had been confined to serving that function, no Fifth Amendment issue would have arisen.

Nor was the interview analogous to a sanity examination occasioned by a defendant's plea of not guilty by reason of insanity at the time of his offense. When a defendant asserts the insanity defense and introduces supporting psychiatric testimony, his silence may deprive the State of the only effective means it has of controverting his proof on an issue that he interjected into the case. Accordingly, several courts of appeals have held that, under such circumstances, a defendant can be required to submit to a sanity examination conducted by the prosecution's psychiatrist. See, *e.g., United States v. Cohen*, 530 F.2d 43, 47–48 (CA5), cert. denied, 429 U.S. 855, 97 S.Ct. 149, 50 L.Ed.2d 130 (1976); *Karstetter v. Cardwell*, 526 F.2d 1144, 1145 (CA9 1975); *United States v. Bohle*, 445 F.2d 54, 66–67 (CA7 1971); *United States v. Weiser*, 428 F.2d 932, 936 (CA2 1969), cert. denied, 402 U.S. 949, 91 S.Ct. 1606, 29 L.Ed.2d

119 (1971); *United States v. Albright*, 388 F.2d 719, 724–725 (CA4 1968); *Pope v. United States*, 372 F.2d 710, 720–721 (CA8 1967) (en banc), vacated and remanded on other grounds, 392 U.S. 651, 88 S.Ct. 2145, 209 L.Ed.2d 1317 (1968).[10]

[8] Respondent, however, introduced no psychiatric evidence, nor had he indicated that he might do so. Instead, the State offered information obtained from the court-ordered competency examination as affirmative evidence to persuade the jury to return a sentence of death. Respondent's future dangerousness was a critical issue at the sentencing hearing, and one on which the State had the burden of proof beyond a reasonable doubt. See Tex.Code Crim.Proc., Art. 37.071(b) and (c) (Vernon Supp. 1980). To meet its burden, the State used respondent's own statements, unwittingly made without an awareness that he was assisting the State's efforts to obtain the death penalty. In these distinct circumstances, the Court of Appeals correctly concluded that the Fifth Amendment privilege was implicated.

(3)

[9] In *Miranda v. Arizona*, 384 U.S. 436, 467, 86 S.Ct. 1602, 1624, 16 L.Ed.2d 694 (1966), the Court acknowledged that "the Fifth Amendment privilege is available outside of criminal court proceedings and serves to protect persons in all settings in which their freedom of action is curtailed in any significant

---

[10] On the same theory, the Court of Appeals here carefully left open "the possibility that a defendant who wishes to use psychiatric evidence in his own behalf [on the issue of future dangerousness] can be precluded from using is unless he is [also] willing to be examined by a psychiatrist nominated by the state." 602 F.2d 705, 707.

way from being compelled to incriminate themselves." *Miranda* held that "the prosecution may not use statements, whether exculpatory or inculpatory, stemming from custodial interrogation of the defendant unless it demonstrates the use of procedural safeguards effective to secure the privilege against self-incrimination." *Id.*, at 444, 86 S.Ct., at 1612. Thus, absent other fully effective procedures, a person in custody must receive certain warnings before any official interrogation, including that he has a "right to remain silent" and that "anything said can and will be used against the individual in court." *Id.*, at 467–469, 86 S.Ct., at 1624–1625. The purpose of these admonitions is to combat what the Court saw as "inherently compelling pressures" at work on the person and to provide him with an awareness of the Fifth Amendment privilege and the consequences of foregoing it, which is the prerequisite for "an intelligent decision as to its exercise." *Ibid.*

The considerations calling for the accused to be warned prior to custodial interrogation apply with no less force to the pretrial psychiatric examination at issue here. Respondent was in custody at the Dallas County Jail when the examination was ordered and when it was conducted. That respondent was questioned by a psychiatrist designated by the trial court to conduct a neutral competency examination, rather than by a police officer, government informant, or prosecuting attorney, is immaterial. When Dr. Grigson went beyond simply reporting to the court on the issue of competence and testified for the prosecution at the penalty phase on the crucial issue of respondent's future dangerousness, his role changed and became essentially like that of an agent of the State recounting unwarned statements made in a post-arrest custodial setting. During the

psychiatric evaluation, respondent assuredly was "faced with a phase of the adversary system" and was "not in the presence of [a] person[ ] acting solely in his interest." *Id.*, at 469, 86 S.Ct., at 1625. Yet he was given no indication that the compulsory examination would be used to gather evidence necessary to decide whether, if convicted, he should be sentenced to death. He was not informed that, accordingly, he had a constitutional right not to answer the questions put to him.

[10, 11] The Fifth Amendment privilege is "as broad as the mischief against which it seeks to guard," *Counselman v. Hitchcock*, 142 U.S. 547, 562, 12 S.Ct. 195, 198, 35 L.Ed 1110 (1892), and the privilege is fulfilled only when a criminal defendant is guaranteed the right "to remain silent unless he chooses to speak in the unfettered exercise of his own will, and to suffer no penalty . . . for such silence."[11] *Malloy v. Hogan*, 378 U.S. 1, 8, 84 S.Ct. 1489, 1493–1494, 12 L.Ed.2d 653 (1964). We agree with the Court of Appeals that respondent's Fifth Amendment rights were violated by the admission of Dr. Grigson's testimony at the penalty phase.[12]

---

[11] While recognizing that attempts to coerce a defendant to submit to psychiatric inquiry on his future dangerousness might include the penalty of prosecutorial comment on his refusal to be examined, the Court of Appeals noted that making such a remark and allowing the jury to draw its own conclusions "might clash with [this Court's] insistence that capital sentencing procedures be unusually reliable." 602 F.2d, at 707. See also *Griffin v. California*, 380 U.S. 609, 85 S.Ct. 1229, 14 L.Ed.2d 106 (1965).

[12] For the reasons stated by the Court of Appeals, we reject the State's argument that respondent waived his Fifth Amendment claim by failing to make a timely,

[12, 13] A criminal defendant, who neither initiates a psychiatric evaluation nor attempts to introduce any psychiatric evidence, may not be compelled to respond to a psychiatrist if his statements can be used against him at a capital sentencing proceeding. Because respondent did not voluntarily consent to the pretrial psychiatric examination after being informed of his right to remain silent and the possible use of his statements, the State could not rely on what he said to Dr. Grigson to establish his future dangerousness. If, upon being adequately warned, respondent had indicated that he would not answer Dr. Grigson's questions, the validly ordered competency examination nevertheless could have proceeded upon the condition that the results would be applied solely for that purpose. In such circumstances, the proper conduct and use of competency and sanity examinations are not frustrated, but the State must make its case on future dangerousness in some other way.

"Volunteered statements . . . are not barred by the Fifth Amendment," but under *Miranda v. Arizona, supra,* we must conclude that, when faced while in custody with a court-ordered psychiatric inquiry, respondent's statements to Dr. Grigson were not "given freely and voluntarily without any compelling influences" and, as such, could be used as the State did at the penalty phase only if respondent had been apprised of his rights and had knowingly decided to waive them. *Id.,* at 478, 86 S.Ct., at 1630. These safeguards of the Fifth Amendment privilege were not afforded

respondent and, thus, his death sentence cannot stand.[13]

(B)

[14, 15] When respondent was examined by Dr. Grigson, he already had been indicted and an attorney had been appointed to represent him. The Court of Appeals concluded that he had a Sixth Amendment right to the assistance of counsel before submitting to the pretrial psychiatric interview. 602 F.2d, at 708–709. We agree.

The Sixth Amendment, made applicable to the states through the Fourteenth Amendment, provides that "[i]n all criminal prosecutions, the accused shall enjoy the right . . . to have the Assistance of Counsel for his defense." The "vital" need for a lawyer's advice and aid during the pretrial phase was recognized by the Court nearly 50 years ago in *Powell v. Alabama,* 287 U.S. 45, 57, 71, 53 S.Ct. 55, 60, 65, 77 L.Ed. 158 (1932). Since then, we have held that the right to counsel granted by the Sixth Amendment means that a person is entitled to the help of a lawyer "at or after the time that adversary judicial proceedings have been initiated against him . . . whether by way of formal charge, preliminary hearing, indictment, information, or arraignment." *Kirby v. Illinois,* 406 U.S. 682, 688–689, 92 S.Ct. 1877, 1882, 32 L.Ed.2d 411 (1972) (plurality opinion); *Moore v. Illinois,* 434 U.S. 220, 226–229, 98 S.Ct. 458, 463–465, 54 L.Ed.2d 424 (1977). And in *United States v. Wade,* 388 U.S. 218, 226–227, 87 S.Ct. 1926, 1932, 18 L.Ed.2d 1149 (1967), the Court explained:

---

specific objection to Dr. Grigson's testimony at trial. See 602 F.2d, at 708, n. 19. In addition, we note that the State did not present the waiver argument in its petition for certiorari. See this Court's Rule 40(1)(d)(2) (1970).

---

[13] Of course, we do not hold that the same Fifth Amendment concerns are necessarily presented by all types of interviews and examinations that might be ordered or relied upon to inform a sentencing determination.

"It is central to [the Sixth Amendment] principle that in addition to counsel's presence at trial, the accused is guaranteed that he need not stand alone against the State at any stage of the prosecution, formal or informal, in court or out, where counsel's absence might derogate from the accused's right to a fair trial." (Footnote omitted.)

See *United States v. Henry*, 447 U.S. 264, 100 S.Ct. 2183, 65 L.Ed.2d 115 (1980); *Massiah v. United States*, U.S. 201, 84 S.Ct. 1199, 12 L.Ed.2d 246 (1964). See also *White v. Maryland*, 373 U.S. 59, 83 S.Ct. 1050, 10 L.Ed.2d 193 (1963); *Hamilton v. Alabama*, 368 U.S. 52, 82 S.Ct. 157, 7 L.Ed.2d 114 (1961).

Here, respondent's Sixth Amendment right to counsel clearly had attached when Dr. Grigson examined him at the Dallas County Jail,[14] and their interview proved to be a "critical stage" of the aggregate proceedings against respondent. See *Coleman v. Alabama*, 399 U.S. 1, 7–10, 90 S.Ct. 1999, 2002–2004, 26 L.Ed.2d 387 (1970) (plurality opinion); *Powell v. Alabama, supra*, 287 U.S., at 57, 53 S.Ct., at 60. Defense counsel, however, were not notified in advance that the psychiatric examination would encompass the issue of their client's future dangerousness,[15] and respondent was denied the assistance of his attorneys in making the significant decision of whether to submit to the examination and to what end the psychiatrist's findings could be employed.

Because "[a] layman may not be aware of the precise scope, the nuances, and the boundaries of his Fifth Amendment privilege," the assertion of that right "often depends upon legal advise from someone who is trained and skilled in the subject matter." *Maness v. Meyers*, 419 U.S. 449, 466, 95 S.Ct. 584, 595, 42 L.Ed.2d 574 (1975). As the Court of Appeals observed, the decision to be made regarding the proposed psychiatric evaluation is "literally a life or death matter" and is "difficult . . . even for an attorney" because it requires "a knowledge of what other evidence is available, of the particular psychiatrist's biases and predilections, [and] of possible alternative strategies at the sentencing hearing." 602 F.2d, at 708. It follows logically from our precedents that a defendant should not be forced to resolve such an important issue without "the guiding hand of counsel." *Powell v. Alabama, supra*, 287 U.S., at 69, 53 S.Ct., at 64.

Therefore, in addition to Fifth Amendment considerations, the death penalty was improperly imposed on respondent because the psychiatric

---

[14] Because psychiatric examinations of the type at issue here are conducted after adversary proceedings have been instituted, we are not concerned in this case with the limited right to the appointment and presence of counsel recognized as a Fifth Amendment safeguard in *Miranda v. Arizona, supra*, 384 U.S., at 471–473, 86 S.Ct., at 1626–1627. See *Edwards v. Arizona*, U.S. _____, 101 S.Ct. 1880, 67 L.Ed.2d (1981). Rather, the issue before us is whether a defendant's Sixth Amendment right to the assistance of counsel is abridged when the defendant is not given prior opportunity to consult with counsel about his participation in the psychiatric examination. But cf. n. 15, *infra*.

Respondent does not assert, and the Court of Appeals did not find, any constitutional right to have counsel actually present during the examination. In fact, the Court of Appeals recognized that "an attorney present during the psychiatric interview could contribute little and might seriously disrupt the examination." 602 F.2d at 708. Cf. *Thornton v. Corcoran*, 132 U.S.App.D.C. 232, 242, 248, 407 F.2d 695, 705, 711 (1969) (opinion concurring in part and dissenting in part).

[15] It is not clear that defense counsel were even informed prior to the examination that Dr. Grigson had been appointed by the trial judge to determine respondent's competency to stand trial. See n. 5, *supra*.

examination on which Dr. Grigson testified at the penalty phase proceeded in violation of respondent's Sixth Amendment right to the assistance of counsel.[16]

C

Our holding based on the Fifth and Sixth Amendments will not prevent the State in capital cases from proving the defendant's future dangerousness as required by statute. A defendant may request or consent to a psychiatric examination concerning future dangerousness in the hope of escaping the death penalty. In addition, a different situation arises where a defendant intends to introduce psychiatric evidence at the penalty phase. See n. 10, *supra*.

Moreover, under the Texas capital sentencing procedure, the inquiry necessary for the jury's resolution of the future dangerousness issue is in no sense confined to the province of psychiatric experts. Indeed, some in the psychiatric community are of the view that clinical predictions as to whether a person would or would not commit violent acts in the future are "fundamentally of very low reliability" and that psychiatrists possess no special qualifications for making such forecasts. See Report of the American Psychiatric Association Task Force on Clinical Aspects of the Violent Individual 23–30,

33 (1974); A. Stone Mental Health and Law: A System in Transition 27–36 (1975); Brief for American Psychiatric Association as *Amicus Curiae* 11–17.

In *Jurek v. Texas*, 428 U.S. 262, 96 S.Ct. 2950, 49 L.Ed.2d 929 (1976), we held that the Texas capital sentencing statute is not unconstitutional on its face. As to the jury question on future dangerousness, the joint opinion announcing the judgment emphasized that a defendant is free to present whatever mitigating factors he may be able to show, *e.g.*, the range and severity of his past criminal conduct, his age, and the circumstances surrounding the crime for which he is being sentenced. *Id.*, at 272–273, 96 S.Ct., at 2956–2957. The State, of course, can use the same type of evidence in seeking to establish a defendant's propensity to commit other violent acts.

In responding to the argument that foretelling future behavior is impossible, the joint opinion stated:

"[P]rediction of future criminal conduct is an essential element in many of the decisions rendered throughout our criminal justice system. The decision whether to admit a defendant to bail, for instance, must often turn on a judge's prediction of the defendant's future conduct. And any sentencing authority must predict a convicted person's probable future conduct when it engages in the process of determining what punishment to impose. For those sentenced to prison, these same predictions must be made by parole authorities. The task that a Texas jury must perform in answering the statutory question in issue is thus basically no different from the task performed countless times each day throughout the American system of criminal justice." (Footnotes omitted.) *Id.*, at 275–276, 96 S.Ct., at 2957–2958.

While in no sense disapproving the use of psychiatric testimony bearing on the issue of future dangerousness, the holding in *Jurek* was guided by recognition that the inquiry mandated by

---

[16] We do not hold that respondent was precluded from waiving this constitutional right. Waivers of the assistance of counsel, however, "must no only be voluntary, but constitute a knowing and intelligent relinquishment or abandonment of a known right or privilege, a matter which depends . . . 'upon the particular facts and circumstances surrounding [each] case. . . .'" *Edwards v. Arizona, supra,* _____ U.S., at _____ , 101 S.Ct., at 1883–1884, quoting *Johnson v. Zerbst*, 304 U.S. 458, 464, 58 S.Ct. 1019, 1023, 82 L.Ed. 1461 (1938). No such waiver has been shown, or even alleged, here.

Texas law does not require resort to medical experts.

III

Respondent's Fifth and Sixth Amendment rights were abridged by the State's introduction of Dr. Grigson's testimony at the penalty phase, and, as the Court of Appeals concluded, his death sentence must be vacated.[17] Because respondent's underlying conviction has not been challenged and remains undisturbed, the State is free to conduct further proceedings not inconsistent with this opinion. Accordingly, the judgment of the Court of Appeals is

Affirmed.

Justice BRENNAN.

I join the Court's opinion. I also adhere to my position that the death penalty is in all circumstances unconstitutional.

Justice MARSHALL, concurring in part.

I join in all but Part II-C of the opinion of the Court. I adhere to my consistent view that the death penalty is under all circumstances cruel and unusual punishment forbidden by the Eighth and Fourteenth Amendments. I therefore am unable to join the suggestion in Part II-C that the penalty may ever be constitutionally imposed.

---

[17] Because of our disposition of respondent's Fifth and Sixth Amendment claims, we need not reach the question of whether the failure to give advance notice of Dr. Grigson's appearance as a witness for the State deprived respondent of due process.

Justice STEWART, with whom Justice POWELL joins, concurring in the judgment.

The respondent had been indicted for murder and a lawyer had been appointed to represent him before he was examined by Dr. Grigson at the behest of the State. Yet that examination took place without previous notice to the respondent's counsel. The Sixth and Fourteenth Amendments as applied in such cases as *Massiah v. United States,* 377 U.S. 201, 84 S.Ct. 1199, 12 L.Ed.2d 246, and *Brewer v. Williams,* 430 U.S. 387, 97 S.Ct. 1232, 51 L.Ed.2d 424, made impermissible the introduction of Dr. Grigson's testimony against the respondent at any stage of his trial.

I would for this reason affirm the judgment before us without reaching the other issues discussed by the Court.

Justice REHNQUIST, concurring in the judgment.

I concur in the judgment because, under *Massiah v. United States,* 377 U.S. 201, 84 S.Ct. 1199, 12 L.Ed.2d 246 (1964), respondent's counsel should have been notified prior to Dr. Grigson's examination of respondent. As the Court notes, *ante,* at 1876, respondent had been indicted and an attorney had been appointed to represent him. Counsel was entitled to be made aware of Dr. Grigson's activities involving his client and to advise and prepare his client accordingly. This is by no means to say that respondent had any right to have his counsel present at any examination. In this regard I join the Court's careful delimiting of the Sixth Amendment issue, *ante,* at 1877, n. 14.

Since this is enough to decide the case, I would not go on to consider the

Fifth Amendment issues and cannot subscribe to the Court's resolution of them. I am not convinced that any Fifth Amendment rights were implicated by Dr. Grigson's examination of respondent. Although the psychiatrist examined respondent prior to trial, he only testified concerning the examination after respondent stood convicted. As the court in *Hollis v. Smith*, 571 F.2d 685, 690–691 (CA2 1978) analyzed the issue, "The psychiatrist's interrogation of [defendant] on subjects presenting no threat of disclosure of prosecutable crimes, in the belief that the substance of [defendant's] responses or the way in which he gave them might cast light on the manner of man he was, involved no 'compelled testimonial self-incrimination' even though the consequence might be more severe punishment."

Even if there are Fifth Amendment rights involved in this case, respondent never invoked these rights when confronted with Dr. Grigson's questions. The Fifth Amendment privilege against compulsory self-incrimination is not self-executing. "Although *Miranda*'s requirement of specific warnings creates a limited exception to the rule that the privilege must be claimed, the exception does not apply outside the context of the inherently coercive custodial interrogations for which it was designed." *Roberts v. United States*, 445 U.S. 552, 560, 100 S.Ct. 1358, 1364, 63 L.Ed.2d 622 (1980). The *Miranda* requirements were certainly not designed by this Court with psychiatric examinations in mind. Respondent was simply not in the inherently coercive situation considered in *Miranda*. He had already been indicted, and counsel had been appointed to represent him. No claim is raised that respondent's answers to Dr. Grigson's questions were "involuntary" in the normal sense of the word. Unlike the police officers

in *Miranda*, Dr. Grigson was not questioning respondent in order to ascertain his guilt or innocence. Particularly since it is not necessary to decide this case, I would not extend the *Miranda* requirements to cover psychiatric examinations such as the one involved here.

[200] DANIEL M'NAGHTEN'S CASE.
May 26, June 19, 1843.

[Mew's Dig. i. 349; iv. 1112. S.C. 8 Scott N.R. 595; 1 C. and K. 130; 4 St. Tr. N.S. 847. The rules laid down in this case have been accepted in the main as an authoritative statement of the law (cf. *Reg.* v. *Townley*, 1863, 3 F. and F. 839; *Reg.* v. *Southey*, 1865, 4 F. and F. 864; *Reg.* v. *Leigh*, 1866, 4 F. and F. 919). But they have been adversely criticised both by legal and medical text writers (see 2 Steph. *Hist. Crim. Law*, 124–186; Mayne *Ind. Crim. Law* (ed. 1896), 368), have been rejected by many of the American States (see e.g. *Parsons* v. *State*, 1887, 81 Ala. 577), and frequently receive a liberal interpretation in England. On point as to questions to the Judges, see note to *London and Westminster Bank Case*, 2 Cl. and F. 191.]

Murder—Evidence—Insanity.

The House of Lords has a right to require the Judges to answer abstract questions of existing law (see London and Westminster Bank Case, *ante* [2 Cl. and F.], p. 191 [and note thereto].

Notwithstanding a party accused did an act, which was in itself criminal, under the influence of insane delusion, with a view of redressing or revenging some supposed grievance or injury, or of producing some public benefit, he is nevertheless punishable if he knew at the time that he was acting contrary to law.

That if the accused was conscious that the act was one which he ought not to do; and if the act was at the same time contrary to law, he is punishable. In all cases of this kind the jurors ought to be told that every man is presumed to be sane, and to possess a sufficient degree of reason to be responsible for his crimes, until the contrary be proved to their satisfaction: and that to establish a defence on the ground of insanity, it must be clearly proved that at the time of committing the act the party accused was labouring under such a defect of reason, from disease of the mind, as not to know the nature and quality of the act he was doing, or as not to know that what he was doing was wrong.

That a party labouring under a partial delusion must be considered in the same situation, as to responsibility, as if the facts, in respect to which the delusion exists, were real.

That where an accused person is supposed to be insane, a medical man, who has been present in Court and heard the evidence, may be asked, as a matter of science, whether the facts stated by the witness, supposing them to be true, show a state of mind incapable of distinguishing between right and wrong.

The prisoner had been indicted for that he, on the 20th day of January 1843, at the parish of Saint Martin in the Fields, in the county of Middlesex, and within the jurisdiction of the Central Criminal Court, in and upon one Edward Drummond, feloniously, wilfully, and of his malice aforethought, did make an assault; and that the said Daniel M'Naghten, a certain pistol of the value of 20s., loaded and [201]

charged with gunpowder and a leaden bullet (which pistol he in his right hand had and held), to, against and upon the said Edward Drummond, feloniously, wilfully, and of his malice aforethought, did shoot and discharge; and that the said Daniel M'Naghten, with the leaden bullet aforesaid, out of the pistol aforesaid, by force of the gunpowder, etc., the said Edward Drummond, in and upon the back of him the said Edward Drummond, feloniously, etc. did strike, penetrate and wound, giving to the said Edward Drummond, in and upon the back of the said Edward Drummond, one mortal wound, etc., of which mortal wound the said E. Drummond languished until the 25th of April and then died; and that by the means aforesaid, he the prisoner did kill and murder the said Edward Drummond. The prisoner pleaded Not guilty.

Evidence having been given of the fact of the shooting of Mr. Drummond, and of his death in consequence thereof, witnesses were called on the part of the prisoner, to prove that he was not, at the time of committing the act, in a sound state of mind. The medical evidence was in substance this: That persons of otherwise sound mind, might be affected by morbid delusions: that the prisoner was in that condition: that a person so labouring under a morbid delusion, might have a moral perception of right and wrong, but that in the case of the prisoner it was a delusion which carried him away beyond the power of his own control, and left him no such perception; and that he was not capable of exercising any control over acts which had connexion with his delusion: that it was of the nature of the disease with which the prisoner was affected, to go on gradually until it had reached a climax, when it burst forth with irresistible [202] intensity: that a man might go on for years quietly, though at the same time under its influence, but would all at once break out into the most extravagant and violent paroxysms.

Some of the witnesses who gave this evidence, had previously examined the prisoner: others had never seen him till he appeared in Court, and they formed their opinions on hearing the evidence given by the other witnesses.

Lord Chief Justice Tindal (in his charge):—The question to be determined is, whether at the time the act in question was committed, the prisoner had or had not the use of his understanding, so as to know that he was doing a wrong or wicked act. If the jurors should be of opinion that the prisoner was not sensible, at the time he committed it, that he was violating the laws both of God and man, then he would be entitled to a verdict in his favour: but if, on the contrary, they were of opinion that when he committed the act he was in a sound state of mind, then their verdict must be against him.

Verdict, Not guilty, on the ground of insanity.

This verdict, and the question of the nature and extent of the unsoundness of mind which would excuse the commission of a felony of this sort, having been made the subject of debate in the House of Lords (the 6th and 13th March 1843; see Hansard's Debates, vol. 67, pp. 288, 714), it was determined to take the opinion of the Judges on the law governing such cases. Accordingly, on the 26th of May, all the Judges attended their Lordships, but no questions were then put.

On the 19th of June, the Judges again attended the House of Lords; when (no argument having been [203] had) the following questions of law were propounded to them:—

1st. What is the law respecting alleged crimes committed by persons afflicted with insane delusion, in respect of one or more particular subjects or persons; as, for instance, where at the time of the commission of the alleged crime, the accused knew he was acting contrary to law, but did the act complained of with a view, under the influence of insane delusion, of redressing or revenging some supposed grievance or injury, or of producing some supposed public benefit?

2d. What are the proper questions to be submitted to the jury, when a person alleged to be afflicted with insane delusion respecting one or more particular subjects of persons, is charged with the commission of a crime (murder, for example), and insanity is set up as a defence?

3d. In what terms ought the question to be left to the jury, as to the prisoner's state of mind at the time when the act was committed?

4th. If a person under an insane delusion as to existing facts, commits an offence in consequence thereof, is he thereby excused?

5th. Can a medical man conversant with the disease of insanity, who never saw the prisoner previously to the trial, but who was present during the whole trial and the examination of all the witnesses, be asked his opinion as to the state of the prisoner's mind at the time of the commission of the alleged crime, or his opinion whether the prisoner was conscious at the time of doing the act, that he was acting contrary to law, or whether he was labouring under any and what delusion at the time?

[204] Mr. Justice Maule:—I feel great difficulty in answering the questions put by your Lordships on this occasion:—First, because they do not appear to arise out of and are not put with reference to a particular case, or for a particular purpose, which might explain or limit the generality of their terms, so that full answers to them ought to be applicable to every possible state of facts, not inconsistent with

those assumed in the questions: this difficulty is the greater, from the practical experience both of the bar and the Court being confined to questions arising out of the facts of particular cases:—Secondly, because I have heard no argument at your Lordships' bar or elsewhere, on the subject of these questions; the want of which I feel the more, the greater are the number and extent of questions which might be raised in argument:—and Thirdly, from a fear of which I cannot divest myself, that as these questions relate to matters of criminal law of great importance and frequent occurrence, the answers to them by the Judges may embarrass the administration of justice, when they are cited in criminal trials. For these reasons I should have been glad if my learned brethren would have joined me in praying your Lordships to excuse us from answering these questions; but as I do not think they ought to induce me to ask that indulgence for myself individually, I shall proceed to give such answers as I can, after the very short time which I have had to consider the questions, and under the difficulties I have mentioned; fearing that my answers may be as little satisfactory to others as they are to myself.

The first question, as I understand it, is, in effect, What is the law respecting the alleged crime, when at the time of the commission of it, the accused knew he was acting contrary to the law, but did the act [205] with a view, under the influence of insane delusion, of redressing or revenging some supposed grievance or injury, or of producing some supposed public benefit?—If I were to understand this question according to the strict meaning of its terms, it would require, in order to answer it, a solution of all questions of law which could arise on the circumstances stated in the question, either by explicitly stating and answering such

questions, or by stating some principles or rules which would suffice for their solution. I am quite unable to do so, and, indeed, doubt whether it be possible to be done; and therefore request to be permitted to answer the question only so far as it comprehends the question, whether a person, circumstanced as stated in the question, is, for that reason only, to be found not guilty of a crime respecting which the question of his guilt has been duly raised in a criminal proceeding? and I am of opinion that he is not. There is no law, that I am aware of, that makes persons in the state described in the question not responsible for their criminal acts. To render a person irresponsible for crime on account of unsoundness of mind, the unsoundness should, according to the law as it has long been understood and held, be such as rendered him incapable of knowing right from wrong. The terms used in the question cannot be said (with reference only to the usage of language) to be equivalent to a description of this kind and degree of unsoundness of mind. If the state described in the question be one which involves or is necessarily connected with such an unsoundness, this is not a matter of law but of physiology, and not of that obvious and familiar kind as to be inferred without proof.

Second, the questions necessarily to be submitted to the jury, are those questions of fact which are [206] raised on the record. In a criminal trial, the question commonly is, whether the accused be guilty or not guilty: but, in order to assist the jury in coming to a right conclusion on this necessary and ultimate question, it is usual and proper to submit such subordinate or intermediate questions, as the course which the trial has taken may have made it convenient to direct their attention to. What those questions are, and the manner of submitting them, is a matter of discretion for the Judge: a discretion to be guided by a consideration of all the circumstances attending the inquiry. In performing this duty, it is sometimes necessary or convenient to inform the jury as to the law; and if, on a trial such as is suggested in the question, he should have occasion to state what kind and degree of insanity would amount to a defence, it should be stated conformably to what I have mentioned in my answer to the first question, as being, in my opinion, the law on this subject.

Third, there are no terms which the Judge is by law required to use. They should not be inconsistent with the law as above stated, but should be such as, in the discretion of the Judge, are proper to assist the jury in coming to a right conclusion as to the guilt of the accused.

Fourth, the answer which I have given to the first question, is applicable to this.

Fifth, whether a question can be asked, depends, not merely on the questions of fact raised on the record, but on the course of the cause at the time it is proposed to ask it; and the state of an inquiry as to the guilt of a person charged with a crime, and defended on the ground of insanity, may be such, that a question as either of those suggested, is proper to be asked and answered, though the witness has [207] never seen the person before the trial, and though he has merely been present and heard the witnesses: these circumstances, of his never having seen the person before, and of his merely been present at the trial, not being necessarily sufficient, as it seems to me, to exclude the lawfulness of a question which is otherwise lawful; though I will not say that an inquiry might not be in such a state, is that these circumstances should have such an effect.

Supposing there is nothing else in the state of the trial to make the questions suggested proper to be asked and answered, except that the witness had been present and heard the evidence; it is to be considered whether that is enough to sustain the question. In principle it is open to this objection, that as the opinion of the witness is founded on those conclusions of fact which he forms from the evidence, and as it does not appear what those conclusions are, it may be that the evidence he gives is on such an assumption of facts, as makes it irrelevant to the inquiry. But such questions have been very frequently asked, and the evidence to which they are directed has been given, and has never, that I am aware of, been successfully objected to. Evidence, most clearly open to this objection, and on the admission of which the event of a most important trial probably turned, was received in the case of *The Queen* v. *M'Naghten*, tried at the Central Criminal Court in March last, before the Lord Chief Justice, Mr. Justice Williams, and Mr. Justice Coleridge, in which counsel of the highest eminence were engaged on both sides; and I think the course and practice of receiving such evidence, confirmed by the very high authority of these Judges, who not only received it, but left it, as I understand, to the jury, without any remark derogating from its [208] weight, ought to be held to warrant its reception, notwithstanding the objection in principle to which it may be open. In cases even where the course of practice in criminal law has been unfavourable to parties accused, and entirely contrary to the most obvious principles of justice and humanity, as well as those of law, it has been held that such practice constitute the law, and could not be altered without the authority of Parliament.

Lord Chief Justice Tindal:—My Lords, Her Majesty's Judges (with the exception of Mr. Justice Maule, who has stated his opinion to your Lordships), in answering the questions proposed to them by your Lordships' House, think it right, in the first place, to state that they have forborne entering into any particular discussion upon these questions, from the extreme and almost insuperable difficulty of applying those answers to cases in which the facts are not brought judicially before them. The facts of each particular case must of necessity present themselves with endless variety, and with every shade of difference in each case; and as it is their duty to declare the law upon each particular case, on facts proved before them, and after hearing argument of counsel thereon, they deem it at once impracticable, and at the same time dangerous to the administration of justice, if it were practicable, to attempt to make minute applications of the principles involved in the answers given by them to your Lordships' questions.

They have therefore confined their answers to the statement of that which they hold to be the law upon the abstract questions proposed by your Lordships; and as they deem it unnecessary, in this peculiar case, to deliver their opinions seriatim, and as all concur in [209] the same opinion, they desire me to express such their unanimous opinion to your Lordships.

The first question proposed by your Lordships is this: "What is the law respecting alleged crimes committed by persons afflicted with insane delusion in respect of one or more particular subjects or persons: as, for instance, where at the time of the commission of the alleged crime the accused knew he was acting contrary to law, but did the act complained of with a view, under the influence of insane delusion, of redressing or revenging some supposed grievance or injury, or of producing some supposed public benefit?"

In answer to which question, assuming that your Lordships' inquiries are confined to those persons who labour under such partial delusions only, and are not in other respects insane, we are of opinion that, notwithstanding the party accused did the act complained of with a view, under the influence of insane delusion, of redressing or revenging some supposed grievance or injury, or of producing some public benefit, he is nevertheless punishable according to the nature of the crime committed, if he knew at the time of committing such crime that he was acting contrary to law; by which expression we understand your Lordships to mean the law of the land.

Your Lordships are pleased to inquire of us, secondly, "What are the proper questions to be submitted to the jury, where a person alleged to be afflicted with insane delusion respecting one or more particular subjects or persons, is charged with the commission of a crime (murder, for example), and insanity is set up as a defence?" And, thirdly, "In what terms ought the question to be left to the jury as to the prisoner's state of mind at the time when [210] the act was committed?" And as these two questions appear to us to be more conveniently answered together, we have to submit our opinion to be, that the jurors ought to be told in all cases that every man is to be presumed to be sane, and to possess a sufficient degree of reason to be responsible for his crimes, until the contrary be proved to their satisfaction; and that to establish a defence on the ground of insanity, it must be clearly proved that, at the time of the committing of the act, the party accused was labouring under such a defect of reason, from disease of the mind, as not to know the nature and quality of the act he was doing; or, if he did know it, that he did not know he was doing what was wrong. The mode of putting the latter part of the question to the jury on these occasions has generally been, whether the accused at the time of doing the act knew the difference between right and wrong: which mode, though rarely, if ever, leading to any mistake with the jury, is not, as we conceive, so accurate when put generally and in the abstract, as when put with reference to the party's knowledge of right and wrong in respect to the very act with which he is charged. If the question were to be put as to the knowledge of the accused solely and exclusively with reference to the law of the land, it might tend to confound the jury, by inducing them to believe that an actual knowledge of the law of the land was essential in order to lead to a conviction; whereas the law is administered upon the principle that every one must be taken conclusively to know it, without proof that he does know it. If the accused was conscious that the act was one which he ought not to do, and if that act was at the same time contrary to the law of the land, he is punishable; and the usual course therefore [211] has been to leave the question to the jury, whether the party accused had a sufficient degree of reason to know that he was doing an act that was wrong: and this course we think is correct, accompanied with such observations and explanations as the circumstances of each particular case may require.

The fourth question which your Lordships have proposed to us is this:—"If a person under an insane delusion as to existing facts, commits an offense in consequence thereof, is he thereby excused?" To which question the answer must of course depend on the nature of the delusion: but, making the same assumption as we did before, namely, that he labours under such partial delusion only, and is not in other respects insane, we think he must be considered in the same situation as to responsibility as if the facts with respect to which the delusion exists were

real. For example, if under the influence of his delusion he supposed another man to be in the act of attempting to take away his life, and he kills that man, as he supposes, in self-defense, he would be exempt from punishment. If his delusion was that the deceased had inflicted a serious injury to his character and fortune, and he killed him in revenge for such supposed injury, he would be liable to punishment.

The question lastly proposed by your Lordships is:—"Can a medical man conversant with the disease of insanity, who never saw the prisoner previously to the trial, but who was present during the whole trial and the examination of all the witnesses, be asked his opinion as to the state of the prisoner's mind at the time of the commission of the alleged crime, or his opinion whether the prisoner was conscious at the time of doing the act that he was acting contrary to law, or whether he was labouring under any and [212] what delusion at the time?" In answer thereto, we state to your Lordships, that we think the medical man, under the circumstances supposed, cannot in strictness be asked his opinion in the terms above stated, because each of those questions involves the determination of the truth of the facts deposed to, which it is for the jury to decide, and the questions are not mere questions upon a matter of science, in which case such evidence is admissible. But where the facts are admitted or not disputed, and the question becomes substantially one of science only, it may be convenient to allow the question to be put in that general form, though the same cannot be insisted on as a matter of right.

Lord Brougham:—My Lords, the opinions of the learned Judges, and the very able manner in which they have been presented to the House, deserve our best thanks. One of the learned Judges has expressed his regret that these questions were not argued by counsel. Generally speaking, it is most important that in questions put for the consideration of the Judges, they should have all that assistance which is afforded to them by an argument by counsel: but at the same time, there can be no doubt of your Lordships' right to put, in this way, abstract questions of law to the Judges, the answer to which might be necessary to your Lordships in your legislative capacity. There is a precedent for this course, in the memorable instance of Mr. Fox's Bill on the law of libel; where, before passing the Bill, this House called on the Judges to give their opinions on what was the law as it then existed.

Lord Campbell:—My Lords, I cannot avoid express-[213]-ing my satisfaction, that the noble and learned Lord on the woolsack carried into effect his desire to put these questions to the Judges. It was most fit that the opinions of the Judges should be asked on these matters, the settling of which is not a mere matter of speculation; for your Lordships may be called on, in your legislative capacity, to change the law; and before doing so, it is proper that you should be satisfied beyond doubt what the law really is. It is desirable to have such questions argued at the bar, but such a course is not always practicable. Your Lordships have been reminded of one precedent for this proceeding, but there is a still more recent instance; the Judges having been summoned in the case of the Canada Reserves, to express their opinions on what was then the law on that subject. The answers given by the Judges are most highly satisfactory, and will be of the greatest use in the administration of justice.

Lord Cottenham:—My Lords, I fully concur with the opinion now expressed, as to the obligations we owe to the Judges. It is true that they cannot be required to say what would be the construction of a Bill, not in existence as a law at the moment at which the question is put to them; but they may be called on to assist your Lordships, in declaring their opinions upon abstract questions of existing law.

Lord Wynford:—My Lords, I never doubted that your Lordships possess the power to call on the Judges to give their opinions upon questions of existing law, proposed to them as these questions have been. I myself recollect, that when I had the honour to hold the office of Lord Chief Justice of the Court of [214] Common Pleas, I communicated to the House the opinions of the Judges on questions of this sort, framed with reference to the usury laws. Upon the opinion of the Judges thus delivered to the House by me, a Bill was founded, and afterwards passed into a law.

The Lord Chancellor:—My Lords, I entirely concur in the opinion given by my noble and learned friends, as to our right to have the opinions of the Judges on abstract questions of existing law; and I agree that we owe our thanks to the Judges, for the attention and learning with which they have answered the questions now put to them.

The People of the State of Colorado, Plaintiff-Appellant, v. Michael Joseph Wright, Defendant-Appellee. No. 80SA256. Supreme Court of Colorado, En Banc. July 26, 1982.

The District Court, El Paso County, Joe A. Cannon, J., entered judgment finding the defendant not guilty by reason of insanity, and the People appealed. The Supreme Court, Lee, J., held that: (1) conclusion of trier of fact that the People had failed to prove sanity beyond a reasonable doubt and that the defendant, though not suffering from an organic brain syndrome, had a comprehension of reality which was too distorted for him to be held legally accountable for his criminal conduct was supported by record, and (2) expert testimony concerning the psychological testing of the defendant, results of those tests, the nature of the condition of minimal brain dysfunction, and its relation to poor impulse control and lack of willpower was admissible as relevant to issue of defendant's sanity despite claim of its unreliability.

Affirmed

1.   CRIMINAL LAW   311, 331

Every criminal defendant is presumed sane, but once any evidence of insanity is introduced at trial, burden of proof is on the People to prove sanity beyond a reasonable doubt. C.R.S.1973, 16–8–101, 18–1–802.

2.   CRIMINAL LAW   740

When evidence of sanity is in dispute, fact finder must resolve conflict in testimony and weigh all relevant evidence to determine whether defendant was legally insane at time of act. C.R.S.1973, 16–8–101, 18–1–802.

3.   CRIMINAL LAW   48

One who is legally insane at time of commission of act which would otherwise be criminal is not criminally accountable and is excused from punishment. C.R.S.1973, 16–8–101, 18–1–802.

4.   CRIMINAL LAW   494

Where expert testimony on the issue of sanity is in conflict, the resolution of

the conflict and the weight to be given to the testimony is solely the province of the trier of fact. C.R.S.1973, 16–8–101, 18–1–802.

5.   CRIMINAL LAW   740

The question of sanity in a criminal case is an issue of fact to be determined by the trier of fact. C.R.S.1973, 16–8–101, 18–1–802.

6.   HOMICIDE   237

Conclusion of trier of fact in prosecution for first-degree murder that the People had failed to prove sanity beyond a reasonable doubt and that the defendant, though not suffering from an organic brain syndrome, had a comprehension of reality which was too distorted for him to be held legally accountable for his criminal conduct was supported by record. C.R.S.1973, 16–8–101, 18–1–802.

7.   CRIMINAL LAW   354, 456

Traditionally, the scope of evidence admissible on the issue of insanity is broad, and even lay persons are free to testify as to the sanity of the defendant if a proper foundation is presented. C.R.S.1973, 16–8–107(2), 16–8–109.

8.   CRIMINAL LAW   488

Expert testimony concerning the psychological testing of the defendant, results of those tests, the nature of the condition of minimal brain dysfunction, and its relation to poor impulse control and lack of willpower was admissible as relevant to issue of defendant's sanity despite claim of its unreliability. C.R.S.1973, 16–8–107(2), 16–8–109.

John Anderson, Special Deputy Dist. Atty., Dennis Faulk, Deputy Dist. Atty., Colorado Springs, for plaintiff-appellant.

J. Gregory Walta, Colorado State Public Defender, Susan L. Fralick, Deputy State Public Defender, Denver, for defendant-appellee.

LEE, Justice.

The defendant, Michael Joseph Wright, was charged with the first degree murder of a child, and he entered a plea of not guilty by reason of insanity. After a trial to the court on the issue of the defendant's sanity, the court entered its order finding the defendant not guilty by reason of insanity. The People bring this appeal of the judgment,[1] arguing that the evidence was insufficient, as a matter of law, to support the trial court's finding of insanity, and that the court improperly considered evidence that the defendant suffered from a minimal brain dysfunction in reaching the conclusion that the defendant was insane. We affirm the judgment.

On the night of July 3, 1979, the defendant was staying in the home of his parents along with his girlfriend, Neva, and her five-month old infant. Neva bathed the infant and put him to bed, then went to bed herself, while the defendant stayed up watching television. In the early morning hours of July 4 the defendant awoke Neva and asked her where the flashlight was, telling her he thought he heard prowlers outside. He took the flashlight and went

out of the house for about twenty minutes. He came back in and engaged in sexual relations with Neva before both fell asleep. The next morning Neva realized that her son was not in his crib. She searched the house and asked the defendant if he knew where the child was. He denied any knowledge of his whereabouts but did not seem concerned. Neva first called relatives and then the police. The defendant sat passively in the house while searchers looked for the child.

The searchers noted that several holes had been recently dug in the field behind the house. The child's body was found buried a short distance from the house. The defendant was questioned by police and eventually confessed to the killing. He described how he had given the baby a bottle of antifreeze to drink, but the child had spit it out. He then took the child into the yard and buried him alive. He later apparently attempted to save the child, but his efforts were too late as the child had already suffocated. He then reburied the child.

The defendant had a history of problems concerning the child. About a week preceding the homicide he took the child for a walk, but returned to the house with the child soaking wet. He told Neva that he had accidentally dropped the child in the creek when he walked across a log bridge. He later admitted that he had attempted to drown the child, but had saved him in time, fearing the wrath of Neva's father should anything happen to the baby. On another occasion he seized the child and refused to give him to his mother when Neva threatened to leave him after an argument. Police were summoned before he finally relinquished the child. On the afternoon prior to the homicide the defendant became angry when he learned that his sister's boyfriend had opened a savings account for the child without his knowledge.

---

[1] Section 16–12–102, C.R.S. 1973 (1978 Repl. Vol. 8), creates a right of appeal in the prosecution regarding any question of law in a criminal case.

After his arrest and incarceration awaiting trial, the defendant repeatedly attempted to contact Neva and wrote to her asking if she still wished to have a baby with him. To the examining psychiatrists he explained that he would be let out of jail if he told his lawyer that he would not do bad things anymore. He expressed his belief that he and Neva could be closer with the child out of the way.

I

[1–3] Every criminal defendant is presumed sane, but once any evidence of insanity is introduced at trial, the burden of proof is on the People to prove sanity beyond a reasonable doubt. *People v. Ware*, 187 Colo. 28, 528 P.2d 224 (1974); *People ex rel. Juhan v. District Court*, 165 Colo. 253, 439 P.2d 741 (1968).[2] When evidence of sanity is in dispute, the fact-finder must resolve the conflict in the testimony, and weigh all relevant evidence to determine whether

---

[2] Legal insanity is defined at section 16–8–101, C.R.S.1973, as follows:

"The applicable test of insanity shall be, and the jury shall be so instructed: 'A person who is so diseased or defective in mind at the time of the commission of the act as to be incapable of distinguishing right from wrong with respect to that act, or being able so to distinguish, has suffered such an impairment of mind by disease or defect as to destroy the willpower and render him incapable of choosing the right and refraining from doing the wrong is not accountable; and this is so howsoever such insanity may be manifested, by irresistible impulse or otherwise. But care should be taken not to confuse such mental disease or defect with moral obliquity, mental depravity, or passion growing out of anger, revenge, hatred, or other motives, and kindred evil conditions, for when the act is induced by any of these causes, the person is accountable to the law.'"

the defendant was legally insane at the time of the act. One who is legally insane at the time of the commission of the act which would otherwise be criminal, is not criminally accountable and is excused from punishment. *See* section 18–1–802, C.R.S.1973 (1978 Repl. Vol. 8).

Both the prosecution and the defense presented considerable evidence regarding the defendant's mental state at the time of the commission of the crime. The People called three psychiatrists, one neurologist, and one psychologist, all of whom concluded that the defendant was sane.

The defendant's cell-mate testified that the defendant had confided to him that he had tricked the doctors into thinking he was insane. The defendant allegedly wished to appear insane so that he would be sent to the state hospital rather than to prison in the hope that he would get out sooner. The experts presented by the prosecution agreed that they thought the defendant was malingering and trying to appear insane to avoid punishment.

The defense presented testimony of experts to the effect that the defendant suffered from minimal brain dysfunction and that he was insane according to the legal definition. Dr. Cole, an expert in forensic psychiatry, testified that the defendant had a "disease or defect of the mind which [rendered] him incapable of distinguishing right from wrong or adhering to the right at the time of the crime." This opinion was developed by relying on the defendant's history, reports of other experts, and personal interviews with the defendant over approximately four and one-half hours. Dr. Cole related the defendant's belief that he would improve his relationship with the child's mother by disposing of the child. He described how the defendant wrote to the child's mother from prison in the apparent belief that their relationship would be ongoing, asking if she would wish to have another child with him. Dr. Cole testified that the defendant suffered from an organic brain syndrome with a psychosis, and as a result he had poor impulse control. This condition was manifested in the defendant's tendency to overreact to irritating forces by striking out in a rage rather than inhibiting his anger more reasonably.

In addition, the defense offered the testimony of Dr. Coutts, a psychologist specializing in neuropsychology. Dr. Coutts testified that the defendant suffered from minimal brain dysfunction, a condition that results when neurotransmitters in the brain do not function normally. As he described it, neurotransmitters such as norepinephrine and seratonin activate "switches" in the brain's "inhibitory command post" to "either turn on or shut off whole behavior." When a person suffers from minimal brain dysfunction, his neurochemical responses do not act properly, either preventing inhibitory cells from turning off or allowing too many excitory cells to turn on. Dr. Coutts testified in terms of the decision-making process of the defendant, stating that the defendant's willpower was destroyed and that his mind was impaired by disease or defect so as to render him incapable of refraining from the wrong and choosing the right.

After hearing all testimony on the issue of the defendant's sanity, the court concluded that the prosecution had failed to prove sanity beyond a reasonable doubt. The court did not find that the defendant suffered from an organic brain syndrome. However, the court was of the opinion that the defendant's comprehension of reality was too distorted for him to be held legally accountable for his criminal conduct.

[4–6] Where expert testimony is in conflict, the resolution of the conflict and the weight to be given to the testimony is solely the province of the trier of fact. *People v. Lowe,* 184 Colo. 182, 519 P.2d 344 (1974). The question of sanity in a criminal case is an issue of fact to be determined by the trier of fact, in this case the trial judge. *Henderson v. People,* 156 Colo. 229, 397 P.2d 872 (1965); *People v. Haines,* 37 Colo.App. 302, 549 P.2d 786 (1976); *see also People v. Ware, supra; Gomez v. District Court,* 179 Colo. 299, 500 P.2d 134 (1972). On review of this record, we find no prejudicial error which would warrant our reversal of the trial court's factual determination.

II

Even though the court did not base its conclusion of legal insanity on a finding that the defendant suffered from an organic brain syndrome, nevertheless, the People argue that the testimony concerning minimal brain dysfunction, also known as organic brain syndrome, should not have been admitted or considered by the trial court in determining whether the defendant suffered from a "mental disease or defect" within the meaning of the statute. The People contend such evidence is unreliable and is not relevant to the issue of sanity.

The People analogize the presence of minimal brain dysfunction to the presence of XYY chromosomal deficiency, which has been rejected as an indication of insanity by other courts. *See, People v. Tanner,* 13 Cal.App.3d 596, 91 Cal.Rptr. 656, 42 A.L.R.3d 1408 (1970). Evidence of XYY chromosomal deficiency has been excluded as irrelevant on the basis that the studies on the subject are inconclusive on the issue of insanity or aggressive behavior as a result of the syndrome, and that not all those who possess the XYY chromosome make-up are involuntarily aggressive.

See People v. Tanner, supra; see also People v. Yukl, 83 Misc.2d 364, 372 N.Y.S.2d 313 (1975); Millard v. State, 8 Md.App. 419, 261 A.2d 227 (1970). We find the People's analogy inapposite.

In this case the expert witnesses, who were qualified without objection, testified that the defendant suffered from a psychosis as well as an organic brain syndrome. Moreover, the prosecution stipulated at trial that the defendant suffered from minimal brain dysfunction. Both defense experts testified that the defendant's minimal brain dysfunction resulted in poor impulse control, and that the defendant was incapable of choosing the right and refraining from doing the wrong.

[7]   Traditionally, the scope of evidence admissible on the issue of insanity is broad. Even lay persons are free to testify as to the sanity of a defendant if a proper foundation is presented. See section 16–8–109, C.R.S.1973 (1978 Repl. Vol. 8); People v. Medina, 185 Colo. 101, 521 P.2d 1257 (1974); Rupert v. People, 163 Colo. 219, 429 P.2d 276 (1967). As we stated in People v. Trujilio, 150 Colo. 235, 238, 372 P.2d 86, 88 (1962):

"A much wider area of conduct on the part of a defendant can be made the subject of inquiry in a trial relating to his sanity, than would be permissible in a trial upon a plea of not guilty. Any abnormal conduct, whether related to the act forming the basis of the accusation or not, may be relevant and important on the issue of his mental condition. Conversely, evidence of normal conduct, and actions reflecting the usual and ordinary under the circumstances, may be shown to prove sanity."

Section 16–8–107(2), C.R.S.1973 (1978 Repl. Vol. 8), also indicates the scope of admissibility of expert testimony in an insanity trial. That subsection provides:

"(2) In any trial or hearing concerning the defendant's mental condition, physicians and other experts may testify as to their conclusions reached from their examination of hospital records, laboratory reports, x-rays, electroencephalograms, and psychological test results if the material which they examined in reaching their conclusions is produced at the time of the trial or hearing."

[8]   The expert testimony concerning the psychological testing of the defendant, the results of the tests, the nature of the condition of minimal brain dysfunction, its relation to poor impulse control and lack of willpower, was clearly admissible in evidence and relevant to the issue of the defendant's sanity. The People have not demonstrated that the court erred in admitting such evidence.

Judgment is affirmed.

Daubert v. Merrell Dow Pharmaceuticals, Inc., 509 U.S. 579. William Daubert, et ux., etc., et al., Petitioners v. Merrell Dow Pharmaceuticals, Inc. Certiorari to the United States Court of Appeals for the Ninth Circuit. No. 92–102. Argued March 30, 1993. Decided June 28, 1993.

Petitioners, two minor children and their parents, alleged in their suit against respondent that the children's serious birth defects had been caused by the mothers' prenatal ingestion of Bendectin, a prescription drug marketed by respondent. The District Court granted respondent summary judgment based on a well-credentialed expert's affidavit concluding, upon reviewing the extensive published scientific literature on the subject, that maternal use of Bendectin has not been shown to be a risk factor for human birth defects. Although petitioners had responded with the testimony of eight other well-credentialed experts, who based their conclusion that Bendectin can cause birth defects on animal studies, chemical structure analyses, and the unpublished "reanalysis" of previously published human statistical studies, the court determined that this evidence did not meet the applicable "general acceptance" standard for the admission of expert testimony. The Court of Appeals agreed and affirmed, citing Frye v. United States, 54 App. D.C. 46, 47, 293 F. 1013, 1014, for the rule that expert opinion based on a scientific technique is inadmissible unless the technique is "generally accepted" as reliable in the relevant scientific community.

Held:

The Federal Rules of Evidence, not Frye, provide the standard for admitting expert scientific testimony in a federal trial. Pp. 4–17.

(a) Frye's "general acceptance" test was superseded by the Rules' adoption. The Rules occupy the field, United States v. Abel, *469 U.S. 45, 49*, and, although the common law of evidence may serve as an aid to their application, id., at 51–52, respondent's assertion that they somehow assimilated Frye is unconvincing. Nothing in the Rules as a [509 U.S. 579, 2] whole or in the text and drafting history of Rule 702, which specifically governs expert testimony, gives any indication that "general acceptance" is a necessary precondition to the admissibility of scientific evidence. Moreover, such a rigid standard would be at odds with the Rules' liberal thrust and their general approach of relaxing the traditional barriers to "opinion" testimony. Pp. 4–8.

(b) The Rules—especially Rule 702—place appropriate limits on the admissibility of purportedly scientific evidence by assigning to the trial judge the task of ensuring that an expert's testimony both rests on a reliable foundation and is relevant to the task at hand. The reliability standard is established by Rule 702's requirement that an expert's testimony pertain to "scientific . . . knowledge," since the adjective "scientific" implies a grounding in science's methods and procedures, while the word "knowledge" connotes a body of known facts or of ideas inferred from such facts or accepted as true on good grounds. The Rule's requirement that the testimony "assist the trier of fact to understand the evidence or to determine a fact in issue" goes primarily to relevance by demanding a valid scientific connection to the pertinent inquiry as a precondition to admissibility. Pp. 9–12.

(c) Faced with a proffer of expert scientific testimony under Rule 702, the trial judge, pursuant to Rule 104(a), must make a preliminary assessment of whether the testimony's underlying reasoning or methodology is scientifically valid and properly can be applied to the facts at issue. Many considerations will bear on the inquiry, including whether the theory or technique in question can be (and has been) tested, whether it has been subjected to peer review and publication, its known or potential error rate and the existence and maintenance of standards controlling its operation, and whether it has attracted widespread acceptance within a relevant scientific community. The inquiry is a flexible one, and its focus must be solely on principles and methodology, not on the conclusions that they generate. Throughout, the judge should also be mindful of other applicable Rules. Pp. 12–15.

(d) Cross-examination, presentation of contrary evidence, and careful instruction on the burden of proof, rather than wholesale exclusion under an uncompromising "general acceptance" standard, is the appropriate means by which evidence based on valid principles may be challenged. That even limited screening by the trial judge, on occasion, will prevent the jury from hearing of authentic scientific breakthroughs is simply a consequence of the fact that the Rules are not designed to seek cosmic understanding but, rather, to resolve legal disputes. Pp. 15–17.

951 F.2d 1128 (CA9 1991), vacated and remanded. [509 U.S. 579, 3]

BLACKMUN, J., delivered the opinion for a unanimous Court with respect to Parts I and II-A, and the opinion of the Court with respect to Parts II-B, II-C, III, and IV, in which WHITE, O'CONNOR, SCALIA, KENNEDY, SOUTER, and THOMAS, JJ., joined. REHNQUIST, C.J., filed an opinion concurring in part and dissenting in part, in which STEVENS, J., joined, post, p. _____.

Michael H. Gottesman argued the cause for petitioners. With him on the briefs were Kenneth J. Chesebro, Barry J. Nace, David L. Shapiro, and Mary G. Gillick.

Charles Fried argued the cause for respondent. With him on the brief were Charles R. Nesson, Joel I. Klein, Richard G. Taranto, Hall R. Marston, George E. Berry, Edward H. Stratemeier, and W. Glenn Forrester.*

---

* Briefs of amici curiae urging reversal were filed for the State of Texas et al. by Dan Morales, Attorney General of Texas, Mark Barnett, Attorney General of South Dakota, Marc Racicot, Attorney General of Montana, Larry EchoHawk, Attorney General of Idaho, and Brian Stuart Koukoutchos; for

the American Society of Law, Medicine and Ethics et al. by Joan E. Bertin, Marsha S. Berzon, and Albert H. Meyerhoff; for the Association of Trial Lawyers of America by Jeffrey Robert White and Roxanne Barton Conlin; for Ronald Bayer et al. by Brian Stuart Koukoutchos, Priscilla Budeiri, Arthur Bryant, and George W. Conk; and for Daryl E. Chubin et al. by Ron Simon and Nicole Schultheis. Briefs of amici curiae urging affirmance were filed for the United States by Acting Solicitor General Wallace, Assistant Attorney General Gerson, Miguel A. Estrada, Michael Jay Singer, and John P. Schnitker; for the American Insurance Association by William J. Kilberg, Paul Blankenstein, Bradford R. Clark, and Craig A. Berrington; for the American Medical Association et al. by Carter G. Phillips, Mark D. Hopson, and Jack R. Bierig; for the American Tort Reform Association by John G. Kester and John W. Vardaman, Jr.; for the Chamber of Commerce of the United States by Timothy B. Dyk, Stephen A. Bokat, and Robin S. Conrad; for the Pharmaceutical Manufacturers Association by Louis R. Cohen and Daniel Marcus; for the Product Liability Advisory Council, Inc., et al. by Victor E. Schwartz, Robert P. Charrow, and Paul F. Rothstein; for the Washington Legal Foundation by Scott G. Campbell, Daniel J. Popeo, and Richard A. Samp; and for Nicolaas Bloembergen et al. by Martin S. Kaufman. Briefs of amici curiae were filed for the American Association for the Advancement of Science et al. by Richard A. Meserve and Bert Black; for the American College of Legal Medicine by Miles J. Zaremski; for the Carnegie Commission on Science, Technology, and Government by Steven G. Gallagher, Elizabeth H. Esty, and Margaret A. Berger; for the Defense Research Institute, Inc., by Joseph A. Sherman, E. Wayne Taff, and Harvey L. Kaplan; for the New England Journal of Medicine et al. by Michael Malina and Jeffrey I. D. Lewis; for A Group of American Law Professors by Donald N. Bersoff; for Alvan R. Feinstein by Don M. Kennedy, Loretta M. Smith, and Richard A. Oetheimer; and for Kenneth Rothman et al. by Neil B. Cohen. [509 U.S. 579, 1]

OJ JUSTICE BLACKMUN delivered the opinion of the Court.

In this case, we are called upon to determine the standard for admitting expert scientific testimony in a federal trial.

I

Petitioners Jason Daubert and Eric Schuller are minor children born with serious birth defects. They and their parents sued respondent in California state court, alleging that the birth defects had been caused by the mothers' ingestion of Bendectin, a prescription antinausea drug marketed by respondent. Respondent removed the suits to federal court on diversity grounds.

After extensive discovery, respondent moved for summary judgment, contending that Bendectin does not cause birth defects in humans and that petitioners would be unable to come forward with any admissible evidence that it does. In support of its motion, respondent submitted an affidavit of Steven H. Lamm, physician and epidemiologist, who is a well-credentialed expert on the risks from exposure to various [509 U.S. 579, 2] chemical substances.[1] Doctor Lamm stated that he had reviewed all the literature on Bendectin and human birth defects—more than 30 published studies involving over 130,000 patients. No study had found Bendectin to be a

human teratogen (i.e., a substance capable of causing malformations in fetuses). On the basis of this review, Doctor Lamm concluded that maternal use of Bendectin during the first trimester of pregnancy has not been shown to be a risk factor for human birth defects.

Petitioners did not (and do not) contest this characterization of the published record regarding Bendectin. Instead, they responded to respondent's motion with the testimony of eight experts of their own, each of whom also possessed impressive credentials.[2] These experts had concluded that Bendectin can cause birth defects. Their conclusions were based upon "in vitro" (test tube) and "in vivo" (live) animal studies that found a link between Bendectin and malformations, pharmacological studies of the chemical structure of Bendectin that purported to show similarities between

---

[1] Doctor Lamm received his master's and doctor of medicine degrees from the University of Southern California. He has served as a consultant in birth-defect epidemiology for the National Center for Health Statistics, and has published numerous articles on the magnitude of risk from exposure to various chemical and biological substances. App. 34-44.

[2] For example, Shanna Helen Swan, who received a master's degree in biostatics from Columbia University and a doctorate in statistics from the University of California at Berkeley, is chief of the section of the California Department of Health and Services that determines causes of birth defects, and has served as a consultant to the World Health Organization, the Food and Drug Administration, and the National Institutes of Health. Id., at degree 113–114, 131–132. Stuart A. Newman, who received his bachelor's in chemistry from Columbia University and his master's and doctorate in chemistry from the University of Chicago, respectively, is a professor at New York Medical College, and has spent over a decade studying the effect of chemicals on limb development. Id., at 54–56. The credentials of the others are similarly impressive. See id., at 61–66, 73–80, 148–153, 187–192, and Attachments 12, 20, 21, 26, 31, and 32 to Petitioners' Opposition to Summary Judgment, in No. 84-20, 3-G(I) (SD Cal.).

the [509 U.S. 579, 3] structure of the drug and that of other substance known to cause birth defects; and the "reanalysis" of previously published epidemiological (human statistical) studies.

The District Court granted respondent's motion for summary judgment. The court stated that scientific evidence is admissible only if the principle upon which it is based is "'sufficiently established to have general acceptance in the field to which it belongs.'" 727 F.Supp. 570, 572 (S.D. Cal. 1989), quoting United States v. Kilgus, 571 F.2d 508, 510 (CA9 1978). The court concluded that petitioners' evidence did not meet this standard. Given the vast body of epidemiological data concerning Bendectin, the court held, expert opinion which is not based on epidemiological evidence is not admissible to establish causation. 727 F.Supp., at 575. Thus, the animal cell studies, live animal studies, and chemical structure analyses on which petitioners had relied could not raise, by themselves, a reasonably disputable jury issue regarding causation. Ibid. Petitioners' epidemiological analyses, based as they were on recalculations of data in previously published studies that had found no causal link between the drug and birth defects, were ruled to be inadmissible because they had not been published or subjected to peer review. Ibid.

The United States Court of Appeals for the Ninth Circuit affirmed. 951 F.2d 1128 (1991). Citing Frye v. United States, 54 App. D.C. 46, 47, 293 F. 1013, 1014 (1923), the court stated that expert opinion based on a scientific technique is inadmissible unless the technique is "generally accepted" as reliable in the relevant scientific community. 951 F.2d, at 1129–1130. The court declared that expert opinion based on a methodology that diverges "significantly from the procedures accepted by recognized authorities in the field . . . cannot be shown to be 'generally accepted as a reliable technique.'" Id., at 1130, quoting United States v. Solomon, 753 F.2d 1522, 1526 (CA9 1985). [509 U.S. 579, 4]

The court emphasized that other Courts of Appeals considering the risks of Bendectin had refused to admit reanalyses of epidemiological studies that had been neither published nor subjected to peer review. 951 F.2d, at 1130–1131. Those courts had found unpublished reanalyses "particularly problematic in light of the massive weight of the original published studies supporting [respondent's] position, all of which had undergone full scrutiny from the scientific community." Id., at 1130. Contending that reanalysis is generally accepted by the scientific community only when it is subjected to verification and scrutiny by others in the field, the Court of Appeals rejected petitioners' reanalyses as "unpublished, not subjected to the normal peer review process, and generated solely for use in litigation." Id., at 1131. The court concluded that petitioners' evidence provided an insufficient foundation to allow admission of expert testimony that Bendectin caused their injuries and, accordingly, that petitioners could not satisfy their burden of proving causation at trial.

We granted certiorari, *506 U.S. 914* (1992), in light of sharp divisions among the courts regarding the proper standard for the admission of expert testimony. Compare, e.g., United States v. Shorter, 257 U.S. App. D.C. 358, 363–364, 809 F.2d 54, 59–60 (applying the "general acceptance" standard), cert. denied, *484 U.S. 817* (1987), with DeLuca v. Merrell Dow Pharmaceuticals, Inc., 911 F.2d 941, 955 (CA3 1990) (rejecting the "general acceptance" standard).

II

A

In the 70 years since its formulation in the Frye case, the "general acceptance" test has been the dominant standard for determining the admissibility of novel scientific evidence at trial. See E. Green & C. Nesson, Problems, Cases, and Materials on Evidence 649 (1983). Although under increasing [509 U.S. 579, 5] attack of late, the rule continues to be followed by a majority of courts, including the Ninth Circuit.[3]

The Frye test has its origin in a short and citation-free 1923 decision concerning the admissibility of evidence derived from a systolic blood pressure deception test, a crude precursor to the polygraph machine. In what has become a famous (perhaps infamous) passage, the then Court of Appeals for the District of Columbia described the device and its operation and declared:

"Just when a scientific principle or discovery crosses the line between the experimental and demonstrable stages is difficult to define. Somewhere in this twilight zone, the evidential force of the principle must be recognized, and while courts will go a long way in admitting expert testimony deduced from a well-recognized scientific principle or discovery, the thing from which the deduction is made must be sufficiently established to have gained general acceptance in the particular field in which it belongs." 54 App. D.C., at 47, 293 F., at 1014 (emphasis added).

Because the deception test had "not yet gained such standing and scientific recognition among physiological and psychological authorities as would justify the courts in admitting expert testimony deduced from the discovery, development, and experiments thus far made," evidence of its results was ruled inadmissible. Ibid.

The merits of the Frye test have been much debated, and scholarship on its proper scope and application is legion.[4] [509 U.S. 579, 6] Petitioners' primary attack, however, is not on the content, but on the continuing authority, of the rule. They contend that the Frye test was

---

[3] For a catalog of the many cases on either side of this controversy, see P. Giannelli & E. Imwinkelried, Scientific Evidence 1-5, pp. 10–14 (1986 and Supp. 1991).

[4] See, e.g., Green, Expert Witnesses and Sufficiency of Evidence in Toxic Substances Litigation: The Legacy of Agent Orange and Bendectin Litigation, 86 Nw. U.L.Rev. 643 (1992) (hereinafter Green); Becker & Orenstein, The Federal Rules of Evidence After Sixteen Years—the Effect of "Plain Meaning" Jurisprudence, the Need for an Advisory [509 U.S. 579, 6] Committee on the Rules of Evidence, and Suggestions for Selective Revision of the Rules, 60 Geo. WashL.Rev. 857, 876–885 (1992); Hanson, James Alphonzo Frye is Sixty-Five Years Old; Should He Retire?, 16 West St.U.L.Rev. 357 (1989); Black, A Unified Theory of Scientific Evidence, 56 Ford.L.Rev. 595 (1988), Imwinkelried, The "Bases" of Expert Testimony: The Syllogistic Structure of Scientific Testimony, 67 N.C.L.Rev. 1 (1988); Proposals for a Model Rule on the Admissibility of Scientific Evidence, 26 Jurimetrics J. 235 (1986); Giannelli, The Admissibility of Novel Scientific Evidence: Frye v. United States, a Half-Century Later, 80 Colum.L.Rev. 1197 (1980); The Supreme Court, 1986 Term, 101 Harv.L.Rev. 7, 119, 125–127 (1987). Indeed, the debates over Frye are such a well-established part of the academic landscape that a distinct term—"Frye ologist"—has been advanced to describe those who take part. See Behringer, Introduction, Proposals for a Model Rule on the Admissibility of Scientific Evidence, 26 Jurimetrics J., 237, 239 (1986), quoting Lacey, Scientific Evidence, 24 Jurimetrics J. 254, 264 (1984).

superseded by the adoption of the Federal Rules of Evidence.[5] We agree.

We interpret the legislatively enacted Federal Rules of Evidence as we would any statute. Beech Aircraft Corp. v. Rainey, *488 U.S. 153, 163* (1988). Rule 402 provides the baseline:

"All relevant evidence is admissible, except as otherwise provided by the Constitution of the United States, by Act of Congress, by these rules, or by other rules [509 U.S. 579, 7] prescribed by the Supreme Court pursuant to statutory authority. Evidence which is not relevant is not admissible."

"Relevant evidence" is defined as that which has "any tendency to make the existence of any fact that is of consequence to the determination of the action more probable or less probable than it would be without the evidence." Rule 401. The Rule's basic standard of relevance thus is a liberal one.

Frye, of course, predated the Rules by half a century. In United States v. Able, *469 U.S. 45* (1984), we considered the pertinence of background common law in interpreting the Rules of Evidence. We noted that the Rules occupy the field, id., at 49, but, quoting Professor Cleary, the Reporter, explained that

---

[5] Like the question of Frye's merit, the dispute over its survival has divided courts and commentators. Compare, e.g., United States v. (Frye is superseded by the Rules of Evidence), Williams, 583 F.2d 1194 (CA2 1978) cert. denied, *439 U.S. 1117* (1979) with Christophersen v. Allied-Signal Corp., 939 F.2d 1106, 1111, 1115–1116 (CA5 1991) (en banc) (Frye and the Rules coexist), cert. denied, *503 U.S. 912* (1992), 3 J. Weinstein & M. Berger, Weinstein's Evidence □ 70203., pp. 702-36 to 702-37 (1988) (hereinafter Weinstein & Berger) (Frye is dead), and M. Graham, Handbook of Federal Evidence 703.2 (3d ed. 1991) (Frye lives). See generally P. Giannelli & E. Imwinkelried, Scientific Evidence 1–5, n. 28–29 (citing authorities).

the common law nevertheless could serve as an aid to their application:

"'In principle, under the Federal Rules, no common law of evidence remains. "All relevant evidence is admissible, except as otherwise provided. . . ." In reality, of course, the body of common law knowledge continues to exist, though in the somewhat altered form of a source of guidance in the exercise of delegated powers.'" Id., at 51–52.

We found the common law precept at issue in the Abel case entirely consistent with Rule 402's general requirement of admissibility, and considered it unlikely that the drafters had intended to change the rule. Id., at 50–51. In Bourjaily v. United States, *483 U.S. 171* (1987), on the other hand, the Court was unable to find a particular common-law doctrine in the Rules, and so held it superseded.

Here there is a specific Rule that speaks to the contested issue. Rule 702, governing expert testimony, provides:

"If scientific, technical, or other specialized knowledge will assist the trier of fact to understand the evidence or to determine a fact in issue, a witness qualified as an expert by knowledge, skill, experience, training, [509 U.S. 579, 8] or education, may testify thereto in the form of an opinion or otherwise."

Nothing in the text of this Rule establishes "general acceptance" as an absolute prerequisite to admissibility. Nor does respondent present any clear indication that Rule 702 or the Rules as a whole were intended to incorporate a "general acceptance" standard. The drafting history makes no mention of Frye, and a rigid "general acceptance" requirement would be at odds with the "liberal thrust" of the Federal Rules and their "general approach of relaxing the traditional barriers to 'opinion' testimony." Beech Aircraft Corp. v.

Rainey, *488 U.S., at 169* (citing Rules 701 to 705). See also Weinstein, Rule 702 of the Federal Rules of Evidence is Sound; It Should Not Be Amended, 138 F.R.D. 631 (1991) ("The Rules were designed to depend primarily upon lawyer-adversaries and sensible triers of fact to evaluate conflicts"). Given the Rules' permissive backdrop and their inclusion of a specific rule on expert testimony that does not mention "general acceptance," the assertion that the Rules somehow assimilated Frye is unconvincing. Frye made "general acceptance" the exclusive test for admitting expert scientific testimony. That austere standard, absent from, and incompatible with, the Federal Rules of Evidence, should not be applied in federal trials.[6]

B

That the Frye test was displaced by the Rules of Evidence does not mean, however, that the Rules themselves place [509 U.S. 579, 9] no limits on the admissibility of purportedly scientific evidence.[7] Nor is the trial judge disabled from screening such evidence. To the contrary, under the Rules, the trial judge must ensure that any and all sci-

entific testimony or evidence admitted is not only relevant, but reliable.

The primary locus of this obligation is Rule 702, which clearly contemplates some degree of regulation of the subjects and theories about which an expert may testify. "If scientific, technical, or other specialized knowledge will assist the trier of fact to understand the evidence or to determine a fact in issue," an expert "may testify thereto." (Emphasis added.) The subject of an expert's testimony must be "scientific . . . knowledge."[8] The adjective "scientific" implies a grounding in the methods and procedures of science. Similarly, the word "knowledge" [connotes more than subjective belief or unsupported speculation]. The term "applies to any body of known facts or to any body of ideas inferred from such facts or accepted as truths on good grounds." Webster's Third New International Dictionary 1252 (1986). Of course, it would be unreasonable to conclude that the subject of scientific testimony must be "known" to a certainty; arguably, there are no certainties in science. See, e.g., Brief for Nicolaas Bloembergen et al. as Amici Curiae 9 ("Indeed, scientists do not assert that they know what is immutably 'true'—they are committed to searching for new, temporary theories to explain, as best they can, phenomena"); Brief for American Association for the Advancement of Science et al. as Amici Curiae 7-8 ("Science is not an encyclopedic body of knowledge about [509 U.S. 579, 10] the universe. Instead, it represents a process for proposing and refining theoretical explanations about the world that are subject to further testing and refinement" (emphasis

---

[6] Because we hold that Frye has been superseded and base the discussion that follows on the content of the congressionally enacted Federal Rules of Evidence, we do not address petitioners' argument that application of the Frye rule in this diversity case, as the application of a judge-made rule affecting substantive rights, would violate the doctrine of Erie R. Co. v. Tompkins, *304 U.S. 64* (1938).

[7] THE CHIEF JUSTICE "do[es] not doubt that Rule 702 confides to the judge some gatekeeping responsibility," post, at 4, but would neither say how it does so nor explain what that role entails. We believe the better course is to note the nature and source of the duty.

[8] Rule 702 also applies to "technical, or other specialized knowledge." Our discussion is limited to the scientific context because that is the nature of the expertise offered here.

in original). But, in order to qualify as "scientific knowledge," an inference or assertion must be [derived by the scientific method.] Proposed testimony must be supported by [appropriate validation]—i.e., "good grounds," based on what is known. In short, the requirement that an expert's testimony pertain to "scientific knowledge" establishes a standard of evidentiary reliability.[9]

Rule 702 further requires that the evidence or testimony "assist the trier of fact to understand the evidence or to determine a fact in issue." This condition goes primarily to relevance. "Expert testimony which does not relate to any issue in the case is not relevant and, ergo, nonhelpful." 3 Weinstein & Berger □ 70202., p. 702–18. See also United

States v. Downing, 753 F.2d 1224, 1242 (CA3 1985) ("An additional consideration under Rule 702—and another aspect of relevancy—is whether expert testimony proffered in the [509 U.S. 579, 11] case is sufficiently tied to the facts of the case that it will aid the jury in resolving a factual dispute"). The consideration has been aptly described by Judge Becker as one of "fit." Ibid. "Fit" is not always obvious, and scientific validity for one purpose is not necessarily scientific validity for other, unrelated purposes. See Starrs, Frye v. United States Restructured and Revitalized: A Proposal to Amend Federal Evidence Rule 702, 26 Jurimetrics J. 249, 258 (1986). The study of the phases of the moon, for example, may provide valid scientific "knowledge" about whether a certain night was dark, and if darkness is a fact in issue, the knowledge will assist the trier of fact. However (absent creditable grounds supporting such a link), evidence that the moon was full on a certain night will not assist the trier of fact in determining whether an individual was unusually likely to have behaved irrationally on that night. Rule 702's "helpfulness" standard requires a valid scientific connection to the pertinent inquiry as a precondition to admissibility.

That these requirements are embodied in Rule 702 is not surprising. Unlike an ordinary witness, see Rule 701, an expert is permitted wide latitude to offer opinions, including those that are not based on firsthand knowledge or observation. See Rules 702 and 703. Presumably, this relaxation of the usual requirement of firsthand knowledge—a rule which represents "a 'most pervasive manifestation' of the common law insistence upon 'the most reliable sources of information,'" Advisory Committee's Notes on Fed. Rule Evid. 602, 28 U.S.C. App., p. 755 (citation omitted)—is premised on an

[9] We note that scientists typically distinguish between "validity" (does the principle support what it purports to show?) and "reliability" (does application of the principle produce consistent results?). See Black, 56 Ford.L.Rev. at, 599. Although "the difference between accuracy, validity, and reliability may be such that each is distinct from the other by no more than a hen's kick," Starrs, Frye v. United States Restructured and Revitalized: A Proposal to Amend Federal Evidence Rule 702, 26 Jurimetrics J. 249, 256 (1986), our reference here is to evidentiary reliability—that is, trustworthiness. Cf., e.g., Advisory Committee's Notes on Fed.Rule Evid. 602, 28 U.S.C. App., p. 755. ("'[T]he rule requiring that a witness who testifies to a fact which can be perceived by the senses must have had an opportunity to observe, and must have actually observed the fact' is a 'most pervasive manifestation' of the common law insistence upon 'the most reliable sources of information.'" (citation omitted)); Advisory Committee's Notes on Art. VIII of Rules of Evidence, 29 U.S.C. App., p. 770 (hearsay exceptions will be recognized only "under circumstances supposed to furnish guarantees of trustworthiness"). [In a case involving scientific evidence, evidentiary reliability will be based upon scientific validity.]

assumption that the expert's opinion will have a reliable basis in the knowledge and experience of his discipline.

C

Faced with a proffer of expert scientific testimony, then, the trial judge must determine at the outset, pursuant to [509 U.S. 579, 12] Rule 104(a),[10] whether the expert is proposing to testify to (1) scientific knowledge that (2) will assist the trier of fact to understand or determine a fact in issue.[11] This entails a preliminary assessment of whether the reasoning or methodology underlying the testimony is scientifically valid, and of whether that reasoning or methodology properly can be applied to the facts in issue. We are confident that federal judges possess the capacity to undertake this review. Many factors will bear on the inquiry, and we do not presume to set out a

definitive checklist or test. But some general observations are appropriate.

Ordinarily, a key question to be answered in determining whether a theory or technique is scientific knowledge that will assist the trier of fact will be whether it can be (and has been) tested. "Scientific methodology today is based on generating hypotheses and testing them to see if they can be falsified; indeed, this methodology is what distinguishes science from other fields of human inquiry." Green, 645. See also C. Hempel, Philosophy of Natural Science 49 (1966) ("[T]he statements constituting a scientific explanation must be capable of empirical test"); K. Popper, Conjectures and Refutations: The Growth of Scientific Knowledge 37 (5th ed. [509 U.S. 579, 13] 1989) ("[T]he criterion of the scientific status of a theory is its falsifiability, or refutability, or testability").

Another pertinent consideration is whether the theory or technique has been subjected to peer review and publication. Publication (which is but one element of peer review) is not a sine qua non of admissibility; it does not necessarily correlate with reliability, see S. Jasanoff, The Fifth Branch: Science Advisors as Policymakers 61–76 (1990), and, in some instances, well-grounded but innovative theories will not have been published, see Horrobin, The Philosophical Basis of Peer Review and the Suppression of Innovation, 263 JAMA 1438 (1990). Some propositions, moreover, are too particular, too new, or of too limited interest to be published. But submission to the scrutiny of the scientific community is a component of "good science," in part because it increases the likelihood that substantive flaws in methodology will be detected. See J. Ziman, Reliable Knowledge: An Exploration of the Grounds for Belief in Science 130–133 (1978); Relman & Angell, How Good Is Peer Review?, 321 New Eng.J.Med. 827

---

[10] Rule 104(a) provides: "Preliminary questions concerning the qualification of a person to be a witness, the existence of a privilege, or the admissibility of evidence shall be determined by the court, subject to the provisions of subdivision (b) [pertaining to conditional admissions]. In making its determination, it is not bound by the rules of evidence except those with respect to privileges." These matters should be established by a preponderance of proof. See Bourjaily v. United States, *483 U.S. 171, 175–176* (1987).

[11] Although the Frye decision itself focused exclusively on "novel" scientific techniques, we do not read the requirements of Rule 702 to apply specially or exclusively to unconventional evidence. Of course, well-established propositions are less likely to be challenged than those that are novel, and they are more handily defended. Indeed, theories that are so firmly established as to have attained the status of scientific law, such as the laws of thermodynamics, properly are subject to judicial notice under Federal Rule Evidence 201.

(1989). The fact of publication (or lack thereof) in a peer reviewed journal thus will be a relevant, though not dispositive, consideration in assessing the scientific validity of a particular technique or methodology on which an opinion is premised.

Additionally, in the case of a particular scientific technique, the court ordinarily should consider the known or potential rate of error, see, e.g., United States v. Smith, 869 F.2d 348, 353–354 (CA7 1989) (surveying studies of the error rate of spectrographic voice identification technique), and the existence and maintenance of standards controlling the technique's operation, see United States v. Williams, 583 F.2d 1194, 1198 (CA2 1978) (noting professional organization's standard governing spectrographic analysis), cert. denied, *439 U.S. 1117* (1979).

Finally, "general acceptance" can yet have a bearing on the inquiry. A "reliability assessment does not require, although [509 U.S. 579, 14] it does permit, explicit identification of a relevant scientific community and an express determination of a particular degree of acceptance within that community." United States v. Downing, 753 F.2d, at 1238. See also 3 Weinstein Berger □ 70203., pp. 702-41 to 702-42. Widespread acceptance can be an important factor in ruling particular evidence admissible, and "a known technique which has been able to attract only minimal support within the community," Downing, 753 F.2d, at 1238, may properly be viewed with skepticism.

The inquiry envisioned by Rule 702 is, we emphasize, a flexible one.[12] Its overarching subject is the scientific validity—and thus the evidentiary relevance and reliability—of the principles that underlie a proposed submission. The focus, of course, must be solely on principles and methodology, not on the conclusions that they generate.

Throughout, a judge assessing a proffer of expert scientific testimony under Rule 702 should also be mindful of other applicable rules. Rule 703 provides that expert opinions based on otherwise inadmissible hearsay are to be admitted only if the facts or data are "of a type reasonably relied upon by experts in the particular field in forming opinions or inferences upon the subject." Rule 706 allows the court at its discretion to procure the assistance of an expert of its own choosing. Finally, Rule 403 permits the exclusion of relevant evidence "if its probative value is substantially [509 U.S. 579, 15] outweighed by the danger of unfair prejudice, confusion of the issues, or misleading the jury. . . ." Judge Weinstein has explained: "Expert evidence can be both powerful and quite misleading because of the difficulty in evaluating it. Because of this risk, the judge, in weighing possible prejudice against probative force under Rule 403 of the present rules, exercises more control over experts than over lay witnesses." Weinstein, 138 F.R.D., at 632.

---

[12] A number of authorities have presented variations on the reliability approach, each with its own slightly different set of factors. See, e.g., Downing, 753 F.2d, at 1238–1239 (on which our discussion draws in part); 3 Weinstein & Berger □ 70203., pp. 7021 to 7022 (on which the Downing court in turn partially relied); McCormick, Scientific Evidence: Defining a New Approach to Admissibility, 67 Iowa L.Rev. 879, 911–912 (1982); and Symposium on Science and the Rules of Evidence, 99 F.R.D. 187, 231 (1983) (statement by Margaret Berger). To the extent that they focus on the reliability of evidence as ensured by the scientific validity of its underlying principles, all these versions may well have merit, although we express no opinion regarding any of their particular details.

III

We conclude by briefly addressing what appear to be two underlying concerns of the parties and amici in this case. Respondent expresses apprehension that abandonment of "general acceptance" as the exclusive requirement for admission will result in a "free-for-all" in which befuddled juries are confounded by absurd and irrational pseudoscientific assertions. In this regard, respondent seems to us to be overly pessimistic about the capabilities of the jury and of the adversary system generally. Vigorous cross-examination, presentation of contrary evidence, and careful instruction on the burden of proof are the traditional and appropriate means of attacking shaky but admissible evidence. See Rock v. Arkansas, *483 U.S. 44, 61* (1987). Additionally, in the event the trial court concludes that the scintilla of evidence presented supporting a position is insufficient to allow a reasonable juror to conclude that the position more likely than not is true, the court remains free to direct a judgment, Fed.Rule Civ.Proc. 50(a), and likewise to grant summary judgment, Fed.Rule Civ.Proc. 56. Cf., e.g., Turpin v. Merrell Dow Pharmaceuticals, Inc., 959 F.2d 1349 (CA6) (holding that scientific evidence that provided foundation for expert testimony, viewed in the light most favorable to plaintiffs, was not sufficient to allow a jury to find it more probable than not that defendant caused plaintiff's injury), cert. denied, *506 U.S. 826* (1992); Brock v. Merrell Dow Pharmaceuticals, Inc., 847 F.2d 307 (CA5 [509 U.S. 579, 16] 1989) (reversing judgment entered on jury verdict for plaintiffs because evidence regarding causation was insufficient), modified, 884 F.2d 166 (CA5 1989), cert. denied, *494 U.S. 1046* (1990), Green, 680–681. These conventional devices, rather than wholesale exclusion under an uncompromising "general acceptance" test, are the appropriate safeguards where the basis of scientific testimony meets the standards of Rule 702.

Petitioners and, to a greater extent, their amici exhibit a different concern. They suggest that recognition of a screening role for the judge that allows for the exclusion of "invalid" evidence will sanction a stifling and repressive scientific orthodoxy, and will be inimical to the search for truth. See, e.g., Brief for Ronald Bayer et al. as Amici Curiae. It is true that open debate is an essential part of both legal and scientific analyses. Yet there are important differences between the quest for truth in the courtroom and the quest for truth in the laboratory. Scientific conclusions are subject to perpetual revision. Law, on the other hand, must resolve disputes finally and quickly. The scientific project is advanced by broad and wide-ranging consideration of a multitude of hypotheses, for those that are incorrect will eventually be shown to be so, and that in itself is an advance. Conjectures that are probably wrong are of little use, however, in the project of reaching a quick, final, and binding legal judgment—often of great consequence—about a particular set of events in the past. We recognize that, in practice, a gatekeeping role for the judge, no matter how flexible, inevitably on occasion will prevent the jury from learning of authentic insights and innovations. That, nevertheless, is the balance that is struck by Rules of Evidence designed not for the exhaustive search for cosmic understanding, [509 U.S. 579, 17] but for the particularized resolution of legal disputes.[13]

---

[13] This is not to say that judicial interpretation, as opposed to adjudicative factfinding, does not share basic characteristics of the scientific endeavor: "The work

IV

To summarize: "General acceptance" is not a necessary precondition to the admissibility of scientific evidence under the Federal Rules of Evidence, but the Rules of Evidence—especially Rule 702—do assign to the trial judge the task of ensuring that an expert's testimony both rests on a reliable foundation and is relevant to the task at hand. Pertinent evidence based on scientifically valid principles will satisfy those demands.

The inquiries of the District Court and the Court of Appeals focused almost exclusively on "general acceptance," as gauged by publication and the decisions of other courts. Accordingly, the judgment of the Court of Appeals is vacated, and the case is remanded for further proceedings consistent with this opinion.

It is so ordered.

CHIEF JUSTICE REHNQUIST, with whom JUSTICE STEVENS joins, concurring in part and dissenting in part.

The petition for certiorari in this case presents two questions: first, whether the rule of Frye v. United States, 54 App. D.C. 46, 293 F. 1013 (1923), remains good law after the enactment of the Federal Rules of Evidence; and second, if Frye remains valid, whether it requires expert scientific testimony to have been subjected to a peer review process in order to be admissible. The Court concludes, correctly in my view, that the Frye rule

_____

of a judge is in one sense enduring, and in another, ephemeral. . . . In the endless process of testing and retesting, there is a constant rejection of the dross and a constant retention of whatever is pure and sound and fine." B. Cardozo, The Nature of the Judicial Process 178–179 (1921).

did not survive the enactment of the Federal Rules of Evidence, and I therefore join Parts I and II-A of its opinion. The second question presented in the petition for certiorari necessarily is mooted by this holding, but the Court nonetheless proceeds to construe Rules 702 and 703 very much in the abstract, and then offers some "general observations." Ante, at 12.

"General observations" by this Court customarily carry great weight with lower federal courts, but the ones offered here suffer from the flaw common to most such observations—they are not applied to deciding whether particular testimony was or was not admissible, and therefore they tend to be not only general, but vague and abstract. This is particularly unfortunate in a case such as this, where [509 U.S. 579, 2] the ultimate legal question depends on an appreciation of one or more bodies of knowledge not judicially noticeable, and subject to different interpretations in the briefs of the parties and their amici. Twenty-two amicus briefs have been filed in the case, and indeed the Court's opinion contains no fewer than 37 citations to amicus briefs and other secondary sources.

The various briefs filed in this case are markedly different from typical briefs, in that large parts of them do not deal with decided cases or statutory language—the sort of material we customarily interpret. Instead, they deal with definitions of scientific knowledge, scientific method, scientific validity, and peer review—in short, matters far afield from the expertise of judges. This is not to say that such materials are not useful or even necessary in deciding how Rule 702 should be applied; but it is to say that the unusual subject matter should cause us to proceed with great caution in deciding more than we have to, because our reach can so easily exceed our grasp.

But even if it were desirable to make "general observations" not necessary to decide the questions presented, I cannot subscribe to some of the observations made by the Court. In Part II-B, the Court concludes that reliability and relevancy are the touchstones of the admissibility of expert testimony. Ante, at 10–11. Federal Rule of Evidence 402 provides, as the Court points out, that "[e]vidence which is not relevant is not admissible." But there is no similar reference in the Rule to "reliability." The Court constructs its argument by parsing the language "[i]f scientific, technical, or other specialized knowledge will assist the trier of fact to understand the evidence or to determine a fact in issue, ... an expert ... may testify thereto. ..." Fed. Rule Evid. 702. It stresses that the subject of the expert's testimony must be "scientific . . . knowledge," and points out that "scientific" "implies a grounding in the methods and procedures of science" and that the word "knowledge" [509 U.S. 579, 3] "connotes more than subjective belief or unsupported speculation." Ante, at 9. From this it concludes that "scientific knowledge" must be "derived by the scientific method." Ante, at 10. Proposed testimony, we are told, must be supported by "appropriate validation." Ante, at 10. Indeed, in footnote 9, the Court decides that "[i]n a case involving scientific evidence, evidentiary reliability will be based upon scientific validity." Ante, at 10, n. 9 (emphasis in original).

Questions arise simply from reading this part of the Court's opinion, and countless more questions will surely arise when hundreds of district judges try to apply its teaching to particular offers of expert testimony. Does all of this dicta apply to an expert seeking to testify on the basis of "technical or other specialized knowledge"—the other types of expert knowledge to which Rule 702 applies—or are the "general observations" limited only to

"scientific knowledge"? What is the difference between scientific knowledge and technical knowledge; does Rule 702 actually contemplate that the phrase "scientific, technical, or other specialized knowledge" be broken down into numerous subspecies of expertise, or did its authors simply pick general descriptive language covering the sort of expert testimony which courts have customarily received? The Court speaks of its confidence that federal judges can make a "preliminary assessment of whether the reasoning or methodology underlying the testimony is scientifically valid, and of whether that reasoning or methodology properly can be applied to the facts in issue." Ante, at 12. The Court then states that a "key question" to be answered in deciding whether something is "scientific knowledge" "will be whether it can be (and has been) tested." Ante, at 12. Following this sentence are three quotations from treatises, which not only speak of empirical testing, but one of which states that the "'criterion of the scientific status of a theory is its falsifiability, or refutability, or testability'" Ante at 12–13. [509 U.S. 579, 4]

I defer to no one in my confidence in federal judges; but I am at a loss to know what is meant when it is said that the scientific status of a theory depends on its "falsifiability," and I suspect some of them will be, too.

I [do not doubt that Rule 702 confides to the judge some gatekeeping responsibility] in deciding questions of the admissibility of proffered expert testimony. But I do not think it imposes on them either the obligation or the authority to become amateur scientists in order to perform that role. I think the Court would be far better advised in this case to decide only the questions presented, and to leave the further development of this important area of the law to future cases. [509 U.S. 579, 1]

Appendix B

Current Training in Psychology and the Law

It can be expected that as psychologists become more aware of the potential for the interaction of psychology and the law, more training will become available. As of this writing, the following programs represent all of the joint-degree, Ph.D. specialty programs, Ph.D. minors, internships, and post-doctoral training opportunities currently available.

DIRECTORY OF PRACTICUM, INTERNSHIP, AND FELLOWSHIP TRAINING OPPORTUNITIES IN CLINICAL-FORENSIC PSYCHOLOGY*

Surveys of Practicum, Internship, and Fellowship Training

Norman Poythress, Ph.D., sent a survey focused on predoctoral clinical–forensic practicum training opportunities to 151 APA-accredited

---

*Reprinted with permission of the American Academy of Forensic Psychology, Summer, 1997. Editors: Gail Vant Zelfde, Ph.D., Psychology Department, Norristown State Hospital, Norristown, PA, and Randy K. Otto, Ph.D., ABPP, Department of Mental Health Law & Policy, Louis de la Parte Florida Mental Health Institute, University of South Florida.

graduate training programs in clinical psychology, of which 71 responded (for a response rate of 47%). Of the 71 programs responding, 61 (86%) reported offering at least one practicum placement at which clinical psychology graduate students received supervised forensic experience, typically in forensic assessment. These 61 programs identified over 200 settings in which students could gain clinical–forensic experience, and included state civil and forensic hospitals, community-based inpatient programs, jails, juvenile detention centers, community mental health centers, and university clinics.

Gail Vant Zelfde, Ph.D., and Andrea Fox Boardman, Ph.D., sent a survey to the 259 internship programs identified in the Association of Psychology and Postdoctoral Internships Centers 1995–1996 Directory (APPIC, 1996) as offering major or minor forensic rotations. Of the 79 internships responding (for a response rate of 31%), 70 reported forensic training opportunities. Of the 70 responding sites which offered forensic training opportunities, 38 (54%) offered major forensic rotations (i.e., 50% or more of the interns' time), and 17 offered minor rotations (i.e., interns spend about 25% of their time in forensic pursuits). The remainder offered more circumscribed and select forensic experience. The majority of forensic experience offered in internship settings occurred with adult, inpatient, and criminal–forensic populations.

Thomas Grisso, Ph.D., and Shannon Wright, Ph.D., used a networking process to identify what appeared to be all of the postdoctoral training programs in clinical–forensic psychology in the United States in 1996. They identified 10 programs, all of which responded to a subsequent mail and telephone survey. Each program accepts yearly applications, provides practicuum experiences that focus exclusively on forensic populations, and offers specialized courses in forensic psychology as part of the fellowship training process. The programs vary somewhat in the breadth and types of forensic activities and populations on which they focus. Admission to these programs is highly competitive, as most programs only accept one to two trainees per year.

The table on pages 468–487 summarizes the surveys compiled by Drs. Poythress, Vant Zelfde, Boardman, Grisso, and Wright. It is anticipated that this directory will serve as a resource for trainees, educators, and administrators interested in training and education in clinical–forensic psychology.

Because revisions and subsequent editions of this directory are anticipated, clinical psychology training directors, internship directors, and fellowship directors who wish to add their programs to this publication or submit corrections should contact the editors.

Other Resources

A number of other resources for professionals or students interested in the interface area of law and psychology are available.

The American Psychology–Law Society/Division 41 (Law and Psychology) of the American Psychological Association

The American Psychology–Law Society is comprised of individuals interested in psychology and law issues. AP–LS encourages APA members, graduate and undergraduate students, and persons in related fields (e.g., sociology, law, psychiatry, criminology) to consider membership. APA membership is not required for membership in the American Psychology–Law Society. If you would like more information about joining AP–LS, write to:

Cathy Oslzly
Department of Psychology
209 Burnett Hall
University of Nebraska-Lincoln
Lincoln, NE 68588-0308
Internet: coslzly@unlinfo.unl.edu

AP–LS also publishes a brochure, titled *Graduate Training in Law and Psychology*. Persons interested in obtaining a copy. of this brochure should send a stamped, self-addressed envelope to:

Edie Greene, Ph.D.
Department of Psychology
University of Colorado
P.O. Box 7150
Colorado Springs, CO 80933

The American Academy of Forensic Psychology

The American Academy of Forensic Psychology (AAFP) is the continuing education and training arm of the American Board of Forensic Psychology (ABFP). Both AAFP and ABFP are part of the American Board of Professional Psychology, which has provided certification in designated psychology specialties since 1947. AAFP was organized for the purpose of contributing to the development and maintenance of forensic psychology as a specialized field of study, research, and practice. Membership in the Academy is limited to persons who are Diplomates of the American Board of Forensic Psychology. AAFP has an Internet home page which you may access at:

http://www.abfp.com/aafp

For information regarding the Diplomate in Forensic Psychology contact:

American Board of Professional
   Psychology
2100 East Broadway, Suite 313
Columbia, MO 65201-6082

Copies of this Directory

Persons interested in obtaining a copy of this directory, which is published by the American Academy of Forensic Psychology, should contact:

Randy K. Otto, Ph.D., ABPP
Department of Mental Health Law &
   Policy
Louis de la Parte Florida Mental
   Health Institute
University of South Florida
13301 Bruce B. Downs Boulevard
Tampa, FL 33612-3899
Internet: otto@hal.fmhi.usf.edu

KEY

The key for the numbered columns in the table on pages 468–487 is:

Column No.	Description
1	APA Accreditation
2	Application Deadline
3	Program Start Date
4	Number of Internship Positions
5	Number of Staff Involved in Forensic Training
6	Number of Major Forensic Rotations
7	Percentage of Time Spent in Forensic Activities (Major Rotations)
8	Number of Minor Forensic Rotations
9	Percentage of Time Spent in Forensic Activities (Minor Rotations)
10	Competition for Forensic Rotations
11	Criminal-Forensic Populations
12	Correctional/Juvenile Justice Populations
13	Civil-Forensic Populations
14	Competence to Proceed
15	Criminal Responsibility
16	Risk Assessment
17	Sentencing/Disposition
18	Neuropsychology
19	Family/Child Custody
20	Personal Injury
21	Other
22	Forensic Treatment Experience
23	Inpatient Civil
24	Inpatient Forensic
25	Outpatient
26	Correctional/Juvenile Justice
27	Court Clinic
28	Other
29	Research Opportunities
30	Forensic Seminars

INTERNSHIPS WITH FORENSIC TRAINING OPPORTUNITIES

Institution
Program
Training Director
Forensic Supervisor
Address
Telephone
E-mail address

	1	2	3	4	5	6	7
ARKANSAS							
Division of Mental Health Services							
Psychology Internship Program	Full	1/15	Aug.	3	4		50%
John R. Anderson, Ph.D.							
Michael J. Simon, Ph.D.							
4313 East Markham St., Little Rock, AR 72205							
501/686-9014 or 9024							
CALIFORNIA							
Atascadero State Hospital							
Psychology Internship Program	Full	11/15	Sept.	3	35	4	75%
Robert Haynes, Ph.D.							
P.O. Box 7001, Atascadero, CA 93423-7001							
805/468-2213							
Kern County Psychology Internship							
Psychology Consortium Program		12/15	Sept.	3	4	1	50%
Kathe D. Lundgren, Ed.D.							
Brad Cloud, Psy.D.							
2920 F St., Ste. B-1, Bakersfield, CA 93301-1829							
805/323-7792							
Metropolitan Detention Center - Los Angeles							
Psychology Internship Program	Full	12/1	Oct.	3	1	1	30%
Selma Reed, Ph.D.							
Ralph Ihle, Ph.D.							
535 N. Alameda St., Los Angeles, CA 90012							
213/485-0439							
Metropolitan State Hospital							
Psychology Internship Program	None	1/17	Sept.	5	4	3	40%
Cheryl A. Kempinsky, Ph.D.							
11400 Norwalk Blvd., Norwalk, CA 90650							
310/863-7011 or 651-4286							
Napa State Hospital							
Psychology Internship Program	Full	11/15	Sept.	4	9		
Richard Lesch, Ph.D.							
2100 Napa – Vallejo Hwy., Napa, CA 94558-6293							
707/253-5631							
Patton State Hospital							
Psychology Internship Program	Full	12/15	Sept.	4	15	4	75%
April Wursten, Ph.D., ABPP							
3102 E. Highland Ave., Patton, CA 92369							
909/425-7511							
San Bernadino County Dept. of Mental Health							
Psychology Internship Program	Full	12/1	July	8	3	1	70%
Christopher Ebbe, Ph.D.							
Maurizio Assandri, Ph.D.							
700 E. Gilbert St., San Bernadino, CA 92415-0920							
909/387-7000							

8	9	10	11	12	13	14	15	16	17	18	19	20	21	22	23	24	25	26	27	28	29	30
		N	Y	N	Y	Y	Y	Y	Y	N	N	N	N		Y	Y	Y	Y	N	N		Y	Y
2		N	Y	N	N	Y	Y	Y	Y	N	Y	N	N		Y	N	Y	N	N	N		Y	Y
N/A	50%	Y	Y	Y	Y	Y	Y	Y	Y	N	Y	Y		Y	N	N	Y	N	N		N	Y
0	N/A	N	Y	Y	N	Y	Y	Y	Y	N	N	N		Y	N	N	N	Y	N		N	N
N/A	N/A	Y	N	N	Y	N	N	N	N	N	N		Y	Y	Y	N	N	N		N	Y
		N	Y	N	N	Y	Y	Y	N	Y	N	N		Y	N	Y	N	N	N		N	Y
0	N/A	N	Y	Y	N	Y	N	Y	N	Y	N	N		Y	Y	Y	N	Y	N		N	Y
1	30%	N	Y	Y	Y	Y	Y	Y	N	N	N	N		Y	Y	N	Y	Y	N		Y	Y

(Continued)

INTERNSHIPS WITH FORENSIC TRAINING OPPORTUNITIES (*continued*)

Institution
  Program
  Training Director
  Forensic Supervisor
  Address
  Telephone
  E-mail address

	1	2	3	4	5	6	7
CALIFORNIA (*continued*)							
VA Medical Center							
Psychology Internship Program	Full	12/8	Sept.	6	2	1	50%
John T. Friar, Ph.D.							
Shoba Sreenioasan, Ph.D.							
11301 Wilshire Blvd., W. Los Angeles, CA 90073							
310/268-4356							
COLORADO							
Adams Community Mental Health Center							
Psychology Internship Program	None	11/30	Oct.	6	5		65%
Catherine Johnston, Ph.D.							
T. J. Price, Psy.D.							
4371 E. 72nd Ave., Commerce, CO 80022-1487							
303/853-3533							
Denver Medical Center							
Psychology Internship Program	Full	11/20	Sept.	7	2	1	50–67%
Martha M. Woods, Ph.D.							
Mike Fitch, Ed.D., 303/375-5611							
777 Bannock St., MC0320 Denver, CO 80204-4507							
303/436-6393							
CONNECTICUT							
Connecticut Valley Psychology Internship							
Psychology Internship Program	Full	11/30	Sept.	2–3	3	0	N/A
David F. Zita, Ph.D.							
Marc Hillbrand, Ph.D.							
River Valley Hospital, Middletown, CT 06457							
203/344-2282							
FLORIDA							
45th St. Mental Health Center							
Psychology Internship Program	Prov.				4		50%
Tom Christiansen, Ph.D.							
Tom Christiansen, Ph.D. & Jan Valentine, MA							
1041 45th St., W. Palm Beach, FL 33407							
407/844-9741							
Florida State Hospital							
Psychology Internship Program	Full	1/1	Sept.	8	12	8	80%
Catherine B. Howell, Ph.D.							
P.O. Box 1000, Chattahoochee, FL 32324-1000							
904/663-7706							
catherine_howell@def.state.fl.us							
Goodman Psychological Services							
Psychology Internship Program	None	1/1	Aug.	4	1	0	N/A
Ana Maria Pi, Ph.D.							
Edda Aponte, Ph.D.							
8180 NW 36 St., Miami, FL 33166							
305/593-1223							

Prov.   Provisional

8	9	10	11	12	13	14	15	16	17	18	19	20	21	22	23	24	25	26	27	28	29	30
2	20%	N	Y	N	Y	Y	Y	Y	N	Y	N	N		Y	Y	Y	N	N	N		N	N
	5%	Y	Y	Y	Y	Y	Y	Y	Y	Y	Y	N		Y			Y	Y			N	Y
	5%	Y	Y	Y	Y	Y	N	Y	Y	Y	Y	N		Y	N	Y	Y	Y	N		Y	N
1	20%	N				Y	Y	Y		Y	N	N		Y	N	Y	Y	N	Y		Y	Y
	25%	N				N	N	Y	Y	N	N	N		Y	N	N	Y	N	N		N	Y
3	20%	Y	Y	N	Y	Y	N	Y	N	Y	N	N		Y	Y	Y	N	N	N		Y	Y
1	10%	N	N	Y	Y	N	N	Y		Y	Y	N		Y	N	N	Y	Y	N		N	N

(Continued)

INTERNSHIPS WITH FORENSIC TRAINING OPPORTUNITIES (*continued*)

Institution
  Program
  Training Director
  Forensic Supervisor
  Address
  Telephone
  E-mail address

	1	2	3	4	5	6	7
FLORIDA (*continued*)							
University of South Florida/Florida Mental Health Institute							
Psychology Internship Program	Full	11/29	Aug.	4	6	1	60%
Richard B. Weinberg, Ph.D.							
Paul Stiles, J.D., Ph.D.							
13301 Bruce B. Downs Blvd., Tampa, FL 33612-3899							
813/974-1992							
INDIANA							
Indiana University School of Medicine							
Psychology Internship Program	Full	12/1	Sept.	7	3	0	N/A
Richard J. Lawlor, J.D., Ph.D.							
Richard J. Lawlor, J.D., Ph.D.							
541 Clinical Dr., Rm. 290, Indianapolis, IN 46202-5111							
317/274-1239							
Park Center							
Psychology Internship Program	Full		Sept.	4	2	0	N/A
Ina S. Carlson, Ph.D.							
Steven Ross, Psy.D.							
909 East State Blvd., Fort Wayne, IN 46805							
219/481-2700							
KENTUCKY							
Federal Medical Center							
Psychology Internship Program	Full	12/1	Aug.	6	4	2	75%
Chris Canon, Ph.D.							
Andrew Simcox, Ph.D.							
3301 Leestown Rd., Lexington, KY 40511-8799							
606/255-6812							
MAINE							
VA Medical Center							
Psychology Internship Program	Full	12/1	July		3	3	30%
Frederick A. White, Ph.D.							
Neil MacLean, Ed.D.							
VAM & ROC, Togus, ME 04330							
207/623-8411, ext. 5383							
MARYLAND							
Crownsville Hospital Center							
Psychology Internship Program	Full		Sept.	3	4	3	90%
Alcides Pinto, Ph.D.							
Peter W. Demuth, Psy.D.							
Crownsville Road, Crownsville, MD 21032							
410/987-6200, ext. 270/319							

* Child Sex Abuse

8	9	10	11	12	13	14	15	16	17	18	19	20	21	22	23	24	25	26	27	28	29	30
0	N/A	N	N	Y	N	N	N	Y	N	Y	N	N		Y	N	N	N	Y	N		Y	Y
1	20%	N	Y	Y	Y	Y	Y	Y	Y	Y	Y	Y	*	Y	N	N	Y	N	N		N	Y
	20%	N	Y	Y	Y	Y	N	Y		Y	Y	N		Y	N	N	Y	N	N		N	Y
0	N/A	Y	Y	Y	N	Y	Y	Y	Y	Y	N	N	N	Y	N	Y	Y	Y	N		N	Y
1	20%	N	Y	Y	N	Y	Y	Y	Y	Y	N	N	N	Y	N	Y	Y	N	Y		Y	Y
3	35%	Y	Y	Y	N	Y	Y	Y	Y	Y	N	N		Y	N	Y	Y	Y	Y		Y	Y

(Continued)

INTERNSHIPS WITH FORENSIC TRAINING OPPORTUNITIES *(continued)*

Institution
Program
Training Director
Forensic Supervisor
Address
Telephone
E-mail address

	1	2	3	4	5	6	7
MARYLAND *(continued)*							
Malcolm Grow Medical Center							
Psychology Internship Program	Full	1/1	Sept.	5	3	0	N/A
Lt. Col. Ronald K. Chapman, Ph.D.							
Lt. Col. Ronald K. Chapman, Ph.D.							
89 MDOS/SGOHY, 1040 Boston Road,							
Andrews AFB, MD 20331-6600							
301/981-7186 301/981-6078							
Springfield Hospital Center							
Psychology Internship Program	Full	12/1	Sept.	3	2	0	N/A
Keith Hannan, Ph.D.							
Lawrence Raifman, Ph.D., J.D.							
Department of Psychology, Sykesville, MD 21784							
410/795-2100, ext. 3943							
MASSACHUSETTS							
Tewksbury Hospital							
Psychology Internship Program	None	1/2	July	2.5	6	0	N/A
Christopher Huvos, Psy.D.							
Steven Nisenbaum, J.D., Ph.D.							
365 East Street, Tewksbury, MA 01876							
617/727-4610, ext. 2645							
chuvos@state.ma.us							
MICHIGAN							
Wayne State University Medical School							
Psychology Internship Program	Full	12/1	Sept.	5	10	0	N/A
Jesse Bell, Ph.D.							
Moses Everette, Ph.D.							
2751 E. Jefferson Ave., Detroit MI 48207							
313/993-3415							
jwbell@wayne st1							
MISSOURI							
Federal Medical Center							
Psychology Internship Program	Full	12/15	Oct.	4	8	1	30%
Christina A. Pietz, Ph.D.							
Dr. Denney, Dr. Frederick, Dr. Mrad, & Dr. Pietz							
1900 West Sunshine, Springfield, MO 65807							
417/862-7041							
St. Louis Psychology Internship							
Psychology Consortium	Full	12/15	Sept.	5	12	5	70%
Joy A. Haven, Ph.D.							
Richard G. Scott, Ph.D.							
5351 Delmar, St. Louis, MO 63112							
314/877-0548							

8	9	10	11	12	13	14	15	16	17	18	19	20	21	22	23	24	25	26	27	28	29	30
5	10%	N	Y	Y	Y	Y	Y	Y	Y	N	Y	N		N	Y	N	Y	N	N		N	Y
1	20%	N	Y	N	N	Y	Y	Y		N	N	N		Y	N	Y	Y	N	N		N	Y
2	20%	N	Y	N	Y	Y	Y	Y	Y	Y	Y	N		Y	Y	Y	N	N	N		Y	Y
2	25%	Y	Y	N	Y	Y	Y	Y	Y		Y	N	N	Y	N	Y	N	N	N		N	Y
1	30%	N	Y	Y	Y	Y	Y	Y	Y	Y	Y	N	N	Y	Y	Y	N	Y	N		Y	Y
0	N/A	N	Y	N	Y	Y	Y	Y	Y	N	N	N		Y	Y	Y	N	N	N		Y	Y

(Continued)

INTERNSHIPS WITH FORENSIC TRAINING OPPORTUNITIES (*continued*)

Institution
Program
Training Director
Forensic Supervisor
Address
Telephone
E-mail address

	1	2	3	4	5	6	7
MISSOURI (*continued*)							
Western Missouri Mental Health Center							
Psychology Internship Program	Full	12/15	Sept.	4	6	4	75%
E. Thomas Copeland, Jr., Ph.D., ABPP							
Steven A. Mandracchi, Ph.D., & Daniel L.							
Birmingham, Ph.D.							
600 East 22nd Street, Kansas City, MO 64108							
816/471-3002							
NEW YORK							
Albany Psychology Internship Consortium							
Psychology Internship Program	Full	11/30	Sept.	7	5	3	65%
Reuban J. Silver, Ph.D.							
Elizabeth Critz Schockmel, Psy.D.							
75 New Scotland Ave., Albany, NY 12205							
518/447-9665							
Crestwood Children's Center							
Psychology Internship Program	Full	12/15	Sept.	5	2	0	N/A
David Corom, Ph.D.							
David Corom, Ph.D.							
2075 Scottsville Road, Rochester, NY 14623							
716/436-4442							
Kings County Hospital Center							
Psychology Internship Program	Full	11/30	July	10	6	2	50%
A. Sandgrund, Ph.D., & N. M. Cohn, Ph.D.							
T. O'Rourke, Ph.D.							
451 Clarkson Ave., Brooklyn, NY 11203							
718/245-2579							
orourke.HSCbrooklyn.edu							
Kings Park Psychiatric Center							
Psychology Internship Program	None	2/1	Sept.	3	2	0	N/A
Allan Smith, Ph.D.							
Allan Smith, Ph.D.							
Box 9000, Kings Park, NY 11754-9000							
516/544-2715							
Kirby Forensic Psychiatric Center							
Psychology Internship Program		11/15	Sept.	3	6	2	40%
Abraham Kuperberg, Ph.D.							
600 East 125th St., New York, NY 10035							
212/427-9003							
Lincoln Medical and Mental Health							
Psychology Internship Program	Full	11/30	Sept.	3	1	0	N/A
Jose A. Valciukas, Ph.D.							
Jose A. Valciukas, Ph.D.							
234 E. 149th St., Bronx, NY 10451							
718/579-5779							

8	9	10	11	12	13	14	15	16	17	18	19	20	21	22	23	24	25	26	27	28	29	30
4	33%	N	Y	Y	N	Y	Y	Y		N	N	N		Y	N	Y	Y	Y	N		Y	Y
0	N/A	Y	N	N	Y	N	N	N	N	N	Y	N		N	N	N	Y	N	N		N	Y
2	5%	N				N	N	Y		N	Y	N		N	N	N	Y	N	N		N	N
0	N/A	Y	Y			Y	Y	Y	Y	Y	N	N		Y	N	Y	Y	Y	Y		Y	Y
1	5%		Y	N	N	N	Y	Y		Y	N	N		Y	Y	Y	Y	N	N		N	N
0	N/A	N																			Y	Y
1	15%	N	Y	Y	Y	Y	Y	Y	Y	N	Y	Y	Y	N	N	N	Y	N	N		N	Y

(Continued)

INTERNSHIPS WITH FORENSIC TRAINING OPPORTUNITIES *(continued)*

Institution
  Program
  Training Director
  Forensic Supervisor
  Address
  Telephone
  E-mail address

	1	2	3	4	5	6	7
NEW YORK *(continued)*							
Manhattan Psychiatric Center							
Psychology Internship Program	Full	11/30	Sept.	6	5	0	N/A
Gerald Perlman, Ph.D.							
Wards Island Complex, New York, NY 10035							
212/369-0500, ext. 2618							
Mount Sinai Services							
Psychology Internship Program	Full	11/30	July	3	2	2	30%
Mark S. Wielgus, Ph.D.							
Lisa Saraydarian, Ph.D. & Anthony Sentoro, Psy.D.							
D10-6 79-01 Broadway, Elmhurst, NY 11373							
718/334-3577							
Ulster County Mental Health Department							
Psychology Internship Program	Full	11/30	July	5	3	0	N/A
David Wheeler, Psy.D.							
Claude Schleuderer, Ph.D.							
Box 1800, Kingston, NY 12401							
914/331-6340							
NORTH CAROLINA							
Federal Correctional Institution							
Psychology Internship Program	Full	11/15	Sept.	4	14	4	50%
Edward "Rhett" Landis, Ph.D.							
Edward "Rhett" Landis, Ph.D.							
P.O. Box 1000, Butner, NC 27509-1000							
919/575-4541, ext. 534							
University of North Carolina, Federal Medical Center, Butner, NC							
Psychology Internship Program	Full	11/30	Sept.	10	18	2	50%
Lee M. Marcus, Ph.D.							
Edward E. Landis, Ph.D.							
Medical School Wing E, CB 7180, Chapel Hill, NC 27599-7180							
919-966-5156							
OHIO							
Child and Adolescent Service Center							
Psychology Internship Program	Full	12/1	July	4	2	0	N/A
Robert M. Brewster, Ph.D.							
Ralph Buterbaugh, M.A.							
1226 Market Ave. N., Canton, OH 44720							
216/454-5161							

* Sex Offenders, Substance Abusers

8	9	10	11	12	13	14	15	16	17	18	19	20	21	22	23	24	25	26	27	28	29	30
1	5%	N																			N	Y
0	N/A	N	Y	N	N	Y	N	N	Y	N	N	N		Y	N	Y	N	N	N		N	Y
5	10%	N	Y	Y	N	Y	N	Y	Y	N	Y	N		Y	N	N	Y	Y	Y		N	Y
4	30%	N	Y	Y	Y	Y	Y	Y	Y	Y	N	N		Y	Y	Y	N	Y	N	*	Y	Y
2	10%	N	Y	Y	N	Y	Y	Y	Y	Y	N	N		Y	Y	Y	N	Y	N		Y	Y
1	5%	N	N	N	Y	N	N	Y		Y	Y			Y	N	N	Y	N	Y		Y	Y

(Continued)

INTERNSHIPS WITH FORENSIC TRAINING OPPORTUNITIES *(continued)*

Institution
Program
Training Director
Forensic Supervisor
Address
Telephone
E-mail address

	1	2	3	4	5	6	7
OHIO *(continued)*							
VA Medical Center							
Psychology Internship Program	Full	1/4	Aug.	9	3	0	N/A
Robert W. Goldberg, Ph.D., ABPP							
10701 East Blvd., Cleveland, OH 44106							
216/791-3800, ext. 4970							
OREGON							
Morrison Center							
Psychology Internship Program	Full		Sept.	5	2	0	N/A
Redmond Reams, Ph.D.							
Orin Bolstad, Ph.D., ABPP							
3355 SE Powell Blvd., Portland OR 97202							
503/232-0191							
PENNSYLVANIA							
Norristown State Hospital							
Psychology Internship Program	Full	12/15	Sept.	4	2	2	35%
Gail Vant Zelfde, Ph.D.							
Gail Vant Zelfde, Ph.D.							
1001 Sterigere St., Norristown, PA 19401-5399							
610/270-1522							
Philadelphia Child Guidance Center							
Psychology Internship Program	Full	11/30	Sept.	4	1	0	N/A
Internship Director							
Andrew Vogelson, Ph.D.							
34th St. and Civic Center Blvd., Philadelphia,							
PA 19104-4322							
215/243-2751							
SOUTH CAROLINA							
William S. Hall Psychiatric Institute							
Psychology Internship Program	Full	1/1	Sept.	4	11	2	100%
William Rothstein, Ph.D., ABPP							
Geoffrey R. McKee, Ph.D., ABPP							
P.O. Box 202, Columbia, SC 29202							
803/734-7246							
GRM70@WSHPI.DMH.STATE.SC.US							
TENNESSEE							
DeBerry Special Needs Facility							
Psychology Internship Program	Full	12/31	Sept.	2	1	2	50%
Lawrence J. Weitz, Ph.D.							
Barbara Bergman, Ph.D.							
7575 Cockrill Bend Industrial Rd., Nashville,							
TN 37209-1057							
615/350-2700							

* Consultation with State Training Schools for Delinquents

† Courtroom Testimony

8	9	10	11	12	13	14	15	16	17	18	19	20	21	22	23	24	25	26	27	28	29	30
2	15%	N	Y	N	Y	Y	Y	Y		Y	N	N		N	N	N	N	N	Y		Y	Y
5	20%	N	N	Y	N	N	N	Y	Y	N	N	N	*	Y	N	N	N	Y	N		N	Y
2	10%	Y	Y	N	N	Y	N	Y	Y	Y	N	N		Y	N	Y	N	N	N		Y	Y
4	10%	N	N	N	Y	N	N	N		N	Y	N		N	N	N	Y	N	N		N	Y
0	N/A	Y	Y	Y	Y	Y	Y	Y	N	N	Y	Y	†	Y	N	Y	Y	Y	N		Y	Y
1	25%	N	Y	N	N	Y	Y	Y	Y	Y	N	N		Y	N	Y	N	N	N		N	Y

(Continued)

INTERNSHIPS WITH FORENSIC TRAINING OPPORTUNITIES *(continued)*

Institution
  Program
  Training Director
  Forensic Supervisor
  Address
  Telephone
  E-mail address

	1	2	3	4	5	6	7
TENNESSEE *(continued)*							
University of Tennessee/VA Medical Center, Knoxville, TN							
Psychology Internship Program	Full			3	2	0	N/A
Karen A. Clark, Ph.D.							
Lynne Zager, Ph.D.							
1030 Jefferson, Memphis, TN 38104							
901/523-8990							
TEXAS							
Federal Medical Center							
Psychology Internship Program	Prov.	12/1	Oct.	4	1	4	40%
Robert Durrenberger, Ph.D.							
Emily Fallis, Ph.D.							
3150 Horton Rd., Fort Worth, TX 76119-5996							
817/535-2111, ext. 370							
University of Texas Medical School of Galveston							
Psychology Internship Program	Full	12/15	Sept.	6	2		10%
Jeff Baker, Ph.D.							
Collier Cole, Ph.D. and Russell Gardner, M.D.							
Galveston, TX 77555-1028							
409/772-9576							
jeffbaker@UTMB.EDU							
University of Texas Medical School at Houston							
Psychology Internship Program	Full	12/15	July	8	6	3	50%
J. Ray Hays, Ph.D., J.D.							
J. Ray Hays, Ph.D., J.D. and Rod Cannedy, Ph.D.							
P.O. Box 20708, Houston, TX 77225							
713/794-4028							
rhays@mind.hcpc.uth.tmc.edu							
UTAH							
University of Utah							
Psychology Internship Program	None	12/31	Sept.	3	3		
Dr. Patricia Hopps							
Dr. Christine Currey							
501 Chipeta Way, Salt Lake City, UT 84108							
801/583-2500							
Wasatch Mental Health—Institute for Psychological Training							
Psychology Internship Program	None	1/15	Sept.	3	3	3	20%
Freeman M. Dunn, Ph.D.							
Thomas C. Wallace, Ph.D.							
750 N. 200 W., Provo, UT 84601							
801/373-4766							

* Competency

8	9	10	11	12	13	14	15	16	17	18	19	20	21	22	23	24	25	26	27	28	29	30
1	15%	Y	Y	Y	N	Y	Y	Y		N	N	N		N	Y	Y	N	Y	Y		N	N
2	20%	Y	Y	Y	Y	Y	Y	Y		N	Y	N			N	N	Y	Y	N		Y	Y
	5	N	Y	Y	Y	Y	N	Y	Y	Y	N	N		Y	N	N	Y	Y	N		Y	Y
0	N/A	N	Y	Y	Y	Y	Y	Y		N	N	N		N	N	N	Y	Y	N		N	Y
		N	N	Y	N	N	Y	N	Y	Y	Y	Y	*	Y	Y	Y	N	N	N		N	Y
0	N/A	N	Y	Y	Y	Y	N	Y	Y	N	Y	Y		Y	Y	N	Y	N	N		N	N

(Continued)

INTERNSHIPS WITH FORENSIC TRAINING OPPORTUNITIES *(continued)*

Institution
Program
Training Director
Forensic Supervisor
Address
Telephone
E-mail address

	1	2	3	4	5	6	7
VIRGINIA							
Eastern Virginia Medical School							
Psychology Internship Program	Full	12/1	July	7	2		20%
Robert P. Archer, Ph.D.							
Donna K. Moore, Psy.D.							
Hofheimer Hall, Norfolk, VA 23507-1912							
757/446-5881							
archer@picard.evans.edu							
Federal Correctional Institution							
Psychology Internship Program	Full	12/18	Oct.	4	1	4	20%
Robert K. Ax, Ph.D.							
Marcus R. Forbes, Ph.D.							
Psychology Services, FCI, Petersburg, VA 23804-1000							
804/733-7881, ext. 248							
University of Virginia Health Sciences Center							
Psychology Internship Program	Full	12/1	July	7		2	67%
Patrick C. Fowler, Ph.D.							
Gary L. Hawk, Ph.D., & David Rawls, Ph.D.							
Drawer C–Blue Ridge Hospital, Charlottesville, VA 22901							
804/924-2252							
pcf7v@galen.med.virginia.edu							
WASHINGTON							
Western State Hospital							
Psychology Internship Program	Full	12/1	Sept.	5	5	2	100%
Mark Soelling, Ph.D.							
Varies							
9601 Steilacoom Blvd., SW, Tacoma, WA 98498-7213							
206/756-2722							
WISCONSIN							
Ethan Allen School							
Psychology Internship Program	Full	12/15	Sept.	5	5		10%
Michael Hagan							
Michael Hagan							
Box 900, Wales, WI 53183-0900							
414/646-3341, ext. 313							
Mendota Mental Health Institute							
Psychology Internship Program	Full	12/15	Sept.	3	14	2	
Rodney K. Miller, Ph.D.							
Several							
301 Troy Dr., Madison, WI 53704							
608/243-2543							
millerk@dhfs.state.wi.us							

* Sex Offender Assessments
† Juvenile Parole Board

8	9	10	11	12	13	14	15	16	17	18	19	20	21	22	23	24	25	26	27	28	29	30
1–2	50%	Y	Y	N	N	Y	Y	Y	Y	Y	N	N		Y	N	Y	N	N	N		Y	N
0	N/A	N	Y	Y	N	Y	Y	Y	N	N	N	N			N	Y	N	Y	N		N	Y
2	33%	Y	Y	Y	Y	Y	Y	Y	Y	Y	N	N		Y	Y	Y	Y	Y	N		N	Y
5	20%	Y	Y	N	Y	Y	Y	Y	Y	Y	N	N		Y	Y	Y	N	N	N		Y	Y
	10%	N	Y	Y	N	N	N	Y	Y	N	N	N	*	Y	N	N	Y	Y	N	†	Y	Y
0	N/A	N	Y	Y	Y	Y	N	Y	N	Y	N	N		Y	Y	Y	N	Y	N		Y	Y

(Continued)

INTERNSHIPS WITH FORENSIC TRAINING OPPORTUNITIES *(continued)*

Institution
Program
Training Director
Forensic Supervisor
Address
Telephone
E-mail address

	1	2	3	4	5	6	7
CANADA							
Alberta Hospital–Edmonton and Glenrose							
Rehabilitation Hospital Consortium							
Psychology Internship Program	Full	12/1	Sept.	4	3	3	66%
Dr. Wendy L. Hawkins							
Drs. Sheila Greer, Dorothy Constable, and Mary-Ann Back							
Box 307, Edmonton, Alberta, Canada T5J2J7							
403/472-5435							
Calgary General Hospital							
Psychology Internship Program	None	12/31	Sept.	2	4	2	90%
Dr. Gene Flessati							
Dr. Tom Dalby							
3500–26 Ave. N.E., Calgary, Alberta, Canada							
TIY 6J4							
403/268-9103							
flessati@acs.ucalgary.ca							
Victoria Hospital							
Psychology Internship Program	Full			3			N/A
Vicky Veitch Wolfe, Ph.D.							
N/A							
800 Commissioners Road E., London, Ontario							
N6A 4G5							
519/685-8144							

* Mock Court Experience

8	9	10	11	12	13	14	15	16	17	18	19	20	21	22	23	24	25	26	27	28	29	30
0		Y	Y	Y	N	Y	N	Y	Y	N	N	N		Y	N	N	Y	N	N	*	Y	Y
0	N/A	Y	Y	Y	N	Y	Y	Y	Y	Y	N	N		Y	N	Y	Y	Y	N		Y	Y
2	20%	N				N	N	N		Y	Y			N	N	N	Y	N	Y		N	N

Forensic Service Settings

Institution	Director	State Mental Health Forensic Hospital or Unit	State Mental Health Civil Hospital	Community Mental Health Center	State Prison	Federal Prison	County Jail	Private Practitioners	Department Clinic	Other
Alabama										
University of Alabama	Beverly Thorn	Y	Y	Y		Y		Y		Y
Arizona										
Arizona State University	Alex Zautra		Y			Y	Y			
California										
Fuller Theological Seminary	Leonardo M. Marmol		Y	Y						Y
University of California Los Angeles	Constance L. Hammen			Y				Y		Y
University of California Santa Barbara	Larry E. Beutler	Y	Y	Y		Y				
University of Southern California	Adrienne Davis	Y	Y	Y	Y		Y	Y		Y
Colorado										
Denver Institute-Adelphi University	Jonathan Jackson	Y		Y						
University of Denver	Wyndol Furman			Y						Y
Connecticut										
University of Connecticut	George J. Allen	Y	Y	Y				Y		
University of Hartford	John G. Mehm		Y	Y						Y
Yale University	Kelly Browne		Y	Y						
Delaware										
University of Delaware	R. Simons		Y	Y						
District of Columbia										
Gallaudet University	Virginia Gutman	Y	Y	Y	Y					
George Washington University	Rolf A. Peterson	Y		Y						Y
Florida										
Florida Institute of Technology	Philip D. Farber		Y			Y	Y	Y		
University of Miami	Donald K. Routh		Y					Y		Y
Georgia										
Emory University	Elaine Walker		Y					Y		
Georgia State University	Michael Milan		Y	Y	Y			Y		
University of Georgia	Karen Calhoun								Y	

Forensic Service Settings

Institution	Director	State Mental Health Forensic Hospital or Unit	State Mental Health Civil Hospital	Community Mental Health Center	State Prison	Federal Prison	County Jail	Private Practitioners	Department Clinic	Other
Hawaii										
University of Hawaii	Tony Marsella	Y	Y	Y				Y		
Illinois										
Chicago Medical School	John E. Calamari			Y	Y		Y	Y		
DePaul University	Sheila Ribordy			Y						
Illinois Institute of Technology	Robert Schleser		Y	Y				Y		
Loyola University of Chicago	Isiaah Crawford			Y						Y
Northern Illinois University	Steve Gold			Y			Y	Y		
Northwestern University	Ian Gotlib									Y
University of Illinois at Chicago	Larry Grimm						Y			Y
Iowa										
University of Iowa	Don Fowles								Y	
Kansas										
University of Kansas	Michael Roberts								Y	
Kentucky										
University of Kentucky	Ruth Baer		Y	Y		Y	Y			
University of Louisville	Suzanne Meeks	Y	Y	Y	Y			Y		
Louisiana										
Louisiana State University	Johnny L. Matson	Y	Y		Y					
San Diego State University/University of California at San Diego	Richard H. Schulte			Y				Y		
Maine										
University of Maine	Geoffrey L. Thorpe		Y				Y		Y	Y
Maryland										
University of Maryland	Robert H. Deluty	Y	Y	Y				Y		
Massachusetts										
Antioch New England Graduate School	Roger Peterson	Y		Y	Y			Y		
University of Massachusetts Amherst	Patricia Wisocki	Y								

(Continued)

Forensic Service Settings

Institution	Director	State Mental Health Forensic Hospital or Unit	State Mental Health Civil Hospital	Community Mental Health Center	State Prison	Federal Prison	County Jail	Private Practitioners	Department Clinic	Other
Michigan										
Michigan State University	Norman Abeles			Y					Y	
University of Detroit Mercy	Karen Chapin	Y	Y				Y			
University of Michigan	Eric Bermann	Y								
Wayne State University	Douglas Whitman	Y							Y	Y
Mississippi										
University of Mississippi	Karen Christoff	Y	Y	Y						
Missouri										
Saint Louis University	Michael J. Ross	Y						Y		
Montana										
University of Montana	David Schuldberg	Y	Y	Y	Y			Y		
North Carolina										
Duke University	Robert Thompson		Y	Y				Y		
University of North Carolina Chapel Hill	Don Baucom	Y	Y	Y						
University of North Carolina Greensboro	Ernest Lumsden			Y				Y		Y
North Dakota										
University of North Dakota	Jeffrey Holm		Y	Y						Y
Nebraska										
University of Nebraska-A102Lincoln	David Hansen	Y		Y	Y			Y		
Nevada										
University of Nevada	Victoria Follette	Y								
New Jersey										
Fairleigh Dickinson University	Robert McGrath									Y
Rutgers University Busch Campus	Stanley B. Messer									Y
Rutgers University New Brunswick	Barbara McCrady									Y
New Mexico										
University of New Mexico	Jane Smith			Y		Y				
New York										
St. John's University	Jeffrey Nevid	Y	Y	Y						Y

Forensic Service Settings

Institution	Director	State Mental Health Forensic Hospital or Unit	State Mental Health Civil Hospital	Community Mental Health Center	State Prison	Federal Prison	County Jail	Private Practitioners	Department Clinic	Other
State University of New York at Binghamton	Stephen A. Lisman		Y	Y					Y	Y
State University of New York at Buffalo	J.S. Shrauger									Y
State University of New York+A2 at Albany	William L. Simmons		Y							Y
Ohio										
Bowling Green State University	Douglas G. Ullman			Y			Y			
Kent State University	Michael Hirt	Y	Y	Y	Y					
Ohio State University	Steven J. Beck	Y		Y			Y	Y		Y
University of Cincinnati	Milton E. Foreman		Y	Y				Y		
Wright State University	James Dobbins	Y	Y	Y	Y		Y	Y		
Pennsylvania										
Allegheny University Dept. of Psychology, Clinical Program	Michael Lowe		Y	Y						Y
Allegheny University Dept. of Psychology, Law and Psychology Program	Don Bersoff	Y	Y	Y				Y		Y
Indiana University of Pennsylvania	Don Robertson			Y		Y			Y	
Pennsylvania State University	William J. Ray			Y	Y		Y			
Temple University	Phillip Kendall		Y	Y	Y					
University of Pittsburgh	Susan Campbell								Y	Y
Widener University	Jules C. Abrams	Y	Y	Y	Y	Y	Y	Y		
South Carolina										
University of South Carolina	Diane Follingstad			Y	Y			Y		Y
South Dakota										
University of South Dakota	Barbara Yutrenka		Y	Y				Y		Y
Texas										
University of Houston	John Vincent			Y	Y	Y	Y	Y		
University of North Texas	Richard Rogers	Y				Y				Y
University of Texas at Austin	Micheal Telch		Y	Y				Y		
Utah										
Brigham Young University	Bert P. Cunick	Y			Y			Y		

(Continued)

Forensic Service Settings

Institution	Director	State Mental Health Forensic Hospital or Unit	State Mental Health Civil Hospital	Community Mental Health Center	State Prison	Federal Prison	County Jail	Private Practitioners	Department Clinic	Other
Virginia										
University of Virginia	Robert Emery	Y	Y	Y						Y
University of Virginia-Curry Programs	Ron Reeve	Y	Y	Y					Y	Y
Virginia Commonwealth University	Don Kiesler	Y		Y	Y	Y				Y
Virginia Polytechnic Institute and State University	Thomas H. Ollendick		Y	Y					Y	
Vermont										
University of Vermont	Bruce E. Compas		Y	Y	Y				Y	
Washington										
University of Washington	Ana Mari Cauce			Y				Y		Y
West Virginia										
West Virginia University	Daniel W. McNeil	Y	Y	Y		Y		Y		
Wisconsin										
University of Wisconsin Madison	Joseph P. Newman	Y			Y	Y				
University of Wisconsin-Milwaukee	David C. Osmon							Y		
Wyoming										
University of Wyoming	Roderick S. Carman	Y	Y	Y						
CANADA										
Alberta										
University of Calgary	Keith Dobson	Y	Y		Y			Y		
British Columbia										
Simon Fraser University	Ronald Roesch	Y	Y		Y	Y	Y			
Ontario										
University of Western Ontario	Rod A. Martin	Y		Y						
Quebec										
McGill University	Blaine Ditto		Y							

Forensic Procedures

Institution	Not Guilty by Reason of Insanity	Child Custody Determination	Guardianship and Conservatorship	Competency to Consent to Treatment	Child Abuse and Neglect	Waiver of Juveniles to Adult Court	Pre-Sentencing Evaluations	Capital Sentencing	Evaluation for Civil Commitment	Competence for Execution	Risk Assessment	Sex Offender Therapy	Restoration of Competence to Stand Trial	Reduction of Violence or Aggressive Tendencies	Competency to Stand Trial
Alabama															
University of Alabama	Y	Y	Y		Y				Y		Y			Y	Y	Y
Arizona															
Arizona State University															
California															
Fuller Theological Seminary		Y	Y	Y	Y				Y		Y	Y		Y	
University of California Los Angeles			Y	Y							Y				
University of California Santa Barbara	Y		Y	Y	Y		Y		Y		Y	Y		Y	Y
University of Southern California	Y	Y	Y	Y	Y	Y	Y	Y	Y		Y	Y	Y	Y	Y
Colorado															
Denver Institute-Adelphi University															
University of Denver		Y	Y		Y		Y		Y		Y			Y	Y
Connecticut															
University of Connecticut	Y	Y	Y	Y	Y		Y		Y					Y	Y
University of Hartford				Y	Y	Y	Y		Y		Y			Y	
Yale University															
Delaware															
University of Delaware		Y	Y		Y						Y				
District of Columbia															
Gallaudet University	Y			Y			Y		Y		Y	Y	Y	Y	Y
George Washington University	Y		Y				Y		Y		Y			Y	Y
Florida															
Florida Institute of Technology		Y			Y						Y	Y		Y	
University of Miami											Y				
Georgia															
Emory University															
Georgia State University									Y		Y	Y		Y	
University of Georgia		Y										Y			

(Continued)

Forensic Procedures

Institution	Not Guilty by Reason of Insanity	Child Custody Determination	Guardianship and Conservatorship	Competency to Consent to Treatment	Child Abuse and Neglect	Waiver of Juveniles to Adult Court	Pre-Sentencing Evaluations	Capital Sentencing	Evaluation for Civil Commitment	Competence for Execution	Risk Assessment	Sex Offender Therapy	Restoration of Competence to Stand Trial	Reduction of Violence or Aggressive Tendencies	Competency to Stand Trial
Hawaii															
University of Hawaii					Y							Y		Y	
Illinois															
Chicago Medical School				Y	Y										
De Paul University		Y			Y									Y	
Illinois Institute of Technology		Y			Y						Y				
Loyola University of Chicago		Y													
Northern Illinois University		Y	Y						Y		Y	Y		Y	Y
Northwestern University															
University of Illinois at Chicago															
Iowa															
University of Iowa															
Kansas															
University of Kansas					Y										
Kentucky															
University of Kentucky	Y					Y			Y		Y		Y	Y	Y
University of Louisville						Y			Y						Y
Louisiana															
Louisiana State University	Y		Y	Y					Y		Y				Y
San Diego State University/University of California at San Diego		Y			Y									Y	
Maine															
University of Maine	Y	Y		Y	Y	Y	Y		Y		Y	Y		Y	Y
Maryland															
University of Maryland				Y	Y				Y		Y	Y		Y	Y
Massachusetts															
Antioch New England Graduate School		Y			Y						Y	Y		Y	
University of Massachusetts Amherst		Y				Y					Y		Y		Y
Michigan															
Michigan State University		Y	Y		Y						Y	Y		Y	Y

Forensic Procedures

Institution	Not Guilty by Reason of Insanity	Child Custody Determination	Guardianship and Conservatorship	Competency to Consent to Treatment	Child Abuse and Neglect	Waiver of Juveniles to Adult Court	Pre-Sentencing Evaluations	Capital Sentencing	Evaluation for Civil Commitment	Competence for Execution	Risk Assessment	Sex Offender Therapy	Restoration of Competence to Stand Trial	Reduction of Violence or Aggressive Tendencies	Competency to Stand Trial
University of Detroit Mercy		Y	Y	Y	Y	Y	Y		Y		Y	Y		Y	Y
University of Michigan					Y									Y	Y
Wayne State University	Y	Y	Y		Y	Y	Y		Y		Y		Y	Y	
Mississippi															
University of Mississippi	Y	Y	Y	Y	Y	Y			Y		Y				Y
Missouri															
Saint Louis University	Y	Y			Y		Y				Y				Y
Montana															
University of Montana	Y	Y			Y						Y	Y		Y	Y
North Carolina															
Duke University		Y	Y		Y						Y			Y	Y
University of North Carolina Chapel Hill		Y		Y	Y				Y		Y	Y			Y
University of North Carolina Greensboro		Y			Y	Y	Y				Y	Y		Y	
North Dakota															
University of North Dakota		Y	Y		Y	Y			Y		Y	Y	Y	Y	Y
Nebraska															
University of Nebraska-A102Lincoln	Y	Y		Y	Y	Y	Y		Y		Y	Y	Y	Y	Y
Nevada															
University of Nevada									Y		Y			Y	Y
New Jersey															
Fairleigh Dickinson University					Y						Y			Y	
Rutgers University Busch Campus			Y		Y										
Rutgers University New Brunswick			Y		Y										
New Mexico															
University of New Mexico															
New York															
St. John's University															
State University of New York at Binghamton					Y										
State University of New York at Buffalo	Y	Y			Y	Y					Y				Y

(Continued)

Forensic Procedures

Institution	Not Guilty by Reason of Insanity	Child Custody Determination	Guardianship and Conservatorship	Competency to Consent to Treatment	Child Abuse and Neglect	Waiver of Juveniles to Adult Court	Pre-Sentencing Evaluations	Capital Sentencing	Evaluation for Civil Commitment	Competence for Execution	Risk Assessment	Sex Offender Therapy	Restoration of Competence to Stand Trial	Reduction of Violence or Aggressive Tendencies	Competency to Stand Trial
State University of New York+A2 at Albany	Y	Y	Y	Y	Y				Y						Y
Ohio															
Bowling Green State University				Y		Y			Y		Y	Y		Y	
Kent State University	Y		Y	Y		Y			Y		Y	Y	Y	Y	Y
Ohio State University			Y		Y	Y	Y					Y			Y
University of Cincinnati															
Wright State University	Y	Y	Y	Y	Y						Y	Y	Y	Y	Y
Pennsylvania															
Allegheny University Dept. of Psychology, Clinical Program	Y	Y	Y	Y	Y		Y		Y		Y	Y	Y	Y	Y
Allegheny University Dept. of Psychology, Law and Psychology Program	Y		Y	Y	Y				Y		Y		Y	Y	Y
Indiana University of Pennsylvania		Y		Y			Y		Y		Y	Y		Y	Y
Pennsylvania State University	Y		Y	Y			Y		Y		Y				Y
Temple University		Y	Y		Y		Y				Y				Y
University of Pittsburgh		Y			Y										
Widener University		Y	Y		Y	Y			Y		Y	Y		Y	
South Carolina															
University of South Carolina						Y	Y					Y		Y	
South Dakota															
University of South Dakota			Y								Y			Y	
Texas															
University of Houston		Y			Y		Y	Y	Y			Y	Y	Y	
University of North Texas	Y										Y		Y	Y	
University of Texas at Austin															
Utah															
Brigham Young University	Y						Y			Y					Y
Virginia															
University of Virginia	Y	Y	Y	Y	Y	Y	Y		Y		Y		Y	Y	Y
University of Virginia-Curry Programs	Y	Y	Y	Y	Y	Y	Y	Y	Y	Y	Y	Y	Y	Y	Y

Forensic Procedures

Institution	Not Guilty by Reason of Insanity	Child Custody Determination	Guardianship and Conservatorship	Competency to Consent to Treatment	Child Abuse and Neglect	Waiver of Juveniles to Adult Court	Pre-Sentencing Evaluations	Capital Sentencing	Evaluation for Civil Commitment	Competence for Execution	Risk Assessment	Sex Offender Therapy	Restoration of Competence to Stand Trial	Reduction of Violence or Aggressive Tendencies	Competency to Stand Trial
Virginia Commonwealth University		Y	Y		Y		Y				Y	Y		Y	
Virginia Polytechnic Institute and State University		Y			Y				Y						
Vermont															
University of Vermont		Y	Y								Y				
Washington															
University of Washington		Y	Y		Y						Y			Y	
West Virginia															
West Virginia University	Y	Y			Y	Y	Y		Y		Y			Y	Y
Wisconsin															
University of Wisconsin Madison		Y	Y	Y	Y						Y	Y		Y	
University of Wisconsin-Milwaukee		Y			Y		Y								
Wyoming															
University of Wyoming	Y	Y	Y	Y	Y	Y			Y		Y				Y
CANADA															
Alberta															
University of Calgary	Y	Y	Y	Y	Y	Y	Y		Y		Y	Y		Y	Y
British Columbia															
Simon Fraser University	Y		Y	Y							Y	Y		Y	Y
Ontario															
University of Western Ontario	Y	Y	Y		Y	Y	Y								Y
Quebec															
McGill University									Y		Y				

Expert Witness Admissibility—Federal Rules of Evidence, 1993

RULE 104. PRELIMINARY QUESTIONS

(a) Questions of admissibility generally. Preliminary questions concerning the qualification of a person to be a witness, the existence of a privilege, or the admissibility of evidence shall be determined by the court, subject to the provisions of subdivision (b). In making its determination it is not bound by the rules of evidence except those with respect to privileges.

(b) Relevancy conditioned on fact. When the relevancy of evidence depends upon the fulfillment of a condition of fact, the court shall admit it upon, or subject to, the introduction of evidence sufficient to support a finding of the fulfillment of the condition.

(c) Hearing of jury. Hearings on the admissibility of confessions shall in all cases be conducted out of the hearing of the jury. Hearings on other preliminary matters shall be so conducted when the interests of justice require, or when an accused is a witness and so requests.

(d) Testimony by accused. The accused does not, by testifying upon a preliminary matter, become subject to cross-examination as to other issues in the case.

(e) Weight and credibility. This rule does not limit the right of a party to introduce before the jury evidence relevant to weight or credibility. (As amended March 2, 1987, effective October 1, 1987.)

RULE 105. LIMITED ADMISSIBILITY

When evidence which is admissible as to one party or for one purpose but not admissible as to another party or for another purpose is admitted, the court, upon request, shall restrict the evidence to its proper scope and instruct the jury accordingly.

RULE 401. DEFINITION OF "RELEVANT EVIDENCE"

"Relevant evidence" means evidence having any tendency to make the existence of any fact that is of consequence to the determination of the action more probable or less probable than it would be without the evidence.

RULE 402. RELEVANT EVIDENCE GENERALLY ADMISSIBLE; IRRELEVANT EVIDENCE INADMISSIBLE

All relevant evidence is admissible, except as otherwise provided by the Constitution of the United States, by Act of Congress, by these rules, or by other rules prescribed by the Supreme Court pursuant to statutory authority. Evidence which is not relevant is not admissible.

RULE 701. OPINION TESTIMONY BY LAY WITNESSES

If the witness is not testifying as an expert, the witness' testimony in the form of opinions or inferences is limited to those opinions or inferences which are (a) rationally based on the perception of the witness and (b) helpful to a clear understanding of the witness' testimony or the determination of a fact in issue.

RULE 702. TESTIMONY BY EXPERTS

If scientific, technical, or other specialized knowledge will assist the trier of fact to understand the evidence or to determine a fact in issue, a witness qualified as an expert by knowledge, skill, experience, training, or education, may testify thereto in the form of an opinion or otherwise.

RULE 703. BASES OF OPINION TESTIMONY BY EXPERTS

The facts or data in the particular case upon which an expert bases an opinion or inference may be those perceived by or made known to the expert at or before the hearing. If of a type reasonably relied upon by experts in the particular field in forming opinions or inferences upon the subject, the facts or data need not be admissible in evidence.

RULE 704. OPINION ON ULTIMATE ISSUE

(a) Except as provided in subdivision (b), testimony in the form of an opinion or inference otherwise admissible is not objectionable because it embraces an ultimate issue to be decided by the trier of fact.

(b) No expert witness testifying with respect to the mental state or condition of a defendant in a criminal case may state an opinion or inference as to whether the defendant did or did not have the mental state or condition constituting an element of the crime charged or of a defense thereto. Such ultimate issues are matters for the trier of fact alone.

Appendix D

Custody Evaluation Guidelines Recommended by the American Psychological Association

INTRODUCTION

Decisions regarding child custody and other parenting arrangements occur within several different legal contexts, including parental divorce, guardianship, neglect or abuse proceedings, and termination of parental rights. The following guidelines were developed for psychologists conducting child custody evaluations, specifically within the context of parental divorce. These guidelines build upon the American Psychological Association's *Ethical Principles of Psychologists and Code of Conduct* (APA, 1992) and are aspirational in intent. *As guidelines, they are not intended to be either mandatory or exhaustive. The goal of the guidelines is to promote proficiency in using psychological expertise in conducting child custody evaluations.*

Parental divorce requires a restructuring of parental rights and responsibilities in relation to children. If the parents can agree to a restructuring arrangement, which they do in the overwhelming proportion (90%) of divorce custody cases (Melton, Petrila, Poythress, & Slobogin, 1987), there is no dispute for the court to decide. However, if the parents are unable to reach such an agreement, the court must help to determine the relative allocation of decision-making authority and physical contact each parent will have with the child. The courts typically apply a "best interest of the child" standard in determining this restructuring of rights and responsibilities.

Psychologists provide an important service to children and the courts by providing competent, objective, impartial information in assessing the best interests of the child; by demonstrating a clear sense of direction and purpose in conducting a child custody evaluation; by performing their roles ethically; and by clarifying to all involved the nature and scope of the evaluation. The Ethics Committee of the American Psychological Association has noted that psychologists' involvement in custody disputes has at times raised questions in regard to the misuse of psychologist's influence, sometimes resulting in complaints against psychologists being brought to the attention of the APA Ethics Committee (APA Ethics Committee, 1985; Hall & Hare-Mustin, 1983; Keith-Spiegel & Koocher, 1985; Mills, 1984) and raising questions in the legal and forensic literature (Grisso, 1986; Melton et al., 1987; Mnookin, 1975; Ochroch, 1982; Okpaku, 1976; Weithorn, 1987).

Particular competencies and knowledge are required for child custody evaluations to provide adequate and appropriate psychological services to the court. Child custody evaluation in the context of parental divorce can be an extremely demanding task. For competing parents the stakes are high as they participate in a process fraught with tension and anxiety. The stress on the psychologist/evaluator can become great. Tension surrounding child custody evaluation can become further heightened when there are accusations of child abuse, neglect, and/or family violence.

Psychology is in a position to make significant contributions to child custody decisions. Psychological data and expertise, gained through a child custody evaluation, can provide an additional source of information and an additional perspective not otherwise readily available to the court on what appears to be in a child's best interest, and thus can increase the fairness of the determination the court must make.

GUIDELINES FOR CHILD CUSTODY EVALUATIONS IN DIVORCE PROCEEDINGS

I. Orienting Guidelines: Purpose of a Child Custody Evaluation

1. *The primary purpose of the evaluation is to assess the best psychological interests of the child.* The primary consideration in a child custody evaluation is to assess the individual and family factors that affect the best psychological interests of the child. More specific questions may be raised by the court.

2. *The child's interests and well-being are paramount.* In a child custody evaluation, the child's interests and well-being are paramount. Parents competing for custody, as well as others, may have legitimate concerns, but the child's best interests must prevail.

3. *The focus of the evaluation is on parenting capacity, the psychological and developmental needs of the child, and the resulting fit.* In considering psychological factors affecting the best interests of the child, the psychologist focuses on the parenting capacity of the prospective

custodians in conjunction with the psychological and developmental needs of each child. This involves (a) an assessment of the adults' capacities for parenting, including whatever knowledge, attributes, skills, and abilities, or lack thereof, are present; (b) an assessment of the psychological functioning and developmental needs of each child and of the wishes of each child where appropriate; and (c) an assessment of the functional ability of each parent to meet these needs, including an evaluation of the interaction between each adult and child.

The values of the parents relevant to parenting, ability to plan for the child's future needs, capacity to provide a stable and loving home, and any potential for inappropriate behavior or misconduct that might negatively influence the child also are considered. Psychopathology may be relevant to such an assessment, insofar as it has impact on the child or the ability to parent, but it is not the primary focus.

II. General Guidelines: Preparing for a Child Custody Evaluation

4. *The role of the psychologist is that of a professional expert who strives to maintain an objective, impartial stance.* The role of the psychologist is as a professional expert. The psychologist does not act as a judge, who makes the ultimate decision applying the law to all relevant evidence. Neither does the psychologist act as an advocating attorney, who strives to present his or her client's best possible case. The psychologist, in a balanced, impartial manner, informs and advises the court and the prospective custodians of the child of the relevant psychological factors pertaining to the custody issue. The psychologist should be impartial regardless of whether he or she is retained by the court or by a party to the proceedings. If either the psychologist or the client cannot accept this neutral role, the psychologist should consider withdrawing from the case. If not permitted to withdraw, in such circumstances, the psychologist acknowledges past roles and other factors that could affect impartiality.

5. *The psychologist gains specialized competence.*

A. A psychologist contemplating performing child custody evaluations is aware that special competencies and knowledge are required for the undertaking of such evaluations. Competence in performing psychological assessments of children, adults, and families is necessary but not sufficient. Education, training, experience, and/or supervision in the areas of child and family development, child and family psychopathology, and the impact of divorce on children help to prepare the psychologist to participate competently in child custody evaluations. The psychologist also strives to become familiar with applicable legal standards and procedures, including laws governing divorce and custody adjudications in his or her state or jurisdiction.

B. The psychologist uses current knowledge of scientific and professional developments, consistent with accepted clinical and scientific standards, in selecting data collection methods and procedures. The *Standards for Educational and Psychological Testing* (APA, 1985) are adhered to in the use of psychological tests and other assessment tools.

C. In the course of conducting child custody evaluations, allegations of child abuse, neglect, family violence, or other issues may occur that are not necessarily within the scope of a particular evaluator's expertise. If this is so, the psychologist seeks additional consultation, supervision, and/or specialized knowledge, training, or experience in child abuse, neglect, and family violence to address these complex issues. The psychologist is familiar with the laws of his or her state addressing child abuse, neglect, and family violence and acts accordingly.

6. *The psychologist is aware of personal and societal biases and engages in nondiscriminatory practice.* The psychologist engaging in child custody evaluations is aware of how biases regarding age, gender, race, ethnicity, national origin, religion, sexual orientation, disability, language, culture, and socioeconomic status may interfere with an objective evaluation and recommendations. The psychologist recognizes and strives to overcome any such biases or withdraws from the evaluation.

7. *The psychologist avoids multiple relationships.* Psychologists generally avoid conducting a child custody evaluation in a case in which the psychologist served in a therapeutic role for the child or his or her immediate family or has had other involvement that may compromise the psychologist's objectivity. This should not, however, preclude the psychologist from testifying in the case as a fact witness concerning treatment of the child. In addition, during the course of a child custody evaluation, a psychologist does not accept any of the involved participants in the evaluation as a therapy client. Therapeutic contact with the child or involved participants following a child custody evaluation is undertaken with caution.

A psychologist asked to testify regarding a therapy client who is involved in a child custody case is aware of the limitations and possible biases inherent in such a role and the possible impact on the ongoing therapeutic relationship. Although the court may require the psychologist to testify as a fact witness regarding factual information he or she became aware of in a

professional relationship with a client, that psychologist should generally decline the role of an expert witness who gives a professional opinion regarding custody and visitation issues (see Ethical Standard 7.03) unless so ordered by the court.

III. Procedural Guidelines: Conducting a Child Custody Evaluation

8. *The scope of the evaluation is determined by the evaluator, based on the nature of the referral question.* The scope of the custody-related evaluation is determined by the nature of the question or issue raised by the referring person or the court, or is inherent in the situation. Although comprehensive child custody evaluations generally require an evaluation of all parents or guardians and children, as well as observations of interactions between them, the scope of the assessment in a particular case may be limited to evaluating the parental capacity of one parent without attempting to compare the parents or to make recommendations. Likewise, the scope may be limited to evaluating the child. Or a psychologist may be asked to critique the assumptions and methodology of the assessment of another mental health professional. A psychologist also might serve as an expert witness in the area of child development, providing expertise to the court without relating it specifically to the parties involved in a cases.

9. *The psychologist obtains informed consent from all adult participants and, as appropriate, informs child participants.* In undertaking child custody evaluations, the psychologist ensures that each adult participant is aware of (a) the purpose, nature, and method of the evaluation; (b) who has requested the psychologist's services; and (c) who will be paying the fees. The psychologist informs adult participants about the nature of

the assessment instruments and techniques and informs those participants about the possible disposition of the data collected. The psychologist provides this information, as appropriate, to children, to the extent that they are able to understand.

10. *The psychologist informs participants about the limits of confidentiality and the disclosure of information.* A psychologist conducting a child custody evaluation ensures that the participants, including children to the extent feasible, are aware of the limits of confidentiality characterizing the professional relationship with the psychologist. The psychologist informs participants that in consenting to the evaluation, they are consenting to disclosure of the evaluation's findings in the context of the forthcoming litigation and in any other proceedings deemed necessary by the courts. A psychologist obtains a waiver of confidentiality from all adult participants or from their authorized legal representatives.

11. *The psychologist uses multiple methods of data gathering.* The psychologist strives to use the most appropriate methods available for addressing the questions raised in a specific child custody evaluation and generally uses multiple methods of data gathering, including, but not limited to, clinical interviews, observation, and/or psychological assessments. Important facts and opinions are documented from at least two sources whenever their reliability is questionable. The psychologist, for example, may review potentially relevant reports (e.g., from schools, healthcare providers, child care providers, agencies, and institutions). Psychologists may also interview extended family, friends, and other individuals on occasions when the information is likely to be useful. If information is gathered from third parties that is significant and may be used as a basis for conclusions,

psychologists corroborate it by at least one other source wherever possible and appropriate and document this in the report.

12. *The psychologist neither overinterprets nor inappropriately interprets clinical or assessment data.* The psychologist refrains from drawing conclusions not adequately supported by the data. The psychologist interprets any data from interviews or tests, as well as any questions of data reliability and validity, cautiously and conservatively, seeking convergent validity. The psychologist strives to acknowledge to the court any limitations in methods or data used.

13. *The psychologist does not give any opinion regarding the psychological functioning of any individual who has not been personally evaluated.* This guideline, however, does not preclude the psychologist from reporting what an evaluated individual (such as the parent or child) has stated or from addressing theoretical issues or hypothetical questions, so long as the limited basis of the information is noted.

14. *Recommendations, if any, are based on what is in the best psychological interests of the child.* Although the profession has not reached consensus about whether psychologists ought to make recommendations about the final custody determination to the courts, psychologists are obligated to be aware of the arguments on both sides of this issue and to be able to explain the logic of their position concerning their own practice.

If the psychologist does choose to make custody recommendations, these recommendations should be derived from sound psychological data and must be based on the best interests of the child in the particular case. Recommendations are based on articulated assumptions, data, interpretations, and inferences based upon established professional and scientific standards.

Psychologists guard against relying on their own biases or unsupported beliefs in rendering opinions in particular cases.

15. *The psychologist clarifies financial arrangements.* Financial arrangements are clarified and agreed upon prior to commencing a child custody evaluation. When billing for a child custody evaluation, the psychologist does not misrepresent his or her services for reimbursement purposes.

16. *The psychologist maintains written records.* All records obtained in the process of conducting a child custody evaluation are properly maintained and filed in accord with the APA *Record Keeping Guidelines* (APA, 1993) and relevant statutory guidelines.

All raw data and interview information are recorded with an eye toward their possible review by other psychologists or the court, where legally permitted. Upon request, appropriate reports are made available to the court.

REFERENCES

American Psychological Association. (1985). *Standards for educational and psychological testing.* Washington, DC: Author.

American Psychological Association. (1992). Ethical principles of psychologists and code of conduct. *American Psychologist, 47,* 1597–1611.

American Psychological Association. (1993). *Record keeping guidelines.* Washington, DC: Author.

American Psychological Association, Ethics Committee. (1985). *Annual report of the American Psychological Association Ethics Committee.* Washington, DC: Author.

Grisso, T. (1986). *Evaluating competencies: Forensic assessments and instruments.* New York: Plenum.

Hall, J. E., & Hare-Mustin, R. T. (1983). Sanctions and the diversity of ethical complaints against psychologists. *American Psychologist, 38,* 714–729.

Keith-Spiegel, P., & Koocher, G. P. (1985). *Ethics in psychology.* New York: Random House.

Melton, G. B., Petrila, J., Poythress, N. G., & Slobogin, C. (1987). *Psychological evaluations for the courts: A handbook for mental health professionals and lawyers.* New York: Guilford Press.

Mills, D. H. (1984). Ethics education and adjudication within psychology. *American Psychologist, 39,* 669–675.

Mnookin, R. H. (1975). Child-custody adjudication: Judicial functions in the face of indeterminacy. *Law and Contemporary Problems, 39,* 226–293.

Ochroch, R. (1982, August). *Ethical pitfalls in child custody evaluations.* Paper presented at the 90th Annual Convention of the American Psychological Association, Washington, DC.

Okpaku, S. (1976). Psychology: Impediment or aid in child custody cases? *Rutgers Law Review, 29,* 1117–1153.

Weithorn, L. A. (Ed.). (1987). *Psychology and child custody determinations: Knowledge, roles, and expertise.* Lincoln: University of Nebraska Press.

OTHER RESOURCES

State Guidelines

Georgia Psychological Association. (1990). *Recommendations for psychologists' involvement in child custody cases.* Atlanta, GA: Author.

Metropolitan Denver Interdisciplinary Committee on Child Custody. (1989). *Guidelines for child custody evaluations.* Denver, CO: Author.

Nebraska Psychological Association. (1986). *Guidelines for child custody evaluations.* Lincoln, NE: Author.

New Jersey State Board of Psychological Examiners. (1993). *Specialty guidelines for psychologists in custody/visitation evaluations.* Newark, NJ: Author.

North Carolina Psychological Association. (1993). *Child custody guidelines.* Unpublished manuscript.

Oklahoma Psychological Association. (1988). *Ethical guidelines for child custody evaluations.* Oklahoma City, OK: Author.

Forensic Guidelines

Committee on Ethical Guidelines for Forensic Psychologists. (1991). Specialty guidelines for forensic psychologists. *Law and Human Behavior, 6,* 655–665.

Pertinent Literature

Ackerman, M. J., & Kane, A. W. (1993). *Psychological experts in divorce, personal injury and other civil actions.* New York: Wiley.

American Psychological Association, Board of Ethnic Minority Affairs. (1991). *Guidelines for providers of psychological services to ethnic, linguistic, and culturally diverse populations.* Washington, DC: American Psychological Association.

American Psychological Association, Committee on Women in Psychology and Committee on Lesbian and Gay Concerns. (1988). *Lesbian parents and their children: A resource paper for psychologists.* Washington, DC: American Psychological Association.

Beaber, R. J. (1982, Fall). Custody quagmire: Some psycholegal dilemmas. *Journal of Psychiatry & Law,* 309–326.

Bennett, B. E., Bryant, B. K., VandenBos, G. R., & Greenwood, A. (1990). *Professional liability and risk management.* Washington, DC: American Psychological Association.

Bolocofsky, D. N. (1989). Use and abuse of mental health experts in child custody determinations. *Behavioral Sciences and the Law, 7*(2), 197–213.

Bozett, F. (1987). *Gay and lesbian parents.* New York: Praeger.

Bray, J. H. (1993). What's the best interest of the child?: Children's adjustment issues in divorce. *The Independent Practitioner, 13,* 42–45.

Bricklin, B. (1992). Data-based tests in custody evaluations. *American Journal of Family Therapy, 20,* 254–265.

Cantor, D. W., & Drake, E. A. (1982). *Divorced parents and their children: A guide for mental health professionals.* New York: Springer.

Chesler, P. (1991). *Mothers on trial: The battle for children and custody.* New York: Harcourt Brace Jovanovich.

Deed, M. L. (1991). Court-ordered child custody evaluations: Helping or victimizing vulnerable families. *Psychotherapy, 28,* 76–84.

Falk, P. J. (1989). Lesbian mothers: Psychosocial assumptions in family law. *American Psychologist, 44,* 941–947.

Gardner, R. A. (1989). *Family evaluation in child custody mediation, arbitration, and litigation.* Cresskill, NJ: Creative Therapeutics.

Gardner, R. A. (1992). *The parental alienation syndrome: A guide for mental health and legal professionals.* Cresskill, NJ: Creative Therapeutics.

Gardner, R. A. (1992). *True and false accusations of child abuse.* Cresskill, NJ: Creative Therapeutics.

Goldstein, J., Freud, A., & Solnit, A. J. (1980). *Before the best interests of the child.* New York: Free Press.

Goldstein, J., Freud, A., & Solnit, A. J. (1980). *Beyond the best interests of the child.* New York: Free Press.

Goldstein, J., Freud, A., & Solnit, A. J., & Goldstein, S. (1986). *In the best interests of the child.* New York: Free Press.

Grisso, T. (1990). Evolving guidelines for divorce/custody evaluations. *Family and Conciliation Courts Review, 28*(1), 35–41.

Halon, R. L. (1990). The comprehensive child custody evaluation. *American Journal of Forensic Psychology, 8*(3), 19–46.

Hetherington, E. M. (1990). Coping with family transitions: Winners, losers, and survivors. *Child Development, 60,* 1–14.

Hetherington, E. M., Stanley-Hagen, M., & Anderson, E. R. (1988). Marital transitions: A child's perspective. *American Psychologist, 44,* 303–312.

Johnston, J., Kline, M., & Tschann, J. (1989). Ongoing postdivorce conflict: Effects on children of joint custody and frequent access. *Journal of Orthopsychiatry, 59,* 576–592.

Koocher, G. P., & Keith-Spiegel, P. C. (1990). *Children, ethics, and the law: Professional issues and cases.* Lincoln: University of Nebraska Press.

Kreindler, S. (1986). The role of mental health professions in custody and access disputes. In R. S. Parry, E. A. Broder, E. A. G. Schmitt, E. B. Saunders, & E. Hood (Eds.), *Custody disputes: Evaluation and intervention.* New York: Free Press.

Martindale, D. A., Martindale, J. L., & Broderick, J. E. (1991). Providing expert testimony in child custody litigation. In P. A. Keller & S. R. Heyman (Eds.), *Innovations in clinical practice: A source book* (Vol. 10, pp. 481–497). Sarasota, FL: Professional Resource Exchange.

Patterson, C. J. (in press). Children of lesbian and gay parents. *Child Development.*

Pennsylvania Psychological Association, Clinical Division Task Force on Child Custody Evaluation. (1991). *Roles for psychologists in child custody disputes.* Unpublished manuscript.

Saunders, T. R. (1991). An overview of some psycholegal issues in child physical and sexual abuse. *Psychotherapy in Private Practice, 9*(2), 61–78.

Schutz, B. M., Dixon, E. B., Lindenberger, J. C., & Ruther, N. J. (1989). *Solomon's sword: A practical guide to conducting child custody evaluations.* San Francisco: Jossey-Bass.

Stahly, G. B. (1989, August 9). *Testimony on child abuse policy to APA Board.* Paper presented at the meeting of the American Psychological Association Board of Directors, New Orleans, LA.

Thoennes, N., & Tjaden, P. G. (1991). The extent, nature, and validity of sexual abuse allegations in custody/visitation disputes. *Child Abuse & Neglect, 14,* 151–163.

Wallerstein, J. S., & Blakeslee, S. (1989). *Second chances: Men, women, and children a decade after divorce.* New York: Ticknor & Fields.

Wallerstein, J. S., & Kelly, J. B. (1980). *Surviving the breakup.* New York: Basic Books.

Weissman, H. N. (1991). Child custody evaluations: Fair and unfair professional practices. *Behavioral Sciences and the Law, 9,* 469–476.

Weithorn, L. A., & Grisso, T. (1987). Psychological evaluations in divorce custody: Problems, principles, and procedures. In L. A. Weithorn (Ed.), *Psychology and child custody determinations* (pp. 157–158). Lincoln: University of Nebraska Press.

White, S. (1990). The contamination of children's interviews. *Child Youth and Family Services Quarterly, 13*(3), 6, 17–18.

Wyer, M. M., Gaylord, S. J., & Grove, E. T. The legal context of child custody evaluations. In L. A. Weithorn (Ed.), *Psychology and child custody determinations* (pp. 3–23). Lincoln: University of Nebraska Press.

Appendix E

Tables and Formulae for Comparing Military Test Performance with Current Test Results

ARMY CLASSIFICATION SCORES: THEIR MEANING AND CLINICAL IMPLICATION*

Psychiatric and psychological evaluation of patients is often subtly, and sometimes not so subtly, related to the clinician's estimate of a patient's level of general intelligence. Behavioral manifestations which are interpreted as "unusual" and/or indicative of behavior pathology (whether characterological,

* Reprinted with permission. Paper prepared by James L. Hedlund, Capt., MSC, Clinical Psychology Service, Walter Reed Army Hospital, for the Conference of Army Clinical Psychologists, sponsored by the Surgeon General, Department of Army, Washington, DC, 2 September 1959. Because the author was unable to attend, the paper was not actually read at these sessions.

The author wishes to express appreciation to Dr. Ardie Lubin and Major Harold L. Williams, both of Walter Reed Army Institute of Research, for their critical reading of this manuscript, for providing additional information, and for making a number of helpful suggestions during its development.

neurotic, or psychotic) in a patient with relatively high intellectual endowment may not be so interpreted with a patient of Borderline or Defective intellectual capacities. Decisions to recommend administrative discharges for acting-out or inadequate performance of duty may also importantly involve considerations of basic intellectual abilities. It is not surprising, then, that psychiatric referrals for psychological testing often involve questions of the patient's general intelligence. If the referring agency, whether psychiatrist, social worker, neurologist or whatever, had a relatively objective and easily obtained basis for ruling out intellectual retardation, diagnosis and disposition of some patients might more easily be accomplished without referral for psychometrics.

With these ideas in mind, the author, a couple of years ago, prepared a mimeographed summary, "Miscellaneous Notes Regarding Army Classification Scores and General Intelligence," which was intended to provide psychiatric staff members with some basic, practical information concerning Army classification scores. These Miscellaneous Notes were so well received, not only by those for whom they were intended, psychiatric staff members who are relatively unsophisticated with regard to problems of tests and measurement, but by clinical psychologists as well, that the author was asked to prepare a somewhat more systematic and comprehensive discussion of the meaning and clinical use of Army classification scores in the military-medical setting. This paper, then, has been developed to that end. It contends to offer nothing original or "new," but only some practical information, brought together in convenient form.

As you know, all Armed Forces inductees currently take the Armed Forces Qualification Test (AFQT) at the time of induction and all Army EM take the Army Classification Battery (ACB) at the Reception Center. Scores obtained on these tests are recorded in each soldier's Field 201-File.

*The "Meaning" of Army
Classification Scores*

1. Armed Forces Qualification
Test (AFQT)

The AFQT is a pre-induction, paper-and-pencil screening test, administered at Armed Forces Induction and Examining Stations, used to estimate general intelligence of inductees. From scores on this test, potential inductees are classified into "Mental Groups" ranging from Mental Group I, reflecting the highest level of intellectual ability, to Mental Group V, the lowest level. Theoretically, inductees scoring in Mental Group V are not actually inducted into the Army. This, however, is not always the case in practice—especially where the induction center has reason to suspect poor motivation for service and "faking bad" on test performance.

AFQT scores are recorded as percentile ranks, ranging from 0 to 100 (see Table 1). If an inductee receives an AFQT score of 78, this means that he has done better on this test than 78% of the general population of inductees; if he attains a score of 13, it means that he has performed better than only 13% (or conversely, that 87% of the general population of inductees have scored better than he).

Caution: It is important to note that other than intellective factors enter into the determination of AFQT scores. Motivation, degree of emotional disturbance, socioeducational-cultural factors, etc., are also very important determiners. Accordingly, it is best to assume the attitude that: (1) any given AFQT score (excluding the possibility of fraudulent posting of scores or some type of "illegal" help in taking the test) reflects "*at least* that much general ability"; and (2) any low AFQT score *may* reflect major motivational, educational-cultural, or

**TABLE 1.   CLASSIFICATION OF INDUCTEES BY
AFQT SCORES**

Mental Group	AFQT Score	Percent Included
I	93–100	8
II	65–92	28
III	31–64	34
IV	10–30	21
V	0–9	9

emotional factors which are, at least at the time of testing, attenuating optimal performance.

2. Army General Classification Test (AGCT) and the Army Classification Battery (ACB)*

Besides the AFQT, two other paper-and-pencil tests or batteries of tests have been used in estimating the general usefulness of a soldier to the service, and in classifying-assigning him to specific training and/or assignment areas.

One of these, the Army General Classification Test (AGCT) was administered to all Army enlisted men from 1940 to 1945 and is no longer in use. Scores for this test, however, are still occasionally available, and it is of some interest to note that the earliest form of the AGCT Form has been released for civilian use, currently being published by Science Research Associates (Burros, 1953, p. 280).

The set of tests which supercedes the AGCT, the Army Classification Battery (ACB), attempts to evaluate various kinds of aptitudes, knowledge, or skills which have been shown to be related to general assignment areas within the military.

---

* Montague's article (1957) also describes each of the ACB subtests as of June 1957, together with some of the technical data relating to each. Although the exact number of items, time limits and 'edition' of the individual aptitude tests now differ from what Montague describes, most of the basic techniques and types of items are the same. Information is currently being gathered regarding the technical data of the newest ACB tests in the hope of bringing the Montague, et al. article completely up-to-date. Some of the more basic differences in the 1958 revision of the ACB, however, will also be touched on in the present paper.

The 1949 ACB was made up of ten separate aptitude subtests, while the 1958 ACB is made up of eleven. It is important to be familiar with both forms of the ACB inasmuch as scores recorded for enlisted personnel prior to 1 October 1958 will refer to the 1949 edition, whereas those recorded thereafter will reflect the 1958 revision. The individual subtests, together with identification as to which edition each belongs, may be briefly summarized as follows:

Reading and Vocabulary Test (RV), 1949. In this test, there were a number of reading passages of one or more paragraphs, with several multiple-choice questions related to the content of each paragraph. 53 items; 25-minute time limit.

Verbal Test (VE), 1958. This test replaces RV described above and is essentially a multiple-choice vocabulary test. Each item presents a complete sentence with one word underlined, and the subject is asked to select a multiple-choice synonym for the underlined word. 50 items; 15-minute time limit.

Arithmetic Reasoning Test (AR), 1949, 1958. Arithmetic problems, verbally presented, with multiple-choice answers. 40 items: 35-minute time limit.*

Pattern Analysis Test (PA), 1949, 1958. "In this test a two-dimensional pattern with numbered lines is presented along with the corresponding three-dimensional figure made by folding the pattern along indicated lines. The edges of the figure are lettered. The examinee is required to identify the lettered edge of the figure corresponding to a numbered

---

* Number of items and time limits refer to the most current edition of any given test.

line in the pattern. The numbers in the pattern are the item numbers and the letters of the figure are used to form five alternative responses for each item." (Montague et al., 1957). 50 items; 20-minute time limit.

Mechanical Aptitude Test (MA), 1949, 1958. Each item in this test consists of a figure illustrating some principle of physics or mechanics, and a verbal question with multiple choice responses. 45 items; 15-minute time limit.

Army Clerical Speed Test (ACS), 1949, 1958. "This test consists of two parts, both highly speeded and administered with separate time limits: (a) In Part I, Number Reversal (125 items), each item consists of two numbers. There are two alternative responses to indicate whether or not the second is exactly the reverse of the first. The time limit is 5 minutes. (b) In Part II, Coding (100 items), there is a key containing 10 words. Each word in the key has a number that is associated with it. Each item presents a word followed by the 10 alternative numbered responses in the key. The time limit is 5 minutes." (Montague et al., 1957).

Army Radio Code Aptitude Test (ARC), 1949, 1958. This is a relatively complicated auditory test, using four phonograph records, which requires subjects to learn code signals to three letters and to then recognize the three coded signals at varying speeds of presentation.

Shop Mechanics Test (SM), 1949, 1958. "In this test each item presents a drawing illustrating some mechanical principle or tool usage, followed by a four-alternative question." (Montague et al., 1957). 40 items; 15-minute time limit.

Automotive Information Test (AI), 1949, 1958. "In this test each item is

a four-alternative question about the identification or operation of automobile parts. Many items are based on pictures or diagrams." (Montague et al., 1957) 40 items; 15-minute time limit.

Electrical Information Test (EI), 1949. "In this test each item is a four-alternative question on some element of electrical information. Many items are based on pictures or schematic diagrams. There are 40 items; the time limit is 15 minutes." (Montague et al., 1957)

Radio Information Test (RI), 1949. "In this test each item is a four-alternative question on some aspect of radio information. Some items are based on schematic diagrams." (Montague et al., 1957) 40 items; 15-minute time limit.

Electronics Information Test (ELI), 1958. A "composite" test replacing 1949 EI and RI, with items similar to those described above. 40 items; 20-minute time limit.

General Information Test (GIT), 1958. Items of this test are multiple-choice, general information questions drawn predominantly from the areas of general Army information and sports. 50 items; 30-minute time limit.

Classification Inventory (CI), 1958. This test, divided into four parts, is essentially a personality-interest inventory. It contains 15 job titles, many of which are somewhat related to military specialties, which require a like-dislike-indifferent choice on the part of inductees; 10 forced-choice, self-description items; 75 self-description items which are very similar to the items of the California Personality Inventory and the items of the MMPI; and 25 words or phrases which must be identified as *least* or *most* descriptive of self. The score which is computed for this test reflects the degree of empirical correspondence to successful combat troops. 125 items; 40-minute time limit.

Scores for both the AGCT and the separate subtests of the Amy Classification Battery are reported in *Army Standard Scores*, not in percentile ranks as is the AFQT. These standard score scales always have a mean of 100 and a standard deviation of 20, and can be roughly interpreted according to Table 2.

In addition to yielding the separate aptitude test scores which are recorded on EM's DA Form 20, his Army Classification Battery also forms the basis for classification of each soldier within eight "aptitude areas," each *aptitude area* score being made up of a composite of two or more aptitude test scores. The aptitude *area* scores are the ones used to help classify and assign EM into various military occupational specialties (or training therefor). The aptitude areas are defined somewhat differently for the 1949 ACB and the 1958 revision, so that separate tables must be used in interpreting aptitude area scores taken from these two batteries. Tables defining aptitude areas for both batteries may be found in Appendix A and B of this paper.

An aptitude area score of especial interest is the *"General Technical" (GT)*, inasmuch as this aptitude area score is now also used to assess over-all general intelligence, and in classifying a soldier into one of the five Mental Groups previously mentioned.*

TABLE 2. RELATIONSHIP BETWEEN ARMY STANDARD SCORES AND PERCENTILE RANKS

Army Standard Score	Percentile Rank
40	0
50	1
60	2
70	7
80	16
90	31
100	50
110	69
120	84
130	93
140	98
150	99
160	100

Table 3 provides, according to the present information, theoretical and empirical, a rough conversion and interpretation guide for evaluating GT scores obtained from the Army Classification Battery.

Caution: Interpretation of the GT scores in terms of percentile ranks and IQ equivalents as given in Table 3 may be helpful, but should be done only with the recognition that such conversions are only rough approximations, "best guesses," as it were, from available information.** Again, the considerations and cautions already mentioned with

---

* Currently other ACB scores are also used in elimination of inductees whose AFQT scores place them in Mental Group IV or V: "The passing score on the ACB was fixed as 90 or higher in any two or more aptitude areas covered by the ACB

tests. Examinees who fail to attain a minimum of 90 are classified as 'Trainability Limited (V-0),' provided they were medically qualified. These examinees are currently not acceptable, though they would qualify under mobilization or emergency conditions." (Reference #9, 1958).

** An appendix provides information on correlations which have been reported between Wechsler IQ and various Army classification scores.

TABLE 3. APPROXIMATE RELATIONSHIPS BETWEEN GT APTITUDE AREA SCORES, PERCENTILE RANK AND WECHSLER IQ EQUIVALENTS

Army Standard Score (GT Score)	Percentile Score (AFQT Equivalent)	Wechsler IQ W–B*	Equivalent WAIS[†]
40	0	—	—
50	1	59	65
60	2	64	68
70	7	77	78
80	16	86	85
90	31	94	92
100	50	101	100
110	69	108	107
120	84	114	115
130	93	120	123
140	98	126	131
150	99	130	135
160	100	—	—

* Wechsler–Bellevue Intelligence Scale for Adolescents and Adults, as described in *Measurement of Adult Intelligence* (1944).
† Wechsler Adult Intelligence Scale, as described in *The Measurement and Appraisal of Adult Intelligence* (1956).

respect to interpreting AFQT scores are completely applicable here.

3. The approximate relationships between Army Mental Groups, AFQT, ACB and Wechsler IQ's can be seen in Table 4.

Use of Army Classification Scores in Estimating Intellectual Impairment

In a recent article, Williams, Lubin and Gieseking (1959) have readministered the first five aptitude tests (RV, AR, PA, MA, and ACS) of the ACB to 64 hospitalized brain-injured patients and to 162 control subjects. They find that there is a significant decline in the scores obtained on each of these tests for the brain-injured patients, as compared with their pre-morbid ACB scores and as compared with the controls. The average decrement totalled over all five subtests, is −66.6 Army standard score points (approximately ⅔ of a standard deviation) for the brain-injured patients, while the score for control groups *increased* slightly, +13.8 Army standard score points for a group of 47 nonbrain-injured and nonpsychiatric patients, and +18.0 points for a group of 115 enlisted duty personnel. When the 64 brain-injured patients were matched with 64 of the 162 controls, such that brain-injured and control subjects were individually matched to within 20 total points of pre-morbid score, a "residual change score" cutoff point was computed such as to yield 82% correct classification of the 64 brain-injured and the total of 162 controls. The authors report that "this seems to be better than the percentage of correct classification reported in most' studies of brain injury" (1959, p. 303).

TABLE 4.   APPROXIMATE RELATIONSHIPS BETWEEN ARMY MENTAL GROUPS, AFQT, ACB AND WECHSLER IQS

Mental Group	AFQT Scores (Percentile Ranks)	AGCT or GT Scores (Army Standard Scores)	Wechsler IQ Equivalents* (Approximate) W–B[†]	WAIS[‡]
I	93–100	130 and over	120 and over	123 and over
II	65–92	110–129	108–119	107–122
III	31–64	90–109	94–107	92–106
IV	10–30	65–89	70–93	73–91
V	0–9	0–64	69 and below	72 and below

* Cronbach (1949, p. 124) presents a table of "Reference Points for Establishing the Meaning of IQ," which may be very useful in helping to interpret the practical significance of various IQ values.

† Wechsler–Bellevue Intelligence Scale for Adolescents and Adults, as described in *Measurement of Adult Intelligence* (1944). Wechsler's classification system, which can be roughly equated with the Army Mental Groups, is given on p. 40 of this reference, and percentile ranks for various IQs are provided on p. 42.

‡ Wechsler Adult Intelligence Scale, as described in *The Measurement and Appraisal of Adult Intelligence* (1958). His classification system is presented on p. 42, and percentile rank equivalents on p. 43.

The clinician, however, faces two major problems in this regard: (1) he does not have ACB tests to readminister;* and, even more critical, (2) the population of patients with which the clinician is involved is not at all the population studied by Williams et al. (i.e., 28% brain-injured and 72% nonpsychiatric and nonbrain-injured).† Very much complicating this whole problem of test prediction of brain-injury is the well recognized dilemma that non-organic psychiatric patients of certain types also evidence significant test impairment in the area of intellectual (cognitive) functions. Indeed, since the study cited above, Williams, et al.‡ have, themselves, found that diagnosed schizophrenics also display a significant decrement in scores when readministered the ACB tests shortly after hospital admission. Their reduced scores on the first five ACB tests are very similar in pattern§ to

---

* As earlier noted, however, one form of the AGCT is now commercially available and could be used by clinicians as a retest instrument.

† Even if the clinician's population were composed of only those two classes of individuals, it is obvious that in order to get better test predictions of organics and nonorganics than by use of base rates alone, the base rate for organics in such a population would have to be greater than 18% (Meehl & Rosen, 1955).

‡ Verbal communication with author.

§ Of incidental note here is that the pattern of deficit for both organics and schizophrenics on the ACB tasks is, at least apparently, quite inconsistent with traditional concepts of intellectual impairment: Williams et al. find a slightly *greater decrement* in the 'verbal' tests of RV, AR, and CS, than in the 'spatial' tests of PA and MA. The authors conclude in this regard, "These results, together with Yates' penetrating analysis, should end the myth that verbal tests such as Reading and Vocabulary are

those of the organics, but are less severe, approximately 1/4 of a standard deviation as compared with the 2/3 of a standard deviation of the brain-injured.

ACB scores, however, can be intelligently used in evaluating the presence and/or extent of general intellectual impairment. Level of pre-morbid (Army entry) functioning as estimated from ACB scores can be compared with current level of functioning as estimated from hospital WAIS performance (or as estimated by retesting with the commercial form of the AGCT). Comparison of GT scores and WAIS IQ can be accomplished by translating both test scores into percentile ranks, or by converting WAIS IQ into score units which are comparable to the Army Standard Scores.* If percentile ranks are used, one must remember that differences in percentile ranks toward the center of the distribution must be interpreted with less significance than equal differences farther out toward the ends of the distribution. Use of the easily converted IQ score may run less risk of confusion and misinterpretation, even though, in some respects, it is a more complex concept.

---

resistant to the effects of brain damage" (1959, p. 304).

* Since WAIS IQ scores for any given age group have a theoretical mean of 100 and a standard deviation of 15, and Army Standard Scores (including GT scores) have a mean of 100 and a standard deviation of 20, the conversion formula for this linear transformation is:

$$\text{Converted IQ Score} = \left[\frac{20}{15}(\text{WAIS IQ}-100)\right]+100$$

$$= \left[\frac{4}{3}(\text{IQ}-100)\right]+100.$$

This "converted IQ score" now has a mean of 100 and a standard deviation of 20, and can be directly compared with the GT score.

Given the correlation between any of the Army Classification scores and WAIS IQ for a particular population, one could also, of course, estimate WAIS IQ at the time of Army entry by using the standard regression equation, $\hat{Y} = a + bX$, where $\hat{Y}$ represents the estimated IQ score at the time of Army entry, $b :: r_{xy} (S_y/S_x)$, and $a = M_y - bM_x$. In this case, S_x and S_y refer to the standard deviations of the Army classification scores and of the WAIS IQ scores, respectively; r_{xy} is the correlation between these two sets of scores; and M_x and M_y are means of the two distributions. The statistical significance of the difference between any patient's estimated Army entry IQ ($\hat{Y}$) and his obtained hospitalization IQ (Y) would be tested by dividing the standard error of estimate (S_{yx}) into their difference ($\hat{Y} - Y'$), and then referring to probability tables for the normal curve. For the general population of inductees, e.g., the Montague, et al. (4) correlation of .81 between RV and Wechsler Full Scale IQ might be used, as well as the theoretical means and standard deviations of the two distributions. For a particular inductee receiving an Army entry RV score of 110 and a later-obtained hospitalization WAIS IQ of 90, we could estimate IQ-at-time-of-entry as follows:

$$b = r_{xy}(S_y/S_x) = .81\,(15/20) = .6075$$

$$a = M_y - bM_x = 100 - (.61)(100) = 39$$

$$\hat{Y} = a + bX = 39 + (.61)(110) = 39 + 67$$
$$= 106.$$

The difference, $\hat{Y} - Y' = 106 - 90 = 16$, is evaluated statistically by the standard error of measurement, S_{yx}, which in this case could be estimated by:

$$S_{yx} = S_y\sqrt{1-r_{xy}^{\,2}} = 15\sqrt{1-(.81)^2} = 8.85$$

The significance ratio of $(106 - 90)/8.85 = 1.81$ indicates that the difference of 16 IQ points obtained for this inductee would have occurred only very rarely by chance alone (i.e., using a one-tailed test, the null hypothesis can be rejected at between the one and two percent levels of confidence). Because this technique, *as exemplified*, makes a number of tenuous assumptions, however—e.g., that the correlation between RV and IQ is the same irrespective of time interval between RV and IQ testing, that Wechsler-Bellevue and WAIS Full Scale IQ scores are interchangeable (i.e., are perfectly correlated), that the correlations between RV and IQ are the same for specific groups of patients as for general inductees, that the means and standard deviations of special groups are the same as the theoretical ones, and so on—it is very likely little or no more precise than the other, somewhat easier and less complicated procedures described above, despite its *apparent* rigor and precision. What is needed for more efficient utilization of the regression equation in this problem is more empirical information concerning the correlations between Army classification scores and WAIS IQ for different time intervals between testings and for different groups of patients.

Although all methods of comparisons suggested here are admittedly crude, and the precautions of translation and interpretation already mentioned must be kept in mind, they may often, nonetheless, be of considerable help in aiding to identify and to estimate extent of impairment. The specific amount of discrepancy between pre-morbid and post-hospitalization scores which constitutes *clinical* significance is, of course, a matter of over-all clinical judgment, and is usually an interacting function of other clinical and/or test data. The particular source or causes of impairment, whether organic or psychogenic, must also be determined from other clinical and/or test data.

REFERENCES

Buros, O. K. *The Fourth Mental Measurements Year Book.* New York: The Gryphon Press, 1953.

Cronbach, Lee J. *Essentials of Psychological Testing.* New York: Harper & Bros., Publisher, 1949.

Meehl, P. E., & Rosen, A. Antecedent probability and the efficiency of psychometric signs, patterns, or cutting scores. *Psychol. Bull.,* 1955, *52,* 194–216.

Montague, E. K., et al. Army tests for assessment of intellectual deficit. *U.S. Armed Forces Med. J.,* 1957, *8,* 883–892.

Murphy, D. B., & Langston, R. D. A short form of the Wechsler-Bellevue and the Army Classification Battery as measures of intelligence. *J. Consult. Psychol.,* 1956, *20,* 405.

Processing of registrants: pre-induction and induction examination results, 1958. *Health of the Army,* Feb 1959, *14,* No. 2.

Wechsler, David. *The Measurement of Adult Intelligence.* Baltimore: Williams and Wilkins Co., 1944.

Wechsler, David. *The Measurement and Appraisal of Adult Intelligence.* Baltimore: Williams and Wilkins Co., 1958.

Williams, H. L., Lubin, A., & Gieseking, C. F. Direct measurement of cognitive deficit in brain-injured patients. *J. Consult. Psychol.,* 1959, *23,* 300–305.

APPENDIX: RELATIONSHIP BETWEEN ARMY APTITUDE AREAS, 1958 ACB TEST SCORES, AND MILITARY OCCUPATIONAL AREAS

Aptitude Area	Abbreviation	Formula	Occupational Area
Infantry–Combat	IN	$\dfrac{AR\pm=2CI}{3}$	11—Combat, Infantry
Armor, Artillery and Engineers—Combat	AE	$\dfrac{GIT\pm=AI}{2}$	10, 12, 13, 14, 16—Combat, other than Infantry
Electronics	EL	$\dfrac{MA+2EI}{3}$	2—Electronics
General Maintenance	GM	$\dfrac{PA+2SM}{3}$	3—Electrical Maintenance 4—Precision Maintenance 5—Military Crafts
Motor Maintenance	MM	$\dfrac{MA+2AI}{3}$	6—Motor Maintenance
Clerical	CL	$\dfrac{VE+2AC5}{3}$	7—Clerical
General Technical	GT	$\dfrac{VE+AR}{2}$	8—Graphic 9—General Technical 0—Special Assignment
Radio Code	RC	$\dfrac{VE+2ARC}{3}$	0—Special Assignment (05 Radio Code) only

Key:

RV	Reading and Vocabulary Test	SM	Shop Mechanics Test
AR	Arithmetic Reasoning Test	AI	Automotive Information Test
PA	Pattern Analysis Test	ELI	Electronics Information Test
MA	Mechanical Aptitude Test	CI	Classification Inventory Test
ACS	Army Clerical Speed Test	GIT	General Information Test
ARC	Army Radio Code Test		

APPENDIX: CORRELATIONS REPORTED BETWEEN WECHSLER IQ SCORES AND VARIOUS ARMY CLASSIFICATION SCORES

Wechsler Scale IQ	Montague et al. (1957).[a] N=100 recruits, ages 20-24			Hedlund (unpublished study).[b] N=122 nonorganic, nonpsychotic, psychiatric patients			Murphy (1956).[c] N=155 consecutive DB releases, ages 16-41 RV+AR+PA / 3	Wechsler 1958, p. 1050 N=400 soldiers, ages 21-30	N=100 soldiers, ages 21-30
	RV	AR	PA	GT	PA	N = 53	3	AGCT	AGCT
Verbal Scale	.81	.79	.60	.64	—	—	—	—	—
Performance Scale	.60	.64	.64	.58	.64	—	—	—	—
Full Scale	.77	.78	.81	.68	.81	.64	.88	.86	.83

[a] In this study, the correlations were actually computed with Wechsler–Bellevue *weighted scores* rather than IQ scores. For any standardization age group, however, Wechsler IQs are linear transformations of the weighted scores, and the correlation coefficients computed for IQ and weighted scores would be the same. Although no time interval between ACB and Wechsler–Bellevue administration was specified, it is presumed to be negligible inasmuch as the Wechsler–Bellevue administration was actually accomplished at the Reception Center.

[b] Although this study includes patients predominantly administered the Wechsler–Bellevue, a number of the patients' IQ scores were obtained from *WAIS* administration. Unfortunately, neither age of the group nor time interval between ACB and hospital testing were computed at the time of this study.

[c] In this study with Disciplinary Barracks population, Murphy estimated Full Scale Wechsler–Bellevue IQs from a short form made up of the Information, Comprehension, and Block Design subtests. In computing his correlations between IQ and ACS scores, he eliminated all subjects whose RV-AR-PA average was less than 75.

Appendix F

Forensic Psychology Specialty Guidelines*

The *Specialty Guidelines for Forensic Psychologists*, while informed by the *Ethical Principles of Psychologists* (APA, 1990) and meant to be consistent with them, are designed to provide more specific guidance to forensic psychologists in monitoring their professional conduct when acting in assistance to courts, parties to legal proceedings, correctional and forensic mental health facilities, and legislative agencies. The primary goal of the *Guidelines* is to improve the quality of forensic psychological services offered to individual clients and the legal system and thereby to enhance forensic psychology as a discipline and profession. The *Specialty Guidelines for Forensic Psychologists* represents a joint

* Reprinted with permission from *Law and Human Behavior*, 15(6) 1991.

The *Specialty Guidelines for Forensic Psychologists* were adopted by majority vote of the members of Division 41 and the American Psychology–Law Society. They have also been endorsed by majority vote by the American Academy of Forensic Psychology. The Executive Committee of Division 41 and the American Psychology–Law Society formally approved these *Guidelines* on March 9, 1991. The Executive Committee also voted to continue the Committee on Ethical Guidelines in order to disseminate the *Guidelines* and to monitor their implementation and suggestions for revision. Individuals wishing to reprint these *Guidelines* or who have queries about them should contact either Stephen L. Golding, Ph.D., Department of Psychology, University of Utah, Salt Lake City, UT 84112, 801-581-8028 (voice) or 801-581-5841 (FAX) or other members of the Committee listed below. Reprint requests should be sent to Cathy Oslzly, Department of Psychology, University of Nebraska–Lincoln, Lincoln, NE 68588-0308.

These *Guidelines* were prepared and principally authored by a joint Committee on Ethical Guidelines of Division 41 and the American Academy of Forensic Psychology (Stephen L. Golding [Chair], Thomas Grisso, David Shapiro, and Herbert Weissman [Co-chairs]). Other members of the Committee included Robert Fein, Kirk Heilbrun, Judith McKenna, Norman Poythress, and Daniel Schuman. Their hard work and willingness to tackle difficult conceptual and pragmatic issues is gratefully acknowledged. The Committee would also like to acknowledge specifically the assistance and guidance provided by Dort Bigg, Larry Cowan, Eric Harris, Arthur Lerner, Michael Miller, Russell Newman, Melvin Rudov, and Ray Fowler. Many other individuals also contributed by their thoughtful critique and suggestions for improvement of earlier drafts which were widely circulated.

519

statement of the American Psychology–Law Society and Division 41 of the American Psychological Association and are endorsed by the American Academy of Forensic Psychology. The *Guidelines* do not represent an official statement of the American Psychological Association.

The *Guidelines* provide an aspirational model of desirable professional practice by psychologists, within any subdiscipline of psychology (e.g., clinical, developmental, social, experimental), when they are engaged regularly as experts and represent themselves as such, in an activity primarily intended to provide professional psychological expertise to the judicial system. This would include, for example, clinical forensic examiners; psychologists employed by correctional or forensic mental health systems; researchers who offer direct testimony about the relevance of scientific data to a psycholegal issue; trial behavior consultants; psychologists engaged in preparation of *amicus* briefs; or psychologists, appearing as forensic experts, who consult with, or testify before, judicial, legislative, or administrative agencies acting in an adjudicative capacity. Individuals who provide only occasional service to the legal system and who do so without representing themselves as *forensic experts* may find these *Guidelines* helpful, particularly in conjunction with consultation with colleagues who are forensic experts.

While the *Guidelines* are concerned with a model of desirable professional practice, to the extent that they may be construed as being applicable to the advertisement of services or the solicitation of clients, they are intended to prevent false or deceptive advertisement or solicitation, and should be construed in a manner consistent with that intent.

I. PURPOSE AND SCOPE

A. Purpose

1. While the professional standards for the ethical practice of psychology, as a general discipline, are addressed in the American Psychological Association's *Ethical Principles of Psychologists*, these ethical principles do not relate, in sufficient detail, to current aspirations of desirable professional conduct for forensic psychologists. By design, none of the *Guidelines* contradicts any of the *Ethical Principles of Psychologists*; rather, they amplify those *Principles* in the context of the practice of forensic psychology, as herein defined.

2. The *Guidelines* have been designed to be national in scope and are intended to conform with state and federal law. In situations where the forensic psychologist believes that the requirements of law are in conflict with the *Guidelines*, attempts to resolve the conflict should be made in accordance with the procedures set forth in these *Guidelines* [IV(G)] and in the *Ethical Principles of Psychologists*.

B. Scope

1. The *Guidelines* specify the nature of desirable professional practice by forensic psychologists, within any subdiscipline of psychology (e.g., clinical, developmental, social, experimental), when engaged regularly as forensic psychologists.

a. "Psychologist" means any individual whose professional activities are defined by the American Psychological Association or by regulation of title by state registration or licensure, as the practice of psychology.

b. "Forensic psychology" means all forms of professional psychological conduct when acting, with definable foreknowledge, as a psychological expert on explicitly psycholegal issues, in direct assistance to courts, parties to legal proceedings, correctional and forensic mental health facilities, and administrative, judicial, and legislative agencies acting in an adjudicative capacity.

c. "Forensic psychologist" means psychologists who regularly engage in the practice of forensic psychology as defined in I(B)(1)(b).

2. The *Guidelines* do not apply to a psychologist who is asked to provide professional psychological services when the psychologist was not informed at the time of delivery of the services that they were to be used as forensic psychological services as defined above. The *Guidelines* may be helpful, however, in preparing the psychologist for the experience of communicating psychological data in a forensic context.

3. Psychologists who are not forensic psychologists as defined in I(B)(1)(c), but occasionally provide limited forensic psychological services, may find the *Guidelines* useful in the preparation and presentation of their professional services.

C. Related Standards

1. Forensic psychologists also conduct their professional activities in accord with the *Ethical Principles of Psychologists* and the various other statements of the American Psychological Association that may apply to particular subdisciplines or areas of practice that are relevant to their professional activities.

2. The standards of practice and ethical guidelines of other relevant "expert professional organizations" contain useful guidance and should be consulted even though the present *Guidelines* take precedence for forensic psychologists.

II.   RESPONSIBILITY

A. Forensic psychologists have an obligation to provide services in a manner consistent with the highest standards of their profession. They are responsible for their own conduct and the conduct of those individuals under their direct supervision.

B. Forensic psychologists make a reasonable effort to ensure that their services and the products of their services are used in a forthright and responsible manner.

III.   COMPETENCE

A. Forensic psychologists provide services only in areas of psychology in which they have specialized knowledge, skill, experience, and education.

B. Forensic psychologists have an obligation to present to the court, regarding the specific matters to which they will testify, the boundaries of their competence, the factual bases (knowledge, skill, experience, training, and education) for their qualification as an expert, and the relevance of those factual bases to their qualification as an expert on the specific matters at issue.

C. Forensic psychologists are responsible for a fundamental and reasonable level of knowledge and understanding of the legal and professional standards that govern their participation as experts in legal proceedings.

D. Forensic psychologists have an obligation to understand the civil rights of parties in legal proceedings in which they participate, and manage their professional conduct in a manner that does not diminish or threaten those rights.

E. Forensic psychologists recognize that their own personal values, moral beliefs, or personal and professional relationships with parties to a legal proceeding may interfere with their ability to practice competently. Under such circumstances, forensic psychologists are obligated to decline participation or to limit their assistance in a manner consistent with professional obligations.

IV. RELATIONSHIPS

A. During initial consultation with the legal representative of the party seeking services, forensic psychologists have an obligation to inform the party of factors that might reasonably affect the decision to contract with the forensic psychologist. These factors include, but are not limited to:

1. The fee structure for anticipated professional services;

2. Prior and current personal or professional activities, obligations, and relationships that

might produce a conflict of interests;

3. Their areas of competence and the limits of their competence; and

4. The known scientific bases and limitations of the methods and procedures that they employ and their qualifications to employ such methods and procedures.

B. Forensic psychologists do not provide professional services to parties to a legal proceeding on the basis of "contingent fees," when those services involve the offering of expert testimony to a court or administrative body, or when they call upon the psychologist to make affirmations or representations intended to be relied upon by third parties.

C. Forensic psychologists who derive a substantial portion of their income from fee-for-service arrangements should offer some portion of their professional services on a *pro bono* or reduced fee basis where the public interest or the welfare of clients may be inhibited by insufficient financial resources.

D. Forensic psychologists recognize potential conflicts of interest in dual relationships with parties to a legal proceeding, and they seek to minimize their effects.

1. Forensic psychologists avoid providing professional services to parties in a legal proceeding with whom they have personal or professional relationships that are inconsistent with the anticipated relationship.

2. When it is necessary to provide both evaluation and treatment services to a party in a legal proceeding (as may be the case in

small forensic hospital settings or small communities), the forensic psychologist takes reasonable steps to minimize the potential negative effects of these circumstances on the rights of the party, confidentiality, and the process of treatment and evaluation.

E. Forensic psychologists have an obligation to ensure that prospective clients are informed of their legal rights with respect to the anticipated forensic service, of the purposes of any evaluation, of the nature of procedures to be employed, of the intended uses of any product of their services, and of the party who has employed the forensic psychologist.

1. Unless court ordered, forensic psychologists obtain the informed consent of the client or party, or their legal representative, before proceeding with such evaluations and procedures. If the client appears unwilling to proceed after receiving a thorough notification of the purposes, methods, and intended uses of the forensic evaluation, the evaluation should be postponed and the psychologist should take steps to place the client in contact with his/her attorney for the purpose of legal advice on the issue of participation.

2. In situations where the client or party may not have the capacity to provide informed consent to services or the evaluation is pursuant to court order, the forensic psychologist provides reasonable notice to the client's legal representative of the nature of the anticipated forensic service before proceeding. If the client's legal representative objects to the evaluation, the forensic psychologist notifies the court issuing the order and responds as directed.

3. After a psychologist has advised the subject of a clinical forensic evaluation of the intended uses of the evaluation and its work product, the psychologist may not use the evaluation work product for other purposes without explicit waiver to do so by the client or the client's legal representative.

F. When forensic psychologists engage in research or scholarly activities that are compensated financially by a client or party to a legal proceeding, or when the psychologist provides those services on a *pro bono* basis, the psychologist clarifies any anticipated further use of such research or scholarly product, discloses the psychologist's role in the resulting research or scholarly products, and obtains whatever consent or agreement is required by law or professional standards.

G. When conflicts arise between the forensic psychologist's professional standards and the requirements of legal standards, a particular court, or a directive by an officer of the court or legal authorities, the forensic psychologist has an obligation to make those legal authorities aware of the source of the conflict and to take reasonable steps to resolve it. Such steps may include, but are not limited to, obtaining the consultation of fellow forensic professionals, obtaining the advice of independent counsel, and conferring directly with the legal representatives involved.

V. CONFIDENTIALITY AND PRIVILEGE

A. Forensic psychologists have an obligation to be aware of the legal standards that may affect or limit the confidentiality or privilege that may attach to their services or their products, and they conduct their professional activities in a manner that respects those known rights and privileges.

1. Forensic psychologists establish and maintain a system of record keeping and professional communication that safeguards a client's privilege.

2. Forensic psychologists maintain active control over records and information. They only release information pursuant to statutory requirements, court order, or the consent of the client.

B. Forensic psychologists inform their clients of the limitations to the confidentiality of their services and their products [see also Guideline IV(E)] by providing them with an understandable statement of their rights, privileges, and the limitations of confidentiality.

C. In situations where the right of the client or party to confidentiality is limited, the forensic psychologist makes every effort to maintain confidentiality with regard to any information that does not bear directly upon the legal purpose of the evaluation.

D. Forensic psychologists provide clients or their authorized legal representatives with access to the information in their records and a meaningful explanation of that information, consistent with existing Federal and state statutes, the *Ethical Principles of Psychologists*, the *Standards for Educational and Psychological Testing*, and institutional rules and regulations.

VI. METHODS AND PROCEDURES

A. Because of their special status as persons qualified as experts to the court, forensic psychologists have an obligation to maintain current knowledge of scientific, professional, and legal developments within their area of claimed competence. They are obligated also to use that knowledge, consistent with accepted clinical and scientific standards, in selecting data collection methods and procedures for an evaluation, treatment, consultation, or scholarly/empirical investigation.

B. Forensic psychologists have an obligation to document and be prepared to make available, subject to court order or the rules of evidence, all data that form the basis for their evidence or services. The standard to be applied to such documentation or recording *anticipates* that the detail and quality of such documentation will be subject to reasonable judicial scrutiny; this standard is higher than the normative standard for general clinical practice. When forensic psychologists conduct an examination or engage in the treatment of a party to a legal proceeding, with foreknowledge that their professional services will be used in an adjudicative forum, they incur a special responsibility to provide the best documentation possible under the circumstances.

1. Documentation of the data upon which one's evidence is based is subject to the normal rules of discovery, disclosure,

confidentiality, and privilege that operate in the jurisdiction in which the data were obtained. Forensic psychologists have an obligation to be aware of those rules and to regulate their conduct in accordance with them.

2. The duties and obligations of forensic psychologists with respect to documentation of data that form the basis for their evidence apply from the moment they know or have a reasonable basis for knowing that their data and evidence derived from it are likely to enter into legally relevant decisions.

C. In providing forensic psychological services, forensic psychologists take special care to avoid undue influence upon their methods, procedures, and products, such as might emanate from the party to a legal proceeding by financial compensation or other gains. As an expert conducting an evaluation, treatment, consultation, or scholarly/empirical investigation, the forensic psychologist maintains professional integrity by examining the issue at hand from all reasonable perspectives, actively seeking information that will differentially test plausible rival hypotheses.

D. Forensic psychologists do not provide professional forensic services to a defendant or to any party in, or in contemplation of, a legal proceeding prior to that individual's representation by counsel, except for persons judicially determined, where appropriate, to be handling their representation *pro se*. When the forensic services are pursuant to court order and the client is not represented by counsel, the forensic psychologist makes reasonable

efforts to inform the court prior to providing the services.

1. A forensic psychologist may provide emergency mental health services to a pretrial defendant prior to court order or the appointment of counsel where there are reasonable grounds to believe that such emergency services are needed for the protection and improvement of the defendant's mental health and where failure to provide such mental health services would constitute a substantial risk of imminent harm to the defendant or to others. In providing such services the forensic psychologist nevertheless seeks to inform the defendant's counsel in a manner consistent with the requirements of the emergency situation.

2. Forensic psychologists who provide such emergency mental health services should attempt to avoid providing further professional forensic services to that defendant unless that relationship is reasonably unavoidable [see IV(D)(2)].

E. When forensic psychologists seek data from third parties, prior records, or other sources, they do so only with the prior approval of the relevant legal party or as a consequence of an order of a court to conduct the forensic evaluation.

F. Forensic psychologists are aware that hearsay exceptions and other rules governing expert testimony place a special ethical burden upon them. When hearsay or otherwise inadmissible evidence forms the basis of their opinion, evidence, or professional product, they seek to minimize sole reliance upon such evidence. Where circumstances reasonably permit, forensic psychologists seek to obtain independent and personal verification of data relied upon as part of their professional services to the court or to a party to a legal proceeding.

1. While many forms of data used by forensic psychologists are hearsay, forensic psychologists attempt to corroborate critical data that form the basis for their professional product. When using hearsay data that have not been corroborated, but are nevertheless utilized, forensic psychologists have an affirmative responsibility to acknowledge the uncorroborated status of those data and the reasons for relying upon such data.

2. With respect to evidence of any type, forensic psychologists avoid offering information from their investigations or evaluations that does not bear directly upon the legal purpose of their professional services and that is not critical as support for their product, evidence, or testimony, except where such disclosure is required by law.

3. When a forensic psychologist relies upon data or information gathered by others, the origins of those data are clarified in any professional product. In addition, the forensic psychologist bears a special responsibility to ensure that such data, if relied upon, were gathered in a manner standard for the profession.

G. Unless otherwise stipulated by the parties, forensic psychologists are aware that no statements made by a defendant, in the course of any (forensic) examination, no testimony by the expert based upon such statements, nor any other fruits of the statements can be admitted into evidence against the defendant in any criminal proceeding, except on an issue respecting mental condition on which the defendant has introduced testimony. Forensic psychologists have an affirmative duty to ensure that their written products and oral testimony conform to this Federal Rule of Procedure (12.2[c]), or its state equivalent.

1. Because forensic psychologists are often not in a position to know what evidence, documentation, or element of a written product may be or may lend to a "fruit of the statement," they exercise extreme caution in preparing reports or offering testimony prior to the defendant's assertion of a mental state claim or the defendant's introduction of testimony regarding a mental condition. Consistent with the reporting requirements of state or federal law, forensic psychologists avoid including statements from the defendant relating to the time period of the alleged offense.

2. Once a defendant has proceeded to the trial stage, and all pretrial mental health issues such as competency have been resolved, forensic psychologists may include in their reports or testimony any statements made by the defendant that are directly relevant to supporting their expert evidence, providing that the defendant has "introduced" mental state evidence or testimony within the meaning of Federal Rule of Procedure 12.2(c), or its state equivalent.

H. Forensic psychologists avoid giving written or oral evidence about the psychological characteristics of particular individuals when they have not had an opportunity to conduct an examination of the individual adequate to the scope of the statements, opinions, or conclusions to be issued. Forensic psychologists make every reasonable effort to conduct such examinations. When it is not possible or feasible to do so, they make clear the impact of such limitations on the reliability and validity of their professional products, evidence, or testimony.

VII. PUBLIC AND PROFESSIONAL COMMUNICATIONS

A. Forensic psychologists make reasonable efforts to ensure that the products of their services, as well as their own public statements and professional testimony, are communicated in ways that will promote understanding and avoid deception, given the particular characteristics, roles, and abilities of various recipients of the communications.

   1. Forensic psychologists take reasonable steps to correct misuse or misrepresentation of their professional products, evidence, and testimony.

   2. Forensic psychologists provide information about professional work to clients in a manner consistent with professional and legal standards for the disclosure of test results, interpretations of data, and the factual bases for conclusions. A full explanation of the results of tests and the bases for conclusions

should be given in language that the client can understand.

   a. When disclosing information about a client to third parties who are not qualified to interpret test results and data, the forensic psychologist complies with Principle 16 of the *Standards for Educational and Psychological Testing.* When required to disclose results to a nonpsychologist, every attempt is made to ensure that test security is maintained and access to information is restricted to individuals with a legitimate and professional interest in the data. Other qualified mental health professionals who make a request for information pursuant to a lawful order are, by definition, "individuals with a legitimate and professional interest."

   b. In providing records and raw data, the forensic psychologist takes reasonable steps to ensure that the receiving party is informed that raw scores must be interpreted by a qualified professional in order to provide reliable and valid information.

B. Forensic psychologists realize that their public role as "expert to the court" or as "expert representing the profession" confers upon them a special responsibility for fairness and accuracy in their public statements. When evaluating or commenting upon the professional work product or qualifications of another expert or party to a legal proceeding, forensic psychologists represent their professional disagreements with reference to a fair and accurate evaluation of the data, theories, standards, and opinions of the other expert or party.

C. Ordinarily, forensic psychologists avoid making detailed public (out-of-court) statements about particular legal proceedings in which they have been involved. When there is a strong justification to do so, such public statements are designed to assure accurate representation of their role or their evidence, not to advocate the positions of parties in the legal proceeding. Forensic psychologists address particular legal proceedings in publications or communications only to the extent that the information relied upon is part of a public record, or consent for that use has been properly obtained from the party holding any privilege.

D. When testifying, forensic psychologists have an obligation to all parties to a legal proceeding to present their findings, conclusions, evidence, or other professional products in a fair manner. This principle does not preclude forceful representation of the data and reasoning upon which a conclusion or professional product is based. It does, however, preclude an attempt, whether active or passive, to engage in partisan distortion or misrepresentation. Forensic psychologists do not, by either commission or omission, participate in a misrepresentation of their evidence, nor do they participate in partisan attempts to avoid, deny, or subvert the presentation of evidence contrary to their own position.

E. Forensic psychologists, by virtue of their competence and rules of discovery, actively disclose all sources of information obtained in the course of their professional services; they actively disclose which information from which source was used in formulating a particular written product or oral testimony.

F. Forensic psychologists are aware that their essential role as expert to the court is to assist the trier of fact to understand the evidence or to determine a fact in issue. In offering expert evidence, they are aware that their own professional observations, inferences, and conclusions must be distinguished from legal facts, opinions, and conclusions. Forensic psychologists are prepared to explain the relationship between their expert testimony and the legal issues and facts of an instant case.

Comparison of Neuropsychological Test Performance in Forensic and Non-Forensic Populations*

The present study compared neuropsychological test performance in a forensic population with data from several community-based normative samples. Means and standard deviations for 225 incarcerated male felons were obtained for 39 neuropsychological measures. Using a series of one sample, two-tailed t-tests, the total forensic sample was found to perform significantly worse (p < .001) on 25 of 39 measures (64%) compared to non-forensic norms adjusted for age and/or education. Although results may be interpreted as indicating the presence of significant cognitive impairment in individuals within a forensic setting, findings are more consistent with the hypothesis that these individuals represent a unique population whose performance on neuropsychological tests is significantly affected by psychosocial and situational factors. Consequently, available normative data which is based largely on the performance of white, well educated, upper middle-class subjects may not provide a valid measure of neuropsychological functioning for forensic populations.

* Reprinted with permission, in press, *American Journal of Forensic Psychology.* Written by Michael J. Selby, Ann S. Airy-Eggertsen, and Gary D. Laver, California Polytechnic State University, San Luis Obispo.

TABLE 1. NON-FORENSIC VS. FORENSIC POPULATIONS

	Non-Forensic	Total Forensic Sample (n=225)				
	μ	n	M	SD	t	p
WAIS-R Fullscale IQ	100.00	112	90.81	12.51	−7.77	.000
Verbal IQ	100.00	112	89.79	12.38	−8.73	.000
Information	10.00	111	7.77	2.80	−8.38	.000
Comprehension	10.00	158.	7.99	2.79	−9.03	.000
Similarities	10.00	118	9.11	3.87	−2.50	.014
Arithmetic	10.00	111	7.95	2.35	−9.17	.000
Vocabulary	10.00	112	8.08	3.00	−6.77	.000
Digit Span	10.00	218	8.24	2.95	−8.79	.000
Performance IQ	100.00	112	93.66	12.95	−5.18	.000
Picture Completion	10.00	113	10.13	3.71	0.37	.704
Picture Arrangement	10.00	158	10.02	3.43	0.00	.944
Block Design	10.00	112	9.18	2.95	−2.95	.004
Object Assembly	10.00	111	7.70	1.88	−12.90	.000
Digit Symbol	10.00	214	7.97	2.70	−10.98	.000
WMS-R Visual Repro	32.95[7]	47	30.23	7.25	−2.56	.014
WMS-R Vis Repro Recall	30.10[7]	47	24.68	9.04	−4.11	.000
WMS-R Logical Prose	25.85[7]	47	20.28	8.50	−4.49	.000
WMS-R Log Prose Recall	22.00[7]	46	14.24	7.88	−6.68	.000
WMS-R Paired Assoc	21.20[7]	29	16.83	4.66	−5.05	.000
WMS-R Paired Assoc Rec	7.65[7]	29	6.62	1.76	−3.15	.004
Rey Complex Fig: Copy	33.20[10]	136	27.71	6.14	−10.42	.000
Rey Complex Fig: Recall	19.50[10]	132	15.26	6.53	−7.47	.000
Trails A*	29.00[14]	217	38.12	14.82	8.56	.000
Trails B*	75.20[14]	213	103.28	55.78	7.35	.000
Wisc Card Sort (1 deck)						
Categories	3.60[16]	33	3.97	4.06	0.52	.604
Persev Responses*	8.40[16]	35	15.00	8.32	4.69	.000
Persev Errors	7.60[16]	37	12.48	7.12	4.15	.000
Grooved Pegboard D*	67.30[14]	86	65.88	14.50	−0.90	.368
Grooved Pegboard ND*	72.30[14]	85	72.18	14.29	−0.10	.937
Finger Tapping D	49.90[14]	38	47.50	8.30	−1.78	.083
Finger Tapping ND	45.20[14]	38	42.08	7.18	−2.68	.011
Rey AVLT Total	46.00[10]	111	43.95	10.77	−2.01	.047
Rey AVLT Trial V	11.40[10]	110	11.04	2.90	−1.32	.192
Rey AVLT Delayed Recall	10.40[10]	108	8.79	3.97	−4.22	.000
Stroop Color-Word	45.00[20]	99	34.34	11.76	−9.01	.000
FAS	49.43[10]	141	37.06	11.35	−13.47	.000
Boston Naming	55.73[22]	27	47.89	5.16	−7.89	.000
Hooper Visual Organization	26.00[10]	25	24.96	3.10	−1.68	.107
Seashore Rhythm	26.10[14]	86	23.84	5.20	−4.03	.000

Note: n-values vary among measures since not all tests were administered to all subjects.
* Lower scores indicate better performance.

TABLE 2.   NON-FORENSIC VS. CAUCASIAN FORENSIC POPULATIONS

	Non-Forensic	Caucasian Forensic Sample (n = 90)				
	μ	n	M	SD	t	p
WAIS-R Fullscale IQ	100.00	38	96.58	13.47	−1.57	.126
Verbal IQ	100.00	38	94.55	12.87	−2.61	.013
Information	10.00	38	8.26	2.73	−3.92	.000
Comprehension	10.00	57	8.54	2.89	−3.80	.000
Similarities	10.00	41	10.51	3.98	0.82	.414
Arithmetic	10.00	38	8.97	2.57	−2.46	.019
Vocabulary	10.00	38	9.18	2.61	−1.93	.062
Digit Span	10.00	87	8.82	2.90	−3.81	.000
Performance IQ	100.00	38	99.74	14.03	−0.10	.909
Picture Completion	10.00	38	11.63	3.32	3.03	.004
Picture Arrangement	10.00	57	11.28	3.82	2.53	.014
Block Design	10.00	38	10.45	3.57	0.77	.445
Object Assembly	10.00	38	7.84	2.37	−5.62	.000
Digit Symbol	10.00	87	8.82	2.84	−3.88	.000
WMS-R Visual Repro	32.95[7]	15	30.53	10.08	−0.93	.369
WMS-R Vis Repro Recall	30.10[7]	15	25.33	9.78	−1.89	.080
WMS-R Logical Prose	25.85[7]	15	18.73	8.40	−3.28	.005
WMS-R Log Prose Recall	22.00[7]	15	14.27	7.23	−4.14	.001
WMS-R Paired Assoc	21.20[7]	11	18.27	2.97	−3.27	.008
WMS-R Paired Assoc Rec	7.65[7]	11	6.82	1.33	−2.08	.064
Rey Complex Fig: Copy	33.20[10]	49	28.76	5.77	−5.39	.000
Rey Complex Fig: Recall	19.50[10]	49	18.00	6.22	−1.69	.098
Trails A	29.00[14]	87	33.97	12.25	3.40	.000
Trails B	75.20[14]	87	85.78	35.28	2.80	.000
Wisc Card Sort (1 deck)						
Categories	3.60[16]	12	3.83	2.55	0.32	.757
Persev Responses	8.40[16]	13	11.46	7.63	1.45	.174
Persev Errors	7.60[16]	13	9.00	5.18	0.97	.349
Grooved Pegboard D	67.30[14]	29	63.29	8.71	−2.23	.034
Grooved Pegboard ND	72.30[14]	29	69.24	10.86	−1.51	.140
Finger Tapping D	49.90[14]	12	47.17	7.79	−1.22	.250
Finger Tapping ND	45.20[14]	12	42.58	5.81	−1.56	.147
Rey ALVT Total	46.00[10]	39	44.08	9.27	−1.30	.203
Rey ALVT Trial V	11.40[10]	38	11.16	2.81	−0.53	.599
Rey ALVT Delayed Recall	10.40[10]	37	8.97	4.04	−2.15	.039
Stroop Color-Word	45.00[20]	36	38.69	12.99	−2.91	.006
FAS	49.43[10]	50	39.86	11.26	−6.32	.000
Boston Naming	55.73[22]	7	52.00	5.48	−1.80	.122
Hooper Visual Organization	26.00[10]	4	24.00	3.37	−1.19	.320
Seashore Rhythm	26.10[14]	42	23.38	5.31	−3.32	.002

TABLE 3.   NON-FORENSIC VS. AFRICAN-AMERICAN FORENSIC POPULATIONS

	Non-Forensic	African-American Forensic Sample (n = 93)				
	μ	n	M	SD	t	p
WAIS-R Fullscale IQ	100.00	49	88.57	11.00	−7.27	.000
Verbal IQ	100.00	49	89.29	10.78	−6.96	.000
Information	10.00	48	8.23	2.87	−4.28	.000
Comprehension	10.00	73	7.93	2.70	−6.53	.000
Similarities	10.00	51.	8.86	3.11	−2.61	.012
Arithmetic	10.00	48	7.71	2.07	−7.66	.000
Vocabulary	10.00	49	8.00	3.15	−4.44	.000
Digit Span	10.00	89	7.98	2.95	−6.48	.000
Performance IQ	100.00	49	89.67	12.06	−5.99	.000
Picture Completion	10.00	50	9.02	3.93	−1.77	.084
Picture Arrangement	10.00	71	9.15	3.05	−2.33	.022
Block Design	10.00	49	8.14	2.45	−5.31	.000
Object Assembly	10.00	48	7.44	1.67	−10.60	.000
Digit Symbol	10.00	86	7.30	2.46	−10.15	.000
WMS-R Visual Repro	32.95[7]	22	28.86	5.47	−3.50	.002
WMS-R Vis Repro Recall	30.10[7]	22	23.82	8.54	−3.45	.002
WMS-R Logical Prose	25.85[7]	22	21.95	6.56	−2.78	.011
WMS-R Log Prose Recall	22.00[7]	22	15.27	8.09	−3.90	.001
WMS-R Paired Assoc	21.20[7]	12	17.42	5.11	−2.57	.026
WMS-R Paired Assoc Rec	7.65[7]	12	6.67	1.83	−1.87	.089
Rey Complex Fig: Copy	33.20[10]	63	25.59	6.36	−9.49	.000
Rey Complex Fig: Recall	19.50[10]	61	12.48	5.76	−9.52	.000
Trails A	29.00[14]	89	40.40	15.39	6.68	.000
Trails B	75.20[14]	86	111.98	65.41	5.21	.000
Wisc Card Sort (1 deck)						
Categories	3.60[16]	13	2.85	1.41	−1.93	.077
Persev Responses	8.40[16]	15	17.00	8.54	3.90	.002
Persev Errors	7.60[16]	16	12.88	6.90	3.06	.008
Grooved Pegboard D	67.30[14]	38	69.18	19.22	0.61	.549
Grooved Pegboard ND	72.30[14]	37	75.76	17.43	1.21	.236
Finger Tapping D	49.90[14]	19	46.68	9.79	−1.43	.169
Finger Tapping ND	45.20[14]	19	40.42	8.47	−2.46	.024
Rey AVLT Total	46.00[10]	48	44.71	10.90	−0.82	.416
Rey AVLT Trial V	11.40[10]	48	11.21	2.66	−0.50	.620
Rey AVLT Delayed Recall	10.40[10]	47	8.94	3.97	−2.53	.015
Stroop Color-Word	45.00[20]	48	31.71	10.16	−9.07	.000
FAS	49.43[10]	67	36.16	11.83	−9.53	.000
Boston Naming	55.73[22]	14	46.50	4.03	−8.59	.000
Hooper Visual Organization	26.00[10]	16	25.75	2.27	−0.43	.665
Seashore Rhythm	26.10[14]	29	25.31	4.29	−0.99	.330

TABLE 4.   NON-FORENSIC VS. HISPANIC FORENSIC POPULATIONS

	Non-Forensic	Hispanic Forensic Sample (n = 42)				
	μ	n	M	SD	t	p
WAIS-R Fullscale IQ	100.00	25	86.44	10.89	−6.23	.000
Verbal IQ	100.00	25	83.52	12.01	−6.86	.000
Information	10.00	25	6.16	2.19	−4.21	.000
Comprehension	10.00	28	7.04	2.63	−5.96	.000
Similarities	10.00	26	7.38	4.37	−3.05	.005
Arithmetic	10.00	25	6.88	1.92	−8.12	.000
Vocabulary	10.00	25	6.56	2.65	−6.50	.000
Digit Span	10.00	42	7.62	2.92	−5.28	.000
Performance IQ	100.00	25	92.24	9.40	−4.13	.000
Picture Completion	10.00	25	10.08	3.09	0.14	.898
Picture Arrangement	10.00	28	9.64	2.79	−0.68	.504
Block Design	10.00	25	9.28	1.97	−1.83	.080
Object Assembly	10.00	25	8.00	1.32	−7.56	.000
Digit Symbol	10.00	41	7.59	2.43	−6.37	.000
WMS-R Visual Repro	32.95[7]	10	32.80	5.37	−0.10	.932
WMS-R Vis Repro Recall	30.10[7]	10	25.60	9.74	−1.46	.178
WMS-R Logical Prose	25.85[7]	10	18.90	12.10	−1.87	.103
WMS-R Log Prose Recall	22.00[7]	9	11.67	8.70	−3.56	.007
WMS-R Paired Assoc	21.20[7]	6	13.00	4.86	−4.13	.009
WMS-R Paired Assoc Rec	7.65[7]	6	6.17	2.48	−1.46	.203
Rey Complex Fig: Copy	33.20[10]	24	31.17	3.93	−2.53	.019
Rey Complex Fig: Recall	19.50[10]	22	16.86	6.29	−1.97	.063
Trials A	29.00[14]	41	41.95	16.66	4.79	.000
Trials B	75.20[14]	40	122.63	60.06	4.99	.000
Wisc Card Sort (1 deck)						
Categories	3.60[16]	8	6.00	7.39	0.92	.389
Persev Responses	8.40[16]	7	17.29	7.91	2.97	.025
Persev Errors	7.60[16]	8	17.25	8.01	3.41	.011
Grooved Pegboard D	67.30[14]	19	62.63	8.55	−2.38	.029
Grooved Pegboard ND	72.30[14]	19	69.68	10.75	−1.05	.303
Finger Tapping D	49.90[14]	7	50.29	3.77	0.26	.796
Finger Tapping ND	45.20[14]	7	45.71	4.03	0.33	.747
Rey AVLT Total	46.00[10]	24	42.21	12.86	−1.45	.162
Rey AVLT Trial V	11.40[10]	24	10.50	3.51	−1.25	.222
Rey AVLT Delayed Recall	10.40[10]	24	8.21	3.97	−2.70	.013
Stroop Color-Word	45.00[20]	15	32.33	11.14	−4.40	.001
FAS	49.43[10]	24	33.75	9.07	−8.74	.000
Boston Naming	55.73[22]	6	46.33	5.32	−4.33	.008
Hooper Visual Organization	26.00[10]	5	23.20	4.76	−1.32	.259
Seashore Rhythm	26.10[14]	15	22.27	6.12	−2.42	.029

Appendix H

Ethical Principles of Psychologists and Code of Conduct*

INTRODUCTION

The American Psychological Association's (APA's) *Ethical Principles of Psychologists and Code of Conduct* (hereinafter referred to as the Ethics Code) consists of an Introduction, a Preamble, six General Principles (A–F), and specific Ethical Standards. The Introduction discusses the intent, organization, procedural considerations, and scope of application of the Ethics Code. The Preamble and General Principles are *aspirational goals* to guide psychologists toward the highest ideals of psychology. Although the Preamble and General Principles are not themselves enforceable rules, they should be considered by psychologists in arriving at an ethical course of action and may be considered by ethics bodies in interpreting the Ethical Standards. The Ethical Standards set forth *enforceable* rules for conduct as psychologists. Most of the Ethical Standards are written broadly, in order to apply to psychologists in varied roles, although the application of an Ethical Standard may vary depending on the context. The

Ethical Standards are not exhaustive. The fact that a given conduct is not specifically addressed by the Ethics Code does not mean that it is necessarily either ethical or unethical.

Membership in the APA commits members to adhere to the APA Ethics Code and to the rules and procedures used to implement it. Psychologists and students, whether or not they are APA members, should be aware that the Ethics Code may be applied to them by state psychology boards, courts, or other public bodies.

This Ethics Code applies only to psychologists' work-related activities, that is, activities that are part of the psychologists' scientific and professional functions or that are psychological in nature. It includes the clinical or counseling practice of psychology, research, teaching, supervision of trainees, development of assessment instruments, conducting assessments, educational counseling, organizational consulting, social intervention, administration, and other activities as well. These work-related activities can be distinguished from the purely private conduct of a psychologist, which ordinarily is not within the purview of the Ethics Code.

---

*Reprinted with permission by the American Psychological Association, Inc.

The Ethics Code is intended to provide standards of professional conduct that can be applied by the APA and by other bodies that choose to adopt them. Whether or not a psychologist has violated the Ethics Code does not by itself determine whether he or she is legally liable in a court action, whether a contract is enforceable, or whether other legal consequences occur. These results are based on legal rather than ethical rules. However, compliance with or violation of the Ethics Code may be admissible as evidence in some legal proceedings, depending on the circumstances.

In the process of making decisions regarding their professional behavior, psychologists must consider this Ethics Code, in addition to applicable laws and psychology board regulations. If the Ethics Code establishes a higher standard of conduct than is required by law, psychologists must meet the higher ethical standard. If the Ethics Code standard appears to conflict with the requirements of law, then psychologists make known their commitment to the Ethics Code and take steps to resolve the conflict in a responsible manner. If neither law nor the Ethics Code resolves an issue, psychologists should consider other professional materials[1]

and the dictates of their own conscience, as well as seek consultation with others within the field when this is practical.

The procedures for filing, investigating, and resolving complaints of unethical conduct are described in the current Rules and Procedures of the APA Ethics Committee. The actions that APA may take for violations of the Ethics Code include actions such as reprimand, censure, termination of APA membership, and referral of the matter to other bodies. Complainants who seek remedies such as monetary damages in alleging ethical violations by a psychologist must resort to private negotiation, administrative bodies, or the courts. Actions that violate the Ethics Code may lead to the imposition of sanctions on a psychologist by bodies other than APA, including state psychological associations, other professional groups, psychology boards, other state or federal agencies, and payors for health services. In addition to actions for violation of the Ethics Code, the APA Bylaws provide that APA may take action against a member after his or her conviction of a felony, expulsion or suspension from an affiliated state psychological association, or suspension or loss of licensure.

---

[1] Professional materials that are most helpful in this regard are guidelines and standards that have been adopted or endorsed by professional psychological organizations. Such guidelines and standards, whether adopted by the American Psychological Association (APA) or its Divisions, are not enforceable as such by this Ethics Code, but are of educative value to psychologists, courts, and professional bodies. Such materials include, but are not limited to, the APA's *General Guidelines for Providers of Psychological Services* (1987), *Specialty Guidelines for the Delivery of Services by Clinical Psychologists, Counseling Psychologists, Industrial/* *Organizational Psychologists, and School Psychologists* (1981), *Guidelines for Computer Based Tests and Interpretations* (1987), *Standards for Educational and Psychological Testing* (1985), *Ethical Principles in the Conduct of Research with Human Participants* (1982), *Guidelines for Ethical Conduct in the Care and Use of Animals* (1986), *Guidelines for Providers of Psychological Services to Ethnic, Linguistic, and Culturally Diverse Populations* (1990), and *Publication Manual of the American Psychological Association* (3rd ed., 1983). Materials not adopted by APA as a whole include the APA Division 41 (Forensic Psychology)/American Psychology–Law Society's *Specialty Guidelines for Forensic Psychologists* (1991).

This version of the APA Ethics Code was adopted by the American Psychological Association's Council of Representatives during its meeting, August 13 and 16, 1992, and is effective beginning December 1, 1992. Inquiries concerning the substance or interpretation of the APA Ethics Code should be addressed to the Director, Office of Ethics, American Psychological Association, 750 First Street, NE, Washington, DC 20002-4242.

This Code will be used to adjudicate complaints brought concerning alleged conduct occurring on or after the effective date. Complaints regarding conduct occurring prior to the effective date will be adjudicated on the basis of the version of the Code that was in effect at the time the conduct occurred, except that no provisions repealed in June 1989, will be enforced even if an earlier version contains the provision. The Ethics Code will undergo continuing review and study for future revisions; comments on the Code may be sent to the above address.

The APA has previously published its Ethical Standards as follows:

American Psychological Association. (1953). *Ethical standards of psychologists.* Washington, DC: Author.

American Psychological Association. (1958). Standards of ethical behavior for psychologists. *American Psychologist, 13,* 268–271.

American Psychological Association. (1963). Ethical standards of psychologists. *American Psychologist, 18,* 56–60.

American Psychological Association. (1968). Ethical standards of psychologists. *American Psychologist, 23,* 357–361.

American Psychological Association. (1977, March). Ethical standards of psychologists. *APA Monitor,* pp. 22–23.

American Psychological Association. (1979). *Ethical standards of psychologists.* Washington, DC: Author.

American Psychological Association. (1981). Ethical principles of psychologists. *American Psychologist, 36,* 633–638.

American Psychological Association. (1990). Ethical principles of psychologists (Amended June 2, 1989). *American Psychologist, 45,* 390–395.

Request copies of the APA's Ethical Principles of Psychologists and Code of Conduct from the APA Order Department, 750 First Street, NE, Washington, DC 20002-4242, or phone (202) 336-5510.

PREAMBLE

Psychologists work to develop a valid and reliable body of scientific knowledge based on research. They may apply that knowledge to human behavior in a variety of contexts. In doing so, they perform many roles, such as researcher, educator, diagnostician, therapist, supervisor, consultant, administrator, social interventionist, and expert witness. Their goal is to broaden knowledge of behavior and, where appropriate, to apply it pragmatically to improve the condition of both the individual and society. Psychologists respect the central importance of freedom of inquiry and expression in research, teaching, and publication. They also strive to help the public in developing informed judgments and choices concerning human behavior. This Ethics Code provides a common set of values upon which psychologists build their professional and scientific work.

This Code is intended to provide both the general principles and the decision rules to cover most situations encountered by psychologists. It has as its primary goal the welfare and protection of the individuals and groups with whom psychologists work. It is the individual responsibility of each psychologist to aspire to the highest possible standards of conduct. Psychologists respect and protect human and civil rights, and do not knowingly participate in or condone unfair discriminatory practices.

The development of a dynamic set of ethical standards for a psychologist's work-related conduct requires a personal commitment to a lifelong effort to act ethically; to encourage ethical behavior by students, supervisees, employees, and colleagues, as appropriate; and to consult with others, as needed, concerning ethical problems. Each psychologist supplements, but does not violate, the Ethics Code's values and rules on the basis of guidance drawn from personal values, culture, and experience.

GENERAL PRINCIPLES

Principle A: Competence

Psychologists strive to maintain high standards of competence in their work. They recognize the boundaries of their particular competencies and the limitations of their expertise. They provide only those services and use only those techniques for which they are qualified by education, training, or experience. Psychologists are cognizant of the fact that the competencies required in serving, teaching, and/or studying groups of people vary with the distinctive characteristics of those groups. In those areas in which recognized professional standards do not yet exist, psychologists exercise careful judgment and take appropriate precautions to protect the welfare of those with whom they work. They maintain knowledge of relevant scientific and professional information related to the services they render, and they recognize the need for ongoing education. Psychologists make appropriate use of scientific, professional, technical, and administrative resources.

Principle B: Integrity

Psychologists seek to promote integrity in the science, teaching, and practice of psychology. In these activities psychologists are honest, fair, and respectful of others. In describing or reporting their qualifications, services, products, fees, research, or teaching, they do not make statements that are false, misleading, or deceptive. Psychologists strive to be aware of their own belief systems, values, needs, and limitations and the effect of these on their work. To the extent feasible, they attempt to clarify for relevant parties the roles they are performing and to function appropriately in accordance with those roles. Psychologists avoid improper and potentially harmful dual relationships.

Principle C: Professional and Scientific Responsibility

Psychologists uphold professional standards of conduct, clarify their professional roles and obligations, accept appropriate responsibility for their behavior, and adapt their methods to the needs of different populations. Psychologists consult with, refer to, or cooperate with other professionals and institutions to the extent needed to serve the best interests of their patients, clients, or other recipients of their services. Psychologists' moral standards and conduct are personal matters to the same degree as is true for any other person, except as psychologists' conduct may compromise their professional responsibilities or reduce the public's trust in psychology and psychologists. Psychologists are concerned about the ethical compliance of their colleagues' scientific and professional conduct. When appropriate, they consult with colleagues in order to prevent or avoid unethical conduct.

Principle D: Respect for People's Rights and Dignity

Psychologists accord appropriate respect to the fundamental rights, dignity, and worth of all people. They respect the rights of individuals to privacy, confidentiality, self-determination, and autonomy, mindful that legal and other obligations may lead to inconsistency and conflict with the exercise of these rights. Psychologists are aware of cultural, individual, and role differences, including those due to age, gender, race, ethnicity, national origin, religion, sexual orientation, disability, language, and socioeconomic status. Psychologists try to eliminate the effect on their work of biases based on those factors, and they do not knowingly participate in or condone unfair discriminatory practices.

Principle E: Concern for Others' Welfare

Psychologists seek to contribute to the welfare of those with whom they interact professionally. In their professional actions, psychologists weigh the welfare and rights of their patients or clients, students, supervisees, human research participants, and other affected persons, and the welfare of animal subjects of research. When conflicts occur among psychologists' obligations or concerns, they attempt to resolve these conflicts and to perform their roles in a responsible fashion that avoids or minimizes harm.

Psychologists are sensitive to real and ascribed differences in power between themselves and others, and they do not exploit or mislead other people during or after professional relationships.

Principle F: Social Responsibility

Psychologists are aware of their professional and scientific responsibilities to the community and the society in which they work and live. They apply and make public their knowledge of psychology in order to contribute to human welfare. Psychologists are concerned about and work to mitigate the causes of human suffering. When undertaking research, they strive to advance human welfare and the science of psychology. Psychologists try to avoid misuse of their work. Psychologists comply with the law and encourage the development of law and social policy that serve the interests of their patients and clients and the public. They are encouraged to contribute a portion of their professional time for little or no personal advantage.

ETHICAL STANDARDS

1.   General Standards

These General Standards are potentially applicable to the professional and scientific activities of all psychologists.

1.01   Applicability of the Ethics Code

The activity of a psychologists subject to the Ethics Code may be reviewed under these Ethical Standards only if the activity is part of his or her work-related functions or the activity is psychological in nature. Personal activities having no connection to or effect on psychological roles are not subject to the Ethics Code.

1.02 Relationship of Ethics and Law

If psychologists's ethical responsibilities conflict with law, psychologists make known their commitment to the Ethics Code and take steps to resolve the conflict in a responsible manner.

1.03 Professional and Scientific Relationship

Psychologists provide diagnostic, therapeutic, teaching, research, supervisory, consultative, or other psychological services only in the context of a defined professional or scientific relationship or role. (See also Standards 2.01, Evaluation, Diagnosis, and Interventions in Professional Context, and 7.02, Forensic Assessments.)

1.04 Boundaries of Competence

(a) Psychologists provide services, teach, and conduct research only within the boundaries of their competence, based on their education, training, supervised experience, or appropriate professional experience.

(b) Psychologists provide services, teach, or conduct research in new areas or involving new techniques only after first undertaking appropriate study, training, supervision, and/or consultation from persons who are competent in those areas or techniques.

(c) In those emerging areas in which generally recognized standards for preparatory training do not yet exist, psychologists nevertheless take reasonable steps to ensure the competence of their work and to protect patients, clients, students, research participants, and others from harm.

1.05 Maintaining Expertise

Psychologists who engage in assessment, therapy, teaching, research, organizational consulting, or other professional activities maintain a reasonable level of awareness of current scientific and professional information in their fields of activity, and undertake ongoing efforts to maintain competence in the skills they use.

1.06 Basis for Scientific and Professional Judgments

Psychologists rely on scientifically and professionally derived knowledge when making scientific or professional judgments or when engaging in scholarly or professional endeavors.

1.07 Describing the Nature and Results of Psychological Services

(a) When psychologists provide assessment, evaluation, treatment, counseling, supervision, teaching, consultation, research, or other psychological services to an individual, a group, or an organization, they provide, using language that is reasonably understandable to the recipient of those services, appropriate information beforehand about the nature of such services and appropriate information later about results and conclusions. (See also Standard 2.09, Explaining Assessment Results.)

(b) If psychologists will be precluded by law or by organizational roles from providing such information to particular individuals or groups, they so inform those individuals or groups at the outset of the service.

1.08 Human Differences

Where differences of age, gender, race, ethnicity, national origin, religion, sexual orientation, disability, language, or socioeconomic status significantly affect psychologists' work concerning particular individuals or groups, psychologists obtain the training, experience, consultation, or supervision necessary to ensure the competence of their services, or they make appropriate referrals.

1.09   Respecting Others

In their work-related activities, psychologists respect the rights of others to hold values, attitudes, and opinions that differ from their own.

1.10   Nondiscrimination

In their work-related activities, psychologists do not engage in unfair discrimination based on age, gender, race, ethnicity, national origin, religion, sexual orientation, disability, socioeconomic status, or any basis proscribed by law.

1.11   Sexual Harassment

(a) Psychologists do not engage in sexual harassment. Sexual harassment is sexual solicitation, physical advances, or verbal or nonverbal conduct that is sexual in nature, that occurs in connection with the psychologist's activities or roles as a psychologist, and that either: (1) is unwelcome, is offensive, or creates a hostile workplace environment, and the psychologist knows or is told this; or (2) is sufficiently severe or intense to be abusive to a reasonable person in the context. Sexual harassment can consist of a single intense or severe act or of multiple persistent or pervasive acts.

(b) Psychologists accord sexual-harassment complainants and respondents dignity and respect. Psychologists do not participate in denying a person academic admittance or advancement, employment, tenure, or promotion, based solely upon their having made, or their being the subject of, sexual-harassment charges. This does not preclude taking action based upon the outcome of such proceedings or consideration of other appropriate information.

1.12   Other Harassment

Psychologists do not knowingly engage in behavior that is harassing or demeaning to persons with whom they interact in their work based on factors such as those persons' age, gender, race, ethnicity, national origin, religion, sexual orientation, disability, language, or socioeconomic status.

1.13   Personal Problems and Conflicts

(a) Psychologists recognize that their personal problems and conflicts may interfere with their effectiveness. Accordingly, they refrain from undertaking an activity when they know or should know that their personal problems are likely to lead to harm to a patient, client, colleague, student, research participant, or other person to whom they may owe a professional or scientific obligation.

(b) In addition, psychologists have an obligation to be alert to signs of, and to obtain assistance for, their personal problems at an early stage, in order to prevent significantly impaired performance.

(c) When psychologists become aware of personal problems that may interfere with their performing work-related duties adequately, they take appropriate measures, such as obtaining professional consultation or assistance, and determine whether they should limit, suspend, or terminate their work-related duties.

1.14   Avoiding Harm

Psychologists take reasonable steps to avoid harming their patients or clients, research participants, students, and others with whom they work, and to minimize harm where it is foreseeable and unavoidable.

1.15 Misuse of Psychologists' Influence

Because psychologists' scientific and professional judgments and actions may affect the lives of others, they are alert to and guard against personal, financial, social, organizational, or political factors that might lead to misuse of their influence.

1.16 Misuse of Psychologists' Work

(a) Psychologists do not participate in activities in which it appears likely that their skills or data will be misused by others, unless corrective mechanisms are available. (See also Standard 7.04, Truthfulness and Candor.)

(b) If psychologists learn of misuse or misrepresentation of their work, they take reasonable steps to correct or minimize the misuse or misrepresentation.

1.17 Multiple Relationships

(a) In many communities and situations, it may not be feasible or reasonable for psychologists to avoid social or other nonprofessional contacts with persons such as patients, clients, students, supervisees, or research participants. Psychologists must always be sensitive to the potential harmful effects of other contacts on their work and on those persons with whom they deal. A psychologists refrains from entering into or promising another personal, scientific, professional, financial, or other relationship with such persons if it appears likely that such a relationship reasonably might impair the psychologist's objectivity or otherwise interfere with the psychologist's effectively perform-

ing his or her functions as a psychologist, or might harm or exploit the other party.

(b) Likewise, whenever feasible, a psychologist refrains from taking on professional or scientific obligations when preexisting relationships would create a risk of such harm.

(c) If a psychologist finds that, due to unforeseen factors, a potentially harmful multiple relationship has arisen, the psychologist attempts to resolve it with due regard for the best interests of the affected person and maximal compliance with the Ethics Code.

1.18 Barter (with Patients or Clients)

Psychologists ordinarily refrain from accepting goods, services, or other non-monetary remuneration from patients or clients in return for psychological services because such arrangements create inherent potential for conflicts, exploitation, and distortion of the professional relationship. A psychologist may participate in bartering *only* if (1) it is not clinically contraindicated, *and* (2) the relationship is not exploitative. (See also Standards 1.17, Multiple Relationships, and 1.25, Fees and Financial Arrangements.)

1.19 Exploitative Relationships

(a) Psychologists do not exploit persons over whom they have supervisory, evaluative, or other authority such as students, supervisees, employees, research participants, and clients or patients. (See also Standards 4.05–4.07 regarding sexual involvement with clients or patients.)

(b) Psychologists do not engage in sexual relationships with students or supervisees in training over whom the psychologist has evaluative or direct authority, because such relationships are so likely to impair judgment or be exploitative.

1.20 Consultations and Referrals

(a) Psychologists arrange for appropriate consultations and referrals based principally on the best interests of their patients or clients, with appropriate consent, and subject to other relevant considerations, including applicable law and contractual obligations. (See also Standards 5.01, Discussing the Limits of Confidentiality, and 5.06, Consultations.)

(b) When indicated and professionally appropriate, psychologists cooperate with other professionals in order to serve their patients or clients effectively and appropriately.

(c) Psychologists' referral practices are consistent with law.

1.21 Third-Party Requests for Services

(a) When a psychologist agrees to provide services to a person or entity at the request of a third party, the psychologist clarifies to the extent feasible, at the outset of the service, the nature of the relationship with each party. This clarification includes the role of the psychologist (such as therapist, organizational consultant, diagnostician, or expert witness), the probable uses of the services provided or the information obtained, and the fact that there may be limits to confidentiality.

(b) If there is a foreseeable risk of the psychologist's being called upon to perform conflicting roles because of the involvement of a third party, the psychologist clarifies the nature and direction of his or her responsibilities, keeps all parties appropriately informed as matters develop, and resolves the situation in accordance with this Ethics Code.

1.22 Delegation to and Supervision of Subordinates

(a) Psychologists delegate to their employees, supervisees, and research assistants only those responsibilities that such persons can reasonably be expected to perform competently, on the basis of their education, training, or experience, either independently or with the level of supervision being provided.

(b) Psychologists provide proper training and supervision to their employees or supervisees and take reasonable steps to see that such persons perform services responsibly, competently, and ethically.

(c) If institutional policies, procedures, or practices prevent fulfillment of this obligation, psychologists attempt to modify their role or to correct the situation to the extent feasible.

1.23 Documentation of Professional and Scientific Work

(a) Psychologists appropriately document their professional and scientific work in order to facilitate provision of services later by them or by other professionals, to ensure accountability, and to meet other requirements of institutions or the law.

(b) When psychologists have reason to believe that records of their professional services will be used in legal proceedings involving recipients of or participants in their work, they have a responsibility to create and maintain documentation in the kind of detail and quality that would be consistent with reasonable scrutiny in an adjudicative forum. (See also Standard 7.01, Professionalism, under Forensic Activities.)

1.24 Records and Data

Psychologists create, maintain, disseminate, store, retain, and dispose of records and data relating to their research, practice, and other work in accordance with law and in a manner that permits compliance with the requirements of this Ethics Code. (See also Standard 5.04, Maintenance of Records.)

1.25 Fees and Financial Arrangements

(a) As early as is feasible in a professional or scientific relationship, the psychologist and the patient, client, or other appropriate recipient of psychological services reach an agreement specifying the compensation and the billing arrangements.

(b) Psychologists do not exploit recipients of services or payors with respect to fees.

(c) Psychologists' fee practices are consistent with law.

(d) Psychologists do not misrepresent their fees.

(e) If limitations to services can be anticipated because of limitations in financing, this is discussed with the patient, client, or other appropriate recipient of services as early as is feasible. (See also Standard 4.08, Interruption of Services.)

(f) If the patient, client or other recipient of services does not pay for services as agreed, and if the psychologist wishes to use collection agencies or legal measures to collect the fees, the psychologist first informs the person that such measures will be taken and provides that person an opportunity to make prompt payment. (See also Standard 5.11, Withholding Records for Nonpayment.)

1.26 Accuracy in Reports to Payors and Funding Sources

In their reports to payors for services or sources of research funding, psychologists accurately state the nature of the research or service provided, the fees or charges, and where applicable, the identity of the provider, the findings, and the diagnosis. (See also Standard 5.05, Disclosures.)

1.27 Referrals and Fees

When a psychologist pays, receives payment from, or divides fees with another professional other than in an employer-employee relationship, the payment to each is based on the services (clinical, consultative, administrative, or other) provided and is not based on the referral itself.

2. Evaluation, Assessment, or Intervention

2.01 Evaluation, Diagnosis, and Interventions in Professional Context

(a) Psychologists perform evaluations, diagnostic services, or interventions only within the context of a defined professional relationship. (See also Standard 1.03, Professional and Scientific Relationship.)

(b) Psychologists' assessment, recommendations, reports, and psychological diagnostic or evaluative statements are based on information and techniques (including personal interviews of the individual when appropriate) sufficient to provide appropriate substantiation for their findings. (See also Standard 7.02, Forensic Assessments.)

2.02 Competence and Appropriate Use of Assessments and Interventions

(a) Psychologists who develop, administer, score, interpret, or use psychological assessment techniques, interviews, tests, or instruments do so in a manner and for purposes that are appropriate in light of the research on or evidence of the usefulness and proper application of the techniques.

(b) Psychologists refrain from misuse of assessment techniques, interventions, results, and interpretations and take reasonable steps to prevent others from misusing the information these techniques provide. This includes refraining from releasing raw test results or raw data to persons, other than to patients or clients as appropriate, who are not qualified to use such information. (See also Standards 1.02, Relationship of Ethics and Law, and 1.04, Boundaries of Competence.)

2.03   Test Construction

Psychologists who develop and conduct research with tests and other assessment techniques use scientific procedures and current professional knowledge for test design, standardization, validation, reduction or elimination of bias, and recommendations for use.

2.04   Use of Assessment in General and With Special Populations

(a) Psychologists who perform interventions or administer, score, interpret, or use assessment techniques are familiar with the reliability, validation, and related standardization or outcome studies of, and proper applications and uses of, the techniques they use.

(b) Psychologists recognize limits to the certainty with which diagnoses, judgments, or predictions can be made about individuals.

(c) Psychologists attempt to identify situations in which particular interventions or assessment techniques or norms may not be applicable or may require adjustment in administration or interpretation because of factors such as individuals' gender, age, race, ethnicity, national origin, religion, sexual orientation, disability, language, or socioeconomic status.

2.05   Interpreting Assessment Results

When interpreting assessment results, including automated interpretations, psychologists take into account the various tests factors and characteristics of the person being assessed that might affect psychologists' judgments or reduce the accuracy of their interpretations. They indicate any significant reservations they have about the accuracy or limitations of their interpretations.

2.06   Unqualified Persons

Psychologists do not promote the use of psychological assessment techniques by unqualified persons. (See also Standard 1.22, Delegation to and Supervision of Subordinates.)

2.07   Obsolete Tests and Outdated Test Results

(a) Psychologists do not base their assessment or intervention decisions or recommendations on data or test results that are outdated for the current purpose.

(b) Similarly, psychologists do not base such decisions or recommendations on tests and measures that are obsolete and not useful for the current purpose.

2.08   Test Scoring and Interpretation Services

(a) Psychologists who offer assessment or scoring procedures to other professionals accurately describe the purpose, norms, validity, reliability, and applications of the procedures and any special qualifications applicable to their use.

(b) Psychologists select scoring and interpretation services (including automated services) on the basis of evidence of the validity of the program and procedures as well as on other appropriate considerations.

(c) Psychologists retain appropriate responsibility for the appropriate application, interpretation, and use of assessment instruments, whether they score and interpret such tests themselves or use automated or other services.

2.09 Explaining Assessment Results

Unless the nature of the relationship is clearly explained to the person being assessed in advance and precludes provision of an explanation of results (such as in some organizational consulting, preemployment or security screenings, and forensic evaluations), psychologists ensure that an explanation of the results is provided using language that is reasonably understandable to the person assessed or to another legally authorized person on behalf of the client. Regardless of whether the scoring and interpretation are done by the psychologist, by assistants, or by automated or other outside services, psychologists take reasonable steps to ensure that appropriate explanations of results are given.

2.10 Maintaining Test Security

Psychologists make reasonable efforts to maintain the integrity and security of tests and other assessment techniques consistent with law, contractual obligations, and in a manner that permits compliance with the requirements of this Ethics Code. (See also Standard 1.02, Relationship of Ethics and Law.)

3. Advertising and Other Public Statements

3.01 Definition of Public Statements

Psychologists comply with this Ethics Code in public statements relating to their professional services, products, or publications or to the field of psychology. Public statements include but are not limited to paid or unpaid advertising, brochures, printed matter, directory listings, personal resumes or curricula vitae, interviews or comments for use in media, statements in legal proceedings, lectures and public oral presentations, and published materials.

3.02 Statements by Others

(a) Psychologists who engage others to create or place public statements that promote their professional practice, products, or activities retain professional responsibility for such statements.

(b) In addition, psychologists make reasonable efforts to prevent others whom they do not control (such as employers, publishers, sponsors, organizational clients, and representatives of the print or broadcast media) from making deceptive statements concerning psychologists' practice or professional or scientific activities.

(c) If psychologists learn of deceptive statements about their work made by others, psychologists make reasonable efforts to correct such statements.

(d) Psychologists do not compensate employees of press, radio, television, or other communication media in return for publicity in a news item.

(e) A paid advertisement relating to the psychologist's activities must be identified as such, unless it is already apparent from the context.

3.03 Avoidance of False or Deceptive Statements

(a) Psychologists do not make public statements that are false, deceptive, misleading, or fraudulent, either because of what they state, convey, or suggest or because of what they omit, concerning their research, practice, or other work activities or those of persons or organizations with which they are affiliated. As examples (and not in limitation) of this standard, psychologists do not make false or deceptive statements concerning (1) their training, experience, or competence; (2) their academic degrees; (3) their credentials; (4) their institutional or association affiliations; (5) their services; (6) the scientific or clinical basis for, or results or degree of success of, their services; (7) their fees; or (8) their publications or research findings. (See also Standards 6.15, Deception in Research, and 6.18, Providing Participants with Information about the Study.)

(b) Psychologists claim as credentials for their psychological work, only degrees that (1) were earned from a regionally accredited educational institution or (2) were the basis for psychology licensure by the state in which they practice.

3.04 Media Presentations

When psychologists provide advice or comment by means of public lectures, demonstrations, radio or television programs, prerecorded tapes, printed articles, mailed material, or other media, they take reasonable precautions to ensure that (1) the statements are based on appropriate psychological literature and practice, (2) the statements are otherwise consistent with this Ethics Code, and (3) the recipients of the information are not encouraged to infer that a relationship has been established with them personally.

3.05 Testimonials

Psychologists do not solicit testimonials from current psychotherapy clients or patients or other persons who because of their particular circumstances are vulnerable to undue influence.

3.06 In-Person Solicitation

Psychologists do not engage, directly or through agents, in uninvited in-person solicitation of business from actual or potential psychotherapy patients or clients or other persons who because of their particular circumstances are vulnerable to undue influence. However, this does not preclude attempting to implement appropriate collateral contacts with significant others for the purpose of benefiting an already engaged therapy patient.

4. Therapy

4.01 Structuring the Relationship

(a) Psychologists discuss with clients or patients as early as is feasible in the therapeutic relationship appropriate issues, such as the nature and anticipated course of therapy, fees, and confidentiality. (See also Standards 1.25, Fees and Financial Arrangements, and 5.01, Discussing the Limits of Confidentiality.)

(b) When the psychologist's work with clients or patients will be supervised, the above discussion includes that fact, and the name of the supervisor, when the supervisor has legal responsibility for the case.

(c) When the therapist is a student intern, the client or patient is informed of that fact.

(d) Psychologists make reasonable efforts to answer patients' questions and to avoid apparent misunderstandings about therapy. Whenever possible, psychologists provide oral and/or written information, using language that is reasonably understandable to the patient or client.

4.02 Informed Consent to Therapy

(a) Psychologists obtain appropriate informed consent to therapy or related procedures, using language that is reasonably understandable to participants. The content of informed consent will vary depending on many circumstances; however, informed consent generally implies that the person (1) has the capacity to consent, (2) has been informed of significant information concerning the procedure, (3) has freely and without undue influence expressed consent, and (4) consent has been appropriately documented.

(b) When persons are legally incapable of giving informed consent, psychologists obtain informed permission from a legally authorized person, if such substitute consent is permitted by law.

(c) In addition, psychologists (1) inform those persons who are legally incapable of giving informed consent about the proposed interventions in a manner commensurate with the persons' psychological capacities, (2) seek their assent to those interventions, and (3) consider such persons' preferences and best interests.

4.03 Couple and Family Relationships

(a) When a psychologist agrees to provide services to several persons who have a relationship (such as husband and wife or parents and children), the psychologist attempts to clarify at the outset (1) which of the individuals are patients or clients and (2) the relationship the psychologist will have with each person. This clarification includes the role of the psychologist and the probable uses of the services provided or the information obtained. (See also Standard 5.01, Discussing the Limits of Confidentiality.)

(b) As soon as it becomes apparent that the psychologist may be called on to perform potentially conflicting roles (such as marital counselor to husband

and wife, and then witness for one party in a divorce proceeding), the psychologist attempts to clarify and adjust, or withdraw from, roles appropriately. (See also Standard 7.03, Clarification of Role, under Forensic Activities.)

4.04 Providing Mental Health Services to Those Served by Others

In deciding whether to offer or provide services to those already receiving mental health services elsewhere, psychologists carefully consider the treatment issues and the potential patient's or client's welfare. The psychologist discusses these issues with the patient or client, or another legally authorized person on behalf of the client, in order to minimize the risk of confusion and conflict, consults with the other service providers when appropriate, and proceeds with caution and sensitivity to the therapeutic issues.

4.05 Sexual Intimacies With Current Patients or Clients

Psychologists do not engage in sexual intimacies with current patients or clients.

4.06 Therapy With Former Sexual Partners

Psychologists do not accept as therapy patients or clients persons with whom they have engaged in sexual intimacies.

4.07 Sexual Intimacies With Former Therapy Patients

(a) Psychologists do not engage in sexual intimacies with a former therapy patient or client for at least two years after cessation or termination of professional services.

(b) Because sexual intimacies with a former therapy patient or client are so frequently harmful to the patient or client, and because such intimacies undermine public confidence in the psychology profession and thereby deter the public's use of needed services, psychologists do not engage in sexual intimacies with former therapy patients and clients even after a two-year interval except in the most unusual circumstances. The psychologist who engages in such activity after the two years following cessation or termination of treatment bears the burden of demonstrating that there has been no exploitation, in light of all relevant factors, including (1) the amount of time that has passed since therapy terminated, (2) the nature and duration of the therapy, (3) the circumstances of termination, (4) the patient's or client's personal history, (5) the patient's or client's current mental status, (6) the likelihood of adverse impact on the patient or client and others, and (7) any statements or actions made by the therapist during the course of therapy suggesting or inviting the possibility of a posttermination sexual or romantic relationship with the patient or client. (See also Standard 1.17, Multiple Relationships.)

4.08 Interruption of Services

(a) Psychologists make reasonable efforts to plan for facilitating care in the event that psychological services are interrupted by factors such as the psychologist's illness, death, unavailability, or relocation or by the client's relocation or financial limitations. (See also Standard 5.09, Preserving Records and Data.)

(b) When entering into employment or contractual relationships, psychologists provide for orderly and appropriate resolution of responsibility for patient or client care in the event that the employment or contractual

relationship ends, with paramount consideration given to the welfare of the patient or client.

4.09 Terminating the Professional Relationship

(a) Psychologists do not abandon patients or clients. (See also Standard 1.25e, under Fees and Financial Arrangements.)

(b) Psychologists terminate a professional relationship when it becomes reasonably clear that the patient or client no longer needs the service, is not benefiting, or is being harmed by continued service.

(c) Prior to termination for whatever reason, except where precluded by the patient's or client's conduct, the psychologist discusses the patient's or client's views and needs, provides appropriate pretermination counseling, suggests alternative service providers as appropriate, and takes other reasonable steps to facilitate transfer of responsibility to another provider if the patient or client needs one immediately.

5. Privacy and Confidentiality

These Standards are potentially applicable to the professional and scientific activities of all psychologists.

5.01 Discussing the Limits of Confidentiality

(a) Psychologists discuss with persons and organizations with whom they establish a scientific or professional relationship (including, to the extent feasible, minors and their legal representatives) (1) the relevant limitations on confidentiality, including limitations where applicable in group, marital, and family therapy or in organizational consulting, and (2) the foreseeable uses of the information generated through their services.

(b) Unless it is not feasible or is contraindicated, the discussion of confidentiality occurs at the outset of the relationship and thereafter as new circumstances may warrant.

(c) Permission for electronic recording of interviews is secured from clients and patients.

5.02   Maintaining Confidentiality

Psychologists have a primary obligation and take reasonable precautions to respect the confidentiality rights of those with whom they work or consult, recognizing that confidentiality may be established by law, institutional rules, or professional or scientific relationships. (See also Standard 6.26, Professional Reviewers.)

5.03   Minimizing Intrusions on Privacy

(a) In order to minimize intrusions on privacy, psychologists include in written and oral reports, consultations, and the like, only information germane to the purpose for which the communication is made.

(b) Psychologists discuss confidential information obtained in clinical or consulting relationships, or evaluative data concerning patients, individual or organizational clients, students, research participants, supervisees, and employees, only for appropriate scientific or professional purposes and only with persons clearly concerned with such matters.

5.04   Maintenance of Records

Psychologists maintain appropriate confidentiality in creating, storing, accessing, transferring, and disposing of records under their control, whether these are written, automated, or in any other medium. Psychologists maintain and dispose of records in accordance with law and in a manner that permits compliance with the requirements of this Ethics Code.

5.05   Disclosures

(a) Psychologists disclose confidential information without the consent of the individual only as mandated by law, or where permitted by law for a valid purpose, such as (1) to provide needed professional services to the patient or the individual or organizational client, (2) to obtain appropriate professional consultations, (3) to protect the patient or client or others from harm, or (4) to obtain payment for services, in which instance disclosure is limited to the minimum that is necessary to achieve the purpose.

(b) Psychologists also may disclose confidential information with the appropriate consent of the patient or the individual or organizational client (or of another legally authorized person on behalf of the patient or client), unless prohibited by law.

5.06   Consultations

When consulting with colleagues, (1) psychologists do not share confidential information that reasonably could lead to the identification of a patient, client, research participant, or other person or organization with whom they have a confidential relationship unless they have obtained the prior consent of the person or organization or the disclosure cannot be avoided, and (2) they share information only to the extent necessary to achieve the purposes of the consultation. (See also Standard 5.02, Maintaining Confidentiality.)

5.07   Confidential Information in Databases

(a) If confidential information concerning recipients of psychological services is to be entered into databases or systems of records available to persons whose access has not been consented to by the recipient, then psychologists use coding or other techniques to avoid the inclusion of personal identifiers.

(b) If a research protocol approved by an institutional review board or similar body requires the inclusion of personal identifiers, such identifiers are deleted before the information is made accessible to persons other than those of whom the subject was advised.

(c) If such deletion is not feasible, then before psychologists transfer such data to others or review such data collected by others, they take reasonable steps to determine that appropriate consent of personally identifiable individuals has been obtained.

5.08   Use of Confidential Information for Didactic or Other Purposes

(a) Psychologists do not disclose in their writings, lectures, or other public media, confidential, personally identifiable information concerning their patients, individual or organizational clients, students, research participants, or other recipients of their services that they obtained during the course of their work, unless the person or organization has consented in writing or unless there is other ethical or legal authorization for doing so.

(b) Ordinarily, in such scientific and professional presentations, psychologists disguise confidential information concerning such persons or organizations so that they are not individually identifiable to others and so that discussions do not cause harm to subjects who might identify themselves.

5.09   Preserving Records and Data

A psychologist makes plans in advance so that confidentiality of records and data is protected in the event of the psychologist's death, incapacity, or withdrawal from the position or practice.

5.10   Ownership of Records and Data

Recognizing that ownership of records and data is governed by legal principles, psychologists take reasonable and lawful steps so that records and data remain available to the extent needed to serve the best interests of patients, individual or organizational clients, research participants, or appropriate others.

5.11   Withholding Records for Nonpayment

Psychologists may not withhold records under their control that are requested and imminently needed for a patient's or client's treatment solely because payment has not been received, except as otherwise provided by law.

6.   Teaching, Training Supervision, Research, and Publishing

6.01   Design of Education and Training Programs

Psychologists who are responsible for education and training programs seek to ensure that the programs are competently designed, provide the proper experiences, and meet the requirements for licensure, certification, or other goals for which claims are made by the program.

6.02   Descriptions of Education and Training Programs

(a) Psychologists responsible for education and training programs seek to ensure that there is a current and accurate description of the program content, training goals and objectives, and requirements that must be met for satisfactory completion of the program. This information must be made readily available to all interested parties.

(b) Psychologists seek to ensure that statements concerning their course outlines are accurate and not misleading, particularly regarding the subject matter to be covered, bases for evaluating progress, and the nature of course experiences. (See also Standard 3.03, Avoidance of False or Deceptive Statements.)

(c) To the degree to which they exercise control, psychologists responsible for announcements, catalogs, brochures, or advertisements describing workshops, seminars, or other non-degree-granting educational programs ensure that they accurately describe the audience for which the program is intended, the educational objectives, the presenters, and the fees involved.

6.03   Accuracy and Objectivity in Teaching

(a) When engaged in teaching or training, psychologists present psychological information accurately and with a reasonable degree of objectivity.

(b) When engaged in teaching or training, psychologists recognize the power they hold over students or supervisees and therefore make reasonable efforts to avoid engaging in conduct that is personally demeaning to students or supervisees. (See also Standards 1.09, Respecting Others, and 1.12, Other Harassment.)

6.04   Limitation on Teaching

Psychologists do not teach the use of techniques or procedures that require specialized training, licensure, or expertise, including but not limited to hypnosis, biofeedback, and projective techniques, to individuals who lack the prerequisite training, legal scope of practice, or expertise.

6.05   Assessing Student and Supervisee Performance

(a) In academic and supervisory relationships, psychologists establish an appropriate process for providing feedback to students and supervisees.

(b) Psychologists evaluate students and supervisees on the basis of their actual performance on relevant and established program requirements.

6.06   Planning Research

(a) Psychologists design, conduct, and report research in accordance with recognized standards of scientific competence and ethical research.

(b) Psychologists plan their research so as to minimize the possibility that results will be misleading.

(c) In planning research, psychologists consider its ethical acceptability under the Ethics Code. If an ethical issue is unclear, psychologists seek to resolve the issue through consultation with institutional review boards, animal care and use committees, peer consultations, or other proper mechanisms.

(d) Psychologists take reasonable steps to implement appropriate protections for the rights and welfare of human participants, other persons affected by the research, and the welfare of animal subjects.

6.07   Responsibility

(a) Psychologists conduct research competently and with due concern for the dignity and welfare of the participants.

(b) Psychologists are responsible for the ethical conduct of research conducted by them or by others under their supervision or control.

(c) Researchers and assistants are permitted to perform only those tasks for which they are appropriately trained and prepared.

(d) As part of the process of development and implementation of research projects, psychologists consult those with expertise concerning any special population under investigation or most likely to be affected.

6.08   Compliance With Law and Standards

Psychologists plan and conduct research in a manner consistent with federal and state law and regulations, as well as professional standards governing the conduct of research, and particularly those standards governing research with human participants and animal subjects.

6.09   Institutional Approval

Psychologists obtain from host institutions or organizations appropriate approval prior to conducting research, and they provide accurate information about their research proposals. They conduct the research in accordance with the approved research protocol.

6.10   Research Responsibilities

Prior to conducting research (except research involving only anonymous surveys, naturalistic observations, or similar research), psychologists enter into an agreement with participants that clarifies the nature of the research and the responsibilities of each party.

6.11   Informed Consent to Research

(a) Psychologists use language that is reasonably understandable to research participants in obtaining their appropriate informed consent (except as provided in Standard 6.12, Dispensing with Informed Consent). Such informed consent is appropriately documented.

(b) Using language that is reasonably understandable to participants, psychologists inform participants of the nature of the research; they inform participants that they are free to participate or to decline to participate or to withdraw from the research; they explain the foreseeable consequences of declining or withdrawing; they inform participants of significant factors that may be expected to influence their willingness to participate (such as risks, discomfort, adverse effects, or limitations on confidentiality, except as provided in Standard 6.15, Deception in Research); and they explain other aspects about which the prospective participants inquire.

(c) When psychologists conduct research with individuals such as students or subordinates, psychologists take special care to protect the prospective participants from adverse consequences of declining or withdrawing from participation.

(d) When research participation is a course requirement or opportunity for extra credit, the prospective participant is given the choice of equitable alternative activities.

(e) For persons who are legally incapable of giving informed consent, psychologists nevertheless (1) provide an appropriate explanation, (2) obtain the participant's assent, and (3) obtain appropriate permission from a legally authorized person, if such substitute consent is permitted by law.

6.12   Dispensing With Informed Consent

Before determining that planned research (such as research involving only anonymous questionnaires, naturalistic observations, or certain kinds of archival research) does not require the informed consent of research participants, psychologists consider applicable regulations and institutional review board requirements, and they consult with colleagues as appropriate.

6.13 Informed Consent in Research Filming or Recording

Psychologists obtain informed consent from research participants prior to filming or recording them in any form, unless the research involves simply naturalistic observations in public places and it is not anticipated that the recording will be used in a manner that could cause personal identification or harm.

6.14 Offering Inducements for Research Participants

(a) In offering professional services as an inducement to obtain research participants, psychologists make clear the nature of the services, as well as the risks, obligations, and limitations. (See also Standard 1.18, Barter [with Patients or Clients].)

(b) Psychologists do not offer excessive or inappropriate financial or other inducements to obtain research participants, particularly when it might tend to coerce participation.

6.15 Deception in Research

(a) Psychologists do not conduct a study involving deception unless they have determined that the use of deceptive techniques is justified by the study's prospective scientific, educational, or applied value and that equally effective alternative procedures that do not use deception are not feasible.

(b) Psychologists never deceive research participants about significant aspects that would affect their willingness to participate, such as physical risks,

discomfort, or unpleasant emotional experiences.

(c) Any other deception that is an integral feature of the design and conduct of an experiment must be explained to participants as early as is feasible, preferably at the conclusion of their participation, but no later than at the conclusion of the research. (See also Standard 6.18, Providing Participants with Information about the Study.)

6.16 Sharing and Utilizing Data

Psychologists inform research participants of their anticipated sharing or further use of personally identifiable research data and of the possibility of unanticipated future uses.

6.17 Minimizing Invasiveness

In conducting research, psychologists interfere with the participants or milieu from which data are collected only in a manner that is warranted by an appropriate research design and that is consistent with psychologists' roles as scientific investigators.

6.18 Providing Participants with Information About the Study

(a) Psychologists provide a prompt opportunity for participants to obtain appropriate information about the nature, results, and conclusions of the research, and psychologists attempt to correct any misconceptions that participants may have.

(b) If scientific or humane values justify delaying or withholding this information, psychologists take reasonable measures to reduce the risk of harm.

6.19 Honoring Commitments

Psychologists take reasonable measures to honor all commitments they have made to research participants.

6.20 Care and Use of Animals in Research

(a) Psychologists who conduct research involving animals treat them humanely.

(b) Psychologists acquire, care for, use, and dispose of animals in compliance with current federal, state, and local laws and regulations, and with professional standards.

(c) Psychologists trained in research methods and experienced in the care of laboratory animals supervise all procedures involving animals and are responsible for ensuring appropriate consideration of their comfort, health, and humane treatment.

(d) Psychologists ensure that all individuals using animals under their supervision have received instruction in research methods and in the care, maintenance, and handling of the species being used, to the extent appropriate to their role.

(e) Responsibilities and activities of individuals assisting in a research project are consistent with their respective competencies.

(f) Psychologists make reasonable efforts to minimize the discomfort, infection, illness, and pain of animal subjects.

(g) A procedure subjecting animals to pain, stress, or privation is used only when an alternative procedure is unavailable and the goal is justified by its prospective scientific, educational, or applied value.

(h) Surgical procedures are performed under appropriate anesthesia; techniques to avoid infection and minimize pain are followed during and after surgery.

(i) When it is appropriate that the animal's life be terminated, it is done rapidly, with an effort to minimize pain, and in accordance with accepted procedures.

6.21 Reporting of Results

(a) Psychologists do not fabricate data or falsify results in their publications.

(b) If psychologists discover significant errors in their published data, they take reasonable steps to correct such errors in a correction, retraction, erratum, or other appropriate publication means.

6.22 Plagiarism

Psychologists do not present substantial portions or elements of another's work or data as their own, even if the other work or data source is cited occasionally.

6.23 Publication Credit

(a) Psychologists take responsibility and credit, including authorship credit, only for work they have actually performed or to which they have contributed.

(b) Principal authorship and other publication credits accurately reflect the relative scientific or professional contributions of the individuals involved, regardless of their relative status. Mere possession of an institutional position, such as Department Chair, does not justify authorship credit. Minor contributions to the research or to the writing for publications are appropriately acknowledged, such as in footnotes or in an introductory statement.

(c) A student is usually listed as principal author on any multiple-authored article that is substantially based on the student's dissertation or thesis.

6.24 Duplicate Publication of Data

Psychologists do not publish, as original data, data that have been previously published. This does not preclude re-publishing data when they are accompanied by proper acknowledgment.

6.25 Sharing Data

After research results are published, psychologists do not withhold the data on which their conclusions are based from other competent professionals who seek to verify the substantive claims through reanalysis and who intend to use such data only for that purpose, provided that the confidentiality of the participants can be protected and unless legal rights concerning proprietary data preclude their release.

6.26 Professional Reviewers

Psychologists who review material submitted for publication, grant, or other research proposal review respect the confidentiality of and the proprietary rights in such information of those who submitted it.

7. Forensic Activities

7.01 Professionalism

Psychologists who perform forensic functions, such as assessments, interviews, consultations, reports, or expert testimony, must comply with all other provisions of this Ethics Code to the extent that they apply to such activities. In addition, psychologists base their forensic work on appropriate knowledge of and competence in the areas underlying such work, including specialized knowledge concerning special populations. (See also Standards 1.06, Basis for Scientific and Professional Judgments; 1.08, Human Differences; 1.15, Misuse of Psychologists' Influence; and 1.23, Documentation of Professional and Scientific Work.)

7.02 Forensic Assessments

(a) Psychologists' forensic assessments, recommendations, and reports are based on information and techniques (including personal interviews of the individual, when appropriate) sufficient to provide appropriate substantiation for their findings. (See also Standards 1.03, Professional and Scientific Relationship; 1.23, Documentation of Professional and Scientific Work; 2.01, Evaluation, Diagnosis, and Interventions in Professional Context; and 2.05, Interpreting Assessment Results.)

(b) Except as noted in (c), below, psychologists provide written or oral forensic reports or testimony of the psychological characteristics of an individual only after they have conducted an examination of the individual adequate to support their statements or conclusions.

(c) When, despite reasonable efforts, such an examination is not feasible, psychologists clarify the impact of their limited information on the reliability and validity of their reports and testimony, and they appropriately limit the nature and extent of their conclusions or recommendations.

7.03 Clarification of Role

In most circumstances, psychologists avoid performing multiple and potentially conflicting roles in forensic matters. When psychologists may be called on to serve in more than one role in a legal proceeding—for example, as consultant or expert for one party or for the court and as a fact witness—they clarify role expectations and the extent of confidentiality in advance to the extent feasible, and thereafter as changes occur, in order to avoid compromising their professional judgment and objectivity and in order to avoid misleading others regarding their role.

7.04 Truthfulness and Candor

(a) In forensic testimony and reports, psychologists testify truthfully, honestly, and candidly and, consistent with applicable legal procedures, describe fairly the bases for their testimony and conclusions.

(b) Whenever necessary to avoid misleading, psychologists acknowledge the limits of their data or conclusions.

7.05 Prior Relationships

A prior professional relationship with a party does not preclude psychologists from testifying as fact witnesses or from testifying to their services to the extent permitted by applicable law. Psychologists appropriately take into account ways in which the prior relationship might affect their professional objectivity or opinions and disclose the potential conflict to the relevant parties.

7.06 Compliance With Laws and Rules

In performing forensic roles, psychologists are reasonably familiar with the rules governing their roles. Psychologists are aware of the occasionally competing demands placed upon them by these principles and the requirements of the court system, and attempt to resolve these conflicts by making known their commitment to this Ethics Code and taking steps to resolve the conflict in a responsible manner. (See also Standard 1.02, Relationship of Ethics and Law.)

8. Resolving Ethical Issues

8.01 Familiarity With Ethics Code

Psychologists have an obligation to be familiar with this Ethics Code, other applicable ethics codes, and their application to psychologists' work. Lack of awareness or misunderstanding of an ethical standard is not itself a defense to a charge of unethical conduct.

8.02 Confronting Ethical Issues

When a psychologist is uncertain whether a particular situation or course of action would violate this Ethics Code, the psychologist ordinarily consults with other psychologists knowledgeable about ethical issues, with state or national psychology ethics committees, or with other appropriate authorities in order to choose a proper response.

8.03 Conflict between Ethics and Organizational Demands

If the demands of an organization with which psychologists are affiliated conflict with this Ethics Code, psychologists clarify the nature of the conflict, make known their commitment to the Ethics Code, and to the extent feasible, seek to resolve the conflict in a way that permits the fullest adherence to the Ethics Code.

8.04 Informal Resolution of Ethical Violations

When psychologists believe that there may have been an ethical violation by another psychologist, they attempt to resolve the issue by bringing it to the attention of that individual if an informal resolution appears appropriate and the intervention does not violate any confidentiality rights that may be involved.

8.05 Reporting Ethical Violations

If an apparent ethical violation is not appropriate for informal resolution under Standard 8.04 or is not resolved properly in that fashion, psychologists take further action appropriate to the situation, unless such action conflicts with confidentiality rights in ways that cannot be resolved. Such action might include referral to state or national committees on professional ethics or to state licensing boards.

8.06   Cooperating With Ethics Committees

Psychologists cooperate in ethics investigations, proceedings, and resulting requirements of the APA or any affiliated state psychological association to which they belong. In doing so, they make reasonable efforts to resolve any issues as to confidentiality. Failure to cooperate is itself an ethics violation.

8.07   Improper Complaints

Psychologists do not file or encourage the filing of ethics complaints that are frivolous and are intended to harm the respondent rather than to protect the public.

Forensic Glossary

AB INITIO. "From the first act." Refers to the validity of statutes and so forth.

ABROGATE. To annul or cancel.

ACQUIT. To set free or judicially discharge.

ACTUS REUS. The criminal act. "The guilty act." The physical act as opposed to the psychical (mens rea).

AD HOC. For a particular or special purpose.

ADMISSIBLE EVIDENCE. Evidence that can be received by the trier of fact (judge or jury).

ADVERSARY PROCESS. A contest by two opposing parties.

ADVERSE PARTY. The person on the opposite side of litigation.

AMICUS CURIAE. Friend of the court. One who gives information to the court on some matter of law that is in doubt. A brief submitted by one who is not a party to a lawsuit.

A POSTERIORI. From the most recent point of view. That which can only be known from experience.

APPELLANT. The party who appeals a decision.

APPELLATE COURT. A court having jurisdiction to review law as a result of a prior determination of the same case.

A PRIORI. To reason from factual and historical knowledge that certain facts are true.

ATTEST. To affirm as true.

BAILIFF. A court attendant.

BAR. The complete body of attorneys.

BENCH. The court; the judges composing the court.

BILL OF PARTICULARS. A statement used to inform the defense of the specific occurrences intended to be investigated on the trial and to limit

558

the course of evidence to the particular scope of the inquiry. An amplification of the pleading.

BONA.   Good or virtuous.

BURDEN OF PROOF.   The duty of a party to substantiate allegation so that dismissal can be avoided. To convince the trier of facts as to the truth of a claim. In civil cases proof must be by a *preponderance* of the evidence, while in criminal cases the state's persuasion burden is met only by proof *beyond reasonable doubt*. In some equity matters and more recent Supreme Court decisions, *clear and convincing evidence* is the standard of proof.

CERTIORARI.   A means of gaining an appellate review. A discretionary writ with the Supreme Court of the United States that may be issued to any court in the land to review a federal question if at least four of the nine justices vote to hear the case.

CIVIL LAW.   Roman law embodied in the Justinian Code.

CIVIL RIGHTS.   Rights given, defined, and specified by positive laws enacted by civilized communities. Note the difference from *civil liberties.* Civil rights are positive in nature, and civil liberties are negative. These are immunities from governmental interference.

CLEAR AND CONVINCING.   A standard of proof beyond preponderance but below reasonable doubt. Less than the degree required in criminal cases but more than that required in ordinary civil actions.

CLEAR AND PRESENT DANGER.   A standard used to determine when one's First Amendment rights may be curtailed or punished. The degree to which a certain act or occurrence is highly likely to bring about substantive evils that the government has a right to prevent.

COLLUSION.   The making of an agreement with another for the purposes of fraud.

COMMON LAW.   Jurisprudence originating in England and applied to the United States. Contrasts with civil law, the descendant of Roman law.

COMPOS MENTIS.   Mentally competent.

CONSPIRACY.   The combination of two or more people who propose to commit a criminal or an unlawful act or to commit a lawful act by criminal and unlawful means or who propose by concerted action to accomplish an unlawful purpose.

CONTEMPT OF COURT.   Either an act or an omission tending to obstruct or interfere with the orderly administration of justice in the court. To impair the dignity of the court or to impair respect for its authority.

CORPUS DELICTI.   The body of the crime. Objective proof that a crime has been committed. *Not* the body of a victim of a homicide. In a murder prosecution, *prima facie* evidence showing that the alleged victim met death by criminal agency. The weight of proof is beyond reasonable doubt.

CORPUS JURIS.   The body of law.

COURT MARTIAL.   Military tribunal that has jurisdiction of offenses against laws of the service in which the offender is engaged. Military status is not sufficient. The crime must be service-connected. (General Court Martial—Presided over by a law officer, has not less than five members, tries defendants on all military offenses, and can prescribe any permitted sanction.) (Special Court Martial—Presided over by three members, may try noncapital offenses, but limited in authority as to sanctions that can be prescribed.) (Summary Court Martial—Presided over by a single commissioned officer, and limited in respect to the personnel over whom it can operate and sanctions it may prescribe. The accused may refuse trial by Summary Court Martial, but the charges can then be referred to a higher level.)

CRUEL AND UNUSUAL PUNISHMENT.   Punishment found to be offensive to the ordinary person. The Eighth Amendment provides "excessive bail shall not be required nor excessive fines imposed nor cruel and unusual punishment inflicted." This term cannot be defined with specificity. It broadens as society pays more regard to human decency and dignity. In general, punishment that amounts to torture or is grossly excessive. Unfair, shocking, or disgusting to people's reasonable sensitivity. Beyond any force needed to maintain order in a prison.

CULPABLE.   Deserving of moral blame. Fault rather than guilt.

CUSTODY.   Applied to property. Not ownership but keeping, guarding, caring for, preserving. Implies that the object is within immediate personal care and control of the person in whose custody the object is subjected. When applied to a person, it may mean to require restraint and physical control.

DAMAGES.   Monetary compensation that the law awards to an injured party.

Actual Damages.   Losses that can be readily proved to have been sustained.

Special (Consequential) Damages.   Loss or injury that is indirect or mediate.

Double (or Treble) Damages.   Two or three times the amount of damages that a court or jury would normally find for a party, awarded for certain kinds of injuries pursuant to statutes authorizing same.

Punitive (Exemplary) Damages.   Compensation in excess of actual damages. A kind of punishment to the wrongdoer. Actual damages must come first before these.

Incidental Damages.   Losses reasonably incident to or conduct giving rise to a claim for actual damages, such as expenses.

Nominal Damages.   A trivial sum as recognition that a legal injury was sustained although slight. The amount is usually so small (one dollar) as not to constitute damages.

DE BENE ESSE.   Provisionally or conditionally.

DE FACTO.   By virtue of the deed. Reality.

DEFAULT JUDGMENT.   A judgment entered against a defendant because of the defendant's failure to respond to a plaintiff's action.

DEFENDANT.   In civil proceedings it is usually the party responding to the compliant. In criminal proceedings it is the accused.

DEFENSE.   Can be denial, or a plea opposing the truth or validity of a plaintiff's case.

Affirmative Defense.   One that serves as a basis for proving some new fact.

Equitable Defense.   One that is recognized by courts of equity.

DE NOVO HEARING.   A new hearing. Usually the judgment of the trial court is suspended, and the reviewing court determines the case as though it originated in the reviewing court.

DEPONENT.   A witness. Facts to be given under oath.

DEPOSITION.   A method of pretrial discovery. It consists of a statement from the witness under oath taken in question-and-answer form. Similar to an appearance at court, with the adversary present and the opportunity for cross-examination. May be taken by any party of any witness. Can be oral (face to face) or written.

DIRECTED VERDICT.   A verdict returned by the jury at the direction of the trial judge. Usually done when the judge feels that the opposing party fails to present a *prima facie* case. May occur when a necessary defense is not presented.

DISCOVERY.   Pretrial procedure. Vital information concerning the case is obtained from the adverse party. Disclosure by adverse party of facts, documents, or information in his or her possession.

DOCKET SOUNDING.   Meeting between the attorneys and the judges to determine the schedule of cases for a particular period of time.

DURHAM RULE.   A test of criminal responsibility adopted by the District of Columbia Court of Appeals (1954). States: "An accused is not criminally responsible if his unlawful act was the product of mental disease or defect" (214 F.2d. 862,874-75). First major modification of M'Naghten's Rule. Many times negated by the American Law Institute's Model Penal Code test (§4.01)(1) Cite 471 F.2d. 969,971 (1972).

EXCULPATORY.   Evidence or statements tending to justify or excuse defendant from fault or guilt.

EXPERT WITNESS.   A witness having "special knowledge of the subject about which he is to testify" (26 A.2d 770,773 [1942]) (22 A.2d 28 [1941]). An expert need not have formal training. The court must be satisfied that the testimony will help the triers of fact.

GRANDFATHER CLAUSE.   Certain legal provisions that permit persons engaged in business or profession before the passage of an act regulating that business or profession to receive a license or prerogative without meeting the criteria of new entrants into the field.

GRIEVANCE. One's charges that something imposes an illegal obligation or burden. A denial of an equitable or legal right or cause of injustice.

HABEAS CORPUS. Used in the criminal and civil contexts. A procedure for obtaining a judicial determination of the legality of an individual's custody. In the criminal context—bringing the petitioner before the court to decide on the legality of confinement. Related to due process of law.

HEARSAY RULE. A statement made other than by a witness while testifying at the hearing offered to prove the truth of a matter stated. This is inadmissible evidence. Oral or written statements are nonadmissible. When witnesses are asked what some other person told them, it is inadmissible if the material being described is for the purposes of determining the truth of the matter asserted. If, however, it is elicited merely to show that the words were spoken, it is admissible.

IMPEACHMENT. To charge a public official with wrongdoing. With reference to the testimony of a witness, to call into question the evidence offered for that purpose. Can also occur by showing that the witness is unworthy of belief. Sometimes by the witness's own statements.

IN CAMERA. Meaning "in chambers." A room adjacent to the courtroom where the judge performs the duties of his office. Also applies if the judge performs a judicial duty or act while the court is not in session.

INCOMPETENCY. Inability. A relative term that is employed to mean disqualification, inability, or incapacity. It may be used to show a lack of physical, intellectual, or moral fitness.

INFORMED CONSENT. Consent given only after a full notice is given as to what is being consented to.

IN LOCO PARENTIS. In the place of the parent.

INSANITY. Not responsible mentally to some degree. The ALI Model Penal Code quotes: "A person is not responsible for criminal conduct if at the time of such conduct as a result of mental disease or defect he lacks substantial capacity either to appreciate the criminality or wrongfulness of his conduct or to conform his conduct to the requirements of the law" (Model Penal Code §4.01 [1]).

JUVENILE COURTS. Judicial systems first established in the late nineteenth century to treat youthful offenders separately from adults. Places the judge in the position of *parens patriae*. Intended to remove the adversary nature of normal proceedings.

LEADING QUESTION. A question posed by a trial lawyer that is improper on direct examination because it suggests to the witness the answer that the witness should deliver.

MANDAMUS.   An extraordinary writ issued from a court to an official compelling the performance of an act that the law recognizes as a duty. Used when other judicial remedies have failed.

MENS REA.   A guilty mind. A general intent to do a prohibited act.

MENTAL ANGUISH.   Compensable injury embracing all forms of mental, as opposed to physical, injury. Can include distress, grief, anxiety, fright, and bereavement.

MISTRIAL.   A trial that is terminated and declared void prior to the jury's returning a verdict. Usually because of some fundamental error prejudicial to the defendant that cannot be cured by instructions to the jury. Sometimes because of the jury's inability to reach a verdict (hung jury). It does not result in a judgment for any party. It indicates a failure of trial. In criminal prosecution it may prevent retrial under the doctrine of double jeopardy.

M'NAGHTEN'S RULE.   Common-law test of criminal responsibility. Acquittal by reason of insanity. "If as a result of a mental disease or defect the defendant did not understand what he did or that it was wrong, or if he was under a delusion (but not otherwise insane) which if true would have provided a good defense. Thus, if one does not understand what one was doing at all or did not know that it was wrong, he is excused. He is also excused if due to an insane delusion he thought he was acting in self-defense or carrying out the will of God. Often called the right/wrong test."

MOTION.   An application to the court requesting an order or a rule in favor of the applicant.

NEGLIGENCE.   Failure to exercise the degree of care that a person should, with ordinary prudence, exercise under similar circumstances.

NON COMPOS MENTIS.   Not having control over the mind or intellect. Insane.

PLEA.   A special answer relying on one or more things as a cause why a suit should be dismissed, delayed, or barred. Technically it is the defendant's answer by matter of fact to the plaintiff's declaration. In a criminal proceeding, the defendant's attorney will enter a plea at the arraignment of either guilty or not guilty. A plea can be *dilatory* (contests grounds other than the merits of the plaintiff's case, such as improper jurisdiction, wrong defendant, or other procedural defects) or *peremptory* (answers to plaintiff's contention).

PLEA BARGAINING.   A process by which the accused and the prosecutor negotiate a mutually satisfactory disposition of the case.

PRECEDENT.   A previously described case that is used as an authority for the disposition of future cases.

PRIVILEGED COMMUNICATIONS.   Communications that occur in a setting of either legal or other professional confidentiality. Allows those who are presenting to resist legal pressure to disclose contents. A breach of the confidentiality can result in a suit.

PRO BONO PUBLICO.   For the public good or welfare. An attorney or other professional takes a case without compensation for the purpose of advancing a social cause or representing a party who cannot afford it.

PROSECUTION.   Pursuing a lawsuit or a criminal trial. Also the state. The criminal equivalent of litigant in a civil suit.

REASONABLE DOUBT.   Refers to the degree of certainty required of a juror for a legally valid determination of the guilt of a criminal defendant. The judge will generally use this term and instructions to the jury to indicate that innocence is to be presumed unless the guilt is so clearly proved that the jury can see no reasonable doubt. It does *not* require proof so clear that no possibility of error exists.

RECESS.   An adjournment of a trial or a hearing that is temporary and occurs after the commencement of the trial. If there is going to be substantial delay, it is called a *continuance*. A temporary dismissal is called *sine die*.

RETAINER.   Compensation paid in advance to an attorney for services to be performed in a specific case. May be a payment simply to get the attorney to be available. It may be the whole sum to be charged or, more often, a deposit.

STAR CHAMBER.   An ancient court of England. No jury present. Abolished in modern jurisprudence.

STRICT LIABILITY.   Liability without a showing of fault. For example, someone who engages in an activity of an ultrahazardous nature is liable for all injuries caused by the enterprise even without negligence being shown. A recently developed area of strict liability concerns *product liability*.

THIRD-PARTY BENEFICIARIES.   Persons who have enforceable rights created by a contract to which they are not parties and for which they give no consideration.

TORT.   A wrong. A private or civil wrong or injury independent of a contract resulting from a breach of a legal duty.

TRIAL.   The offering of testimony before a competent tribunal according to established procedures.

VENUE.   A neighborhood, and synonymous with "place of trial." If refers to the possible place or places for the trial of a suit. Among several places where jurisdiction could be established.

VERDICT.   The opinion of a jury or a judge sitting as a jury on a question of fact.

VOIR DIRE.   To speak the truth. Examination by the court or by attorneys of prospective jurors to determine their qualification for jury service. To determine if cause exists for a challenge to excuse them.

WAIVER.   An intentional and voluntary giving up or surrender of a known right.

WEIGHT OF THE EVIDENCE.   The relative value of the totality of evidence presented on one side of a judicial dispute in light of the evidence presented by the other side. Refers to the persuasiveness of testimony of witnesses.

WITNESS.   One who gives evidence of a cause before a court and who attests or swears to the facts.

WORK PRODUCT.   Work done by an attorney in the process of representing a client that is ordinarily not subject to discovery. It can generally be defined as writings, statements, or testimony that would substantially invade an attorney's legal impressions or legal theories about pending litigation. An attorney's legal impressions and theories would include his tactics, strategy, opinions, and thoughts.

WRIT.   A mandatory precept issued by an authority in the name of the sovereign or the state for the purpose of compelling a person to do something.

References

Abarbanel, A. (1979). Shared parenting after separation and divorce: A study of joint custody. *American Journal of Orthospsychiatry, 50,* 320–329.

ABA Standing Committee on Association Standards for Criminal Justice. (1983). *First tentative draft—criminal justice mental health standards* (pp. 7-259–7-297). Washington, DC: American Bar Association.

Acker, J. (1990). Social science in Supreme Court criminal cases and briefs. *Law and Human Behavior, 14,* 25.

Ackerman, M. J., & Ackerman, M. C. (1977). Custody evaluation practices: A survey of experienced professionals (revisited). *Professional Psychology: Research and Practice, 28,* 137.

Adams, D. (1993). Factitious disorders and malingering. *Psychotherapy Bulletin, 27,* 10.

Ainsworth, M. (1973). The development of infant-mother attachment. In B. Caldwell & H. Riccioti (Eds.), *Review of child development research* (Vol. 3). Chicago: University of Chicago Press.

Ajzenstadt, M., & Burtch, B. (1990). Medicalization and regulation of alcohol and alcoholism. *International Journal of Law and Psychiatry, 13,* 127.

Akers, R. (1991). Addiction: The troublesome concept. *Journal of Drug Issues, 21*(4), 777.

Alexander, M. (1988). Clinical determination of mental competence. *Archives of Neurology, 45,* 23.

Alpert, J., Brown, L., Cece, S., Courtois, C., Loftus, E., & Ornstein, P. (1996). *Working group on investigation of memories of childhood abuse: Final report.* Washington, DC: American Psychological Association.

American Bar Association. (1989). *Criminal justice mental health standards.* Washington, DC: Author.

American Educational Research Association, American Psychological Association, & National Council on Measurement in Education. (1985). *Standards for educational and psychological testing.* Washington, DC: Author.

American Psychological Association. (1974). *Standards for educational and psychological tests.* Washington, DC: Author.

American Psychological Association. (1986). *Guidelines for computer-based tests and interpretations.* Washington, DC: Author.

American Psychological Association. (1992). Ethical principles of psychologists and code of conduct. *American Psychologist, 47*(1), 1597.

American Psychiatric Association. (1994). *Diagnostic and statistical manual of mental disorders* (4th ed.). Washington, DC: Author.

American Psychological Association. (1994). Guidelines for child custody evaluations in divorce proceedings. *American Psychologist, 49,* 677.

American Psychological Association. (1994). Interim report of the APA Working Group on the investigation of memories of childhood abuse. *Shepard's Expert and Scientific Evidence Quarterly, 2,* 465.

American Psychological Association. (1994). *Risk management with potentially dangerous patients.* Washington, DC: Author.

Anastasi, A. (1981). *Psychological testing* (4th ed.). New York: Macmillan.

Anderson, K. (1982). American prisons. *Time, 11*(120), 38–82.

Anthony, N. C. (1971). Comparison of client's standard, exaggerated, and matching MMPI profiles. *Journal of Consulting and Clinical Psychology, 36,* 100–103.

Antonuccio, D. (1994). Will nicotine patch really stick? *Archives of Internal Medicine, 154,* 927.

Arnett, P., & Franzen, M. (1997). Performance of substances abusers with memory deficits on measures of malingering. *Archives of Clinical Neuropsychology, 12,* 513.

Austerlitz, J. (1986). The use of psychological evaluations in political asylum hearings. *Immigration Newsletter, 15,* 7.

Axelrod, B., Brines, B., & Rapport, L. (1997). Estimating full scale IQ while minimizing the effects of practice. *Assessment, 4,* 221.

Bailis, D., Darley, J., Waxman, T., & Robinson, P. (1995). Community standards of criminal liability and the insanity defense. *Law & Human Behavior, 19,* 425.

Baker, R. (1968). The effects of psychotropic drugs on psychological testing. *Psychological Bulletin, 69*(6), 377.

Barkdoll, G., & Bell, J. (Eds.). (1989). *Evaluation and the federal decision maker* (New Directions for Program Evaluation, No. 44). San Francisco: Jossey-Bass.

Barrett, J. (1995). Historical influences effecting the behavioral actions of abused drugs. In J. Frascella & R. Brown (Eds.), *Neurobiological approaches to brain-interaction* (NIDA Research Monograph No. 124). Rockville, MD: Public Health Service.

Bartlett, J. (1968). *Familiar quotations* (14th ed.). Boston: Little, Brown.

Bartram, M., Kirkpatrick, D., Hecker, L., & Prebis, J. (1996, August). *Strengths and vulnerablities of grandfamily functioning.* Paper presented at the 104th annual convention of the American Psychological Association, Toronto.

Bathurst, K., Gottfried, A., & Gottfried, A. (1997). Normative data for the MMPI-2 in child custody litigation. *Psychological Assessment, 9,* 205.

Bazelon, D. (1974). Psychiatrists and the adversary process. *Scientific American, 230,* 18–23.

Beal, E. W. (1979). Children of divorce: A family systems perspective. *Journal of Social Issues, 35*(4), 140–154.

Beckham, J., Annis, L., & Gustafson, D. (1989). Decision making and examiner bias in forensic expert recommendations for not guilty by reason of insanity. *Law & Human Behavior, 13,* 79.

Belli, M. (1982). The expert witness. *Trial, 17*(7), 35–37.

Belsky, J. (1981). Early human experience: A family perspective. *Development Psychology, 17*(1), 3–23.

Benedict, J., & Donaldson, D. (1996). Recovered memories threaten all. *Professional Psychology: Research and Practice, 27,* 427.

Berman, A., & Cohen-Sandler, R. (1983). Suicide and malpractice: Expert testimony and the standard of care. *Professional Psychology: Research and Practice, 14,* 6.

Bernard, L., McGrath, M., & Houston, W. (1993). Discriminating between malingering and closed head injury on the Wechsler Memory Scale Revised. *Archives of Clinical Neuropsychology, 8,* 539.

Bernstein, C. (1994). Winning trials nonverbally. *Trial, 30,* 16.

Bersoff, D. (1981). Testing and the law. *American Psychologist, 36*(10), 1047–1059.

Berube, M. (Ed.). (1982). *The American heritage dictionary* (2nd college edition). Boston: Houghton Mifflin.

Binder, L. (1993). An abbreviated form of the Portland Digit Recognition Test. *Clinical Neuropsychologist, 7,* 104.

Black, H. (1979). *Black's law dictionary.* St. Paul, MN: West.

Blackburn, R. (1996). What is forensic psychology? *Legal and Criminological Psychology, 1*(1), 3.

Blau, T. H. (1959). *Private practice in clinical psychology.* New York: Appleton-Century-Crofts.

Blau, T. H. (1982). *The psychologist as expert witness: Compendium* (pp. 169–171). Tampa, FL: Psychological Seminars.

Blau, T. (1984). An evaluative study of the role of the grandparent in the best interests of the child. *America Journal of Family Therapy, 12,* 46.

Blau, T. H. (1994). *Psychological services for law enforcement.* New York: Wiley.

Blau, T. H., & Blau, R. (1988). The competence and credibility of children as witnesses. In J. Reese & J. Horn (Eds.), *Police psychology: Operational assistance.* Washington, DC: U.S. Government Printing Office.

Bockman, R. (1982, December 13). Expert: Leave insanity defense alone. *Tampa Tribune,* pp. B1–2.

Boenhert, C. (1989). Characteristics of successful and unsuccessful insanity pleas. *Law & Human Behavior, 13,* 31.

Boffey, P. M. (1983, January 20). Psychiatric group urges stiffer rules for insanity pleas. *New York Times,* p. 8.

Bonnie, R., & Slobogin, C. (1980). The role of mental health professionals in the criminal process. *Virginia Law Review, 66,* 427–522.

Bornard, L., McGrath, M., & Houston, W. (1993). Discriminating between simulated malingering and closed head injury on the Wechsler Memory Scale–Revised. *Archives of Clinical Neuropsychology, 8,* 539.

Borum, R., & Grisso, T. (1995). Psychological test use in criminal forensic evaluations. *Professional Psychology: Research & Practice, 26*(5), 465.

Borum, R., Swartz, M., & Swanson, J. (1996, July). Assessing and managing violence risk in clinical practice. *Journal of Practice and Behavioral Health,* 205.

Bradley, B., Gossop, M., Brewin, C., Phillips, G., & Green, L. (1992). Attributions and relapse in opiate addicts. *Journal of Consulting and Clinical Psychology, 60*(3), 470.

Braunstein, B., & Schuman, T. (1996). Child custody guidelines: Psychologists working together with other professionals. *The California Psychologist, 29,* 6.

Brekke, N., & Borgida, E. (1988). Expert psychological testimony in rape trials: A social-cognitive analysis. *Journal of Personality and Social Psychology, 55,* 372.

Brody, J. E. (1983, March 29). Bonding at birth: A major theory being questioned. *New York Times, Science Times,* pp. 15, 16.

Brooks, C., & Milchman, M. (1991). Child sexual abuse allegations during custody litigation: Conflicts between mental health witnesses and the law. *Behavioral Sciences and the Law, 9,* 21.

Brooks, J. (1985). Polygraph testing: Thoughts of a skeptical legislator. *American Psychologist, 40,* 348.

Brooks, N., McKinlay, W., Symington, C., Beattie, A., & Campsie, L. (1987). Return to work within the first seven years of severe head injury. *Brain Injury, 1,* 5.

Buckhout, R. (1974). Eyewitness testimony. *Scientific American, 231*(6), 23–31.

Burk, S. (1986). The defense of voluntary intoxication: Now you see it, now you don't. *Indiana Law Review, 19,* 147.

Buros, J. E. (Ed.). (1933–1978). *Mental measurement yearbooks: Tests in print—Educational, psychological and personality tests of 1933 and 1934* (Vols. 1–8). Highland Park, NJ: Gryphon Press.

Butcher, J. (1987). *Computerized psychological assessment: A practitioner's guide.* New York: Basic Books.

Butschky, M., Bailey, D., Henningfield, J., & Pickworth, W. (1995). Smoking without nicotine delivery decreases withdrawal in 12-hour abstinent smokers. *Pharmacology Biochemistry and Behavior, 50*(1), 91.

California State Psychological Association. (1980). Standards for professional services on court panels and other legal consultations. *California State Psychologist, 14*(2), 21–22.

California State Psychological Association. (1981). Two professionals urge ban on psychiatric testimony. *California State Psychologist, 15*(5), 1, 16.

Callahan, K. (1988). Voluntary intoxication in limited circumstances may reduce second-degree murder to voluntary manslaughter. *Suffolk University Law Review, 22,* 476.

Callahan, L., Mayer, C., & Steadman, H. (1987). Insanity defense reform in the United States–Post Hinckley. *Mental and Physical Disability Law Reporter, 11,* 54.

Ceci, S., & Bruck, M. (1995). *Jeopardy in the courtroom.* Washington, DC: American Psychological Association.

Chambers, M. (1983, January 21). Insanity defense backed by panel. *New York Times,* p. 15.

Clark, H. H. (1974). *Cases and problems in domestic relations.* St. Paul, MN: West.

Cleary, T., Humphreys, L., Kendrick, S., & Wesman, A. (1975). Educational uses of test with disadvantaged students. *American Psychologist, 30,* 15.

Clingempeel, W. G., & Reppucci, N. D. (1982). Joint custody after divorce. *Psychological Bulletin, 91*(1), 102–127.

Cofer, C. N., Chance, J. E., & Judson, A. J. (1949). A study of malingering on the MMPI. *Journal of Psychology, 27,* 491–499.

Cohen, A. (1984). The "urge" of the narcotic addict: A review of psychiatric classification. *International Journal of the Addictions, 19*(3), 335.

Collins, G. (1982, December 20). Some broken families retain many bonds. *New York Times,* p. 17.

Committee on Ethical Guidelines for Forensic Psychologists. (1991). Specialty guidelines for forensic psychologists. *Law and Human Behavior, 15,* 655–665.

Committee on Pattern Jury Instructions. (1979). *Pattern jury instructions (Criminal cases).* St. Paul, MN: West.

Conoley, J., & Impara, J. (Eds.). (1933–1995). *Mental measurement yearbooks* (Vol. 1–12). Lincoln: The Buros Institute of Mental Measurements, University of Nebraska Press.

Conoley, J., & Impara, J. (Eds.). (1995). *The twelfth mental measurements yearbook.* Lincoln: University of Nebraska Press.

Conoley, J., & Kramer, J. (Eds.). (1989). *The tenth mental measurements yearbook.* Lincoln: University of Nebraska Press.

Cope, V. (1989). Predicting future violence. *Trial, 25,* 82.

Cornell, D. (1987). Role conflict in forensic clinical psychology: Reply to Arcaya. *Professional Psychology: Research & Practice, 18,* 429.

Cornell, D., & Hawk, G. (1989). Clinical presentation of malingerers diagnosed by experienced forensic psychologists. *Law and Human Behavior, 13,* 375.

Cowden, V., & McKee, G. (1995). Competency to stand trial in juvenile delinquency proceedings. *University of Louisville Journal of Family Law, 33,* 629.

Cox, V., Paulus, P., & McCain, G. (1984). Prison crowding research. *American Psychologist, 39,* 1148.

Dahlstrom, W. G., Welsh, C. S., & Dahlstrom, L. E. (1975). *An MMPI handbook* (p. 164). Minneapolis: University of Minnesota Press.

Davis, D. (1991). Executing the mentally retarded. *Florida Bar Journal, 65,* 12.

Denney, R. (1996). Symptom validity testing of remote memory in a criminal forensic setting. *Archives of Clinical Neuropsychology, 11,* 589.

Dennis, M. (1989). Assessing the neuropsychological abilities of children and adolescents for personal injury litigation. *Clinical Neuropsychologist, 3,* 203.

DiCarlo, M., Gfeller, J., & Drury, J. (1997). Assessing feigned cognitive impairment with Rey's 15-Item Test: Is this task easy or what? *Archives of Clinical Neuropsychology, 12,* 309.

Dix, G. (1977). The death penalty, "dangerous," psychiatric testimony and professional ethics. *American Journal of Criminal Law, 5,* 151–214.

Dullea, G. (1983, February 7). Wide changes in family life are altering the family law. *New York Times,* pp. 1, 12.

Eddy, N., Hallbach, H., Isbell, H., & Seevers, M. (1965). Drug dependence: Its significance and characteristics. *Bulletin of the World Health Organization, 32,* 721.

Egeth, H. (1993). What do we *not* know about eyewitness identification? *American Psychologist, 48*(5), 577–580.

Ehrle, G., & Day, H. (1994). Adjustment and family functioning of grandmothers rearing their grandchildren. *Contemporary Family Therapy, 16,* 67.

Eiser, J., & Gossop, M. (1979). "Hooked" or "sick": Addicts perceptions of their addiction. *Addictive Behaviors, 4,* 185.

Ekman, P., Friesen, W., & O'Sullivan, M. (1988). Smiling when lying. *Journal of Personality and Social Psychology, 54,* 414.

Ekman, P., & O'Sullivan, M. (1991). Who can catch a liar? *American Psychologist, 46,* 913.

Executive Committee, Family Law Section, NJSBA. (1983). Mediation committee report. *New Jersey Family Lawyer, 11*(5), 75–80.

Falk, J. (1983). Drug dependence: Myth or motive? *Pharmacology, Biochemistry and Behavior, 19,* 385–391.

Faust, D., Hart, K., & Guilmette, T. (1988). Pediatric malingering: The capacity of children to fake believable deficits on neuropsychological testing. *Journal of Consulting and Clinical Psychology, 56,* 578.

Faust, D., Hart, K., Guilmette, T., & Arkes, H. (1988). Neuropsychologists' capacity to detect adolescent malingerers. *Professional Psychology: Research and Practice, 19,* 508.

Federal Rules of Evidence for United States Courts and Magistrates. (1975). St. Paul, MN: West.

Feiner, R., Terre, L., Farber, S., Primavera, J., & Bishop, T. (1985). Child custody: Practices and perspectives of legal professional. *Journal of Clinical Child Psychology, 14,* 27.

Finkel, N. (1988). *Trials and tribulations of the insanity defense.* New York: Plenum Press.

Fitch, W., Petrella, R., & Wallace, J. (1987). Legal ethics and the use of mental health experts in criminal cases. *Behavioral Science and the Law, 5,* 105.

Fowler, J., Volkow, N., Wang, G., Pappas, N., Logan, J., MacGregor, R., Alexoff, B., Shea, C., Schlyer, D., Wolf, A., Warner, D., Zezulkova, I., & Cilento, R. (1996). Inhibition of monoamine oxidase B in the brains of smokers. *Nature, 379*(567), 733.

Franzen, M., & Martin, N. (1996). Do people with knowledge fake better? *Applied Neuropsychology, 3*, 82.

Freed, D. J., & Foster, H. H., Jr. (1981). Divorce in the fifty states: An overview. *Family Law Quarterly, 14*, 229–284.

Freiberg, P. (1995). Pathological gambling turning into epidemic. *APA Monitor, 26*(12).

Frye, E. (1968). A readability formula that saves time. *IRA Journal of Reading, 11*(7).

Fuchsberg, A. (1991). Ten commandments for successful evaluation and settlement. *Trial, 27*, 52.

Fulconer, D. M. (1942). *The adjustive behavior of some recently bereaved spouses.* Doctoral dissertation, Northwestern University.

Gardner, R. (1987). *The parental alienation syndrome and the differentiation between fabricated and genuine child sex abuse.* Creekskill, NJ: Creative Therapeutics.

Gardner, R. A. (1982). *Family evaluation in child custody litigation.* Creekskill, NJ: Creative Therapeutics.

Gardner, W., Lidz, C., Mulvey, E., & Shaw, E. (1996). Clinical versus actuarial predictions of violence in patients with mental illnesses. *Journal of Consulting and Clinical Psychology, 64*, 609.

Gibbs, M., Sigal, J., Adams, B., & Grossman, B. (1989). Cross-examination of the expert witness: Do hostile tactics affect impressions of a simulated jury? *Behavioral Sciences and the Law, 7*, 275.

Gibeaut, J. (1997). Sobering thoughts. *ABA Journal, 83*, 56.

Glaser, G. (1979). Discretion in juvenile justice. In L. Abt & I. R. Stuart (Eds.), *Social psychology and discretionary law.* New York: Van Nostrand-Reinhold.

Glasser, I. (1989, November 20). We can control drugs but we can't ban them. *The New York Times.*

Glick, I. O., Weiss, R. S., & Parkes, C. M. (1974). *The first year of bereavement.* New York: Wiley.

Glick, P. C. (1979). Children of divorced parents in demographic perspective. *Journal of Social Issues, 35*(4), 170–181.

Glueck, S. S. (1925). *Mental disorder and the criminal law.* Boston: Little, Brown.

Golding, J., Sanchez, R., & Sego, S. (1996). Do you believe in repressed memory? *Professional Psychology: Research and Practice, 27*, 429.

Golding, J., Sego, S., Sanchez, R., & Hassemann, D. (1995). The believability of repressed memories. *Law and Human Behavior, 19*, 569.

Golding, S. (1990). Mental health professionals and the courts: The ethics of expertise. *International Journal of Law and Psychiatry, 13*, 281.

Goldofski, O. B. (1904). The psychology of testimony. *Vyestnik Prava*, No. 16-18, 185.

Goodman, A. (1991). *The addictive process: A psychoanalytic understanding.* Paper presented at the 15th annual meeting of the American Academy of Psychoanalysis.

Goodman-Delahunty, J. (1997). Forensic psychological expertise in the wake of *Daubert. Law and Human Behavior, 21*(2), 121.

Gordon, B., Jens, K., Hollings, R., & Watson, T. (1994). Remembering activities performed versus those imagined. *Journal of Clinical Child Psychology, 23*, 239.

Gothard, S., Viglone, D., Meloy, J., & Sherman, M. (1995). Detection of malingering in competency to stand trial evaluations. *Law and Human Behavior, 19*, 493.

Gough, H. G. (1954). Some common misconceptions about neuroticism. *Journal of Consulting Psychology, 18*, 287–292.

Gourvitz, E. H. (1983). Divorce mediation—An alternative to the adversary approach. *New Jersey Family Lawyer, 11*(5), 81–85.

Gozansky, N. (1976). Court-ordered investigations in custody casts. *Willamette Law Journal, 12,* 511–526.

Grand Jury Defense Office. (1982). The witness' appearance before the grand jury. In National Lawyer's Guild (Ed.), *Representation of witness before federal grand juries.* New York: Clark Boardman.

Grassie, J. (1990). *Lucky number.* PBS Television Production, Maryland Public Television.

Greenberg, S., & Shuman, D. (1997). Irreconcilable conflict between therapeutic and forensic roles. *Professional Psychology: Research and Practice, 28,* 50.

Gregory, C. O., Kalven, H., & Epstein, R. A. (1977). *Cases and materials on torts* (3rd ed.). Boston: Little, Brown.

Greif, J. B. (1979). Fathers, children, and joint custody. *American Journal of Orthopsychiatry, 50,* 311–319.

Greiffenstein, M., Baker, W., & Gola, T. (1996, August). *What kind of faking does the Fake Bad Scale measure?* Poster session presented at the annual convention of the American Psychological Association, Toronto.

Griffith, R., Brady, J., & Bigelow, G. (1981). Predicting the dependence liability of stimulant drugs. In T. Thompson & C. Johnson (Eds.), *Behavioral pharmacology of human drug dependence* (NIDA Research Monograph No. 37). Washington, DC: U.S. Government Printing Office.

Grisso, T., Miller, M., & Sales, B. (1987). Competency to stand trial in juvenile court. *International Journal of Law and Psychiatry, 10,* 1.

Gualtieri, T., & Cox, D. (1991). The delayed neurobehavioral sequelae of traumatic brain injury. *Brain Injury, 5,* 219.

Guilmette, T., & Hagan, L. (1997). The ethical neuropsychologist: Courting the clinician. *Clinical Neuropsychologist, 11,* 287.

Guilmette, T., Hart, K., Guiliano, A., & Leinenger, B. (1994). Detecting simulated memory impairment. *Clinical Neuropsychologist, 8,* 283.

Gulliver, S., Hughes, J., Solomon, L., & Achintya, N. (1995). An investigation of self-efficacy, partner support, and daily stresses as predictors of relapse to smoking self-quitters. *Addiction, 90,* 767.

Hall, G., & Crowther, J. (1991). Psychologists' involvement in cases of child maltreatment: Additional limits of assessment methods. *American Psychologists, 46,* 79.

Hall, S., & Havassy, B. (1986). Commitment to abstinence and relapse to tobacco, alcohol and opiates. In F. Tims & C. Leukefeld (Eds.), *Relapse and recovery in drug abuse* (NIDA Research Monograph No. 72). Rockville, MD: Public Health Service.

Haney, C. (1984). Death qualification [Special issue]. *Law and Human Behavior, 8*(½), 1–193.

Haney, C., Banks, W., & Zimbardo, P. (1973). Interpersonal dynamics in a simulated prison. *International Journal of Criminology and Penology, 1,* 69.

Hartman, D. (1995). *Neuropsychological toxicology* (2nd ed.). New York/London: Plenum Press.

Hasker, P., King, J., Bloodworth, M., Spring, A., & Klebe, K. (1997). The detection of simulated malingering using a computerized category classification test. *Archives of Clinical Neuropsychology, 12,* 191.

Hasker, P., King, J., Klebe, K., Bajszar, G., Bloodworth, M., & Wallicks, S. (1997). The detection of simulated malingering using a computerized priming test. *Archives of Clinical Neuropsychology, 12,* 145.

Heath, D. (1988). Quasi-science and public policy: A reply to Robin Room about details and misrepresentations in science. *Journal of Substance Abuse, 1,* 121.

Heilbrun, K. (1987). The assessment of competency for execution: An overview. *Behavioral Sciences and the Law, 5,* 383.

Heilbrun, K. (1996). When is an "expert" an expert? *American Psychology Law Society News, 16*, 5.

Heilbrun, K. (1997). Prediction versus management models relevant to risk assessment: The importance of legal decision-making context. *Law and Human Behavior, 21*, 347.

Heinze, M., & Grisso, T. (1996). Review of instruments assessing parenting competencies used in child custody evaluations. *Behavioral Sciences and the Law, 14*, 241.

Henningfield, J., Cohen, C., & Slade, J. (1991). Is nicotine more addictive than cocaine? *British Journal of Addiction, 86*, 565.

Hess, A. (1987). The ethics of forensic psychology. In I. Weiner & A. Hess (Eds.), *Handbook of forensic psychology.* New York: Wiley.

Hetherington, E. M., Cox, M., & Cox, R. (1979). Play and social interaction in children following divorce. *Journal of Social Issues, 35*(4), 26–49.

Hilts, P. (1994, August 2). Is nicotine addictive? It depends on whose criteria you use. *New York Times Science.*

Hiscock, M., & Hiscock, C. K. (1989). Refining the forced-choice method for the detection of malingering. *Journal of Clinical and Experimental Neuropsychology, 11*, 967.

Holland, T. R., Holt, N., & Beckett, G. E. (1982). Prediction of violent versus nonviolent recidivism from prior violent and nonviolent criminality. *Journal of Abnormal Psychology, 91*(3), 178–182.

Holmes, T. H., & Masuda, M. (1973). Life change and illness susceptibility. In *Separation and depression* (pp. 161–186, AAAS Publication No. 94). Washington, DC: American Association for the Advancement of Science.

Honaker, L. (1988). The equivalency of computerized and conventional MMPI administration: A critical review. *Clinical Psychology Review, 8*, 561.

Howell, R. J. (1982). In defense of the insanity plea. *Bulletin of the American Academy of Forensic Psychologists, 3*(1), 1–2.

Humphreys, L. (1973). Statistical definitions of test validity for minority groups. *Journal of Applied Psychology, 58*, 1.

Institute of Judicial Administration (American Bar Association). (1977). *Juvenile justice standards project.* Cambridge, MA: Ballinger.

Isaacson, W. (1982, July 5). Insane on all counts. *Time,* pp. 22–26.

Isbell, H. (1958). Clinical research on addiction in the United States. In R. Livingston (Ed.), *Narcotic drug addiction problems.* Bethesda, MD: U.S. Public Health Service.

Iverson, G., Franzen, M., & Hammond, J. (1995). Examination of inmates ability to malinger on the MMPI-2. *Psychological Assessment, 7*, 118.

Iverson, G., Slick, D., & Franzen, M. (1997). Evaluation of a Wechsler Memory Scale–Revised, malingering index in a non-litigating clinical sample. *Archives of Clinical Neuropsychology, 12*, 341.

Jaffe, J. (1985). Drug addiction and drug abuse. In L. Goodman, T. Rall, & F. Murad (Eds.), *The pharmacological basis of therapeutics* (7th ed.). New York: Macmillan.

Jaffe, J. (1990). Drug addiction and drug abuse. In L. Goodman, T. Rall, A. Nies, & P. Taylor (Eds.), *The pharmacological basis of therapeutics* (8th ed.). New York: McGraw-Hill.

Jaffe, J., & Jaffe, F. (1989). Historical perspectives on the use of subjective effects measures in assessing the abuse potential of drugs. In N. Fischman & M. Mello (Eds.), *Testing for abuse liability of drugs in humans* (NIDA Research Monograph No. 92). Rockville, MD: Public Health Service.

Jaffe, S. (1903). Ein psychologisches experiment in Kriminalistischen seminar der universitaet Berlin [A psychological experiment in criminality seminar at the University of Berlin]. *Beitraege zur Psychologie der Aussage, mit besonderer Bereuecksrchitigung der Rechtspflege, Paedogogik, Psychiatrie und Geschichts forschung, 1*, 79.

James, H. (1881). *The portrait of a lady.* New York: Modern Library.

Jameson, B., Ehrenberg, M., & Hunter, M. (1997). Psychologists' ratings of the best-interest-of-the-child custody and access criteria: A family systems assessment model. *Professional Psychology: Research and Practice, 28,* 253.

Jones, A. (1977). Suicide by aircraft: A case report. *Aviation Space, Environmental Medicine, 48,* 454–459.

Kahn, M., Fox, H., & Rhode, R. (1988). Detecting faking on the Rorschach: Computer versus expert clinical judgment. *Journal of Personality Assessment, 52,* 516.

Kalven, H., & Zeisel, H. (1966). *The American jury.* Boston: Little, Brown.

Katkin, E. (1985). Polygraph testing, psychological research, and public policy. *American Psychologist, 40,* 346.

Kauffman, J., Shaffer, H., & Burglass, N. (1984). A strategy for the biological assessment of addiction. In H. Shaffer & B. Stimmel (Eds.), *The addictive behaviors.* New York: Haworth Press.

Kaufman, R., & English, F. W. (1979). *Needs-assessment: Concept and application.* Englewood Cliffs, NJ: Educational Technology.

Kayloe, J. (1993). Food addiction. *Psychotherapy, 30*(2), 269.

Kazdin, A. (1996). The myth of repressed memory: Comments and reactions. *Clinical Psychology: Science and Practice, 3*(14), 366.

Kazen, B. A. (1977). *When father wants custody: A lawyer's view.* Austin: State Bar of Texas.

Keilin, W., & Bloom, L. (1986). Child custody evaluation practices: A survey of experienced professionals. *Professional Psychology: Research and Practice, 17,* 338.

Kerr, N. L., & Bray, R. M. (Eds.). (1982). *The psychology of the courtroom.* New York: Academic Press.

King, C. (1934, December). Non-narcotic addictions. *Clinical Medicine and Surgery,* 563.

Klassen, D., & O'Connor, W. (1989). Assessing the risk of violence in released mental patients: A cross validation study. *Psychological Assessment, 1,* 1.

Knapp, S., Vandecreek, L., & Zirkel, P. (1985). Legal research techniques: What the psychologist needs to know. *Professional Psychology: Research and Practice, 16,* 363.

Koelega, H. (1993). Stimulant drugs and vigilance performance: A review. *Psychopharmacology, 111*(1), 1.

Kornetsky, C., & Bain, G. (1995). Brain-stimulation reward: A model for the study of the rewarding effects of abused drugs. In J. Frascella & R. Brown (Eds.), *Neurobiological approaches to brain-interaction* (NIDA Research Monograph No. 124). Rockville, MD: Public Health Service.

Kozlowski, L., Wilkinson, A., Skinner, W., Kent, C., Franklin, T., & Pope, M. (1989). Comparing tobacco cigarette dependence with other drug dependencies. *Journal of the American Medical Association, 261*(6), 898.

Kramer, J., & Conoley, J. (Eds.). (1992). *The eleventh mental measurements yearbook.* Lincoln: University of Nebraska Press.

Ladd, J. (1952). Expert testimony. *Vanderbilt Law Review, 5,* 414, 419.

Lagenbucher, J., Morgenstern, J., Labouvie, E., & Nathan, P. (1994a). Diagnostic concordance of substance use disorders in *DSM-III, DSM-IV* and *ICD-10. Drug and Alcohol Dependence, 36,* 193.

Lagenbucher, J., Morgenstern, J., Labouvie, E., & Nathan, P. (1994b). Lifetime *DMS-IV* diagnosis of alcohol, cannabis, cocaine and opiate dependence: Six months reliability in a multi-site clinical sample. *Addiction, 89,* 1115.

Lamb, M. E. (1977). The development of mother-infant and father-infant attachments in the second year of life. *Developmental Psychology, 13*(6), 637–648.

Landsman, S. (1995). Of witches, madmen, and products liability: An historical survey of the use of expert testimony. *Behavioral Sciences and the Law, 13,* 131.

Lee, G., Loring, D., & Martin, R. (1992). Rey's 15-Item Visual Memory Test for the detection of malingering: Normative considerations. *Psychological Assessment: A Journal of Consulting and Clinical Psychology, 4,* 43.

Leesfield, I. (1987). Negligence of mental health professionals. *Trial, 23,* 57.

Lees-Haley, P. (1989). MMPI and F-K scales: Questionable indices of malingering. *American Journal of Forensic Psychology, 7,* 81.

Lees-Haley, P. (1990). Vocational neuropsychological requirements of U.S. occupations. *Perpetual and Motor Skills, 70,* 1383.

Lees-Haley, P. (1992). Efficacy of MMPI-2 validity scales and MCMI-II modifier scales for detecting spurious PTSD claims: F, F-K, Fake-Bad Scale, Ego Strength, Subtle-Obvious Subscales, DIF, and DEB. *Journal of Clinical Psychology, 48,* 681.

Lees-Haley, P. (1997). Ethical issues in forensic neuropsychology. *California Psychologist, 30,* 24.

Lees-Haley, P., English, L., & Glenn, W. (1991). A fake bad scale on the MPI-2 for personal injury claimants. *Psychological Reports, 68,* 203.

Lehman, D., Wortman, C., & Williams, A. (1987). Long-term effects of losing a spouse or child in a motor vehicle crash. *Journal of Personality and Social Psychology, 52,* 218.

Lehrman, F. (1996). Factoring domestic violence into custody cases. *Trial, 32,* 32.

Leo, J. (1982a, July 5). Insane on all counts. *Time,* pp. 22–27.

Leo, J. (1982b, July 5). Is the system guilty? *Time,* pp. 26–27.

Levine, A. (1990, February 5). America's addiction to addictions. *U.S. News and World Report.*

Lewis, A. (1996, February 12). Prohibition folly. *The New York Times.*

Lewis, C. (1987). Minors: Competence to consent to abortion. *American Psychologist, 42,* 84.

Lezak, M. D. (1976). *Neuropsychological assessment* (pp. 476–477). New York: Oxford University Press.

Lezak, M. D. (1995). *Neuropsychological assessment* (3rd ed.). New York: Oxford University Press.

Lichter, D. H. (1981). Note: Diagnosing the dead. *American Criminal Law Review, 18,* 617–635.

Lim, J., & Butcher, J. (1996). Detection of faking on the MMPI-2: Differentiation among faking bad, denial, and claiming extreme virtue. *Journal of Personality Assessment, 67,* 1.

Lindley, M. (1990, August 23). TV viewing is fourth legal addiction. *The News Herald.*

Lindsay, D., Memon, A., Poole, D., & Bull, R. (1996). Rejoinder to Pope's 1995 comments regarding Poole, Lindsay, Memon, & Bull, 1995. *Clinical Psychology: Science and Practice, 3,* 355.

Lipsitt, P. D. (1970). *Competency Screening Test.* Boston: Competency to Stand Trial and Mental Illness Project.

Lipsitt, P. D., Lelos, D., & McGarry, A. L. (1971). Competency for trial: A screening instrument. *American Journal of Psychiatry, 128*(1), 137–141.

Litwak, T. R., Gerber, G. L., & Fenster, C. A. (1980). The proper role of psychology in child custody disputes. *Journal of Family Law, 18,* 269–300.

Lobsien, M. (1904). Veber psychologie der aussage. *Zeit schrift feur Paedagogische Psychologie, VI,* 161.

Loftus, E. (1979). *Eyewitness testimony.* Cambridge, MA: Harvard University Press.

Loftus, E. (1981). Eyewitness testimony: Psychological research and legal thought. In M. Tonry & N. Morris (Eds.), *Crime and justice: An annual review of research* (Vol. 3). Chicago: University of Chicago Press.

Loftus, E. (1983). Silence is not golden. *American Psychologist, 38,* 564–572.

Loftus, E. (1996). The myth of repressed memory and the realities of science. *Clinical Psychology: Science and Practice, 3,* 356.

Loftus, E., & Monahan, J. (1990). Trial by data: Psychological research as legal evidence. *American Psychologist, 35*(3), 270.

Lopez, S., & Romero, A. (1988). Assessing the intellectual functioning of Spanish-speaking adults: Comparison of the EIWA and the WAIS. *Professional Psychology, Research and Practice, 19,* 263.

Louisell, D. W. (1955). The psychologist in today's legal world. *Minnesota Law Review, 39*(3), 235–272.

Lowery, C. R. (1981). Child custody decisions in divorce proceedings: A survey of judges. *Professional Psychology, 4*(12), 492, 498.

Lubet, S. (1993). Eight techniques for direct examination of experts. *Trial, 29,* 57.

Luepnitz, D. A. (1978). Children of divorce: A review of the psychological literature. *Law and Human Behavior, 2*(2), 167–169.

Lykken, D. (1979). The detection of deception. *Psychological Bulletin, 86,* 47.

Mack, T. (1994, August). Scientific testimony after *Daubert:* Some early returns from lower courts. *Trial, 23.*

Mahon, C. (1986). Intoxication and the law: Drunk driving. *Annual Survey of American Law,* 229.

Martell, D. (1992). Forensic neuropsychology and the criminal law. *Law & Human Behavior, 16,* 313.

Martin, R. C., Franzen, M., & Orey, S. (1996). Magnitude of error as a strategy to detect feigned neuropsychological impairment. *Journal of the International Neuropsychological Society, 2,* 25.

Marx, M. L. (1977). Prison conditions and diminished capacity—A proposed defense. *Santa Clara Law Review, 17,* 855–883.

Maudsley, H. (1898). *Responsibility in mental disease.* New York: Appleton.

McCann, J., & Dyer, F. (1996). *Forensic assessment with the Millon Inventories.* New York: Guilford Press.

McCloskey, M., & Egeth, H. E. (1983). Eyewitness identification: What can a psychologist tell a jury? *American Psychologist, 38,* 550–563.

McIntosh, J., & Prinz, R. (1993). The incidence of alleged sexual abuse in 603 family court cases. *Law and Human Behaviour, 17,* 95.

McKinzey, R., Dodd, M., Krebbiel, M., Mensch, A., & Trombka, C. (1997). Detection of malingering on the Luria-Nebraska Neuropsychological Battery: An initial and cross-validation. *Archives of Clinical Neuropsychology, 12,* 505.

McKinzey, R., & Russell, E. (1997). Detection of malingering on the Halstead-Reitan Battery: A cross-validation. *Archives of Clinical Neuropsychology, 12,* 585.

Melton, G., & Limber, 'S. (1989). Psychologists' involvement in cases od child maltreatment. *American Psychologist, 44,* 1225.

Melton, G., & Wilcox, B. (1989). Changes in family law and family life. *American Psychologist, 44,* 1213.

Melton, G. B. (1983). More on insanity reform. *Division of Psychology and Law Newsletter, 3*(2), 6–8.

Miele, G., Tilly, S., Furst, N., & Frances, A. (1990). The definitions of dependence and behavioral addictions. *British Journal of Addictions, 85,* 1421.

Milkman, H., & Shaffer, H. (Eds.). (1985). *The addictions. Multi-disciplinary perspectives and treatments.* Lexington, MA: Lexington Books.

Millon, T. (1982). *Millon clinical multiaxial inventory.* Minneapolis: Interpretive Scoring Systems.

Mitchell, J. (Ed.). (1985). *The ninth mental measurements yearbook.* Lincoln: University of Nebraska Press.

Mitchell, J. (1992). Self-regulation and "addictive behavior" some theoretical remarks. *International Journal of the Addictions, 27*(6), 743.

Mittenberg, W., Azrin, R., Milsaps, C., & Heilbronner, R. (1993). Identification of malingered head injury on the Wechsler Memory Scale-Revised. *Psychological Assessment, 5,* 34.

Mittenberg, W., Rothole, A., Russell, E., & Heilbronner, R. (1996). Identification of malingered head trauma on the Halstead-Reitan Battery. *Archives of Clinical Neuropsychology, 11,* 271.

Mittenberg, W., Theroux-Fichera, S., Zielenski, R., & Heilbronner, R. (1995). Identification of malingered head injury on the Wechsler Adult Intelligence Scale–Revised. *Professional Psychology: Research and Practice, 26,* 491.

Molinoff, D. (1977, May 22). Life with father. *New York Times Magazine.*

Monahan, J. (1975). The prevention of violence. In J. Monahan (Ed.), *Community mental health and the criminal justice system.* New York: Pergamon Press.

Monahan, J. (1981). *Predicting violent behavior: An assessment of clinical techniques.* Beverly Hills, CA: Sage.

Monahan, J. (1988). Risk assessment of violence among the mentally disturbed. *International Journal of Law and Psychiatry, 11,* 249.

Monahan, J. (1992). Mental disorder and violent behavior. *American Psychologist, 17,* 511.

Monahan, J. (1996). Violence prediction: The past twenty and the next twenty years. *Criminal Justice & Behavior, 23,* 107.

Monahan, J., & Steadman, H. (1994). Toward a rejuvenation of risk assessment research. In J. Monahan & H. Steadman (Eds.), *Violence and mental disorder: Developments in risk assessment.* Chicago: University of Chicago Press.

Morganstern, J., Lagenbucher, J., & Labouvie, E. (1994). The generalizability of the dependence syndrome across substances: An examination of some properties of the proposed *DSM-IV* dependence criteria. *Addiction, 89,* 1105.

Morris, N., & Miller, M. (1987). *Prediction of dangerousness in the criminal law* (Research in brief). Washington, DC: National Institute of Justice.

Morris, R. (1997). Child custody evaluations: A risky business. *Register Report, 23,* 6.

Morris, S. (1989). Grandparents, uncles, aunts, cousins, friends. *Family Advocate, 12,* 11.

Morse, S. (1978). Law and mental health professionals: The limits of expertise. *Professional Psychology, 9,* 389–399.

Morse, S. (1995). The "new syndrome" excuse syndrome. *Criminal Justice Ethics, 14,* 3.

Mossman, D., & Hart, K. (1996). Presenting evidence of malingering to courts. *Behavioral Sciences and the Law, 14,* 271.

Mullen, J. M., & Dudley, H. K., Jr. (1981). Development of an actuarial model for predicting dangerousness of patients in maximum-security mental hospitals. In J. R. Hays, T. K. Roberts, & K. S. Solway (Eds.), *Violence and the violent individual.* New York: SP Medical and Scientific Books.

Mulvey, E. P. (1982). Family courts: The issue of reasonable goals. *Law and Human Behavior, 6*(1), 49–64.

Munsterberg, H. (1908). *On the witness stand*. New York: Doubleday.

Myers, J. (1996). Applying *Daubert* to psychological evidence. In S. Poulter (Ed.), *Scientific evidence in the courts: A post-Daubert assessment*. Washington, DC: American Bar Association, Science and Technology Section.

Narayanan, L., Menon, S., & Levine, E. (1995). Personality structure: A culture-specific examination of the five-factor model. *Journal of Personality Assessment, 64*(1), 51.

Nathan, P. (1980). Etiology and process in the addictive behaviors. In W. Miller (Ed.), *The addictive behaviors: Treatment of alcoholism, drug abuse, smoking and obesity*. Oxford, England: Pergamon Press.

National Conference of Commissioners on Uniform State Laws. (1971). Uniform marriage and divorce act. *Family Law Quarterly, 5*, 205–251.

Nelson, J., Pearson, H., Sayers, W., & Glynn, T. (1982). *A guide to drug abuse research terminology* (NIDA Research Issues 26). Washington, DC: Superintendent of Documents.

Nicholson, R., Briggs, S., & Robertson, H. (1988). Instruments for assessing competency to stand trial: How do they work? *Professional Psychology, Research and Practice, 19*, 383.

Nicholson, R., Robertson, H., Johnson, W., & Jensen, G. (1986, August). *A comparison of instruments for assessment of competency to stand trial*. Poster session presented at the annual convention of the American Psychological Association, Washington, DC.

Norton, J. E. (Ed.). (1981). *The anatomy of a personal injury law suit* (2nd ed.). Washington, DC: Association of Trial Lawyers of America.

Nottingham, E. J., & Mattson, R. E. (1981). A validation study of the competency screening test. *Law and Human Behavior, 5*(4), 329–335.

Nurco, D. (1981). Precursors of addiction and problems of drug dependence. In L. Harris (Ed.), *Drug dependence* (NIDA Research Monograph No. 41). Washington, DC: U.S. Government Printing Office.

O'Brien, C. (1996). Drug addiction and drug abuse. In J. Hardman & L. Limbird (Eds.), *Goodman and Gilman's the pharmacological basis of therapeutics* (9th ed.). New York: McGraw-Hill.

Ogloff, J. (1990). The admissibility of expert testimony regarding malingering and deception. *Behavioral Sciences and the Law, 8*, 27.

Olekains, N., & Bardsley, P. (1995). Caffeine dependence syndrome. *Journal of the American Medical Association, 273*(18), 1417.

Orthner, D. K., & Lewis, K. (1979). Evidence of single father competence in child-rearing. *Family Law Quarterly, 13*, 27–47.

Otto, R. (1992). Prediction of dangerous behavior: A review and analysis of "second generation" research. *Forensic Reports, 5*, 103.

Overholser, J. (1990). Differential diagnosis of malingering and factitious disorder with physical symptoms. *Behavioral Sciences and the Law, 8*, 55.

Paniak, C., Shore, D., & Rourke, R. (1989). Recovery of memory after severe closed head injury. *Journal of Clinical and Experimental Neuropsychology, 11*, 631.

Parachini, A. (1988, August 18). Researcher identifies "fetal soap addiction." *The Tampa Tribune*.

Parry, J. (1997). Civil commitment of sexual predators. *Mental and Physical Disability Law Reporter, 21*, 435.

Peele, S. (1975). *Love and addiction*. New York: TapLinger.

Peele, S. (1985). *The meaning of addiction*. Lexington, MA: Heath.

Peirce, N. (1989, May 10). Fighting the lottery addiction. *The Tampa Tribune*.

Perdue, J. (1993). The five-question rule: Cross examination simplified. *Trial, 29*, 40.

Perline, M. L. (1980). The legal status of the psychologist in the courtroom. *Mental Disabilities Law Review, 3*(4), 194–200.

Petrella, R. C., & Poythress, N. G., Jr. (1983). The quality of forensic evaluations: An interdisciplinary study. *Journal of Consulting and Clinical Psychology, 51*(1), 76–85.

Petrich, J., & Holmes, T. H. (1977). Life changes and onset of illness. *Medical Clinics of North America, 61*(4), 825–838.

Pomazal, R. (1985). Addiction Zenachlor—drug issues from a to z. *Journal of Drug Education, 15*(1), 73.

Pope, A. (1992). An essay on criticism. In J. Bartlett *Familiar quotations* (p. 298). Boston: Little, Brown. (Original work published 1688–1744)

Pope, K., Butcher, J., & Seelen, J. (1993). *The MMPI, MMPI-2 and MMPI-A in court.* Washington, DC: American Psychological Association.

Poythress, N. G. (1980). Coping on the witness stand: Learned responses to "learned treatises." *Professional Psychology, 1,* 139.

Poythress, N. G. (1982). Concerning reform in expert testimony. *Law and Human Behavior, 6,* 39–43.

Press, A. (1983, January 10). Divorce American style. *Newsweek,* pp. 42–48.

Price, R. (1990). *Developments in psychological evaluation for malingering and symptom exaggeration.* Compendium for workshop at the 6th annual Mental Health and Law Conference, Tampa, FL.

Prigatano, G., Smason, I., Lamb, D., & Bortz, J. (1997). Suspected malingering and the Digit Memory Test: A replication and extension. *Archives of Clinical Neuropsychology, 12,* 609.

Pritchard, D., & Rosenblatt, A. (1980). Racial bias in the MMPI: A methodological review. *Journal of Consulting and Clinical Psychology, 48,* 263.

Quas, J., De Cicco, V., Bulkley, J., & Goodman, G. (1996). District attorneys' views of legal innovations for child witnesses. *AP-LS News, 16,* 5.

Racine, R., Lindeman, J., & Davis, K. (1995). The battle over science in the courtroom. *The Federal Lawyer, 42*(2), 37.

Rahe, R. H. (1972). Subjects' recent life changes and their near-future illness reports. *Annals of Clinical Research, 4,* 250–265.

Ray, E., Engum, E., Lambert, E., Bane, G., Nash, M., & Bracy, O. (1997). Ability of the Cognitive Behavioral Driver's Inventory to distinguish malingerers from brain-damaged subjects. *Archives of Clinical Neuropsychology, 12,* 491.

Reed, J. (1996). Fixed vs. flexible neuropsychological test batteries under the *Daubert* standard for the admissibility of scientific evidence. *Behavioral Sciences and the Law, 14,* 315.

Reed, S. (1997). Disqualifying as an expert witness. *Trial, 33,* 26.

Reitan, R., & Wolfson, D. (1997). Consistency of neuropsychological test scores of head-injured subjects involved in litigation compared with head-injured subjects ot involved in litigation. *Clinical Neuropsychologist, 11,* 69.

Rey, A. (1941). L'examen psychologique dans las cas d'encephalopathie traumatique [Psychological testing in the case of traumatic brain disorder]. *Archives de psychologie, 28*(112), 286–340.

Richmond, D. (1996). Bad science: Repressed and recovered memories of childhood sexual abuse. *University of Kansas Law Review, 44,* 517.

Roache, J., & Griffith, S. (1989). Abuse liability of anxiolytics and sedative/hypnotics: Methods assessing the likelihood of abuse. In N. Fischman & N. Mello (Eds.), *Testing for abuse liability of drugs in humans* (NIDA Research Monograph No. 92). Rockville, MD: U.S. Department of Health and Human Services.

Robbins, C. (1987, September 28). Hordes of New Mexico chile addicts are bracing for the long cold winter. *New York Times*, p. 8.

Robinson, D. N. (1982, June 23). The *Hinckley* decision: Psychiatry in court. *The Wall Street Journal*, p. 5.

Robitscher, J. (1980). *The powers of psychiatry*. Boston: Houghton Mifflin.

Roesch, R. (1979). Determining competency to stand trial: An examination of evaluation procedures in an institutional setting. *Journal of Consulting and Clinical Psychology, 47*(3), 542–550.

Roesch, R., & Golding, S. L. (1978). Legal and judicial interpretation of competency to stand trial statutes and procedures. *Criminology, 16*, 420–429.

Rogers, R. (1987). Ethical dilemmas in forensic evaluations. *Behavioral Sciences and the Law, 5*, 149.

Rogers, R. (Ed.). (1997). *Assessment of malingering and deception*. New York: Guilford Press.

Rogers, R., Bagby, R., & Dickens, S. (1992). *Structured interview of reported symptoms: Professional manual*. Odessa, FL: Psychological Assessment Resources.

Rogers, R., Harrell, E., & Liff, C. (1993). Feigning neuropsychological impairment: A critical review of methodological and clinical considerations. *Clinical Psychology Review, 13*, 255.

Rogers, R., Sewell, K., & Goldstein, A. (1994). Explanatory models of malingering. *Law and Human Behavior, 18*, 543.

Rossi, P. H. (Ed.). (1982). *Standards for evaluation practice* (Publication No. 15, New Directions for Program Evaluation: Evaluation Research Society). San Francisco: Jossey-Bass.

Rotgers, F., & Barrett, D. (1996). *Daubert v. Merrell Dow* and expert testimony by clinical psychologists. *Professional Psychology: Research and Practice, 27*(5), 467.

Rothke, S., Friedman, A., Dahlstrom, W., Greene, R., Arrendondo, R., & Mann, A. (1994). MMPI-2 normative data for the F-K Index: Implications for clinical, neuropsychological, and forensic practice. *Assessment, 1*, 1.

Ruback, R. B. (1982). Issues in family law. In J. C. Hanson & L. Abade (Eds.), *Values, ethics, legalities and the family therapist*. London: Aspen Systems.

Rudestam, K. E. (1977). Physical and psychological responses to suicide in the family. *Journal of Consulting Clinical Psychology, 45*(2), 162–170.

Rutter, M. (1971). Parent-child separation: Psychological effects on the children. *Journal of Child Psychology and Psychiatry and Allied Disciplines, 12*, 233–260.

Rutter, M. (1972). Maternal deprivation reconsidered. *Journal of Psychosomatic Research, 16*, 241–250.

Saks, M. J., & Hastie, R. (1978). *Social psychology in court*. New York: Van Nostrand-Reinhold.

Sales, B. D. (Ed.). (1981). *The trial process*. New York: Plenum Press.

Sanborn, N., & Sanborn, J. (1976). The psychological autopsy as a therapeutic tool. *Diseases of the Nervous System, 37*(4), 7.

Sanders, A. (1987). Intoxication and the law: Drug testing in the workplace. *1987 Annual Survey of American Law*, 167.

Santruck, J. W., & Warshak, R. A. (1979). Father custody and social development in boys and girls. *Journal of Social Issues, 35*(4), 112–115.

Saunders, T., Gindes, M., Bray, J., Shellenberger, S., & Nurse, A. (1996). Should psychotherapists be concerned about the new APA child custody guidelines? *Psychotherapy Bulletin, 31*, 28.

Savitzky, J., & Karras, D. (1984). Competency to stand trial among adolescents. *Adolescence, 14*, 349.

Saxe, L., Dougherty, D., & Cross, T. (1985). The validity of polygraph testing: Scientific analysis and public controversy. *American Psychologist, 40,* 355.

Scanlon, J. C., & Weingarten, K. (1963). The role of statistical data in the functioning of courts. *Buffalo Law Review, 2*(12), 522–527.

Schacter, D. (1986a). Amnesia and crime. *American Psychologist, 41,* 286.

Schacter, D. (1986b). Feelings-of-knowing ratings distinguish between genuine and simulated forgetting. *Journal of Experimental Psychology: Learning, Memory and Cognition, 12,* 30.

Schacter, D. (1986c). On the relation between genuine and simulated amnesia. *Behavioral Sciences and the Law, 4,* 47.

Schaler, J. (1991). Drugs and free will. *Social Science and Modern Society, 28*(6), 42.

Schaler, J. (1993). *Addiction beliefs of treatment providers: Factors explaining variance.* Unpublished doctoral dissertation, University of Maryland.

Schaler, J. (1995). The addiction belief scale. *International Journal of the Addictions, 30*(2), 117.

Schinka, J., & Borum, R. (1994). Readability of normal personality inventories. *Journal of Personality Assessment, 62*(1), 95.

Schoenfeld, L. S., & Lehmann, L. S. (1981). Management of the aggressive patient. In C. E. Walker (Ed.), *Clinical practice of psychology.* New York: Pergamon Press.

Schretlen, D. (1988). The use of psychological tests to identify malingered symptoms of mental disorder. *Clinical Psychology Review, 8,* 451.

Schutte, J., & Howell, M. (1997). Refuting common defenses in traumatic brain injury cases. *Trial, 33,* 32.

Schwartz, M. (1987). Limitations on neuropsychological testimony by the Florida appellate decisions. *Clinical Neuropsychologist, 1,* 51.

Schweber, C. (1981). Criminalization and incarceration: The federal response to drug addiction among women 1914–1934. *Mason University Law Review, 4,* 71.

Selby, M., Airy-Eggertsen, A., & Laver, G. (in press). Comparison of neuropsychological test performance in forensic and non-forensic populations. *American Journal of Forensic Psychology.*

Selby, M., Yuspeh, R., Ririe, J., & Quiroga, M. (1994). Neuropsychological test norms for forensic populations. *Clinical Neuropsychologist, 8,* 343.

Shah, S. (1963). Crime and mental illness: Some problems in defining and labeling deviant behavior. *Mental Hygiene, 53,* 21–33.

Shah, S. (1977, February). Editorial. *APA Monitor,* p. 2.

Shah, S. (1978). Dangerousness. A paradigm for exploring some issues in law and psychology. *American Psychologist, 33,* 224–238.

Shakespeare, W. (1604). *Othello, Act II, Scene II.*

Sheridan, R. (1990). The false child molestation outbreak of the 1980s: An exploration of the cases arising in the divorce context. *Issues in Child Abuse Accusations, 2,* 146.

Shneidman, E. S. (1967). Some current developments in suicide prevention. *Bulletin of Suicidology, 33,* 41.

Shneidman, E. S. (1976). *Suicidology: Contemporary developments* (pp. 351–352, 540–544). New York: Grune and Stratton.

Shneidman, E. S. (1978). *Voices of death.* New York: Bantam Books.

Siegler, M., & Osmond, H. (1968). Models of drug addiction. *International Journal of the Addictions, 3,* 3.

Simon, R. (1993). A preliminary analysis of *Daubert. ATLA Section Newsletter: Supplement, 2*(4), 2.

Slovenko, R. (1973). *Psychiatry and law.* Boston: Little, Brown.

Slovenko, R. (1983, February 14). Pleading insanity is here to stay: Insanity plea or not. *New York Times,* p. 18.

Slovic, P., & Monahan, J. (1995). Probability, danger and coercion. *Law and Human Behavior, 19,* 49.

Smith, G., & Hall, J. (1983, March 30). Study: "Guilty but mentally ill" verdict having no effect on insanity cases. *Atlanta Journal,* p. 25-A.

Sommers, C. (1995, July 10). The flight from science and reason. *The Wall Street Journal.*

Span, M., & Cantor, D. W. (1983). Caution: Joint custody. *New Jersey Family Lawyer, 2*(5), 88–96.

Spar, J., Hankin, M., & Stodden, A. (1995). Assessing mental capacity and susceptibility to undue influence. *Behavioral Science and the Law, 13,* 391.

Spaulding, W. (1985). Testimentary competency. *Law and Human Behavior, 9,* 113.

Stall, R., & Biernacki, P. (1986). Spontaneous remission from the problematic use of substances: An inductive model derived from a comparative analysis of the alcohol, opiate, tobacco, and the food/obesity literature. *International Journal of the Addictions, 21*(1), 1.

Steadman, H. J., & Morrissey, J. P. (1981). The statistical prediction of violent behavior. *Law and Human Behavior, 3*(4), 263–274.

Steinman, S. (1981). The experience of children in a joint custody arrangement. *American Journal of Orthopsychiatry, 51*(3), 403–414.

Stockton, M., Jason, L., & McMahon, S. (1995, August 12). *Health beliefs and smoking cessation in a worksite program involving groups, incentives and self-help manuals.* Paper presented at the annual meetings of the American Psychological Association, Toronto.

Stolberg, A., & Anker, J. (1983). Cognitive and behavioral changes in children resulting from parental divorce and consequent environmental changes. *Journal of Divorce, 7,* 23.

Stolberg, A., & Bush, J. (1985). A path analysis of factors predicting children's divorce adjustment. *Journal of Clinical Child Psychology, 14,* 49.

Strickland, T., Stein, R., Khalsa-Denison, B., & Andre, K. (1996). *Neuropsychological effects of chronic cocaine use following sustained abstinence.* Poster session presented at the annual meeting of the National Academy of Neuropsychology, New Orleans, LA.

Stromberg, C., Lindberg, D., & Schneider, J. (1995). A legal update on forensic psychology. *The Psychologist's Legal Update, 6,* 3.

Strout, R. L. (1982, August 30). The American family: Winds of change. *Tampa Tribune,* p. 11-A.

Suggs, D. L. (1979). The use of psychological research by the judiciary. *Law and Human Behavior, 3*(1/2), 135–148.

Sutherland, G., Stapleton, J., Russell, M., & Feyerabend, C. (1995). Naltrexone, smoking behavior and cigarette withdrawal. *Psyhcopharmacology, 120,* 418.

Sutker, P., & Allain, A. (1988). Issues in personality conceptualizations of addictive behaviors. *Journal of Consulting and Clinical Psychology, 56*(2), 172.

Swanson, J., Lee, J., & Hopp, J. (1984). Caffeine and nicotine: A review of their joint use and possible interactive effects in tobacco withdrawal. *Addictive Behaviors, 19*(3), 229.

Sweet, J., Moberg, P., & Westergaard, C. (1996). Five-year follow-up survey of practices and beliefs of clinical neuropsychologists. *Clinical Neuropsychologist, 10,* 202.

Symptom Validity Tests [Computer software]. (1998). Woodsboro, MD: Cool Spring Software.

Talbott, G. (1989). The judicial system and addictions–1989: A medical perspective. *Georgia State Bar Journal, 25*(3), 134.

Taylor, R. E. (1983, January 20). Insanity defense should be narrowed, psychiatrists say. *The Wall Street Journal*, p. 18.

Tenhula, W., & Sweet, J. (1996). Double cross-validation of the Booklet Category Test in detecting malingered traumatic brain injury. *Clinical Neuropsychologist, 10*, 104.

Terman, L. M. (1931). Psychology and the law. *Los Angeles Bar Association Bulletin, 6*, 142–153.

Terman, L. M. (1935). Psychology and the law. *Commercial Law Journal, 40*, 639–646.

Terry, C., & Pellens, N. (1928). *The opium problem*. New York: Bureau of Social Hygiene.

Thompson, G., Arruda, J., Javorsky, D., Dahlen, D., Somerville, J., Guilmette, T., & Stern, R. (1997). The effects of coaching on the detection of malingering using the abbreviated Hiscock Forced Choice Procedure. *Archives of Clinical Neuropsychology, 12*, 414.

Thompson, R., Tinsley, B., Scalora, M., & Parke, R. (1989). Grandparents' visitation rights. *American Psychologist, 44*, 1217.

Tierney, J. (1982). Doctor, is this man dangerous? *Science, 3*(5), 28–31.

Twiford, J. (1986). Joint custody: A blind leap of faith? *Behavioral Sciences and the Law, 4*, 157.

U.S. Department of Health and Human Services. (1988). *Nicotine addiction: A report of the Surgeon General* (Office on smoking and health). Washington, DC: U.S. Government Printing Office.

U.S. Department of Health and Human Services. (1994). *The international classification of diseases, 9th revision, clinical modification. ICD•9•CM* (5th ed., Vol. 1). Washington, DC: U.S. Government Printing Office.

Ustad, K., Rogers, R., Sewell, K., & Guarnaccia, A. (1996). Restoration of competency to stand trial: Assessment with the Georgia Court Competency Test and the Competency Screening Test. *Law and Human Behavior, 20*, 131.

Von Schiller, J. (1798). *Wallenstein's Tod Act I, Scene IV.*

Vranizan, N. (1995, June 6). Groups studying on-line addictions. *The Tampa Tribune.*

Wakefield, H., & Underwager, R. (1991). Sexual abuse allegations in divorce and custody disputes. *Behavioral Sciences and the Law, 9*, 451.

Wakefield, H., & Underwager, R. (1996). Commentary on Kenneth Pope's review. *Clinical Psychology: Science and Practice, 3*, 366.

Wald, P. M. (1982). Become a real "friend of the court." *APA Monitor, 13*(2), 5.

Wallerstein, J. (1983). Children of divorce: The psychological task of the child. *American Journal of Orthopsychiatry, 53*, 80.

Wallerstein, J. (1985). Children of divorce: Report of a ten-year follow-up of older children and adolescents. *Journal of the American Academy of Child Psychiatry, 24*, 545.

Wallerstein, J. S., & Kelly, J. B. (1975). The effects of parental divorce: Experiences of the pre-school child. *Journal of the American Academy of Child Psychiatry, 14*, 600–616.

Walters, H. A. (1981). Dangerousness. In J. R. Moon (Ed.), *Encyclopedia of clinical assessment* (Vol. 2). San Francisco: Jossey-Bass.

Wasyliw, O., Grossman, L., Haywood, T., & Cavanaugh, J. (1988). The detection of malingering in criminal forensic groups: MMPI validity scales. *Journal of Personality Assessment, 52*, 321.

Webster, C., Harris, G., Rice, M., Cormier, C., & Quinsey, V. (1994). *The violence prediction scheme: Assessing dangerousness in high risk men*. Toronto: University of Toronto.

Wehman, P., Kreutzer, J., West, M., Sherron, P., Diambra, J., Fry, R., Groah, C., Sale, P., & Killam, S. (1989). Employment outcomes of persons following traumatic brain injury. *Brain Injury, 3*, 397.

Weiner, I., Exner, J., & Sciara, A. (1996). Is the Rorschach welcome in the courtroom? *Journal of Personality Assessment, 67*, 422.

Weissman, H. (1990). Distortions and deceptions in self presentation: Effects of protracted litigation in personal injury cases. *Behavioral Sciences and the Law, 8*, 67.

Weitzman, L. J., & Dixon, R. B. (1979). Child custody awards: Legal standards and empirical patterns for child custody, support, and visitation after divorce. *University of California, Davis Law Review, 12*, 473–521.

Wells, G. L., Leippe, M. R., & Ostrom, T. (1979). Guidelines for empirically assessing the fairness of a lineup. *Law and Human Behavior, 3*, 285–294.

Wenke, E. A., Robison, J. O., & Smith, G. W. (1972). Can violence be predicted? *Crime and Delinquency, 18*, 393–402.

Wetter, M., & Corrigan, S. (1995). Providing information to clients about psychological tests: A survey of attorneys' and law students' attitudes. *Professional Psychology: Research and Practice, 26*, 474.

Wewers, M., Tejwani, G., & Anderson, J. (1994). Plasma nicotine, plasma ß-endorphin and mood states during periods of chronic smoking, abstinence and nicotine replacement. *Psychopharmacology, 116*, 98.

White, G. (1990). Deposing the treating psychotherapist. *California Trial Lawyer's Association Forum, 20*, 61.

White, L. (1987). The mental illness defense in the capital penalty hearing. *Behavioral Sciences and the Law, 5*, 411.

Wiggins, E., & Brandt, J. (1988). The detection of simulated amnesia. *Law and Human Behavior, 12*, 57.

Wigmore, J. H. (1909). Professor Munsterberg and the psychology of testimony. *Illinois Law Review, 3*(7), 399–445.

Wigmore, J. H. (1940). *On evidence* (3rd ed., pp. 367–368). Boston: Little, Brown.

Wirthlin, J. (1987). Information and suggestions relating to testimony and discovery proceedings and trial. *Public Service Psychology, 12*, 12.

Wolchick, S., Braver, S., & Sandler, I. (1985). Maternal verses joint custody: Children's postseparation experiences and adjustment. *Journal of Clinical Child Psychology, 14*, 5.

Wolinsky, J. (1982). Programs join "distrustful" disciplines. *APA Monitor. 13*(2), 15.

Wolman, R., & Taylor, K. (1991). Psychological effects of custody disputes on children. *Behavioral Sciences and the Law, 9*, 399.

Worsnop, R. (1982, November 16). Video game fever. *Congressional Quarterly.*

Youngjohn, J., Davis, D., & Wolf, I. (1997). Head injury and the MMPI-2: Paradoxical severity effects and the influence of litigation. *Psychological Assessment, 9*, 177.

Ziskin, J. (1981a). *Coping with psychiatric and psychological testimony* (3rd ed.). Marina del Ray: Law and Psychology Press.

Ziskin, J. (1981b). Use of the MMPI in forensic settings. *Clinical Notes on the MMPI, 9*, 1–13.

Ziskin, J. (1991). *Coping with psychiatric and psychological testimony* (5th ed.). Marina del Ray: Law and Psychology Press.

Ziskin, J., & Coleman, L. (1981). Two professionals urge ban on psychiatric testimony. *California State Psychologist, 15*(5), 1–13.

Author Index

Subject Index